First published in the United States of America in 2021 by Rizzoli International Publications, Inc.

300 Park Avenue South,
New York, NY 10010
www.rizzoliusa.com

Copyright © 2021 OMA

OMA NY: Search Term
Shohei Shigematsu, Jason Long

Editor: Sophia Choi
Associate Editor: Timothy Ho
Team: Jeremy Wolin, Patricio Fernandez, Yiyao Wang,

Design: Studio Lin

For Rizzoli

Editor: Ian Luna
Project Editor: Meaghan McGovern
Production Managers: Barbara Sadick and Maria Pia Gramaglia
Copy Editor and Proofreader: Angela Taormina and Natalie Danford
Design Coordination: Olivia Russin

Publisher: Charles Miers

All rights reserved. No part of this publication may be reproduced, stored in a retrieval system, or transmitted in any form or by any means, electronic, mechanical, photocopying, recording, or otherwise, without prior consent of the publishers.

Every effort has been made to gain permission from copyright holders and or photographers, where known, for the images reproduced in the book, and care has been taken to caption and credit those images correctly. Any omissions are unintentional and appropriate credit will be included in future editions if further information is brought in writing to the publisher's attention.

Printed in Italy

2021 2022 2023 2024 2025 /
10 9 8 7 6 5 4 3 2 1
ISBN: 978-0-8478-6920-6
Library of Congress Control Number: 2021938185

Visit us online: Facebook.com/
RizzoliNewYork
Twitter: @Rizzoli_Books
Instagram.com/RizzoliBooks
Pinterest.com/RizzoliBooks
Youtube.com/user/RizzoliNY
Issuu.com/Rizzoli

OMA NY search term

RIZZOLI
NEW YORK

New York · Paris · London · Milan

Acknowledgments:
Without Rem Koolhaas, OMA wouldn't have a culture of relentless research and design. Without the other partners—Ellen van Loon, Reinier de Graaf, David Gianotten, Iyad Alsaka, Chris van Duijn—OMA wouldn't be the eclectic entity it is today. The work within is indebted to the dedication of our Associates: Scott Abrahams, Jake Forster, Christy Cheng, Yusef Ali Dennis, and Chris Yoon. Project leaders Lawrence Siu, Caroline Corbett, Salome Nikuradze, and Takeshi Mitsuda brought ideas for buildings to life. We thank Helen Billson and every individual who supported the creative anarchy. Not to forget those who left their marks— Associates: Charles Berman, Ziad Shehab, Luke Willis, Laura Baird, and Ted Lin; and project leaders: Michael Smith, Christin Svensson, Patrick Hobgood, Sandy Yum, Clarisa Garcia Fresco, Paxton Sheldahl, Ceren Bingol, Yolanda do Campo, Matthew Haseltine, and Jackie Woon Bae.

We are grateful for the clients who inspired our work: Mohsen Mostafavi, Kent Kleinman, Rabbi Steve Leder, Alberto Valner, Rebecca Rugg, Judith De Jong, Line Ouellet, Pierre Lassonde, Janne Sirén, Jeffrey Gundlach, Joe Lin-Hill, Lisa Phillips, Massimiliano Gioni, Cai Guo-Qiang, Lulu Zhang, Taryn Simon, Alan Faena, Ximena Caminos, Karen Sutton, Allan Schwartzman, Andrew Bolton, Anna Wintour, Florence Müller, Christoph Heinrich, Agustín Arteaga, Olivier Bialobos, Frank Stephan, Ichiro Enomoto, Yoshihiro Amamoto, Shingo Tsuji, Midori Omori, Frank and Kirby Liu, Thao Nguyen, David Martin, George Perez, Phoebe Yee, David von Spreckelsen, George Klein and Marian Klein Feldt, John Durschinger, Megan Brothers, Stephen Riley, Konnie Eskender, and Scott Kratz.

Kendall/Heaton Associates, Provencher_Roy, Gruen Associates, Cooper Robertson, Revuelta, Beyer Blinder Belle, Maeda Corporation, Nihon Sekkei, Kume Sekkei, Arquitectonica, HKS, Y.A. Studio, Powers Brown, and SLCE Architects have helped bring our visions into reality. Arup, Thornton Tomasetti, DeSimone, Front, 2x4, MTWTF, Tillotson Design, L'Observatoire, and Dot Dash have been consistent co-conspirators.

Sophia Choi refined chaos into the form of this book and was crucial to its momentum. Timothy Ho was critical in the assemblage of a mountain of content. Jeremy Wolin, Patricio Fernandez, and Yiyao Wang collected and refined the drawings. Christopher Hawthorne, Lisa Phillips, Massimiliano Gioni, Taryn Simon, Iris van Herpen, Virgil Abloh, David Byrne, Alice Waters, and Cecilia Alemani injected new perspectives to our preoccupations. We owe much to Michael Rock for his critical voice; Beatrice Galilee for input on our own narrative; Diana Murphy for guidance on the publishing world. Ian Luna and Meaghan McGovern of Rizzoli trusted us on this massive undertaking.

Alex Lin and his team at Studio Lin conceived a creative direction to find and tell our story. This book, with all the questions, ideas, and speculations it has posed, would not exist without him.

OMA NY

Search Term

This book is an index of twenty-three works by OMA New York—built, lost, and in progress.

Over the last thirteen years, our identity has materialized through our growth as a satellite office within the unique circumstance of OMA's lineage. We went from working on one institutional project in New York to thirty projects ongoing simultaneously across diverse scales and typologies—masterplans, parks, towers, museums, exhibitions, and more....

We started as a small office of five and grew to a full-fledged operation of eighty. We reached a point where it made sense to ask: What is OMA New York?

We began our search by diving deep into our archives, rediscovering projects and compiling materials that exist in between the brief and the final product. We distilled their narratives into booklets to organize our efforts and outputs. We made zines to assemble aesthetic consistencies: blue foam towers, heterogenous square plans, and cut-and-paste concept collages. We transcribed lecture recordings and presentation PowerPoints into a slew of thumbnail images and captions to build an engine for transmitting narratives with unequivocal candor. This process of studying our studies slowly grew into an obsession, like being in an internet black hole before you even begin to realize that hours (for us, years) had passed.

It led to this book, which is a humble effort for us to find answers, or define ourselves by what isn't immediately apparent. The book is the result of a search term: a time frame—from before the 2007 financial crisis through the 2016 Trump era to the 2020 Covid-19 pandemic—for tracing our now-extensive body of work to discern and reflect on its consequences; and a set of particular terms for revealing the latent coherence that has been the driving force behind our projects.

The book is metadata—an illuminating index revealing inherent frameworks. It is an open-source archive that reflects our openness as an office and depicts the impact of individual influences, interests, and curiosities. Embedded within the chaotic array of images are a set of narratives for each project that provide a rational and seemingly inevitable path toward a final resolution. From big-picture to anecdotal, formal to playful, conceptual to technical, and authoritative to unrestrained, multiple narratives can be extracted from the matrix of images while leaving room for outside interpretation. Materials from ongoing observations and research of larger issues in specific domains show our drive in mining signs of typological evolution. The diversity of projects within each territory—institution, art, fashion, mixed-use, residential, workspace, and public realm—underlines how we observe the way typologies change over time and how we push ourselves and others to redefine them.

Through this search term, we are challenging ourselves with new queries while trying to come to terms with our steadfast convictions. But, most importantly, through its sheer energy and attitude, we hope that this book will serve as a source of inspiration and a springboard for further explorations.

Shohei Shigematsu and Jason Long,
OMA NY Partners

Attitudes

1 Pre-conception is worse than post-rationalization.

2 Making options is easy but deciding is difficult.

3 Don't repeat yourself (unless it didn't get built).

4 A specific response has the most general impact.

5 Ugliness can be more promising than "beauty."

6 Not every project needs a cantilever.

7 The most efficient form is a box. Or is it a sphere?

8 Ego and consensus are not mutually exclusive.

9 Sometimes the client has good ideas.

10 Good conclusions are often obvious.

11 Learn by embracing unintended consequences.

12 Downturns are just as profitable as upturns.

13 Make unknown from the known.

Milstein Hall

Milstein Hall

Milstein Hall was one of the first projects we worked on as OMA New York (ca. 2006-2007), and one that was able to sustain creative momentum amid the turbulence of the 2007–2009 financial crisis. It was small in scale, but rich in context—navigating preservation of a historic campus, the changing environments of education for creative disciplines, and the complex puzzle of diverse programmatic pieces that exist in multi-disciplinary learning.

The main ambition for the new building for Cornell's College of Architecture, Art, and Planning (AAP), was to create a new interdisciplinary studio for the architecture school and unite the AAP campus without demolishing its existing buildings. What should an architecture school designed by an architect be? How can a building embody the nature of collaboration and continuous experimentation that is crucial to architecture education and actual practice? Could the building itself be a pedagogical instrument?

AAP was fragmented as a campus, dislocated from the energy of university life—situated on the northern periphery of Cornell's historic Arts Quad. Its programs were spread across four existing buildings—Rand Hall, Sibley Hall, The Foundry, and Tjaden Hall—linear, corridor-based buildings that segregated the disciplines in closed rooms behind a labyrinth of entrances, security codes, and dead ends. We wanted to connect the buildings and propose a type of space currently absent from the campus: a wide-open expanse that stimulates interdisciplinary interaction and allows flexibility over time. The site and form are defined entirely by the existing buildings and campus alignments. The result is not a symbolic, isolated addition but a connecting structure: an elevated horizontal plate that links the second levels of Sibley and Rand Halls and reaches across University Avenue toward The Foundry. Like a mini Arts Quad, it transforms an ad hoc cluster of buildings into a continuous landscape of spontaneous activities and encounters.

In order to create a large, flexible space for studios conducive to improvisational interaction among AAP programs, we had to cantilever the upper plate 48 feet over University Avenue. The desire for a single open space and the required perimeter and interior trusses to cantilever were conflicting propositions. We developed a hybrid truss system—Vierendeel to conventional—to balance structural efficiency and maintain open circulation. The truss is exposed so that students can see its transition and understand areas of stress. To encourage flow and interaction through a diverse repertoire of studio environments, the upper plate is not defined by walls but by movable furniture and a central program band for gathering. Within the band, a stepped auditorium and flexible lounge provide social spaces that can also be used for informal meetings, presentations, crits, and exhibitions.

Below the upper plate, the lower plate contains public programs that serve the entire AAP. More often than not, there is persistent warfare between the box and the blob. Here, we merge the two by adding a landscape-like element: a concrete dome rises to puncture the upper plate and dissect the lower plate. It simultaneously creates a flexible, double-height crit space and opens a direct route from studios to lower levels. Embedded on top of the dome's sloping surface is a double-height auditorium with panoramic views to the street and campus. Where the dome does not intersect the upper plate, it defines two public plazas under the north and southeast cantilevers, attracting "urban" activity that was nonexistent before.

Over the decade following its completion, we'd been observing the different uses of the building, discovering both intended and unexpected post-occupancy—an art installation in the dome, a student riding his bike in the studio while others play badminton, one napping in a hammock strung across the truss, a dance performance on the stairs, informal lectures on architectural model exhibitions. Milstein Hall may not necessarily be an iconic building, but perhaps it's an iconic place that is defined by the playful activities and creative interactions that it fosters.

Location	Ithaca, NY, USA		
Status	Completed, 2011		
Typology	Institution		
Program	Flexible Studio	25,000 ft²	2,320 m²
	Crit Space/Gallery	6,400 ft²	600 m²
	Auditorium	3,400 ft²	320 m²
	Support/Services	12,200 ft²	1,130 m²
	Total Area	47,000 ft²	4,370 m²

OMA NY   Milstein Hall

Milstein Hall

Milstein Hall

OMA NY   Milstein Hall

Milstein Hall

OMA NY   Milstein Hall

Milstein Hall

OMA NY   Milstein Hall

Milstein Hall

OMA NY

Milstein Hall

Milstein Hall

8 Cornell University is located in Ithaca, New York. With over 20,000 students, the college campus has the highest population density in the city.

9 Cornell's College of Architecture, Art, and Planning (AAP) is an isolated campus in nature, just south of the Finger Lakes. The lake's tributary and gorge is right above the northern campus.

10 Cornell's initial development addressed the town of Ithaca below it.

11 Falls Creek Gorge

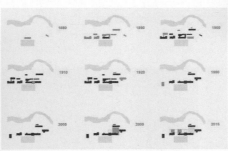

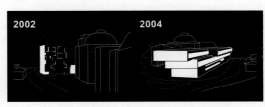

12 Today, the areas of Ithaca with the highest population density are Cornell's west and north residential areas. The Thurston Avenue Bridge has become the university's de facto gateway.

13 Campus development history—unlike the relative stability enjoyed by the rest of the Arts Quad, the zone between the northern edge of the quad and the gorge has seen perpetual building, demolition, adaptations, and additions.

14 Milstein Hall was awarded to Steven Holl in 2002. In 2004, the project was re-commissioned to Barkow Leibinger until 2005. Both schemes assumed demolishing Rand Hall and were canceled after overwhelming requests from alumni and students to preserve the building in the expansion of the AAP facilities. OMA was approached in late 2005 and asked to develop a proposal that preserved the existing AAP buildings.

15 The first view of the campus upon entering via the Thurston Avenue Bridge is of Rand Hall.

16 The site of the new AAP building is situated at the entry to the northern end of the campus, between Cornell's historic Arts Quad and the Falls Creek Gorge on a surface parking lot adjacent to Sibley Hall, Rand Hall, Tjaden Hall, and The Foundry.

17 Together with the Johnson Museum of Art, the AAP forms the "backside" of the Arts Quad—detached from the larger campus.

18 The northern site of the campus has been neglected and underused. It didn't feel a part of the campus.

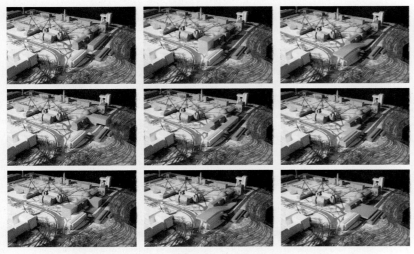

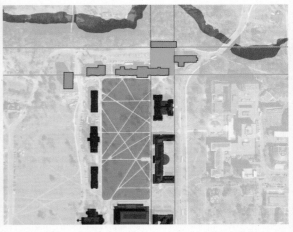

19 From the beginning the site for the new building was undetermined. Initial studies for siting and massing aimed to create an addition that would form a united complex with the existing buildings.

20 The site was conceived entirely based on existing buildings and campus alignments.

Milstein Hall

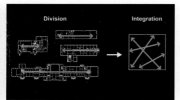

22   Plate as tool for integration

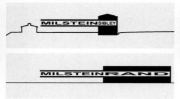

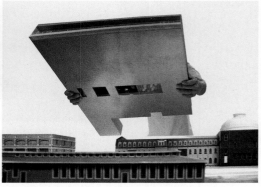

23   Integration with Rand and Sibley

21   Rather than creating a new freestanding building, Milstein Hall is a connective addition to the AAP. A horizontal plate connecting F2 of Rand and Sibley is like a mini Arts Quad for the AAP campus.

24   The box, modern architecture's typology par excellence, typically stands in isolation. In Milstein Hall, it acts as a connector, transforming an ad hoc cluster of buildings into a continuous space with the scale to facilitate collaboration.

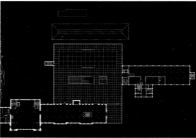

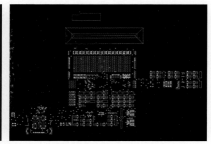

25   The new building links Rand and Sibley and extends over University Avenue to establish an urban relationship to The Foundry.

26   Milstein's plate introduces a zone of lesser definition. Largely determined by furniture, it allows for pedagogical experimentation.

27   Within the horizontal plate, subtle manipulations define zones that suggest and trigger particular uses. Meanwhile, the openness allows activity to flow freely both within the plate and to and from Rand and Sibley.

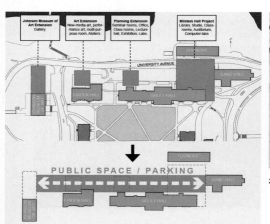

29   Milstein Hall becomes the hinge between the eastern edge and the new AAP campus to the north.

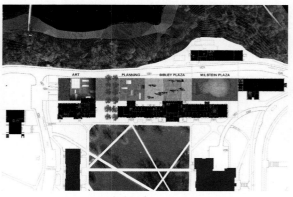

28   The siting and conception of Milstein Hall catalyzed a masterplan for AAP that integrates underground parking and future growth of the campus.

30   By connecting Milstein Hall and the Johnson Museum of Art extension with landscape and parking, a public band is created where open space and future extensions for the art and city and regional planning departments are placed.

31   A new public band

32   An integrated corridor of program and open space, with connection to the Johnson Museum of Art.

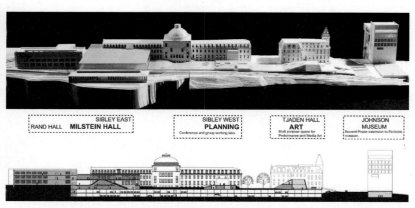

33   The lower plate of Milstein Hall would form the beginning of a new landscape of public space. This gesture would provide space for seminars and a computer lab for the city and regional planning department, as well as a large black-box space for media, conceptual, and performance arts for the art department.

34 Elevation model of masterplan connecting the disparate buildings of the AAP campus

35 The masterplan not only emphasizes the entire college and the Johnson Museum as a creative center, but also creates a newly vibrant campus edge oriented toward the gorge. Milstein Hall rotates the north-south axis to east-west.

36 After the masterplan phase, we returned to more formal studies specific to the plate. How can the design of the plate further enhance connections within the AAP campus?

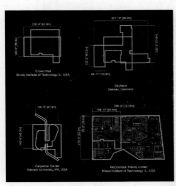

37 Scale comparison to other educational centers—clockwise from top left: Crown Hall, Illinois Institute of Technology; Bauhaus, Dessau, Germany; McCormick Tribune Campus Center, Illinois Institute of Technology; Carpenter Center, Harvard University

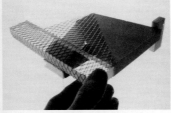

38 Plate studies—contiguous programs, structural wrapper, studio clusters

41 A cantilever reaching toward The Foundry over University Avenue was considered to maintain the road access while opening up the ground plane for both transportation and student activities.

42 Plate as connective datum—the cantilevering plate would be seen on either side of Rand Hall when approaching the new complex from the east.

39 The plate option was the best way to provide a typology entirely absent from the campus—a vast horizontal expanse allowing for multiple simultaneous occupations. Its open studios and crit spaces would provide high flexibility over time.

40 Plate study models

43 The ambition was for the form to complete the northern edge of the campus and create a unified expanse facing the gorge.

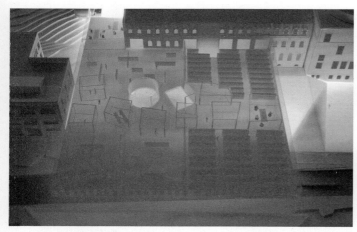

45 Plate interior model

46 Plate study—interior partition for potential library

47 Initial concept model—two plates

48 Initial structural study for plate—no trusses

49 The initial design called for a transfer portal over University Avenue for the building's structure.

44 Inside the plate is an open zone of less definition, contrasting to the other parts of the college, which are fairly fixed. The interior is intended for experimentation and reinterpretation over time.

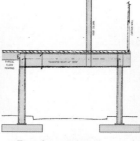

50 The transfer portal clearly defines University Avenue.

51 It creates a colonnade-like gateway beneath the plate.

52 Transfer portal section

53 Concept collage of initial structural scheme with portals

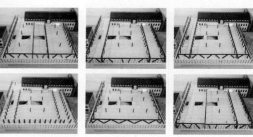

54 View down University Avenue

55 However, due to the proximity between high vehicular activity on the road and important pedestrian zones, the transfer portal was eliminated to provide better visual openness and safety.

56 Initial structural study for plate—structure on top

57 New options for various truss systems were explored that would allow the building to cantilever over University Avenue.

59 Structure study models stacked

58 Truss system study models stacked in crate

60 Final structure—hybrid truss

61 The final structure is a hybrid Vierendeel and conventional truss system that enables the building to efficiently cantilever over University Avenue while maintaining flexibility inside the building.

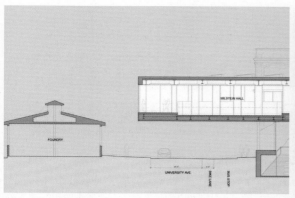

62 The building reaches out over University Avenue and interacts with the bus route, bike lane, and building entrances to form a dynamic space below.

63 The cantilevered upper plate hovers above a bus stop.

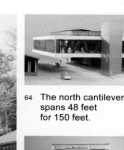

64 The north cantilever spans 48 feet for 150 feet.

65 Model view of plate datum from Rand

66 The continuous 12-foot-high band of glass facade establishes a floating studio. The activities within are visible to the public from the road, creating a recognizable gateway.

67 Given the building's limited height (33 feet grade), the plate preserves views of the existing AAP buildings.

68 View from under the north cantilever—connection to The Foundry

69 The plate gradually reveals itself as one moves from the Arts Quad to East Avenue. Its minimal appearance maintains the historically preserved character of the Arts Quad.

70 The building reclaims the north area by placing a symbol within the site.

71 The plate becomes a gateway that creates a connection between north and south.

72 It radiates activity and occupation.

73 It is a singular, panoramic beam of modernity.

74 The cantilevered plate liberates the ground level and maintains the flow of cars and pedestrians beneath the plate.

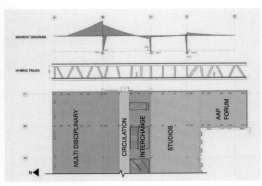

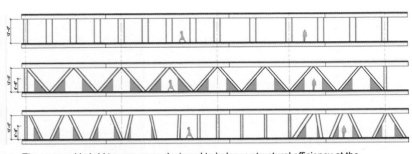

75 By analyzing the circulation and program as well as actual stress patterns of the building, a hybridized truss was developed—Vierendeel trusses are employed in areas of circulation and transition to conventional trusses.

76 The exposed hybrid trusses were designed to balance structural efficiency at the cantilevers and maintain open circulation within the large open plan. From top to bottom: Vierendeel truss maximizes circulation, minimizes structural efficiency; conventional truss maximizes structural efficiency, minimizes circulation; hybrid truss balances structural efficiency with circulation.

77 The open plate allows flexible furniture configurations to define areas of activity.

78 The open plan provided an opportunity for us as architects to be involved in pedagogical discussion. Together with the building committee and university stakeholders, a variety of upper plate zones supporting the physical and programmatic vision of collaborative learning were explored.

79 Nearly 1,200 tons of steel are used to frame Milstein Hall and support its two cantilevers.

80 Shohei presenting the final model to building committee and university stakeholders.

81 Truss frame construction

82 The truss travels along the facade from conventional to straight.

83 Students can actually see the transition of the truss and understand where the stress is occurring in the building.

84 A composite image of the 25,000-square-foot studio taken by photographer Brett Beyer— approximately 250 photos were captured by a camera suspended 12 feet above the floor. The image depicts the upper plate as a mini-Arts Quad supporting diverse activities.

85 Enclosed by floor-to-ceiling glass, Milstein Hall's upper plate features panoramic views of the surrounding environment and is directly connected to additional studio spaces in Rand and Sibley Halls.

86 The upper plate provides a large flexible space for studios that are conducive to improvisational interaction among the AAP programs.

87 Low pin-up wall

88 Break-out desk

89 High pin-up wall

90 Upper plate with views to the campus and greenery

91 The studio includes 25,000 square feet of flexible space that is home to approximately 16 architecture studios (220 students) each semester.

92 Desk crit

93 An open display of studio production

94 Individual workstations

95 Informal discussions at the break-out desks

96 Flexible low pin-up walls loosely define work zones while allowing for casual interaction from passersby.

97 Sibley Hall's exterior facade becomes an interior wall.

98 A playful moment of interaction between students and building

99 Installation or domestication? Students capitalize on the truss.

100 Optimized use of building structure— a hammock amenity

101 Architecture inspires creative display.

Lounge/Crit Space   Stepped Auditorium   Stairs   Moving Room

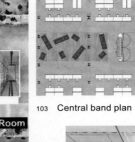

103   Central band plan

102   Within the upper plate, a programmed central band supports the studio by providing a lounge area, stepped auditorium, and circulation from the ground level.

104   The stepped auditorium is an informal presentation space set within the studios.

105   The auditorium is created by lifting the slab of the upper plate, which also establishes the entry to the main auditorium from the studio floor.

106   Maria Claudia Clemente, Francesco Isidori, and Professor Val Warke (Fall 2018)

107   The upper plate's only electrical closet is hidden within a polished stainless steel shell that also opens up to reveal pin-up walls and a large LCD screen for presentations.

108   Students watch a lecture remotely in the informal auditorium.

109   Amanda Williams and Andrea Simitch Lecture (Spring 2018)

110   It is also used as a social space.

111   View of electrical closet from stepped seating of the auditorium

112   Lounge model

113   On the other side of the electrical closet is a flexible lounge area that provides an informal meeting space and encourages interaction.

114   Lounge area as additional pin-up or exhibition space

115   Michelle Young and Mitch Glass give a lecture to the students in the lounge area (Spring 2019).

116   Spring 2018 final thesis reviews

117   The main stair, also within the band, brings students down to the bridge and B1 crit space.

118   The stairway visually connects the upper plate to the activities happening in the crit space below.

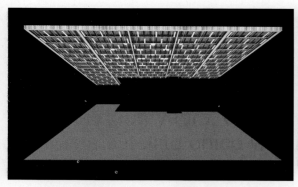

119 In the upper plate, chilling, air circulation, data, and electricity are placed in the ceiling to ensure flexibility. The high tech ceiling contrasts with a basic floor.

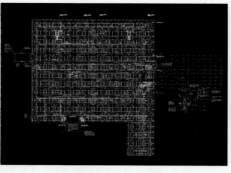

120 A field of custom-designed lights and chilled beams were carefully coordinated with the structural and mechanical systems to define the ceiling plane using normally hidden functional elements.

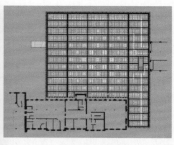

121 Ceiling utilities include low-velocity HVAC, acoustic insulation, passive chilled beam, skylights with light-diffusing interlayers, custom light fixtures with daylight sensors, continuous electrical busway, and exposed structural steel.

122 This ceiling infrastructure allows for a truly open and flexible studio floor that can be adapted at any time. The floor contains radiant heating and heat is distributed through the concrete floor slab.

123 The lighting is programmed by a highly customizable and efficient Lutron control system connected to daylight sensors.

124 Constant light levels are maintained, balancing daylight with artificial light.

125 The open expanse brings typical exterior campus activities indoors.

126 Students playing badminton

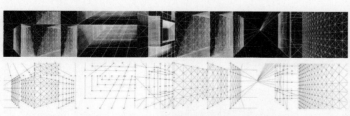

127 The curtains in the studios were designed by Inside Outside. The concept uses architectural drawings from the Dutch Renaissance artist/architect Hans Vredeman de Vries (1527–1607) to suggest another space outside of Milstein Hall. The enlarged perspectival drawings are digitally printed onto white vinyl mesh and perforated with holes along the perspective lines. (Top: perforation system. Bottom: marking crossing points of perspective lines.)

128 The custom-designed curtain preserves views out from the studios toward the Arts Quad, maintains natural daylight without glare, and presents a striking image at this northeast entry to the quad.

130 Signage study on the north cantilever

131 The building signage is integrated into the marble.

129 On the exterior facade, two simple bands of Turkish marble define the extent of the upper plate. The naturally-occurring vertical bands of gray and white enrich the exterior with a specific scale and material that is unique yet unites the different buildings across the proliferation of architectural styles in this area of campus.

132 Blocks of stone were custom quarried to orient the veins vertically along the short dimension, then cut and polished outside Carrara, Italy.

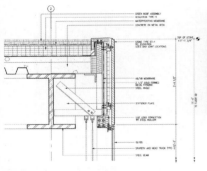

133 The building name was CNC routed ⅛-inch into the stone and painted white.

134 Marble band installation

135 Marble band installation

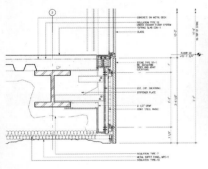

136 West facade detail

137 The vertically oriented marble veining was necessary to achieve achieving the appearance of a continuous horizontal band of stone that emphasizes the cantilevers and floating nature of the upper plate.

138 The building name is engraved directly into the full height of the lower fascia marble panels in vertical bands.

139 The vertical bands at once disappear into the stone and reveal themselves as distinct barcode lettering.

140 The uniqueness of the naturally striated marble directly influenced 2x4's design of the custom Milstein Hall building sign located on the south cantilever's east facade.

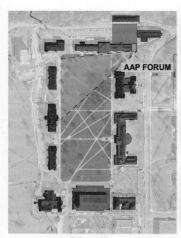

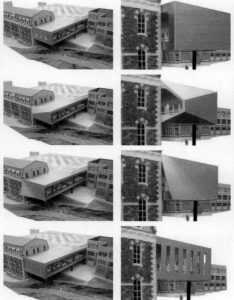

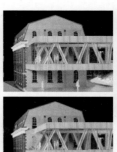

141 The southeast cantilevered area of the studios, named the AAP Forum, is considered a unique space within the upper plate. It is the area of the plate most visible from the pedestrian walkways of the Arts Quad and from East Avenue, approximately the same elevation as the studio floor.

142 AAP Forum facade studies

143 AAP Forum corner articulation studies— from top to bottom: straight facade, sloped facade, balcony

144 In order to preserve the cornice of the adjacent building, one study proposed a negative impression onto the facade.

145 The final design for the forum is a straight facade that respects the adjacent Sibley Hall.

146 The facade is set back to preserve the cornice.

147 The Forum's visibility from the Arts Quad establishes a new gateway.

148 The upper plate defines a covered outdoor plaza beneath it. Considering the cold climate of Ithaca and the expanse of the plate above, we wanted to create a more humane feeling below for a more interior-like experience.

149 To create a room–like feeling, the underside of the plate references traditional tin ceilings but in a larger size.

150 The panels are custom-stamped perforated aluminum.

151 The metal panels are fabricated on an automotive stamping machine.

152 Panel fabrication

153 View from B1

154 A stolen ceiling panel in a student's dorm room

155 The ceiling panels are continuous, extending through both interior and exterior spaces, de-emphasizing the boundary between them.

156 The ceiling panels begin from inside the auditorium and extend outside toward The Foundry.

157 Above the grid of perforated metal panels, acoustic blankets tune specific zones. Above the road, the blankets absorb noises from passing vehicles. In the auditorium, they improve audible performance. In the covered plaza, they reduce noise transmittance to the adjacent offices, classrooms, and auditorium.

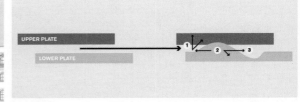

158 Beneath the upper plate, a half-submerged lower plate contains a cluster of public programs—an auditorium and exhibition and crit spaces—that serve the entire AAP.

159 The roof of the lower plate rises to form a bump, a single manipulation that simultaneously provides (1) access into the upper plate, (2) an open, double-height crit space and foyer within the lower plate, and (3) the required slope of the auditorium.

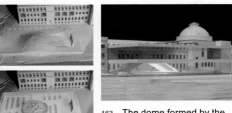

160 Initial study of lower plate and bump

161 Early dome concept from AAP masterplan

162 Lower plate and bump concepts developed during the master-planning phase

163 The dome formed by the bump creates a relationship to the dome of Sibley Hall.

164 Lower plate model—B1

165 Lower plate model—auditorium

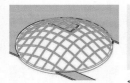

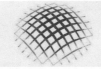

167 Dome structure study—grid

168 Dome structure study—displacement, ring

169 Dome structure study—displacement, no ring

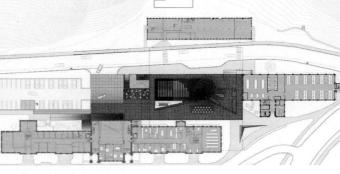

166 Ground level plan

171 The dome was formed using two layers of ⅜-inch plywood with a finish layer of ⅜-inch MDO board.

172 The concrete was poured in a single twelve-hour period.

173 Topping slab

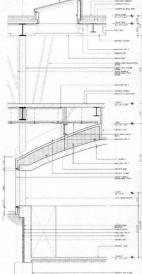

170 Dome formwork construction

175 Shohei Shigematsu presenting the model of dome and auditorium

174 The dome is a double-layered concrete system. The exposed underside is a cast-in-place structural slab spanning the main critique space beneath the dome.

176 Unlike the steel construction of the trusses, building the dome was a very heavy-handed concrete construction. It had to be cast in a single night, in one shot. Five different concrete cars were used. The concrete dome contrasts with the upper plate's glass and steel character.

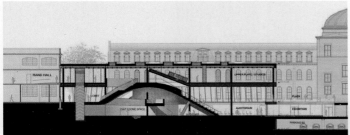

177 The dome intersects the upper plate to create an opening to the studios.

178 Where the dome does not intersect the upper plate, it creates additional covered outdoor spaces.

179 Under the northern cantilever, the dome is sliced to create a window that looks down into the activities of B1.

180 The covered space is also a bus stop.

181 On the south side of the building, the dome and upper plate together create a covered area that is an extension of the outdoor plaza.

182 Initial concept collages for programs activating the exterior covered plaza

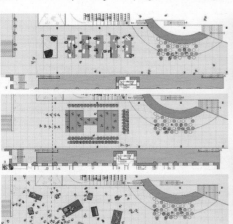

183 Outdoor plaza program scenarios

184 Cocktail event in the covered plaza

185 Franny's Food Truck in the outdoor plaza

186 Seating pods situated on the south side of the concrete dome add a public, urban quality to the covered space.

187 The translucent seating pods invite informal gathering.

188 Lounging pod

189 The dome extrudes from the inside to outside, becoming a space that attracts urban activity on the campus that was not present before.

190 Integrated bike rack

191 The pod seating is constructed of acrylic shell with a polyurethane outer layer illuminated by LED lights.

192 On the south side, the custom designed mullions are integrated with light fixtures. Juxtaposing the organic forms of the dome and the pod seating with the orthogonal plate creates a varied landscape.

193 Milstein Hall provides the AAP with the first auditorium and large-scale lecture hall within its own facilities. It is designed for maximum flexibility.

194 The clearly defined upper plate floating above gives way to an auditorium that is enclosed in glass on three sides, providing a panoramic view.

195 The seating was custom-designed by OMA and developed and manufactured by Martela Oy of Finland.

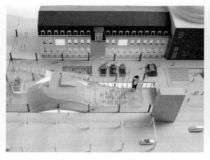

196 The auditorium is embedded within the top of the concrete dome.

197 The glass-enclosed auditorium provides a permeable boundary between academic space and the public.

198 A panoramic view of the surrounding campus

201 Performance

199 The auditorium is divided into two halves—fixed seats on the raked section of the dome and loose seats on the level section. When the auditorium is not used at its full capacity of 300 people, the lower level can be used for studio critiques and smaller meetings.

200 The cantilevered fixed seat backs fold down to form a continuous bench for higher-capacity seating. The bench configuration can also be used as tables for exhibition and display.

202 A full-house lecture

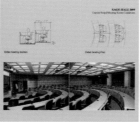

204 The existing boardroom had long rows of desks that made it inconvenient to get in and out of the seats.

205 We wanted to provide first-class seats for board members and looked at personal seating references.

203 Howard Milstein, the main donor, wanted to use the auditorium as a boardroom for the university and decided to retrofit the space during construction. OMA custom-designed the solution to integrate the boardroom into the auditorium and the resulting seats were developed and manufactured by Figueras International of Spain.

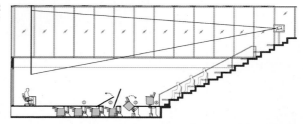

206 Since board meetings happen only twice a year, a deployable system was needed. The boardroom is assembled at the touch of a button, which deploys sixty-one seats by automatically raising them from below the raised floor of the level floor section.

208 Boardroom seating activated in discussion configuration–voting systems, microphones, and electricity are all integrated within each seat.

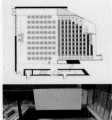

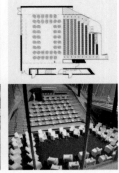

209 Speaker configuration

210 Discussion configuration

207 Each of the sixty-one individual seats can be raised or lowered independently and is integrated with power, an oversized tablet, and a storage bin.

211 Twice a year, the seats rise from beneath the floor like zombies to host a board meeting.

212 Boardroom seating activated in speaker configuration–each seat is attached to a post that allows 360-degree rotation with locking positions every 7.5 degrees.

214 View of curtain from outside through a sloped glass facade

213 When privacy or blackout is required, a custom-designed curtain unfurls from the auditorium in one continuous panel that surrounds the auditorium.

215 The curtain is digitally printed on both surfaces. It is made of black-out fabric with perforated holes following the perspective lines of the digitally printed drawing of Hans Vredeman de Vries.

216 A field of columns "support" the large cantilever of the upper plate and suggest a classical landscape on the interior and exterior of the building. It is one continuous curtain 150 feet long and is stored around the balcony stair when not in use.

Milstein Hall

219 B1 model in plan view

218 B1 model

220 Models of program scenarios in the B1 crit space

217 Adjacent to the auditorium but under the concrete dome is a 5,000-square-foot circular critique space. It is a large, flexible open space that is connected to the upper plate as well as the auditorium by a concrete stair and bridge.

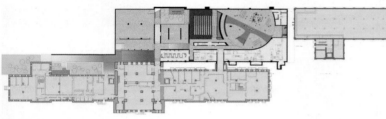

221 B1 plan

222 The materiality of the lower level, constructed of exposed, cast-in-place concrete, adds a contrast to the upper plate's glass and steel character.

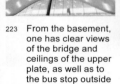

223 From the basement, one has clear views of the bridge and ceilings of the upper plate, as well as to the bus stop outside below the cantilever.

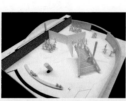 

224 Crit configurations—clockwise from top left: three crit spaces, room, exhibition, and stored.

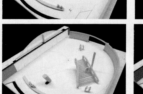

225 A felt-lined pin-up wall stored along the north facade can be retracted and configured into a number of divisions for exhibitions or multiple critiques.

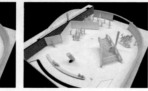

226 The movable walls include three 30-foot panels and one 16-foot panel.

227 The flexible, movable wall allows faculty to divide the space and host activities simultaneously.

228 Critique in session

229 Architecture spring 2015 final reviews

230 Introduction to Architecture summer program 2018

231 An intimate exhibition within the vast, open crit space

232 Architecture fall 2015 final reviews

233 Students can look down to the crit space and pin-up walls from a bridge piercing the dome space.

Milstein Hall

234 A concrete bridge spanning 70 feet across the dome space punctuates the organic form of the dome. Students can access the B1 crit space directly from the upper plate studio and the bridge is also an observation platform for spectating the activities below.

235 Bridge as a mezzanine

236 Sculptural stair

237 The bridge aligns with the ground level outside.

238 Model view of bridge and crit space below

239 The structural concrete truss railing and stair allow the bridge to span across the dome column-free.

240 Much like a landscape element, the dome, bridge, and stairs provide unpredictable spaces in between the upper plate and the ground floor.

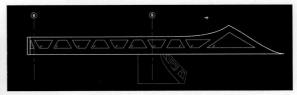

241 Bridge elevation

242 Bridge formwork

243 Bridge construction

244 Two separate crits in session

245 Structural concrete truss railing and stair

246 The bridge penetrates the concrete dome, creating a multi-dimensional space.

247 Celebrate Milstein Hall event

248 Because of the bus stop located right outside of the building, the dome space experiences high foot traffic. Architecture students and non-architectural crowds alike can look down into the activity at Cornell AAP. From the crit space, students can also look up to the bridge and bus stop.

249 Installation view

250 Berndnaut Smilde, *Nimbus Milstein Hall* (2014)

251 Many different activities occur in the space, from more intimate gatherings to larger events.

252 Connecting the three levels of Milstein Hall, a vertical moving room (12 feet 3 inches by 6 feet 4 inches) serves as the elevator.

253 The moving room is built from standard plywood panels, fully assembled in Québec City, dismantled, and reassembled on site in Ithaca.

254 Elevator viewed from the covered exterior passageway

255 The elevator is large enough to allow the transport of models between the studios and the dome critique space.

256 Further vertical circulation within the plate includes an exterior stair tower that is also a vertical trellis.

267 The stair tower is composed of expanded aluminum mesh panels covered with Akebia quinata vines.

262 Gallery wall configuration 3

258 The "living wall" brings greenery up the building and onto the roof, a gesture toward the natural gorge to the north.

259 View of the upper plate, ground level entry, auditorium, and B1 gallery—different program layers that touch upon each other and function together.

260 Gallery wall configuration 1

261 Gallery wall configuration 2

263 The movable walls accommodate multiple gallery configurations.

264 Gallery installation in progress

265 On B1 is a gallery with rotating walls and a round window connected to the entrance from University Avenue.

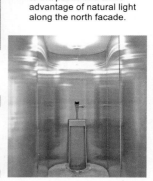

266 The adjacency to the sunken garden gives the gallery maximum exposure to the public and takes advantage of natural light along the north facade.

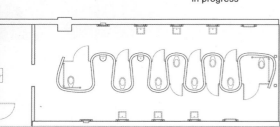

267 The B1 bathrooms are defined by a continuous ribbon that interlocks two separate rooms.

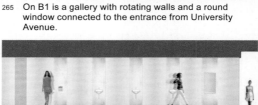

268 Elevation

269 Urinal

270 Bathroom model

271 Bathroom model

272 B1 bathroom

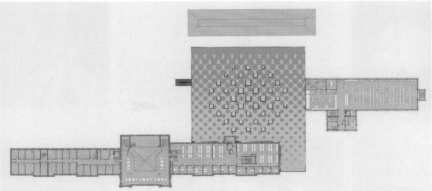
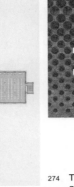

273   Roof plan—the exterior of the upper plate responds with different materials to the performative demands of their position on the building. The 25,000-square-foot roof is a sedum-covered green roof punctuated by a cluster of northern facing skylights that gradually increase in size toward the darker center of the plate.

274   Two different types of sedum create a gradient pattern of dots that transition from articulated small circles near the man-made Arts Quad on the south, to a dense, larger pattern of dots toward the natural landscape of the gorge on the north.

275   Roof model—varying scale and configuration of skylights

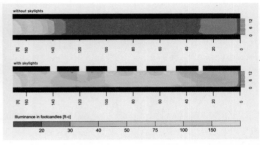

276   Daylight calculation—distribution of daylight in building section without skylights versus with skylights

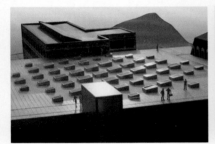

277   Roof model

278   Roof model with landscape

279   Construction sequence—left to right, by column: steel structure, roof structure, waterproofing, green roof planting

280   The green roof integrates Milstein Hall into the natural context of Ithaca and the Falls Creek Gorge.

281   The skylights enable the building to have consistent, natural light levels across the entire second floor of the studio space.

282   Three sizes of skylights are arranged in a radial pattern on the roof with the larger ones at the center and smaller ones toward the perimeter of the building.

283   The vegetated roof creates a varied, living landscape far more appealing than a ballast roof. It also absorbs water rather than channeling it to the existing storm water system.

284   285   286   287   288   289

290   291   292   293   294   295

296   297   298   299   300   301

302   303   304   305   306   307

308   309   310   311   312   313

314   315   316   317   318   319

320   321   322   323   324   325

Milstein Hall

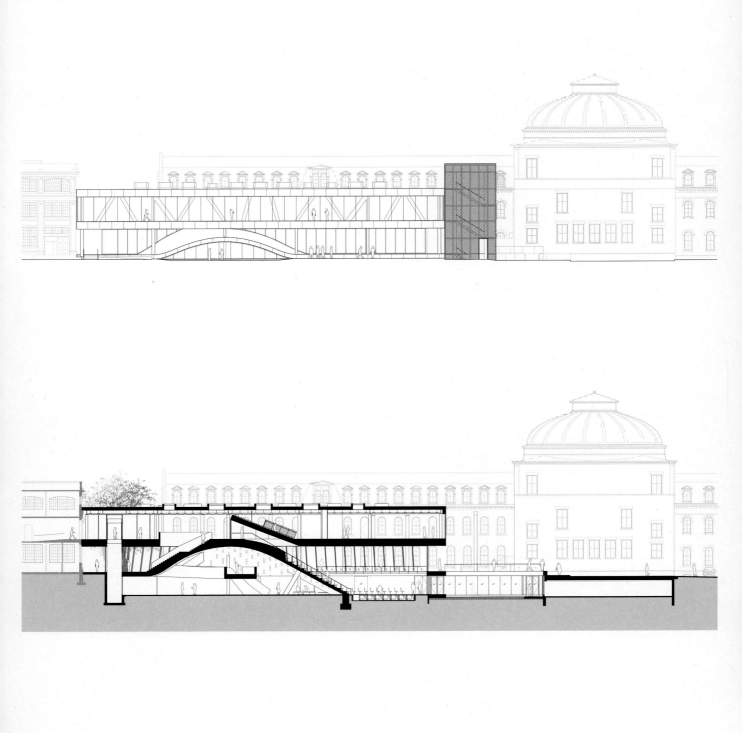

Milstein Hall

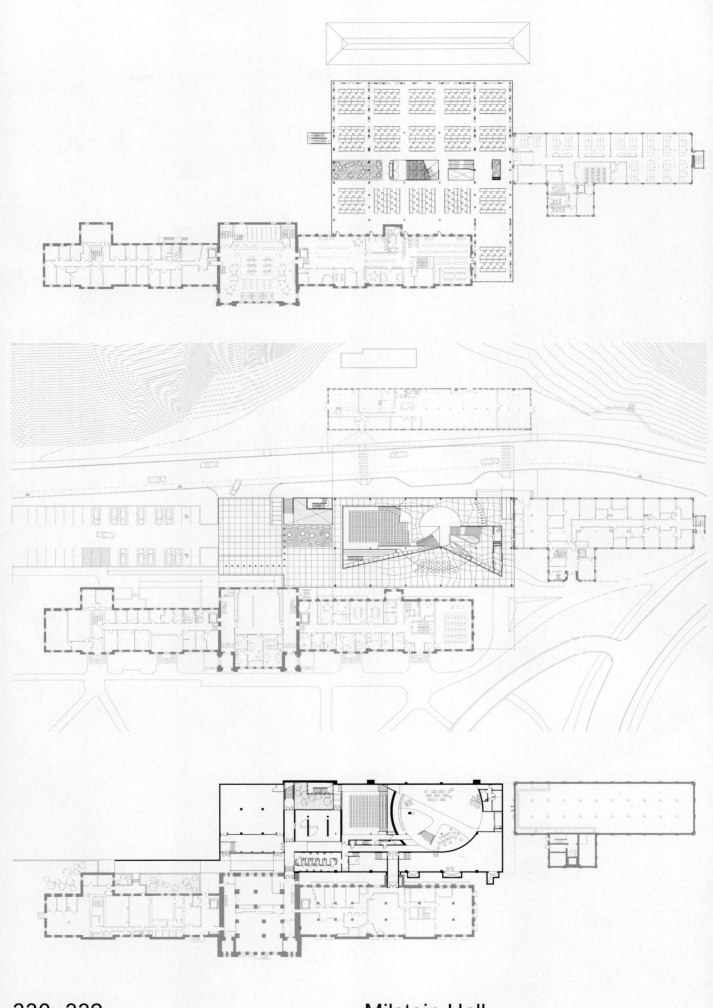

Milstein Hall

Audrey Irmas Pavilion

Audrey Irmas Pavilion

We have been trying to build in Los Angeles for more than a decade and the Audrey Irmas Pavilion for the Wilshire Boulevard Temple marks our first cultural building in the city. It is also our first religious institution. Religious institutions have always played a critical role in civic life as places for communal activities in and out of worship. The temple's vision for its campus was to create a space to host the multiple ways in which people convene. How can the new pavilion harness the energy of gathering that is simultaneously respectful to historic traditions and reflective of modern civic needs?

The pavilion is designed to be a machine for gathering, forging new connections with the existing campus activities and inviting the urban realm in to create a new civic anchor. We wanted the building to be iconic enough to be recognized as a new civic entity but subtle enough to complement the iconicism of the existing temple. Our approach is simple yet contextual. The starting point was a box: the all-too-generic model for an event space. The basic box is shaped with forms out of respect to the adjacent historical buildings on the campus.

On the west side, the building slopes away from the existing temple, creating a thoughtful buffer and framing a new courtyard between the two buildings. The pavilion leans south, away from the historic school, opening an existing courtyard to the sky and bringing light in. The parallelogram simultaneously reaches out toward the main urban corridor, Wilshire Boulevard, to establish a new urban presence. The resulting form is carved by its relationship to its neighbors. It is both enigmatic and familiar, creating a counterpoint to the temple that is at once deferential and forward-looking.

The facade draws from the geometries of the temple's dome interior. A single hexagon unit with a rectangular window is rotated to reflect the program within and aggregated to create a distinct pattern. The panels enhance the building's volumetric character while adding a human-scaled texture that breaks down its mass.

Event spaces often sacrifice character for flexibility. Here, flexibility is provided through diversity in scale and spatial characters for gathering. The pavilion consists of three distinct gathering spaces expressed as voids punctured through the building—a main event space (large), a chapel and terrace (medium), and a sunken garden (small). The three spaces are interlocked and stacked one atop another to establish vantage points in and out of each space. Within each space are a series of openings that filter light and frame views to the temple and historic school, reorienting visitors to the complex and beyond.

At the ground level, the main event space echoes the temple dome by lowering the arc and extruding it north across the site to connect Wilshire Boulevard to the school courtyard. In its full length, the vaulted, column-free expanse has the capacity to host diverse programs such as banquets, markets, conventions, performances, and art events. An oculus provides a view through the void above to the dome of the historic temple.

On the second level is a more intimate chapel and outdoor terrace. The trapezoidal room and terrace face west, framing the arched stained glass windows of the historic temple. A third void is a sunken garden that connects smaller meeting rooms on the third floor to the rooftop event space with expansive views of Los Angeles, the Hollywood sign, and the mountains to the north. Together, the voids establish a diverse collection of spaces for multiple purposes—from sermons and studies, to b'nai and b'not mitzvah and concerts, to work and relaxation.

Due to the 2020 Covid-19 pandemic, the opening of the building has been delayed and the crisis has suspended the very act of congregating. Can the pavilion reassure the value of gathering, and even support the changing notion of gathering?

Location	Los Angeles, CA, USA		
Status	Completed, 2021		
Typology	Institution		
Program	Event Space	13,900 ft²	1,300 m²
	Chapel/Terrace	10,200 ft²	940 m²
	Office	6,600 ft²	610 m²
	Sunken Garden	1,000 ft²	100 m²
	Roof Terrace	7,300 ft²	680 m²
	Service/Back-of-House	15,600 ft²	1,440 m²
	Total Area	54,600 ft²	5,070 m²

Audrey Irmas Pavilion

Audrey Irmas Pavilion

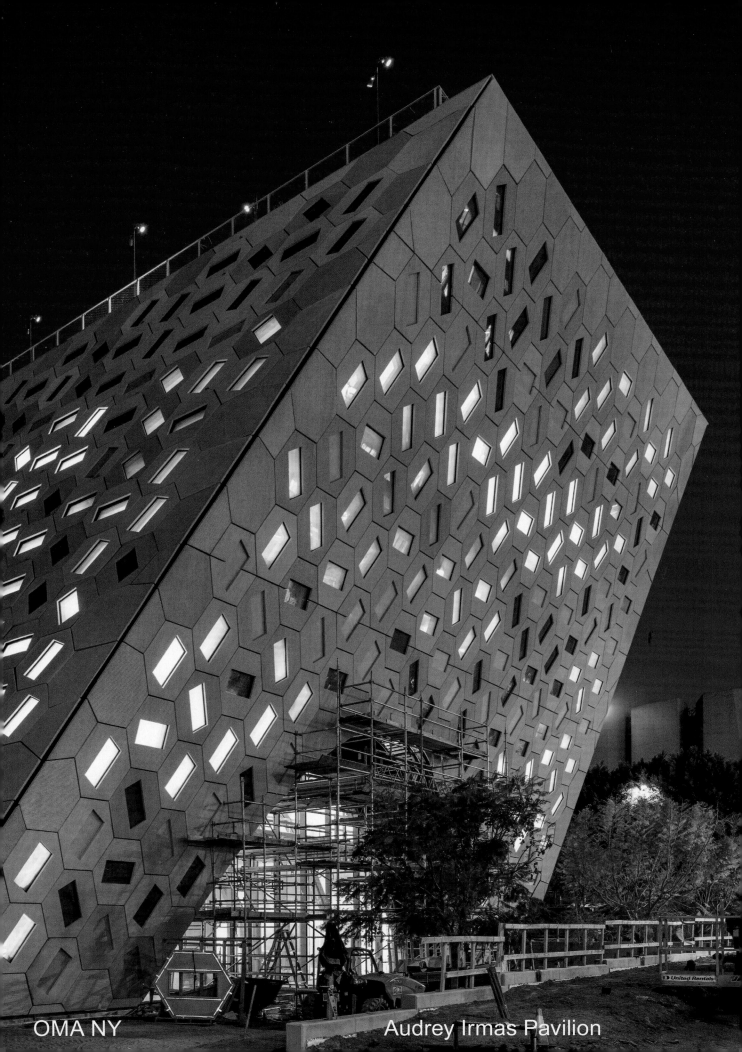

OMA NY

Audrey Irmas Pavilion

Audrey Irmas Pavilion

OMA NY

Audrey Irmas Pavilion

Audrey Irmas Pavilion

OMA NY

Audrey Irmas Pavilion

Audrey Irmas Pavilion

339 Founded in 1862, Wilshire Boulevard Temple is the oldest Jewish congregation in Los Angeles, California, and was the city's first synagogue.

340 "Wilshire Boulevard Temple is more than a synagogue. It is a place of worship that also offers its members a place of community and education." —Tony and Jeanne Pritzker

341 The domed structure is inspired by the great cathedrals of Europe and combines elements of Byzantine and Romanesque styles. Its interior is patterned after the pantheon in Rome.

342 View from Harvard Boulevard

343 View of temple from the corner of Wilshire Boulevard and Harvard Boulevard

344 Located on the corner of Wilshire and Harvard, the Audrey Irmas Pavilion enables the campus to establish a new aura and scale of receptivity to the city around it.

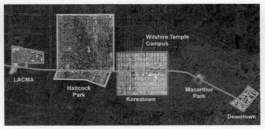

345 Site context—Wilshire Boulevard Campus lies on a main axis that runs through major civic, cultural, and public domains of Los Angeles.

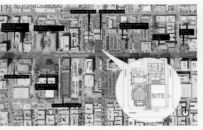

346 Facing Wilshire Boulevard, the addition to the campus is a rare opportunity to establish a new face for the temple on an active thoroughfare.

347 Existing spaces at the temple were limiting and unable to accommodate the desired scale and diversity of programs. Conference rooms were bleak and uninspiring and gathering spaces were too small to accommodate the large congregation.

348 Mass gathering in K-town—World Cup celebration on Wilshire Boulevard.

349 Can the site be a new gathering place for the neighborhood?

350 Precedents of admired spaces— after discussions with the temple on the types of desired spaces, we researched a number of admired spaces that were both beautiful and inspiring but also practical.

351 The new gathering place has a responsibility to the rest of the complex to act, together with the sanctuary, as a new center for the temple.

352 The Wilshire Boulevard Temple site is located on the dividing line between a residential neighborhood to the north and civic/commercial areas to the south. This positions the addition to become both civic and intimate.

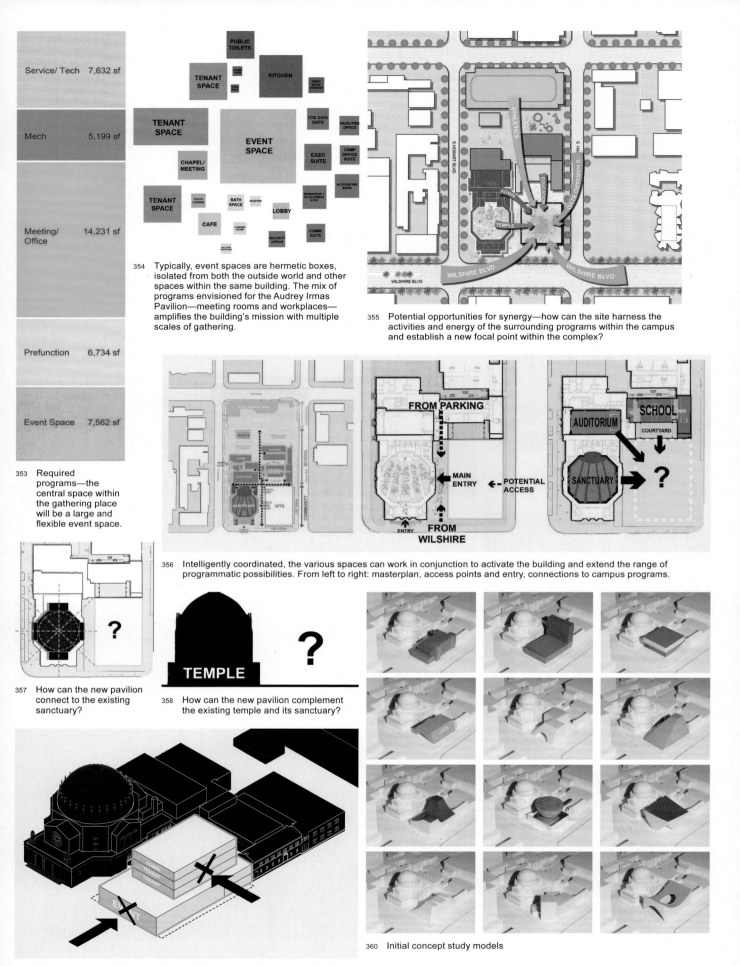

Service/ Tech   7,632 sf

Mech   5,199 sf

Meeting/ Office   14,231 sf

Prefunction   6,734 sf

Event Space   7,562 sf

353   Required programs—the central space within the gathering place will be a large and flexible event space.

354   Typically, event spaces are hermetic boxes, isolated from both the outside world and other spaces within the same building. The mix of programs envisioned for the Audrey Irmas Pavilion—meeting rooms and workplaces—amplifies the building's mission with multiple scales of gathering.

355   Potential opportunities for synergy—how can the site harness the activities and energy of the surrounding programs within the campus and establish a new focal point within the complex?

356   Intelligently coordinated, the various spaces can work in conjunction to activate the building and extend the range of programmatic possibilities. From left to right: masterplan, access points and entry, connections to campus programs.

357   How can the new pavilion connect to the existing sanctuary?

358   How can the new pavilion complement the existing temple and its sanctuary?

359   How can we establish a level of porosity that connects the new pavilion both visually and physically to the existing campus?

360   Initial concept study models

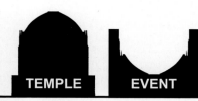

362　Temple dome versus inverted arch

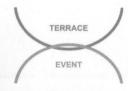

363　Intersection of two arch programs

361　An earlier scheme that was explored during the concept phase was "parting the sea," where the levels above the event space are cleft into two blocks to create an inverted arch.

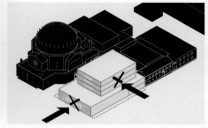

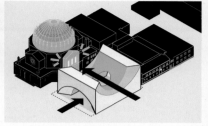

364　Two extruded arches are carved out of a single volume. The terrace arch above establishes visual connections to the Temple's arches while the event arch below establishes a physical connection to the existing school.

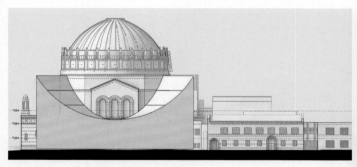

365　Elevation view of the Parting scheme

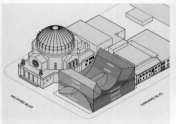

366　At the intersection of the two program arches, a skylight frames a view of the temple's dome.

367　Program diagram

368　The inverted arch would simultaneously frame the upper arches and dome of the temple and create a dramatic outdoor space for the pavilion.

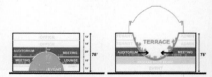

369　Program section—program bands are stacked vertically. The arch event space connects to the first three levels while the terrace connects to the top floors.

370　Terrace view

371　The form creates a visible open space for gathering directly from Wilshire Boulevard.

372　Terrace arch facade study

374　While the inverted arch of the Parting scheme clearly addressed the historic temple, it disconnected the upper level programs. The goal for the final concept was to reconnect the building's top floor to create a programmatic loop that envelops the new terrace in active spaces.

373　Aerial view

361–374　　　　　　　　　　　　　　　Audrey Irmas Pavilion

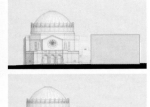
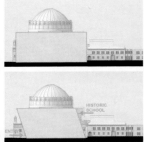

375 For the final scheme, the pavilion massing is an expression of respect, responding to the significance of the existing temple and historic school.

376 The building slopes away from the temple, deferring to the campus's primary center and allowing light to enter the courtyard between the two buildings.

377 View from Wilshire Boulevard and South Harvard Boulevard (1:64 scale model)

378 View from South Harvard Boulevard (1:64 scale model)

379 From Harvard Boulevard, the new massing shifts away from the historic school to open up to the sky and bring light into the school's existing courtyard.

380 Aerial view of Audrey Irmas Pavilion and Ashley Glazer Family Campus

381 While the northern facade of the building leans away from the school, its southern facade angles toward Wilshire, creating a small covered plaza in front of the building.

382 Respecting the Temple, the height of the pavilion does not exceed that of the dome, preserving views to the Temple dome while creating a usable roof.

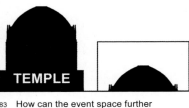

383 How can the event space further complement the existing sanctuary? How can the new building draw visual connections to the existing temple while creating a new identity?

384 Arch precedents, from left to right: Union Station Wedding Venue, Hollywood Bowl, Second Street Tunnel Fashion Show

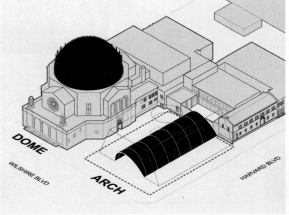

385 By lowering the arch of the Temple's dome and extruding it north across the site, a vaulted space is created. It clearly addresses Wilshire Boulevard, while connecting Wilshire to the existing school's courtyard to create a thoroughfare of events and activities.

386 Extruded arch space—Étienne-Louis Boullée, Bibliothéque du Roi (1785)

387 This thoroughfare establishes a seamless transition from the interior environment to the exterior, taking advantage of the climate in Los Angeles to create a vibrant space for gathering.

Audrey Irmas Pavilion

388 Rendered view from Wilshire Boulevard

390 The pavilion also provides meeting rooms of various sizes in proportion to the sizes of the three event spaces. They are organized by size from large to small as one moves up the pavilion.

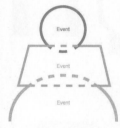

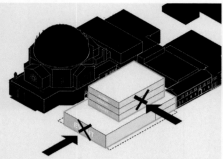

389 Three event spaces are carved out of the pavilion's monolithic volume and iconic moments of the temple, such as its dome and arched windows, are framed while views across the site are preserved.

391 Three distinct views, from top to bottom: view to the hills from the roof, view toward the temple from F2, view and invitation to the city

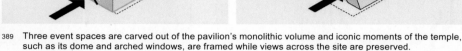

392 Elevation view looking toward the temple

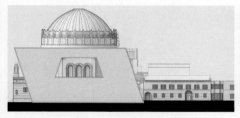

393 View of the temple's arched windows from the F2 event space

394 Through the introduction of multiple voids within the volume, a series of interconnected event spaces are formed: a large arched event space, a medium-sized chapel and outdoor terrace, and a formal and intimate sunken garden.

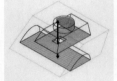

395 The main arched event space is located on the ground floor. On F2 there is a medium-sized chapel space with an outdoor terrace. A sunken garden on F3 connects up to the landscaped roof terrace.

396 Concept model—void negatives as three formally distinct gathering spaces

397 Each of the three distinct spaces will have different material characters.

398 Three interconnected event spaces with views from one space to another

399 The diverse spaces for gathering can be separate or connected to accommodate a range of events. From left to right: four events, three events, two events, one event.

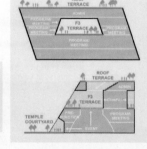

400 Every interior event space has a corresponding exterior courtyard or terrace.

401 Section view cutting through the main event space, F2 chapel, and F3 sunken garden

402 Section view cutting through the lobby, main event space, F2 chapel lobby, and F3 meeting rooms

388–402   Audrey Irmas Pavilion

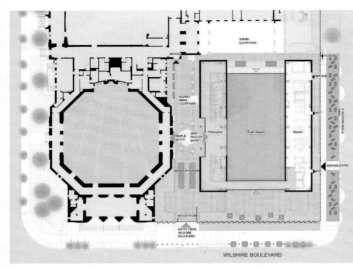

403 Around the pavilion are three courtyards—Audrey Irmas, Wilshire, and Siegel. The Audrey Irmas Courtyard is a key connective space between the main entry to the pavilion and the temple.

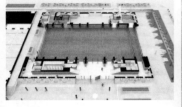

405 Rendered plan—F1

406 View of Siegel Courtyard open to the event space

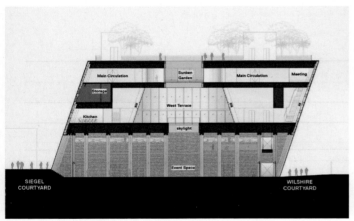

410 Long section through F1 event space

412 View of Audrey Irmas Courtyard

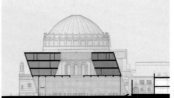 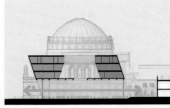

404 The main event space extends across the entire ground level, out into the courtyard facing Wilshire Boulevard but also to that of the school.

407 At the south end of the site adjacent to Wilshire Boulevard, the Wilshire Courtyard becomes an extension of the pavilion's event space and an asset for the community. Lush plantings, a sculpture garden, and shade provided by the pavilion's canted facade provide an oasis along the busy road.

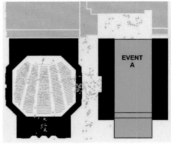 

408 The Wilshire Courtyard becomes an extension of the event space.

409 Removing the Seigel Courtyard's southern wall integrates the two spaces and allows the event space to spill out into the courtyard.

411 Section diagrams—from left to right: north–south section, east-west section, east–west section.

413 The main pavilion entry is located directly across from the temple's east entry, allowing for a seamless transition from the sanctuary to the new main event space.

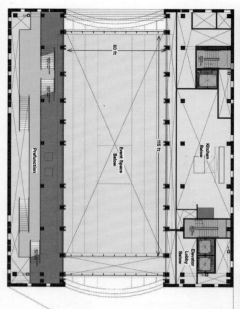

414　F1 Plan

416　The wall, arches, and coffers are made of book-matched sassandra veneer.

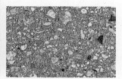

415　The main event space is long and expansive, figuratively extending to the temple to create both programmatic and visual connections. The column-free space can host a wide variety of events, ranging from lectures to banquets to exhibitions and conventions.

417　The floor is red terrazzo to create a consistent tonality within the space.

418　Event space construction, 2021

419　Event scenarios—clockwise from top left: banquet, wedding, lecture, film screening

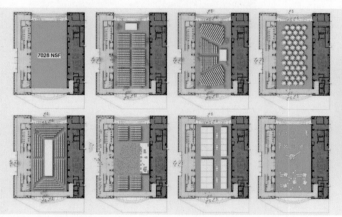

420　Event configurations

421　Conventional theater boxes

422　Theater boxes as coffers

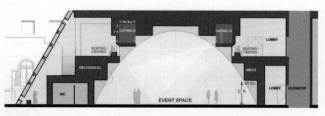

425　Built-in benches and windows on the third tier of the event space allow for viewing opportunities into the main event hall.

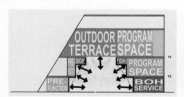

423　Activated arch—on the upper levels, the event space is surrounded by and engaged with meeting rooms and balconies.

424　Windows within the arches that support the event space and the floors above create a series of interactive coffers.

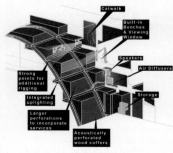

426　Mechanical, audio, and lighting are built into the wooden coffers.

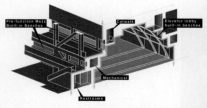

427　Prefunction mezzanine with integrated benches and viewpoints into the central event space

428　At the apex of the event space, an oculus brings light into the space from above and provides a view through the upper terrace to the dome of the historic temple.

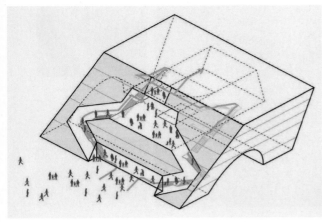

429 Circulation strategy through three event spaces—a grand stair facing the temple extends up from the courtyard and leads visitors to the upper-level balconies and meeting spaces around and above the event space.

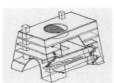

430 Circulation study— ramped theater boxes

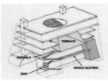

431 Circulation study— programmed platforms

432 Circulation study— objects on path

433 Informal vs. formal circulation—while two cores on the east side of the building provide service access and egress, the building's primary circulation is created by a series of grand stairs that face the temple on the west side.

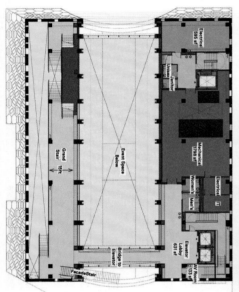

437 Stacked program volumes surround the event spaces. On the two lower levels, prefunction, service, and meeting spaces wrap the event-space arch, acting both as a mediator between interior and exterior and as a mezzanine with views into the activities of the main event space.

434 Circulation concept sketch—program loop

435 Circulation concept sketch—program section

436 Circulation paths

438 Across all three levels, the pavilion's public circulation has a unified material palette to aid with wayfinding.

439 Reference—Chand Baori stepwell in Rajasthan, India (c.800–1800)

440 The prefunction space and mezzanine double as circulation.

441 From the western prefunction mezzanine, a continuous stair along the south facade leads visitors up to F2 and F3.

442 Central circulation from lobby to prefunction and mezzanine

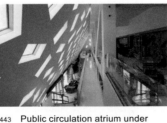

443 Public circulation atrium under construction, December 2020

444 Grand stair

445 F2 elevator lobby

446 Section model

447 The circulation originates from the west entry and is carried through the prefunction mezzanines, which are programmed with informal meeting spaces and built-in seating. The mezzanine offers views down to the main event space and out to the campus and city through unique facade windows.

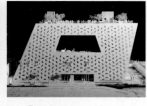

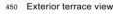

448 F2 contains an exterior terrace facing west toward the temple. The terrace is surrounded on three sides by program spaces—to the east the chapel, to the south additional smaller meeting spaces, and to the north, administrative offices that have access to the outdoor terrace.

449 Chapel view

450 Exterior terrace view

452 The chapel ceiling is green expanded metal mesh.

453 Glazing is green SEFAR glass—laminated mesh.

451 Chapel and terrace event scenarios, from left to right: presentation (168 seats), banquet (184 seats), presentation and banquet (256 seats), lecture (313 seats).

454 The floor is precast green paver.

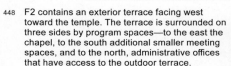

455 On F2, an outdoor terrace acts as a prefunction space for the entire floor.

456 The chapel and east and west terraces form the trapezoidal void on the second level that frames a view of the distinctive triple arched windows of the temple's east facade. The walls of the chapel open up to the exterior terrace to create a continuous indoor-to-outdoor volume.

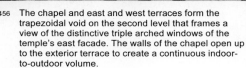

457 F2 terrace construction, February 2021

458 Conference room construction, 2021

459 F2 lobby

460 F2 lobby

461 The chapel has views to the outdoor terrace and Harvard Boulevard.

462 The outdoor terrace physically connects the chapel and meeting spaces and visually connects to the event space below.

463 The exterior terrace is covered, but the building's slope brings more light to the space and opens it up to views of the city, the temple, and the sky above.

464 Light is filtered through the terrace to the main event space below via the skylight that connects the event space and west terrace.

465 F2 meeting room

466 F2 boardroom

467 The F2 conference room maintains visual connections to both the covered terrace and the chapel.

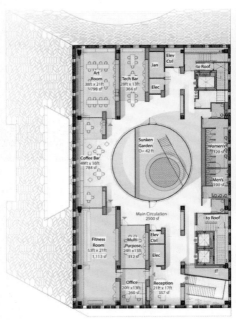

469 The F3 corridor doubles as a lounge/reception space.

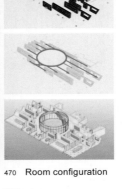

470 Room configuration

468 F3 contains various programs, to be occupied by the Annenberg Foundation, that are centered around a central sunken garden.

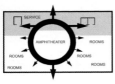

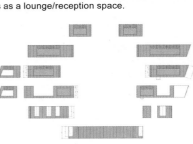

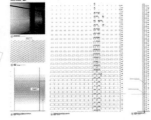

471 All spaces on F3 are accessible from the main circulation loop. That loop connects to both north and south public stairs, passenger elevators, and service elevator.

472 Interior elevations of F3 walls and millwork

473 The glass walls act as privacy screens with frit patterns that resonate with the geometry of the building.

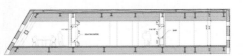

474 Art room and tech bar section

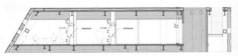

475 Fitness and multi-purpose rooms section

476 Solid walls running north–south define the spaces on F3. The walls provide a kit of parts, including a built-in credenza and storage space.

477 Fitness room

478 The spaces throughout F3 carry blue accents to match the tone of the sunken garden.

479 F3 sunken garden view, February 2021

480 The sunken garden is defined by its blue glazing.

481 The floor is blue concrete.

482 F3 coffee bar

483 Construction view, February 2021

484 Bathroom view with facade window and interior tiles emulating the pattern of the exterior facade

485 View into the sunken garden from the corridor

486 The sunken garden is visible upon arrival on the third level and can be accessed from the main circulation space as well as the roof terrace above.

468–486

Audrey Irmas Pavilion

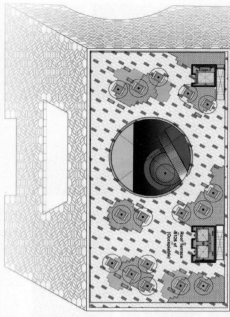

487 Roof plan—an exterior staircase extends from F3 to the roof.

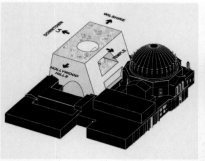

488 The roof provides panoramic views out to downtown Los Angeles, the Hollywood Hills, Wilshire Boulevard, and the adjacent temple dome.

490 Concept sketch—F3 and roofscape integration

489 Rendered perspective roof plan

491 Sunken garden accessible from F3 and the roof

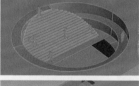
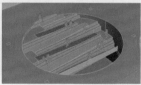

492 Roof access ramp studies—clockwise from top left: ramp inside circle opening (1¾ turns), ramp outside circle opening (1¼ turns), ramp integrated with seating, ramp folded along Harvard facade.

493 Sunken garden stair studies

494 The void seen from the roof garden creates dynamic views of the temple's dome, down to the F3 activities, the F2 terrace, and into the main event space.

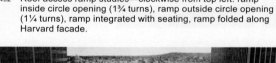

496 Sunken garden shading studies

497 Sunken garden under construction, February 2021

495 The exterior sunken garden acts as a focal point, providing a vertical visual and spatial connection down, in contrast to the horizontally expansive roof terrace.

498 Elevators provide direct access from the ground floor to the roof.

499 The roof garden can be used as informal breakout space for the entire pavilion.

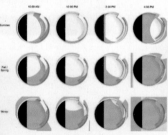

500 The roof garden becomes an elevated park within the neighborhood.

502 Found patterns throughout the Wilshire Boulevard Temple campus were used as reference.

501 The facade of the pavilion is formed of a field of hexagonal panels that subtly reference the signature pattern of the octagons found on the ceiling of the historic sanctuary.

503 Octagonal panels of the sanctuary dome

504 Wilshire Boulevard Temple sanctuary oculus

505 Facade studies

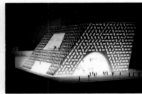

506 The hexagonal pattern frames and accentuates the sloped openings of the building, highlighting primary spaces while providing light and air to the smaller spaces around them.

507 The panels add a more human scale to the building.

508 The overall facade also acts as a screen that, when internally lit, creates a lantern-like glowing effect.

509 The structure is comprised of a single geometric unit, and rotating the standard hexagonal panel creates a dynamic texture across the overall facade.

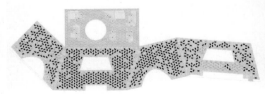

510 Unrolled facade

511 Because of the hexagonal geometry, there are no readily apparent vertical lines in the facade, creating an overall impression that emphasizes the volumetric character of the building.

501–511

Audrey Irmas Pavilion

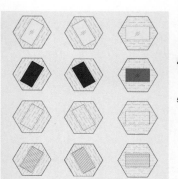

514 The tonality and materiality of the GFRC facade resonates with the tones and textures of the temple and the rest of the campus.

513 Window types, from top row to bottom row: clear vision glass window, shadow box, glass fiber reinforced concrete (GFRC) infill, mechanical louver

512 The facade is grouped in unitized panels following the hexagon geometry. A panel has 3 by 3–foot hexagons and is approximately 14 feet by 14 feet from floor to floor.

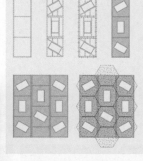

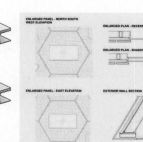

518 Installation method

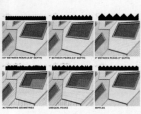

515 The facade unit is composed of 3-inch GFRC panels with inset windows, attached to prefabricated panels that are mounted onto the building slab.

516 Panels are suspended from floor edges and consist of precast thermal installation and waterproofing, pre-installed within each integrated sandwich panel.

517 The regular rectangular shape of the window openings can host clear windows, shadow boxes, or louvers, as required by program.

519 The panels' ridged surface affects the tone depending on their rotation.

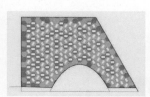

520 Three rotation directions establish three panel types.

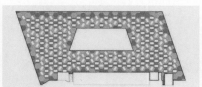

521 Facade panel rotation directions— blue: horizontal; pink: -60 degrees; green: +60 degrees.

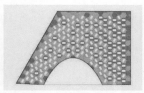

522 The three panel types are spread evenly across the facade.

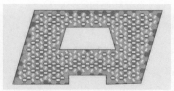

523 Over-aggregation of a single tone is avoided, while a dynamic facade is created.

525 View from Wilshire Boulevard

524 Joining options for facade edge

526 The pavilion's windows are reflected onto the face of the temple.

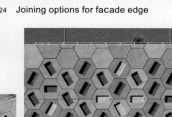

527 In certain lighting conditions, the panels appear more similar in tone.

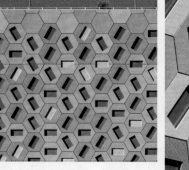

528 Throughout the day, the three angles of rotation utilize the ridged surfaces to create varying tones on the facade.

512–528   Audrey Irmas Pavilion

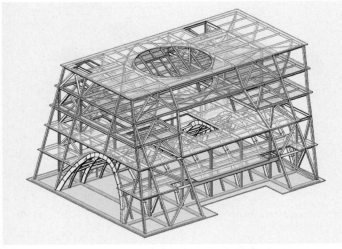

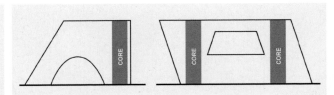

529 The building has a footprint of approximately 160 feet by 120 feet and is five stories tall, with a typical story height of 14 feet. The unconventional shape is supported by a structure that is both simple and conventional, with a series of columns organized on an approximately 30-by-30-foot grid.

530 Two cores located along the vertical east wall provide access and egress from two points in the building.

531 Structure section—a 70 foot-long plate girder spans the width of the event space

532 Site photo, July 2019

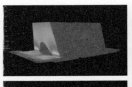

533 The building envelope incorporates passive solar design principles in order to reduce heating and cooling loads as much as possible.

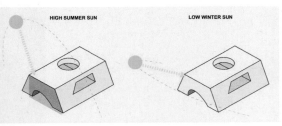

534 The slanted southern facade combined with the inset glazed curtain wall is designed to self-shade the windows to limit unwanted solar heat gains from the summer sun high in the sky. Meanwhile, the envelope will allow the lower winter sun to penetrate beneath the overhang, benefiting the space through reduced heating requirements.

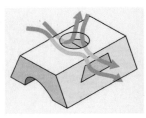

535 The building's F2 and F3 levels will benefit from natural ventilation through programmatic openings, providing occupant comfort while reducing energy use.

536 Panel installation, July 2020

538 Panel installation, October 2020

539 Panel installation, February 2021

537 Facade construction, September 2020

540 Construction timelapse, December 2018–March 2021

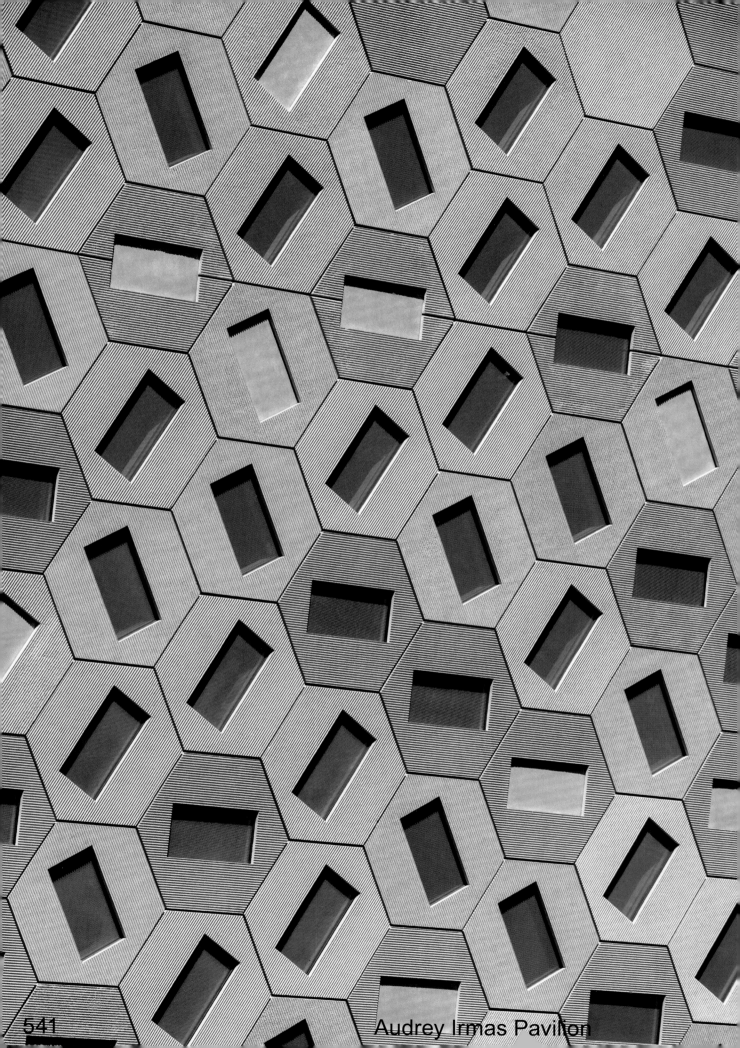

Audrey Irmas Pavilion

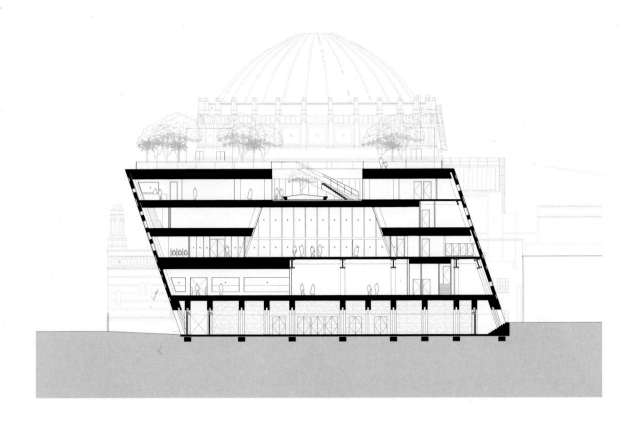

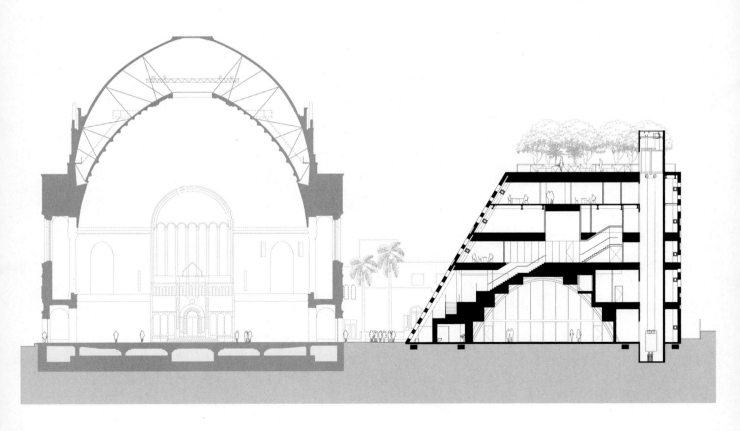

Audrey Irmas Pavilion

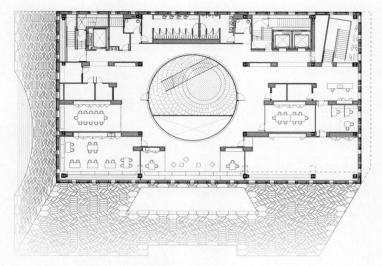

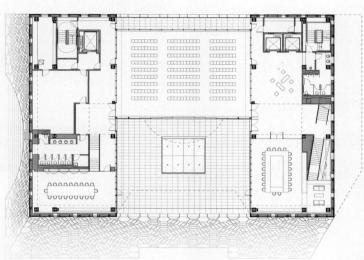

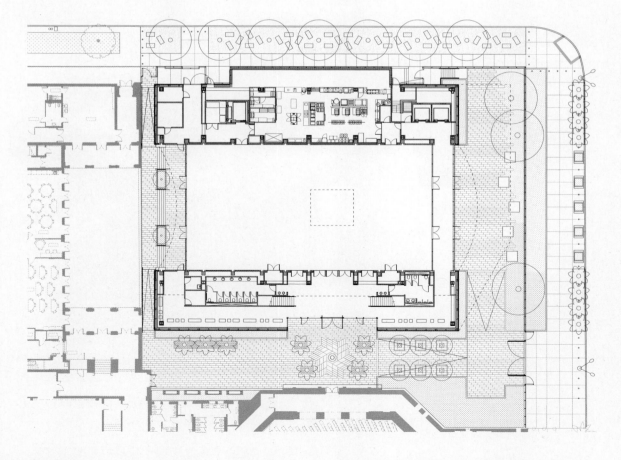

544–546

Audrey Irmas Pavilion

UIC Center for the Arts

UIC Center for the Arts

The UIC Center for the Arts (the Center) is our first performing arts center. We were faced with an interesting challenge to merge a concert hall and theater, both typically highly controlled and concealed boxes, with a public university, whose mission is to create radical openness and extreme accessibility. Can we turn the performing arts center inside-out, creating a building that communicates performance making?

The campus is located at a junction of three major neighborhoods: the cultural center of the Loop; Greektown, a tech and live/work center; and University Village, a research center. The existing campus designed by Walter A. Netsch (SOM) was built around a Central Forum. Its inward-facing, closed-off concrete deck was later demolished to open up the center of the campus. The resulting porosity to the surrounding neighborhood conveyed the start of UIC's ambition to integrate the campus into the city and provide a connected network for its students and the public.

The site for the Center is a vacant lot (currently used for events) located outside Netsch's original radial organization, on the northeast corner of the campus with immediate adjacency to the city. We were inspired by the site's potential to create a new connector between the city and campus that could foster a dialogue between performance and the public, which aligned with the institution's desire to create a receptor to the increasingly diverse student population within and outside of the College of Architecture, Design, and the Arts (CADA), as well as Chicago's communities.

Our approach was to create a building that communicates the Center's wide range of activities out to its surrounding neighborhoods. The Center is anchored by two towers—a student tower that faces the campus and opens to a performance park, and a public tower that looks to the cityscape and opens to a screening plaza. Large ramps flow from the street into the building, connecting outdoor and indoor performance spaces, including the concert hall and the main stage theater (Phase 2). Production spaces and back-of-house facilities line Harrison Street on the ground floor, rendering the activities of performance production and CADA's core programs visible to pedestrians on the street.

In response to UIC's fundraising and development planning, we conceived a unique flexibility for phasing. The 500-seat concert hall is sandwiched by the two towers that house rehearsal spaces, exhibition spaces, and foyers. Together they make up Phase 1, which can function on its own with crucial programs while awaiting further phases.

The concert hall establishes flexibility with vineyard-style seating surrounding the stage, composed of a series of rotated squares. The resulting layout defines spaces that accommodate different scales of performance, from intimate solo recitals to a grand symphony. A black box theater can be deployed within the shell of the concert hall, efficiently merging the two crucial types of venue and alleviating the need for a theater prior to Phase 2. In Phase 2, the main theater is added on the eastern edge of the site, with additional production shops and an elevated roof deck that connects to the public tower. The theater's operable doors allow performance to spill out toward the city and surrounding landscape.

A translucent veil stretched between the two towers creates an interstitial space around the concert hall. This improvisational space is a platform for a variety of gatherings—from impromptu performances, class sessions, and exhibitions, to public events—catalyzing interdisciplinary activities within CADA and beyond. By making the life within visible to the outside, the Center communicates its openness and establishes a welcoming environment—one that symbolizes the Center as a connector between UIC and the greater community.

Location	Chicago, IL, USA		
Status	2019–Ongoing		
Typology	Institution		
Program	Concert Hall	24,000 ft²	2,230 m²
	Theater	16,400 ft²	1,520 m²
	Rehearsal Studios	15,000 ft²	1,400 m²
	Production Shops	11,000 ft²	1,020 m²
	Lobbies/Gallery/Cafe	18,600 ft²	1,730 m²
	Admin/Support	3,000 ft²	280 m²
	Total Area	88,000 ft²	8,180 m²

548

UIC Center for the Arts

UIC Center for the Arts

UIC Center for the Arts

551   Chicago, Illinois, is one of the largest metropolises in the Midwestern United States and is the country's third-largest city.

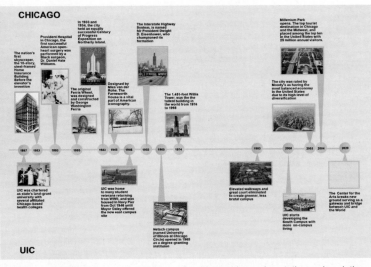

552   The city of Chicago has a long history of architectural experimentation and evolution.

553   The World's Columbian Exposition was held in Chicago in 1893 and had a profound effect on architecture, the arts, and Chicago's self-image, especially after the Great Chicago Fire of 1871 that destroyed much of the city.

554   The layout of the exposition was designed, in part, by Daniel Burnham, Frederick Law Olmsted, John Wellborn Root, and Charles B. Atwood.

555   The city itself was developed along the Lake Michigan waterfront.

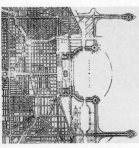

556   The 1909 Burnham Plan of Chicago, Daniel Burnham and Edward H. Bennett

557   Sky Ride, Chicago World's Fair (1933)—the Century of Progress Exposition also took place in Chicago.

558   Chicago was an experimental ground for modern architecture in the 1960s. Mies van der Rohe heavily influenced the city's architecture when he developed his modern style of using glass and steel, like the S.R. Crown Hall for IIT College of Architecture.

559   Frank Lloyd Wright Home and Studio, Oak Park—Chicago was also the city where Frank Lloyd Wright began his career.

560   Bertrand Goldberg, Marina City (1967)

561   SOM, Willis Tower (1973)

562   Millennium Park (2004)

563   Chicago is also home to the Chicago Bulls, with Michael Jordan playing fifteen seasons and winning six championships.

564   Music and the performing arts have a long history in the city of Chicago. In the 1920s, a distinctive Chicago Jazz style evolved from the migration of Black musicians from Southern cities, specifically New Orleans.

565   Chicago is the birthplace of experimental storefront theater and modern improvisational theater.

566   Home to more than 200 small theater companies, the city is a destination for touring productions and is one of the major theater capitals of the United States.

567   At the center of Millennium Park is the Jay Pritzker Pavilion designed by Frank Gehry. The outdoor venue is home to the Grant Park Symphony Orchestra and Chorus and the Grant Park Music Festival and also hosts a diverse range of outdoor concerts and public activities.

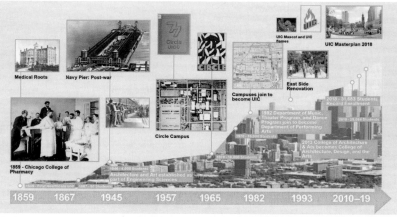

568 The University of Illinois at Chicago (UIC) is the city's largest institution for higher learning and ranks among the top Research One (R1) universities.

570 A precursor to UIC, the Chicago Undergraduate Division, later the University of Illinois at Navy Pier, was founded by the State of Illinois in 1946 to educate GIs returning from World War II, demonstrating the need for a large public university in the city.

569 The private Chicago College of Pharmacy (1859), College of Physicians and Surgeons (1882), and Columbian College of Dentistry (1891) affiliated with the University of Illinois in 1913 and merged with the University of Illinois at Congress Circle in 1982 to become today's University of Illinois at Chicago.

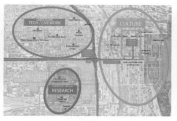

571 Mayor Richard J. Daley with supporters of the Harrison-Halsted Campus—the university's mission has always been to provide a first-class education as a public good.

572 Michael D. Amiridis, UIC chancellor—UIC's location is in and of the city of Chicago.

573 UIC sits at the intersection of three major neighborhoods in the city: the cultural center of the Loop, tech and live/work-centered Greektown, and research-centered University Village, home to UIC.

574 The existing university campus was designed by Walter A. Netsch of SOM.

575 Netsch's concentric campus plan created a center with a fortress-like condition surrounding it. The site lies outside the radial organization, abutting the city.

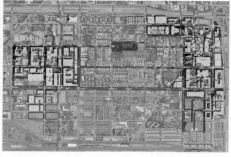

576 Netsch's original plan for Congress Circle centered the campus around a Great Court, Central Forum, and a series of raised walkways that were closed off and inward-facing.

577 In 1993, the large concrete deck was replaced with a grassy plaza that opened up the center of campus and established porosity to the surrounding neighborhood.

578 In 2018, a new masterplan was proposed to create a connected network of all-season, sustainable open spaces that knit the campus together.

579 This masterplan has allowed the campus to grow in parallel with record-breaking student enrollment in recent years. The new center will combine art, education, and public activities to accommodate students as well as the general public.

580 Within UIC, the College of Architecture, Design, and the Arts (CADA) is a multidisciplinary institution combining creative and technical curriculums. Many of its classes and musical ensembles are filled by non-CADA majors, serving the broader student population of the university. The current campus lacks a centralized space dedicated to CADA.

581 The university currently does not have a dedicated concert hall. UIC ensembles perform in various venues throughout Chicago—clockwise from top left: Benito Juarez High School, Notre Dame de Chicago, Lecture Center Quad, Studebaker Theater.

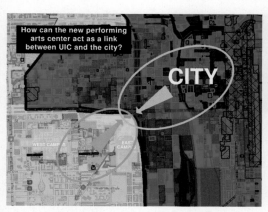

How can the new performing arts center act as a link between UIC and the city?

CITY

582 UIC resolved to create a new Center for the Arts to act as a gateway between the university and the world. The site for the performing arts center would be located at a critical junction between the city and the campus.

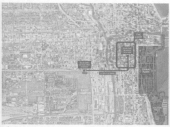

583 The Blue Line and UIC Halsted Station is conveniently located in front of the site and connects to the Loop, Chicago's main cultural and commercial core, in six minutes.

584 Contrasted against the high-rise skyline of the nearby Chicago Loop, the UIC campus remains dominated by mid- and low-rise architecture.

585 Harrison Field, the site for CADA's new Center for the Arts, is adjacent to downtown Chicago with a spectacular view of the skyline.

586 With Chicago's skyline in the background, the grassy lawn is well used for public events, like the annual Spark in the Park.

587 The site's selection as the location for the finalist UIC Obama Library proposal in 2015 underscores its urban significance.

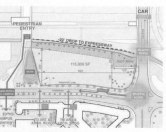

588 Site plan with critical adjacencies—pedestrian passages via the Peoria Street Overpass and the pass-through to the art and architecture building; traffic noise; car and bus transit.

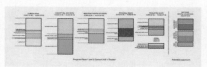

589 Program requirements

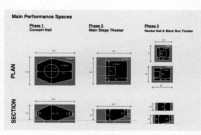

592 Ideal dimensions of the major performance spaces

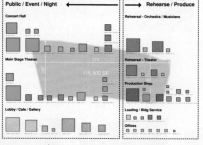

590 As a public urban hub for performance gathering, the project required an 88,000-square-foot building with a 500-seat concert hall and 270-seat theater, as well as rehearsal halls, production shops, supporting facilities, lounge, cafe, and exhibition space.

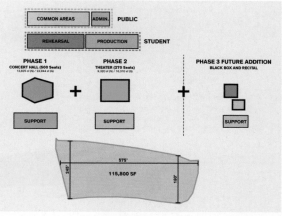

591 The broader programs for the new performing arts center include a concert hall in Phase 1, a theater in Phase 2, and a black box and recital hall in Phase 3.

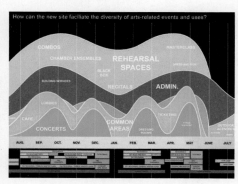

593 Throughout the year, the programmatic requirements of the Center for the Arts will wax and wane, demonstrating a need for a high degree of flexibility that can accommodate maximum occupancy during large-scale events as well as casual, daily use.

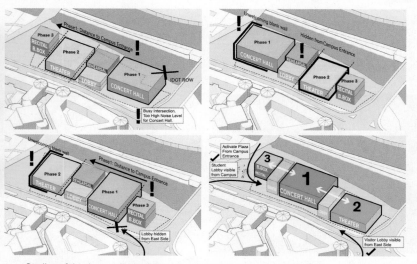

594 Studies of the three main performance spaces, their required adjacencies, and site access. Due to budget constraints, the final design would need to support phased construction, affecting the complexity of the venues' placement on the site.

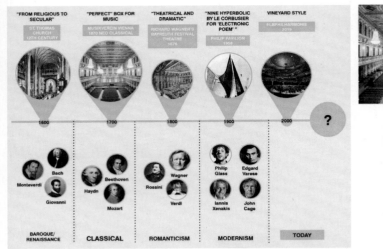

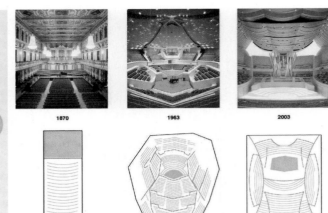

595   In designing Phase 1 for the Center for the Arts—a 500-seat concert hall— we first examined the changing history of the venue. Each major movement in Western architecture has offered an evolution on the concert hall, from the religious architecture of the Baroque to contemporary vineyard-style halls.

596   The classical shoebox-style hall, often called a "perfect box for music," places the performers at one end of a rectangular volume, while the more modern vineyard-style arrangement places them in a sunken center area with the audience seated on stepped platforms on all sides. The contemporary vineyard 2.0 marries the vineyard's audience-performer relationship with the shoebox's stellar acoustics.

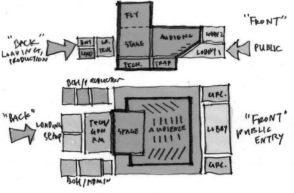

597   A typical theater building has a distinct front and back, with lobby and public circulation stacked with the front entrance and back-of-house equipment, loading, storage, and practice spaces stacked behind the stage.

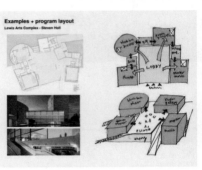

598   Recent campus arts centers provide alternative models. Steven Holl's Lewis Arts Complex features a large central lobby and plaza encircled by performance spaces.

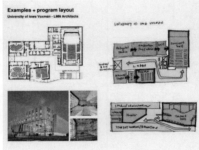

599   LMN's Voxman Center threads the lobby around and underneath the theaters.

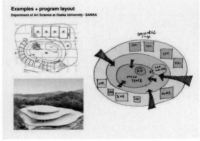

600   SANAA's Osaka University Department of Arts and Science radially surrounds a central theater with lobby and back-of-house spaces.

601   The site designated for the future UIC Center for the Arts is generous compared with the footprints of many notable theaters and recent campus performing arts centers. From left to right: University of Iowa Voxman (Iowa, USA), Alice Tully Hall (New York, USA), Princeton Lewis Arts Complex (New Jersey, USA), Osaka University Department of Arts and Science (Osaka, Japan).

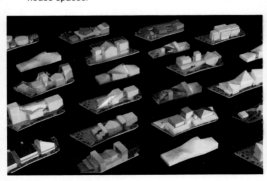

602   Concept model army

603   Various studies were developed to explore the relationships between key programs, the connectivity of those programs to the city, and the optimization of a phased construction schedule.

605 Historic proposal for Chicago's multi-level streets

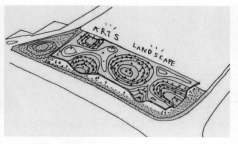

606 Plinth as arts landscape

604 An initial study, the Plinth, placed student back-of-house programs along the I-290 highway and public programs along Harrison Street.

607 Plinth concept collage à la Superstudio

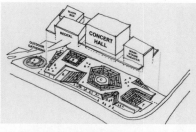

608 Programs embedded within the Plinth create a landscape of activities.

609 Programs are organized horizontally, creating a new type of campus landscape in the style of Netsch's Central Forum.

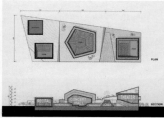

610 Plinth study plan and section

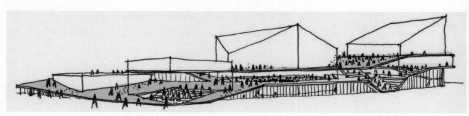

611 A continuous public platform, the Plinth steps up toward downtown to create higher vantage points. However, the expansive exterior space would be unusable half the year in Chicago's extreme winters.

612 Plinth study aerial view

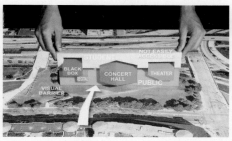

613 Another study, the Wall, stacked public and student back-of-house spaces into a slim vertical structure to maximize efficiency.

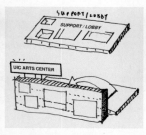

614 Wall study concept sketch, à la Robert Venturi and Denise Scott Brown, resembles a billboard.

615 Wall concept collage à la Nam June Paik

616 Wall study concept collage

617 CADA activities are broadcast to the city.

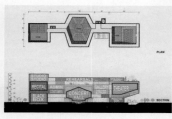

618 Wall—plan and section

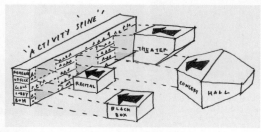

619 Programs are plugged into a vertical activity spine.

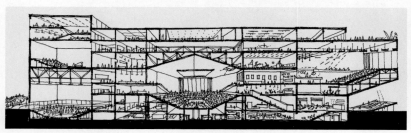

620 Wall study section sketch

621 The Wall literally broadcast the activities of the center out to the city, but also created a lack of porosity between the city and campus.

622 For the final scheme, spaces for students and the public are split into two towers, creating porous north-south connections between the city and the campus.

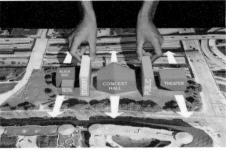

623 The towers are flanked by the three performance spaces, which allows them to delineate the distinct venues and efficiently serve both sides.

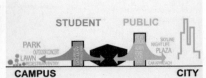

624 The two vertical towers act as piers in a bridge connecting the campus and the city.

625 Broadcasting towers

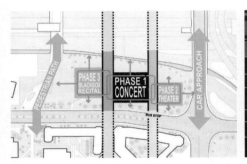

626 Surrounding these "bars" of common space, the placement of the center's major program elements reacts to the two main approaches: a campus and student approach from the west, and a city/public approach from the east.

627 The towers' directionality extends Chicago's street grid into the campus, increasing connectivity between the university and the surrounding neighborhood.

628 The site and the towers' directionality resonate with the many bridges found throughout Chicago, knitting various areas and communities.

629 Chicago River bridges (1939)

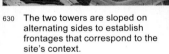

630 The two towers are sloped on alternating sides to establish frontages that correspond to the site's context.

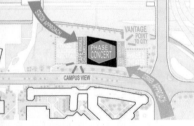

631 The sloping towers create opposing peaks. The Public Tower peak establishes views toward the city and the Student Tower peak looks out onto the campus.

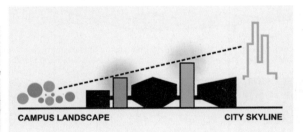

632 The two towers provide a tiered transition between the low campus landscape and the elevated city skyline.

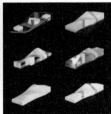

633 Study models for the final two-tower scheme with early envelope studies.

634 At the intersection of Harrison and Halsted, an entry is defined at the Public Tower and activity within is immediately visible.

635 Aerial view of two towers and Concert Hall

UIC Center for the Arts

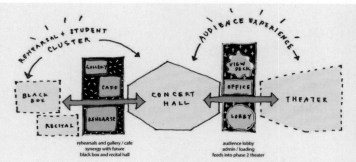

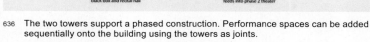

rehearsals and gallery / cafe
synergy with future
black box and recital hall

audience lobby
admin / loading
feeds into phase 2 theater

638   Spacecraft

637   Club sandwich

639   Kebab

636   The two towers support a phased construction. Performance spaces can be added sequentially onto the building using the towers as joints.

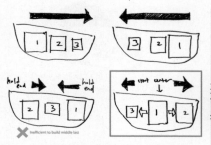

640   Tests showed that it would be inefficient to build the center last, so the phasing sequence would begin at the center, then continue to east and west.

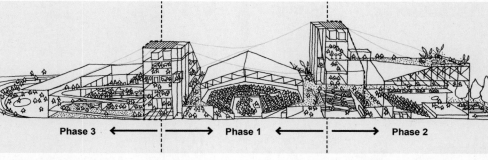

641   Phase 1 consists of the Concert Hall and towers, Phase 2 adds on the Theater, and Phase 3 finishes the complex with the Black Box and Rehearsal Studios.

PHASE 1

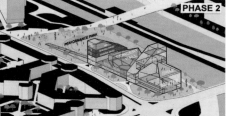

PHASE 2

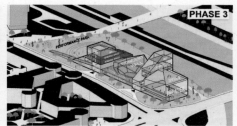

PHASE 3

642   Phase 1 leaves two open spaces on the east and west of the site. By developing the site's eastern portion with the Theater in Phase 2, a strong presence can be established along the primary approach that most visitors will take to campus.

643   In Phase 1, the rest of the site is used as a new park and plaza.

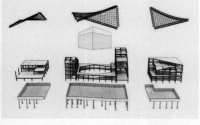

644   Each phase is its own discrete structure, allowing each performance space to be acoustically separated from the rest.

645   The structural independence of each component allows for phasing flexibility.

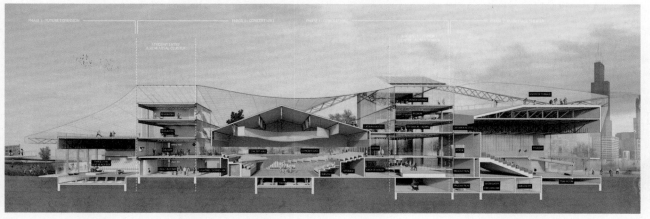

646   Perspective section—all phases complete

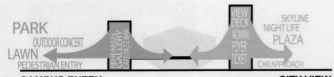

647 The first phase includes the Concert Hall as well as the student back-of-house and public tower. The Student Tower sits next to an outdoor concert area and primary pedestrian paths, while the Public Tower sits adjacent to an urban plaza and car approach.

648 Chicago Skyway Bridge

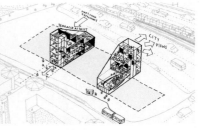

649 The Student Tower slopes away from the expressway and the Public Tower rises up toward the city.

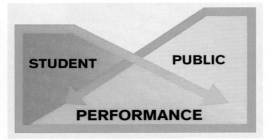

650 Together with the three performance spaces, the two towers create an infinite loop of activity within the Center for the Arts.

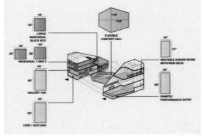

651 Phase 1 programs

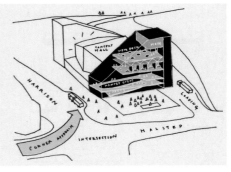

652 The Public Tower is located off of Halsted Street.

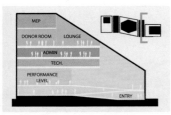

653 The tower contains a lobby entry, administrative/tech spaces, and an upper level donor room/lounge.

654 Public Tower user group—concertgoers

655 Public Tower user group—administrators and donors

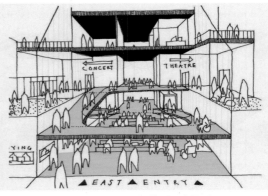

656 The ground level of the Public Tower features a grand lobby defined by a curving ramp that delivers the audience to the Concert Hall and Theater on the second level.

657 The lobby and ramp establish extreme accessibility to key arts programs and public areas. The ramped lobby is an additional flexible performance and rehearsal space.

658 Lobby as an intimate venue for small-scale performances

659 Lobby as a grand gathering space and waiting area

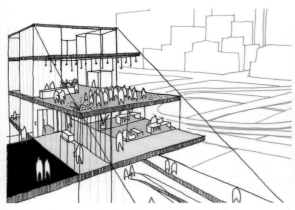

660 The donor room boasts a view of the Chicago skyline.

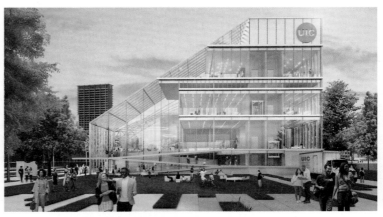

661 Public Tower from Halsted Street

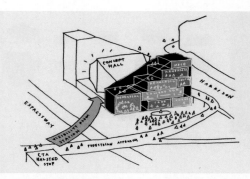

662 The Student Tower is visible and easily accessible from the CTA Halsted Station.

663 During the day, the Cafe/Jazz Bar at the base of the Student Tower attracts students and pedestrians.

664 Gallery 400 provides necessary exhibition space on campus.

665 Gallery 400 is relocated into the Student Tower from across I-290.

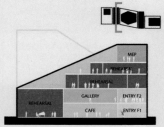

667 Program section

668 User group— student musicians

669 User group— art and architecture students

670 The Student Tower contains multiple rehearsal spaces, galleries, and a cafe.

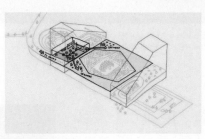

666 Gallery 400 spills out onto F2 around the Concert Hall.

671 A long, sweeping ramp brings pedestrians from the CTA station to the Student Tower.

672 A secondary ramp leads from the campus to the Student Tower.

673 By placing the student production spaces at ground level, the full activity of CADA's core curriculum is made visible to pedestrians on the street.

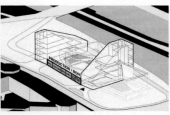

674 Back-of-house—costume, set design, prop studios, and storage form the base between the towers.

675 User group—theater crews, costume designers

676 The Student Tower contains a large rehearsal space that can be used before the Black Box and Rehearsal Studios are constructed in Phase 3.

677 Evening view

678 Student Tower and outdoor amphitheater plaza from Peoria Street Overpass

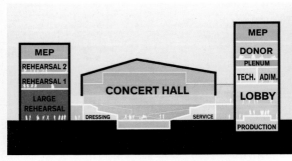

679 The two towers will be built at the same time as the Concert Hall, which lies between the Student and Public Towers.

680 There has been a growing trend toward vineyard-style concert halls. Clockwise from top left: Berliner Philharmonie, Berlin, Germany; Walt Disney Concert Hall, Los Angeles, California; Philharmonie de Paris, Paris, France; DR Koncerthuset, Copenhagen, Denmark.

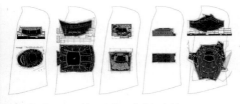

681 Scale comparison—from left to right: Stanford University Bing Concert Hall, Walt Disney Concert Hall, New World Center Miami, Wiener Musikverein, Berliner Philharmonie.

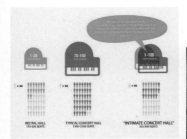

682 How can a single space support a range of scales to accommodate a large performance but not feel empty for a small one?

683 An intimate space is created at the center.

684 By rotating it, multiple scales of space can be established.

685 The result is a dynamic layer of small to extra-large spaces.

686 Concert Hall model

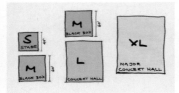

687 CADA-required performance scales of spaces ranging from an intimate solo stage to a grand concert hall.

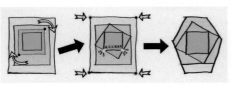

688 Like a Russian nesting doll, a series of squares are rotated to allow for entryways and access.

689 Terraced seating wraps around a central stage. The vineyard-style hall is optimized for acoustics and views.

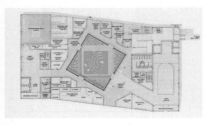

690 Plan—L1

691 Plan—L2

692 Concert Hall with full orchestra and audience

693 The volume of the Concert Hall is bisected horizontally and a glazed window wraps the space, opening the hall up to the public area that surrounds it. The slit establishes views down into the performance space and creates views out from the central stage.

694 Vertical surfaces can be deployed to provide area for projections.

695 At full capacity, the Concert Hall feels both full and intimate.

696 A black box theater configuration is provided within the shell of the Concert Hall, alleviating the need prior to Phase 3.

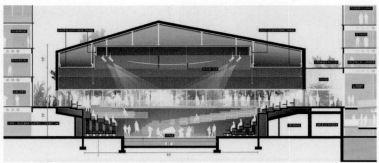

698 The interior of the Concert Hall has been shaped to maximize sound reverberation and reflection.

699 The shell has been placed on sound isolators for optimal acoustic performance.

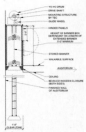

700 Draperies and acoustic panels are stored above and deployed.

697 Elements such as draperies, acoustic panels, and removable seats facilitate flexibility within the Concert Hall venue.

701 XL—orchestral or other full house with perimeter acoustic curtains (535 seats)

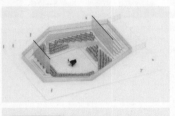

702 L—chamber or recital with rollup acoustic banners that double as projection surfaces (420 seats)

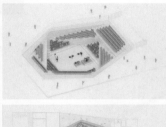

703 M—rehearsal/open concerts or classes (200 seats or optional)

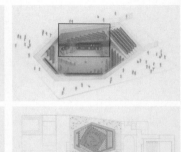

704 S—black box configuration with rollup acoustic banners

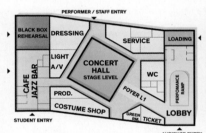

705 At ground level, the Concert Hall is surrounded by shops, dressing rooms, and service spaces, with student and audience entries in the Student and Public Towers.

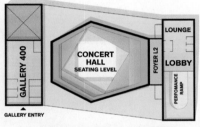

706 The ramp leads visitors up to the F2 lounge and lobby and a secondary foyer connects to upper-level seating within the Concert Hall.

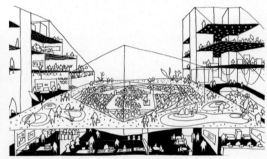

707 The Concert Hall is a central space that connects the various activities of the two towers flanking it.

708 Phase 1 elevation—two towers and Concert Hall

709 By providing multiple accessible routes into and around the Concert Hall, radical accessibility is at the core of the design.

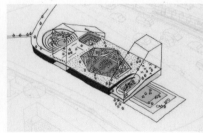

710 Axon sketch

711 After the completion of Phase 1, the open sites flanking the Concert Hall can be used as exterior performance plazas for the campus and the city.

712 Phase 1 build-out creates a park stage and a city stage on the two ends of the site, maintaining use of the site for outdoor performances and doubling the potential for simultaneous concerts.

713 The three volumes are connected by a singular roofscape that stretches between the two towers.

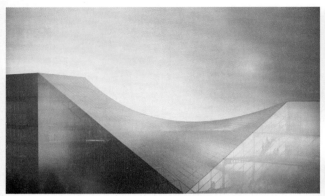

714 For the facade, we proposed an envelope that would introduce a softness not yet found on UIC's campus.

715 Like a veil, the facade is stretched over the building blocks of the arts center.

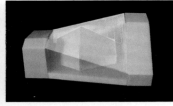

716 The expressive roof encloses the interstitial space between the towers and Concert Hall.

717 From left to right: rectangular site extrusion, dividing the block with North-South Bars, pushing bars down to address southeast and northwest approach, final form with two peaks

718 Conducting movements

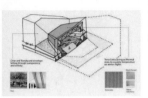

722 Materiality sketch

719 The roof defines a semi-conditioned space that can be enjoyed throughout Chicago's cold season.

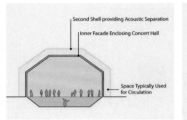

720 A typical concert hall has a double shell composed of an inner facade enclosure in an outer shell for acoustic separation.

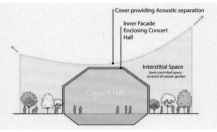

721 Performance embedded in nature—the cover providing acoustic separation is expanded, creating a new, semi-controlled interstitial space.

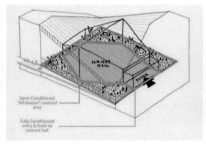

723 The all-season garden and the Concert Hall provide both semi-conditioned and conditioned spaces.

724 The garden provides a landscaped common space with views into the Concert Hall.

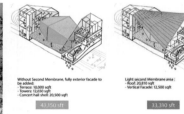

725 By enclosing this all-season area, the amount of total facade to be added is actually less than if these volumes were considered separately.

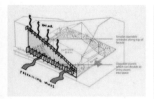

726 Operable panels open to allow natural ventilation during the summer and close to retain warmth during the winter.

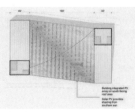

727 Roof plan

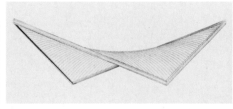

728 The double-ruled surface of the hyperbolic paraboloid allows for easy, efficient construction.

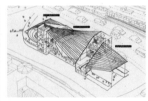

729 In the later phases, the envelope can be further "stretched" across new additions.

730 Phase 1 from the Peoria Street Overpass

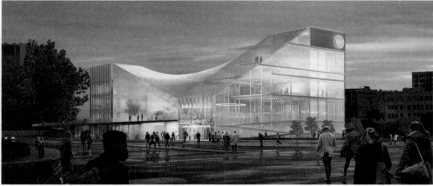

731 Phase 1 from Harrison and Halsted, with envelope

714–731   UIC Center for the Arts

734 Phonograph

732 The organization of programs also easily allows for expansion. Phase 2 includes the addition of a Theater on the eastern edge of the site, along with additional production shops and an elevated roof deck.

CAMPUS LANDSCAPE   CITY SKYLINE

733 The Theater takes advantage of its frontage toward the city and the skyline to create an open performance space that can directly engage the public.

735 Plan—L2 in Phase 2

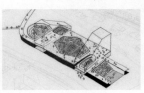

736 The Theater shares the existing Lobby from Phase 1 and is accessible from the same ramp.

737 The skin of the building extends to cover the Theater, creating an additional interstitial zone.

738 From black box to outdoor stage—an operable wall opens the Theater to the city.

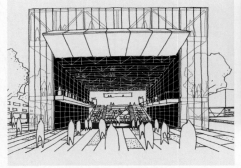

739 The operable door allows for performance to spill out toward the city and surrounding landscape, creating a literal connection between the city and the Theater.

740 Performance—closed configuration

741 Performance—open configuration

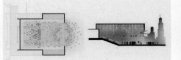

742 In warm weather, the Theater opens up for large gatherings and diverse performances that integrate UIC with the city.

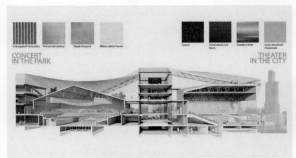

743 The color and materiality of the Theater complement the Concert Hall. The Concert Hall is warm and earthy, while the Theater is cool in tone to reflect the industrial nature of the catwalks and theater equipment.

744 Theater view from main approach from downtown Chicago at Halsted looking south.

745 View of Theater from Harrison and Halsted

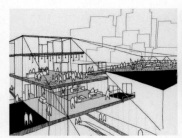

746 The addition of Phase 2 also creates a new roof deck on top of the Theater, connected to the donor room in the Public Tower.

747 The amount of usable donor space is expanded to the exterior and an additional "outdoor" all-season space is created.

748 Final Model—Phases 1 and 2

732–748   UIC Center for the Arts

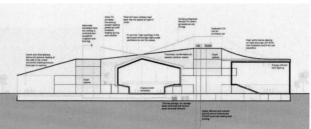

750 Phase 3 rehearsal space and black box studies

749 Phase 3 is the most open-ended, but the current programmatic needs call for rehearsal spaces and a Black Box theater for use by theater and music students.

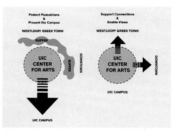

753 Energy-efficient strategies will be deployed in the Concert Hall to efficiently heat and cool the crowded space.

751 Unified under a sloping roof, the mix of rehearsal spaces is both intimate and collective, covered and exposed.

752 The Center for the Arts will be climate controlled through a mix of campus utilities and geothermal heating opportunities.

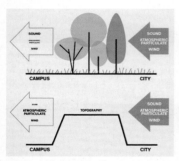

754 Radiant heating and cooling would keep public and rehearsal spaces comfortable, even with expansive glazing.

755 It was important to consider landscape as both a connector and a buffer for the campus.

756 The outdoor area facing West Loop and downtown could be landscaped to provide a buffer and support connections.

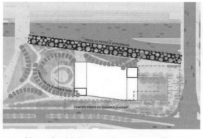

759 Landscape plan—Phase 1

757 The landscape strategy uses both planting and topography to create a buffer between I-290 and the UIC campus.

758 Along the highway edge, trees will serve as an air filter and windbreak. Landform will act as a natural buffer around the west amphitheater plaza. Canopy trees for summer shading will surround the east plaza and the southern edge of the site.

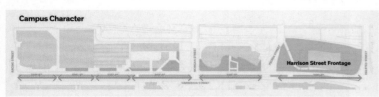

Campus Character

760 The landscape serves as a continuation of the UIC campus's Harrison Street frontage.

761 Landscaped view along the Harrison Street entry ramp to the Concert Hall

762 View of site from the Willis Tower Skydeck—the completed Center for the Arts will create a new arts landscape embedded in both nature and the city.

763 Aerial view of all three phases complete— the competition for the UIC Center for the Arts was a unique process that engaged stakeholders and the community from the start of the competition.

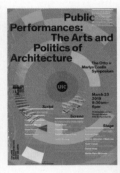

764 During the design competition, UIC held a public symposium with the shortlisted firms.

765 Throughout the selection process, the team participated in a series of public presentations in Chicago.

766 Transporting the final presentation model in Chicago

767 Unpacking models for final presentation

768 Setting up for the final presentation

769 Concept models on public view at the final presentation, April 2019

770 Model setup

771 Attendees inspecting the final model after the public presentation

772 Final model

773 Final model with projection

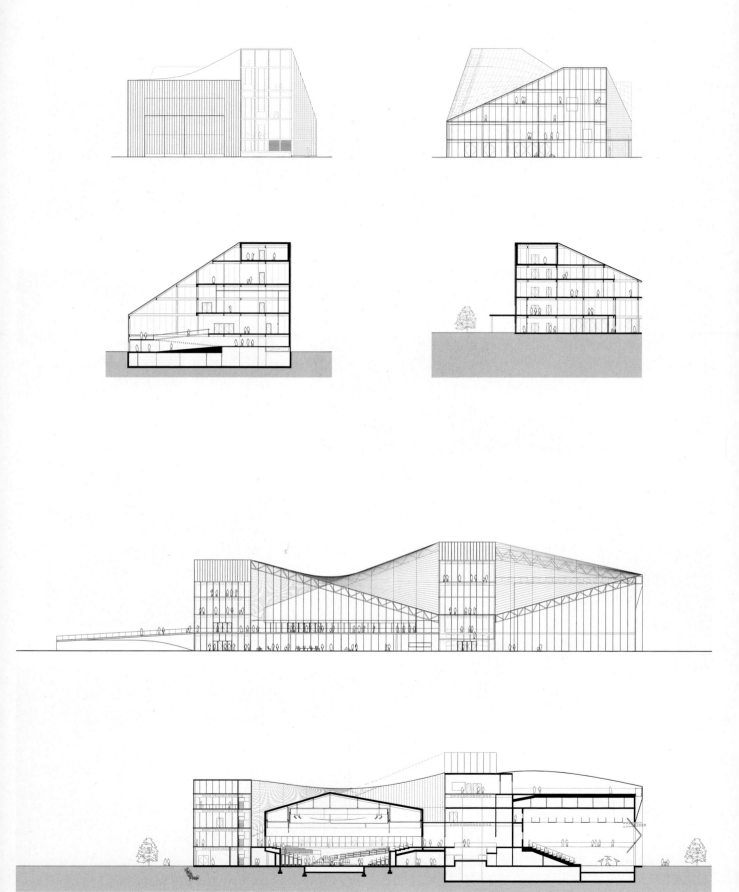

UIC Center for the Arts

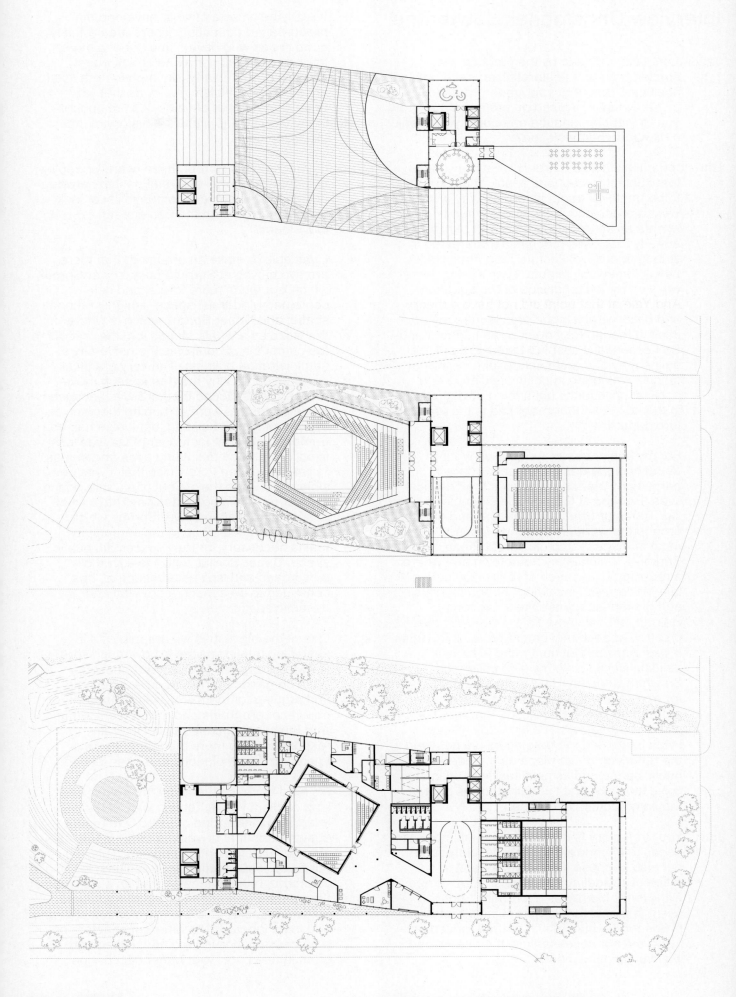

UIC Center for the Arts

Interview Christopher Hawthorne

Jason Long: I'm intrigued by the fact that you studied both architectural history and political science. I read that your undergraduate thesis actually focused on protest. What drew you to that combination and could you speak a bit about the thesis too?

Christopher Hawthorne: Largely what drew me to that subject matter was a lack of design skill, to be frank. Or to put it another way, I was very interested in architecture when I arrived at Yale as an undergraduate, but I knew already that I was much more interested in writing about architecture than practicing it. I think I knew my talents, such as they were, were on the editorial side of the equation. And Yale at that point did not have a theory and history track in the architecture major itself, although they do now, as I understand. So I essentially cobbled together a political philosophy and architecture joint degree by officially majoring in political science and political philosophy but finding advisors both in the poli-sci department and in the architecture department.

For my senior essay, I ended up writing about how the design of public spaces, particularly plazas, influences their political lives. I looked at the obvious examples, like Trafalgar Square in London, and others around the world. In the end I focused most of my research on Sproul Plaza at UC Berkeley, which is my hometown and where a redesign by a bunch of really fascinating late Modernists, including Vernon DeMars and the landscape architect Lawrence Halprin, almost immediately predated the first free speech movement protests in 1964. It was a space that continued to have a political life well into my own childhood. So when Berkeley High School students, for example, marched against apartheid, or for other political protests, that was the place in Berkeley that everybody went to. I was interested in the relationship between the remaking of the plaza as a modernist public space and its political life. And in some ways the work that I'm doing now is right at that intersection, of course.

JL: Your trajectory is interesting, I think, not just because anyone's biography is interesting, but also because it parallels a trend in our office of straddling disciplines. That started with Rem's history as a journalist, but you see it in many people here. I initially studied philosophy, which I think has influenced my work, but not necessarily in the one-to-one way you might expect.

CH: It really helps as a critic to have had that broad-based education. There are certainly good critics who have come out of a more traditional and constrained architectural education. But clearly, like architecture itself, architectural criticism demands that you draw on a number of fields. It's not enough, in my view, just to know the history of the discipline itself.

JL: In your study of Sproul Plaza, were you able to identify a one-to-one relationship between design moves and the compatibility or lack of compatibility with the free speech movement?

CH: I was able to make an argument that there are two halves of Sproul Plaza: Lower Sproul, which is a much more formal and self-contained Modernist space, a highly rational space; and Upper Sproul, which is where the plaza as a whole bleeds into the rest of the campus and confronts the university's administration building. The very practical explanation for why the free speech movement protests wound up there was because those protestors were arranging themselves at the foot of that building, but it also helped tremendously that the upper plaza was less fixed, more open to shifting uses and moods. I think the lesson I drew was that it was possible to squeeze the life out of a public space by over-determining its design. That's what continues to plague Lower Sproul, which does not open itself up to the serendipity that is necessary for truly successful public space. Upper Sproul, which is a kind of crossroads and isn't as prescriptive, has continued to be a much more vital and dynamic space.

JL: One of the big issues we grapple with in designing public spaces is how much specificity to introduce. The process of design often demands proposing novel elements and arguing for them—creating zones or objects or programs and giving them a name. And the client and the public naturally respond to fixity more than they respond to something ambiguous and open-ended.

CH: It's hard because the client, no matter what kind of client you're dealing with, is typically interested in that kind of fixity. One recent design trend that drives me crazy is the labeling of every element of a design. This is a particular issue in memorial designs, leading you through the stages of grief as it were. I remember as a critic writing about several 9/11 memorials, where every element of it had to be labeled. The different chapters of a procession through memorial space are often labeled now with rather saccharine capitalized titles, which I think is a sign of over-determination, particularly where emotion is concerned. But this is also true in more general public-space design. So I agree with you; there's all kinds of evidence that the open-ended serendipitous space, if well designed and if attractive enough, can be more truly public. But there is very much a trend, as you're suggesting, to have not just an emphasis on programming, but to have an overly close relationship between programming and fixed, physical sections of a public space. I think having some undefined or un-programmed spaces and really striking that balance is important and tends maybe not to be talked about enough.

JL: Maybe it also aligns with something you've said about cities like LA and Houston. You've pointed out that their vastness and lack of differentiation makes it hard for people and for critics to immediately get their heads around them. I think there is a parallel between that discomfort and some short-sighted decisions in the design of public space. It's easier to feel like you understand something when it is broken down into pieces and labeled.

CH: Yes, and to me this is a great strength of LA, and why I would argue that really understanding LA on its own terms requires more sophistication than reading or analyzing a more traditionally organized city. Particularly if you've been educated as I have in a Eurocentric tradition that privileges a certain kind of city and a certain kind of organization of civic space. Those expectations are really confounded by Los Angeles. Whereas if you understand Asian or Latin American cities, you tend to find Los Angeles more legible. It's really less a question of legibility or lack thereof, than the perspective from which one approaches LA. Being flummoxed by LA and its urbanism often reveals a kind of parochialism, a lack of exposure to cities globally that don't look like New York or Paris.

The larger question you ask is a really important one, which is how to preserve or embrace this quality of Los Angeles, which in some ways can be alienating in terms of the lack of fixity and the openness, and the lack of defined edges between—whether it's between neighborhoods or even between cities in LA County. There's a fluid nature to the urbanism here, which I think people who appreciate LA on its own terms really value. But it can sometimes be effectively tempered by spaces that are a little bit more precisely fixed that take you out of that fluid, undifferentiated landscape and at least for a time into someplace more contained. Striking that right balance is really the challenge of designers in LA for the next generation.

JL: Is there a difference in the way that public space operates in LA that's identifiable? What makes a public space in LA successful versus what might make public space successful somewhere else?

CH: LA has not produced enough particularly well-designed spaces. Largely because the ways in which we redesigned the city— around the car, freeway, and the single-family house during the middle of the twentieth century—were more wide ranging and aggressive than in other cities. We have a lot of work to undo those changes, and that work has all kinds of implications for public space.

For a long time, there were amenities, largely in private space, that were available to a wide cross-section of Angelenos and did help democratize the private realm to a certain degree. By which I mean as a middle-class family, and even for parts of the twentieth century as a working-class family, you could arrive in LA and buy into that idea of California, the LA dream, which would allow you to build the kind of open space in your own garden that you might have expected to find in a park of a more crowded city. Instead of building one big Central Park as New York did, we essentially built tens of thousands of miniature Central Parks in people's backyards.

It's crucial to note that access to that dream was first limited by race, then limited by supply as the city grew. We have a deficit of park space in Los Angeles. At the same time, we have a legacy from before mid-century of really successful public spaces and denser multifamily architecture, going back to the nineteenth century. Both in my writing and my work in the mayor's office I have tried to talk about and find ways to reconnect to that.

JL: Can you talk about your current role as LA's chief design officer—what the role entails and how it facilitates conversations between different communities and city agencies? It puts you at the intersection of a lot of things we just talked about—the fixity and specificity of public space as well as the complexity of public space in how it's intertwined with political, social, and economical structures.

CH: I was the architecture critic at the *Los Angeles Time*s for about fourteen years, from 2004 to early 2018. And in the last few years of that position I would say I was concentrating more and more on the city of Los Angeles itself—questions of urbanism as well as questions of architecture. Mayor Eric Garcetti decided early in 2018 that he wanted to create a new position called "chief design officer," which would coordinate our architecture and design initiatives across the city within a single office, and asked me if I would take it on. On the one hand it was a tough decision because being an architecture critic was the only job I'd really ever aspired to—and I felt really fortunate to have a full-time position as a critic in a city like Los Angeles, which to me remains the most compelling city in the United States to be writing about. On the other hand, it wasn't an especially tough decision to take this new job just because it seemed like such a fascinating challenge. And because of the way the mayor had framed the position, which was ambitious and wide-ranging. Los Angeles has been a terrific place for advancing individual ambitions, but we have struggled to advance a collective vision or set of visions about where the city itself should go. We have had relatively few institutions or platforms for talking about civic identity, particularly as it relates to architecture and urban design. The mayor created this position in part to address that. And so engagement in a variety of forms, helping frame questions about where Los Angeles is headed in terms of its built environment and civic identity, is a significant part of my work.

JL: And once you found yourself in this new position, how did you decide where to focus your efforts? The territory is incredibly vast, and I imagine that the myriad of different overlapping agencies in any city government could make it difficult to maneuver.

CH: It is a vast city and I did have a lot to learn. I still do! I think I was helped by having written about the city for as long as I have, particularly given the focus in my criticism on urbanism and on the ways in which Los Angeles was transforming itself. It did take some time and careful thinking to decide where to focus my time and energy. I have found two things to be particularly effective. One is looking for chances to work directly with individual city departments, which has resulted in some very specific initiatives. Then, at a much broader macro level, to step back and think about the larger questions related to civic identity that this job gives me a chance to put on the table for a civic discussion. I think that has particularly included the future of housing policy and our relationship to history in civic memory. In those two cases I've tried to think about initiatives in a broader, open-ended way.

JL: Watching the Black Lives Matter protests over the summer and also, in a more bucolic way, the introduction of restaurant sheds into streets across New York, I've been reminded that the street is, more than parks or plazas, our largest and maybe primary public space. But the things that define it are largely quotidian, from curbs to streetlights, and in general its design is driven by practicality. I was struck by the fact that several of the specific initiatives that you've launched directly engage with the street and those seemingly banal elements.

CH: It's really a combination of the banal and the transformative, or even the revolutionary, that you find along the street, particularly in Los Angeles. This line of thinking for me goes back to work I did as a critic. In some ways the most important single event that I covered was the immigration rights marches of 2006. There are remarkable photographs of those marches, which attracted hundreds of thousands of people, all wearing white, and went down Wilshire Boulevard and down Broadway in downtown. One part of the crowd then gathered at the foot of City Hall, where there is no traditional plaza. The marchers adapted amoeba-like to that lack of traditional space. We have, on one hand, a deficit of traditional open and public space, but an excess of street space, which we have largely over-determined as automotive space. The Black Lives Matter and other protests of 2020 have all demonstrated that this vast reservoir of really powerful public space is pre-made, as it were, ready-mixed, and just waiting to be redefined. It doesn't require anything more than human intervention or activation—only a crowd to decide that it wants to use that space in a different way. It's always an important lesson when a crowd instantly can give us a glimpse of another way of using the city or the streets.

JL: In addition to public space, one of the things I've been engaged with a lot lately is housing. Partly because of the economics and partly because of the kind of design that we do, we're typically being asked to design high-rises and often in dense urban centers or at their periphery. Now we are working on our first 100 percent affordable housing project in San Francisco, where there's much more of a debate or discussion about, or even outright hostility toward, density. How do you think LA is coping with the need for density or the need for housing in an environment that isn't known for high-rises?

CH: The crisis in housing in LA is due in large part due to the fact that we stopped building enough housing in the 1980s and we under-built housing across the 1990s and beyond. It's only been the last five years or so that we've begun to address the deficit, and there have been other factors that have really exacerbated the crisis.

It's important to say that just in terms of scale and housing typology we need a broad-based series of changes and reforms to tackle this crisis. The mayor has really supported the production of accessory dwelling units, or ADUs, and now ADUs make up a solid 20 percent of our housing production every year. On the other end of the spectrum, we've seen a really strong number of affordable units produced in large or multifamily buildings near transit thanks to our Transit Oriented Communities initiative. In a larger sense, there has been for more than a generation a sort of gentleman's agreement, a policy bargain, that housing production would be confined to these two ends of the spectrum: incremental change in low-rise neighborhoods and more intense development along transit corridors. We haven't really had a debate about any more significant changes to low-rise neighborhoods, and indeed there has been very little political incentive for elected officials to put the question of single-family or low-rise neighborhoods on the agenda.

The opposition to change in those neighborhoods is quite diverse. It does come, to a certain degree, from wealthy homeowners in the hills. But it also comes from communities of color who have legitimate and well-founded concerns about what any changes to zoning or land use policy in their neighborhoods would mean, especially in terms of opening up the floodgates to speculative investment, displacement, and so forth. So to make broader progress on the housing in LA is going to require putting those low-rise neighborhoods on the agenda but in a way that fully addresses those concerns. Despite the rhetoric in so much of the press coverage—and I was probably guilty of some of this myself as a critic—of deep polarization between Yimbys (or housing advocates) on one end of the spectrum and Nimbys (or housing opponents) on the other, we find that most people are somewhere in the middle. As they learn more about redlining and histories of racial exclusion and racist lending practices, and as they understand the urgency of addressing climate change and building new housing closer to jobs and transit, there is a growing consensus that this land-use pattern that we spent the twentieth century developing in Los Angeles is simply not a sustainable one for contemporary twenty-first-century Los Angeles. At the same time, people have legitimate and reasonable concerns about what any changes

will mean for their communities, and I think those concerns are particularly acute, for reasons rooted in history, in communities of color. We organized Low-Rise: Housing Ideas for Los Angeles, a design challenge we launched in 2020, around this set of ideas. We really tried to rethink how design competitions worked in a fundamental way. We started with a series of community-engagement listening sessions about housing and used those to shape the brief. And we made the sessions required viewing for every competitor. Instead of architects telling communities what their housing should look like, we wanted Low-Rise to be a vehicle for communities to tell architects what they need, how they want to see their neighborhoods grow and evolve.

JL: My experience recently with this affordable housing project in San Francisco tracks to a lot of what you are saying. The community meetings that we've had have not been dominated by people opposing the project altogether. The people who do express concern are more worried about the potential impact of homeless services than the housing itself. In fact, I would say the majority of people are very much in favor of bringing affordable housing to the site, and maybe even a plurality want us to go higher than we are being allowed to build.

CH: A lot of this, I have found, has to do with framing. The single-family model, offering this California dream lifestyle, is increasingly rigid and limiting. It forecloses a lot of options that people are interested in adding to their neighborhoods. We found the engagement sessions for Low-Rise to be quite interesting from that point of view—that increasingly people, particularly younger people, but also older people, see the limitations of the rigidity of that model.

I think Covid has only clarified this for people—if you're interested in being able to separate yourself from the family during the day to work from home or quarantine without leaving the household altogether; if you're older and interested in aging in place or downsizing without leaving your community; if you want to live in a larger multigenerational household—in all kinds of ways our low-rise zoning forecloses a lot of those options. People are also seeing the things they would like to have in their neighborhood—the ability to walk to local retail, having closer connections with neighbors, and a stronger sense of resilience and community. All those things can be facilitated by some thoughtful updates to how we organize low-rise neighborhoods. Then that begins to open up the conversation in ways that we see as being very fruitful, rather than two very closed positions. The distinctions between density and overcrowding have also been clarified by this crisis. Some people early on thought sprawl and lack of density would save us. And then we had a terrible Covid surge in the winter of 2020 into 2021 that really preyed on overcrowded multigenerational households, especially where at least one member of the household had a job that couldn't be done remotely. We are both a horizontal and an overcrowded city—again, LA doesn't fit neatly into expectations many people have about cities.

JL: The shifting Covid situation in New York and Los Angeles over the last few months seems to reveal a lie as to what density means or what crowding means. There's always a link between health and housing. At the turn of the twentieth century it was about ventilation and combating unhealthy density. Now it is perhaps more about supply on the one hand but also the need for a different kind of typological thinking on the other—serving communities in a way that they're not being served by the housing that is there, by both how much of it there is but also how it functions.

CH: I think we're far enough into the pandemic to begin to draw some lessons about how people want to live. We are beginning to have lots of conversations in City Hall about what the demand for office space will look like and whether there might be some ways to streamline the conversion of some office space to residential over time. There are ways in which we need to bring elements of the workplace into the home. There are ways in which, to get back to your question about open space, the pandemic has clarified the appeal of well-designed shared outdoor space, public or private. We've been projecting our interior spaces via Zoom to the rest of the world while working at home, and as we think about the next generation of residential architecture, there will be a desire to expand the programs or elements of the residential sphere.

I think there's something very similar to be said about multigenerational living and the ways in which people will want to live in places which will allow them to move flexibly across many years between living alone, having children, having a growing family, having children go away, come back as an adult, have extended family living for short or long stays, all in a compound that exceeds the ability of the single-family house to change and adapt. We have not had,

in recent decades, a housing policy that has reflected the desire to create those kinds of domestic spaces.

JL: One thing I really appreciated in your writing as a critic was the way you often challenged current preconceptions by invoking history to set the present in a broader context and reveal the narrowness of what we assume to be inevitabilities. And I'm interested in how in your current role you see the place of history and of issues related to preservation in a city like LA.

While our office is always striving to create new buildings and new ways of thinking and designing, over the last two decades we have also been engaging with how to deal with history. I actually began my career at OMA looking at issues of preservation in Beijing, and I'm currently working on the adaptive reuse of an enormous building in Houston. The Houston building was a post office, but not a grand public hall like the Farley Post Office in New York. It was primarily a huge concrete warehouse where all the mail for southeast Texas was sorted. Especially in a context where most things feel provisional, its expansiveness and its durability as a concrete monolith make it unique, but it is not a building you would think to preserve at first glance.

Whether it's the generic character of our post office, or the lightweight construction that makes up the majority of the city fabric, it can be especially difficult to figure out what merits preservation in a place like Houston, and of course also LA.

CH: I think it's fair to say we have a singular, perhaps peculiar, relationship to history and the notion of civic memory in LA. For reasons that have to do with our history of boosterism, of myth-making, of connections to Hollywood and the so-called dream factory, I believe we have been more aggressive in the erasure or whitewashing of the histories of certain communities of LA.

That was one of the reasons we launched the Mayor's Office Civic Working Group with a number of the leading historians of LA and the American West, as well as architects, designers, artists, community leaders, and Native leaders, among others. The goal was to produce some policy recommendations for how the city could engage, particularly in its public design work, more forthrightly and honestly with the complicated history of the city, particularly where that history is fraught or has been buried or whitewashed.

OMA NY   Christopher Hawthorne

The initiative began with a full group meeting in City Hall. Then we broke into subcommittees looking at particular themes like labor, process, indigenous land acknowledgement, historic preservation, an inventory of monuments and markers around the city, and so forth. The discussions were meant to make room for contradiction, even paradox. Eric Avila, a professor at UCLA, very early on made the provocative point that one of the things that we need to preserve in Los Angeles is a history of iconoclasm, even a history of forgetting to a certain degree— a history of operating free of the weight of history. That has long been a central part of the appeal of Los Angeles. How can we preserve that as the city's institutions grow and mature? It's a great and confounding question.

JL: So, not caring about history.

CH: Exactly. LA was appealing as a destination particularly for artists and architects, but for people in all kinds of industries across the twentieth century, because it was a place where you could escape the weight of history that you feel in other cities. I was glad that we were reminded of that because the last thing any of us wanted to do is slip into a series of discussions about how to set the city in amber and freeze any kind of progress, which would be antithetical to the basic idea of LA. It's a tricky set of questions, but one idea that helped bring focus to the work was to address the histories in Los Angeles that have been actively erased rather than productively or creatively set aside. Being open to two different approaches—one to recapture histories that have been aggressively erased, and the other to capture and preserve LA's history of standing apart from an obligation to a certain kind of history—those two things in concert really helped move the project forward.

JL: It has been great to speak with you so much about Los Angeles, because while this whole book is about OMA New York, and we are living and working in New York, we are also striving to make an impact in Los Angeles and to learn from being there.

CH: I love New York and lived there for several years. I'm sure some New Yorkers would disagree with this, but to me the great thing about LA is just how much—and this is true as a critic and it's certainly true in the work I'm doing now—is up for grabs in terms of these basic building blocks of civic identity that we've been talking about. In some ways, in terms of architecture and urbanism, New York has probably changed more

dramatically than LA in the two last decades, for good and ill. More new capital-A architecture has gone up in New York than in LA. But in terms of how a city understands itself, its basic identity and shape, that all seems up for grabs in LA in a way that is incredibly complicated and sometimes fraught but really exciting. I don't think the same is true in many American cities. Historically, as I've said, we have a lot to answer for. But as we look ahead, most of the major meta questions are up for debate: What kind of housing defines LA? How much will we embrace verticality? Is this still a place best understood, or made legible, through movement? What is the relationship between Hollywood, the entertainment industry, and the city itself? And so on. And that, for a city as old and as big and as complex as LA, is a really unusual thing.

JL: LA is constantly in the state of becoming.

CH: Exactly. I'll steal a line from the great LA critic Esther McCoy. She said of Rudolph Schindler's work, "A Schindler house is in movement. It is becoming." LA is the same way.

Christopher Hawthorne is the chief design officer for the city of Los Angeles, California. Prior to working in City Hall, he served as the architecture critic for the *Los Angeles Times* for fourteen years.

OMA NY   Christopher Hawthorne

Pierre Lassonde Pavilion

Pierre Lassonde Pavilion

The museum is fated to extend. The number of artworks is increasing, mediums are diversifying, and collections are expanding. The exponential growth of art and what that means for museum extensions is a known dilemma. Le Corbusier imagined a museum that "contained everything"—the "Museum of Unlimited Growth" (1931)—a museum of "limitlessness" in the form of a spiraling ziggurat that could infinitely expand. Quite a large number of museum extensions are being built around the world—some are competitive, some are subservient, others completely seamless.

We've noticed that the question of how to extend the museum is becoming more complex, due to the diversification of art and the increase of public activities and civic ambitions. There is a discrepancy between the speed of activity growth and the speed of physical growth, or evolution, of the spaces for accommodating those activities. The *new* new extensions must provide spaces for multiple purposes and improvisation. How can we identify and create those unprogrammed spaces that are often not explicitly in the brief?

For the Pierre Lassonde Pavilion, an addition to the Musée National des Beaux-Arts du Québec (MNBAQ), we wanted not to create an iconic imposition, but rather an extension that embodies new links between the museum and its context. MNBAQ is located in Champs de Bataille Park, embedded in nature but lacking a direct interface to the city. For the first time, it acquired a site in the park facing a main boulevard (Grande Allée). Our approach was to extend not only the museum, but also the city and park simultaneously. By bringing the city and park into the building, we saturate the museum with an overabundance of flexible public surfaces, addressing the need for spaces that can accommodate growing public engagement.

We "peel" up the museum from the park ground—the city slides under and the park goes over, with art as a catalyst between the two entities. We stacked three gallery volumes that decrease in size as they step up—temporary exhibits (50m x 50m), permanent modern and contemporary collection (45m x 35m), and design/Inuit exhibits (42.5m x 25m)—creating a cascade ascending from the park to the city. As they step up in section, the gallery boxes step toward the city in plan, framing the existing courtyard of the church cloister.

OMA NY   Pierre Lassonde Pavilion

The stacking creates a Grand Hall sheltered under a dramatic cantilever. It is an extension of the street into the museum, an urban plaza for public functions, from large-scale installations and performances to weddings and galas. A glass curtain-wall enclosure allows the lush greenery of the park to visually flood the room. The Grand Hall marks the beginning of a network of flexible spaces that complement the quiet reflection of the galleries.

On the museum's edge, foyers, lounges, shops, and gardens offer a hybrid of activities, art, and promenades. Along this spine, orchestrated views from a monumental spiral stair and an exterior "pop-out" stair reconnect visitors with the park, the city, and the museum complex. Within the boxes, mezzanines and overlooks link temporary and permanent exhibition spaces. Roof terraces provide space for outdoor displays and bring visitors out into the park. This three-dimensional public domain establishes layers of "unprogrammed" zones that are flexible enough to be activated with art or events.

A facade of varying degrees of transparency reinforces the building's relationship to its rich context. Moments of clear glass provide an ever-present view to the neighborhood, the surrounding trees, and the existing museum pavilions. In the galleries, a translucent facade captures the light and shadows of the trees. At night, the building is softly lit like a lantern.

While the new building provides a 90 percent increase in exhibition surfaces, it is the expansion of the "other" spaces that make the museum truly a civic amenity. The galleries, in conjunction with the activities of the Grand Hall and the spine of flexible zones, transform the museum into a highly public assemblage of art, city, and park.

Location	Québec City, Canada		
Status	Completed, 2016		
Typology	Museum		
Program	Museum/Gallery	29,500 ft²	2,740 m²
	Public space	61,700 ft²	5,730 m²
	Theater	4,800 ft²	450 m²
	Museum Shop	2,800 ft²	260 m²
	Restaurant	4,300 ft²	400 m²
	Services	60,000 ft²	5,570 m²
	Total Area	163,100 ft²	15,150 m²

Pierre Lassonde Pavilion

785

Pierre Lassonde Pavilion

OMA NY

Pierre Lassonde Pavilion

Pierre Lassonde Pavilion

OMA NY   Pierre Lassonde Pavilion

Pierre Lassonde Pavilion

OMA NY

Pierre Lassonde Pavilion

Pierre Lassonde Pavilion

OMA NY

Pierre Lassonde Pavilion

Pierre Lassonde Pavilion

790 The Musée National des Beaux-Arts du Québec (MNBAQ) is a museum in Québec City, Canada with approximately 25,000 works produced in, but not limited to, Québec or by Québec artists.

791 Prior to the Pierre Lassonde Pavilion, the museum campus was composed of three distinct buildings connected within Battlefields Park: the Charles Baillairgé Pavilion, Central Pavilion, and Gérard-Morriset Pavilion.

792 The museum, for the first time, bought a site that faces the main urban boulevard of the city. It is next to an existing church.

793 The new site's location facing a main thoroughfare provided an opportunity to establish a better connection to the city and its activities.

794 Concept study models— as the museum's fourth building in the complex, the new pavilion aims to complete the interconnected yet disparate museum complex while forming new links between the park and the city.

795 In between city and park

796 Initial concept study— Ant Farm: one big multi-story wall where the movement of people is visible to the city.

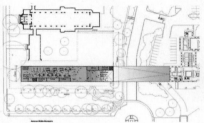

797 Ant Farm—ground floor plan

798 Ant Farm—long section

799 Another initial concept was the Two Towers scheme.

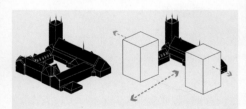

800 Two towers would liberate the site and create a direct link to the park.

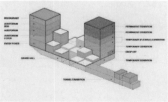

801 The Two Towers scheme divides the museum extension into spaces with public functions, such as the auditorium and Grand Hall (a rentable space) and gallery spaces.

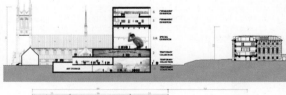

802 Two Towers—long section

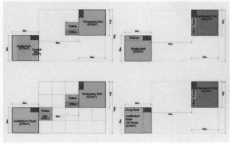

803 Two Towers—upper level plans

804 Two towers—aerial view

805 Two Towers—study models

Pierre Lassonde Pavilion

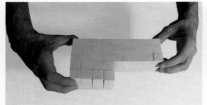

806 Another scheme that was explored was the Grid scheme.

807 Extruded sloped volumes in a grid would bring natural light down to the galleries.

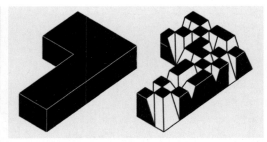

808 Grid—maximizing skylights

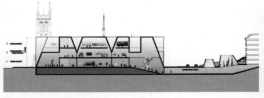

809 Grid—long section

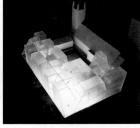

810 Grid—physical model

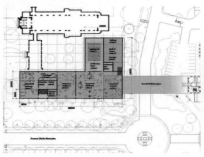

811 Grid—ground floor plan

812 Grid—massing rendering

813 Grid—upper-level programs

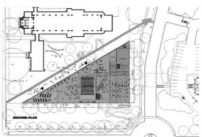

814 Grid—upper-level plans shown in axo

815 Triangle scheme—the form brings people directly to the park through the church courtyard, not to the museum. It creates an interesting tension between the church and the existing museum complex.

816 Triangle—study model

817 Triangle—study model

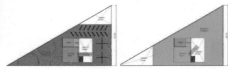

818 Triangle—ground floor plan and direct path to park

819 Triangle—upper level plans

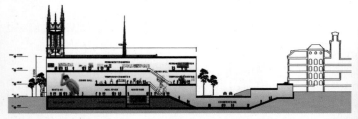

820 Triangle—section

821 Triangle—view from Grande Allée

822 Triangle—view south

823 The Triangle scheme would maximize openness to the existing church and courtyard.

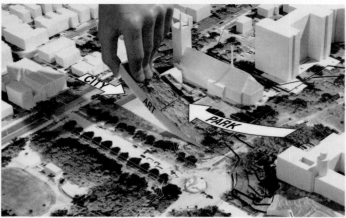

824 The final scheme is based on the narrative of three entities—the city, art, and park—converging on site.

825 Three entities extend onto the site, and art becomes the catalyst between the city and park.

826 Final scheme resin model

827 Stacked galleries

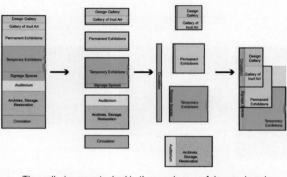

828 The galleries are stacked in three volumes of decreasing size: temporary exhibitions (164 by 164 feet), permanent modern and contemporary collections (148 by 115 feet), and the design/Inuit exhibits (139 by 82 feet).

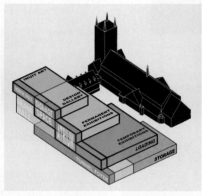

829 This concept creates a cascading form that descends out toward the park.

830 Shohei Shigematsu presents the final scheme model to John R. Porter and Pierre Lassonde.

831 A new gateway that opens up to the city with a dramatic cantilever

832 The landscape of the park continues overhead while city activity slides under.

833 Echoing the topography of the hills beyond, the gallery boxes form a slope that extends the museum to the park and opens it to the city.

834 Rotation view of final form

835 Aerial view from southwest

836 Aerial view from northwest

837 Aerial view from west

838 Aerial view from southeast

839 Gallery boxes step out in plan reaching out onto Grande Allée while simultaneously orienting the building toward the park.

840 Southwest elevation

841 Northeast elevation

842 Northwest elevation

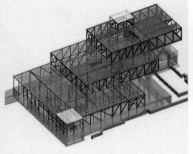

843 A total of 1,090 tons of steel was used for the structure to support the cantilever.

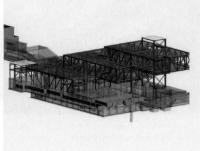

844 The Howe truss structure employed is typically used for long-span bridges.

845 Construction view

846 View from southwest

847 The connection plates are hidden in the floor thickness.

848 The stepping creates a covered plaza and "slides" the city under the building.

849 The park slides up onto the terraces of the stacked boxes.

852 The form of the building allows the museum to weave together the city, the park, and the museum.

850 The height is maintained to parallel and respect the lower roof of the adjacent church.

851 The building frames the existing courtyard of the Saint-Dominique Church cloister.

853 Building within the existing museum context

854 View from southeast at dusk

855 The stepped form breaks down the scale of the building and preserves views of the church tower when viewed from the park, becoming a respectful addition to the museum campus.

Pierre Lassonde Pavilion

856 The stacking of gallery boxes creates the Grand Hall below the resulting cantilever that interfaces Grande Allée.

857 Concept model view from the front plaza looking into the Grand Hall

858 The Grand Hall is sheltered under a 41-foot-high cantilever.

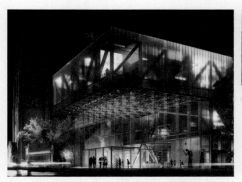

859 The competition scheme proposed a wooden construction for the underside of the cantilever.

860 This scheme would use a hybrid structure of steel trusses for the cantilever support and glulam (glue laminated timber).

861 Final concept rendering—the cantilever is structurally independent of the glass wall that encloses the Grand Hall located underneath the cantilever.

862 Cantilever construction

863 Construction view from Grande Allée

864 The double-height Grand Hall lobby opens up the museum to the city and establishes an inviting presence.

865 View from Avenue de Bourlamaque

868 The Grande Allée cantilever creates a covered plaza that draws the city into the museum.

866 The cantilever spans more than 65 feet over the Grand Hall.

867 View from the church side on Grande Allée

869 Day-to-night view of the building from Grande Allée

870 The plaza and Grand Hall work together to provide an urban platform for the museum's public functions.

871 Shohei Shigematsu and Justin Trudeau shake hands at the opening day ceremony in the outdoor plaza.

872 Visitors await entry into the museum on opening day (June 24, 2016).

873 Opening day

874 Opening day view from southwest

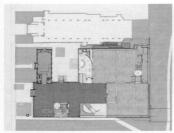

875 The ground level houses the Grand Hall lobby, coat check, ticketing, boutique, and an open cafe.

876 Galleries and programs are easily accessible from the Grand Hall and the glass facade establishes a series of visual connections among the museum programs, courtyard, city, and the park.

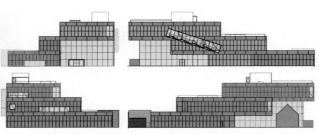

877 The Grand Hall is enclosed by a glass curtain wall with glass fins that allow unobstructed views to the city and park.

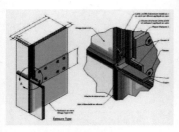

878 Structural glass fins

879 The fins are 31 inches deep and spaced 63 inches on center.

880 The all-glass facade preserves maximum transparency and simultaneously connects the museum to the park, city, and the historical church.

881 View toward the park

882 View from the park, looking into the Grand Hall

883 View toward the park

884 The restaurant and cafe are located in the Grand Hall and are new public amenities for the city. The location allows visitors to enjoy the scenery of both the park and the city.

885 The ceiling is continuous from inside to outside, creating a covered outdoor plaza that invites the city in.

886 View toward the city

887 Rafael Lozano-Hemmer, *Solar Equation* (2019)—the Grand Hall can also accommodate large-scale art installations.

888 The space also establishes a connection to the existing Saint-Dominique Church visually, with the presbytery extending into the Grand Hall.

889 The Grand Hall's expansive glass facade creates a panoramic view of Grande Allée and Battlefields Park, bringing the urban and natural elements into the large open interior space.

Pierre Lassonde Pavilion

890   Under the cantilever, the Grand Hall serves as an interface to the Grande Allée and an urban plaza for the museum's public functions.

891   Rendering of Grand Hall lobby

893   Grand Hall—banquet/fundraiser

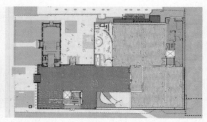

892   The column-free Grand Hall is an extension of the street and is surrounded by different programs and events.

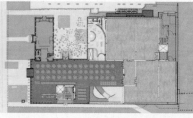

894   Grand Hall plan—banquet/fundraiser

895   The Grand Hall acts as an extension of the street that interacts with the museum's various programs.

896   View of presbytery wall, courtyard, and bookstore from the Grand Hall.

897   From the Grand Hall, visitors can access entrance points to all of the museum's amenities.

898   Opening day event

899   Opening day event

900   Presentation/lecture

901   Dance performance

902   Museum gala

903   Concert

904   Party

905   Wedding

906   People and activities flow seamlessly from the Grand Hall onto the atrium stair.

907   View of Grand Hall and connection to main atrium stair

890–907

Pierre Lassonde Pavilion

908 The existing presbytery intersects the Grand Hall and its facade is an abstraction of the old presbytery wall.

909 The existing presbytery facade could not bear the loads imposed by the new glass structure and had to be demolished.

910 The back side of the presbytery wall was poured on the ground and raised into place with the formwork. Once raised, the front portion of the formwork was built and the concrete pour was made in place during a single pour period.

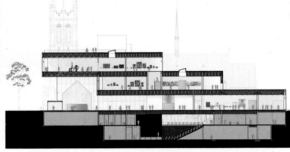

911 In section, the presbytery creates a moment of visual connection to the existing church from within the new building.

913 The concrete presbytery highlights the moment of connection between the Pierre Lassonde Pavilion and the former Saint Dominique Church and acknowledges the existing elements of the site in a playful way.

912 Facade detail through presbytery wall

914 The presbytery now houses the coat check and restrooms.

915 Detail view of presbytery wall and Grand Hall glazing

916 The presbytery wall captures the varying light conditions through the Grand Hall's glass facade and maintains a view of the church tower beyond.

917 Wedding ceremony

918 The liquid polyurethane membrane of the interior was applied to the formwork before it was raised into place.

919 Adding a pop of color establishes the green as signage that is easily recognized upon entry.

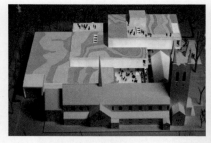

920 The stacking of the gallery boxes frames an exterior courtyard that is partially covered.

921 The courtyard is on an intimate scale that orients the museum toward the existing church.

922 View of courtyard from the park side

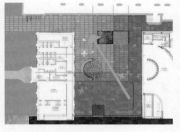

923 The courtyard materiality transitions from full stone coverage by the museum to smaller stones and greenery toward the church.

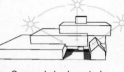

924 Sun and shadow study carefully looking at the building's impact on the courtyard space

925 Courtyard model looking toward Grand Hall

926 Courtyard model looking toward Grand Hall and boutique

927 Courtyard in the winter

928 Construction

929 Construction

930 The courtyard is a connective space that ties the new building to its historic context.

931 View into the boutique

932 The courtyard can also accommodate large-scale installations and various events, including a sixty-person wedding.

933 The courtyard offers multiple vantage points—to the adjacent church, the boutique on the ground level, and the gallery box stacked above.

934 A semi-circular bench in the courtyard follows the shape of the bookshelves found in the boutique, creating a dialogue between exterior and interior spaces.

935 Adjacent to the courtyard is the boutique, the museum's bookstore and retail space, which can be accessed directly from the Grand Hall.

936 View into the boutique from the courtyard

937 The boutique takes the form of an amphitheater, oriented toward the courtyard.

938 Final concept rendering

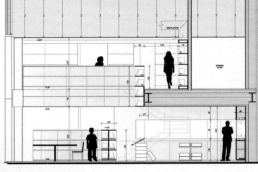

939 The boutique is composed of multiple layers, including a smaller mezzanine reading room.

940 Courtyard view from the boutique

941 The boutique is expressed as an excavated solid block from which programmatic double-height voids are carved to create an entry and the shop/library.

942 The boutique's integrated shelving uses unpainted, sealed pine plywood on all of the curved surfaces.

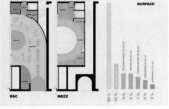

943 Voids and surface types range from display, counter/workstation, reading, storage, and vertical circulation.

944 Boutique display area with vitrines and views of the rounded entrance and library beyond

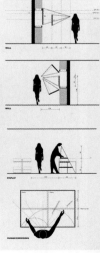

945 Vitrine types for display, storage, and use

946 Entrance to the boutique from the Grand Hall

947 Entry view

948 Boutique entrance from the Grand Hall

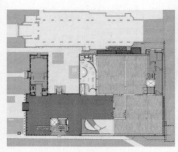

949 Three levels of galleries surround the Grand Hall. The temporary gallery space is located on the ground floor, enabling easy access from the museum's entry hall and loading area.

950 In the F1 Gallery, two distinct exhibition spaces create two interconnected yet easily separable volumes to accommodate a range of temporary shows.

951 When divided for separate exhibitions, each gallery is independently accessible from both the gallery foyer and the delivery entrance, ensuring flexibility in the museum's operations, as one temporary exhibition can be installed or dismantled without impacting the other's continued use.

952 The F1 Gallery includes a unique window from the mezzanine.

953 In 2018, the F1 Gallery hosted an Alberto Giacometti exhibition.

954 F2 Gallery—the second level houses the post-World War II modern and contemporary art collections of the museum.

955 Every gallery space throughout the museum continues to frame exterior moments to achieve a sense of orientation to the existing complex.

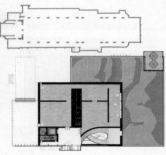

956 F2 Gallery plan

957 F2 Gallery

959 F2 Gallery and Sculpture Terrace—terraces on top of each gallery box provide spaces for outdoor displays and installations.

960 F2 Gallery and Sculpture Terrace—the design of the galleries prioritizes optimal dimensions for hanging and viewing art.

958 F2 Gallery—an efficient five-meter grid that allows curators to easily plan wall partitions in the galleries.

962 F3 Design Gallery

963 F3 Inuit Gallery

961 F3 gallery plan—the third level splits into two to present Design and Inuit collections.

964 Shohei Shigematsu escorting Prime Minister Justin Trudeau through the F3 Inuit Gallery.

965 In one of the rooms of the F3 Design Gallery, a large window looks out onto the terrace and the museum campus beyond.

966 F3 gallery—the galleries have a contemplative quality, designed to thwart museum fatigue through strategically placed rest areas and the use of natural light.

949–966   Pierre Lassonde Pavilion

967 Complementing the defined gallery spaces, the circulation spine activates a chain of programs.

968 Foyers, lounges, bridges, and gardens along the spine offer an array of activities, art, and public promenades along the museum's edge.

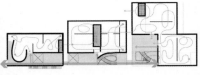

969 A chain of programmatic elements are strung across a circulation spine on the museum's edge and direct both fast and slow circulation.

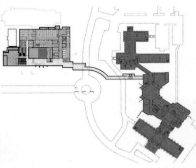

970 Section model of the atrium stair

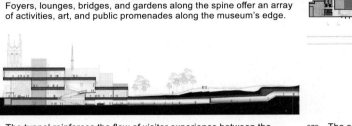

971 The tunnel reinforces the flow of visitor experience between the different buildings of the museum campus.

972 The shape of the tunnel is informed by the roundabout above.

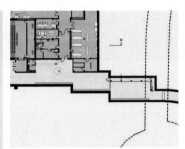

973 The tunnel has a five-meter grade in elevation.

974 Through its sheer length and changes in elevation, the curved passage slowly reveals the next destination, building anticipation while acting as a palate cleanser between the museum spaces.

975 At the terminus of the tunnel is a unique gallery leading into the Pierre Lassonde Pavilion, accommodating a large scale triptych by Jean-Paul Riopelle.

977 Jean-Paul Riopelle, *Tribute to Rosa Luxemburg* (1992)

976 The three long pieces of the Riopelle mural have never previously had the opportunity to be displayed side by side with continuity.

978 The tunnel gallery is dedicated to the single Riopelle triptych.

979 The new 426-foot-long tunnel is broken up by a multi-purpose space/bar and a permanent gallery for the 131-foot-long mural.

980 The tunnel gallery can also be used as an additional programming space for the museum's community activities, such as student multidisciplinary performances in collaboration with Bouillon d'Art Multi (BAM) in 2017.

Pierre Lassonde Pavilion

982   Early concept for tunnel and grand stair

981   View to the grand atrium stair on B1 from the Tunnel Gallery

983   The atrium formed by the spiral stair is a spinning wheel—visitors coming through the tunnel from the existing complex and those coming from the street meet and traverse.

984   The stair is composed of three sections, each measuring 49 feet in length. Each section was dropped in place with a crane before the roof was built.

985   Stair construction

986   The main atrium stair begins at the entry to the auditorium and the tunnel at the B1 level.

988   Looking up from the B1 Lounge

987   The stair is a conduit for museum activities.

989   A lounge area beneath the atrium stair can be used as an additional exhibition space.

990   It can also be used as a pre-function space for events happening in the auditorium or tunnel.

992   The auditorium is located in B1 where the tunnel and the grand atrium stair meet. Large windows allow visitors to view the activities within.

991   Basement level plan—the building has two basement levels that contain the auditorium, public bathrooms, tunnel entrance, art storage, and other back-of-house spaces, such as kitchens, offices, wood shop, and mechanical rooms.

993   Curtain closed

994   Curtain open

995   Construction

996   Auditorium

997   Walls and ceiling are finished with an industrial black expanded metal that covers reflective and absorptive surfaces as required by the acoustics. The floor has a blue rubber finish to match the seating upholstery in order to express the auditorium as a single continuous plane folded down.

998   The glass wall creates a luminous auditorium for events that do not need blackout. The auditorium can seat 266. The stage is designed for a variety of performances and is easily accessible from back stage and the freight elevator.

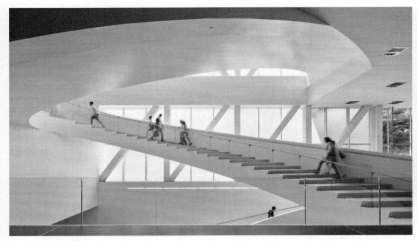

999 The atrium stair combines a solid exterior balustrade and transparent interior guardrail, exposing the circulation up to the gallery levels while maintaining its sculptural form.

1000 The grand atrium stair leads visitors up from the B1 auditorium and the tunnel gallery.

1001 Atrium stair studies—from top to bottom: excavated cube, programmatic landings, serpentine stair

1002 Gallery and atrium model

1003 Gallery and atrium model

1004 Atrium stair rendering

1008 On the first mezzanine, carefully placed windows establish views into the F1 temporary exhibitions gallery and the Charles Baillairgé Pavilion outside.

1005 OMA New York staff on museum opening day

1006 Sculptural stair

1007 Atrium stair leading up to the first mezzanine

1009 Visitors moving along the stairs on opening day

1010 Aerial view of atrium stair looking down onto the B1 lounge

1011 View from the first landing mezzanine between ground and second levels

1013 Museum gala procession and photo op

1014 Dance performance

1012 Chamber music performance on the stairs—the stair itself becomes programmable space.

1015 The atrium stair terminates in a second lounge on F2, from which the circulation spine continues up vertically via an exterior stair.

1016 Pop-out stair construction

1017 The stair begins from the F2 lounge and leads visitors up to the F3 galleries and outdoor terrace.

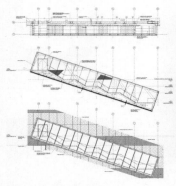

1018 Pop-out stair plan, section, and elevation

1019 The pop-out stair is intended to help overcome museum fatigue and orient visitors to the park and the museum.

1020 The stair is essentially an extruded window that allows visitors to step outside the gallery box and look out onto the adjacent park.

1021 Justin Trudeau descending the pop-out stair

1022 Visitors are given an expansive view of the trees of the adjacent park.

1023 Pop-out stair construction—stair treads

1024 Pop-out stair construction—stair box

1025 The underside of the stair is polished stainless steel.

1026 Having the stair step out of the building's skin provides more internal space for circulation.

1027 Dance performance

1028 View of the park's winter scenery

1029 Aluminum treads and risers with LED strips are integrated into the nosing.

1030 The circulation is made visible from the outside.

1031 Flanking the pop-out stair above and below are the F2 mezzanine lounge and F3 multi-purpose room.

1032 The F2 mezzanine lounge offers visitors a place to rest in between the gallery floors, with views out onto the park.

1033 The mezzanine lounge is large enough to accommodate smaller-scale installations and can be used as an additional gallery space.

1034 At the terminus of the pop-out stair on F3 is the multi-purpose room, an open flexible space that acts as a lounge but can also be used as an extension of gallery exhibitions or for other events and programs.

1035 The multi-purpose room acts as the final space for respite along the museum's chain of programs.

1036 The glass facade along the multi-purpose room brings light into the space.

1037 A large opening strategically placed along the facade reorients visitors to the city.

1038 The room supports the museum's diverse range of public programs, including a drawing class.

1039 Education

1040 Party

1041 The multi-purpose room can also be used as a reception area for exhibition openings.

1042 Daytime performance

1043 Evening performance

1044 View of terrace from the F3 multi-purpose room

1045 The F3 multi-purpose room extends to the exterior terrace with an outdoor sculpture and a lookout point toward the park, reorienting visitors to the rest of the museum campus.

1031–1045   Pierre Lassonde Pavilion

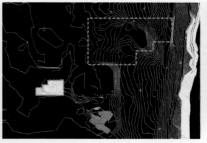

1047   By using the topographic lines of the park, we strengthened the intention that the museum be a continuation of the park.

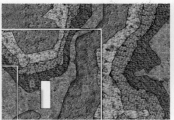

1048   The contour lines were carried to the planting patterns on the terrace, and different zones were defined based on a survey of plantings in the park.

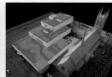

1049   Roof terrace landscape

1050   August 19, 2015

1051   August 19, 2015

1052   August 22, 2015

1053   August 26, 2015

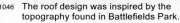

1046   The roof design was inspired by the topography found in Battlefields Park.

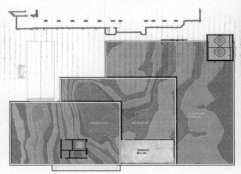

1054   Roof plan

1055   The park topography extends onto the museum's roof.

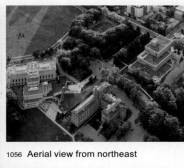

1056   Aerial view from northeast

1057   The landscape on the roof and terrace is composed of 90,000 plants and five different types of succulents, all selected based on their efficiency and high availability in Québec.

1058   F2 sculpture terrace—the landscaping is a warm palette with contrasting heights, avoiding intense colors to create harmony with the park and the museum's exterior materiality.

1059   View from the park

1060   Five main plants were used: Oktoberfest stonecrop, Fuldaglut stonecrop, chive, tricolor stonecrop, and white stonecrop.

1061   F3 terrace exterior view

1062   The planting palette and pattern of the roof landscape establish a visual continuity from park to museum.

1063 The design of the facade began with conceptualizing the gesture of peeling the park up to slide the city underneath.

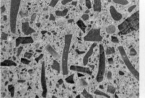

1065 Recycled glass terrazzo

1066 Blue aggregate facade

1069 Facade study models

1070 Solidworks

1071 Perforations

1064 We first explored layering colored aggregates to simulate the strata of the land beneath.

1067 Blue aggregate facade—courtyard

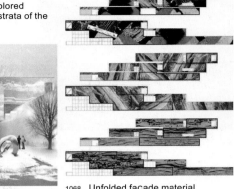

1068 Unfolded facade material concept studies

1072 Orthogonal strata

1073 Organic strata

1074 Facade study models

1077 Puffer facade—exterior view

1078 Puffer facade—interior view

1076 Puffer facade model detail

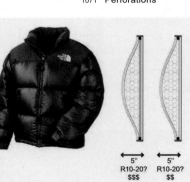

3"	1.5"	1.5"	5"	5"
R20	R10	R5	R10-20?	R10-20?
$$$$	$$	$	$$$	$$

1075 In order to respond to the cold climate of Québec City, the puffer facade study was proposed as a strategy for improving insulation.

1079 Daytime elevation

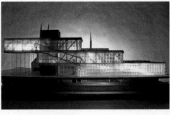

1080 Evening elevation

1081 How can the facade improve insulation and have an appearance that is cohesive with the park and existing campus?

1063–1081   Pierre Lassonde Pavilion

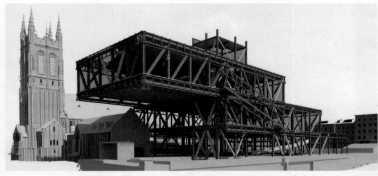

1082 The final facade was informed by the cantilevered structure, using the hybrid steel truss system as a base for the layered facade.

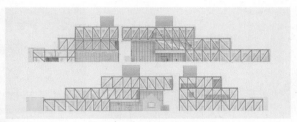

1083 A fritted pattern follows the hybrid steel truss system, subtly emphasizing the structural form of the museum.

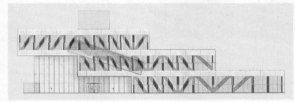

1084 Facade frit pattern standardization

1085 Standard three panels

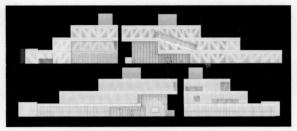

1086 A "truss frit" projecting the structure accentuates the expression of the steel trusses by varying the density of frits according to the rhythm of the structure, incrementally grading from 80 percent density to 20 percent.

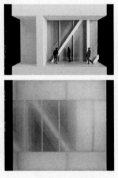

1087 The glass echoes the structure behind. An inverse shadow of the structure appears behind the glass.

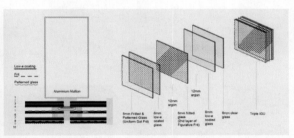

1088 Triple-laminated IGU panels with patterned glass, low-E coating, two layers of fritting and a layer of diffuser glass were used to improve the facade's thermal performance, prevent solar gains in the summer, and allow diffused natural light.

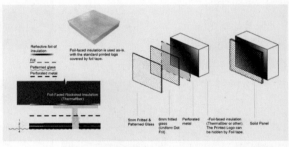

1089 In the rest of the gallery spaces, an insulated wall is located behind the translucent glass system.

1091 The fritting is both a means of glare control and pattern making, with light-diffusing qualities that create an even tone of natural light in the gallery spaces.

1090 The outer layer of patterned glass captures sunlight in different conditions, transforming the building's appearance at various times of day.

1092 The trusses are coated in intumescent fire-retardant paint and white powder coating.

1093 Frit pattern visibility test, creating depth on the facade

1094 At night, the trusses are visible on the facade.

1095 The multilayered patterned and fritted glass facade creates a double reading for the building that fluctuates from solid in the day to translucent at night.

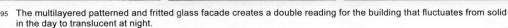

1096 The textured glass creates a frosted appearance that blends in with the park in Québec's snowy climate.

1097   1098   1099   1100   1101   1102

1103   1104   1105   1106   1107   1108

1109   1110   1111   1112   1113   1114

1115   1116   1117   1118   1119   1120

1121   1122   1123   1124   1125   1126

1127   1128   1129   1130   1131   1132

1133   1134   1135   1136   1137   1138

1097–1138   Pierre Lassonde Pavilion

Pierre Lassonde Pavilion

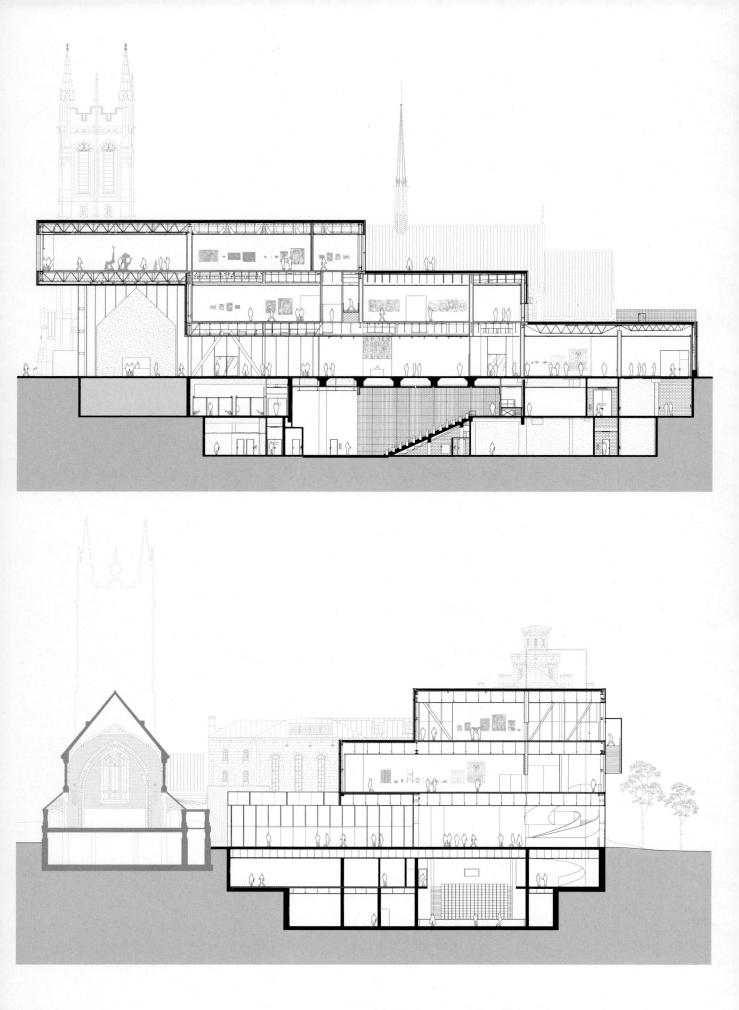

Pierre Lassonde Pavilion

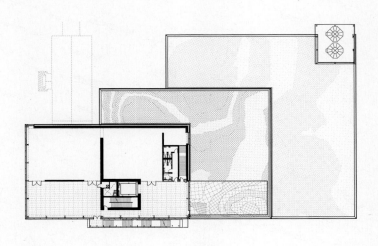

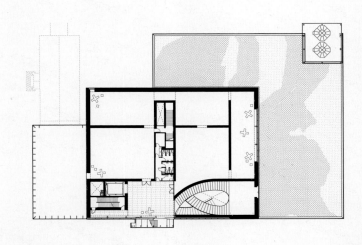

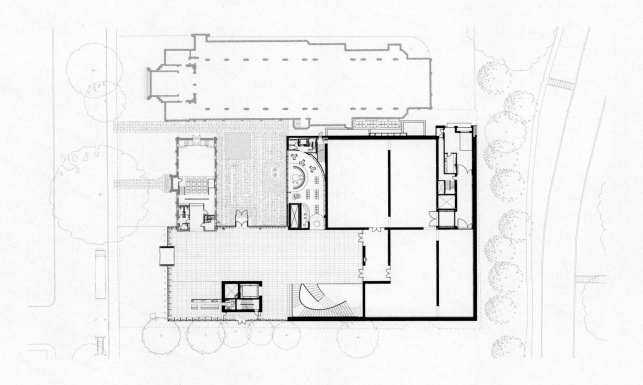

1142–1144   Pierre Lassonde Pavilion

Buffalo AKG Art Museum

Buffalo AKG Art Museum

We often say that there are only two types of museums: a museum in the park, embedded in the tranquility of nature, and a museum in the city, implanted within the energy of urbanism. The Albright-Knox Art Gallery in Buffalo is both. It sits at the northern edge of the historic Delaware Park, designed by Frederick Law Olmsted. The city is known for its history of industrial revolution and the current revitalization of remnants from that past. It has a rich architectural history—from silos and manufacturing facilities to buildings by Eero Saarinen, Louis Sullivan, and Frank Lloyd Wright.

  The museum itself has two connected historic buildings: a 1905 solid, neo-classical building by Edward B. Green originally planned for the 1901 Pan-American Exposition and a 1962 Modernist extension by Gordon Bunshaft that included a new auditorium box and an outdoor courtyard. Despite being in the park, the two buildings side-by-side sever views and access to it from the city, and even from inside the museum itself. Our ambition for the extension was not only to expand the complex to accommodate the museum's growing art collection and diversifying programs, but also to reconnect it to the park and city and establish a new openness to public activities.

  The 1905 and 1962 buildings command a clear separation, closed off from their surroundings. In contrast, the approach for the new pavilion is to unlock the full potential of being in the park. We started with a gallery in the shape of a cross, or a plus sign (because it's an addition). The gallery lies at the heart of the building while four transparent corners—containing lobby, media gallery, office, and loading—bring the park in and surround the museum in nature. While the scale of the cross galleries is akin to that of the intimate rooms of the 1905 structure, two larger, more efficient gallery boxes that resonate with Bunshaft's box are stacked above. A double-height gallery in the front of the building connects the cross and flexible boxes.

  We had been observing how museums are evolving to provide diverse avenues of public engagement through expanded gallery activities and non-exhibition programs. We felt that museums now need to strike the right balance between programmed and programmable space, and must find new relationships between them. Our response was to wrap the second-level gallery with a promenade, an unprogrammed space for various activities—from sculpture exhibitions and galas to educational programs and wellness classes. The promenade and stack of efficient galleries are enveloped by a transparent facade that achieves an open and ephemeral quality. This "veil" covers the promenade to form a double-height buffer zone between nature and art. The resulting winter garden simultaneously embeds visitors in the park and exposes the museum's activities to the campus and city. It is an inverse of the Bunshaft: while he captured nature at the center of art, we place art at the core surrounded by nature.

In addition to the new pavilion, the existing campus as a whole is preserved and improved. A scenic bridge connecting the north building to the 1905 building weaves through, and immerses visitors in, the historic park landscape. We bury the surface parking lot underground and place a large park lawn at the center of the campus and restore the historic steps of the 1905 building facing the lawn. The Bunshaft building becomes a new education wing and a roof added to the courtyard creates an enclosed town square. Most importantly, a new point of entry on the east facade of the Bunshaft establishes a through-connection from the city to the park.

While the existing buildings are hermetic, the new pavilion opens itself up to its surroundings—a transparent entity that contributes a new profile and language to the lineage of architectural history of the institution. Together, the complex offers an array of programs and spatial experiences—from classic to modern to contemporary, gallery to classroom, intimate rooms to grand halls, lawn to courtyard to winter garden. The result is a true campus-like museum that aspires to integrate art, architecture, and nature.

Location	Buffalo, NY, USA		
Status	Construction, 2016–Ongoing		
Typology	Museum		
Program	New Galleries	27,200 ft²	2,530 m²
	Promenade/Terrace	6,100 ft²	570 m²
	Indoor Public Space	13,800 ft²	1,280 m²
	Services/Loading/Storage	7,000 ft²	650 m²
	MEP/Back-of-House	16,800 ft²	1,560 m²
	Parking	27,400 ft²	2,550 m²
	Total Area	98,300 ft²	9,140 m²

OMA NY   Buffalo AKG Art Museum

Buffalo AKG Art Museum

Buffalo AKG Art Museum

1149 Buffalo, New York, is the second-largest city in the state, located at the border of the United States and Canada.

1150 The City of Buffalo started in the late 1700s as a small trading settlement.

1151 With the completion of the Erie Canal in 1825, Buffalo's prominence as the canal's western terminus led to increased commerce and a population boom for the city.

1152 At the start of the twentieth century, Buffalo became an industrial hub, a center for hydroelectric power, shipbuilding, and railway shipping.

1153 Industrial shutdowns and suburban migration in the latter half of the twentieth century caused a dramatic population decline, which continued through the early twenty-first century.

1154 In recent years, Buffalo's affordability has made it a magnet for millennial home-buyers and younger residents.

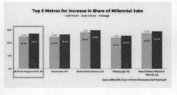

1155 This increase in millennial homeownership has paralleled a rise in millennial-held jobs, contributing to the city's revival.

1156 Architectural remnants of Buffalo's period of industrial prominence are found throughout the city, such as Frank Lloyd Wright's Martin House (1905).

1157 Eliel and Eero Saarinen, Kleinhans Music Hall (1940)

1158 Louis Sullivan, Guaranty Building (1896)

1159 Henry Hobson Richardson-designed asylum, now the Hotel Henry (1870)

1160 Buffalo's former industrial buildings and landscapes are being adapted for new destinations, further adding to the city's resurgence.

1161 In 1868, Frederick Law Olmsted designed a city-wide system of parks and parkways in Buffalo.

1162 The idea behind Olmsted's parks, including the Buffalo park system, was to immerse visitors in the landscape. The parks were to create a "specific antidote" to the tensions created by the urban environment.

1163 Delaware Park, the largest of the three original parks, is considered the centerpiece of the Buffalo park system.

1164 In 1901, the Pan-American Exposition was held along the western edge of Delaware Park. The Albright Art Gallery was designed in conjunction with the fairgrounds to house principal art exhibitions.

1165 Edward B. Green was commissioned to design the structure in a neoclassical style.

1166 Though it was originally intended to serve as the Fine Arts Pavilion for the 1901 World's Fair, delays at the quarries postponed construction and it remained incomplete until 1905.

1167 In 1905, the Albright Art Gallery opened to the public as the Buffalo Art Academy's first permanent home dedicated to showcasing art.

1168 With the opening of the Room of Contemporary Art in 1939, Albright Art Gallery became an arts destination, establishing itself at the forefront by showing the most radical art of the time.

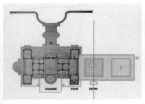

1169 Identifying the need for expansion, the museum hired Gordon Bunshaft to design an addition. The SOM building was completed in 1962 for the renamed Albright-Knox Art Gallery.

1170 The 1962 Building's priorities were to add a new auditorium, additional gallery space, an outdoor sculpture court, and a members' room with a view out to the park.

1171 Along with the Modernist building came the addition of a surface parking lot, and with it the demolition of the 1905 Building's original western stair, thus shifting the museum's entrance to the 1962 Building.

1172 The 1962 Building added a 348-seat auditorium and 6,000 square feet of exhibition space.

1173 1962 Building gallery

1174 Additional exhibition spaces extended out into the corridors.

1175 Visitors in the 1962 building's west corridor

1176 Art was also displayed in the courtyard between the 1905 and 1962 buildings.

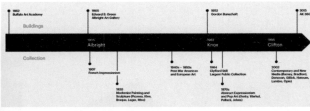

1177 Classical 1905 facade

1178 Modernist 1962 facade

1179 The Albright-Knox Art Gallery has expanded its footprint once every sixty years, steadily growing its collection since its opening in 1905.

1181 Albert Bierstadt, *The Marina Piccola, Capri* (1859) was the first painting and first work gifted by an artist to enter the museum's collection.

1182 The collection includes one of the most substantial public repositories of the works of American artist Clyfford Still (1904–1980).

1183 Albright-Knox also holds the most significant collection of the works of Venezuelan-American sculptor Marisol (1930–2016), including *Baby Girl* (1963).

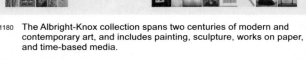

1180 The Albright-Knox collection spans two centuries of modern and contemporary art, and includes painting, sculpture, works on paper, and time-based media.

1188 Paul Gaugin, *Le Christ jaune (The Yellow Christ)* (1889) is part of the museum's extensive Impressionist and Post-Impressionist collection.

1189 Modern works from the collection, as seen in the 2014 exhibition "Sincerely Yours: Treasures of the Queen City"

1184 Site-specific integrated works by Sol LeWitt

1185 Multimedia audio-visual works by Kelly Richardson

1186 Rachel Whiteread, *Untitled (Domestic)* (2002)—this large-scale work is on display in the Sculpture Court.

1187 Nam June Paik, *Piano Piece* (1993), part of Albright-Knox's Room for Contemporary Art.

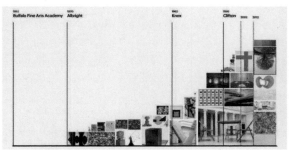

1190 As the collection has grown with diverse and large-scale works, a new addition to the campus was once again needed.

1191　The Albright-Knox Art Gallery campus in 2016, consisting of the adjoining 1905 and 1962 buildings, surface parking lot, and standalone Clifton Hall.

1192　The original building circulation imagined a through connection from city to park. The building would be freestanding, surrounded by the landscape of the park.

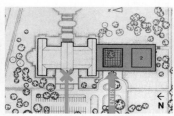

1193　The 1962 Building addition relocated the gallery entrance to the modern wing. Direct access from the city to the park through the 1905 Building was severed.

1194　The 1905 Building entrance was replaced by a parking lot.

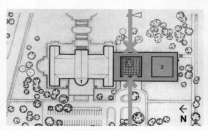

1195　The addition also blocked off the path to the park that had been accessible along the sides of the 1905 Building.

1196　View toward the plinth wall from the park

1197　1905 Building and 1962 addition today

1198　In 2012, we entered a masterplan competition for the expansion of the Albright-Knox campus, studying short- and long-term goals to address the shortage of space for the growing art collection.

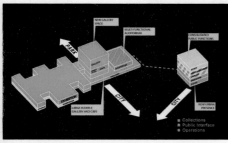

1199　One proposed study replaced Clifton Hall and the Bunshaft courtyard with new public and gallery volumes, respectively.

1200　New gallery volume in the courtyard and public volume in Clifton Hall

1201　New gallery volume completes the Knox plinth

1202　View from the park

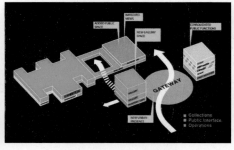

1203　Another study proposed public functions in Clifton Hall and a gallery volume parallel to it, creating a gateway from the city to the park.

1204　The new volumes add much-needed space while preserving the Bunshaft courtyard.

1205　A gateway and new urban campus condition is established between the two volumes.

1206　Unfortunately, we lost the masterplan competition.

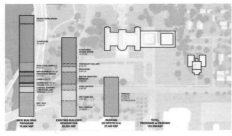

1209 North-South cantilever scheme

1207 In 2016, the vision for a campus expansion was renewed, and we entered the AK360 competition to design a new campus building.

1208 By adding a new building to the campus, the museum would gain 30,000 square feet of prime gallery space, while expanding its education spaces within the 1962 addition and updating galleries in the 1905 Building.

1210 The north-south axis is extended to create one long gallery bar, with a three-story-high stack of galleries anchoring the cantilever on its northern side.

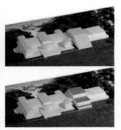

1211 The Landscape scheme submerged the gallery volume underground.

1212 The museum is expanded without enlarging its footprint.

1213 The Bridge scheme pulled landscape up over the Bunshaft courtyard, reconnecting the city to the park while adding a new gallery volume underneath.

1214 Bridge scheme study models

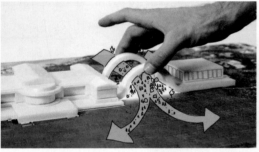

1217 The galleries of the 1905 building and the education spaces of the 1962 addition meet and merge on the bridge.

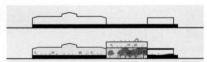

1215 Our final competition scheme reestablished a gateway to Delaware Park, lifting the 1962 courtyard to create a continuous public space underneath.

1216 The new gateway references a signature Olmsted element—picturesque bridges that frame the landscape beyond.

1218 The floating volume introduces a framed connection from the city to the park.

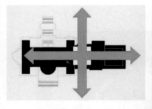

1219 This new public pathway adds an east-west axis to the existing north-south axis that currently defines the campus.

1220 The expansive Entry Hall below the floating gallery becomes a new town green, framed on both sides by the 1905 and 1962 buildings.

1221 The floating scheme connects the gallery spaces between the two buildings, while adding a passage through the courtyard where there was once a wall.

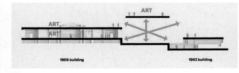

1222 Multidirectionality of views

1223 Competition scheme section

1224 Voids in the floating volume enable views and natural light to penetrate into the Entry Hall.

1225 The raised volume creates new vantage points to the city and park from within the gallery spaces and the rooftop sculpture garden.

1226 The newly connected building engages the landscape, ensuring porosity between the city and the park around it, as well as the existing buildings of the campus.

1207–1226   Buffalo AKG Art Museum

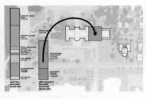

1229 The updated scheme located two new galleries, one raised above the courtyard and the other sunken on the city side of the 1905 Building. One lifted to be seen, establishing views to the surrounding context, and the other lowered, with a clear connection to the landscape, preventing the obstruction of any of the existing facades.

1228 The competition scheme had to be further developed to meet the specific amount of new gallery space.

1227 We won the competition in June 2016, which was featured on the first page of The Buffalo News below Dolly Parton.

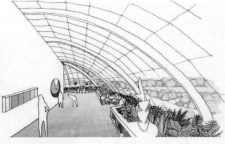

1230 Dome scheme

1231 Dome scheme view

1232 A domed volume covers the Bunshaft courtyard, creating an opportunity for a grand public space below.

1233 The dome creates a greenhouse-like gallery around the perimeter.

1234 Veil scheme

1235 A veiled volume acts as a physical landscaped bridge from city to park.

1236 The landscaped "veil" brings visitors up and over the building.

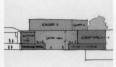

1237 Arch schemes explored adapting the single floating volume to create a stepped and vaulted "tunnel" that acts as a gateway.

1238 The current outdoor courtyard serves as the hinge to connect city to park and the 1905 and 1962 buildings. Lifting the volume creates a passage underneath from city to park.

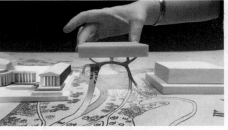

1239 The organic landscape and pedestrian paths that intersect in the courtyard will also have a three-dimensional quality, creating vertical connections to the floating volume.

1240 Design developments extended circulation up the building's facade and integrated the face of the lifted volume.

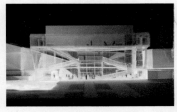

1241 Making activities visible

1242 360-degree wrapped scheme

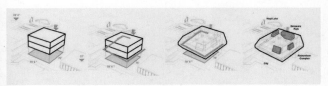

1243 Circulation wraps around the galleries and is then enveloped by a translucent veil that exposes the activities to the campus.

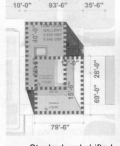

1244 Stacked and shifted scheme

1245 Galleries are offset and joined with circulation.

1246 New gallery spaces above the courtyard and sunken into the landscape are integrated seamlessly with the existing 1905 Building's galleries, minimizing the footprint of intervention.

1227–1246

Buffalo AKG Art Museum

1247 Architecture critics and members of Buffalo's preservation community widely panned the floating volume scheme. They argued that the courtyard between the 1962 and 1905 buildings was a critical feature of Bunshaft's work and should not be eliminated.

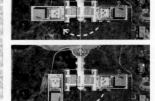

1248 As a result, new sites were tested, and the northern portion of the site was selected to preserve the character of the existing buildings.

1249 Turning the North-South cantilever scheme 90 degrees created an L-shaped gallery arrangement along the site's northern edge.

1250 Contiguous galleries on a single level

1251 Further scheme developments consolidated the extended single floor gallery of the L-shaped site into a detached, two-level gallery in the northwest corner.

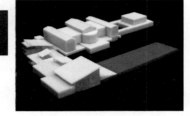

1252 L-shaped scheme

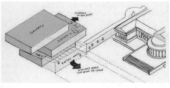

1253 Stacked boxes scheme—efficient gallery boxes are stacked to cascade toward park and lawn.

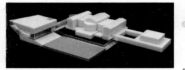

1254 Loop scheme—stacked galleries with a continuous loop of circulation

1255 The tower of gallery boxes is wrapped by circulation, connecting to the 1905 Building to create a loop.

1256 Pinecone scheme—the gallery tower is broken down to create individual rooms with distinct views.

1257 Introverted vs. extroverted

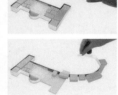

1258 Gallery rooms spiral upward to peak east toward park views.

1259 Rooms are merged with a continuous circulation loop.

1260 Individual galleries wrap around a central flexible box

Flexible Box   Rooms   Hybrid

1261 Pinecone scheme

1263 The Pinecone scheme departs from the axial quality of the existing buildings and introduces multidirectional galleries to the campus.

1264 Terraces between the galleries combine landscape and art.

1265 The terraced spaces act as visual breaks between the gallery rooms.

1266 Central atrium surrounded by galleries

1262 The 1905 galleries are unfurled and wrapped around a central atrium.

1267 Pinecone with 1905 and 1962 buildings

1268 Further developments of the Pinecone scheme placed a single flexible gallery on top to combine a large box with smaller rooms and minimized exterior occupiable spaces.

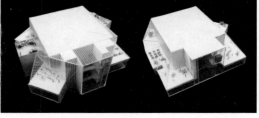

1269 Other concerns of the Pinecone scheme were its height, lack of directionality and sense of arrival, excessive terraces, and orthogonality. A new direction was explored.

1270 The need for a more diversified gallery experience and a softer appearance led the design toward a more streamlined and iconic silhouette for the north building.

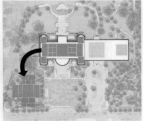

1271 Drawing from the scale of the 1905 galleries, rooms were translated and rearranged in a plus-shaped configuration on the first floor.

1272 The plus-shaped plan places art at the core, while creating four distinct corner programs.

1273 Landscape permeates the building from all sides, while visually opening the corners enhances the sense of porosity.

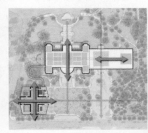

1274 The plus-shaped plan combines the singular axes of the 1905 and 1962 buildings, puncturing through the walls to create a sense of multidirectionality.

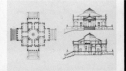

1275 Andrea Palladio, Villa Rotonda (1567)

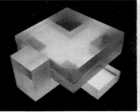

1276 The F1 galleries are topped with two efficient gallery boxes, with a double-height gallery placed in front of the building.

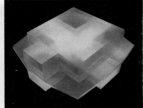

1277 A promenade wraps around the F2 gallery to accommodate the diverse programs increasingly expected of museums.

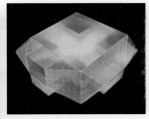

1278 The galleries and promenade are enveloped by a veil, creating a year-round winter garden that allows visitors to enjoy the park during Buffalo's harsh winters.

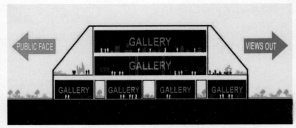

1279 While the rooms and galleries are stacked efficiently, connecting the points between them establishes an interstitial space that surrounds and creates an image for the new museum addition.

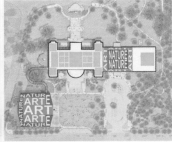

1280 The north building is the inverse of the 1962 courtyard—where the courtyard captured nature in the center of art, the north building places art at its core with nature and flexible spaces surrounding it.

1281 North building model

1282 A glass veil and a hermetic gallery box

1283 Site

1284 Gallery rooms

1285 Flexible box

1286 Promenade

1287 Double-height gallery

1288 Veil

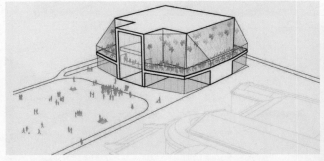

1289 The promenade and new lawn act as a new public venue for the museum campus, and can also be used as exhibition space.

1290 A new icon for the Albright-Knox Art Gallery campus

1291 The north building addition and new lawn complement the 1905 and 1962 buildings, creating a campus of the individual—yet visually and physically connected—buildings in the park.

1292 The building's veil creates a new public presence for the campus. In contrast to the more solid and hermetic 1905 and 1962 buildings, the north building is open all around, exposing the museum's activities to the city and park.

1293 Wrapping the building to create a transparent museum

1294 Giovanni Strazza, *The Veiled Virgin* (1850s)

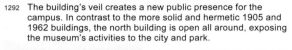

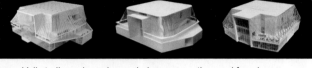

1295 Veil studies—draped, rounded corners, orthogonal facade

1296 The veil-enclosed promenade allows for flexible activities against the backdrop of the park.

1297 Large-scale artworks can be displayed on the double-height gallery walls.

1298 The promenade offers expansive views of Delaware Park.

1299 The promenade can also be used for auxiliary programs like seating and a cafe.

1300 The veil creates a space that can be used as an elevated, all-weather sculpture court for permanent or temporary installations.

1301 ¼ inch = 1 foot scale model (2019)

1302 Sculpture court

1303 Event space

1304 Large-scale mural

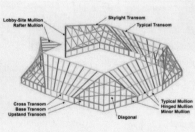

1305 The veil's frame acts as infrastructural support for the galleries.

1306 Sprinkler lines, track lighting, art hanging, and shades are integrated into the veil mullion structure.

1308 Marble facade and veil mock up, November 2020

1307 Annual sun exposure, from left to right—south facade; east facade; north facade; west facade

1309 Veil mockup

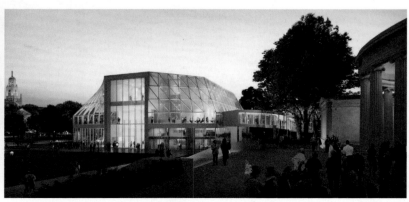

1310 The veil and promenade continuously exhibit the activity of the north building, contributing to an enhanced campus experience from both inside and outside the museum.

Buffalo AKG Art Museum

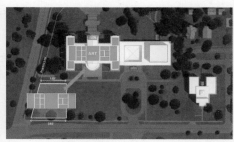

1311 The three floors of galleries, which reference the scale of the 1905 Building, are reorganized to make a diversified art-viewing experience.

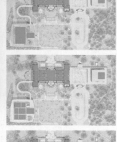

1312 Reorganized gallery spaces

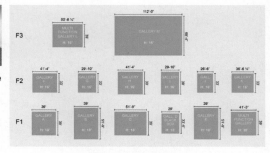

1314 North building gallery dimensions

1313 As part of the AK360 plan, the galleries of the 1905 Building will also be renovated.

1318 A bridge punctuates the upper level of the multifunction gallery, offering views down to the art and out toward the lawn.

1315 The ground floor consists of a square central gallery connected to four wings, forming the plus-shaped gallery plan.

1316 Museum visitors arrive at an entry vestibule that faces the double-height multifunction gallery, then enter the lobby to the left.

1317 The double-height gallery provides a space for displaying large-scale installations.

1321 The plus configuration creates enfilade galleries, with marble portals between rooms echoing the marble on the building's facade.

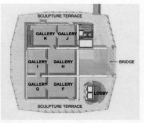

1322 Visitors access the second-floor galleries via the stair or elevators that start in the lobby. On F2, the promenade provides a space outside the galleries to relax and enjoy the park.

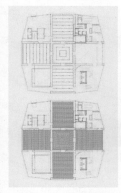

1319 The plus-shaped plan is enhanced by the pattern of the ceiling lighting and wood floors.

1320 The F1 central gallery is accessible from all four sides.

1324 The F3 galleries can be accessed from the F2 promenade stairs at the opposite end of the lobby circulation core.

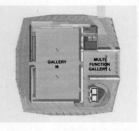

1325 Occupying the third floor, a large open gallery provides extreme flexibility.

1326 Third floor multifunction gallery

1323 The second-floor galleries offer a suite of adjoining rooms ideal for multi-section exhibitions.

1327 Section model

1328 The expansive F3 gallery introduces a portal view toward the park to the north, reinforcing the connection not just to the existing Albright-Knox campus, but to the Buffalo History Museum and the city beyond.

1311–1328   Buffalo AKG Art Museum

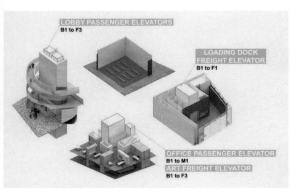

1329 The first floor's plus-shaped galleries create four corner conditions, each occupied with a different program—lobby, office, Black Box gallery, and loading.

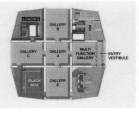

1330 F1 corner programs

1331 The lobby reception desk, entrance from the underground parking, and access to the galleries are located in the southwestern corner.

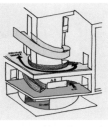

1332 Lobby and B1–F3 circulation core

1333 Lobby early model

1337 F1 office plan

1334 View of lobby, reception, and circulation core, with stair access up to the F2 galleries and down to the underground parking.

1335 Lobby view from outside

1336 Office spaces and meeting rooms for the museum's staff occupy the F1 and mezzanine levels in the southeast corner.

1338 Office concept sketch

1339 F1 meeting rooms and mezzanine level offices

1340 F1 office reception

1341 Large meeting room

1342 The mezzanine level offices have views out toward the museum campus and lawn.

1343 The Black Box space is located at the northwestern corner.

1344 Black Box plan

1345 A curtain-clad flexible gallery space, the Black Box can be used for multimedia art, performances, and small events.

1346 Black Box gallery view from outside

1347 The north building loading dock is located in the northeastern corner adjacent to Iroquois Drive.

1348 Loading dock plan

1349 Loading dock view

1350 The loading dock holds a large freight elevator for transporting art between floors.

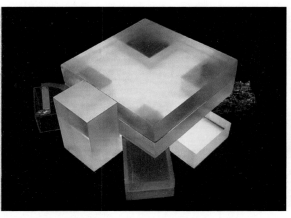

1351 Concept model of four distinct corner programs that support the gallery spaces

1353 Campus elevation from Elmwood Avenue

1354 Elevation unwrapped to show bridge connection

1355 Bridge plan

1352 A bridge, clad in reflective glazing and highly polished metal, connects the north building to the 1905 Building via a winding path through existing trees on the site, facilitating both art and pedestrian movement.

1356 The bridge enters into the 1905 Building through a new opening cut to the size of an existing bay.

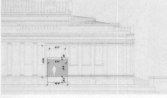

1357 The 9 by 9–foot clearance facilitates both pedestrian movement and art handling between the old and new gallery spaces.

1358 Bridge connection studies

1359 Bridge connection from inside the 1905 Building

1360 The bridge creates an opportunity to view outdoor sculptures in the round while still inside the museum.

1361 Bridge connection from the inside of the north building

1362 View along the bridge

1363 View entering 1905 Building

1364 The bridge column supports are different sizes and are placed randomly to blend in with the surrounding trees.

1365 The bridge path wraps around the trees on site, preserving the historic oaks that are part of Olmsted's Delaware Park.

1366 At night the bridge can be lit on both the interior and exterior to create an iconic form in the landscape.

1367 Bridge model

1368 Winding through the trees on the campus, the bridge connects the two buildings and allows visitors to be immersed in the park at a higher vantage point.

1352–1368   Buffalo AKG Art Museum

1369 Moving the museum's parking underground creates a large lawn at the center of the campus, returning the landscape to the park that once surrounded the museum at its founding.

1370 The historic steps of the 1905 Building were demolished to make way for the parking lot during the construction of the 1962 addition.

1371 The existing surface parking lot obstructs the view of the 1905 Building from Elmwood Avenue.

1372 Current 1905 Building condition, as seen from the parking lot.

1373 As part of the AK360 campus-wide overhaul, the 1905 Building stairs will be restored, with improvements to provide direct access from the lawn.

1374 The new lawn improves sight lines to the 1905 Building and provides a space for relaxation and recreation.

1375 Evening concert on the steps of the 1905 Building

1376 Winter lawn

1377 Located at the opposite end of the lawn, a proposed Head House connects visitors to the underground parking.

1378 A proposed Jeppe Hein installation of mirrored columns surrounds the Head House, integrating art with architecture.

1379 Head House connection from the underground parking lot

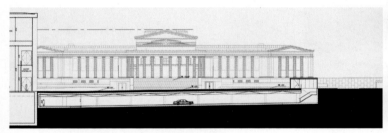

1380 Underground parking and Head House section

1381 The underground parking lot provides access to both the 1905 and the north buildings.

1382 Environmental graphics help visitors locate the museum entrances.

1383 Visitors enter the north building via a circular lobby underneath the building's main lobby.

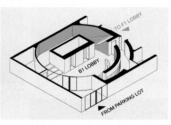

1384 The B1 lobby is characterized by a textile wall installation by Miriam Bäckström and a terrazzo floor in a complementary color palette.

1385 The terrazzo tones gradate in color leading from the B1 to the F1 lobby. The color sequence continues up to F2 and F3, highlighting the visitor's path vertically through the building.

1386 Miriam Bäckström's woven artwork echoes Sol LeWitt's Wall Drawing #1268: Scribbles: Staircase (AKAG), installed in the staircase of the 1905 Building.

1387 The continuous artwork, which maintains Albright-Knox's integration of art with transitional public spaces, draws visitors up the stair from the B1 lobby into the north building.

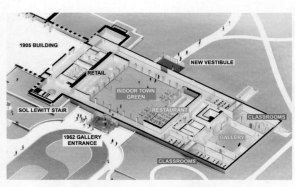

1389 1962 Building renovation—classroom

1390 1962 Building renovation—gallery

1388 As part of the AK360 renovation, the 1962 Building, already the location of the museum's primary auditorium space, will become a wing solely dedicated to education.

1391 Vehicular drop-off roundabout

1392 The vehicular drop-off designed for the 1962 Building will remain, renovated to provide entry into the underground parking structure.

1393 View toward 1962 Building entrance and vehicular entrance into the underground parking structure.

1394 Existing 1962 Building entrance

1395 The park side of the 1962 Building was originally a blank wall, eliminating a connection to the park.

1396 With the addition of a second entry vestibule that mirrors the 1962 original, visitors will be able to pass through the museum to the park.

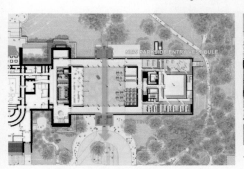

1397 Establishing a through-connection

1398 The addition of large swinging windowed doors allows activity in the 1962 Building to spill out into the courtyard.

1399 The retail space opens up to the north end of the courtyard.

1400 Restaurant seating extends out on the south end of the courtyard.

1401 In an inversion of the veil placed on the north building, the 1962 Building courtyard will be covered by a glass roof.

1402 Enclosing the currently open-air courtyard will allow it to be used year-round.

1403 The glass roof will be a site-specific installation, titled *Common Sky*, by Olafur Eliasson and his Studio Other Spaces. It reflects and refracts the activity of the courtyard below in a kaleidoscopic display and reintroduces our original intent to create a public town square enveloped in art and a new gateway to the park.

1388–1403   Buffalo AKG Art Museum

1404   AK360 architect announcement, June 2016

1405   OMA selection, June 2016

1406   Kickoff meeting, September 2016

1407   Community engagement—public meeting, November 2016

1408   Public meeting

1409   State Historic Preservation Office (SHPO) meeting

1410   Albright-Knox committee meeting

1411   Shohei Shigematsu with AK director Janne Sirén, donor Jeffrey Gundlach, and board president Alice Jacobs

1412   AK360 groundbreaking

1413   AK360 groundbreaking, December 2019

1414   1905 Building renovation

1415   1905 Building marble cleaning

1416   1905 Building historic western stair restoration

1417   1905 Building ornamentation removed and stored for preservation during renovation

1418   1962 Building's offices facing the courtyard are removed to make way for the restaurant.

1419   Full-scale facade mockup

1420   Full-scale gallery mockup to test materials/lighting, located in the 1905 Building's Sculpture Court

1421   Site excavation, August 2020

1422   1,500 cubic yards of concrete were poured in an 8-hour period for the 15,000-square-foot foundation, January 2021

1423   The completed museum campus is expected to open in 2022.

Buffalo AKG Art Museum

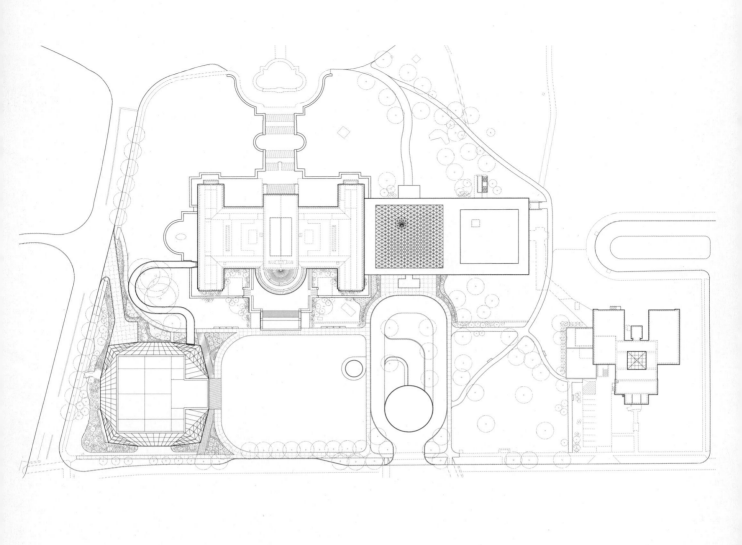

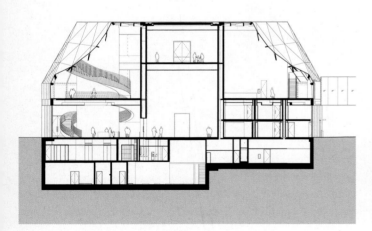

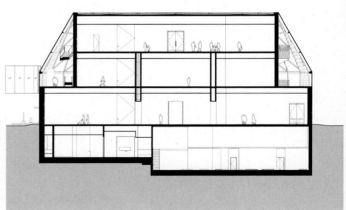

1425–1427   Buffalo AKG Art Museum

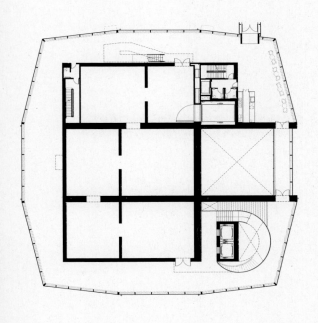
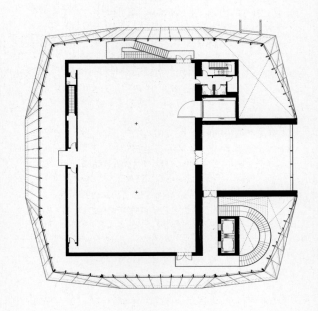
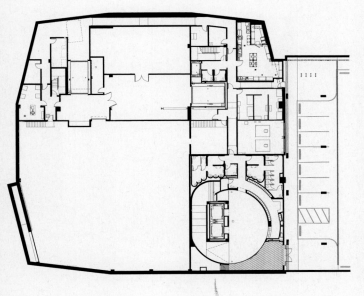
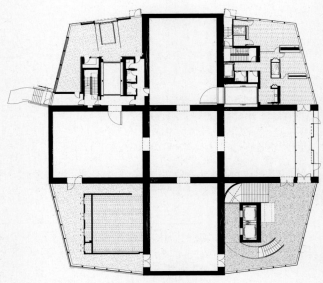

1428–1431   Buffalo AKG Art Museum

1432

New Museum

New Museum

We were finally given an opportunity to build a cultural institution in New York, a new addition to the New Museum next door to its iconic SANAA-designed building at 235 Bowery (fortuitously resembling the conditions we faced back in 2001, for the Whitney Museum extension to the beloved Brutalist building by Marcel Breuer). The New Museum has been growing in visitors, exhibitions, and activities. Its diverse engagements, including an incubator, education programs, and events like IdeasCity, have been transforming the institution into a cultural laboratory. We were asked to add a new building that provides much-needed space for its expanded activities and simultaneously reflects increasingly public ambitions—duplicating the program and square footage on a site immediately adjacent to the existing building—part and counterpart, side-by-side.

   This condition was deeply entrenched in dichotomies. While dichotomies are inherent to museum expansions—old versus new, better versus worse, ugly versus beautiful—they can suppress the full potential of the pair. We looked to less didactic, more unexpected and maybe even romantically entangled relationships that could exist between two parts of a whole. Can one be highly infrastructural to give support and free agency to the other? Can it be two equal entities in complete harmony? Can the two be distinct and independent but reciprocal as a pair? Our approach complements and respects the integrity of the adjoining SANAA building, while asserting its own distinct identity. The new New Museum will be a synergistic pair working spatially and programmatically in tandem, offering a repertoire of spaces for the institution's curatorial ambitions and diverse programs.

   We stack the required programs exactly at the same level of the existing building—three floors of galleries, a permanent home for NEW INC, offices, multifunctional education and event spaces—new and old conjoined. Ceiling heights of the newly connected galleries align on each floor, creating expanded space for exhibitions and horizontal flow between the buildings. Galleries can be used singularly across the floorplate to host larger exhibitions or separately for diversity and curatorial freedom. Due to the horizontality of the site, the galleries in the new building increase in size on the upper levels while the galleries in the existing building decrease in size—the total area per connected floor remains balanced.

A distinction between the two buildings is created by taking advantage of our site's depth to insert an interstitial space, in between art and city, containing a stair atrium and dedicated gallery elevators for improved vertical circulation. This highly public face—starting from the exterior plaza and atrium stair to terraced multi-purpose rooms at the top—is a conduit of art and activities that provides an openness to engage the Bowery and the city.

The existing tower's verticality treats the different programs within in the same expression. We wanted to create a healthy contrast by expanding the galleries horizontally and introducing two setbacks. An angled setback starting from the top of gallery stack to the street defines a new public plaza at the terminus of Prince Street that becomes a focal point and a buffer zone between existing and new. A second setback above the galleries makes the top of the building disappear, while opening up the upper-level terraces to the sky. Clad in laminated glass with a layer of metal mesh, the building appears monolithic during the day, establishing a unified exterior alongside the existing building's metal mesh facade. In the evening, the transparency of the facade is enhanced as light permeates through its openings, exposing the museum's anatomy.

The new New Museum is a partnership of two different personalities with high compatibility—independent but in constant dialogue. The result is an expanded platform that provokes even more dynamic interactions between art, artists, and people, which are then exposed to communicate the museum's civic ambitions to the city. The new building is visible, even from our office on the thirteenth floor of 180 Varick Street, across Prince Street over SoHo.

Location	New York, NY, USA		
Status	2016–Ongoing		
Typology	Museum		
Program	Gallery	10,500 ft²	970 m²
	Public Spaces	8,600 ft²	800 m²
	Education/Event/NEW INC	6,400 ft²	590 m²
	Studio/Support/Admin	8,400 ft²	780 m²
	MEP	14,600 ft²	1,360 m²
	Total Area	48,500 ft²	4,500 m²

OMA NY   New Museum

New Museum

New Museum

OMA NY

New Museum

1435

New Museum

New Museum:
EXPANSION & OUTREACH

1437 "Carsten Höller: Experience" (2011)

1438 "The Keeper" (2016)

1439 "Pipilotti Rist: Pixel Forest" (2016)

1440 "Sarah Lucas: Au Naturel" (2018)

1436 The New Museum of Contemporary Art was founded in 1977 by Marcia Tucker and positioned between a traditional museum and an alternative space, existing in small gallery spaces in lower Manhattan and focusing on exhibitions that would catalyze a broader dialogue between artists and the public. In 1999, under director Lisa Phillips, the expansion of museum programs and increased visitorship led to the completion of its first building. The vertical museum designed by SANAA opened in 2007 at 235 Bowery.

1442 "Festival of Ideas for the New City" (2011)

1443 IdeasCity was founded in 2011 and transformed the New Museum into a public platform with collaborative initiatives between the arts, design, education, and the community.

1441 Over the past forty years the New Museum has been growing, not only in the number of exhibitions and visitors, but also its activities and ambitions. With initiatives like NEW INC and IdeasCity, the institution is becoming a platform and multi-faceted entity and sought a new building addition to address current and future needs.

1444 The biennial catalyzed the institution to extend beyond its walls and into the public realm.

1445 IdeasCity

1446 NEW INC, the world's first museum-led incubator, created a collaborative and experimental community.

1447 The New Museum is located in the Bowery neighborhood of lower Manhattan.

1448 The Bowery is the oldest thoroughfare in Manhattan, with a history of commerce and culture, but it began to decline in the late nineteenth century and came to be considered a dangerous and drug-ridden neighborhood.

1449 CBGB, 315 Bowery (1973)

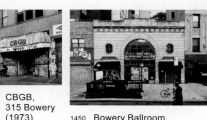

1450 Bowery Ballroom, 6 Delancey Street (2019)

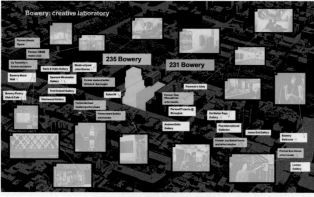

1451 Eva Hesse worked on her sculptures in a small studio at 134 Bowery.

1452 Mark Rothko's former studio at 222 Bowery

1453 The Bowery is also home to many restaurant equipment vendors.

1454 The Bowery has historically been home to artists and galleries and the New Museum has, in a way, catalyzed the revival of the neighborhood as a creative laboratory. We wanted to reflect both the history and present cultural effervescence with the new addition.

OMA New York

Prince Street

New Museum

1456 The site is close to the OMA New York office, a straight shot along Prince Street.

1457 While the New Museum created a new cultural center, the Bowery can be criticized for its gentrification.

1455 The site for the expansion is at 231 Bowery, a former restaurant supply store adjacent to the existing museum building by SANAA.

1458 Juxtaposition of Bowery's existing grit, like one of the last remaining flophouses, Bowery Mission, and Freeman's Alley, with new gallery, hospitality, and residential developments.

1459 231 Bowery is located at the terminus of Prince Street, a major thoroughfare, and is authentic to the neighborhood character. We were interested in the idea of preservation, especially given Bowery's history of art spaces in such buildings.

1460 Coincidentally, "Cronocaos," an exhibition on preservation, was held at 231 Bowery in 2011.

1461 One side of the exhibition was "preserved" as it was while inhabited by the store, while the other was renovated into a typical white cube museum space.

1462 View south on Bowery

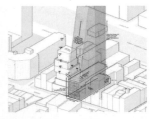

1463 View north on Bowery

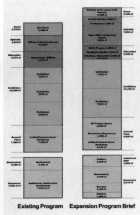

Existing Program   Expansion Program Brief

1465 The program brief for the expansion was to almost double the square footage of the existing programs—lobby/common area/bookshop, galleries, education, NEW INC, and event space.

70.5 ft / 21.4m   50.0 ft / 15.2m

235 BOWERY 7,700 sf   231 BOWERY 8,840 sf

Existing   Expansion

1466 The site for the expansion itself is much longer, deeper, and narrower than the existing building's site, which was a consideration.

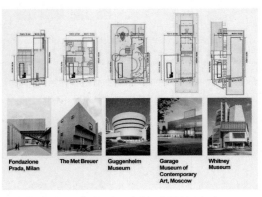

Fondazione Prada, Milan | The Met Breuer | Guggenheim Museum | Garage Museum of Contemporary Art, Moscow | Whitney Museum

1467 Scale comparisons, from left to right: Fondazione Prada (Milan), the Met Breuer (New York City), Guggenheim Museum (New York City), Garage Museum of Contemporary Art (Moscow), and Whitney Museum (New York City)

1464 Zoning envelope

COMPETITIVE
AKRON ART MUSEUM
COOP HIMMELB(L)AU, 2007

SUBSERVIENT
GUGGENHEIM NEW YORK
FRANK LLOYD WRIGHT, 1959
GWITHMEY SEIGEL, 1992

AUTONOMOUS
JEWISH MUSEUM BERLIN
DANIEL LIBESKIND, 2001 & 2007

1468 Before designing the building, we thought about the kinds of relationships that could exist between the existing and new. Extensions can be autonomous or competitive or, as is the case with the Guggenheim, completely subservient.

1469 Our proposal for the 2001 Whitney Museum Extension tried to simultaneously preserve a historic brownstone while providing a new vertical extension, creating a trio of buildings of three different generations.

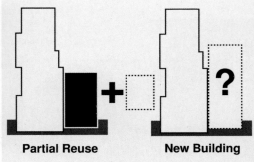

Partial Reuse   New Building

1470 Despite the mandated duplication of program, how can the expansion renew the museum—rather than redo the museum—as a distinct yet complementary pair? Would a partial reuse or an altogether new building be most effective for the renewal?

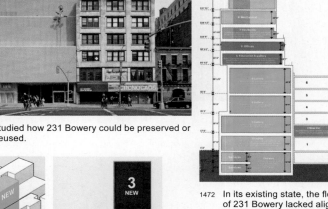

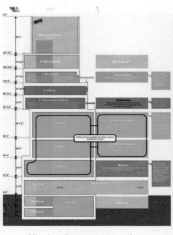

1471 We first studied how 231 Bowery could be preserved or partially reused.

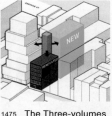

1475 The Three-volumes scheme divides the site into a collection of buildings, with the front of the 231 building preserved.

1476 At the conjunction of the three volumes is a circulation and service crossing, connecting the three parts.

1477 Three-volumes scheme model

1472 In its existing state, the floorplates of 231 Bowery lacked alignment to the museum building, a condition antithetical to creating synergy between the two sites.

1473 Aligning the program and floorplates between 231 Bowery and the SANAA building, the pair could form a lower cluster of galleries with education and event space above, clarifying circulation throughout the museum.

1474 Study models for preservation and partial reuse

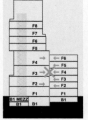

1478 Mismatched floorplates prohibit connectivity.

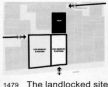

1479 The landlocked site posed construction challenges and new activities would be hidden from public view.

1480 Sketch from Chrystie Street revealing the junction between buildings.

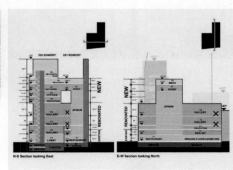

1481 Three-volumes scheme sections—education and NEW INC and the existing museum programs are at the front and new galleries are in the back volume.

1484 Expressed Core scheme model

1482 Sketch from Prince Street—a variation of the three-volumes scheme was an option that would have to reveal the connection between the two buildings and expose the new activities.

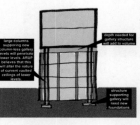

1483 Another option for selective preservation was the Expressed Core scheme. Existing lower levels of the 231 building are preserved, with new column-free gallery floors added above.

1485 Expressed Core scheme sections

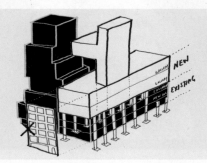

1486 To accommodate the new galleries, a new structure would have to be surgically threaded through the existing floors. The original facade would likely have to be abandoned.

1487 Large columns to support the new column-free galleries will penetrate the lower levels and the structure will require new foundations, posing a complex and costly construction.

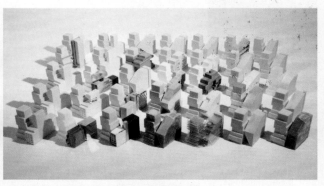

1488 While selectively preserving 231 Bowery seemed conceptually promising, it proved practically difficult, with limited connectivity, constrained heights, and disjointed floorplates with the existing museum building. A new building, rather than preservation, allowed for a reassessment of priorities so we began to think critically about the relationship between new and existing pairs with further studies.

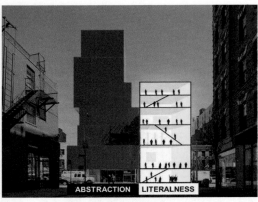

ABSTRACTION LITERALNESS

1489 We looked beyond dichotomies, at relationships between pairs.

1490 Marina Abramović and Uwe Laysiepen (Ulay), *Imponderabilia* (1977)—tension between two entities

1491 Rocket launcher and rocket—one highly infrastructural and the other to be launched

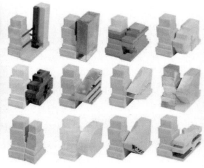

1492 Study models—distinct and complementary pairs

1493 The final concept was conceived first by cloning the program and stack to align with 235 Bowery.

1494 Taking advantage of the site's depth, a public face is added to the program stack.

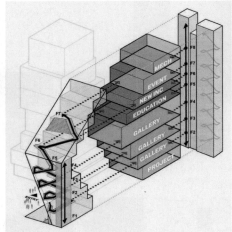

1495 The resulting interstitial space introduces a buffer zone that contains a stair atrium extending up beyond the gallery floors, a new auditorium, and circulation between programs, including dedicated elevators for galleries.

1496 Program model

1497 Circulation model

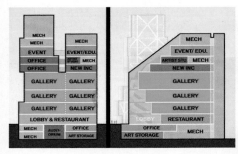

1498 The galleries, NEW INC, education rooms, and event spaces align to the existing building's programs while an angled articulation of the programmatic split between gallery and production zones defines a new form.
The pair is completely merged in one section but takes the form of two distinct buildings in the other section.

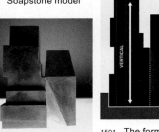

1499 Soapstone model

1500 Concrete model

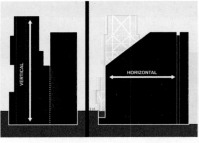

1501 The form introduces a horizontal counterpart to the existing building's verticality.

1502 Horizontal and vertical components balancing and supporting each other.

1503 Meeting with Kazuyo Sejima—coordination was required because the two buildings would be highly connected, and the new building would expose an unseen facade of SANAA's building.

1504 Daylit vs. controlled

1505 Production vs. exhibition

1506 Experimental vs. efficient

1507 Accessibility

1508 Accommodation

1509 Studio vs. loft

1510 A new spatial diversity is generated: an urban plaza for events like IdeasCity; flexible, loft-like gallery floors that can act in combination or independently; and terraced studio-like incubator, education, and event spaces.

1511 The new form is shaped by its relationship to the existing building's organization. While SANAA treats the entire building with a consistent formal and material expression, the datum of the new building clarifies the organization between public and private spaces. Aligning with the height of the existing building's galleries, the building sets back above the datum and disappears from street view. Below the datum, the volume sets back diagonally to introduce a triangular plaza as a shared space between the two buildings.

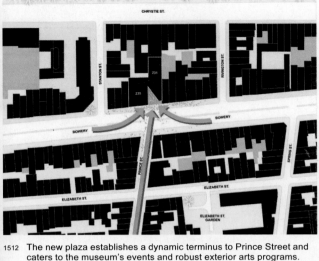

1512 The new plaza establishes a dynamic terminus to Prince Street and caters to the museum's events and robust exterior arts programs.

1513 Existing view from Prince Street

1514 New building view from Prince Street

1518 360-degree view of exposed model

1515 In contrast to the hermetic existing SANAA building, activities within the new building are revealed and are made visible to Prince Street.

1516 Barbara Hepworth, *Two Forms (Apolima)* (1969)— contrast of differing stones emphasizes opposing forms

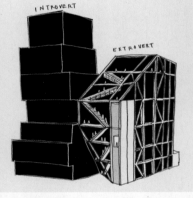

1517 A healthy contrast between introversion and extroversion.

1519 Model in site, public face exposed

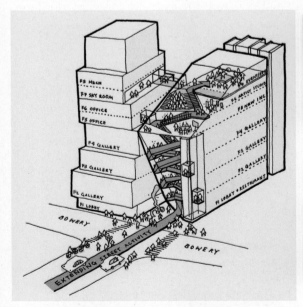

1520 The interstitial public face acts as an extension of Prince Street and the neighborhood's movement and energy.

1521 Model in site

1522 Lisa Phillips and Artistic Director Massimiliano Gioni, inspecting the ¼ inch = 1 foot model

1523 ¼ inch = 1 foot section model

1524 The plaza at the terminus of Prince Street becomes a focal point and a buffer zone between the new and old.

1525 The plaza accommodates the museum's increase in capacity, as the museum's annual attendance has grown from 60,000 to more than 400,000 since 2007.

1526 The plaza also becomes the anchor for the museum's outdoor public activities, and supports the institution's mission to expand beyond museum walls.

1527 IdeasCity scenario before

1528 IdeasCity scenario after

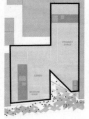

1529 IdeasCity

1530 Pop-up

1531 Performance

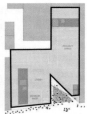

1532 Installation

1533 Early sketch of public plaza and exposed circulation

1536 The plaza acts as an informal gathering space.

1534 The angled articulation at the plaza reveals an unseen portion of SANAA's stepped profile.

1535 The public plaza flexes to accommodate the New Museum's diverse agendas.

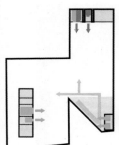

1537 Upon entering the building, visitors are met with multiple modes of circulation. Internalized circulation core of the existing building is complemented by outward-facing modes of circulation.

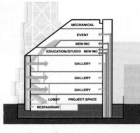

1538 Two efficient passenger elevators dedicated to the gallery levels are paired with a grand stair at the building's entry. Freight elevators in a machine-like circulation tower at the back of the building expose movement along an otherwise-hidden eastern elevation.

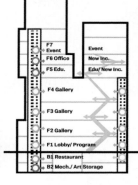

1539 An experiential stair positioned between the new and existing buildings serves gallery levels and links upper-level programs.

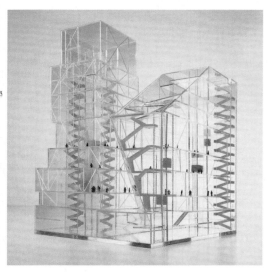

1540 The dual system of efficient and experiential circulation at either end of the building broadcasts the New Museum's mission as an activity-based, public institution.

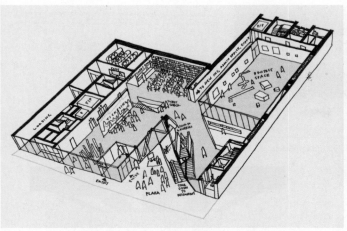

1541   One of the main challenges of the expansion was to clarify the entry and ground-floor lobby area.

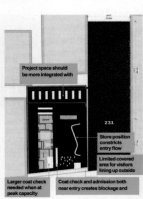

1542   The existing ground level had a limited area for visitors and constricted flow and visibility.

1543   Lobby ticket queue

1544   The existing ticketing is close to the street, causing congestion near the entry.

1545   Lobby study plan—angled

1546   Lobby study plan—bookshelf reuse

1547   Lobby study—curtain closed as space divider

1548   Lobby study—curtain open

1549   Lobby model

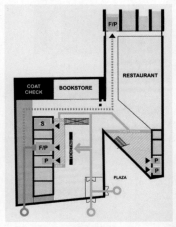

1550   With the expansion, the two buildings shared a unified ground floor. Programs such as ticketing, bookstore, and cafe are consolidated toward the back of the existing lobby to provide easy and clear connection to both buildings.

1551   F1 axon—entry is provided into both buildings.

1552   Gallery elevators in 231 Bowery with view out onto the street

1553   Relocation of the coat check, bookstore, and ticketing desk frees up the lobby space. Direct access to elevators and stairway to galleries are located on either side of ticketing. To maximize flexibility, a retractable screen is used to create a simple and light ticketing zone and barrier to the elevators behind.

1554   View from the existing ground floor looking across to 231 Bowery

1555   View behind ticketing screen

1556   The screen behind the ticketing desk can be used for projections that display ticketing information, art, or for events when the lobby is rented.

1558 Despite moving the bookstore to the back, we wanted to maintain its visibility from the street.

1559 Cafe and book store plan

1557 Adjacent to the coat check at the back is the cafe and bookstore in the space formerly used as the project space gallery.

1561 Existing cafe bar reconfigured to integrate with the bookstore.

1560 View of existing cafe from the project space gallery.

1562 A series of existing skylights above the bookstore is exposed to illuminate the space.

1564 Existing coat check

1563 The space is naturally day-lit and becomes a garden-like waiting and lounge area.

1565 The new coat check is consolidated with the new location of the cafe.

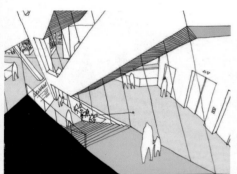

1567 An exterior stair in the plaza traces the facade down to a B1 entry.

1568 Section showing proposed B1 restaurant—a courtyard is positioned on the front facade to increase visibility and light from the plaza.

1569 View from B1 restaurant—direct access from the plaza is established and the opening brings light from the exterior down into the lower level.

1566 For the restaurant, we initially proposed its location on B1 so it could become both a part of and discrete from the museum lobby.

1570 The restaurant was moved to the ground floor to consolidate public amenities and activate the ground floor while providing more visibility.

1571 Sketch of ground floor restaurant looking out onto museum entrance, F1 lobby, and atrium stair.

1572 From F1 lobby, visitors can directly access the galleries through a highly visible stair.

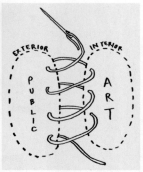

1574 The stair stitches together the exterior public domain with the art interior.

1575 The act of stitching art and public transforms the stair into an interstitial zone that establishes a public face for the museum and communicates its activities to the neighborhood.

1573 The gallery stair within the new building establishes a clarity in circulation that did not exist in the museum before.

1576 Typical building fire escape stair found on Bowery

1577 While public movement is made visible to the outside, the stair also creates a sense of orientation for the visitors, both to the city and the existing museum building.

F2 Gallery Stair   **F3 Gallery Stair**   **F4 Gallery Stair**

1578 Stair relationships to existing and new galleries

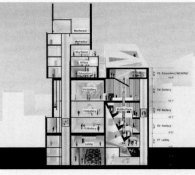

1579 The stair acts as a public face while clearly connecting the new and existing galleries. The clarified access and connection also allow for curatorial freedom across the two buildings.

1581 Stair study model

1582 Stair study model

1583 Stair and gallery section model

1584 Client meeting for gallery stair

1580 A new public zone is established in between the old and new buildings.

1585 Urs Fischer, *Horses Dream of Horses* (2004)—atrium installation

1586 Urs Fischer, *Spinoza Rhapsody* (2006)— the stair form creates a dramatic atrium that can accommodate large-scale installations.

1587 F2 stair landing looking out to the street—the activated atrium becomes its own gallery space.

1573–1587   New Museum

1590 Stair view from landing on F5, leading up to NEW INC.

1589 The gray metallic cladding of the staircase echoes the facade materiality of the SANAA building.

1588 Gallery stair view from F3 with works by Urs Fischer. The gallery stair's circulation corridor provides additional wall space for display.

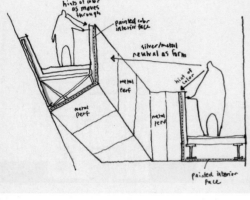

1592 Outside face—anodized aluminum

1593 The color treatment is seen or unseen based on the viewer's position.

1591 The cold material of the staircase is treated with color on surfaces behind the perforated metal cladding to create a hint of color.

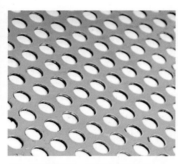

1594 Inside face—color-treated or painted

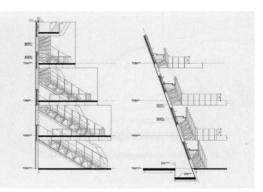

1595 The stair consists of a triangular steel truss spanning floor to floor with intermediate support provided by a sloping column at the western facade fold.

1596 In addition to the gallery stair, there are two dedicated gallery elevators within the interstitial, public face of the new building.

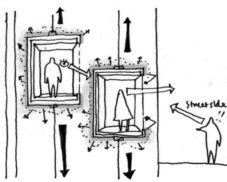

1597 The elevators of 231 Bowery aim to have a more outward presence, given their position.

1598 The outside of the elevators is treated with reflective thermal insulation.

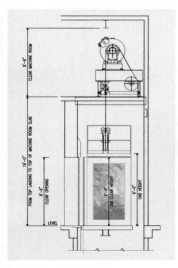

1600 View from outside

1601 View from inside

1599 A monitor inside the elevator activates circulation with art.

1602 Visitor activity within the museum is broadcast to the street and plaza.

1603   The monumental stair provides relief from the limited circulation space in the existing galleries of 235 Bowery while providing access to the galleries of the new building.

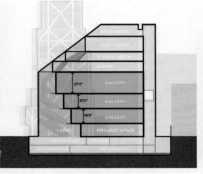

1604   Galleries are located on F2, F3, and F4 to expand upon the existing spaces in 235 Bowery. The new galleries are highly connected to the existing, and they will work together both spatially and programmatically.

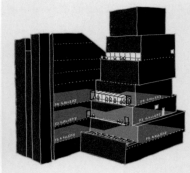

1605   Connections between the two buildings are carefully coordinated at each level to avoid structural bracing. A number of strategies for the type and nature of connection points is provided for curatorial flexibility.

1606   Gallery connection

1607   F4 gallery—performance

1608   Section view of 235 and 231 galleries—the depth of the new building provides an expansive, horizontal gallery space that complements the existing museum tower's verticality.

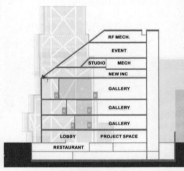

1609   Horizontal gallery connections— (A) direct access from both galleries to atrium stair and elevator circulation, (B) discrete openings from gallery to gallery, (C) potential large openings to create horizontal flexibility, as well as a separate tube on F4.

1610   A glass tube at the back of F4 galleries utilizes an existing window opening adjacent to the core to avoid puncturing the main "presentation" wall and creates discrete circulation between the two buildings.

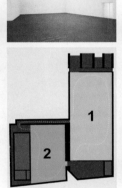

1611   No opening—two separate exhibitions with limited opening between two buildings

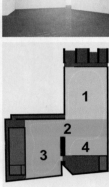

1612   Half opening—one column bay can be opened to create a series of connected exhibitions across the two buildings.

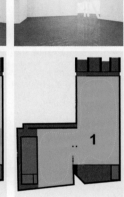

1613   Full opening

1614   Diverse gallery configurations—from left to right: two distinct exhibitions, triennial, retrospective.

1615   F4 gallery closed

1616   F4 gallery open and connected

1617   The dividing concrete masonry unit (CMU) wall between the two buildings will be removed during construction. Plaster gallery walls will be built, allowing them to be removed to fit different exhibitions.

1618 The F2–F4 galleries of 231 Bowery are efficient yet diverse.

1619 F2–F4 plans—each gallery level has different spatial parameters and plan dimensions, due to the horizontality of the site and the lower setback created for the plaza and the sloping interstitial space. In 235 Bowery, the galleries decrease in size on the upper levels, whereas in 231, galleries increase in size. The total gallery area per floor remains balanced.

1620 F2–F4 sections—as the floorplates expand, the heights of the gallery ceilings increase from the bottom to the top of the gallery stack.

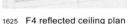

1625 F4 reflected ceiling plan

1622 Wall configuration study—east-west wall

1623 Wall configuration study—north-south walls

1624 Wall configuration study—organic

1621 Temporary gallery wall configuration studies showing connection points between wall and ceiling—from left to right: east-west walls, north-south walls, organic shapes.

1626 F3 gallery perimeter study using color to test relationship between wall and ceiling

1627 Study of temporary gallery partition to exposed ceiling relationship

1628 Test fit—"Thomas Bayrle: Playtime" (2018) show inside the new gallery

1630 Ceiling of existing 235 Bowery

1631 Early gallery ceiling study emulating the existing 235 Bowery ceiling

1629 The simple floor and an efficient ceiling system provide a flexible strategy for display and lighting.

 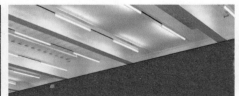

1632 Ceiling with structure and integrated mechanical, walls, and polished concrete floor slabs.

1633 Simple, linear tracks with a busway can accommodate both fluorescent and LED strip lighting, as well as directional point lights.

1634 Mechanical ducts evenly spaced in alternating structural bays

1618–1634

New Museum

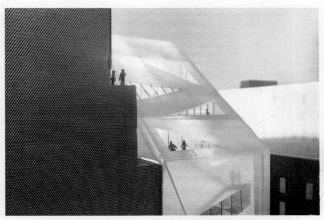

1635 On the upper levels, the circulation on the face of the building forges new connections between NEW INC, education, and event programs.

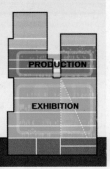
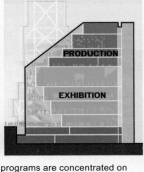

1636 Exhibition and public programs are concentrated on the lower levels while collaborative programs are accumulated on the upper levels. The interstitial space and stair connect the two entities and tie together the different types of production, work, and learning spaces.

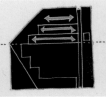

1637 Open and flexible

1638 Destination at top

1639 Eva Hesse's works on display (1965)

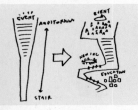

1640 We propose a series of interchangeable, flexible spaces along the stair.

1641 Upper level studies—from left to right: double-height spaces, continuous circulation with auditorium connected to event, straight stair as element.

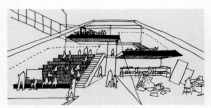

1642 Study—double-height spaces

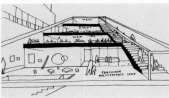

1643 Study—straight stair

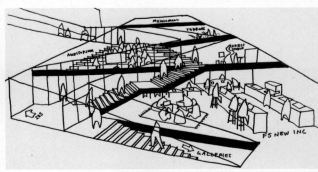

1644 By stringing the various office and collaborative programs along a continuous circulation that weaves back and forth from the ground level, a series of active landings are established whose configurations enhance visibility of programs.

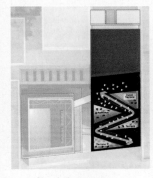

1645 Circulation weaves between programs.

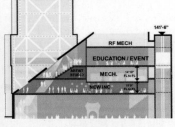

1646 The NEW INC program occupies a full office floor on F5 while a flexible open space is used for both education and event functions. F6 houses the mechanical with a small artist-in-residence studio.

1647 F5 plan—NEW INC

1648 NEW INC main workspace

1649 NEW INC social space

1650 NEW INC media lab

1651 NEW INC fabrication lab

1635–1651   New Museum

1652 On F6 is a simple volume dedicated to the museum's artist-in-residence program. The studio enjoys privacy as the only enclosed space in the sixth-floor expansion, and is located in close proximity to the New Museum administrative offices via a skybridge.

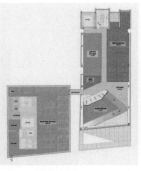

1653 F6 plan

1654 A large north-facing window in the studio provides ambient light and a view down to the alleyway.

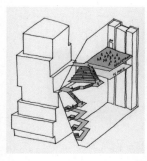

1655 Axon sketch of destination spaces

1656 On the public facing side of the sixth and seventh floors is a sloped, double-height auditorium.

1657 Auditorium model

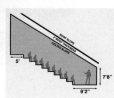

1658 Seating section

1659 The multi-use auditorium can be used independently for events, talks, banquets, and installations, or in synergy with adjacent programs like the Sky Room and the education/event space.

1660 View of auditorium looking out to Prince Street—the double height of the auditorium gives way to a flexible use as it is easily accessible and visible from both NEW INC below and the multi-purpose education/event space above on F7.

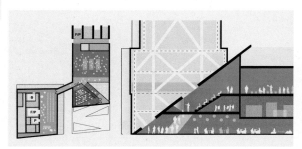

1661 Daytime—lecture space for education program or NEW INC

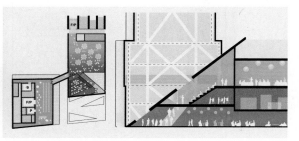

1662 Evening—conference or product launch

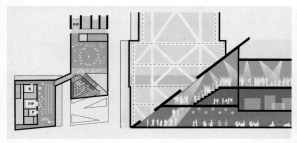

1663 Single event—connected event in the Sky Room and F7 event space

1664 View of auditorium with blackout shades

1665 View of F6 terrace and auditorium from the informal lounge space.

1666 The carpeted alcove lounge is articulated as its own space through the material change. In between the F6 auditorium and lounge, a corridor leads up to F7.

1667 Section model

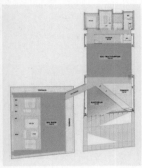

1668 F7 plan

1669 At F7, a flexible space that complements the existing Sky Room is programmed to accommodate both education initiatives and events. The walls and ceiling are oriented strand board (OSB) washed silver, establishing a neutral palette for the flexible space.

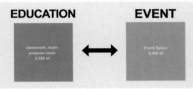

1670 Flexibility between education and event programs

1671 Typical programs in the existing New Museum Sky Room—from left to right: First Saturdays for Families, school and teen programs, reception/cocktail, private events

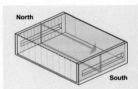

1672 The clear and flexible space is surrounded by windows on three sides and also opens up to the atrium stair.

1673 During the day, the floor can be closed off from the public for classes, reviews, and children's programs.

1674 The space can also be rented for private events, either discrete from or supplemental to other rentable areas like the Sky Room or the auditorium.

1675 View of event space from auditorium, partition open

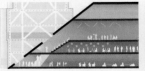

1676 The height of the event space is increased from the existing Sky Room to allow for enhanced flexibility of use.

1677 A skybridge connects to the Sky Room terrace in 235 Bowery

1678 View of 231 Bowery and event space from the Sky Room.

1665–1678

New Museum

1679 On the upper levels, the shape of the staircase creates a void on every level from F5 to F7. The voids become terraces that open up to the city and sky.

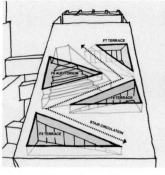

1680 Each terrace has a different materiality suited to the program on its floor, reinforcing an individual identity per floor and providing a colorful moment of respite along the circulation path.

1681 The terraces are extensions of the upper-level programs and provide an outdoor space that simultaneously reorients visitors to Prince Street and Bowery.

1682 Terrace model

1683 F5 NEW INC—experimental

1684 F5 NEW INC terrace—fiberglass-reinforced grating

1685 F6 ancillary—semi public, relief

1686 F6 auditorium and artist studio terrace—baroque zinc panels

1687 F6 auditorium—blue-stained plywood

1688 F7 event/education—playful but serious

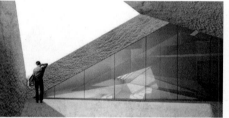

1689 F7 event and education terrace—metal panel with shotcrete finish

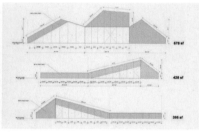

1690 Unfolded terrace elevations

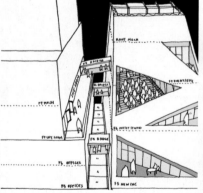

1691 Skybridges on the upper levels provide connections between the two buildings, creating access from the existing building to programs like NEW INC, auditorium, education, and the terraces.

1692 New York sky bridges

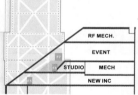

1693 Upper-level openings between the two buildings

1694 Model view from the backside—on F7, the skybridge connects the Sky Room, event, and auditorium space for a single function.

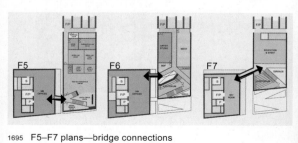

1695 F5–F7 plans—bridge connections

1696 Roof view of terraces and skybridges

1698 Infrastructural core study models

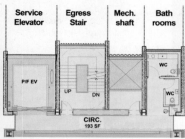

Service Elevator	Egress Stair	Mech. shaft	Bath rooms

1699 As a counterpart to the more public atrium stair, the support for the building is pushed to the back and acts as a functional appendage.

1700 The building is the body and the core is the backpack

1701 Back core workshop session

1697 At the back of the building is an expressive infrastructure befitting the streetscape of Chrystie Street, to support the vertical transportation for the museum's operations.

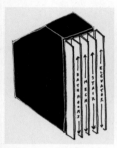

1702 The back core houses the back of house elements—service elevator, egress stair, mechanical shaft, and bathrooms.

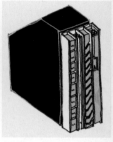

1703 The back-of-house programs are expressed as volumes within a series of fins.

1704 Model view from backside

1705 A discreet yet articulated back contrasts to the front body of the building form.

1706 Section model

1709 Service elevator

1708 Gallery view facing the back core

1710 View out from service elevator

1714 F4 bathroom

1707 Back corridor view

1711 Back corridor view of entry to restrooms

1712 Isolated spaces within the back core, like the elevator and the bathrooms, have surprising moments of color.

1713 On the gallery floor bathrooms, clerestory windows take advantage of the high ceilings to let natural light in. On F5 and F7, windows are located at eye level, providing views out to the Lower East Side.

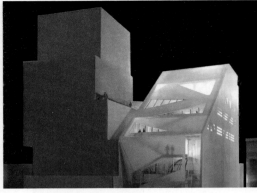

1715 For the facade concept, we wanted to create a counterpoint to the introverted, abstract 235 Bowery.

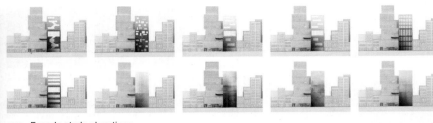

1716 Facade study elevations

1717 Facade study collages

1718 Earlier facade concept (aka Pompidou scheme), where the entire front facade was transparent.

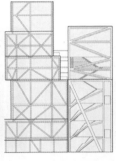

1719 X-ray drawing of elements beyond the facades

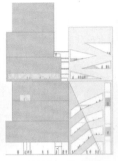

1720 231 facade defined by the circulation elements within

1721 Skeleton model of 235 and 231 Bowery

1722 The stair that continues from the ground to the top defines the solid portions of the street-facing facade.

1723 Facade materiality studies—how can we maximize the extroverted nature of the expansion and create a light, translucent volume?

1724 We tested different ways that mesh could be integrated with glass.

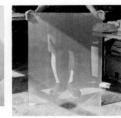

1725 A metallic appearance that is also transparent

1726 SEFAR glass sample, testing subtle transparency.

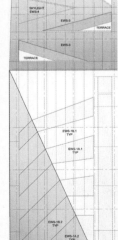

1727 West elevation glass paneling

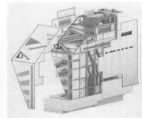

1728 A unitized curtain wall with fabric glass wraps the west facade, opening up to Prince Street. The north-south lot line walls are clad in insulated metal panels.

1729 Facade mock-up

1730 In the evening, the activity and the anatomy of the museum are exposed.

1731 During the day, the building appears metallic and abstract, having a synergy with the existing SANAA building.

New Museum

1732 Evening view from Bowery

1733 The SEFAR glass wraps from the west facade to the north and south facades, stepping to follow the profile of the public face.

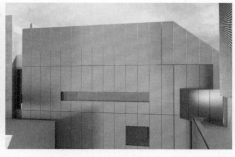

1734 The north and south facades are clad with metal panels with windows.

1735 A total of twenty-five exterior wall systems, varying in build-up

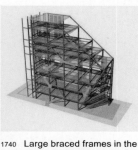

1736 Model view from southwest

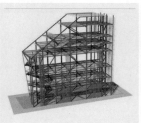

1737 North elevation

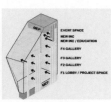

1738 South elevation

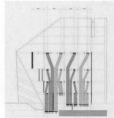

1739 For the structure, we collaborated with Arup. The two long north and south walls have structure integrated with MEP services with a series of braced and non-braced bays.

1740 Large braced frames in the east-west direction resolve east-west sloping column forces, braced or moment frames in north-south direction.

1741 Two walls are stiffened by brace frames at the front and back cores, creating column-less spans in the interior.

1742 The MEP and sustainability approach is unique as it is an extension and adaptation of the existing building systems.

1743 All of the ducts run along the south wall, creating clear horizontal spans throughout the building.

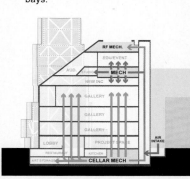

1744 The plenum space of the south facade acts as a service wall that distributes both from the bottom-up and top-down. This efficient configuration creates a shorter distance for services to reach a given floor and reduces loads placed on the system.

1745 From top to bottom: F8 mechanical; F6 mechanical; B1 POE, electrical, MDF rooms; B2 mechanical

1746 Axial force under dead load

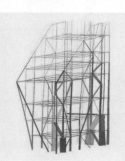

1747 Axial force and deflection under lateral load

1748 The project aims to integrate sustainability strategies to work toward LEED and WELL certification and meet high sustainability, as well as health and safety, ratings.

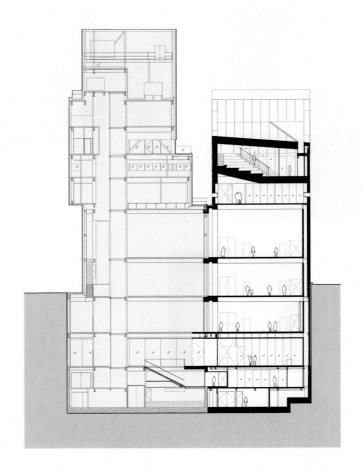

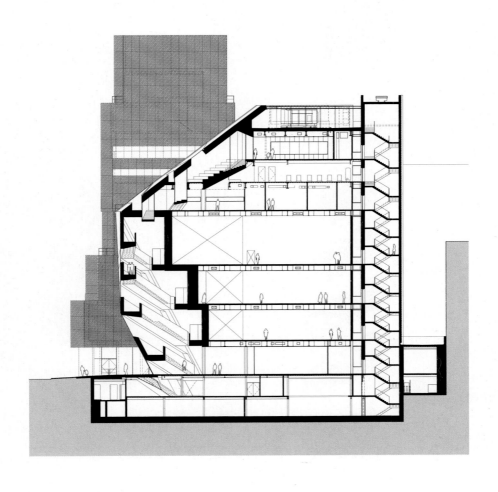

New Museum

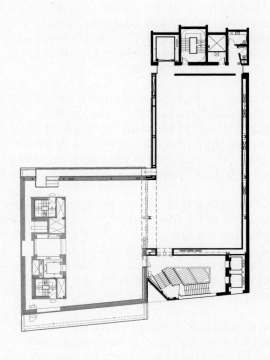

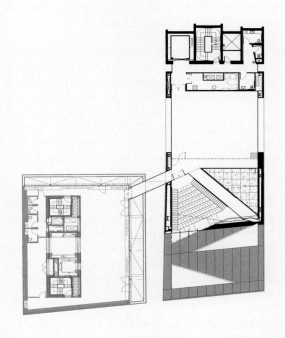

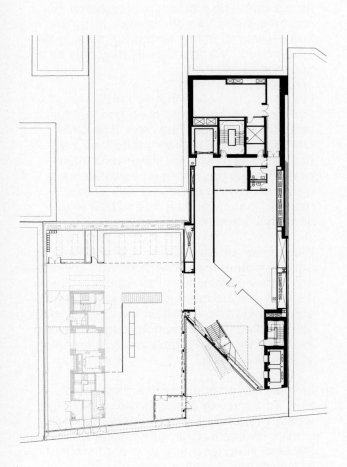

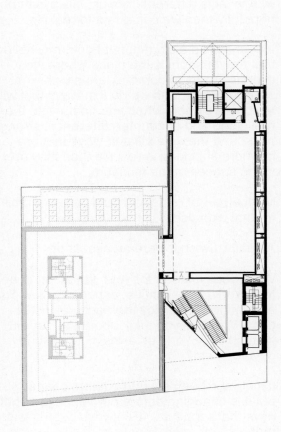

New Museum

Interview Lisa Phillips & Massimiliano Gioni

Shohei Shigematsu: What do you think is the role of the museum in this moment?

Lisa Phillips: Museums are educational institutions first and foremost, with art and culture at their center. We understand culture in its broad sense at the New Museum, encompassing many different kinds of activities and media. "Art and culture" is also constantly being redefined and an important part of our museum's mission is to respond to culture in the making and as it's changing.

We focus on how artists and other cultural creators open our eyes to the world around us through their practice and activities. For us, the museum can open minds, hearts, and eyes—elevating understanding, challenging our assumptions, and fostering tolerance.

Massimiliano Gioni: My definition of a museum, which is maybe a little too catchy, is that it's a gym of the soul, the mind, and the senses. It's a place where we practice freedom and where we learn to coexist with the unknown. It is an experimental and experiential setting where we learn how to come to terms with what is different from us, in ways that hopefully then we can adapt to real life.

It sounds like a slogan, but I do firmly believe that the museum is the place where we exercise ways to come to terms with what we don't know, and we do it in ways that will become valuable when you go out into the real world and encounter difference, strangeness, and the unfamiliar in ways that are far more shocking in real life than they are in the spaces of the museum.

SS: Maybe part of our stair could be a treadmill for that exercise.

MG: Actually, I wish it were an escalator.

SS: What does it mean for your institution to be in New York? I think cities, especially New York, are defined in part by their cultural institutions. What do you think about the current state of New York, in terms of its cultural development?

LP: It's always been a world cultural capital, but it is changing before our very eyes right now, that's for sure. It's always been a place that has attracted people from all over the world for what it has to offer and that has to do with the density, the activity, and the youth population—the dynamism of the city in the way that it's physically constructed.

SS: The city, especially in the downtown areas like the Bowery, had a period of time where it was known as a place where artists lived, worked, and hung out. Do you think New York has the same energy, relevance, and focus on culture as it once had?

LP: In a more globalized world that's connected digitally, physical location may be less important. We're certainly feeling that most intensely right now. Our audience is located all over the world and is very engaged even if not physically present.

MG: I think the fact that we're having this conversation today by video is just the most evident signal that we are at the cusp of a moment that is very different from pre-pandemic. So many of our assumptions about what the city is, and what density even means, are different today.

LP: The crisis could actually turn things back to a point where the city is more accessible. It could open up possibilities for new populations to move in with affordable housing. New York may not survive in the same way as this glittering emblem of commerce, but maybe it will be something else. It's in transition. How is all of this verticality going to be repurposed? Vertical density may now be in question.

MG: I think it's interesting that you are asking this question because there is no firm that has thought more about New York than OMA. OMA is founded on the myth of New York. Are those assumptions still alive in 2021 when the city has not been as dense as it was pre-Covid? How do we reflect this moment in the work we do and how long does this moment last?

SS: We've been observing and operating in different cities other than New York, and now there are more critical issues than density. I think it's a bit early to make specific assumptions about how Covid will affect the city, and difficult to reflect this moment through our work in a meaningful way that is not just grasping at an initial hunch.

In your conversations with artists about New York, pre- or during Covid, what is the typical response you get from both those who've had their studios here for a while and the new, younger artists who are trying to establish their practice here?

LP: The city has been less and less hospitable to young artists. They've had to go farther and farther away from the center and that's true of many cities, not just New York. The creative communities get pushed to the fringes and are part of the gentrification process. Areas transform, artists get pushed out, and they move somewhere else where there is more opportunity. Maybe that's ironically now the suburbs!

Now it feels like New York is no longer the preeminent cultural capital of the world but just part of a constellation of places. With globalization and increased mobility, I think many artists feel that they are citizens of multiple places.

MG: In New York you will always meet somebody who will tell you, "New York was really great ten years ago." In ten years, even looking back at this moment of crisis we think is its lowest point, I'm sure someone will say, "Oh, but New York was really great in 2020." It's an interesting antidote to any fixed idea of New York.

SS: It's interesting to think about that notion or sentiment toward the city over generations of change as a way to combat a fixed idea of the city. You also said OMA is founded in part on the myth of New York and that made me think about the myth of OMA itself. There is a fixed idea of who we are as an office, but it has been evolving throughout the last decade.

This book is in a way for us to reflect the voice of my generation through OMA New York's work. Lisa, you've been running an art museum in New York for quite some time. And Mass, while you also have a quite extensive career in the art world, the two of you are perhaps considered to come from different generations. What do you think about the notion of generations?

LP: At the New Museum, we have so many different generations involved on staff and board. On staff, as a boomer, I'm the outlier for sure. There are a number of Gen X-ers, millennials, Gen Z-ers… so at least four generations. If you count the board, maybe five. That's a lot. But we've always felt young at heart, and we are a young institution.

But with the recent major cultural shifts taking place—particularly after the Great Recession of 2008 and fallout from that, and the Occupy Wall Street movement, and later Times Up and Black Lives Matter—it's clear that there are increasing pressures and demands from a younger generation to shift priorities.

That's an important cultural shift, and very important for the future of museums.

SS: It's true that downturns stimulate shifts in many, if not all, aspects of culture. I've always been interested in and have researched the post-crisis phenomenon, where major events like economic crises or natural disasters are followed by moments in which people think more deeply about pre-existing systems. Often, this timeframe catalyzes new inventions or modes of living. More immediately, I think the pandemic is changing the street-scape of New York. Some people are enjoying the activated street experience that feels more like European streets.

LP: I love the way the street has been reinvented for outdoor dining. It took a crisis for the street to be used that way. The nature of public space is changing.

SS: Absolutely. It's refreshing to see unexpected activities revitalizing public space in a way that's different from the recent trend of parks being over-programmed. I think parks were losing the sense of being a place for people to hang out without knowing exactly what to do. It reflects a certain fear of breaking away from the collective action and pre-scribed activity, which can take away a sense of freedom that's vital to the core value of a public space.

And I think this can apply to rethinking programming in museums too. There are a lot of planners who whisper into the ears of cities, encouraging a cookie-cutter approach to cultural planning that renders the art experience into a checklist.

I think art events are an example of this and we've done some research on perennialogy and what that means for architecture. It used to be that cities coveted iconic museums for a certain economic effect, but now art events have become the new engine. What do you think about this shift and its implications on the role of the museum?

LP: I feel the biennales and fairs were really about bringing art to other communities. It's a redistribution of activity around capital and very much dependent on ease of transport and travel. But I think what people have found out during this crisis is that the art fair model is not the only one. Costs were getting extreme—of transport and of proper staffing—and there were so many fairs that to participate in all of them became a huge investment. Maybe there will be other alternatives that rise up now. I'm not sure that the online models are working the way

OMA NY   Lisa Phillips & Massimiliano Gioni

people hoped, but pop-ups seem to be working. So there's still that idea of bringing art to other places and to where people are, but maybe just not through the art fair setting.

MG: Because I'm partial to them I do want to distinguish between biennales and fairs. A biennale lasts around three to six months and is an educational enterprise. Obviously biennials still operate within an economy of spectacle, but they are very different from art fairs. I think for all cultural institutions today it's important to understand their relationship to this culture of spectacles.

Even the New Museum—and maybe this is also important in relation to the architecture—exists in an event economy because we are a museum with no permanent collection and we change our shows periodically and that is part of our power of attraction. So we are certainly complicit with a certain idea of spectacle, but I hope our exhibitions analyze and deconstruct ideas of passive spectacularization.

In a sense, the architecture offers the anchor for the event and that is also something we should think about critically. We can have a perennial change of shows because we have a building that is recognizable and telegraphs our identity and mission. The balance is established by having something that is attractive and recognizable and that drives people there, and the perennial change of shows.

I think we are witnessing, as we speak, museums like MoMA understanding that they can achieve the temporary event effect with their permanent collection. The newest expansion at MoMA is based on a hybrid combination of permanent collection and temporary exhibition. They found that the public doesn't seem to distinguish so much between the collection and a temporary show, and now they are thinking of a canon that is permanently under construction and shifting.

I think in our case, paradoxically, we need an iconic building to ground our temporary shows: the building provides a sense of permanence. I'm not saying that this is the reason why we're doing a new building, but I think even our current building helped us sustain this perennial sense of motion and dynamism that our program is built on.

SS: That's interesting. I've never heard the potential of iconic architecture framed that way before. And to respond to Lisa's comment on the challenges of transporting art and traveling for it at this time, do you think there will be more distinction between global and local scenes?

LP: I think it might. I think there's definitely more focus on the local than there has been. We're just part of a constellation of communities that are spread out, so there is that too. But I don't think we're going to go back to regionalism or a provincial idea of local.

MG: At the same time, as it happened after 9/11, even though this current Covid transition is lasting much longer, you also realize how rooted you are in a neighborhood, even in a city as big as New York. It's the city less as a mirror of global transaction and more the city as a neighborhood. This is really an empirical and personal experience.

The ecosystem of galleries in New York City, for example, and specifically the ones around the New Museum in the Lower East Side, appears to be so much more rooted in the city than I think it ever appeared to me before Covid. The galleries in the Lower East Side have done monthly late nights. It's both endearing and also firghtening to see how their survival is connected to the neighborhood, to people who are willing to go out, see each other, continue a dialogue. Sadly, you don't see many collectors on those nights, but you get a sense that those connections are now more valuable and more important than ever.

SS: So for you, iconicism is about providing a sense of permanence to the temporariness of your exhibitions and it's rooted to the idea of creating an anchor for the community around it.

MG: What really struck me when I came to New York was that the museum is like a contemporary cathedral. In the Middle Ages great works of architecture were produced that also acted as gravitational centers around which different communities gathered. Similarly, museums are the expression of an ecosystem that is quite intricate, built on the participation of artists, visitors, donors, staff, and many other communities.

SS: Then is the notion of iconic even relevant?

LP: It's going to be questioned more than it has been. What is it? It's where the form of the building aligns with the brand of the institution, or defines a cultural moment. But I think right now, there's less interest in the iconic, which is the instant image that represents something, as opposed to more distributed

OMA NY   Lisa Phillips & Massimiliano Gioni

forms or functions. Those are qualities that are more and more valued. But even an anti-iconic form could become iconic.

Similarly, Mass's idea of the museum as a place of worship is something that many people are questioning. Both the church and the museum are also important community and education centers—focal points for the community and for the transmission of information. This is a different paradigm that may lead to a different kind of architecture.

MG: I think the irony is that when we selected you guys for the competition, I don't think we went to OMA for its ability to create an icon. We were more fascinated by your conversations and your work around preservation and urbanism. The SANAA building is also not an icon in the way in which Frank Gehry's instant spectacle is.

In the brief for the new building we said we wanted to have a recognizable building, but it was never necessarily a picture or a spectacle. I think the new building you designed is interesting because it is photogenic but it's not immediately visual. This new building of yours, I don't know what it is exactly, and I mean that as a compliment.

SS: It's true. We also have a hard time describing it.

LP: I think, in fact, you're right, Mass. We were attracted to OMA's work precisely because it was not going to be iconic. I think the SANAA building did give an image to the museum's mission, but is not as functional as we need it to be now. As we've grown our needs have grown too, so we were looking to expand the functionality of the museum.

SS: We were interested in the diversification of public engagement, both at the New Museum and museums in general, and how that shift could be captured through the architecture. But, of course, the extension was also about responding to new needs and accommodating growth.

I'm sure you have been observing the successes and challenges of the increasing number of museum extensions happening around the world. What do you think about museum extensions in general? Can you tell us more about your research and thinking when you were envisioning your museum extension?

MG: In a sense it was very pragmatic. Although the interiors will be completely integrated, we liked the idea of an expansion that could also function as a campus. It's one joint building when it needs to be, but it can also be separate entities. I think that it is unusual for an expansion to have that flexibility. It was born from a pragmatic need because the museum is quite constricted and it maximizes the floorplate to the greatest extent.

LP: What's interesting is that we used 231 Bowery as more of an experimental space—for creating new works, for knowledge production, for NEW INC. It has contained a lot of experimental programming that now will be incorporated into the museum and integrated into our public display and public flow. Then the challenge is how to continue those experimental programs in a space that's finished.

SS: I agree that a raw space of a typical Bowery building felt almost intrinsic to experimental programming. It was a challenge to maintain a level of that informality in a new building, which is why we really wanted to try to preserve 231.

You said the expansion is like a campus. Maybe it's somewhat at odds with the desire to preserve the authenticity of the neighborhood, but could you foresee even more extensions with new buildings?

LP: I'm less interested in bricks and mortar and more interested in partnerships, distribution, and finding new ways of doing what we do.

MG: Which I think has been a successful model on our part and a form of innovation. Maybe because we were previously constricted within a single space, we developed a lot of other ideas that were less physical. So I think the two developed in parallel—the much needed expansion with an experimental vocation and a series of activities that were less specifically attached to physical spaces. They were happening in a parasitic or symbiotic function elsewhere.

But to think of expansion today, in November 2020, it's a whole different game. The question we're asking ourselves and you, is "What is the function or definition of expansion in the middle of a historical contraction?" I don't think we have an answer to that yet, but maybe the answer is what Lisa is alluding to—more immaterial content and less physical. I always like to say that museums first of all are softwares, not hardware. I think that's a big question that is still pending.

SS: I think in this moment, it makes sense to create a place for contemplation and exchange, even more so than before.

OMA NY   Lisa Phillips & Massimiliano Gioni

You mentioned earlier that the museum is first and foremost an educational space. In that sense, it seems appropriate to expand the museum to provide a platform for learning and discourse. The museum is also a public space, and the current state of division in our society has highlighted the need for a new public realm that fosters dialogue and openness. How can the museum space itself evolve to reflect the changing role of today's institutions?

MG: I can say that—and forgive me for being sincere—it's not the easiest time to be in a museum because there is an incredible level of questioning and responsibility that we are held to. On the other hand, this is happening because the public recognizes that museums are central to civic and civil life. It's also because museums are now speaking to audiences of millions and we are seen as places where criticism is still welcome. It's not repressed. All this scrutiny around museums suggests that the museum is still a healthy place of self-discovery and self-invention.

LP: Many see museums as neoliberal institutions, which may not always be a positive thing, particularly since they're also the result and support of the so-called ruling class, or at least the moneyed class. There's a fundamental tension between how we are structured and supported and our values and ability to question those things. There are fundamental contradictions. Tax dollars partially support museums as well, and so the public feels a great sense of ownership, as they should. So there is also this tension between the museum being in the public trust and being supported by wealthy donors, because that's the system in capitalist America.

SS: And that system can, in a way, slow down experimentation or evolution of the museum typology.

LP: Yes, it could be at odds with that idea of radical reinvention. Because in some ways museums uphold the status quo, with their neoliberal ideas. But do you see radical experimentation of museum typologies in other cultures?

SS: Maybe it's not a radical experimentation, but I think museums in the U.S. are embracing a radical openness. In the projects we've been working on—including the New Museum but also our extension for the Albright-Knox Art Gallery—we were able to expose the activities of the institutions to create a new openness that acknowledges the public demand for transparency.

In other cultures, I think there've been some interesting models. Naoshima and Inhotim are alternatives to museums in the city—by transplanting art to specific, remote, and often natural settings, they developed a culture of art pilgrammage that is opposite to the immediacy of the art experience in the city. But I wouldn't say they represent a radically evolved museum. Do you think there is enough experimentation or evolution happening in the format or system of the gallery or museum?

LP: That's a really good question. I was taken with those SESC [Social Service of Commerce] models in Brazil. The massive community cultural centers include all kinds of activities, from poetry to sports to cooking. They really are used by the community to a huge extent and are supported by companies that are taxed a percentage of their profits to support those centers. I really liked what I saw in working with them and visiting several in Brazil. I thought that was an interesting model.

MG: Something similar can be said about Azkuna Zentroa in Bilbao, which is also a combination of community center and museum. You mentioned Inhotim and Naoshima— great, amazing experiences. They're both conceived of as places of leisure, which is also something to think about. Museums are assumed to be a part of leisure, and that also comes with specific assumptions. As a European, I was always shocked that the *New York Times* weekend section is called "Arts and Leisure." When I was growing up, art was not meant to be leisure—it was meant to be friction, opposition, criticism, change. Then again, I personally compare it to a gym, so I guess I'm a victim of the same assumptions.

From a very practical point of view, I was expecting something more provocative on your part on the question of whether or not the white cube is still the ideal place to see art. It might just be an aesthetic question, but it's an interesting question.

SS: I think that question has been asked many times, to the degree that whenever we provided a non-white cube, we lost a competition.

LP: Not in our case.

MG: Because they proposed a white cube, it's interesting.

SS: We were more interested in evolving the relationship between the white cube and non-gallery programs. By nature of their very public use, the non-galleries can become unexpectedly potent areas of the museum that then has the potential to redefine the use or significance of the white cube.

Speaking of provoking the white cube, what do you think about the rise of mega-galleries—like the galleries in Chelsea erecting museum-sized buildings; museums run by a single collector; or auction houses that now have museum-quality galleries that can be programmed?

LP: The mission is so different and that's always going to be a distinction. But certainly it blurs a lot of boundaries and lines that had been previously so separated, which forces you to articulate your distinctions. I think we can learn from each other.

MG: In one of our recent meetings we were discussing the consolidation of mega-galleries as a threat to the museum system. With the pandemic, I think galleries are facing their own threats. In recent months I've thought a lot about how the relationships between galleries and museums might change after the pandemic.

SS: Typically post-crisis there would be a shared sentiment to exchange ideas, and I'm curious about whether that moment will bring the two entities closer together or push them further apart and create a deeper distinction.

Do you think your relationships with artists might change as well? How do you find that artists are reflecting on the current moment?

MG: I was speaking to a successful, or formerly successful artist—fashion and success change so quickly now—and today there is this assumption that success equals selling out, compromise, or privilege. So I think artists are also doing a lot of soul searching these days, just trying to understand their role. There are also many conversations around ethics, which are healthy, but that can easily turn very moralistic, to the extent that any position that doesn't conform to certain expectations is deemed suspicious. In the past, the role of the artist was not to conform and to do so violently.

So I think a lot of artists are asking: what is their responsibility today? Are they meant to point in the direction of nonconformism, which right now would mean being ostracized for not aligning with ethical issues that all recognize as important? Or is it to mobilize their success in support of ethical change? Even though not many artists might

necessarily articulate it that way, I think there is a strong indecision about their role.

LP: I would say it's a period of intense questioning that actually is a very positive thing, too. Everything is being questioned. What does expansion look like? What does progress look like? What does success mean as an artist? I think everything is being thrown into question and that is the moment we are in.

SS: That's a great way to put it. Our book is also a search term. We're searching our own ideas within the work, but also searching for relevance to the zeitgeist. It's a rabbit hole, but productive in that many questions and topics are being discussed. In a way, it's a type of self-quarantine.

LP: I like that. That's a great idea for a title for a show—"Self-Quarantine."

Lisa Phillips is a curator, author, and director of the New Museum in New York since 1999. Prior to joining the New Museum, she worked as a curator for the Whitney Museum for twenty-three years.

Massimiliano Gioni is a curator, contemporary art critic, and artistic director of the New Museum. Gioni was the director of the 55th Venice Biennale.

OMA NY   Lisa Phillips & Massimiliano Gioni

Cai Studio

Cai Studio

We often fantasize about what it would be like to be artists.
As architects, we set our agenda and ambition at the influence of
the client—designs are rarely generated entirely of our own volition.
When working with artists, we are inspired by their unique ways of
advancing their agendas, philosophies, and feelings.

What artist Cai Guo-Qiang created with his staff within the
converted 1885 schoolhouse on New York's Lower East Side was a
real community, a rare sight. As his practice grew more diverse
and international, his studio had to respond. Although the project
brief to renovate and expand the existing studio was rooted in practical concerns, Cai thought about the larger role of the studio at a
time when "not many artists spend all day in their studios creating
art themselves," and how the studio can reflect the changing scope
of art.

We were drawn to his interest in the evolving interface of the
art world and wanted to create a multi-faceted artist's headquarters
while continuing to reflect Cai's intimate studio culture. So while the
different functions of the studio are organized independently, it was
important that the flow be continuous—in its entirety, the studio acts
as one entity and one space through a constant sense of awareness
between its diverse activities.

Cai's lack of gallery representation means that his studio must
play a crucial role in the artist's operations, acting as his main work,
archive, gallery, reception, and office space. The studio previously
consisted of one floor on the ground level. The expansion includes
the basement level and an adjacent storefront on First Street.

Our approach was to create a space centered around light
and openness, in response to Cai's love for the existing courtyard
and his desire to make the basement feel less subterranean. Twice
the original square footage, the studio is operationally enhanced with
multiple functions organized around a central, light-filled courtyard.

A set of vertical connections from the street level illuminate
the cellar level below, which had once been a cavern-like nightclub.
Daylight from the courtyard filters down through a series of light wells
comprised of walkable glass panels and a reflective bamboo vault.
A central stairwell leads to the lower level and provides a double-

height display space. An existing structural vault was repurposed as a periscope, offering views to the street from the basement.

The porous boundaries between the programs unite the studio through continuous materials and light. A resin wall spans both levels along the courtyard edge, creating a central spine distributing natural light. Historic elements of the building are preserved: the red school door that continues to serve as the main entry; original brick and stone masonry and archways; the existing stairs and iron railings.

Each room can function as both a workspace and public venue. Two ateliers with museum quality lighting are used for daily exhibitions as well as receptions. In the cellar, a room with A/V capabilities and a sixteen-foot solid Douglas fir table hosts large meetings and film screenings. A library provides a dedicated space for interviews with Cai's collection of books close at hand.

Cai's recollection of experiences in and of Japan inspired elements of the studio (we were even able to present to him in Japanese). A Tea Room composed of the essential elements of a customary Japanese tea house acts as a traditional ceremonial space for visitors and a contemplation space for the studio. The Tea Room is also Cai's quiet hiding place where no one can find him.

Location	New York, NY, USA		
Status	Completed, 2015		
Typology	Artist Collaboration		
Program	Gallery	2,800 ft²	260 m²
	Office	2,100 ft²	195 m²
	Services	3,800 ft²	355 m²
	Total Area	8,700 ft²	810 m²

1756

Cai Studio

1757

Cai Studio

1758

Cai Studio

OMA NY   Cai Studio

Cai Studio

1760 Cai Guo-Qiang is a prolific artist who crosses multiple mediums within art, including drawing, installation, video, and performance art. While living in Japan from 1986 to 1995, he explored the properties of gunpowder in his drawings, which led to his experimentation with explosives on a massive scale and also led to the development of his signature works.

1764 Gunpowder is a key medium used by Cai.

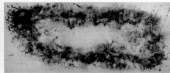

1765 *Head on Vortex* (2006)

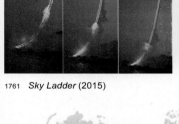

1761 *Sky Ladder* (2015)

1762 Gunpowder painting process

1763 Drawing upon Eastern philosophy and contemporary social issues as a conceptual basis, these projects and events aim to establish exchange between viewers and the larger universe around them, utilizing a site-specific approach to culture and history.

1766 *Transient Rainbow* (2006)

1767 Cai has developed a number of large-scale spaces to produce and store his work around the world.

1768 Suburban Center & Fabrication— Beijing, China

1769 Warehouse for fabrication and gunpowder— Long Island, New York, USA

1770 Storage, residence, fabrication, horse farm— northern New Jersey, USA

1772 Cai's New York studio pre-renovation, set for an exhibition

1771 The artist's studio serves as the headquarters for himself and his staff of ten and accommodates various programs and functions.

1773 Reception

1774 Studio tour

1775 Lecture

1776 Tea ceremony

1777 As Cai is not represented by a gallery, his New York studio plays a crucial role as the operational base for internal exhibition and administration.

1760–1777

Cai Studio

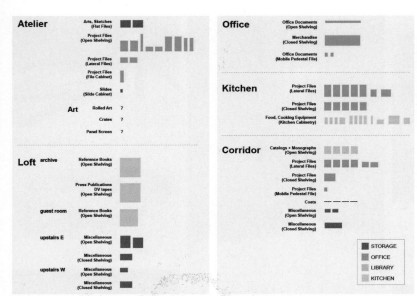

Atelier

Arts, Sketches (Flat Files)	
Project Files (Open Shelving)	
Project Files (Lateral Files)	
Project Files (File Cabinet)	
Slides (Slide Cabinet)	
Art Rolled Art	?
Crates	?
Panel Screen	?

Loft

archive	Reference Books (Open Shelving)
	Press Publications DV tapes (Open Shelving)
guest room	Reference Books (Open Shelving)
upstairs E	Miscellaneous (Open Shelving)
	Miscellaneous (Closed Shelving)
upstairs W	Miscellaneous (Open Shelving)
	Miscellaneous (Closed Shelving)

Office

Office Documents (Open Shelving)	
Merchandise (Closed Shelving)	
Office Documents (Mobile Pedestal File)	

Kitchen

Project Files (Lateral Files)	
Project Files (Closed Shelving)	
Food, Cooking Equipment (Kitchen Cabinetry)	

Corridor

Catalogs + Monographs (Open Shelving)	
Project Files (Lateral Files)	
Project Files (Closed Shelving)	
Project Files (Mobile Pedestal File)	
Coats	
Miscellaneous (Open Shelving)	
Miscellaneous (Closed Shelving)	

Legend: STORAGE / OFFICE / LIBRARY / KITCHEN

1778 The renovation of Cai's studio aims to address the growing need for additional storage and to provide specialized artwork archive and inventory through a new library space.

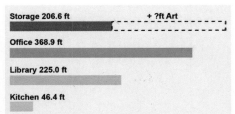

Storage 206.6 ft	+ ?ft Art
Office 368.9 ft	
Library 225.0 ft	
Kitchen 46.4 ft	

1779 Enhanced storage, office, and library

S   M   L   XL

1780 Living gallery—accommodating larger quantity and scale of display

1781 We explored different artist studios in New York that served functions beyond production—Louise Bourgeois studio (2000–2010).

1782 Bourgeois held Sunday salons at her studio where artists seeking feedback on their work could meet with her.

1783 Bourgeois with *Femme Maison* (1947) in the front parlor of her workspace.

1784 Super public/interdisciplinary—Andy Warhol's Factory (1962–1968)

1785 Andy Warhol's Factory served production, archive, and display functions.

1786 Donald Judd's studio was one of the first artist lofts in SoHo (1968–1996).

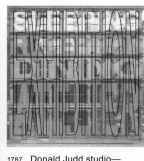

1787 Donald Judd studio—programs separated by floor are tied together as a "permanent installation."

1788 Donald Judd in his studio (1968–1996)

1789 For Judd, the making and viewing of art were coextensive with the other activities of living. Judd's New York studio is now open to visit by reservation, where visitors can experience the installations and architecture he created.

1790 From the functionality of Donald Judd's SoHo studio to the Factory's hive of social activity, how can Cai's studio build upon the heritage of New York artist studios?

Cai Studio

1791 Cai Studio is located in a former schoolhouse on Manhattan's Lower East Side.

1792 The original red school door and a wedge-shaped courtyard remain.

1793 Original studio space and newly acquired ground level storefront and basement (yellow)

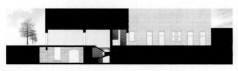

1794 Site section through the courtyard

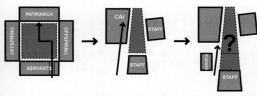

1797 The new organization of Cai's studio uses the wedge-shaped extension of the courtyard as the central space in the tradition of historic Chinese courtyard layouts. From left to right: traditional Chinese courtyard house, original studio, OMA proposal.

1795 Cai's acquisition of the building's 1st Street storefront allows for a continuous wedge, optimizing the courtyard's public space to the full extent of the site.

1796 Original courtyard

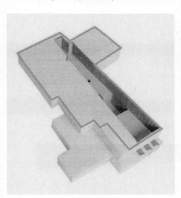

1798 Concept model of light wedge extending through the entire depth of the site

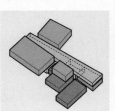

1799 Layout centered around the light wedge

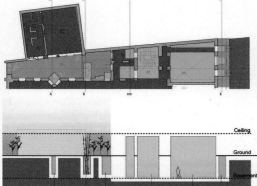

1800 Voids—the light wedge provides both horizontal and vertical distribution of light, excavating voids to the basement level of the studio.

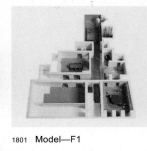

1801 Model—F1

1802 Model—B1

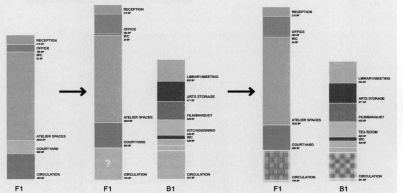

1803 The expansion of Cai's studio to the 1st Street storefront and basement provides an opportunity to rethink the overall organization of Cai's operations and create enhanced zones of interaction and display.

1804 Enhanced program—B1

1805 Enhanced program—F1

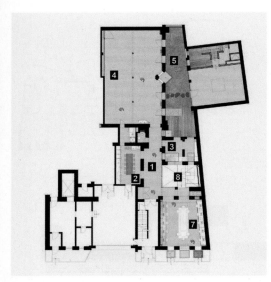

1806 Ground floor—proposed: (1) entrance corridor, (2) reception, (3) Cai's office, (4) West Atelier, (5) Courtyard, (6) Atelier East, (7) office, (8) Atrium/Central Void

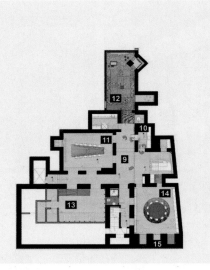

1807 Basement level—proposed: (9) basement corridor, (10) bar, (11) Banquet/Media Room, (12) Tea Room, (13) art storage, (14) Library, (15) Periscope

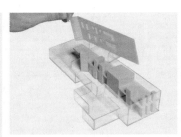

1808 To reinforce the light wedge, a resin wall is inserted into the central spine.

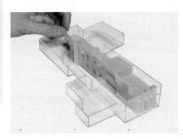

1809 This translucent wall provides the opportunity for multiple functions.

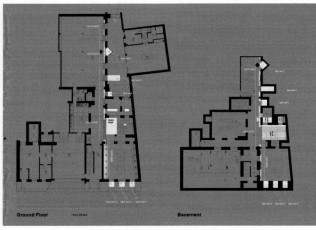

1810 Light wedge functions—organizing disparate spaces of the studio, distributing light and mechanical services, acting as a wayfinding element, providing new storage opportunities

1811 Unfolding space—the central spine revives the idea of unfolding space inherent in Chinese paintings and referenced in Cai's works. The wall can be seen as a canvas within which different scenes take place.

1813 *I Want to Believe* (2002)

1812 Three paintings by Dong Qichang (1555–1636)

1814 Section model

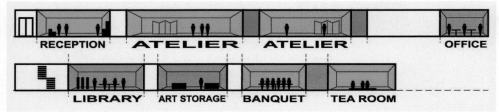

RECEPTION ATELIER ATELIER OFFICE

LIBRARY ART STORAGE BANQUET TEA ROOM

1815 The organization of programs reflects Cai Guo-Qiang's reference to the "temporal experience of viewing Chinese hand scroll paintings, whose narratives unfold horizontally."

1816 Section model

1817 Reference—shoji wall

1818 For the light wedge, we referred to the ambient translucency of a traditional shoji wall.

1819 Rendering—West Atelier resin wall

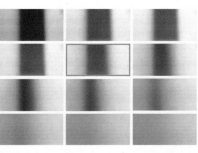

1820 Light reaction studies—a translucent resin material was chosen to line the light wedge. The resin provides a light-reactive element that simultaneously showcases the studio's structure, creating a built-in art installation.

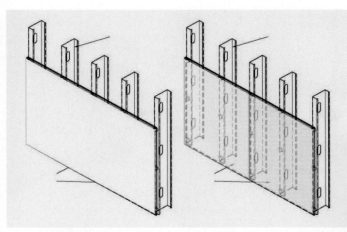

1821 The use of a resin wall in place of the standard gypsum board is a subtle difference that enhances the light from the courtyard while revealing the building's original character. The ¾-inch resin panels are offset from the existing walls by 3⅝ inches—the width of a standard metal stud.

1822 Drywall installation

1823 Framing

1824 Resin panel with metal stud

1825 Resin with framework

1826 Metal stud substructure

1827 B1 Tea Room model

1828 West Atelier resin wall model

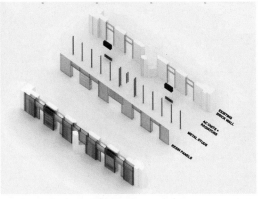

1829 Exploded axonometric of resin wall

1830 Model testing light filtration

1831 East Atelier resin wall model

1832 Concept rendering of resin wall along studio corridor

1833 View of resin wall along studio corridor

1834 The resin wall stretches across the ground-level corridor, unifying the program spaces it connects.

1835 Concept rendering of resin wall at the Atrium/Central Void

1836 The porous boundaries between the programs unite the studio through continuous materials and light.

1821–1836

Cai Studio

1838 The resin wall allows daylight to fill the West Atelier.

1837 The resin wall spans both levels along the courtyard edge, acting as a central spine that distributes natural light.

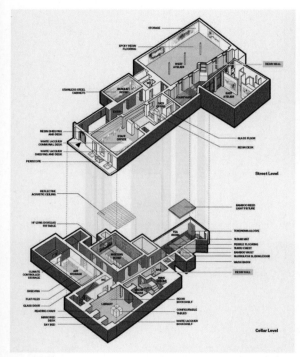

1839 Exploded axonometric of the two studio levels

1840 The lighting system is integrated between the brick wall and the resin wall.

1841 Resin wall detail

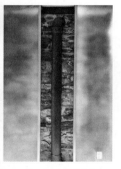

1842 Resin wall detail

1843 The resin wall integrates bookshelves and counterspace, while also embedding infrastructural services.

1844 Material for existing walls—silver paint, white painted brick, translucent ice resin

1845 Library view through the resin wall

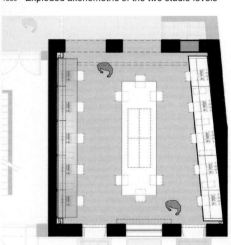

1846 Next to the entry on the ground level is the office, where the resin wall becomes integrated with bookshelves.

1847 Office model

1848 Main office on the ground level

1849 The office ceiling and all the spaces within the light wedge are coated with a light-reflective finish. The shelving integrated into the resin wall and beneath the central desk accommodates project file storage.

1850 The staff office features an open plan with a central meeting space.

1851 Shelving—white paint with lacquer finish

1852 The studio manager's office is located across the Atrium from the staff office.

1853 The Atrium between the offices establishes a visual connection from one space to the other.

1854 Studio manager in her office

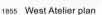
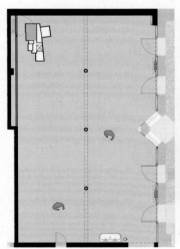

1855 West Atelier plan

1856 Sketch rendering of West Atelier—the ground level's West Atelier is simultaneously a gallery space, working studio, meeting room, and event space.

1857 Study model—West Atelier

1858 Material for flooring—epoxy resin

1859 West Atelier—meeting

1860 West Atelier—meeting and display

1861 West Atelier—meeting

1862 The West Atelier functions as the main gallery space for the studio. Its exhibition features have been enhanced with museum-quality lighting and light from the courtyard diffused through the resin wall.

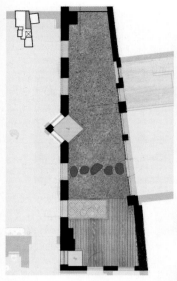

1863　Courtyard plan—the courtyard is fully accessible from both Ateliers

1864　Concept model—courtyard

1865　The courtyard is optimized to allow maximum light and air to filter into the Ateliers.

1866　A bamboo planting is inserted in a basement level vault, topped by a grated cover that allows for growth into the courtyard level.

1867　Courtyard view of bamboo vault and office

1868　Direct entry to courtyard from office

1869　The courtyard materiality exploits the existing red brick walls of the building's exterior, with landscaping to match its tonality and texture.

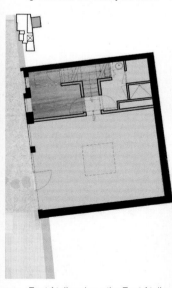

1870　East Atelier plan—the East Atelier is located across the courtyard from the West Atelier and is a secondary gallery that features three walls for exhibition.

1871　Sketch rendering of East Atelier

1872　East Atelier interior view

1873　View through courtyard from East Atelier to West Atelier

1874　Used for both exhibition and production, the space is able to accommodate artworks of impressive height.

Cai Studio

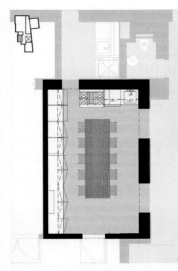

1875 Reception plan—the reception area combines a functioning kitchenette with ample seating to accommodate a range of functions.

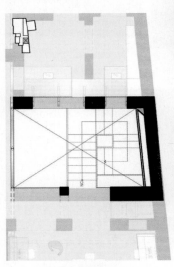

1878 Central Void/Atrium plan—the Central Void functions as the main access to the lower level, as well as a casual gathering area.

1876 Receptions and gatherings previously took place within the existing studio space without a designated room for food service and entertaining.

1879 Original stair

1877 From visitor reception to Cai's weekly staff meetings to a catered event, the reception room accommodates diverse functions with convenient access to the West Atelier.

1880 Early study models of Central Void and Atrium stair

1881 Central Void model

1882 Model of final Central Void

1883 The double height expanse of the Central Void provides openness and visual connection throughout the two levels.

1884 The Central Void utilizes the original ironwork stair and railing, retaining the cellar-like details of the basement level.

1885 The height of the void also provides a unique opportunity for large-scale artwork.

1875–1885   Cai Studio

1886 View down Central Void and stair from F1

1887 We wanted to preserve some elements of the original building.

1888 The Central Void uses the original ironwork of the stairs and railing.

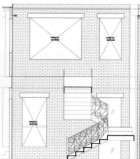

1889 Central Void/Atrium stair north elevation

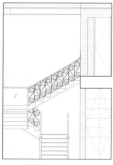

1890 Central Void/Atrium stair east elevation

1891 The mix of original and contemporary elements transitions between the upper and lower levels.

1892 Completed stair view

1893 Completed stair view

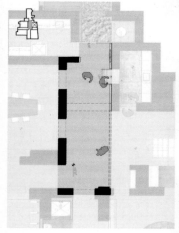

1894 Basement corridor plan

1895 Basement rendering

1896 View of basement corridor and bar

1897 The basement corridor retains the existing masonry of the basement level with minimal interventions.

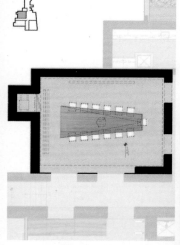

1898 Banquet Room plan—the Banquet Room is the central space in the basement.

1899 The Banquet Room is equipped to accommodate meetings, lectures, catered events, and film screenings.

1886–1899   Cai Studio

1901 The solid wood posed challenges for delivery and installation.

1902 The table had to be slid down the double-height Central Void space into the basement.

1900 Cai Guo-Qiang and Shohei Shigematsu in the Banquet Room—the central table in the Banquet Room was specifically made with a single slab of solid wood.

1903 The ceiling creates an ideal room for screenings and audiovisual presentations.

1904 The materiality of the acoustic ceiling creates a soft texture against the hard stone and brick of the original cellar.

1905 The ceiling is made up of custom acoustic pillows.

1906 Cai giving a tour to Dia Foundation

1910 Library model

1911 Library shelving installation

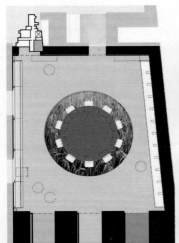

1907 Library plan—across the Banquet Room is the Library that houses Cai's collection of publications.

1908 Library rendering

1909 Library model

1912 The resin wall shelving integrates light fixtures.

1913 Cai giving a tour to Dia Foundation

1914 Cai sketching in the Library

1915 A tour and reception for Rhode Island School of Design board of trustees and guests at Cai Foundation in February 2020

1916 The Library has the flexibility to function as both a reading room and a more private workshop/studio.

1917 The bookshelf is a lighting fixture that brightens the basement room and is a feature in itself.

1918 Within the Library, three nooks offer distinct configurations for reading. The nooks double as voids punctured through the two floors to bring light down into the basement level.

1919 Within one of the voids, an integrated Periscope creates a vertical connection from First Street to the studio life below using a mirrored desk surface.

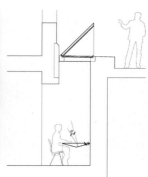

1920 Section at Periscope

1921 Exterior view of light wells down to the Library

1922 Beistegui Apartment, Le Corbusier, Paris (1930)

1923 Beistegui Apartment rooftop camera obscura

1924 Submarine periscope

1925 Periscope mock-up on 1st Street

1926 Periscope mock-up

1927 Periscope mock-up

1928 Testing Periscope visibility levels

1929 Testing Periscope visibility levels

1930 Periscope assembly

1931 Periscope assembly

1932 Periscope assembly

1933 Passersby on the street glimpse views down into the studio.

1934 Periscope details

1935 Periscope installation

1936 Interior view

1937 Periscope installation

1938 The Periscope doubles as a mirrored desk.

1939 The Periscope makes use of an existing structural vault to offer views to the street from the basement.

1918–1939

Cai Studio

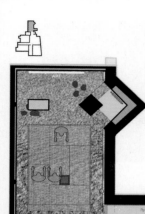

1941 Entry to the Tea Room from the basement corridor

1942 Tea Room rendering

1940 In B1, a Tea Room acts as an additional reception space, as well as a contemplative area within the studio.

1944 The Tea Room is composed of the essential elements of a customary Japanese tea house. Above the mat is a floating light fixture made of woven bamboo reed. A freestanding tokonoma is located opposite the tea room entrance and features art from Cai's father, Cai Ruiqin.

1945 Lighting integrated under the tatami enhances the floating effect.

1943 Tea Room before ceiling fixture installation–the tatami mat appears to be floating off the ground.

1946 Light fixture installation

1947 Bamboo reed installation

1948 Ceiling fixture detail

1949 Ceiling fixture detail

1950 Tatami mat

1951 Tea ceremony

1952 Museo Bilbao board members in repose

1953 The Tea Room acts as a traditional ceremonial space for visitors.

1954 The space provides a modern contemplation space for the studio.

1940–1954

Cai Studio

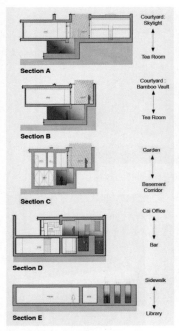

Section A

Courtyard: Skylight

Tea Room

Section B

Courtyard: Bamboo Vault

Tea Room

Section C

Garden

Basement Corridor

Section D

Cai Office

Bar

Section E

Sidewalk

Library

1955   Light well sections—natural light from the courtyard filters down through a series of light wells composed of walkable glass panels.

1956   Each vault has its own distinct identity. One is a bamboo vault with trees that extend vertically up into the central courtyard on the ground level.

1957   View of bamboo vault from the Tea Room

1958   Reflective walls create an expanse of bamboo within the small space.

1959   View up the vault into the courtyard

1960   View of bamboo vault from the courtyard

1961   A vault with a water basin accompanies the Tea Room's ceremonial functions and creates reflections that enhance the light.

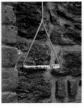

1962   Water basin lever

1963   Art storage plan—in the basement is a climate-controlled art storage room that provides inventory and archiving space.

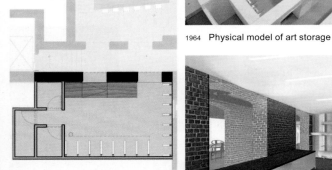

1964   Physical model of art storage

1965   Sketch rendering of art storage

1966   The storage contains both Cai's work and his personal collection.

1967   Glass doors provide visual access to the inventory, while providing a hermetic seal for air quality.

1968   The storage establishes ease of access to works and materials to support the activities of the studio.

1969
1970
1971
1972
1973
1974
1975
1976
1977
1978
1979
1980
1981
1982
1983
1984
1985
1986
1987
1988
1989
1990
1991
1992
1993
1994
1995
1996
1997
1998
1999
2000
2001
2002
2003
2004
2005
2006
2007
2008
2009
2010

1969–2010

Cai Studio

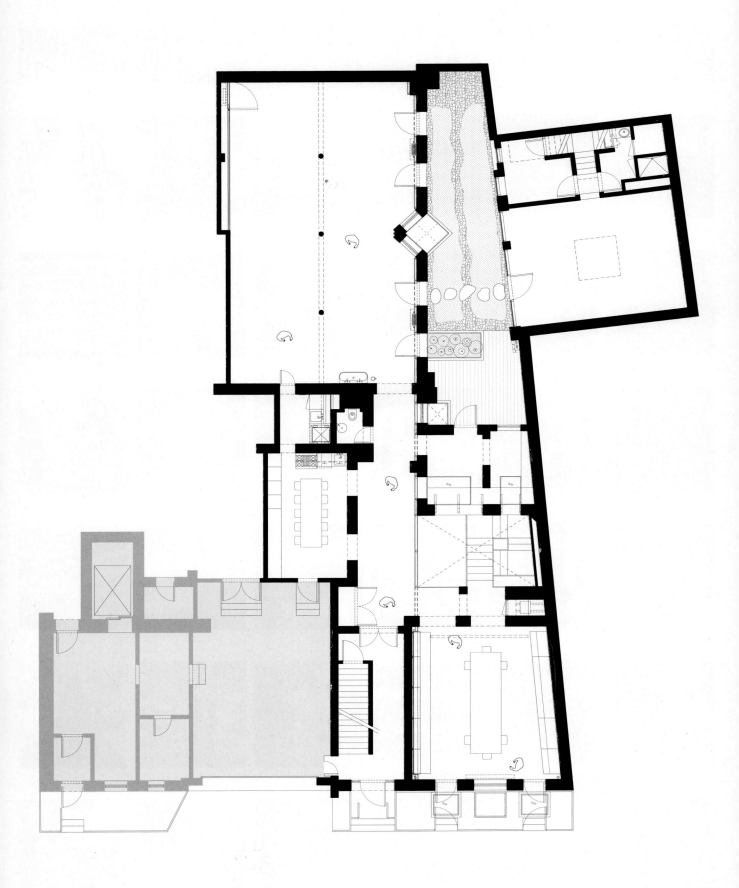

2011   Cai Studio

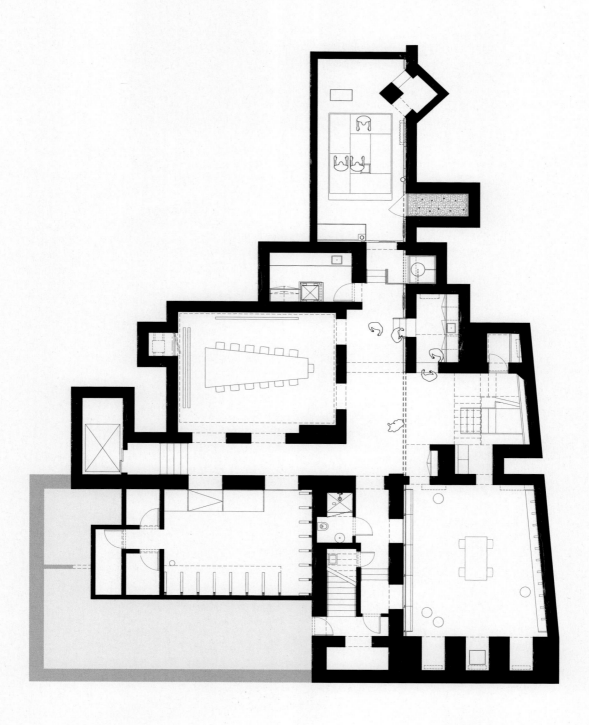

2012   Cai Studio

2013

An Occupation of Loss

Taryn Simon: An Occupation of Loss

In recent years, we've witnessed a rise in artist-led installations and staged performances, in which immersive experiences often pose art as an event. These works can provide environments that allow freedom of interpretation and engagement, redefining the relationship between art and audience. The scale of such environments—lying somewhere between architecture and sculpture—presents an interesting challenge we don't get to experience very often in our practice.

For our collaboration with artist Taryn Simon on the New York performance of *An Occupation of Loss* (co-commissioned by Park Avenue Armory and Artangel) for the Armory's Wade Thompson Drill Hall, Simon takes a different approach to the staging of performance. She devised a monumental sculptural setting in which she considers the anatomy of grief and the intricate systems we construct to contend with uncertainty and the contingencies of fate. She invited professional mourners to simultaneously broadcast lamentations within the sculpture—including northern Albanian laments, which seek to excavate "uncried words"; Wayuu laments, which safeguard the soul's passage to the Milky Way; Greek Epirotic laments, which bind the story of a life with its afterlife; and Yazidi laments, which map a topography of displacement and exile.

The practices of the professional mourners, the scale of the structures and the hall, and the temporality of performance inspired the team to enhance and push the intangible aspects of installation design. We focused on the visceral effects of sound, the scale of grief, and their spatial implications. The design was sonically motivated, focusing on the performance of loss rather than its physical manifestation, which has been historically marked by multiple scales.

Informed by the subterranean form and sonic properties of a well, the eleven concrete structures were excavated and inverted to make their scale visible above ground. Each well measures 45 feet in height and is composed of eight stacked custom concrete rings. A continuous base raises the ellipses of the wells to distribute their structural loads, while integrated lift holds allow cranes to easily stack the rings and facilitate transportation. The readymade ruin responds to both personal and monumental dimensions. Like the Zoroastrian "towers of silence" that informed Simon's vision for the project, the installation makes explicit the never-ending human need to give structure to death in order to understand it. Despite the wells' monumental scale, the enclosed intimacy and confrontation within them heightens the tension between authenticity and performance.

Within each towering structure, mourners enacted rituals of grief that resounded throughout the vast hall. Their lamentations were orchestrated by the collective presence, absence, and movement of the audience. Together, the inverted wells functioned as a discordant instrument, resembling an organ in which each pipe produced its own distinct sound. Ranging from purely vocal to instrumental, distinct mourning rituals echoed from within each well to produce a cacophony of sound whose dissonance reverberated within the installation's eleven-voice polyphonic sound module. During the daytime, the public was invited to activate the sculpture with their own sounds, as a low drone produced from recordings of the mourners' rituals provided echoes of the evening laments.

The installation makes palpable the tensions between the audience, sculpture, and performance through a balance of monumental scale and unexpected intimacy. The resulting occupiable sculpture leaves room for both intentional uncertainties and unexpected engagements and emotions.

Location	New York, NY, USA		
Status	Completed, 2016		
Typology	Artist Collaboration		
Program	Exhibition	38,200 ft²	3,550 m²

2014   An Occupation of Loss

An Occupation of Loss

OMA NY

An Occupation of Loss

2016

An Occupation of Loss

OMA NY

An Occupation of Loss

An Occupation of Loss

2018 Taryn Simon is a multidisciplinary artist who works primarily in photography, text, sculpture, and performance. She lives and works in New York City.

2019 *An American Index of the Hidden and Unfamiliar* (2007)

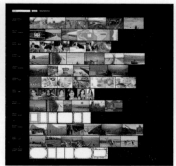

2020 *Image Atlas* (2012)

2021 *The Picture Collection* (2013, 2020)

2022 *Paperwork and the Will of Capital* (2016)

2025 For *An Occupation of Loss*, Simon spent years researching the practice of professional mourning.

2026 *An Occupation of Loss* investigates boundaries of grief between the living and the dead, the past and the present, the performer and the viewer. The performance underscores the tension between authentic and staged emotion, memory and invention, spontaneity and script.

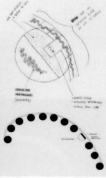

2027 Simon's idea was to create above-ground wells that would be sonically activated by professional mourners within them.

2023 *A Cold Hole* (2018–2019)

2024 *Black Square* (2006–present)

2028 The installation and performance took place in Park Avenue Armory's Wade Thompson Drill Hall, which was designed in 1880 Gothic Revival style by architect Charles Clinton.

2029 View of Wade Thompson Drill Hall

2030 The large open space posed an opportunity to create a monumental installation.

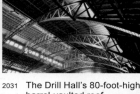

2031 The Drill Hall's 80-foot-high barrel-vaulted roof is the oldest of such scale in America and features eleven elliptical wrought-iron arches.

2032 Roof structure and clerestory windows

2033 Ernesto Neto, *anthropodino* (2009)—large-scale art installations have typically taken place in the daytime, with vibrant activations.

2034 Ryoji Ikeda, *the transfinite* (2011)

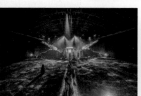

2035 The space also supports theater productions, such as Rob Ashford and Kenneth Branagh's *Macbeth* (2014).

2036 Philippe Parreno, "H{N}Y P N{Y}OSIS" (2015)

2037 Paul McCarthy, "WS" (2013)

2018–2037   An Occupation of Loss

2038 Taryn Simon and Shohei Shigematsu taking initial measurements for potential size and scale of the aboveground wells within the Park Avenue Armory's Wade Thompson Drill Hall.

2039 Testing shape and scale

2040 A condition of the design was transportability of the large-scale installation. We looked into ready-made, prefabricated concrete pipes as potential materials.

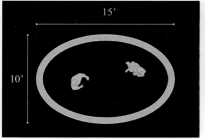

2041 Taryn initially conceptualized an elliptical shape for the pipes.

2042 Reinforced concrete elliptical pipe

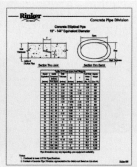

2043 However, the desired elliptical pipe was too large and would require a cost-prohibitive mold; its form was also difficult to transport. We looked to other forms.

2044 Donald Judd, *15 untitled works in concrete* (1980–1984)

2045 Ready-made, reinforced-concrete rings

2046 Site visit

2047 Site visit

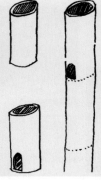

2048 We decided to precast modular pipe segments and transport them to the site.

2049 1:1 corrugated cardboard scale models in the Wade Thompson Drill Hall

2050 A custom mold was created.

2051 Custom mold assembly in progress

2052 Outer layer around rebar

2053 The custom mold

2054 Concrete pipes with latches, which would be useful for transportability and assembly.

2055 Site visit

2056 Interior of pipe

2057 The installation's concrete pipes were custom-made to be light, which facilitated transportation and installation.

2058 We explored various paths of circulation among the wells, including bridges and ramps from which viewers could look down into the wells from above.

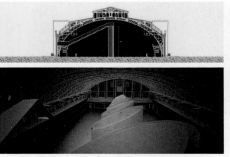

2059 Configuration study 1—linear path

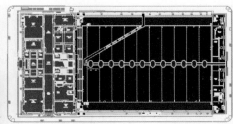

2060 Configuration study 1—linear path

2061 Configuration study 2—multi-cluster

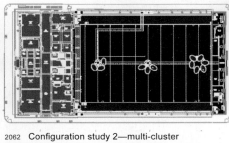

2062 Configuration study 2—multi-cluster

2064 Configuration study 3—grid in linear paths

2065 Configuration study 3—grid in linear paths

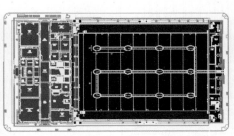

2063 Configuration study 2—multi-cluster

2066 Configuration study 3—grid in linear paths

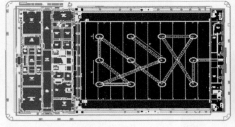

2067 Configuration study 4—grid in a network of paths

2068 Configuration study 4—grid in a network of paths

2069 Configuration study 4—grid in a network of paths

2070 Configuration study 4—grid in a network of paths

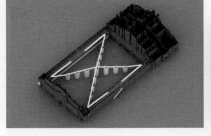

2071 Configuration study 5—intersecting linear paths

2072 Configuration study 5—intersecting linear paths

2073 Configuration study 5—intersecting linear paths

2074 Configuration study 5—intersecting linear paths

2075 Configuration study 6—arc

2076 Configuration study 6—arc

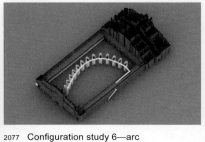

2077 Configuration study 6—arc

An Occupation of Loss

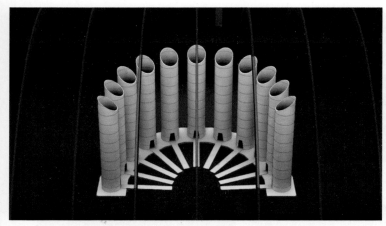

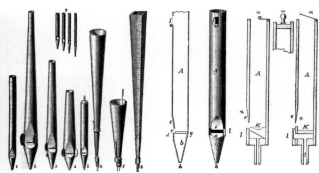

2079 Organ pipe studies

2078 The final configuration takes the form of an arc, resembling a pipe organ.
Guided by the subterranean form and sonic properties of a well, the eleven pipes
are inverted to make their scale visible above ground.

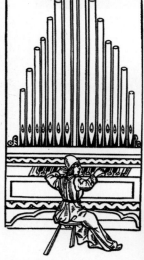

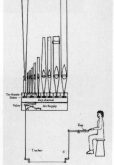

2081 Organ components

2082 Final configuration rendering

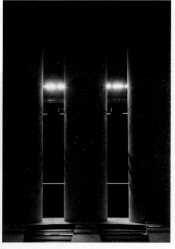

2083 Final configuration rendering

2080 As with a pipe organ,
each pipe produces its
own distinct sound.
The mourners' simulta-
neous laments from within
the pipes produce
a cacophony of grief.

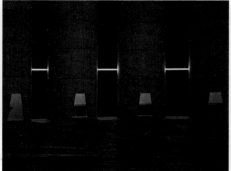

2085 Each visitor's experience of the
laments is unique, orchestrated by
their undirected circulation among
the pipes.

2084 The space generated by grief is often marked by an absence of language.
Individuals and communities pass through the unspeakable consequences of loss
and can emerge transformed, redefined, reprogrammed.

2086 View south from behind the towers

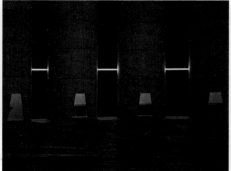

2087 The void opened up by loss can be filled by
religion, nihilism, militancy, benevolence—
or anything.

2088 The eleven pipes function together as a discordant
instrument, amplifying the performance of grief.

2078–2088   An Occupation of Loss

2089   Mockup installation on site in the Park Avenue Armory's 55,000-square-foot Wade Thompson Drill Hall.

2091   The concrete rings were stacked and assembled on site.

2090   Each well is composed of eight vertically stacked concrete rings. Integrated lift holds allow cranes to easily stack the rings and facilitate transportation.

2092   Each ring is 5 feet high (the top and base rings are 7 feet high).

2093   Zoomed-in view of integrated lift hold

2094   During the daytime, visitors are free to wander and activate the sculpture with their own sounds.

2095   Daytime installation view

2096   In the daytime, a quiet drone created from the recordings of the mourners' rituals provides echoes of the evening performance.

2097   The angled tops of the pipes

2098   A sliver of the hall's clerestory window is revealed during the day. The natural light seeping in transforms the installation experience.

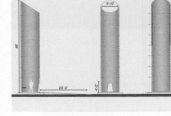

2099   Pipe sections

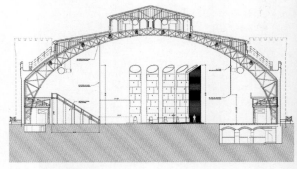

2100   Overall section

2101   By day, the installation reverberates with the call-and-response of the living as visitors interact with one another and with the pipes themselves.

2089–2101   An Occupation of Loss

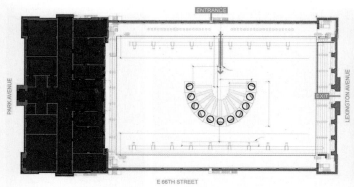

2102 Visitors enter the Park Avenue Armory by ascending an anonymous fire escape on 67th Street—an unprecedented entry strategy for the Armory that bypassed familiar entrances and architectural reference points. The public first sees the installation in its entirety from the Armory's second level mezzanine (20 feet above ground level) before descending a narrow staircase. After the mourners stop performing, a roll gate clangs open and visitors exit the Drill Hall through a large loading-dock style portal onto Lexington Avenue.

2103 View from second-floor mezzanine to ground-floor installation

2104 Visitors view installation from second-floor mezzanine.

2105 Visitors descend the stairs to the ground floor.

2106 Visitors descend the stairs to the ground floor.

2107 Visitors enter the installation.

2108 Professional mourners direct and exercise agency over the abstract space that opens up after loss. Threatened by this authority, governments and organized religions have often marginalized their practices.

2111 Two lines of light demarcate the entry into the installation. Simon collaborated with lighting designer Urs Schönebaum on the lighting design.

2112 Visitors enter through a light portal at the base of the stairs. The LED lines suspended from the ceiling appear weightless alongside the monolithic installation.

2109 Final concept rendering—light lines

2110 Installation view

2113 Daytime installation view

2114 There is no prescribed path by which visitors must circulate. Each person's movements and sonic experience are unique and unscripted.

An Occupation of Loss

2115 Eleven narrow ramps incline gradually toward entrances so low that visitors must bow their heads to enter.

2116 The ramp design was inspired by Simon's research on the Tower of Silence, a raised structure built by Zoroastrians for excarnation, enacted by exposing the dead to carrion birds.

2117 Site visit—ramp

2118 Site visit—well entry

2121 The sloping ramps invite a slow, deliberate entrance into the wells.

2119 Installation view—ramps

2120 Installation view—ramps

2122 Daytime installation view

2123 Daytime installation view

2124 Daytime installation view

2125 Each pipe is illuminated with a single LED light-line held in place by a custom groove at the top of the pipe.

2126 Simon inspects a pipe.

2127 Looking up from inside the well

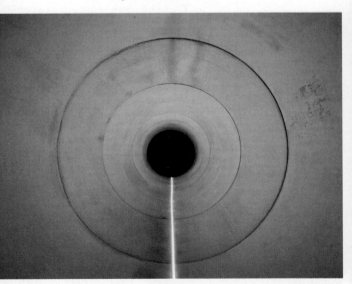

2128 Each concrete pipe rises 45 feet in height, re-creating the sensation of being at the bottom of a well.

2115–2128   An Occupation of Loss

2129 Simon wanted to establish a space in which the mourners could control the psychological and emotional experience of the public within each pipe.

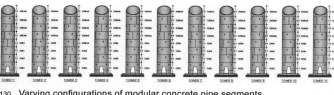

2130 Varying configurations of modular concrete pipe segments

2131 Studies—professional mourners broadcast their laments from a large concrete platform inside each pipe. Their unscripted laments direct the sonic and psychological experiences within the spaces.

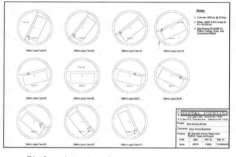

2132 Platform layout study

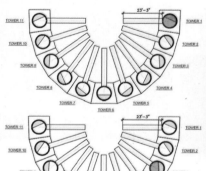
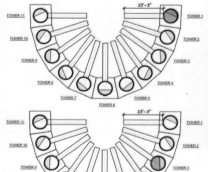

2133 Platform study

2134 Study—rotated platforms front view

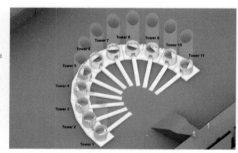

2135 Study—rotated platforms axon view

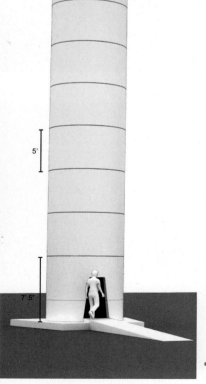

2136 The trapezoidal opening to each concrete pipe, at 4 feet, 2 inches, is shorter in height than the typical door.

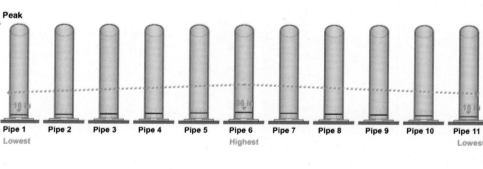
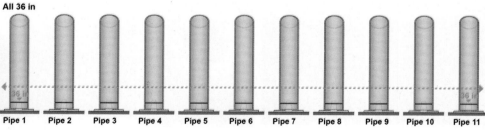

2137 Platform height studies—top: peak; bottom: level

2138 View from inside the pipe

2139 Installation view—
entrance to pipe.
Each pipe is occupied
by a professional mourner
or mourner ensemble.

2140 Haji Rahila Jafarova and Lala Ismayilova from
Azerbaijan, where mourning is a profession
for which women are greatly esteemed. Only
female visitors are allowed to enter this pipe.

2141 Aníbal González, from Ecuador,
performs a yaravi, a lament that
speaks to the dead.

2142 Kalas Tossouni Boudoyan, Aziz
Tamoyan, and Amar Ozmanian, Yezidi
professional mourners.

2143 Installation view—entrance
to pipe

2144 The mourners' laments resound throughout the vast hall.

2145 Installation view—
entrance to well

2146 P-3 visa petitions—
Simon documented the
performers' application
processes to reveal
structures governing global
exchange, the movement
of bodies, and the hierar-
chies of art and culture.

2147 On exiting, visitors receive booklets with excerpts of supporting
documents for the P-3 visa
application process. Simon notes
that the work was curated by
the U.S. government, whose
permissions determined the
presence and absence of
performers.

2148 Simon's double album,
published in 2019 by
The Vinyl Factory, includes
both live and studio
recordings of the laments
performed by the profes-
sional mourners.

2149 The pipes have since
moved to the
Massachusetts Museum
of Contemporary Art
(MASS MoCA), where they
will be installed outdoors
as a freestanding and
interactive sculpture.

2150 Modular pipe segments
(pre-installation view) on
site at MASS MoCA.

2151 Rendering—installation of the wells at MASS
MoCA.

An Occupation of Loss

2152 2153 2154 2155 2156 2157
2158 2159 2160 2161 2162 2163
2164 2165 2166 2167 2168 2169
2170 2171 2172 2173 2174 2175
2176 2177 2178 2179 2180 2181
2182 2183 2184 2185 2186 2187
2188 2189 2190 2191 2192 2193

2152–2193   An Occupation of Loss

An Occupation of Loss

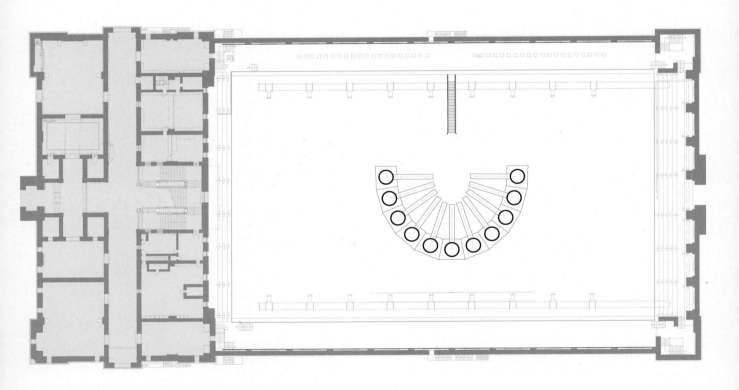

An Occupation of Loss

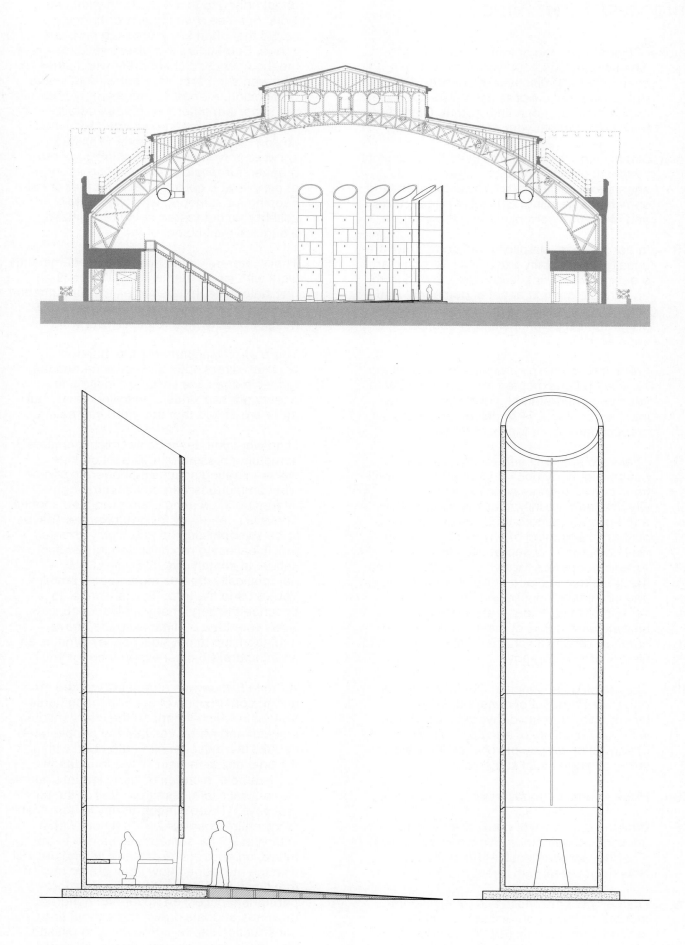

An Occupation of Loss

Interview Taryn Simon

Shohei Shigematsu: You are a collector of sorts, when it comes to your work. There's an intense drive to discover or unearth stories or truths, and that process itself also seems to inform the thesis of a final output. Could you tell us more about your research method?

Taryn Simon: I consciously try to keep it ridiculously simple at the start of each project. But it seems to quickly shatter into a complex (and sometimes grueling) constellation of efforts and ideas that control me and the process.

SS: In our process, simplicity and complexity are usually not mutually exclusive. We can start a design with a simple gesture derived from an intricate context or set of demands. And a seemingly simple design can have complex programmatic relationships or spatial experiences.

From floral centerpieces to cold-water plunges, you find unexpected topics and translate your own understanding of those subjects into new contexts. How do you arrive at your preoccupations, or topics of research?

TS: There are so many different departure points—an early book documenting competitions between grass species, a novel in which a leading character's emotional state and tears are generated by payment, alongside an imagination of physically inverting a well, the pursuit of secret sites beyond American borders following 9/11, the certainties imagined in blood colliding with chance and circumstance, eliciting the gasp only seen in birth and death, applause as a barometer of public opinion, and a woman named Romana Javitz who helmed an untold history of photography.

SS: They're all quite specific. Our architectural output is a product of observations driven by our own interests or hypotheses, mixed with the specificity of each project. What kind of conviction do you have when jumping into some of those initial subjects?

TS: Huge swaths of doubt mixed with insistence.

SS: When in doubt, we're more open to embrace unexpected outcomes. We prefer to accept a certain awkwardness or unfamiliarity. How do you deal with unanticipated results?

TS: I use empty portraits in a lot of my works to mark moments of resistance, failures to access, bureaucratic red tape, and cultural and personal limitations. They are partly about adhering to the systems within the work, but also a way to put forth friction points that often say more than an actual image. Sometimes this visual absence gives me the chance to collaborate with someone who wants to participate but without visual recognition. Alongside these empty portraits are important otherwise hidden details— for example, someone incarcerated who I couldn't access, or someone in military service, or women who couldn't be photographed for religious or cultural reasons, or people who couldn't travel for fear of kidnapping, or someone who wanted to collaborate but feared being recognized alongside the subject of the work.

SS: That's interesting because you predominantly work with visual mediums, but there is an "invisible" side that becomes the fundamental premise. How do your own notions of ugliness or beauty then relate to your work?

TS: There are misalignments that happen between direct optical experience and the "ghost images" we carry. Ugliness and beauty are two kinds of misalignments, but there are others that are more interesting.

SS: I find what you describe as "misalignments" something present across a lot of your work—creating spaces that operate somewhat ambiguously. In architecture, I am interested in creating unprogrammed spaces. There is a tendency for programmed spaces to be so sophisticated and highly charged that it leaves no room for freedom or improvisation. In some ways, the uncertainty paradoxically creates more spatial stability. You've used the term "liminal space" to describe the zone that your work occupies. Does your idea of "liminal space," have a relationship to physical space? What is an architecturally liminal experience for you?

TS: *A Polite Fiction* was a project I worked on during construction of the Fondation Louis Vuitton in which I mapped the interventions, objects, and narratives that the people hired to build the museum had entombed within the final polished walls of the foundation. For example, pictures of world leaders buried behind walls; a message written in the safe that says, "There's more money in here than in my entire country–DRC"; a note with a cigarette left for someone to smoke in the future; an abstract oil painting behind drywall with the message "Now I can put on my CV that I'm in the Louis Vuitton Foundation's permanent collection"; over one hundred drawings of goats drawn throughout the construction site by someone who missed the goats on his parents' farm in Portugal.

There was privilege and power, but also all these latent economic and social pressures pushing up against them, simultaneously silenced and preserved.

SS: I think most, if not all of architecture is shaped by invisible structures and influences. I've personally been interested in how crises influence architecture and urbanism. I found that historically, upturn and modernization were coupled and downturn and de-modernization, or stagnancy, were coupled. Today, we're dealing with more complex correlations between those binary conditions, and at a much higher frequency of fluctuations.

Architects are often pushed to catch up with a rapidly changing society, but the industry is inherently slow. I admit, I sometimes value that speed because it often thwarts expectations, especially in this time, of immediacy, efficiency, profitability from production to consumption. There's more time to digest those changes, so the work is not purely reactive, but proactive in assessing any new values more diligently.

You spend a lot of time on some of your projects, sometimes more than four years. How do you observe the speed of society today? Do you consciously try to capture the zeitgeist of the time?

TS: My process has always been slow—taking a lot of time to look at something. Although I work in the current moment, I don't see the work as operating within it in real time. It's usually the result of a long period of thinking about something that is gone, but that through the act of photography is re-linked to the current, colliding with the unknown present in some unexpected mashup.

Or time collapses with a distant future—in the year 3015, 1,000 years after its creation, a black square made from vitrified nuclear waste will be dug up. I made this square with Russia's State Atomic Energy Corporation, and it's being stored in a nuclear waste disposal plant in Sergiev Posad until its radioactive properties diminish to levels deemed safe for human exposure and exhibition. Cast within the black square is a steel capsule with a photograph and a handwritten letter to the future.

SS: What do you think about the relationship between the time you spend on your work and the outcome?

TS: It's absurd.

SS: Love the three-dimensional Malevich's *Black Square* you've created with the Energy Corporation.

Do you value collaboration with different fields? For us, it's almost a given. Although challenging at times, we enjoy collaborating with other disciplines because the convergence of those different perspectives is what helps us achieve something new or unexpected.

TS: I've always collaborated with individuals, scattered domains, and institutions in different ways. It's at the core of all my projects. One that stands out is my collaboration with Aaron Swartz on *Image Atlas*, which is a search engine that investigates cultural differences and similarities by indexing the top image results for given search terms across local engines throughout the world.

SS: With this book, we're trying to investigate similarities and differences across our own work and in that process try to find inherent frameworks that underline our diverse output. It's also interesting to see the different narratives we've crafted over the course of the projects in context with one another. What is the role of the text or narrative in your work?

TS: Text is at the center of my work, although in small font and off to the side. It serves as both an anchor and a disruptor. It fixes things in different ways than the image. And the two play off each other in a never-ending performance.

SS: How do you then reflect that dynamic in the form of a book? Through an ultimate exposure of our process and a sense of open-endedness, we hope this book serves as a search engine for us, and as an open-source platform for anyone else to find their own—as you say—departure points. Although, that intention has resulted in over 6,000 images in the book. A lot of your work deals with massive archives and image collections as well. How do you structure that effort in printed matter?

TS: Bookmaking is always an attempt to make sense of too much and to hold it all together figuratively and literally. Books give the appearance of being comprehensive and authoritative or complete—a fantasy of legibility.

Taryn Simon is a multidisciplinary artist who works primarily in photography, text, sculpture, and performance. She lives and works in New York City.

OMA NY

Taryn Simon

Faena District

We've been investigating how the art world has been evolving, specifically how the latent influence of soft power has led to a rise in the art fair as a model for reinvigorating cities: there are almost 200 perennials and fairs per year, with 22 art events occurring on the same month in some years. The success of Art Basel in cities like Miami is a great example of the profound and complex effect that art fairs can have in transforming a city into an art destination. It has even led to programs like Art Basel Cities, where the model of Art Basel is adopted by cities looking to accelerate international recognition of their very own art scenes.

We began working on Faena District at a time when Miami's cultural scene was evolving and becoming more layered. The city's cultural center of gravity was shifting from the global reach of Art Basel toward local scenes, establishing a permanent foothold not bound by the art fair calendar. A strong movement of Latino investors seeing the city as a safe haven for their funds has also contributed to Miami's growth and status as a gateway between Latin America and the United States. It has become a new Latin American capital, building itself out of its diversity.

Alan Faena is an Argentinian fashion designer turned hotelier and developer who came to Miami Beach with a vision to build a new mixed-use neighborhood. His range of investments in culture, in addition to commercial developments, posed an opportunity for the project to take a holistic approach. Our creative partnership began with researching Faena's brand identity and evolved into urban design, programming, buildings, and scenography. It was like designing a small universe in a pocket of the city.

Located in the heart of the Miami Beach peninsula, the site for Faena District presented three lots encompassing both sides of Collins Avenue, with direct waterfront views of the Atlantic Ocean and Indian Creek. We designed the district with three buildings—Faena Forum, Bazaar, and Park—to complement Faena's hotel and residential components.

The Forum claims the heart of the complex by addressing both the quieter, residential zone along Indian Creek and the commercial and cultural thoroughfare on Collins. We conceived two volumes—a cube and a cylinder—that generate distinct frontages while achieving the same intimate scale as the Bazaar and Park. The cube houses a black box and the cylinder has a space with a classical dome ceiling, further accentuating the identity of each volume.

The juxtaposition of the two types of spaces provides flexibility for the diverse programming of Faena's multi-faceted ambitions. Combined, the full layout has the capacity for large-scale events. Independently, the spaces can be divided to accommodate different events simultaneously. Below the main assembly level, a lobby that takes on the form of an amphitheater can function as a third event space for additional programming. With this flexibility, the Forum can host multiple combinations and a range of events—from concerts to conventions, lectures to banquets, exhibitions to art fairs—all within a single evening.

The circular plan of the cylinder volume allows the sidewalks to expand around it, activating the public domain within the district. Below the cylinder, a shaded exterior plaza is formed by removing a wedge from the front of the building, providing a dramatic sense of arrival under a 45-foot cantilever. The cantilever is supported by a structural facade that also allows for vast column-free spaces on the building's two main levels. The facade is created by a series of arches and catenary curves overlaid with a hurricane grid, resulting in a pattern resembling an organic form like a palm tree or a seashell, which we found appropriate for Miami Beach.

Liberated from obligations to operate as a strictly institutional or a strictly commercial entity, the Forum presents a new typology for interaction. It is an event machine that is independent from yet complementary to the art fair, creating a focal point for the city's increasingly diverse art and cultural activities.

Location	Miami, FL, USA		
Status	Completed, 2016		
Typology	Art Platform		
Program	Cultural Forum	43,000 ft²	4,000 m²
	Theater	6,700 ft²	600 m²
	Parking	28,300 ft²	2,600 m²
	Retail	20,100 ft²	1,900 m²
	Total Area	98,100 ft²	9,100 m²

2200

Faena District

2201

Faena District

OMA NY

Faena District

Faena District

OMA NY   Faena District

Faena District

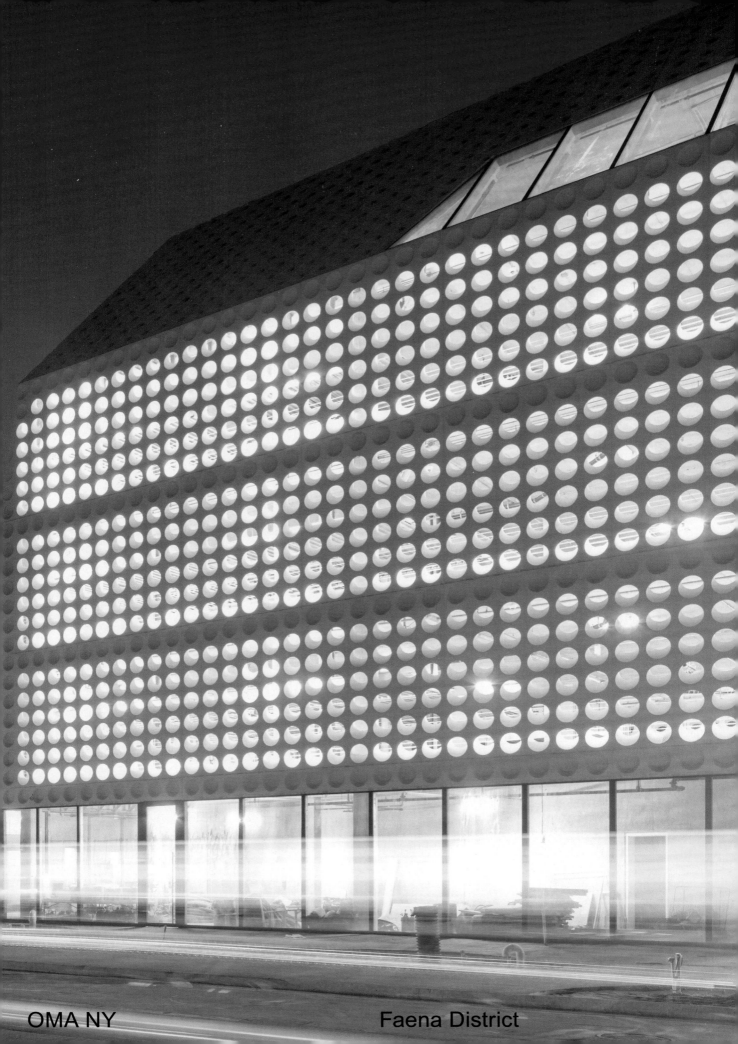

OMA NY   Faena District

Faena District

2205 Alan Faena is an Argentinian fashion designer turned hotelier and developer who has developed properties in his native Buenos Aires and now Miami. He is the founder and president of Faena Group.

2206 Faena Group's portfolio ranges from hotel and residential to cultural and curatorial domains, such as the Faena Art Center in Buenos Aires (2011).

2207 We began with an investigation into the constellation of its brands and activities.

2208 Faena Group's diverse parts could be defined by a duality of commercial and cultural identities.

2209 The duality was further explored to define an intertwined path between its cultural and commercial activity.

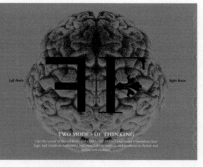

2210 Two modes of thinking: like the union of the left and right brain, the combination of Faena and the Faena District is poised to fuse logic and intuition, rationality and imagination, analysis and synthesis.

2211 The branding exercise helped direct the project and identify the ambition to forge a new type of multifunctional arts space, one that balances Faena's cultural activities with its commercial activities.

2212 Saxony Hotel on Collins Avenue, Miami Beach, Florida (1949)

2213 Saxony and Versailles Hotels along Golden Sands, Miami Beach, Florida (1950s)

2214 The site for Faena's new vision was in the middle of a long stretch of Miami Beach, in an area that was active in the '50s but is no longer as vibrant. When the project was commissioned, the site was not in the most active part of Miami Beach.

2215 Unlike other developments along the beach such as the Fontainebleau, an enclosed resort, this project offered an opportunity to create an entirely new neighborhood that would feel more urban and less like a compound.

2216 The existing site presented three conditions—a large, wedge-shaped site for a multifunctional arts space, a historic art deco hotel that had to be preserved, and an empty lot allocated for parking and retail.

2217 The three site conditions with three distinct programs posed a challenge.

2218 The site is also located on a unique stretch where the beach is at its widest and the peninsula at its narrowest. Indian Creek and the Atlantic Ocean are very close to each other with clear views to and from one another. The two waterways and their different characters and conditions presented an opportunity for the design to respond to and address the urban context and distinct frontages.

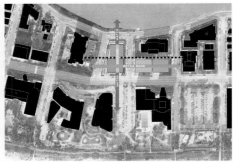

2219 The wedge-shaped site for the arts space straddles two areas with different characters—one quiet and residential, the other clearly linked to the hotels and condos around it.

2220 One of the first models made, with buildings like chocolates in a box. Each volume can have a distinct character while together they create a neighborhood.

2221 Three buildings create a frontage to Collins Avenue. Rather than creating one big volume on the site, two separate volumes similar in size are created, one that addresses Indian Creek and another that addresses Collins Avenue.

2222 Three volumes

2223 Four volumes

2224 While the two volumes address the site's distinct frontages, another challenge was in claiming the "heart" of the complex. We looked at the plan repeatedly and found that the old Saxony Hotel has a curved facade facing Collins Avenue and Norman Foster's Miami Beach Condominium has a wedge shape, both opening up toward Collins.

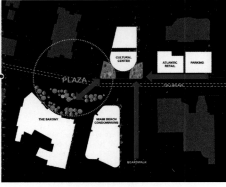

2225 By creating a circle with the volume facing Collins Avenue, a larger central plaza is created.

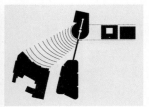

2226 The curved volume creates a new focal point while simultaneously orienting and linking the building to the rest of the complex.

2227 We started with the idea that the various components of the complex were meant to fit together, like a Pangaea supercontinent.

2228 The whole complex is then separated into different buildings.

2229 Barbizon Hotel, Ocean Drive— the concept also drew from the famous streamline buildings in Miami Beach; the round shape resonated with the Miami Beach Modernist style.

2230 Reference— Cardozo Hotel South Beach, 1300 Ocean Drive

2231 Reference—Miami Beach Post Office, Washington Avenue

2232 Saxony, Miami Beach Condominium, and Forum

2233 Faena District

2234 Aerial view of the Faena Hotel (formerly Saxony Hotel) and Faena House condominiums across Collins Avenue from the Faena Forum

2237 Compared to a large cultural institution like the Metropolitan Museum of Art, the Guggenheim embodies a magical scale because it's embedded into a residential area, making it similar to the Forum in character and context.

2236 New York's Guggenheim Museum was used as a reference for its scale.

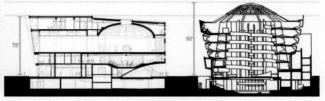

2235 View down Collins—once the split volume and urban connectivity for the district were established, we looked to precedents for size and shape in response to the client's request for a forum for public interaction.

2238 Scale comparison between Faena Forum and the Guggenheim

2241 Sphere

2239 Roman Forum—the most celebrated meeting place in the world. Capitalizing on its scale and programmatic diversity, the aptly named Faena Forum is not so much an art space as it is a meeting space. It is a public domain where interaction occurs.

2240 The open-ended programmatic ambition of the Forum presented a challenge in giving a form. The concept began with collaging vision-oriented architecture onto the site (Étienne-Louis Boullée, Cenotaph for Newton, 1784).

2242 More classical forms were considered and collaged onto the site as well.

2243 Cylinder

2244 Concept collage— circular theater (Bruno Taut, Glass Pavilion, 1914)

2245 Cone

2246 Teatro Colón, Buenos Aires, Argentina (1908)

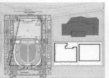

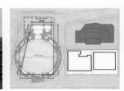

2247 Scale comparison— Teatro Colón

2248 Pantheon, Rome, Italy (125 A.D.)

2249 Scale comparison— Pantheon

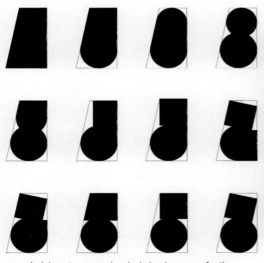

2250 Arriving at a more classical circular space for the volume facing Collins, we looked at complementary shapes for the volume facing Indian Creek.

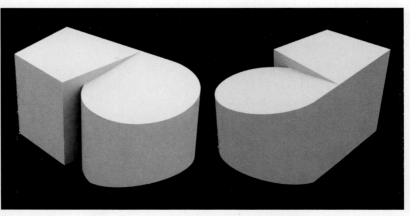

2251 We arrived at the combination of a cylindrical volume with a contemporary black box. The final form appears simple yet deceptive—on one side it appears as two volumes, while on the other side it is merged into a single mass.

2252 With minimal intervention, the space can operate as two contrasting halves with two entirely different activities.

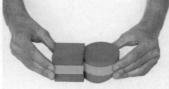

2253 Or, the two volumes can work together to form a symbiotic relationship.

2254 View from Collins and 33rd Street—two distinct volumes that are attached

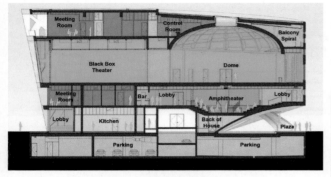

2255 The two volumes can be combined or separated, providing the ultimate flexibility for Faena's diverse programming. The form's interiors are further designed to create distinctions. The cylindrical volume contains a classical dome section, while the square volume contains a more straightforward black box theater.

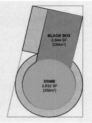

2256 Combined, the two spaces create a 6,676-square-foot Assembly Hall. Separated, the 3,832-square-foot dome and 2,844-square-foot black box can host two different events simultaneously.

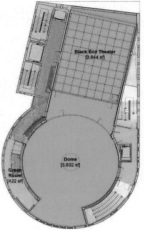

2257 Level 3 Plan—the Assembly Hall can be configured as a unified space that can easily accommodate a variety of large scale events.

2258 Assembly Hall, viewed from the dome space

2261 The space can be divided using partition walls that enclose the Forum into two distinct spaces, physically and acoustically independent from one another.

2262 Dance rehearsal—partition closed

2263 Dance rehearsal—partition open

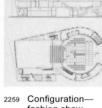

2259 Configuration—fashion show, 201 seats

2260 Configuration—lecture, 762 seats

2264 The Forum is like a cultural machine, with a number of different events occurring simultaneously.

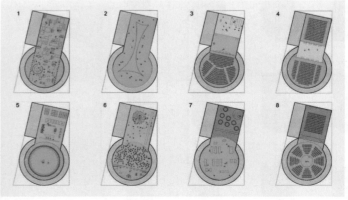

2265 Assembly Hall Configurations—(1) Convention (2) Exhibition (3) Performance: 500-seat auditorium, stage, back of house (4) Double-sided Stage: 600-seat auditorium (5) Convention: 100-seat round table, pre-function space (6) Concert: performance space, pre-function lounge (7) Two separate events: exhibition and ballroom (8) Two separate events: 370-seat arena and 200-seat lecture.

2266 The side of the Assembly Hall facing Collins Avenue has a distinct domed ceiling with an oculus that is reminiscent of historic spaces for gathering.

2267 Dome geometry and oculus

2268 Dome mock-up

2269 Dome construction

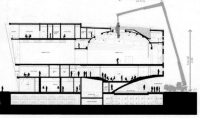

2270 In the dome, the opening of the oculus is large enough to allow transport of large-scale exhibition content and other objects.

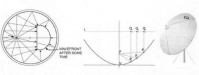

2271 The dome is structural but it is also an acoustic device that provides specific conditions for events with varying requirements.

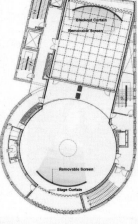

2272 Assembly Hall—staging features

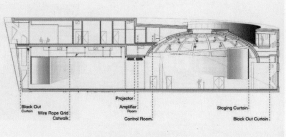

2273 Staging features in the Assembly Hall include a blackout curtain, wire rope grid catwalk, projector, control room, and staging curtain.

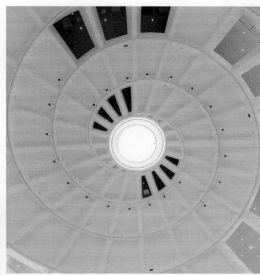

2274 Rather than a pure dome, the Faena dome's design is a spiral integrated with infrastructure and a lighting rig to accommodate multiple events.

2275 The black-box theater is the counterpart to the dome. The space is integrated with a range of staging features and a tension grid catwalk ceiling that can accommodate a typical theater performance and allow for a quick turnaround for a diverse range of events.

2276 Installation

2277 Dance performance

2278 Film screening

2279 Black box construction

2280 View of closed partition from black box

2281 Facing Indian Creek, the black-box space features a floor to ceiling window that can be blacked out with curtains or open for ample daylighting and views.

2282 Evening performance utilizing the floor to ceiling window as a backdrop

2283 Around the dome, a walkway spirals up along the building's facade to form a balcony space that looks down to the Assembly Hall and out to the surrounding context.

2284 Spiral Balcony model

2285 The balcony provides visitors with a range of perspectives and additional seating.

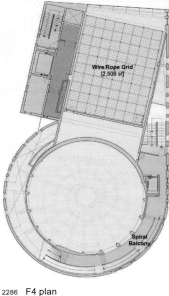

2286 F4 plan

2287 The spectators on the balcony are visible from below

2288 The balcony is integrated with the dome's structure.

2289 The ambition of the balcony was to create an opportunity for performance and architecture to merge.

2290 The ceiling of the Spiral Balcony is lined with an acoustic buffer.

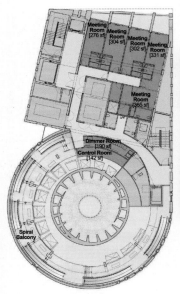

2291 F5 plan

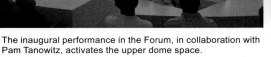

2292 The inaugural performance in the Forum, in collaboration with Pam Tanowitz, activates the upper dome space.

2293 Activities within the black box are also visible from the balcony.

2295 While the main Assembly Hall can be two spaces working together or separately, the Collins side lobby doubles as a third space—the Amphitheater.

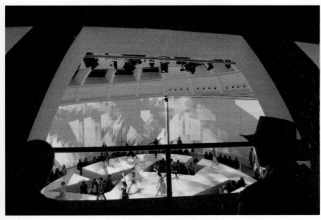

2294 View of Pam Tanowitz performance from the Spiral Balcony

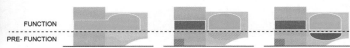

2296 Maximizing potential usability—in the most extreme moment, the Forum can host three events simultaneously and two pre-event functions (from left to right—one event, two events, three events).

2297 Amphitheater in the F2 lobby is an inverse of the dome of the Assembly Hall.

2301 Material studies

2302 Pre-function lounge

2298 Verona Arena, Verona, Italy (30 A.D.)

2299 Mirroring the dome, the lobby features a sunken pit for pre-function or smaller events.

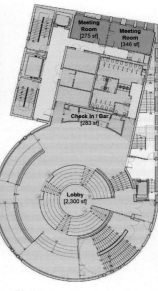

2300 F2 plan

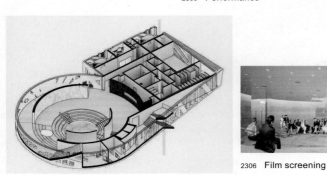

2303 Performance

2304 The space can serve as a pre-function lounge as well as an independent space for intimate film screenings and smaller performances.

2305 F2 lobby axonometric diagram

2306 Film screening

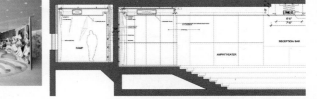

2307 Staging features in the lobby/pre-function area include blackout curtain, acoustic projecting curtain, silver screen curtain, rotating projector, and coffer.

2308 The sunken Amphitheater is partially enclosed.

2309 Small lecture in the Amphitheater

2310 Performance in the Amphitheater during Miami Music Week 2018

2311 Isabel Lewis performance during 2018 Miami Art Week

2312 The central space for gathering is circumscribed by the daylit corridor, establishing a layer of activities within F2.

2313 F1 plan—at the ground level are two lobbies. The main entry faces Collins Avenue while a second lobby faces Indian Creek.

2314 The arrival for a building is quite important in Miami Beach. The city's hotels have historically had glamorous arrivals. We wanted to create a sense of arrival that would also extend the public domain.

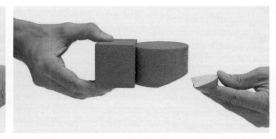

2315 Rather than adding a canopy to the pure volume of the building, we created one with the building itself by removing a "wedge" from the cylinder to expand Collins Plaza while creating the building's covered Entry Plaza.

2316 Beneath the canopy, the greenery extends from Collins Plaza and slides under the Forum.

2317 The landscape penetrates deeper into the Entry Plaza and adds to the network of public spaces within the district.

2318 Canopy construction

2319 Entry Plaza and canopy construction

2320 2018 Miami Music Week performance

2321 A parade passes through the Entry Plaza.

2322 A shallow pool of water under the wedge helps cool the Entry Plaza and reflects light toward the cantilevered canopy.

2323 Activated plazas along Collins Avenue

2324 By removing the wedge, a 45-foot cantilever allows a seamless connection between the Entry Plaza and Collins Plaza.

2325 Faena District aerial view during inaugural celebration. The Entry Plaza is illuminated in red.

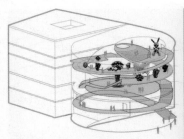

2326 The entry and circulation of the building are simple—visitors walk around the perimeter, circling a flexible central space.

2327 Main access into the Forum is located on Collins Avenue.

2328 The main entrance brings visitors into the Forum through a covered stairway.

2329 View down to Collins Plaza

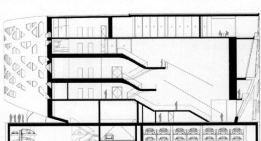

2330 Rendered section showing Indian Creek Lobby, Atrium, and circulation.

2331 The perimeter stair always provides a sense of orientation by offering views out to the ocean.

2332 Perimeter circulation from the F2 lobby to the F3 Assembly Hall.

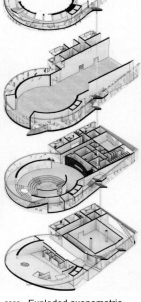

2333 Exploded axonometric diagram

2335 The Indian Creek side lobby is compressed and utilitarian.

2334 A second, small lobby at Indian Creek provides an additional "front door" that can be exclusively dedicated to the black-box theater, separate from the dome space entrance and the Collins entry.

2339 The concrete provides a contrast from the lighter-hued materiality of the Forum's active spaces.

2336 The Indian Creek side lobby opens to the Atrium, located where the cylinder and cube volumes join.

2337 The wall of the Atrium is activated with large scale works.

2338 The walls of the egress stairway were left as raw cast-in-place concrete.

Faena District

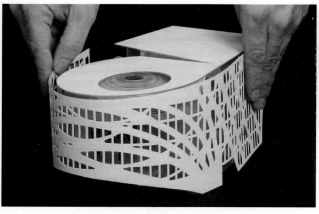

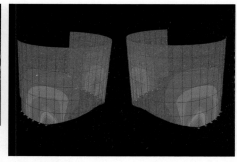

2340　The Forum's facade is structural and was conceived by the need to support the cantilever sheltering over the exterior Entry Plaza.

2341　Cantilever diagram showing the directionality of force on the structural facade

2342　Stress diagram

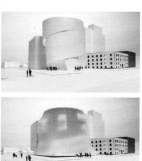

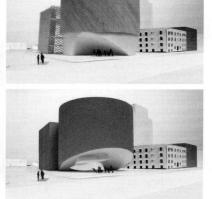

2343　Early study models of the cylinder volume

2344　Early entry study models

2345　Despite the need to utilize a structural facade, we explored more common elements, such as punched windows, resonating with the banality of the residential buildings around the site.

2346　We decided to express the facade's structure.

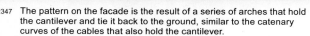

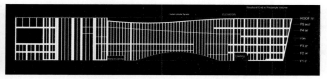

2347　The pattern on the facade is the result of a series of arches that hold the cantilever and tie it back to the ground, similar to the catenary curves of the cables that also hold the cantilever.

2348　The pattern of arches was superimposed with a typical grid that was necessary for the anti-hurricane commission of the area.

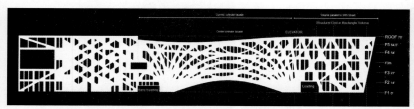

2349　The result is an overlay of two structural and environmental patterns that create a unique skin specific to urban conditions.

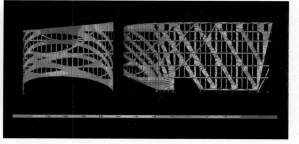

2350　By analyzing the stress on the building due to the cantilevered form, the skin is mobilized as structure.

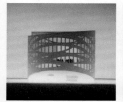

2351　View from Collins Avenue

2352　View from 34th Street

2353　View from Indian Creek

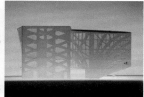

2354　View from Indian Creek

2355　View from 33rd Street

2356 Aerial view of Faena District under construction

2357 For the facade windows, unique plywood formwork was created for each individual window.

2358 Formwork and rebar

2359 The plywood molds were placed in the concrete floor by floor to create the structural pattern.

2360 North wall formwork

2361 Window formwork

2362 South facade

2363 South wall

2364 Spiral walkway interior wall under construction

2365 Concrete was poured floor by floor as false window frames were cast in place within the molds to have a perfect one-to-one match for the windows that were manufactured simultaneously as each floor was poured.

2366 Facade construction from inside the dome space of the Forum

2367 The structural facade has 350 distinct windows and allows for vast column free spaces on the building's two main levels.

2368 The distinct pattern of the skin resembles a seashell on the beach, connecting it to tropical images of Miami while creating a unique face that stands out from its surroundings.

2369 View from Collins Avenue and 33rd Street

2370 The facade from the Indian Creek side offers a subtle yet dramatic presence when the building is approached from the street.

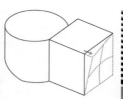

2371 The facade "curls" outward, slightly reaching out onto Indian Creek.

2372 View from 34th Street and Indian Creek

2373 View from 33rd Street and Indian Creek

2374 View from Indian Creek

2375 View of the Indian Creek Atrium's mural through the facade

2376 The facade gently peels out to follow the curve of Indian Creek.

2377 Aerial view from the Indian Creek side

2378 Balconies on the top level and at the core and lobby frame the single larger opening to the Assembly Hall.

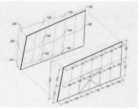

2379 The over-sized window opening to the black box is composed of twelve individual glass elements.

2380 The large window is a removable facade that facilitates art loading for large-scale installations.

2381 In between beach and creek

2382 On 34th Street is a single facade that unifies the two volumes. While the facade's pattern is distinct, the building's scale and color match with the surrounding neighborhood.

2383 Upon completion, we were tasked with designing the scenography for "Once With Me, Once Without Me," the inaugural performance for Faena Forum. The idea was to simulate the condition of a beautiful moment during construction, when the parting walls had not yet been built.

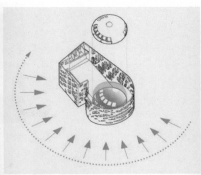

2384 Using projections, the scenography simulated the passage of time, represented by shadows cast by the building's fenestration onto the Assembly Hall when it was an open floor free of parting walls.

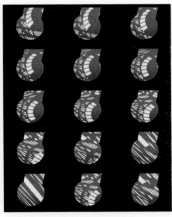

2385 We looked at the shadow patterns the facade would project within the building at various times on the day of the performance.

2386 Overlay of shadows throughout the day.

2387 We wanted to create a dialogue between people and the building. Audience members are embedded within seating that merges with the stage, which occupies the entire space.

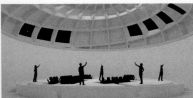

2388 The viewers become part of the stage and are completely immersed in the performance.

2389 Seating embedded within a raised stage

2390 The shadows that would be cast by the facade were simulated by projections, moving throughout the entire space in conjunction with the dancers. The building and scenic design acts as one with the performers and audience.

2391 Architecture and choreography work together to expand the domain of the stage and liberate the dancers to engage with the building.

2392 The shadows are projected beyond the stage onto the 360-degree wall of the performance space.

2393 The performance activated the building by utilizing the Assembly Hall in its entirety. It began solely in the dome space, and then the walls in between the two volumes opened mid-performance.

2394 View from the black box

2395 View from the black box onto the dome space

2396 View from the Spiral Balcony

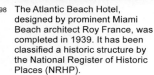

2399 View along Collins Avenue

2398 The Atlantic Beach Hotel, designed by prominent Miami Beach architect Roy France, was completed in 1939. It has been classified a historic structure by the National Register of Historic Places (NRHP).

2397 In addition to the Forum, OMA designed two additional buildings on Collins Avenue to complete the Faena District. In between the Forum and Faena Park is Faena Bazaar, the retail component that would be activated by commercial programs.

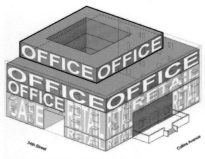

2400 The Bazaar provides curated ground-floor retail space and event/office space on the upper levels.

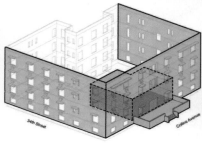

2401 The existing hotel lobby and three facades (north, south, and east) were preserved and renovated.

2402 The existing building's facades feature typical Miami Beach art deco details such as cantilevered "eyebrows" above most windows. The east facade, which is the location of the main entry, includes bands of vertical fluting.

2043 A new opening on the south facade of the Bazaar provides access to the courtyard directly from 34th Street.

2404 With the exception of the original hotel's lobby, the interior floors were demolished and rebuilt. The renovated Bazaar raises the level of the half basement to grade level in order to accommodate parking below the building (pictured above—existing lobby).

2405 View of completed lobby looking toward courtyard

2409 F1 plan

2410 F2 plan

2411 F3 plan

2412 Roof plan

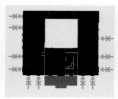

2406 Existing access to Atlantic Beach Hotel courtyard

2407 Proposed access to Bazaar

2408 Activated courtyard

2413 In order to provide better access to light and improve the layout of the Bazaar, a new external courtyard is positioned on the ground level, linking retail spaces along the south and north sides of the building and providing a sheltered function space.

2414 The courtyard space and interior program elements of the Bazaar are unified by a continuous screen.

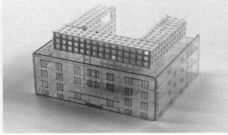

2415 The screen also provides privacy and wayfinding.

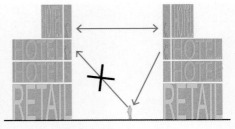

2416 Screen requirements

2417 Early screen studies

2418 Study—grid screen

2419 The preferred scheme was a vertical screen that would allow for subtle visual connection at the upper levels while providing privacy.

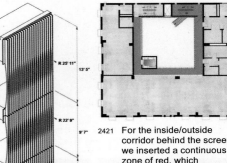

2420 It is fifty percent open as an exterior corridor while acting as a balustrade.

2421 For the inside/outside corridor behind the screen, we inserted a continuous zone of red, which resonates with Faena's brand.

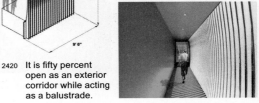

2422 Courtyard corridor

2424 Elevators, pop out stairs, and corridors are accentuated in Faena's distinctive corporate red.

2423 Looking down to the courtyard from F3

2425 The screen establishes porosity, preserving views out toward the beach from multiple points within the building.

2426 The external courtyard opens up to the sky.

2427 Courtyard view

2428 Upper floor levels maintain the approximate position of the existing floor levels. The second level is removed to allow greater floor-to-ceiling heights on the ground floor.

2429 The Rooftop Pavilion and outdoor terrace provide additional event spaces with views of the Atlantic Ocean and a unique overview of the entire Faena District and Miami Beach.

2430 MIXMAG X Winter Music Week at Faena Bazaar rooftop

2431 DJ set on the rooftop

2432 Faena Park, OMA's first freestanding garage, is a state-of-the-art parking structure programmed with street level retail, three levels of parking, and a penthouse event space with views to the Atlantic Ocean and the surrounding Faena District.

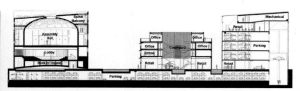

2433 Plan of underground parking across the Forum, Bazaar, and Park

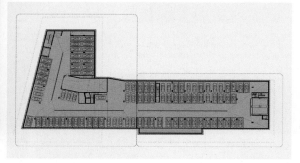

2434 Faena Park accommodates 285 cars, with an 81-car capacity above ground and 154-car capacity in a subterranean level of parking that spans the Faena Forum, Bazaar, and Park.

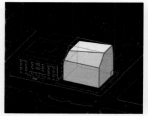

2435 Zoning

2436 Program and access

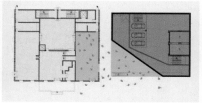

2437 The ground-floor retail in the parking garage is located in proximity to the Bazaar to establish connection and flow from one building to the other.

2438 Ground-level retail

2439 Final concept model

2440 We explored various forms and levels of perforations for the facade.

2441 The twenty-foot-deep underground parking level—three feet above Miami's high ground-water table—was constructed by dewatering the site using a bathtub construction method that combines steel sheet piles and a concrete tremie slab to seal the site.

2442 We wanted to create a breathing facade for the cars within that is porous enough yet maintains some privacy.

2443 View of Faena Park down Collins Avenue

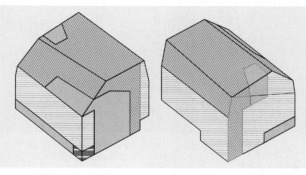

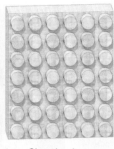

2445 Open—with liner   2446 Closed—glass plug   2447 Closed—plug

2444 Due to the form of the garage, different panel types were developed depending on the program type.

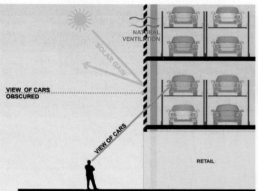

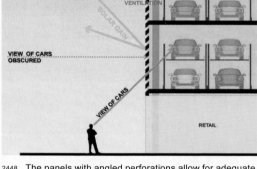

2449 Early mock-up for perforation size comparison

2450 The panels were produced from rubber molds. Each rubber mold had to have a "lip" on the plug that sat in a small recess in the plywood form.

2451 Each type of hole or recess required a unique mold detailed in CAD then made out of rubber.

2448 The panels with angled perforations allow for adequate natural ventilation and controlled views.

2454 The increased surface area inside the angled perforations captures a greater amount of daylight than a simple punched opening.

2452 Mock-up testing on 180 Varick Street   2453 Final panel mock-up

2455 Panel installation

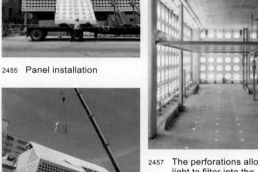

2457 The perforations allow light to filter into the space without causing overwhelming heat within the structure.

2458 In order to maximize efficiency, the valet-operated system utilizes parking lifts that stack two cars per space.

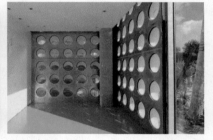

2459 Parking lobby with signature Faena red epoxy flooring

2456 Panels were hoisted by cranes and pieced together on site.

2460 In the evening the parking structure glows.

2461 The precast concrete facade with angled perforations controls views of the building's contents while subtly revealing the colors of cars parked within.

2462 The upper level is a multi-purpose space that can be programmed with events or retail pop-ups, with views to the Atlantic Ocean.

2463 Upper level multi-purpose space

2464 The strategic windows from the top floor make activities visible from the rest of the district.

2465 Upper level east window

2466 East window facing Collins

2467 South window facing Bazaar and Forum

2469 View from upper level looking down Collins Avenue toward the Bazaar and Forum

2470 View from the upper level toward Faena Bazaar and Forum

2471 View down Collins Avenue

2468 A glimpse of a film screening on the upper level during Faena's Biennial of Moving Images

2472 Exposing movement of the cars

2473 On 35th Street, an exposed glass elevator shaftway reveals the vehicular and passenger movement within the building.

2474 Faena Park, Bazaar, and Forum are working to establish a new neighborhood that integrates the multiple facets of Faena into the existing character of Miami Beach.

2475 2476 2477 2478 2479 2480
2481 2482 2483 2484 2485 2486
2487 2488 2489 2490 2491 2492
2493 2494 2495 2496 2497 2498
2499 2500 2501 2502 2503 2504
2505 2506 2507 2508 2509 2510
2511 2512 2513 2514 2515 2516

2475–2516   Faena District

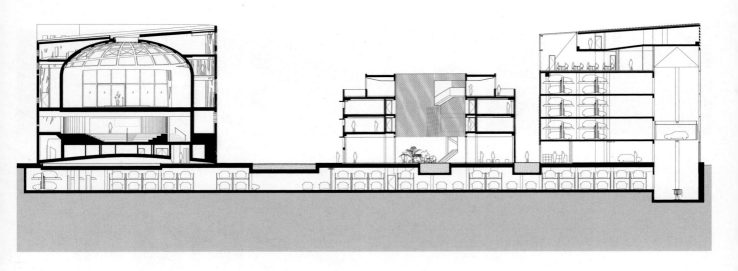

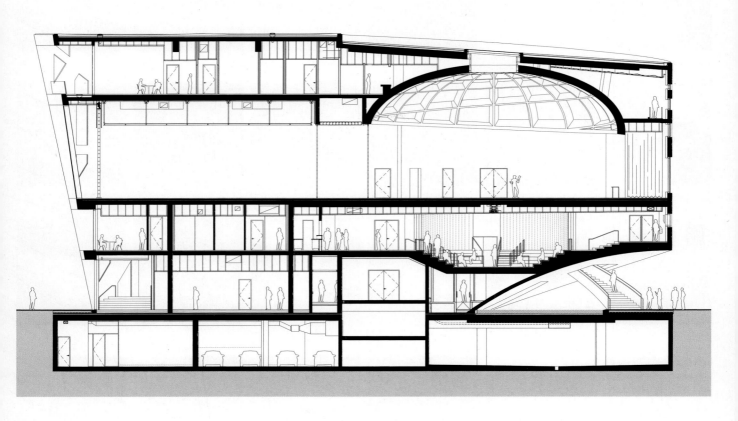

Faena District

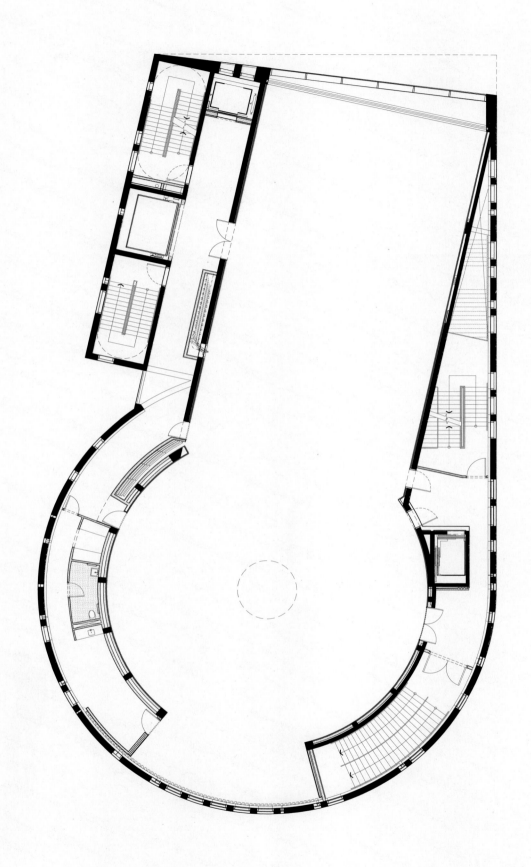

2519   Faena District

2520

Sotheby's Headquarters

Sotheby's Headquarters

Over the years, we had been investigating shifts in the art market, specifically art events such as perennials and art fairs. The domination of global art fairs not only represents a strength in private sales, but also the power of the art event to draw in other creative-adjacent industries like fashion, design, food, music, and others. The auction house typology has also been absorbing the structural changes of the art market. It is now a multi-faceted art and business entity increasingly influenced by private and online sales; digital technology; and diversification of customers, goods, and services.

We were lucky to be approached by Sotheby's to redesign its global headquarters at a time when the multinational corporation was contemplating its organizational structure and business model. This gave us an opportunity to create a building to reflect that ambition and change the entity itself from within. Can the auction house—a typology typically perceived as insulated and exclusive—be an accessible art destination? How can the headquarters support a new mix of programs and be a catalyst for activities beyond art transactions?

Located at 1334 York Avenue in New York between the Upper East Side and Lenox Hill, the building sat quietly within a hospital district, with most people unaware that it was home to Sotheby's global headquarters. The stocky, palazzo-like building was poorly utilized—various programs wildly mixed and dispersed throughout without specific intentions. Existing conditions and locations of employee, client-serving, and back-of-house spaces were sprawled across the building with unclear circulation and a lack of efficiency.

Our approach was surgical—starting with a reorganization of programs throughout the building. We clarified the overall building flow by restacking and consolidating complementary programs while freeing up space for improved connectivity and openness—new retail, gallery, and client spaces span the first four floors to better engage clients and visitors, placing public accessibility at the forefront.

Flexibility in architecture is often defined through adaptable or movable elements within blank spaces, so that anything can happen anywhere. What results are, more often than not, characterless environments that fail to work perfectly for any specific program or use. Sotheby's required extreme flexibility, due to its sales model and fast-paced calendar. We created a system of gallery clusters that allow for quick transformation from big exhibitions to private sales rooms. Rather than flexibility through genericity, we establish flexibility through diversity.

Forty new galleries of twenty distinct types ranging in size, scale, material, and form tailor to different types of sales, exhibitions, and events. A repertoire of spatial conditions for display—including white cube, double-height, enfilade, corridor, cascade, octagonal, and L-shaped—can be used individually or as clusters to accommodate various programming and display of Sotheby's diverse portfolio. Each cluster can be closed for art installation while the majority of the floor remains open for exhibition, enabling a rapid and efficient turnover of exhibition spaces, which typically occurs every three to four days.

We wanted to introduce a new aura for the renewed headquarters with contextual materiality. Entry into each gallery cluster is defined with custom-stained walnut panels and doors, a nod to the woodwork found at Sotheby's London. The history of the building itself is not ignored. Existing concrete columns are exposed, stripped, and hand stippled to reveal their material character. The column is typically the enemy of the gallery, but here columns are embraced and accentuated as a notable feature. Steel beams in open ceiling galleries are left exposed, acknowledging the building's former industrial life as a cigar factory and Kodak warehouse.

Upon opening, the renovated headquarters served as a backdrop for record-breaking sales at the Contemporary Art Auctions. It has also hosted an array of programs that are not auction-related—from runway shows for New York Fashion Week to performances by the New York City Ballet—reemerging as a cultural destination on Manhattan's eastern edge, an area once devoid of active art presence.

Location	New York, NY, USA		
Status	Completed, 2019		
Typology	Art Platform		
Program	Gallery/Retail	64,200 ft²	5,970 m²
	Client Spaces	8,200 ft²	760 m²
	Office	5,600 ft²	520 m²
	Back-of-House	67,300 ft²	6,250 m²
	Total Area	145,300 f²	13,500 m²

Reception

2521

Sotheby's Headquarters

Sotheby's Headquarters

Sotheby's Headquarters

Sotheby's Headquarters

OMA NY   Sotheby's Headquarters

Sotheby's Headquarters

2525   As we continue to work within the art realm with artists and institutions, we are investigating how the art market is shifting.

2526   In recent years there has been a trend of smaller galleries expanding, blurring the line between gallery and museum. Diversification of programs and spaces seemingly correlates to increased sales.

2527   According to the 2019 Art Basel and UBS Global Art Market Report, dealer sales in 2018 reached an estimated 35.9 billion dollars, up 7 percent year-on-year.

2528   Sales at public auction of fine and decorative art and antiques (excluding private sales) reached 29.1 billion dollars in 2018, an increase of 3 percent year-on-year, and up 30 percent over 2016.

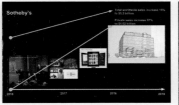

2529   The global sales in the online market reached an estimated 6 billion dollars in 2018, up 11 percent year-on-year.

2530   Total worldwide sales for Sotheby's increased 15 percent from 2016 to 2019, reaching 5.3 billion dollars and its private sales increased 37 percent, to 1.02 billion dollars.

2531   Sotheby's headquarters renovation came at a time when the company was contemplating its own business model. Its building had the potential to reflect that ambition and catalyze change within the entity itself.

2532   The auction house used to be focused primarily on the grand auction. In a way, it was a space for that one spectacle and few activities beyond that.

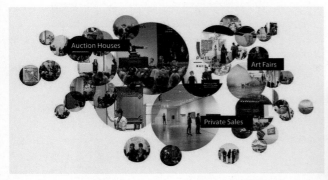

2533   Now the auction house itself is a multi-faceted art entity.

2535   Sotheby's has locations all over the world, including Paris, London, Zurich, Milan, Geneva, and Hong Kong.

2534   The old model of Sotheby's as a fine art auction house has been changing.

2536   With the globalization of the art market and growing use of technology, Sotheby's adapted a wide array of digital tools for buying and selling.

2537   Goods for sale have also been diversified, breaking through new markets by partnerships, such as one with RM for the sale of vintage cars.

2538   Sotheby's has also partnered with eBay for art sales.

2539   'I Like It Like This' Auction in collaboration with Drake (2015)—artists and celebrities curate namesake auctions.

2540   As global art fairs have increased in number and gained visibility, the commercial art market has grown busier, which in turn has impacted auction house calendars. Sotheby's will curate art auctions around the time of fairs such as Art Basel and Frieze.

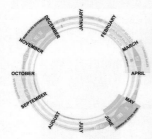

2541   These factors contribute to a fast-paced calendar for the auction house, with rotating exhibitions, auctions, events, and a stream of private sales, in addition to the two major auction seasons per year.

2542   Most of the year, the existing main auction room in the New York headquarters is underutilized. The large space is designed to serve the largest auctions with little flexibility for the smaller, more frequent sales.

2543   How can the headquarters of Sotheby's reflect its historic legacy while enabling adaptation to a changing business model?

2544 The auction house is located at 1334 York Avenue. The building sits in the hospital district of 72nd Street and York, where no one really knew it was the global headquarters of Sotheby's. It was a big, fat, underutilized building.

2545 Timeline of major events in the history of Sotheby's above, timeline of its building history below—Sotheby's opened its New York office at Bowling Green near Wall Street in 1955. In 1964, the company acquired Parker Bernet in New York, America's largest fine auction house, and moved to 980 Madison Avenue, then 171 East 84th Street the following year. In 1980 operations moved to 1334 York Avenue. Two years later, the Madison Avenue and 84th Street galleries closed and all exhibits were consolidated.

2546 1334 York was once a four-story building built for P. Lorillard Tobacco Factory in 1921.

2547 In 1949, the building served as a Kodak warehouse.

2548 News clipping of the opening of Eastman Kodak Company's New York branch at 1334 York (1949)

2549 Sotheby's purchased the building in 1982, making small renovations.

2550 In 1999, the building was renovated dramatically with KPF, adding six new floors to the existing four-story building.

2551 Key gallery fit-outs were designed by Gluckman Tang.

2552 The existing office of traditional cubicles, private offices, and—more recently—some collaborative working environments.

2553 Despite the renovations, the building had its challenges, with ample square footage but deep floorplates that were inefficiently divided.

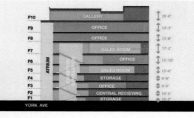

2556 Vertical circulation was not optimal because of the disarray of programs and their distribution throughout the building.

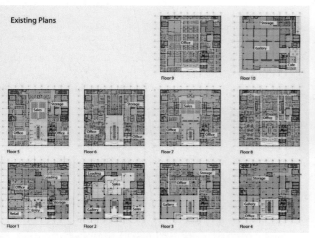

Existing Plans

2554 Public functions like galleries and retail spaces were interspersed with office and back-of-house spaces, resulting in a lack of communication between similar functions.

2555 As a result of rapid exhibition turnover, galleries facing the main escalators were often "under construction" and exposed to visitors on their way to open exhibition spaces.

2557 The existing client service rooms lacked consistency and were spread out through the building, some in locations that were not easily accessible.

2558 Sotheby's had considered moving out of the 1334 York location to 432 Park Avenue because of Park's more central location and proximity to other cultural entities.

2559 An initial study for the Park Avenue location explored consolidating public-facing spaces and galleries across the site with an art bridge.

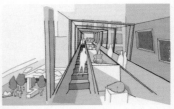

2560 The art bridge sought to join the disconnected areas of the site, but the Park Avenue location offered less square footage than the current building. The move would have required Sotheby's to lease additional space on other sites.

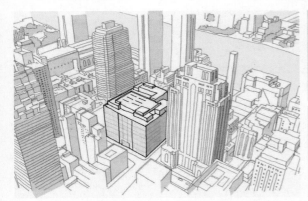

2561 During this phase, options for remaining in 1334 York and renovating the existing building were proposed.

2562 The schemes were driven by the key need to reorganize and identify clear program areas and accessible space for public-serving activities.

2563 The Tower scheme proposed slicing the proportionately square building into four towers that were distinct yet connected, each housing different programs.

2564 Appropriately sized sales rooms and intimate galleries

2565 Towers are connected by programmatic bridges. The physical cuts allow light and air to penetrate the existing deep floorplates.

2566 Another scheme proposed inserting an activity atrium in the front of the building and explored centralizing storage for efficient adjacency to all programs.

2567 The Super Atrium scheme proposed a central atrium visually connecting all program floors.

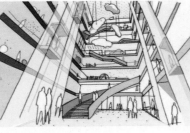

2568 Super atrium

2569 Storage access from gallery, office, and sales

2570 The Public-Face scheme communicates the art, sales, and office townhall activities to the city, while creating a smaller atrium and entry on the ground floor.

2571 Public gallery atrium leading up to sales

2572 Atrium exterior view

2573 Office townhall

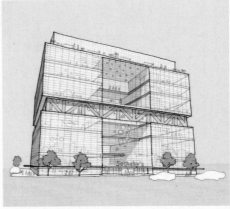

2574 The early proposals for the location at 72nd and York proved that the existing space could provide more clarity, flexibility, and freedom to transform operations at Sotheby's. Thus, Sotheby's decided to remain in its current location.

2558–2574   Sotheby's Headquarters

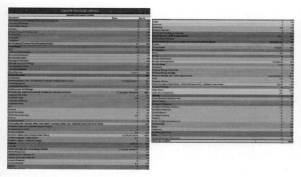

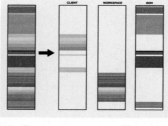

2576 Programs were grouped into three general categories—client, workspace, and back-of-house.

2577 Program bar

2575 A seven-month-long programming and concept design study analyzed every component of programs in the Sotheby's building by floor and square footage to determine how best to reorganize and consolidate the multi-faceted functions.

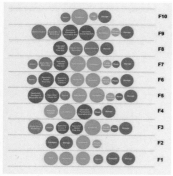

2580 Because of program dispersal throughout the building, there were few adjacencies between programs, and departments were separated on different floors.

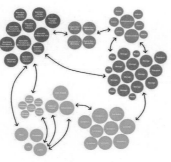

2581 Concentrating program types together in relation to the overall business flow would enable increased efficiencies and collaboration.

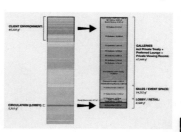

2578 The client environment is defined by the spaces where clients are received, including galleries, sales floor/auction rooms, private viewing rooms, and retail spaces.

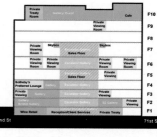

2579 Client-related programs were dispersed throughout the building, exacerbating client circulation throughout the space.

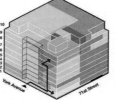

2583 The entry sequence, especially for clients, was unclear. Escalators and elevators were slow and ill-equipped to transport clients to private viewing rooms and the sales room floor.

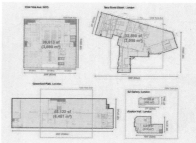

2584 The programming study also looked closely at Sotheby's operations in London, which is a network of smaller galleries and warehouses.

2582 Surveys were conducted with the Sotheby's staff on items such as client experience, design, events, lobby, retail, and digital tools.

2586 Staff and specialists also desired improved client spaces and galleries that would accommodate the rapid exhibition turnover rate and benefit from more natural light.

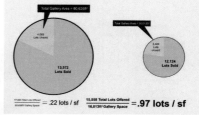

2587 Number of lots sold is often used as an indicator of how much gallery square footage is necessary. However, with significantly less gallery space, Sotheby's London was able to sell almost the same number of lots as New York.

2585 Tracking a typical visitor's path through the building revealed a disconnected and inefficient experience.

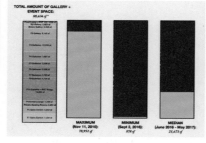

2588 There was a need for galleries that could be used as spaces for client interaction.

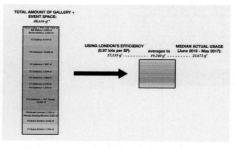

2589 The programming studies of the auction house's operations showed that performance was not based on total client-serving square footage, but on an efficient use of space.

2590 The programming and concept studies helped determine an ambition for the design to clarify the dispersed activities within the building.

2591 How can key programs be consolidated and organized efficiently, while providing the optimal configuration for public engagement?

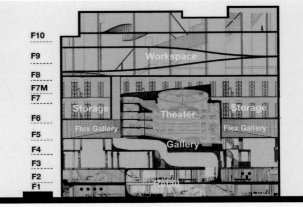

2592 Early concept section—the main auction room is reimagined as a cultural anchor, surrounded by zones of programs restacked to establish sectional clarity. The reorganization strengthens communication both within and between the previously detached program types.

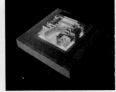

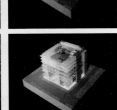

2593 Early concept model

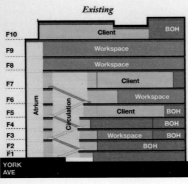

2594 Public galleries were formerly sandwiched between back-of-house and workspaces.

2595 The client spaces were brought down and consolidated from F1 to F4, streamlining circulation for visitors.

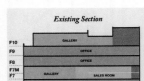

2596 Existing section

2597 Phase 1 section

2598 Resin and acrylic model of gallery configurations from F1 to F4

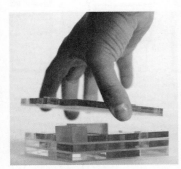

2599 F1-F4 gallery stack

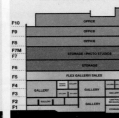

2600 Gallery model

2601 The first phase would bring public galleries to the lower levels to create a more accessible cultural destination. It also included gallery fit-out, storage, and structural work to create new, double-height galleries.

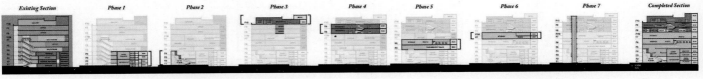

2602 One of the parameters of the project was keeping the building fully operational during the renovation. The concept design was divided into seven different phases, allowing Sotheby's to "repair the airplane while it was flying."

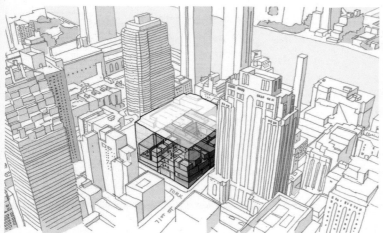

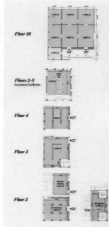

2605 Unconventional signage—(RED) Charity Auction, New York (2008)

2603 Exhibition spaces tend to be large, white boxes that can be partitioned as needed. While a typical museum gallery may have exhibition turnover every few months, Sotheby's had turnover every three to four days, which meant that spaces were continually being reconfigured. The wide variety of both types of objects and selling environments also required a high diversity of spaces.

2604 The existing galleries were not only disjointed but formally inefficient and uniform. The typical plans would often require the construction of temporary walls in order to serve various needs.

2606 Evocative display—At Home: Designer Showhouse and Auction, New York (2016)

2607 Immersive event—Bunny Mellon Interiors event, New York (2014)

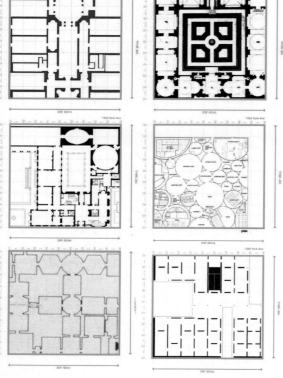

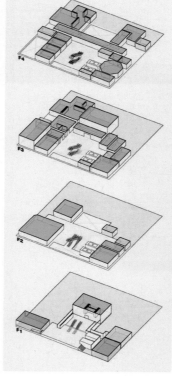

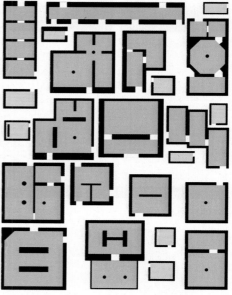

2608 Scale comparison, clockwise from top left: Tate Britain (London), Glyptothek (Munich), Tomihiro Art Museum (Gunma, Japan), North Carolina Museum of Art (Raleigh, North Carolina), National Gallery (London), Frick Collection (New York). We looked to diverse types of gallery sizes, shapes, and purpose—both contemporary and historical—in response to Sotheby's diverse requirements.

2609 Flexibility is achieved through diversity of unique galleries per floor. Clear orientation points assist circulation throughout.

2610 Gallery taxonomy—a mix of galleries can be organized in clusters, used individually or as a unified space. The clusters accommodate various programming needs as well as the display of the diverse Sotheby's portfolio.

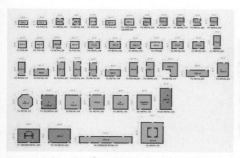

2611 There are a total of forty new galleries of twenty distinct types ranging in size, scale, material, and form.

2612 While providing a range of specific gallery types, spaces are further grouped into clusters with unique routes of circulation. This allows one cluster to remain open while another is closed for art installation, preventing visitors from walking through under-construction spaces as they previously did.

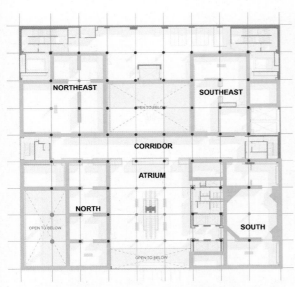

2614 A cove detail exposes the column cap within the finished dropped ceiling.

2613 The ambition of creating a diverse range of gallery clusters didn't initially match the building's existing column grid. The column is typically an enemy of the gallery but in this case, the columns are embraced as an element of the building's history and are left exposed as a key feature of the galleries.

2615 The ceiling needed to be dropped for services, but the column caps are as much an architectural feature as the columns themselves.

2616 The original columns are structurally reinforced in double-height spaces.

2617 Section of coved ceiling details

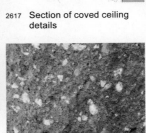

2618 The new reinforced concrete is hand stippled to match existing columns.

2619 The contrast between the existing column cap and the reinforced concrete in the F3 double-height gallery highlights the building's renovation history.

2620 While the columns enhance the building's industrial past, the portals draw on the global status of Sotheby's. Entry into gallery clusters is defined at their thresholds with custom-stained walnut panels and doors.

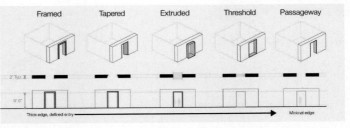

2621 Gallery portal studies—framed, tapered, extruded, threshold, passageway

2622 Portal studies, clockwise from top left: convex profile (mirrored), simple profile (wood), faceted (wood), banded (concrete), abstracted columns (concrete), abstracted molding (reflective white).

2623 The use of stained walnut is a nod to the traditional woodwork found at Sotheby's in London, where the company was founded.

2624 The rich material denotes entry into each gallery cluster.

2625 To establish seamless transitions, the portals are flush to the wall with a minimal edge.

2613–2625

Sotheby's Headquarters

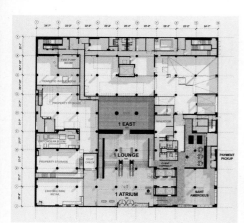

2627 Public-facing programs like the cafe have been relocated to the first floor.

2628 The first floor hadn't had dedicated exhibition space and primarily served as a transit point to spaces located elsewhere. The new floorplan combines more client and public-facing retail and gallery programs.

2626 The galleries begin on the first level and aim to create a seamless connection between the street and exhibition space.

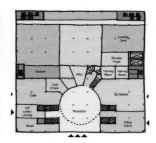

2629 Preliminary lobby studies—funnel, islands, radial

2630 Existing entry and lobby

2631 Lobby model

2632 The level of the first floor has been raised to reduce the existing height difference, creating a more continuous floor and establishing clear views down to the new first-floor galleries.

2634 The new double-height gallery can be seen upon entering the building.

2633 Bands of digital screens designed by 2x4 add dynamic signage that emphasizes the depth and funneling effect toward the F1 signature gallery.

2637 With the removal of a floor slab to create the double-height space, the columns in this space were structurally reinforced. The new concrete aggregate matches existing historic columns.

2635 This gallery is visually connected to the second floor through interior windows.

2636 The wood flooring is unique to this gallery, giving it a distinct character of its own.

2638 Visitors on F2 look down into the double-height gallery.

2639 Thom Browne x Samsung performance, "I'm Not Ready Yet" (2020)—the space is large enough to host different events.

2626–2639   Sotheby's Headquarters

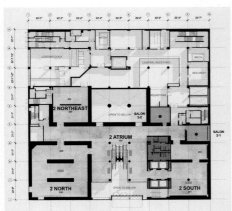

2640 The F1 lobby and gallery are immediately connected to the second floor via escalator. Two windows facing the elevator lobby orient the visitors to the F1 double-height gallery.

2641 F2 model

2642 The escalator lobby on F2 provides additional space for display, but can also be used as a pre-function space for openings and events. From here, one can look out onto the city and vice versa.

2643 F2 houses three main galleries as well as two private sales rooms.

2644 F3 escalator gallery

2645 F1 double-height gallery from F3

2646 Sotheby's and New York City Ballet: Festival of Wonder (December 2020)

2647 Opening reception

2648 The majority of the galleries feature polished concrete flooring. Artifacts where previous walls and columns existed are revealed in the floor texture.

2649 Walls, necessary for exhibition display, are set proud of the existing window wall to enable natural, non-mechanical ventilation of the facade.

2650 There are two large picture windows at the northwest corner of F2 that had previously been underutilized. The new gallery frames these openings to establish a new connection to the street. Because of the grade change, these windows are highly visible to passersby and sculptural works can be placed in position to be seen from outside.

2651 In some galleries, steel beams are exposed in an open ceiling to acknowledge the building's industrial past. New mechanical ducts and existing ceiling and beams are painted gray, highlighting the exhibition walls.

2652 Private viewing rooms throughout feature either carpeted or epoxy flooring, providing a more refined personal viewing environment.

2653 Strategically placed openings bring natural light into galleries, while also maximizing the total linear footage of exhibition space. A poured-in-place resin epoxy floor, in addition to the finished ceiling and cove column detail, demarcates this as a signature gallery.

Sotheby's Headquarters

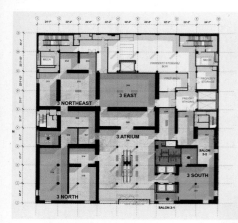

2654 From F2, one seamlessly transitions up to F3 via the escalator and is met with three distinct clusters of uniquely shaped and sized galleries.

2655 Early gallery cluster study—taking into consideration the flow of visitors by either escalator or elevator, contained paths of circulation establish the three clusters. Within each cluster is a diverse range of gallery sizes, including one larger signature gallery.

2656 F3 model

2657 Escalator gallery

2658 F3 double-height gallery model

2659 In the north cluster of F3, the signature gallery is a double-height space.

2661 Key features are two large reinforced columns and two windows with views out onto 72nd Street.

2662 F3 gallery view with art

2660 An interior window in the double-height space provides a visual connection to a gallery on F4.

2663 "LINES," performance by artist Shantell Martin (May 2019)

2665 A band of clerestory windows brings more natural light into the expansive space.

2664 Sotheby's and New York City Ballet: Festival of Wonder (December 2020)

2666 The clusters are sequenced carefully so visitors pass first through smaller, more compressed spaces before entering larger, more expansive ones.

2667 A smaller, transitional gallery connects the north signature gallery to the northeast cluster.

2668 Alfa Romeo Berlina Aerodinamica Tecnica Concepts, Contemporary Art Evening Sale (October 2020)—the main gallery within the northeast cluster is more traditional, but flexible enough to exhibit diverse collections.

2669 The northeast cluster connects to another signature gallery. The double-height space is located centrally on F4, connected to an intermediary gallery that faces the escalators.

2670 Reception in the escalator gallery with portals leading to intermediary gallery and east signature gallery

2671 Centrally located and without columns, the east signature gallery is a double-height, flexible space optimal for large events like dinners.

2672 Contemporary Art Evening Auction exhibition view

2673 Shohei Shigematsu speaking at a private dinner reception (May 2019)

2674 Set up for private dinner honoring Shohei and recognizing Mark Rothko's Untitled, which was being sold during the Contemporary Art Evening Auction (May 2019)

2675 Reception dinner for Massimo Bottura Contemporary Curated Sale (September 2019)

2676 In the south cluster, the signature gallery is a cascade of rooms.

2677 Impressionist and Modern Art Auction exhibition (May 2019)

2678 The cascade gallery creates an open and overlapping view from one gallery to another.

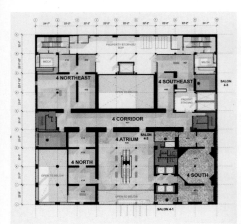

2679 The galleries on F4 respond to the diverse range of items displayed at Sotheby's. Four clusters on each corner are accessed through a long corridor gallery.

2680 Early gallery cluster study—four clusters on each corner of the floor

2681 F4 model

2682 F4 corridor gallery model

2683 The first gallery approached from the escalators is the corridor gallery, an expansive, linear space for diverse exhibitions.

2684 Unlike museums, Sotheby's Sotheby's stages exhibitions that are extremely dense with art. The experience of display density is emphasized in the corridor gallery, allowing for a different type of exhibition.

2685 All of the artwork laid on the floor during installation. It was interesting to see so many valuable works strewn along the floor.

2686 Mario Buatta: Prince of Interiors Auction exhibition (January 2020)

2687 In the south cluster, the signature gallery is an octagon that was informed by jewelry collections auctioned at Sotheby's.

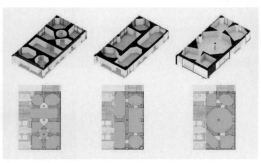

2688 Early gallery studies—cellular, elongated cell, octagon

2689 An exposed column occupies the center of the octagon gallery.

2690 The column cove is recessed into the ceiling to enhance the presence of the column.

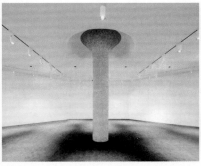

2691 The flooring is carpet and the eight-sided room provides multiple facets for art display.

2692 American Art Auction exhibition (July 2019)

2693 The column punctuates the gallery space.

2694 The northeast gallery is designed in four quadrants by dividing walls in a cross configuration.

2695 The four quadrants are anchored by an original column.

2696 Northeast gallery pre-installation

2697 The cross shape creates four rooms that exchange views.

2698 Within each cluster are private viewing rooms that can be used strategically to host clients during walking tours of the public exhibitions. In the past, private sales rooms were disconnected from the galleries and the outside.

2699 In the north cluster's private salon, a window reconnects the space to the outside.

2700 The signature gallery in the north cluster follows an enfilade configuration.

2701 Enfilade gallery model

2702 The enfilade gallery supports a sequential exhibition experience.

2703 At the terminus of the enfilade gallery is a carefully placed interior window that looks down into the F3 north double-height gallery.

2704 View of the enfilade gallery through the F3 north gallery's interior window

2705 Contemporary Art Auctions exhibition (May 2019)

2706 Mario Buatta: Prince of Interiors Auction exhibition (January 2020)

2707 Expressionism and Modern Art Auction exhibition (July 2020)

2708 The enfilade gallery culminates in a carefully framed, off-center opening to the window wall, framing the existing facade at a key location that does not compromise art display and bringing light into the length of the space. Following the opening of the new galleries in May 2019, Sotheby's hosted a record-breaking 350-million-dollar auction in their Impressionist & Modern Art Evening Sale.

2694–2708   Sotheby's Headquarters

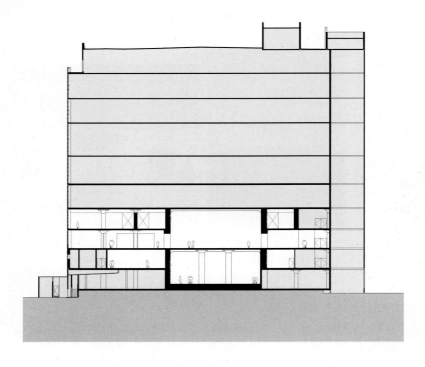

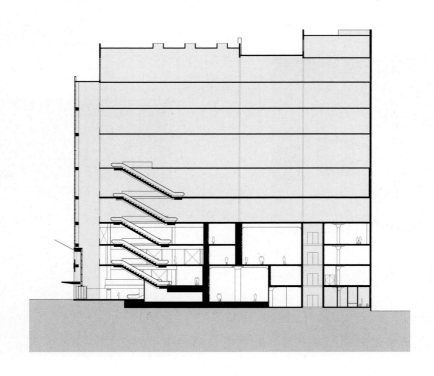

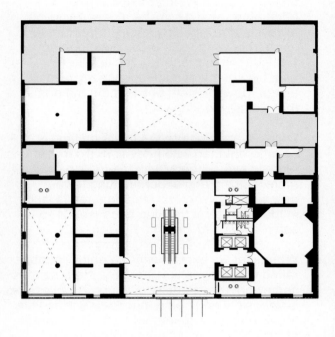
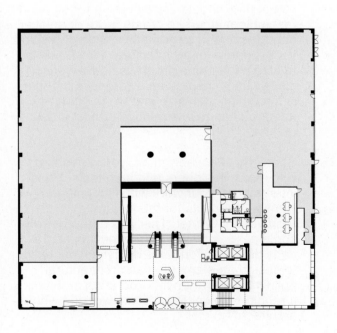
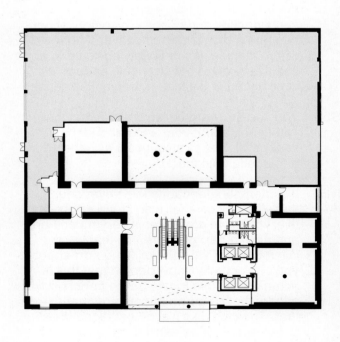

2711–2714   Sotheby's Headquarters

Interview Iris van Herpen

Shohei Shigematsu: What is your relationship to architecture?

Iris van Herpen: I think there are obviously a lot of differences but a lot of overlap in the disciplines of fashion and architecture. On the edge of my own discipline a new discipline always starts, so I find it very important to learn from what I see in the development within architecture. And I really take that as a big source of inspiration in my own texture development but also the materials that we are working with.

I think in architecture the focus on time is so different than within fashion. It's much more in sync already with the future—much more syncing and experimenting toward new visions. Whereas fashion often is stuck in the short-term thinking because it's so season focused.

SS: Whenever we explain why we enjoy collaborating with the fashion industry, the reason is somewhat the opposite of yours. Architecture is very slow and heavy-handed, leaving little room for rapid experimentation. The speed of fashion allows us to be more frivolous and playful.

IvH: I love the speed of fashion. It creates a lot of space for experimentation and also mistakes. That's very different from the large scale, long-term projects in architecture. I do think the focus on the future and therefore also the sustainability and change in society should become a bigger part of conversations within fashion. It's definitely en route to a positive change but strangely enough it's slow because it's fast. If that makes sense.

SS: You use the word future quite often when you speak about your work and fashion in general. You're also, in a way, labeled as a futuristic designer.

IvH: It's interesting because I've never seen myself really as a futurist, in the sense that everything we create feels very much here and now, a part of the reality that we are living today. That's the exciting part about it. you can actually show people that this is actually possible today. Some people have no idea how a garment could be made like that. They feel like it's almost digitally rendered or it doesn't really exist, but it does. It shows in a way that with our craftsmanship and technology, and by blending those two, we can actually go much further than what we see every day within fashion. It's about

opening up that perspective for people—about what fashion can mean and be, and how it can evolve. In my mind, my work is more connected to the here and now than toward the future. But I understand that people see the future in it, because it's so distinct from what they know.

SS: We are often asked what the future of architecture or the city is. Everyone is interested in the future now more than ever, but it used to be that the present and the future had a very big gap. People were envisioning a distant future—200 or more years away from their time. Society moves at such a fast speed now that people are speculating about a future as imminent as tomorrow. Why do you think people are increasingly focused on the future? What do you think about when you are asked to envision the future?

IvH: The future, now more than ever, is uncertain to people and I think there is a growing communal consciousness that a lot needs to change. That feeling of change is growing within every culture and every country. That's what is really driving the curiosity for people to better understand how they can participate in that change. The creators and the makers of today in different disciplines perhaps play the role of inspiration and innovation in showing possible changes within our industries. That's why I think this conversation is so important. We need more and more collaboration across disciplines and it's the only way that we can be quick enough in creating change. Like biologists and scientists— I think they should start working together with fashion designers to create more or quicker changes on the sustainability side of fashion. It's the same for architecture. We should try to invent the same progress in every discipline. I think there is an awareness that time is becoming sensitive and we're going to need to change in a relatively short amount of time.

SS: Speaking of collaboration, you've worked with many designers and architects. I was interested in your work with Neutelings Riedijk Architects for the Naturalis Biodiversity Center. This was different from some of your previous architect collaborations because you were applying your skill to design an element of an architectural building rather than incorporating architecture into fashion. Do you like working with architects?

IvH: [laughs] If I didn't like it, I wouldn't have been doing it for ten years! Even before starting my own label, I was always doubting which discipline I would go into because there are so many worlds that fascinate me. I come from dance originally, so dance is still very much part of my inspiration. But architecture continues to fascinate me for different reasons. There is so much to learn from each project that I work on with an architect that it's always reflected in my own work even if it's a totally different scale. It became part of my design language and creates a new perspective for my own discipline.

SS: The boundary between architecture and fashion has definitely been dissolving. They've become more intertwined and more recently, maybe in the last twenty years, that relationship has been escalating commercially. In the beginning, it was more limited to the shop, but now there's a diverse range of avenues for the two disciplines to work together. I think that crossover has also led to questioning previous notions of retail, branding, and fashion shows. Do you see yourself working with architects on your own brick-and-mortar retail, runway, or other environments?

IvH: Yeah, absolutely. It's an interesting topic that you're raising because I've been in conversation for a while now about the design for my exhibition that is coming up, so more on the scenography side of things. But also for the runway in Paris. They are projects at different scales but are perfect to involve architects because it's a different process than when I work on a garment. With garments, it's very focused on my own craftsmanship, very much following my own approach of creation— so it's a different conversation. But for scenography, a show, or an installation, it feels like the dynamics are a little bit the other way around, which I like a lot. I become part of their mind, their way of thinking, and their values within architecture. I would love to engage with architects to conceive a retail store. I probably would go more in the direction of a museum-like place because everything we create is like haute couture, so it's very much focused on art. A museum setting would be really exciting to conceptualize together.

SS: That's a great segue to talking about how your work could be exhibited. We have been looking at fashion exhibitions as an interesting domain. In art exhibitions, art is "holy" and as an architect it's difficult to reimagine the white cube, as it is considered the ideal setting. But in fashion, objects and garments have a multitude of narratives that can influence the spatial experience. The storytelling element of fashion really requires the environment to also participate. And of course, there's the tired dilemma or ambiguity between art and fashion nowadays. What do you think about fashion exhibitions nowadays? How would you approach an exhibition for your own work?

IvH: When I start working on things I like to start with the difficulties, or the problems that I would like to dive into. And one of the areas that I haven't yet figured out completely but want to focus on within exhibition, is how to embed the essence of transformation and movement into it. Movement and transformation are the key elements that describe everything that I do. That comes from my dance background but also this ode to nature, living in this breathing world, is really translated into my work. So in a way, a museum or exhibition is a hard way to present a work. On the runway, that soul of the collection is really shown by seeing it moving and breathing the way it should.

I am continuously asking myself how we can translate that into an exhibition. The most foreseeable ways of doing that are not ideal yet—garments can be presented on robots or infrastructure of that kind, although, then the human side of the work is not really represented. It's a challenge that hasn't been solved and I think that's the exciting part of it because that's precisely the moment to think about approaching it from the perspective of another discipline. Perhaps with architects themselves, but also with kinetic artists. I recently worked with Anthony Howe, a kinetic artist who made a sculpture for a show that is wind powered, so very much in dialogue with the elements of nature. It really transformed the space and gave me the inspiration to look to architecture. Perhaps in the future there will be more elements that are in sync with nature or this feeling of transformation of a breath, or a heartbeat. That idea of living architecture is continuously fascinating to me. I think as designers we are trained to design toward a finished product, but if you look at the processes within nature, everything comes in the emotion, and dialogue. I imagine within ten, twenty, thirty years, our designs will also become more organic and transformative. That's very exciting because then you can start designing for time and for how a concept or even the material is responsive and morphing with the zeitgeist, so to say.

SS: Maybe we can talk more about your process. You deal with dichotomies and often say you are inspired by them. Architecture also operates in dichotomies—geometric versus organic, fixed versus flexible, solid versus void. How do you see beyond the typical notion of dichotomies?

OMA NY   Iris van Herpen

IvH: I think it's all about scale, or zooming in. The more you zoom into a certain dichotomy, the more you find new relationships within them. A lot of people see the most present dichotomy within my own work, the traditional craftsmanship process and techniques. But once you start combining these two in a garment you start seeing all the relationships or the conversations between them. Then, suddenly, that whole dichotomy is gone. That goes for a lot of dichotomies that we have polarized in our minds. Once you start combining them or looking into them, there are often a lot of new narratives to find there.

SS: In our process we value accidental findings. Sometimes we even value unfamiliar ugliness more than obvious beauty. Do you have a similar tendency? Do you embrace accidents or ugliness?

IvH: Yeah. I think that's especially important for me because I'm looking for new forms of femininity. The whole notion of femininity has become so boxed that I'm really trying to get free from that and find those new forms of what femininity can mean. It is really about bravery, I would say—to start on the process without knowing where it will end. I would say 50 percent of my work comes throughout the concept, when I have an idea of where to go to. And then it always ends up going somewhere else anyway. The other half really starts from experimentation. And all that means is that the beginning of the process is a mess and a lot of mistakes, are happening. So we're trying to solve these mistakes when you realize—okay, this is actually such an interesting mistake, we are going to dive into this more—and we start learning about something that you really couldn't foresee. Half of the collection is grown from those mistakes and I think those are often the most valuable looks and, to me, they often present a new femininity in silhouettes, softness, and in movement, that I could not have imagined if I hadn't gone through the messy process.

SS: We also do a lot of studies and make many models, and something surprising can be born out of a kind of intended disarray. But we sometimes go back to that messy stage and rethink the status of the project, so it's not always a linear process. Even beyond the life of a project, we revisit our archive of rejected options and sometimes they are transformed into something new. I'm sure you must have rejected designs, but do you sometimes revisit them and use them for another inspiration?

IvH: Absolutely. I have a big archive of failures. It's all the little experiments, the material tests, and everything we do in a collection. Often I just go through them. But it's all perspective anyway. Sometimes I really rejected a sample for it not being good enough, then when you look at it two or three years later then you suddenly see a possibility for it and new ideas often grow from that rediscovery.

SS: The process of experimentation is fascinating for architects because it's a little bit speculative. We can never really test the space we are creating at the scale of the final product. In fashion, the experimentation can happen at the scale of what the finished product will be. Could you speak about the notion of experimentation in the fashion industry at large?

IvH: I think experimentation has become a little bit extinct in the last two or three decades. That's mainly because of the scale most companies are operating in, with mass production definitely guiding the system. Within haute couture there is some experimentation, though in my perception it's pretty limited.

SS: Are you alarmed by that situation?

IvH: I'm amazed by it. I have a natural instinct for experimentation. It's in my nature. I could not create in a different way. If the process wasn't there, if I wasn't able to experiment the way I can do it now, I would not be in fashion. I'm just not product driven in that sense, so to me, it's interesting to see that experimentation or innovation, even within craftsmanship, because it has always been a big part of fashion. It's a little lost nowadays. But on the other hand, if you start zooming in you see all these new designers who are completely into it. It's more that the industry is so largely driven by mass production. At that scale, there is not a lot of time and space to freeform.

SS: I'm sure you get this question a lot, but can we talk about technology? You often talk about your work as extended forms of the human body. I'm interested in what you think about human devices outside of fashion as we've been discussing—from wearable technology like headphones, Apple Watch, Google Glass to health and wellness devices like stress canceling neck bands and LED skincare face masks. There are even medical prosthetics that are mind-controlled to provide sensations of touch. I imagine in the future, people will be wearing everyday devices that extend the senses and enhance the experience of daily life. What do you think about this sector of design and how it can cross into your domain?

IvH: There are so many levels to it and it depends on each device. I think for something like headphones, in terms of design, we can go much further than where we are at the moment. A lot of these devices, when they are electronic, you can really see that they are designed by a different category of designers almost. They are often very masculine as well. Even when they try to make something feminine, it's often a failure because they just add some pink or some cuteness to it. But obviously femininity is so much more layered and so much more complex and diverse that in terms of design, 99 percent of the time I'm disappointed in the wearable tech corner. But I guess it's also a very new discipline. So it's really a matter of time, and again, a matter of collaboration. Tech companies should collaborate more with designers and be a bit braver.

SS: That's precisely why we would like to see someone like you participating in that arena. How you use technology in your practice for more than just production and efficiency, but for experimentation, is fascinating. On that topic, I wanted to discuss 3D printing, a process that you often merge with crafting by hand. I think the 3D printer is an interesting tool because you can model something quite simple or something very intricate, but both are printed with the press of a button. In some ways, objects were considered complex because of the labor and difficulty of making them in real life. So the hierarchy and people's notions of simplicity and complexity are subject to change. I think the two actually start to blend—structure and ornamentation, for example. How do you deal with simplicity or complexity?

IvH: I'm looking for a balance, in both the design itself and the process; it always feels like dancing. In my designs, the most prominent elements are shape and silhouette; material; texture and technique; and colors. When going for complexity in some of those elements, I choose simplicity in others. And it's the same for the process. When the technique and material development is very complex I will choose a simpler pattern. When you start making every step of the project very complex, the flow gets stuck. Even while we're in the making process, my design process is ongoing—I am always refining, tweaking, and adjusting. I can only do that well when there is an organic flow and I can keep on dancing and tuning.

SS: I'm intrigued by how your dance background relates to the fluidity of your process and the dynamism of your designs themselves. I definitely agree that a less linear

progression can lead to more unanticipated outcomes, even though it can seem laborious or lacking a clear direction at times. For us, making models by hand is a process to test our conviction in a design, but more so to discover the unimagined. So we're also constantly designing and physically testing simultaneously. The various output is not easily recognizable for its coherence, but we would like to believe that the rigor of the process defines our identity and culture.

This book is a way to look at those methods and outcomes from a bird's-eye-view to reveal or confirm our affinities and attitudes. You seem to have such a strong conviction in your own interests and identity, which is conveyed in the work. What do you think about the fact that we are actively searching for an identity?

IvH: Even though my designs come from me and the identity is very personal, the creative process is very communal. I feel a big influence from the people around me, in the atelier, and outside it from everyone we collaborate with. They shape me, widen my view, expand my horizon, which feels so important and inspiring. And although OMA is a lot bigger, it's probably similar on a broader level. It's a symbiotic identity, grown on dependence, much like nature. It's an evolving identity of a community and that's really beautiful.

Iris van Herpen is a fashion designer of haute couture who merges craftsmanship with diverse domains of interest. Her multidisciplinary work spans collaborations with artists, architects, and scientists.

OMA NY   Iris van Herpen

2715

Manus x Machina

Manus x Machina: Fashion in an Age of Technology

Fashion exhibitions have become effective modes of communicating the historical and cultural narratives of fashion. The Costume Institute has been at the forefront of maximizing this potential, drawing interest from a wide audience—from high society to the layperson. Objects of fashion are also considered an art form, but one that is more accessible and has a higher degree of connection to people because clothing is something we deal with every day. This radical accessibility compels us to rethink the relationship between curation and the audience experience. The exhibition design itself should be devoted to communicating the diverse narratives of objects and garments.

 Manus x Machina explores how designers are reconciling the handmade and the machine-made in the creation of haute couture and avant-garde ready-to-wear. The theme investigated a multitude of techniques, specifically the similarities and differences across various designers. Given the necessary attention to intricacy, our instinct told us that this exhibition would require a neutral and tranquil environment to draw people's focus to the detail of the garments.

 The exhibition took place in the Robert Lehman Wing of the Metropolitan Museum of Art, a double-height, octagonal addition constructed in 1975. The Lehman Wing is not a real gallery space, but a light-filled atrium and a series of corridors. The space posed environmental challenges: excessive daylighting unconducive to textile exhibition, split levels, a corridor condition lacking dedicated display walls, and an eclectic material palette. Given the challenges, luckily or not, we had to create our own environment within.

 From the Met entrance to the Lehman Wing, the setting is classical in language, especially the church-like character of the Medieval Gallery. Our approach relates to that language, but creates something temporary and light in contrast to the heavy masonry. We wanted to build an ethereal temple to fashion. A white, translucent volume was inserted into the existing brick and stone corridors and atrium, softening the hard geometries and materiality. The armature of scaffolding wrapped with a translucent fabric echoes the sectional relationship of a central clerestory and perimeter naves, creating a "ghost cathedral." It introduces temporality within a historic institution.

A raised platform built across the double-height atrium provides continuous circulation and a central gallery. Our intervention was a single circle in plan—the gap between the circular perimeter and the structure of the existing building was used to create a series of poches for display. Although temporary, it was the first time the museum had added new square footage to the building. Upon arrival, the central dome space orients visitors with a Chanel wedding dress that embodies the exhibition's theme. Details of the train's intricate pattern are projected on the dome's black-out scrim, recalling the frescoes of the Sistine Chapel that compel one to look up. Four chapel-style poches provide an area to focus on case studies.

A single material covers the ghost cathedral for a continuous, neutral backdrop for the entire exhibition. A scrim, typically used for theater sets, provides a complex transparency. When lit from the front, the scrim appears opaque and functions as a projection backdrop for garment details. Lit from behind, it appears transparent, exposing a sense of the Lehman Wing's existing material palette and language. The spatial depth allows for visual connections to the wedding dress from all quadrants of the Lehman Wing, while revealing silhouettes of the temporary scaffolding structure within. The scrim doubles as a medium to integrate lighting, signage, and projection into the architecture. Rather than relying on overpowering media screens that too often distract the audience from the garments themselves, details of the garments were projection-mapped to the poche scrim.

A testament to the popularity of fashion exhibitions, *Manus x Machina* was the Met's eighth most visited exhibition, attracting 752,995 visitors and ranking it alongside exhibitions dedicated to Picasso and *Mona Lisa*. We also designed the centerpiece and "red" carpet for the Met Gala, "the party of the year" in conjunction with the exhibition. The gala design conveyed a much different experience than the exhibition, a colorful and dazzling environment for celebrities rather than a neutral and contemplative setting for the everyday visitor—memorable, but in a different sense.

Location	New York, NY, USA		
Status	Completed, 2016		
Typology	Fashion		
Program	Exhibition	18,300 ft²	1,700 m²

OMA NY   Manus x Machina

Manus x Machina

Manus x Machina

OMA NY

Manus x Machina

Manus x Machina

OMA NY

Manus x Machina

Manus x Machina

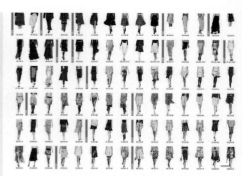

2720 Fashion exhibitions pose an opportunity for architects to be more experimental in exhibition design and explore new ways in which people engage with objects on display.

2721 Shohei Shigematsu and OMA have had a history of working within this realm, notably with Prada on the "Waist Down" exhibition, which took place in five different cities—Tokyo, Shanghai, Seoul, New York, and Los Angeles.

2722 The exhibition design set a stage where viewers engaged with more than 100 skirts and their dynamic movements.

2724 Skirts displayed as sculpture

2723 "Waist Down" Tokyo—viewers interact with a skirt that has been motorized to sway from side to side.

2725 Vacuum-sealed skirts

2726 A magnifying glass allows viewers to examine the details of craft.

2727 The enlarged scale of the skirts creates a visual focus on the dynamic movement of the skirts captured on the catwalk.

2728 Cutout mannequins create a forest of skirts and legs.

2729 Skirt cutouts are mirrored on one side to create an immersive field of reflections.

2730 Skirts on motors spin 360 degrees to reveal pleated and embroidered details.

2731 "Waist Down" Los Angeles—exterior projection visualizes a skirt laid out flat, like a plan view.

2732 "Waist Down" New York

2733 "Waist Down" Shanghai—skirt cutouts draw attention to the objects displayed at a surprising scale.

2734 The exhibition took place within the suites of the Peace Hotel on The Bund.

2735 "Waist Down" Seoul—the exhibition took place in the OMA-designed Prada Transformer.

2736 Cutouts of skirts and legs walk up the sides of the rotating Prada Transformer.

2737 "Manus x Machina: Fashion in an Age of Technology" was an exhibition put together by the Costume Institute of the Metropolitan Museum of Art in New York.

2738 Led by curator Andrew Bolton, the Costume Institute is responsible for the ambitious exhibitions that are produced annually at the museum, each year under a distinct theme.

2739 The Costume Institute's previous exhibitions have been diverse in themes and content, taking place in various spaces throughout the museum where typically white-cube galleries provided flexibility for spatial transformation.

2740 Met Costume Institute 2012 exhibition—"Schiaparelli and Prada: Impossible Conversations"

2741 Met Costume Institute 2013 exhibition—"PUNK: Chaos to Couture"

2742 Met Costume Institute 2014 exhibition—"Charles James: Beyond Fashion"

2743 Met Costume Institute 2015 exhibition—"China: Through the Looking Glass"

2744 The theme of our commission was "Manus x Machina," exploring how designers are reconciling the handmade and the machine-made in the creation of haute couture and avant-garde and ready-to-wear.

2745 Left: Christian Dior (1949); right: Sarah Burton for Alexander McQueen (2012)

Even when I work with computers, with high technology, I always try to put in the touch of the hand.
Issey Miyake (Designer)

The art challenges the technology, and the technology inspires the art.
John Lasseter (Director)

Science and technology revolutionize our lives, but memory, tradition, and myth frame our response.
Arthur Schlesinger (Historian)

One machine can do the work of fifty ordinary men. No machine can do the work of one extraordinary man.
Elbert Hubbard (Author)

2746 We began with looking at how the relationship between man and technology has been understood and perceived by creative individuals across disciplines.

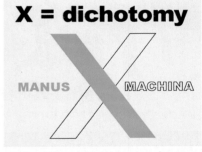

X = dichotomy

2747 The exhibition addresses the beginning of haute couture in the nineteenth century, when the sewing machine was invented, and the emergence of a distinction between the hand (manus) and the machine (machina) at the onset of mass production.

2748 We wanted to explore the dichotomy and the relationship between the viewer and the garments to present the wide range of garments created by two methods.

2749 The ambition was to encourage visitors to question the relationship and distinction between the two.

2750 Typically, a fashion exhibition is dedicated to a single designer or follows a visually consistent theme. Here, the contents are diverse and based on comparisons, so we wanted to create an ideal condition where visitors could focus on the detail of the garments.

2751 The exhibition features more than 170 garments.

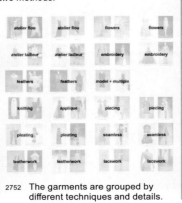

2752 The garments are grouped by different techniques and details.

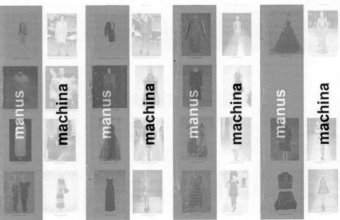

2753 Garments are further organized by juxtaposing the man-made and machine-made.

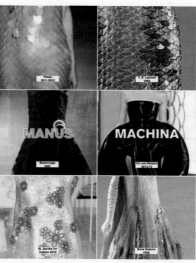

2756 How can the exhibition design create an environment where the viewers can inspect and draw relationships among the garments displayed?

2754 Exhibition content, from top to bottom: Issey Miyake (1984) and Madame Gres (1937–39), Junya Watanabe (2015) and Mila Schön (1968), Junya Watanabe (AW 2015–16) and Pierre Cardin (1968)

2755 Exhibition content, from top to bottom: Prada (2011–12) and Yves Saint Laurent (1983), Balenciaga (1927) and Iris van Herpen (2012–13), Marc Jacobs for Louis Vuitton (2012) and Boue Soeurs (1928)

2757 Early concept collage, a level of abstraction in the environment that enhance the garments

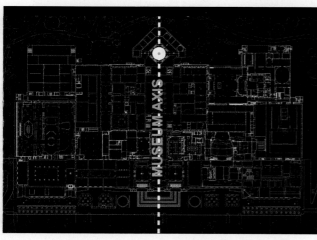

2758 The exhibition takes place in the Lehman Wing, a bright atrium and corridor for which a new exhibition space was created.

2759 Lehman Wing atrium—existing condition

2760 Robert Lehman Wing, Kevin Roche, John Dinkeloo, and Associates (1967)

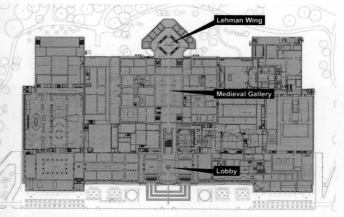

2761 The somewhat underutilized atrium intersects the main museum axis, giving it potential to become a focal point of the museum.

2762 From the lobby to the Lehman Wing, the spaces along the exhibition trajectory transition from a classical language to one that is highly modern.

2763 From the museum lobby

2764 Medieval Gallery

2765 View into Lehman Wing

2766 Exhibition entry

2754–2766   Manus x Machina

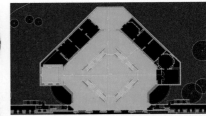

2767 The Lehman Wing posed many challenges for displaying art, including an over-abundance of sunlight, contrasting styles between the atrium and corridors, and lack of wall space.

2768 The conditions forced us to create our own environment within the existing space.

2769 Lehman Wing top floor plan—the 19-foot corridors of the existing Lehman Wing are more like hallways than gallery spaces.

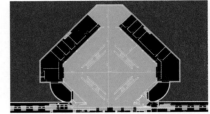

2770 The lower level echoes the upper level but does not have a skylight.

2771 Cathedral Reference—Santa Maria Miracolo e Montesanto, Rome, Italy (1681)

2772 Christo and Jeanne-Claude, *Big Air Package*, Gasometer Oberhausen, Germany (2013)

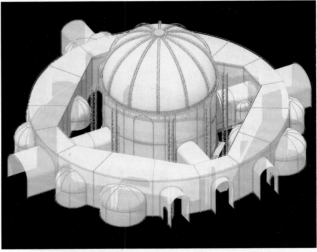

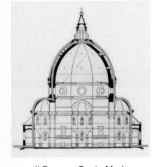

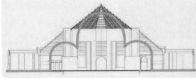

2773 Il Duomo, Santa Maria del Fiore, Florence, Italy (1436)

2774 The section of the Lehman Wing's atrium and perimeter galleries has a latent Cathedral quality, echoing the relationship of a central clerestory and perimeter naves.

2775 In order to create a black-out condition more suited for delicate garments, a ghost cathedral following the shape of the existing space is inserted into the Lehman Wing and takes the form of a chapel.

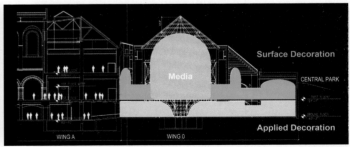

2776 Lehman Wing section (existing condition)

2777 Ghost cathedral concept diagram

2778 Existing Lehman Wing with abundance of natural light from the skylight.

2779 Building within a building—a new building skin is imposed within the existing atrium of the Lehman Wing.

2780 The surfaces of the new structure are covered in a translucent membrane to create a neutral and contemplative space, allowing viewers to focus on the delicately detailed pairings of garments within the exhibition.

2767–2780   Manus x Machina

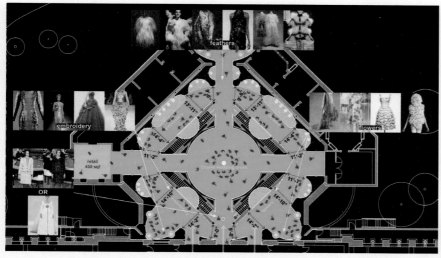

2782 Process niche—Basilica di San Domenico, Bologna, Italy (1228)

2781 On the top floor, each of the four main corridors contains a different technique. Each corridor has integrated poches that focus on garment details and process, which are at times projected onto the scrim surface. From the central space, visitors can access the four corridors freely, rather than being limited to walking around the perimeter.

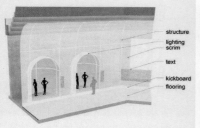

2783 In order to create exhibition space in the corridors, we used the space in between the existing wall and the perimeter of the ghost cathedral to create poches.

2784 Poche concept renderings

2785 A combination of readily available and custom scaffolding is employed as an armature for the scrim membrane.

2786 Stretching scrim over the scaffolding armature

2787 Installation view

2788 Installation view

2789 More opaque scrim is used for the case study poches for clarity in projection, while a more translucent scrim is used for other areas to make both the scaffolding structure and the other exhibition spaces more visible throughout the galleries.

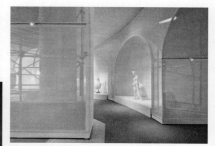

2790 The scrim has different levels of transparency depending on lighting conditions.

2791 View of flower garment poche

2793   The scrim defines the spaces within the cathedral and can be stretched without leaving visible seams. When lit from behind, the scrim appears transparent, exposing the exhibition armature.

2792   The scrim is a custom perforated membrane, developed and supplied by NEWMAT, adding a complex translucency with varying levels of light and opacity throughout the exhibition.

2794   When lit from the front, the membrane appears opaque, becoming a backdrop that enhances the color and details of the garments.

2795   The delicate and abstract surface provides a high contrast to the rough scaffolding.

2797   Lehman Wing corridor existing condition

2798   Completed corridor, with a series of poches

2796   The scrim can be used as a display surface, with some exhibition texts printed directly onto it.

2799   Lehman Wing corridor existing condition

2800   Approximately 30,000 square feet of scrim was used to achieve the ghost cathedral.

Manus x Machina

2801 Concept rendering of featherwork gallery in the northern niche of the Lehman Wing

2802 The featherwork garments are displayed in a more traditional setting due to their sensitivity.

2803 Rather than displaying information on screens or boards, the exhibition integrates text subtly onto the plinths.

2804 Recent fashion exhibitions often focus heavily on LED screens rather than actual garments. Instead of relying on screens, videos of garment details are projected onto the scrim in four poches, drawing attention to the details only when necessary.

2805 Projection study on different types of scrim material

2806 Projection studies

2807 Central atrium projection study model

2808 Projection study on mock-up model

2809 Projection mapping test on a full size poche mock-up

2810 Throughout the exhibition, when media is required, it is integrated into the architecture using projection mapping. Rather than displaying runway videos, which are typically shown in fashion exhibitions, the only media content is of garment details.

2811 Media is not an afterthought and is integrated into the architecture.

2812 Projection mapping

2813 Projection is carefully integrated into the form of the poche.

2814 Projection test with human model

2815 Four distinct projections of different technique details are projected onto each case study poche—embroidery, beadwork, flowers, and featherwork.

2816 Featherwork details projection mapped into the poche form

2817 Embroidery corridor

2818 The petal detail is enhanced in the projection.

2819 Flower case study poche

2820 The exhibition signage designed by 2x4 is the only other media feature aside from the projections.

2821 Details of the craft used in creating the garments displayed are magnified and projected onto the scrim.

2822 Projection in the central dome is visible through the translucent scrim.

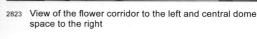

2823 View of the flower corridor to the left and central dome space to the right

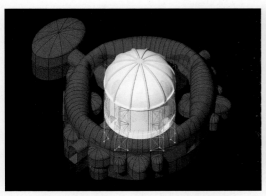

2824 For the central atrium, a black-out condition was most necessary to cover the skylight above the space. Our concept is likened to a soft cocoon sheltering the centerpiece of the exhibition theme.

2825 Altar/pulpit—Saint Peter's Basilica, Rome, Italy (1615)

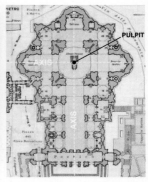

2826 Pedestal—Saint Peter's Basilica, Rome, Italy (1615)

2827 Our proposal builds a temporary floor bisecting the atrium and creating a new gallery space at the center of the Lehman Wing.

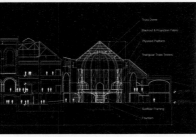

2828 Principle section diagram of cocoon structure in the central atrium

2829 Cocoon study—F1 view

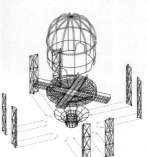

2831 Cocoon structure exploded axon

2830 Cocoon structure axon

2832 Existing view of central atrium from Lehman Wing entry

2833 By adding a new floor, we establish a sense of arrival to the exhibition.

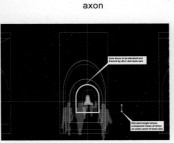

2834 Central atrium study—visibility from Lehman Wing entry

2835 Central atrium entry study—view from exhibition entrance

2836 The raised platform built across the double height atrium provides a continuous 2,300-square-foot gallery and circulation—an unprecedented intervention in the history of the Met.

2837 View of central gallery from featherwork perimeter gallery

Manus x Machina

2838 The exhibition's centerpiece is a 2014 Chanel wedding dress by Karl Lagerfeld that embodies the exhibition's theme.

2839 The scuba knit ensemble stands as a superlative example of the confluence between the handmade and machine-made.

2840 The pattern on the train is hand-painted with gold metallic pigment, machine-printed with rhinestones, and hand-embroidered with pearls and gemstones.

2841 We looked to the decorative elements of cathedrals for a way to display details of the dress. Siena Cathedral of Santa Maria, Siena, Italy (1264)

2842 Stained glass—Canterbury Cathedral, Canterbury, England (1077)

2843 The Stations of the Cross

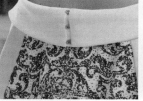

2844 Train detail

2845 Train detailing process

2846 An initial concept for the central atrium included wall projections that draw upon the Catholic Stations of the Cross, each step in the making of the Chanel wedding dress represented as a Station.

2847 Pedestal study for cocoon wedding dress—ellipsoid mound

2848 For the final concept, projection was limited to the dome in order to preserve a pure central space that would focus on the centerpiece dress.

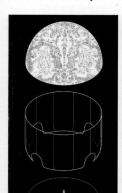

2849 The dress was designated to act as the centerpiece on a central pulpit.

2850 The dome itself is self-supporting and custom-made, comprised of a ring beam, twelve arch beams, and an oculus, all fabricated as CNC-milled plywood box sections with steel connector plates.

2851 The dome was lifted by hoists attached to eight scaffolding towers and placed onto corbels attached to those towers throughout the exhibition.

2852 Scrim stretched onto the dome

2838–2852   Manus x Machina

2853 Upon arrival, the central gallery orients visitors with the Chanel wedding dress by Karl Lagerfeld.

2854 Lehman Wing atrium—before

2855 Central atrium after completion

2856 Details of the 20-foot train's baroque pattern are projected on the dome's blackout scrim, recalling the Sistine Chapel.

2857 The projected video of the dress detail creates a new way for the viewer to engage with the object displayed.

2858 A custom pedestal was designed to accentuate the length of the train.

2862 View of central atrium and Chanel wedding dress

2859 Lehman Wing atrium—existing central atrium skylight

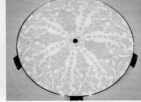

2860 The dome creates a black-out condition.

2861 View of the train's detail projected onto the dome

2863 View of the central atrium and dome with the structure of the case study poches visible through the scrim

2864 Central atrium view

2865 Shohei Shigematsu and head curator of Metropolitan Museum of Art's Costume Institute, Andrew Bolton

2866 Two stairways located on either side of the north-facing entry to the central gallery bring visitors down to the lower level gallery, which exhibits garments with structural decoration.

2853–2866

Manus x Machina

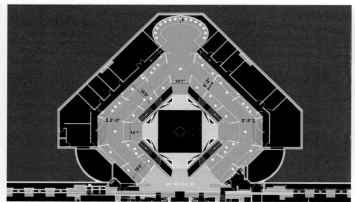

2867 The lower level is transformed into a disparate gallery as a result of the new floor built across the atrium. The layout is composed of angled niches and an exterior gallery similar to the featherwork gallery on the floor above.

2868 View of stairway to lower level corridor

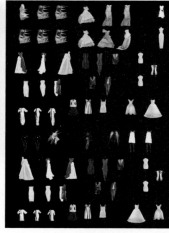

2869 The lower level exhibits garments of structural decoration.

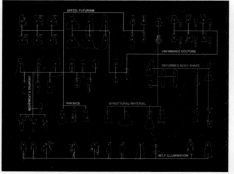

2870 Organizational study of garments for display

2871 The design of the lower level gallery aims to provide a contrast from the upper level. The scrim is deployed in flat planes that provide a new orthogonality.

2872 Reference for double blind—Robert Irwin, *Secession* (2013)

2873 Reference for double blind—Dan Graham, *Tunnel of Love* (2014)

2874 The angled niches are located at the junctions where the corridors meet.

2875 Pleating niche by the entry to the lower level gallery

2876 Pleating niche

2877 Tailoring niche

2878 The more orthogonal niches contrast with the organic forms of those on the upper level.

2880 Existing view of lower level corridor

2881 In the corridor gallery, planes of scrim create an enfilade of rooms.

2879 View of lower level corridor gallery

2882 Draped scrim "walls" create angled niches that establish a layered view corridor with moments from complete transparency to opacity.

2883 Contrary to the soft curves of the upper level galleries, the angled niches subtly yet effectively elevate the colorful garments and their more structural qualities.

2884 Shohei with Anna Wintour—we were also commissioned to design the annual Met Gala in conjunction with the exhibition.

2885 2012 centerpiece—"Schiaparelli and Prada: Impossible Conversations"

2886 2013 centerpiece—"PUNK: Chaos to Couture"

2887 2014 centerpiece—"Charles James: Beyond Fashion"

2888 2015 centerpiece—"China: Through the Looking Glass"

2889 Shohei Shigematsu, Anna Wintour, and Andrew Bolton

X = dichotomy

MANUS X MACHINA

MANUS X MACHINA

2890 The design for the gala drew upon the same concept as the exhibition design—reconciling the dichotomy between the man-made and machine-made.

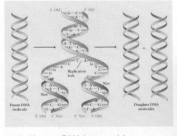

2891 Human DNA base pairing

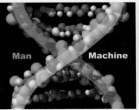

2892 Human DNA molecular mode

2893 Cotton fiber at x5000 zoom

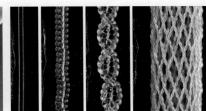

2894 Nylon after twist insertion for artificial muscle

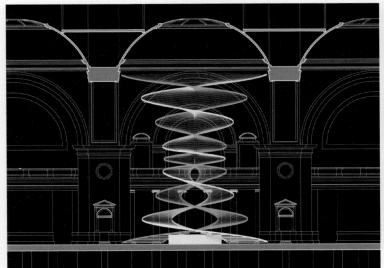

2895 The double helix centerpiece represents the dichotomy that is the theme of the exhibition: one strand is man-made and the other machine-made.

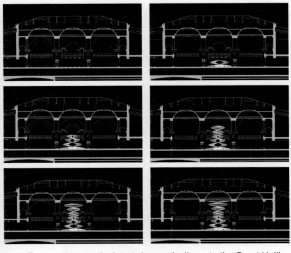

2896 Two separate paths intertwine vertically up to the Great Hall's domed ceiling.

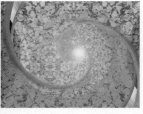

2899 The initial concept paired a red path of real rose petals with a pink path of laser-cut petals.

2898 The Great Hall centerpiece—DNA hourglass net of flowers

2897 Concept rendering of the Great Hall centerpiece

2900 Arrival view of the centerpiece

2901 The Great Hall—before

2902 The Great Hall—after with completed centerpiece

2904 The Great Hall stairs

2903 Completed view of the Great Hall centerpiece

2905 An early proposal continuation of the Grand Hall centerpiece onto the Great Hall stairs.

2906 We also designed elements for the Gala environment, including an entry wall in the Temple of Dendur comprised of real and laser-cut petals.

2908 Gala seating—original chair

2909 Gala seating—MxM-themed chairs

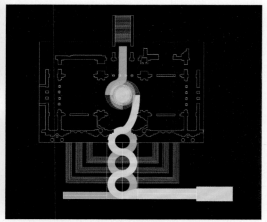

2910 The concept for the exhibition and gala centerpiece was deployed for the entry and tent, as well as the red carpet, establishing a cohesive event procession.

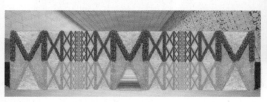

2907 Entry wall concept study

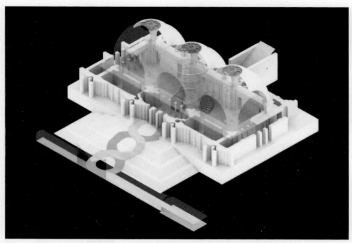

2911 The gala's red carpet design is a reflection and continuation of the centerpiece installation's intertwining of two different colors.

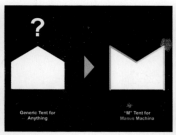

2912 *Vogue* Gala portal—tent transformation

2913 *Vogue* Gala tent—exterior view

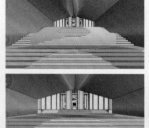

2915 *Vogue* Gala tent—entry sequence

2916 The carpet design, which rejected the typical red or single-color format, was heavily criticized by the media for being distracting during the event.

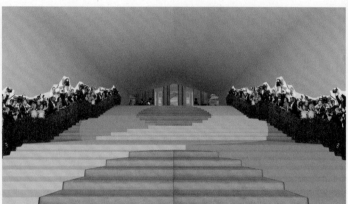

2914 *Vogue* Gala tent—concept collage

2917 The helix pattern of the carpet created a series of white, central zones that celebrities were naturally drawn to for photo moments. Here, the dress even matched the colors of the carpet.

2918 Taylor Swift

2919 Editor-in-chief of *Vogue* who is also a chairwoman of the Gala poses with another celebrity guest.

2920 Another celebrity guest stops to pose in the central zone.

2921 Lupita Nyong'o

2922 While the exhibition design provided a neutral and contemplative setting, the gala design was colorful and glamorous.

2923 2924 2925 2926 2927 2928

2929 2930 2931 2932 2933 2934

2935 2936 2937 2938 2939 2940

2941 2942 2943 2944 2945 2946

2947 2948 2949 2950 2951 2952

2953 2954 2955 2956 2957 2958

2959 2960 2961 2962 2963 2864

2923–2864   Manus x Machina

Manus x Machina

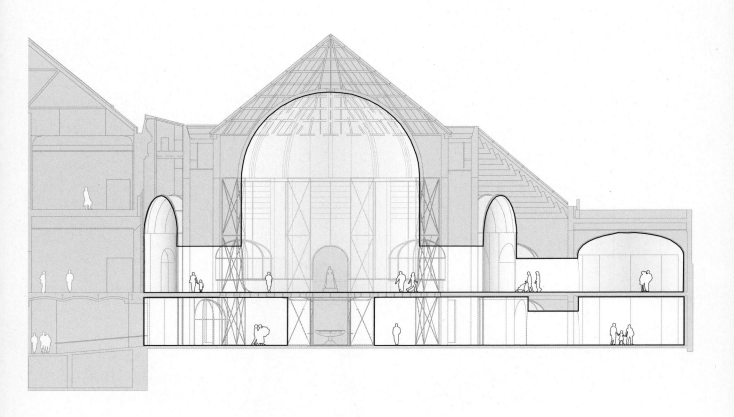

Manus x Machina

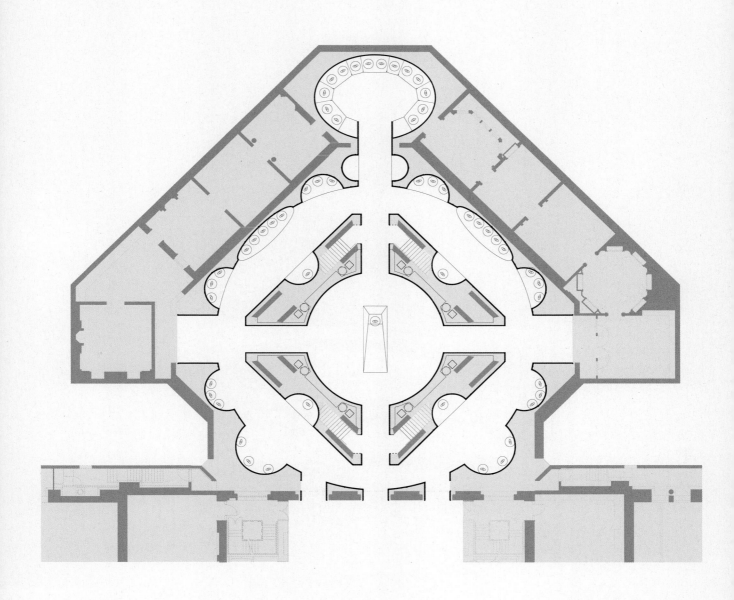

Manus x Machina

Dior: From Paris to the World

Dior: From Paris to the World

Fashion is becoming simultaneously relatable (fast fashion) and distant (couture) now more than ever. The display of couture in the highly public museum setting inherently captures both familiarity and glamour, which has led to a recent rise in the popularity of fashion exhibitions in museums. Luxury garments themselves have layers of stories to tell—from the designer's concepts and techniques to the commercial and cultural contexts in which they were created. The fashion exhibition, we believe, is a stimulating domain that poses us to rethink the relationship between the audience and display and create a narrative-driven environment that pushes the convergence of spatial and communication design.

We were asked to design Dior's first retrospective in the United States at the Denver Art Museum, following its success at the Musée des Arts Décoratifs in Paris, home of Dior. Featuring more than 200 couture garments, artworks and artifacts, accessories, jewelry, photographs, sketches, and videos, the exhibition surveys more than 70 years of the House of Dior's legacy and global influence in themes stemming from inspirations that have been predominant in the history of the house and its creative directors. We were inspired by the creative continuity and consistent identity of the House despite its diversity of artistic visions, and challenged by the drastic change in the environment—from Europe to America and from a classical to a contemporary museum.

We conceived a continuous backdrop to serve as individual enclosures for different themes and creative directors, creating cell-like rooms that expand and contract to fit within the atypical geometries of the galleries. Each cell is defined in response to the diverse themes of the exhibition content—aluminum panels of varying curvatures, textures, and profiles that echo Dior's feminine figures, classic silhouettes, and textures—from the feminine silhouette of the New Look to floral shapes in garden-inspired designs. While materiality of the display armature takes cues from the titanium cladding of Daniel Libeskind's Hamilton Building, the organic forms break from the building's stark industrial quality. The undulating structures provide not a direct mirror, but a multiplied reflection and abstract enhancement of the garments. Although the rooms are different in character, the continuous materiality ties the individual themes together.

To reinforce a uninterrupted narrative through Dior, the diverse rooms are interconnected. A nod to Christian Dior's obsession for his Granville garden, a meandering pathway carves through the various exhibition themes and artistic directors. The path defines enfilade rooms with a double-sided presentation within each, and clear sightlines to adjacent spaces.

The Martin and McCormick Gallery is given over to a single theme, "From Paris to the World", that highlights Dior's global influence. The pathway continues through a dramatic valley, where all garments can be viewed from a single vantage point. Here, the aluminum material shifts from a vertical backdrop to a horizontal one, in response to the unconventional shape and height of the gallery. Petal-shaped platforms, echoing a recurring form in Dior ball gowns, crawl up the inclined walls to create an immersive topography.

From Paris to Colorado to Texas, the global voyage of the exhibition is reminiscent of Christian Dior's own expedition. After Denver, the show traveled to the Dallas Museum of Art and took place in a Modernist museum designed by Edward Larrabee Barnes. Much like in Denver, our approach was to be specific to the architecture of the main gallery, the Barrel Vault. By inverting the vault—the audience walks the catwalk while "models" are staged on bleachers—we flipped the typical narrative of fashion voyeurism.

Location	Denver, CO, USA/Dallas, TX, USA		
Status	Completed, 2018/2019		
Typology	Fashion		
Program	Denver Exhibition	13,800 ft²	1,300 m²
	Dallas Exhibition	12,100 ft²	1,100 m²

Dior: From Paris to the World

OMA NY

Dior: From Paris to the World

Dior: From Paris to the World

Dior: From Paris to the World

2973 Christian Dior was an art gallerist turned courtier who revolutionized fashion in Paris and around the globe after World War II.

2974 His haute couture was revolutionary in its expression of modern femininity, which shed the masculine silhouette that was commonplace during the war.

2975 Dior's iconic look featured soft shoulders, accentuated busts, and cinched waists, elements that led to a new movement in fashion history.

2976 The House of Dior was founded in 1946 and its first collection was presented in 1947.

2977 Dior headquarters at 30, avenue Montaigne in Paris

2978 The iconic staircase of 30, avenue Montaigne

2979 Dior's first exhibition in thirty years, "Christian Dior: Couturier du Rêve," took place in 2017 against the classical backdrop of the Musée des Arts Décoratifs in Paris.

2980 Entrance to the Dior exhibition, modeled after 30, avenue Montaigne

2981 The museum's classical architecture was well suited to Dior's couture garments.

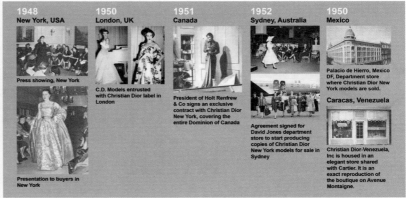

2982 After World War II, Dior traveled the world and his expedition through North and South America expanded the house's global influence.

2983 The exhibition's central theme, "From Paris to the World," focuses on the house of Dior's enduring legacy and global influence. In the same way that Dior himself toured the United States, establishing connections in New York, Los Angeles, Dallas, and Chicago, the exhibition would travel to the United States and present Dior's first U.S. retrospective.

2984 The show features the designs of Dior and the creative directors who followed him—Yves Saint Laurent, Marc Bohan, Gianfranco Ferré, John Galliano, Raf Simons, and Maria Grazia Chiuri.

2985 The exhibition also explores the House's thematic history, including Dior's own inspirations from the garden of Les Rhumbs, his pink villa in Normandy. These themes are repeated by subsequent creative directors.

2986 The exhibition surveys 70 years of Dior and showcases more than 200 couture dresses, as well as accessories, costume jewelry, photographs, drawings, runway videos, and other archival material.

PARIS

DENVER

2989 Florence Müller and Shohei Shigematsu in front of the Hamilton Building

2987 After the Paris exhibition, Florence Müller, the exhibition's co-curator, joined the Denver Art Museum (DAM) as the Avenir Foundation Curator of Fashion & Textile Art. She would bring the retrospective to Denver, with a new vision focusing on Dior's worldwide reach and influence.

2988 In stark contrast to the Paris exhibition, the site of Dior's first retrospective in the United States is the contemporary Frederic C. Hamilton Building by Daniel Libeskind.

CONTEMPORARY

NON-TRADITIONAL

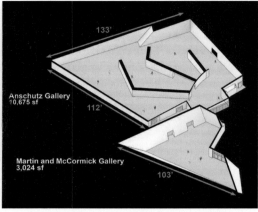

Anschutz Gallery 10,675 sf

Martin and McCormick Gallery 3,024 sf

2990 How can the exhibition fit into a contemporary setting?

2991 How can the exhibition design maneuver the specificity of the architecture and its non-traditional spaces?

2992 The site consists of two galleries—Anschutz Gallery, with existing angular walls, and the Martin and McCormick Gallery, a smaller column-free space with sloping walls.

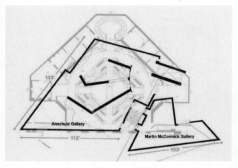

2993 Scale comparison to "Manus x Machina"

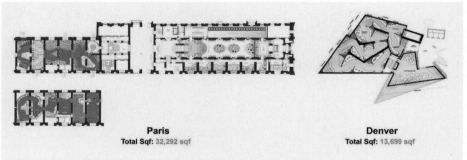

Paris
Total Sqf: 32,292 sqf

Denver
Total Sqf: 13,699 sqf

2994 Scale comparison of the exhibition at the Musée des Arts Décoratifs and at DAM

Christian Dior Couturier du Rêve Curatorial Themes

1 Christian Dior 1905–1957
2 Christian Dior Galleriste
3 Christian Dior et la Photographie
4 Les Affinités Artistiques
5 Colorama
6 Paris
7 Trianon
8 Le Tour du Monde en Dior
9 Les Jardins Dior
10 Dior, Couturier Parfumeur
11 30, Avenue Montaigne
13 Le New Look
14 Yves Saint Laurent
15 Marc Bohan
16 Gianfranco Ferré
17 John Galliano
18 Raf Simons
19 Maria Grazia Chiuri
20 Les Ateliers de 1947 à 2017
21 L'Allure Dior
22 Versailles et J'Adore
23 Le Bal Dior
24 Stars en Dior

2995 The Paris exhibition featured twenty-four different themes.

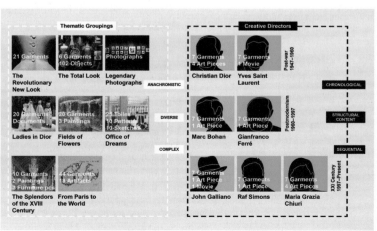

2996 The Denver exhibition showcases fifteen themes. Thematic Groupings are more anachronistic and diverse, while the Creative Directors section is more chronological and structured.

2987–2996   Dior: From Paris to the World

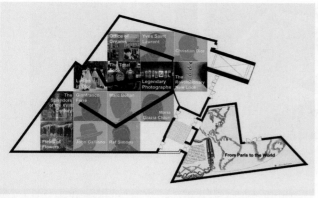

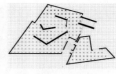

2998 Grids defined by lighting effects

2999 Small grid with garments at axes

3000 Enfilade and grid hybrid

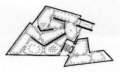

3001 Couture salons

3002 Classic galleries

3003 Curved rooms

2997 The challenge was to clarify the diverse themes within a clearly defined space with sloping and angled walls.

3004 The goal was to create a series of intimate room-like enclosures that also drew upon the sensual silhouettes of Dior's garments.

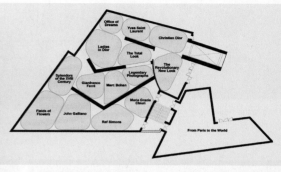

3005 The resulting rooms are organic, conforming to the highly specific gallery architecture.

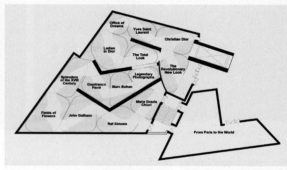

3006 In order to enhance the curatorial narrative, a winding path is carved through the cluster of enclosures.

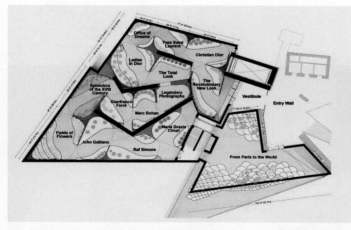

3007 The exhibition conveys curatorial themes as a series of enfilade rooms that expand and contract to fit within the irregular gallery plan while optimizing spaces for display.

3008 Enfilade—Dulwich Picture Gallery, London, UK

3009 Paths—Dior Haute Couture Spring 2013, Paris Fashion Week

3010 The three distinct moves create a spatial journey through the brand's long history.

3011 The organic pathway is a nod to the gardens of Christian Dior's childhood home—Les Rhumbs, a pink villa in Granville, Normandy.

3012 Diverse contents are further unified through materiality, conceived specifically to fit the contemporary context of the Hamilton Building.

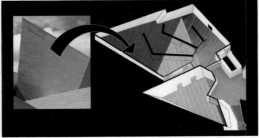

3013 The materiality of the display takes cues from the titanium cladding of the building. Aluminum surfaces become backdrops for the exhibition's displays.

3014 Dior reference for reflective backdrops

3015 In the essence of Dior, the undulating backdrops are drawn from classic and feminine silhouettes.

3016 The raw undulated metal reflects and abstracts the garments on display, enhancing the colors of the pieces.

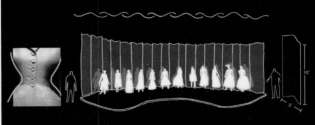

3017 Sketch of metal panel undulation, informed by the iconic Dior Bar Jacket's nipped waist.

3018 Backdrop reflectivity and undulation studies—concave vs. convex panels

3019 Large, medium, and small scales of undulation

3020 Aluminum finish samples

3021 Rose-toned aluminum with semigloss finish

3022 Mock-ups comparing aluminum finishes

3023 DAM's Jennifer Pray and curator Florence Müller during installation

3025 Each room is defined by aluminum panels of varying curvatures, textures, and profiles that echo the signature shapes of Dior garments. While the rooms are unique in either form, color, or undulation, the material consistency runs throughout the exhibit.

3024 Organic rooms with aluminum enclosures

3027 When Dior first debuted the Bar Suit in 1947, the emphasis on the female form and material construction after a period of global austerity was immediately shocking. The form has been refined by subsequent creative directors.

3028 Plan view

3026 The first room is the Revolutionary New Look, featuring Christian Dior's first collections that redefined and reconstructed the female figure.

3029 Exhibition content—8 Line

3030 Exhibition content—Bar Suit and Corolle Line

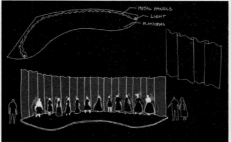

3031 Plan, elevation, and axon sketch—the profile of the panels echoes the feminine silhouette of the New Look.

3032 Axon view

3033 Sheets of mill-finish aluminum 6 millimeters thick are run through an industrial roller.

3034 This process creates precise radiuses and curves for each panel.

3035 The aluminum panels are hung from a steel tube structure that defines the overall room shape.

3036 The rawness of the aluminum juxtaposes with the garments' soft textures. A synergy exists between the curves of both the subject and backdrop.

3037 Each silhouette is subtly reflected.

3039 The organic pathway leads visitors into the next room. A projection above highlights enlarged details of construction and form from various New Look garments over time.

3038 Looking toward the exhibition entrance

3040 The Christian Dior room showcases his relationship to art and artists, displaying artwork from his past exhibitions.

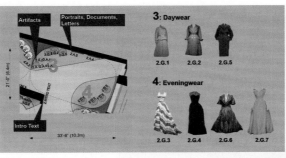

3041 Exhibition content—daywear, eveningwear, artifacts, portraits, documents, and letters.

3042 Axon view—Christian Dior

3043 Christian Dior's pieces juxtaposed with a painting by Yan Pei-Ming, *Mr. Christian Dior* (2011). The garments' colors are subtly reflected on the backdrop.

3044 Dior's "Surrealist Exhibition: Sculptures, Objects, Paintings, Drawings" (1933)

3045 Dior's own gallery is recreated for the display of artworks and artifacts. A Man Ray photo of Dior's 1933 Surrealist exhibition is printed on translucent vinyl and adhered to a corrugated aluminum panel.

3046 Test print of images on corrugated panels

3047 The smaller scale of corrugation creates a dynamic reflection across the panels.

3048 Axon view—Yves Saint Laurent, The Little Prince of Fashion, 1957–1960

3049 View from Christian Dior to Yves Saint Laurent

3050 The contemporary backdrop for a classic garment subtly reflects the garment's silhouette.

3051 Yves Saint Laurent

3052 Movie poster for *The Wild One* (1953)—Saint Laurent's "Beatnik" collection took cues from Marlon Brando in the László Benedek film.

3053 Exhibition content—dresses, portrait, and video

3054 Rendering of Yves Saint Laurent gallery

3055 View entering the Yves Saint Laurent gallery

3056 The path directs visitors from one to another while establishing enfilade views.

Dior: From Paris to the World

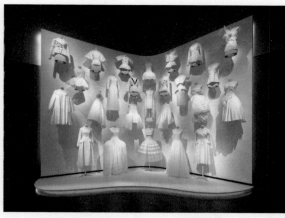

3057 The Office of Dreams gallery is a reimagination of Christian Dior's atelier, displaying toiles and patterns for prototyping.

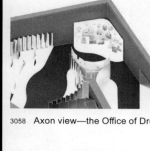

3058 Axon view—the Office of Dreams

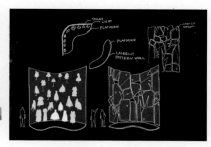

3059 One wall features a collection of toiles and another wall is composed of laser-cut patterns.

3060 The ateliers of the House of Dior, circa 1948

3061 Patterns in Dior's Paris atelier

3062 Mannequins in Dior's Paris atelier

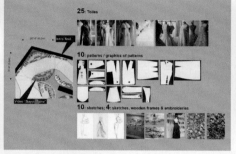

3063 Exhibition content—toiles, patterns/graphics of patterns, sketches, and embroideries

3064 Rendering—pattern wall with display case

3065 The pattern wall is powder coated white aluminum.

3066 Axon view—Ladies in Dior

3067 View from The Office of Dreams toward Ladies in Dior

3068 Ladies in Dior is a presentation of garments worn by famous women, from celebrities to American socialites.

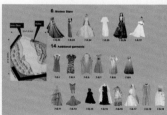

3069 Exhibition content—garments worn by modern/past stars, including video

3070 The panels for Ladies in Dior are like those for of The Revolutionary New Look. The larger scale of the undulations enhances the sensuality of the theme.

3071 Sketch of projection canopies

3074 Rooms are subtly distinguished by narrow strips of light.

3072 Further defining the room is a ribbon of scrim for video projection mounted above the aluminum panels.

3073 The room's elongated shape serves as a long backdrop reminiscent of a red carpet procession.

3075 The Total Look is the culmination of Christian Dior's expansive idea of offering a complete look from head to toe.

3076 Axon view—the Total Look

3077 In the Paris exhibition, color-coordinated, complete-look ensembles were intricately displayed against a black backdrop.

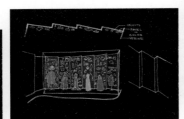

3078 Exhibition content—six complete looks, from hats and shoes to make-up and jewelry, organized by color

3079 A staggered composition of individual panels create a three-dimensional display within a vitrine.

3080 Content layouts for each color were carefully tested and composed before mounting locations were set within each panel.

3081 Colored panel mock-ups

3082 Opening day

3083 The color-matched panels enhance the color of the garment and objects. In order to fully saturate the display with each theme's colors, this space does not include the aluminum panels used elsewhere.

3084 Enfilade view of the Total Look from the next room, Legendary Photographs

3085 The Christian Dior years coincided with the golden age of fashion photography, producing a multitude of photographic works that convey Dior's expression.

3086 Axon view—Legendary Photographs

3087 Exhibition content—photographs only

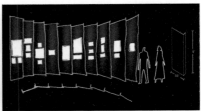

3088 The form of the display armature is the same as that of The Total Look.

3089 The black panel frames create a subtle texture within the dark space.

3090 The texture does not compete with the photographs but rather enhances them by creating depth within the display.

3091 The backdrop is a play on Dior's refined cuts and skilled draping.

3075–3091   Dior: From Paris to the World

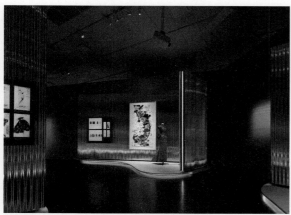

3092 Much like Christian Dior, Marc Bohan valued classical references and was inspired by the art world. His garments are accompanied by artworks that inspired him.

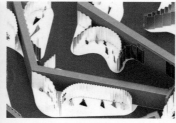

3093 Axon view—Mark Bohan, Classicism Revisited, 1961–1989

3094 Marc Bohan dressing Sophia Loren (1963)

3095 Bohan drew inspiration from art, especially American Abstract Expressionism and Jackson Pollock's drip paintings.

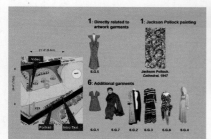

3096 Exhibition content—garment directly related to artwork, Jackson Pollock painting, and additional garments that captured the essence of the 1960s

3097 The wall takes on a more angular shape, following the existing angled gallery wall.

3098 The stripes of the dress are reflected and amplified, yet the reflection does not compete with the garment.

3099 Rendering view

3100 The panels are 10 feet high and have a mill finish.

3101 Enfilade view of Gianfranco Ferré from Marc Bohan

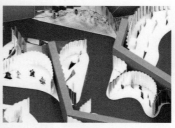

3102 Axon view—Gianfranco Ferré, The Postmodern Couturier, 1989–1996

3103 The first non-French designer to head Dior, Gianfranco Ferré brought Italian extravagance, inspired by seventeenth-century Baroque architecture and art.

3104 Giovanni Benedetto Castiglione, *Deucalion and Pyrrha* (1655)

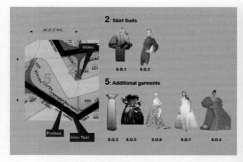

3105 Exhibition content—skirt suits, additional garments, portrait, sketches, and video.

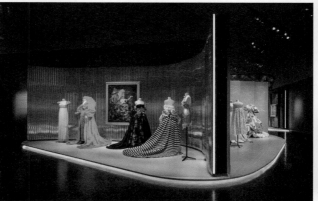

3106 The vivid red of the dress as well as the textures and figurative movements of all the garments stand out against the monochromatic backdrop.

3107 One side of the room displays his skirt suits accompanied by sketches and a video.

3108 Garments paired with Castiglione painting

3109 The Splendors of the XVIII Century features garments from a time when Christian Dior sought to bring the flamboyance of eighteenth-century France into the present day.

3110 Axon view—The Splendors of the XVIII Century

3111 Hall of Mirrors, Palace of Versailles

3112 The elaborate ornamentation and decadence of the eighteenth-century architecture and interior is decoded into a graphic appliqué for the backdrop of the room.

3113 Exhibition content—garments, furniture and objects, garments related to portraits and paintings

3114 An initial idea was to create gold metallic curtain-like panels etched with abstract ornamentation.

3115 The ornate elegance of eighteenth-century France is reimagined with abstract graphics inspired by the Hall of Mirrors at Versailles applied to gold-painted, faceted walls, creating a backdrop that is both contemporary and resonant.

3116 From the Splendors of the XVIII Century, visitors wind up in Fields of Flowers, showcasing Christian Dior's passion for flowers and gardening.

3117 Pergola and pool at the villa Les Rhumbs, Christian Dior's childhood home

3118 Christian Dior drew inspiration from his passion for gardening and botanical anatomy.

3119 Axon view—Fields of Flowers

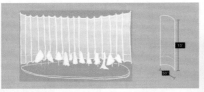

3120 The panels take after the shape of flower petals as well as the silhouettes of the skirts and dresses.

3123 Juxtaposing art of Impressionist painting and garments—Pierre-Auguste Renoir, *Young Woman in a Garden* (1916)

3121 Exhibition content—garment accompanying artwork, Marc Quinn painting, additional garments and paintings

3122 The panels are powder-coated pink (the technical name is penny dust).

3124 Fields of Flowers garments exhibited with Renoir painting and Claude Monet, *Water Lilies* (1904). Above, a scrim ribbon follows the organic shape of the room and displays a photo print from Granville. Projections of dappled flowers and leaves hang over the enclosure.

3125 Garments and accompanying painting Marc Quinn, *Colorado Spring* (2009).

3126 After Fields of Flowers, visitors are led to John Galliano, first of the most contemporary grouping of creative directors.

3127 Galliano drew references from various art and cultural inspirations, including the classic films of Jean Cocteau.

3128 Axon view—John Galliano, The Storyteller, 1997–2011

3129 Exhibition content—film, garments, Cocteau film, and Marchesa Casati portrait

3130 Rendered view testing garment reflectivity

3131 The details and colors of Galliano's garments are reflected and amplified by the panels.

3132 Garment paired with artwork, Arturo Martini, *Marchesa Casati as Cesare Borgia* (1925)

3133 Garment (left) inspired by Surrealism and the works of Jean Cocteau.

3134 Raf Simons, although known for his minimalism, channeled Dior's romanticism and transformed classic curves into sculptural silhouettes.

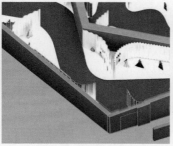

3135 Axon view—Raf Simons, The Shapeshifter, 2012–2015

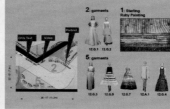

3136 Exhibition content—garments accompanying artwork, Sterling Ruby painting, additional garments

3137 One side of the room displays a spray painted artwork from Sterling Ruby, *SP262* (2013), paired with garments inspired by the piece.

3138 The verticality of the backdrop enhances the abstract horizontality of the painting and textiles while accentuating their silhouettes.

3139 The textures and colors of the garments are abstracted and reflected, bringing attention to details without overwhelming the display.

3140 The meandering pathway provides a seamless view back toward the John Galliano exhibit, while the consistent backdrops enhance the exhibition's continuity and flow.

3141 The last alcove exhibits the work of Maria Grazia Chiuri, Dior's creative director from 2016 to the present.

3142 *"Her Dior: Maria Grazia Chiuri's New Voice," Rizzoli, 2021*—Chiuri is the first female head of Dior.

3143 Milliner Stephen Jones, Maria Grazia Chiuri, and Shohei Shigematsu during the exhibition's opening.

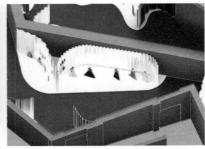

3144 Axon view—Maria Grazia Chiuri, The New Femininity, 2016–Present

3145 Exhibition content—garments, artworks, mood boards, and video

3146 Rendering

3147 Garment displayed with Man Ray sculpture

3149 The vertical pattern of the corrugated panel provides a neutral yet tactile backdrop for the garments.

3151 The corridor connecting the Anschutz and Martin and McCormick Galleries is transformed into a display space itself, featuring Dior's scarves from the 1950s through the 1970s.

Man Ray, *Non-Euclidean Object* (1932)

3148

3150 The pathway winds through the last alcove and leads visitors to Chiuri's mood boards on the back wall before entering the corridor to the Martin and McCormick Gallery.

3152 Scarf corridor plan

3153 More than fifty-six scarves from Dior Heritage line both walls of the corridor leading to From Paris to the World.

3155 Christian Dior was often inspired by his travels and his trips informed many collections.

3156 He was also a pioneer in globalizing fashion, establishing an international network of locations for the brand and its boutiques.

3154 The pathway continues to the Martin and McCormick Gallery. From Paris to the World focuses on Dior's global legacy. Displays take the form of a dramatic valley, where an overview of Dior's global inspirations can be viewed from a single vantage point.

3160 Exhibition content—garments organized by their geographical location of influence: Americas, Europe, Asia, and Africa

3157 To showcase the diversity of influence, the design would take on the idea of a Wunderkammer.

3158 Archival museum storage on display

3159 Dior's Paris atelier

3161 Early concept sketch— cabinet-like valley

3162 Study— orthogonal valley

3163 Landscape topography

3164 One study explored the details of folds and pleats in Dior garments.

3165 Study— topography/pleats

3166 The final concept is inspired by the petal motif repeatedly used in many of Dior's garments.

3167 In opposition to the vertical backdrop of the Anschutz Gallery, aluminum panels shift to a horizontal surface for display.

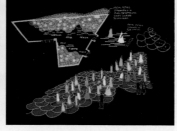

3168 Petal-shaped platforms climb up the inclined walls of the gallery.

3169 Final concept model

3170 Final concept model

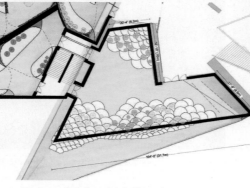

3171 Martin and McCormick Gallery plan

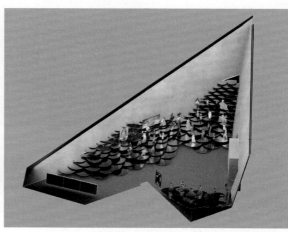

3172 The climbing petals create an immersive topography specific to the architecture. The cascading platforms respond to the height of the gallery.

3154–3172

Dior: From Paris to the World

3173 From Paris to the World—layered horizontal platforms seen from above.

3174 From left to right, the garments are organized by their location of influence—Americas, Asia, and Africa.

3175 The garments inspired by Europe are organized on the opposite end of the valley.

3176 View from the corridor entry into the valley

3177 Early rendering view of northern wall

3178 Early rendering view of southern wall

3179 Full-scale mock-up of single petal form work

3180 The framework of the petals had to be specified to the sloping walls of the gallery.

3181 Some petals were custom made and had to be cut to specific sizes to fit the sloping angles of the gallery walls.

3182 Installation

3183 There are a total of 134 petals in the gallery, with 5 different sizes of typical petals—45 inches, 56 inches, 68 inches, 78 inches, and 90 inches wide.

3184 The valley of petals creates a dynamic condition for display, as some objects can be seen up close while others draw visitors to new vantage points.

3185 Shohei Shigematsu and Florence Müller, the Avenir Foundation Curator of Fashion & Textile Art, in the Martin and McCormick Gallery on opening day.

3186 Colors and silhouettes are subtly reflected and enhanced on the horizontal surfaces of the metal petals.

Dior: From Paris to the World

3187 The entry to the exhibition was conveniently located on the second level, immediately up the grand staircase at the building's entry.

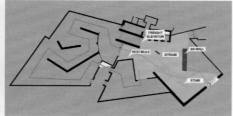

3188 The circulation route from the museum entry to the exhibition provided an opportunity to activate the stair and create a formal entrance into the galleries.

3189 An earlier study explored the option to utilize the stairway as an additional exhibition space.

3190 Earlier study of activated atrium

3191 Stair studies—options for projection of garment details or the classic facade of Dior headquarters at 30, avenue Montaigne

3192 The final stair design takes a more literal approach, recreating the iconic stair moment of the Dior atelier.

3193 Wall decals of ladies in Dior line the stairway

3194 Because of the sloping wall, the installation required careful maneuvering.

3195 The atrium stair is transformed into a contemporary counterpart to the Dior atelier stair, reminiscent of Dior's beginnings.

3196 Christoph Heinrich, Denver Art Museum's Frederick and Jan Mayer Director, gives opening remarks during the Gala.

3197 Visitors are led up the stairs to the entrance to the exhibition.

3198 For the entrance, it seemed appropriate to reimagine the iconic facade of 30, avenue Montaigne in Paris.

3199 Taking cues from Dior's use of reflectivity in many of their runway shows while providing continuity with the exhibition design that lies ahead, the facade is combined with a reflective surface.

3200 The entrance simultaneously reflects the activities within the museum and the atrium space in front.

3201 The image of the atelier facade and entrance is overlaid on a mirrored surface.

3202 Like stepping into the Dior atelier itself, the entryway marks the beginning of a journey through the House of Dior's history and all of its inspirations, influences, and passions.

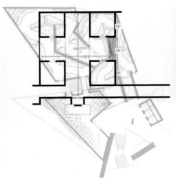

3205 The show has gone from a contemporary building as venue to a Modernist one.

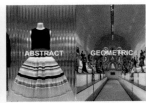

3206 The transition from a more abstract interior to a geometric one required rethinking the exhibition design.

3203 The show traveled from DAM to the Dallas Museum of Art (DMA) in Texas. The exhibition design in Denver was conceived through specificity to the contemporary context of the Hamilton Building. The starkly different Modernist architecture of DMA required an entirely new exhibition design.

3204 Scale comparison overlay of DAM and DMA

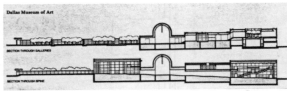

3207 The Modernist building was designed by architect Edward Larrabee Barnes.

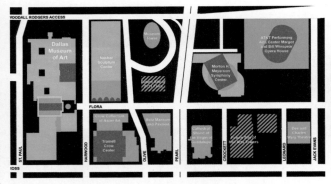

3208 DMA is a cultural anchor within the Dallas Arts District, located at the terminus of Flora Street, a major cultural axis. A key feature of the building is its barrel vault, which can be activated as an extension of Flora Street.

3209 Barnes took reference from Claude Ledoux's ideal and visionary architecture in conceiving the barrel vault space.

3210 How can we extend the reductive geometry and enhance elements of grandeur and fantasy?

3211 Isa Genzken installation in the barrel vault space (2014)

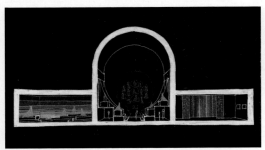

3212 The central barrel vault space stages From Paris to the World, figuratively drawing on the museum's site context and the exchange of cultures and inspirations. Attached to the barrel vault are a series of well-defined galleries that house the other exhibition themes.

3213 Mirroring the vault along both the X and Y axes emphasizes the existing architecture of the gallery while creating an infinite "catwalk."

3214 The catwalk concept draws upon Christian Dior's Fall 1999 couture show in the orangerie at Versailles.

3215 Rendered view of garments displayed in the mirrored barrel vault

3216 Versailles x DMA, Grand Canal, and adjoining Bosquets

3217 Quad taxonomy

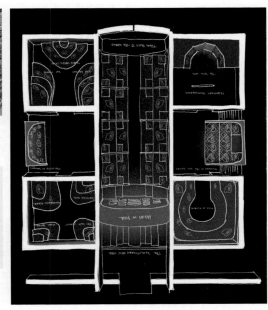

3218 The rooms take cues from Christian Dior's obsession with gardens and the taxonomy of the garden at Versailles. The result is a dramatic central space punctuated with bosquet-like rooms.

Dior: From Paris to the World

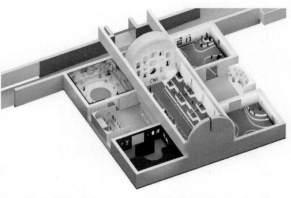

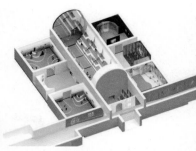

3220 The back wall of the barrel vault is a mirror that further enhances the length and loftiness of the space.

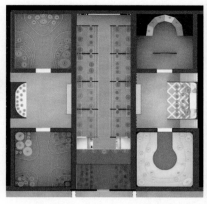

3219 Curatorial themes are re-sequenced for a new narrative of the retrospective and a number of themes are organized in relation to the museum context.

3221 After entering through the Revolutionary New Look, which marks the beginning of the brand, visitors are taken through a polycarbonate tunnel to then emerge at the dramatic reveal of the barrel vault midway through the exhibition.

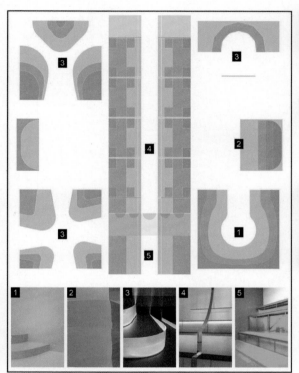

3222 Display platform topography

3223 As at the exhibition in Denver, the exhibition entry is a mirrored recreation of the Dior Paris atelier facade.

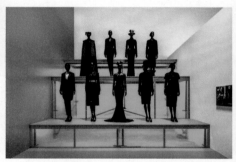

3224 The Revolutionary New Look is juxtaposed against a red polycarbonate and scrim background

3225 Office of Dreams is placed in a transept gallery, creating a relationship to the geometric Ellsworth Kelly sculpture in the adjacent courtyard.

3227 Total Look

3226 The seven creative director sections are housed in two rooms, on individual cascading platforms.

3228 Fields of Flowers features an abstract background of pink roses, with a gradient of pink tiered platforms highlighting the key color of Miss Dior.

3230 The reimagined barrel vault becomes a reversed catwalk where the positions of the spectator and the garments are flipped.

3229 Splendors of the XVIII Century is placed adjacent to the museum's permanent exhibition of European works.

3231 The barrel vault displays the exhibition's central theme, "From Paris to the World." The space is large enough to display the diverse range of Dior's garments continuously, providing visitors with a seamless narrative of the brand's cultural influences over time. Similar to the DAM exhibit, the methods of display are specific to their context, utilizing the architectural characteristics of the space to create a unique viewing experience.

3219–3231

Dior: From Paris to the World

Dior: From Paris to the World

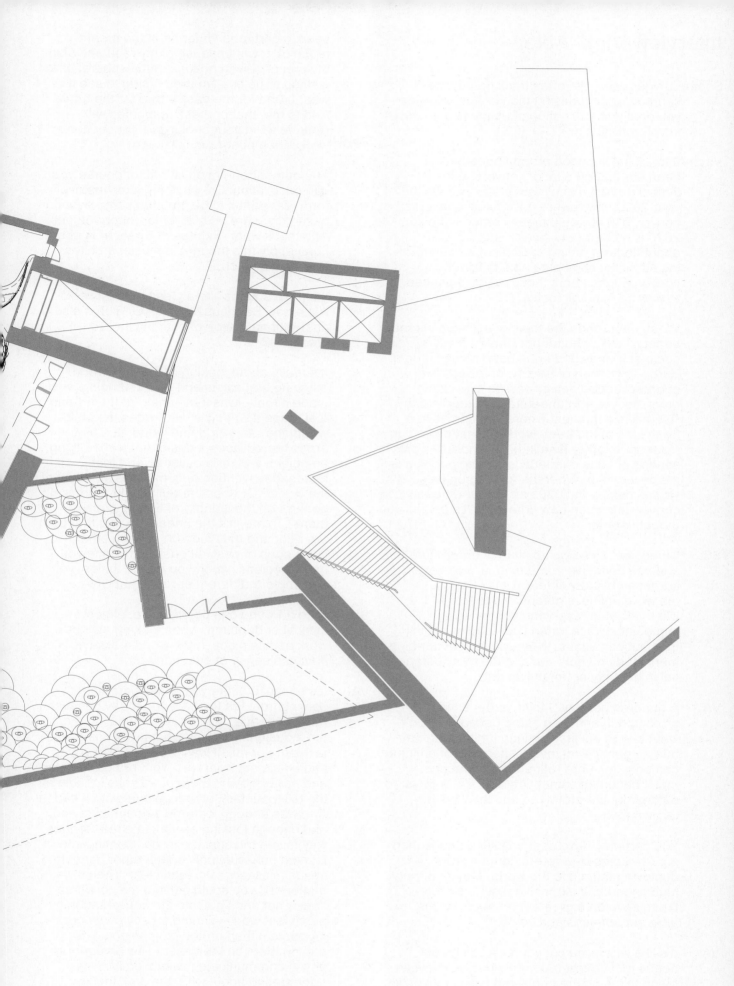

OMA NY   Dior: From Paris to the World

Interview Virgil Abloh

Shohei Shigematsu: We often think that ugliness can be more promising than beauty. How do you deal with the notion of ugliness or beauty in your production?

Virgil Abloh: That's a good prompt because I've been starting off a lot of conversations by almost putting a copyright stamp on "It's the year 2020." If we were having this conversation in 2019, it would mean something else. 2020 is a civil rights awakening. 2020 is about understanding capitalism, understanding ethnicity, and being able to have conversations about those topics that used to only be in small rooms.

When I approach the topic of ugliness verses beauty, I ask, who taught what? I think my circle of friends and I had been focusing on a European canon of beauty, of rationalism, of order... good design verses everything other, as a way to understand human hand. But this is a moment where you can have a fresh look at the framework of what makes up a canon. In other timelines, it's more like presenting an idea of beauty or ugliness to make it a new canon. Whereas, putting ugliness verses beauty in 2020 can trigger different conversations on new timelines. It's a thought starter.

SS: When you're designing clothes or furniture, and you conceive something, are you ever surprised by how different it is? For us, the word ugliness means unexpected. We think when everyone finds a design immediately nice, often it already exists in their subconscious. When we look at our blue foam study models, we see the most potential in the ugly or unfamiliar one.

VA: A hundred percent. I think about an idea, prototype it, and then I stop because I don't want to ruin my first instinct. I think that the human gesture on the first iteration of an idea can only get more refined, which means that it becomes something else. I'm always putting out the prototype and let it live on its own track.

SS: You certainly have been initiating and launching raw ideas in different domains and deploying them into the world. Maybe through high speed and extensiveness, the prototypes develop a greater presence across different domains and contexts.

VA: It's like when you cut yourself, the blood needs to hit oxygen before what we know as blood takes on the bright-red form that you've seen in cartoons. In terms of the creative realm of now—because of my race and also my preconceived notions of the spheres that I wanted to be in—I'm prototyping to see if what I read for the past is true for the future. And to me, that process resonates with Attitude #1 in your book ("pre-conception is worse than post-rationalization.")

The number one myth is that, of course you can post-rationalize anything into whatever form you want it to be, but that same equation has to measure up over different prototypes. And that's what "Figures of Speech" is about. I can apply this thought in music, architecture, and fashion.

SS: It almost sounds like a Gesamtkunstwerk, like a new Bauhaus thinking. Or is that also a post-rationalization of your instinctive creations?

VA: It's really about looking at the built world, anything that exists and understanding what made it that—was it the chair, or the iPhone that made it what it is. How does the built world, the real world, the world as a fact, arrive there? Does a designer invent a thing, an object, tool, or a building, and that manmade invention becomes the architect of the world? Or does the built world organically go through the laundry of time and arrive there? To me, it's the understanding that both are right and they feed off of each other, like a soup of post-rationalizing. Once you have that lens, when you create things, you can implore different parts of that DNA.

SS: I like how you can be objective, almost cynical or doubting, when looking at your work and its place in the world—always having a sense of questioning.

VA: It's because of the year I was born and coming from left field. I laugh today because I remember at a point an editor would not call me a designer or think what I was doing was fashion. For me, it was like—hey, I'm young and black, not from New York or Los Angeles and never moving there. It was like looking at the tall mountain, at architecture with a capital A. It was enough lectures, enough studying, and enough looking at work in a real serious way to see the space missed. Coming into fashion unassumingly on the other hand, that space missed was crystal clear. Then it was a matter of if you could get into the conversation or not and I got into the conversation by persistent work—finding out my own operating system then prototyping objects and putting them on the table. I saw an opportunity to communicate my subversive reformatting about what the architect is.

SS: I wish I had taken actions to doubts about the system of architecture myself.

VA: The only reason I have a voice is because I saw the smaller inconsistencies within the bigger picture. It was like looking closer at the grass to find the smaller interruptions while I was immersed in a generation that was looking up at the mountain.

SS: Now I understand why you went to fashion—it was more tangible to go through a smaller trail than to scale the big mountain.

VA: Eloquently put, exactly that. I was at IIT watching OMA's student center go up, sitting in a lecture about it. And of course, Michael Rock and the OMA team said—'okay, we're building this radical new student center and you guys are going to like it. It relates to Mies, whatever that is, so it's radical.' But then in the same sentence they said, 'Prada epicenters are going to be this and this is the rationale.' So I'm there thinking: fashion takes a hundred less hours, a hundred less days, and a hundred less people, to communicate an architectural idea to it being in the real world.

Then I was looking at the fashion industry and could see the generation that it wasn't speaking to. I could see the value from that generation bestowed on the practice, on the fashion designer. I could see that fashion was law. You say a name, Louis Vuitton or Gucci, and it almost supersedes the brand. It becomes a religion—is it real or is it made up? Of course it's real. 1854 is when Louis Vuitton made the innovation—the branded trunk and the monogram print.

He debuted it in Chicago, ironically, at the World's Fair. Trunks before then were like treasure chests. The top was curved and you couldn't stack them, so he made it flat and made a waterproof edge around it. The competitors started copying that so the trunk evolved—he made the innovation. He made a monogram print so that you could see it from afar and you knew that the right brand made that.

Fast forward to now, I was going to the Louis Vuitton store because rappers rapped about it and it was an aspirational thing. I was in architecture school and I would go to the store and buy a wallet or something. So you can feel how obvious it was for me to take what was happening and ask, how many buildings can I build in my lifetime with this much willingness to think, investigate, and prototype? And I thought of fashion as the generational hard-lined infrastructure to constantly communicate. It's like high-fi,

high-speed internet. In comparison to architecture it's a different practice, but I like to think my whole operating system of logic comes completely from architecture, the only formal training I had.

SS: You said something important here—that its infrastructure. How does your notion of fashion as infrastructure in a wider context of society reconcile with the commercial pressure to constantly regenerate and participate in a marketing cycle of brands like Off-White and Louis Vuitton?

VA: It's literally like an equation. Whatever you input greatly affects the output. In all of our creative industries, if you remove the "façade" of everyone's machine, it's the greatest story ever told. It's the common thread between all systems. Any work or product veers from relevant to irrelevant only once temporal constraints are imposed.

SS: The speed of fashion is then a byproduct of inputting the constantly shifting values and modes of contemporary times. Is that equation itself your idea of the zeitgeist?

VA: For me the zeitgeist is the broad term for what you input, which is formed by the internet, the algorithm, social media, travel, the political situation—either in a very apparent way or subconsciously. And the younger generation is in the driver's seat and responsible for that micro-trend or micro-blip. I was born in 1980 which gives me this before the internet, rational mind.

SS: Just in time [laughs].

VA: Just in time. If I were born ten years later, it would be a different story. We didn't have the things that my kids have now. Skateboarding stuck to me and a CD was music as a tangible object. But I also spent twenty years with an iPod and I remember the first one. So, I am aware of how an algorithm affects my own personal taste. I've seen the transition from when Google didn't exist to Google feeling like an honest transaction, to now, when I Google something and something I already like pops up on the screen. That perspective forms my zeitgeist about how the political world works, how we all work, and how humans are adapting. That's why the year 2020 is important.

But I'm also able to empathize and put myself in the shoes of different stratospheres of people. That's why Chicago is important. I live here for that very reason. It's not a cosmopolitan city. I'm not jaded by a scene. As soon as I walk outside there's not anyone

OMA NY

Virgil Abloh

who really knows a heightened experience of the work I do or what Louis Vuitton means, or what architecture is, or what "design" design is. So it's zeitgeist plus reality, but also keeping tabs on what are the amazing innovations that are happening, in the most capital letter sense of the word, Art and Architecture. Constantly zig-zagging across those different positions or frameworks provides me a personal zeitgeist.

SS: We think that the new zeitgeist, as an architect, is not necessarily delivering contemporary design but trying to create a new typology to capture the changing society. Architectural evolution, as you know, is very slow, but there are subtle changes. And as you say, 2020 will probably trigger some changes in human behavior and the way we understand or question the system of cities. But architecture has the luxury to be specific to each project—different client, different city, different program—so I never get bored. Your work inherently has a strong relationship to a wide consumer market. Is specificity important to you? If so, how do you embrace specificity in your work?

VA: I often take a step back and look at the broader picture and I look at it from the younger generation's perspective—we've been sold these brands, myths, and "facades." How I view my role to some extent is to be the guy that makes these big "facades" feel like there's a human behind there. It could be something as simple as someone looking at my Instagram to see and know there's rap music playing in the Louis Vuitton atelier. What that creates is a specificity.

When I look through the content in your book, the language is relevant. There's a line you can draw between familiar materials and forms that veer from the norm, which speaks to the common person's existing understanding but simultaneously subverts their idea of what a material should be used for and how it can embrace them. I think this is a parallel link to what I do with fashion or objects.

Sophia Choi: This book is an attempt to use a language that resonates with a younger generation that now understands architecture through social media platforms and search engines. But at the same time, this rapid mode of consumption maybe questions the relevance of the actual building. How do you communicate without diluting the complexities and context of the work?

VA: There's a language of reality and a language within high society. Before Y2K and the

internet was supposed to implode our real life, those two worlds were supposed to be forever separate. When I look at these spreads, the identity of OMA has moved closer toward the line of naturally occurring everyday language and that's a very big deal. It's almost the same as in fashion. I was putting a hoodie, a t-shirt, and jeans on a Parisian runway, which is very radical. But it actually comes from looking at the zeitgeist of the reality at the time. The heart of the fashion consumer was no longer just the fashion lady of 5th Avenue with the handbag. It was also the kid downtown on Canal Street trying to buy a Louis Vuitton hat. SoHo was an interesting mix, because one block off Canal it's bootleg, but then there's Supreme, that just sold for two billion dollars—out of the smallest retail footprint, selling skateboard clothes on a rack. Something had changed.

It's about speaking a language in a vernacular that doesn't just cater to high society but sustains value for both in ways that don't have to be congruent with each other. That's where the weight of this book comes into play and the weight of why architecture should be contemporary. You're not just making old buildings or basing the new off the old, but there's a provocative sensibility to have an effect on the current ecosystem without dismantling what came before. With my fashion, I used to get called a disruptor, which is funny. But in actuality, I'm trying to take the knowledge and practice of a previous generation and put it in a transistor so that a young generation knows that I'm trying to prop up the past.

SS: In architecture, there's definitely a growing demand to engage with a broader and more public audience across all typologies. But maybe finding a more specific demographic that we're losing touch with and responding to it can instigate some kind of evolution, as you are doing in fashion by creating a link for the younger generation and streetwear culture.

VA: There are people building a practice basically trying to unravel the value of a whole canon before you but we're humans and our nature is to evolve and build off the past.

SC: Is that kind of evolution you're pushing toward in fashion, effectively happening in architecture? Do you find that architecture today, the built environment, is effectively speaking to a new generation?

VA: I think that this book is like a crowbar. I often say that about my career. I make crowbars— literally tools to open stuff up with. I think architecture has been a genre to do exactly that, just as much as fashion. If you look at it in those terms, I left formal architecture to make architecture in a new costume called fashion. To your question, the way that the industry respects the past has traditionally held it back from being super agile—to speak the language of today. Though there are a few variables of architecture you can change and it starts being more at the eye level of people. This book is one, which is controlling the rhetoric around a material, a context, or even history.

But for me, the biggest variable that I changed was time, in terms of permanence. When I look at photos of the "Manus x Machina" exhibit in the book, I see the analysis of the existing architecture and the logic of the diagrams that then ultimately manifests itself in a new architecture, which has its own new system to look at fashion. It's temporary but anyone who went through the exhibit has now felt architecture and has felt the diagram. That's the realm that I operate in more so than my "fashion design." The fashion show is temporary architecture to me. It's again, about borrowing that logic of fashion as hyper infrastructure for communication and applying it to space.

SS: Ironically, in our fashion exhibitions the approach was to make the architecture less felt. But I agree, it's an interesting domain precisely because it pushes us to come up with new ways to look at fashion, but also enhance its narratives in a way that redefines the relationship between people and the exhibition space. It's also a relatively new domain that is becoming blockbuster content for museums. What do you make of how fashion exhibitions have recently emerged at the forefront of museum shows?

VA: On the macro scale, the idea of museum as civic space is something that we're working with in my practice. From a curatorial standpoint, it's the same as any other exhibition—how do we translate it to reflect the current generation? Ten years ago it could have been a Warhol show that would draw a fraction of the attendance today at the Met or my show "Figures of Speech." I think it says a lot about the change in times and society, just as much as it says about whatever work is being exhibited. It's interlaid with the question of, what is a museum supposed to be? Who is it catered for?

Then you have the forever tension—is fashion art? Is art fashion? That, to me is a bit tired. Those are hefty words. But the stumbling block isn't the object itself, it's the generation

coming to terms with something that they swore would never question. So are you trying to prop up a value system to keep things separate so that worlds stay the same? Or is the younger generation just going to bulldoze over these walls or make the whole thing irrelevant?

I think more of what we see today with museums is from the other side—the budget, attendance, and the blockbuster show. When "Figures of Speech" was at the High Museum in Atlanta, the attendance was so high that they didn't have to furlough one employee during the initial Covid lockdown. For a museum in this moment, what could have been done to make as much money to sustain a place? That to me, is the 3D thinking of architecture, versus the 1D thinking where the "proper artist" is there to just exhibit. A part of the "Figures of Speech" rationale was also the retail shop. Being honest about the museum gift shop. Could the exhibited items be in the shop and could the shop stuff be in the exhibit and is there a distinguishable part? It was making a total show. Putting the whole building in quotes is just the prototype.

SS: That show is quite diverse because it inherently reflects your personal modes and output across disciplines. For us, it was an interesting experience to first design "Manus x Machina," which was an investigation of techniques across multiple designers, brands, and timelines. Then we designed a retrospective for Dior which, as a fashion house with multiple creative directors, lends its own type of diversity to the content. But as an experience, the exhibition design had to express a continuous narrative through Dior. If you were asked to design a fashion exhibition for a singular brand, would you take a similar approach as you did for "Figures of Speech," or would that require a different approach of immersing yourself in the culture of that brand or entity?

VA: I would push it further. Like you said, these blockbusters are going to be the norm. For me, the fundamental problem with clothes is how they arrive in these spaces. It's very hard to make them feel different than in the retail environment. You always have this dilemma: mannequin or no mannequin, on the floor or on the table or in the air. Can you touch them? I always say that these objects aren't precious. I like to consider the theater of museums as well, like including the museum guards as a part of the exhibition. I think my future exploration in that realm will be more interactive—am I breaking the rules? Am I allowed to do that? I put the

OMA NY   Virgil Abloh

same chip in my head when thinking about a fashion collection.

SS: It seems like your architectural approach enables you to remove any boundaries between programs. What is then your current thinking of retail design? Do you see the role of retail changing to reflect changes in society? The Off-White stores are quite diverse and I get the sense that you're thinking about it programmatically but also with specificity to the different locations.

VA: Again, I'm "stamping" the year 2020 here, but it's important because of the current prevalence of the Starbucks model, where any location in the world you go to you're supposed to feel a familiar experience. In some ways, the Off-White stores are meant to be a counter culture to that.

SS: To globalization?

VA: Globalization, uniform experience. Another strong reference point of mine is a story from one of my mentors, the graphic designer Peter Saville. An important part of both of our careers was designing album covers. He told me the story about Joy Division's iconic cover, the cover with the line graphs on the front. He took that graphic from an art book and brought it to the meeting, showed it to the band, and they loved it. He said, "I didn't even do anything." It's my favorite analogy, and this is the logic of the Off-White stores that I found as a parallel—he asked the band 'ok, now we have the artwork, should we put your name on it?' And the band said 'no, that's not cool.' Then he asked, 'should we put the names of the songs?' and they said no. It was a series of questions that made the design. It ended up being iterations of under-designing. Then that cover becomes iconic because it didn't have anything else to throw it off. So for me, a large part of the Off-White stores don't have the name on it—I was undoing the Louis Vuitton or the big brand.

The Off-White store in Tokyo, behind Prada Aoyama, is technically called "Something and Associates" and its meant to be an office cubicle. My idea for retail in Tokyo comes from its history, and how the space shows up next to big brands that have a bigger budget. But also asking, what can I do in that square footage that makes it important? It was about not putting "Off-White" on it and calling it something else. Which ties into a more contemporary thought of mine, which is the power of cryptic-ness and not being literal.

SS: You manage to generate a new mode of communication and a platform for discourse within any context. Almost like place making but through communication that implores the gray areas. You use quotation marks to frame something with irony or a straightforwardness, which is similar to how we think about architecture program. We quite literally label section drawings with big bold text calling out the program because without that seemingly obvious label, no one can really tell what the space actually is for because it's quite generic.

But now, architecture is becoming highly programmed so we're interested in "unprogramming" aspects of a building. Do you think there's room in fashion to un-program things or make it ambiguous?

VA: I think the big question is what is true and false. What's ugly and what's beautiful? Then zooming into program, looking at a building with a roof deck at the top and retail at the bottom—my brain will explode trying to figure out what part of that "norm" is the truth. But asking these questions changes the output. OMA's graphic representation is a style of building a project. It's an internal office language for rationalizing and explaining. It's a style that's honored to your own, but more so it's a way of understanding in a new language.

That's why I use quotes. I started it as a means of being able to be cryptic, literal, and figurative at the same time. To me it was freedom, my own space. I don't have to say Off-White and it's running away from the branding of it into something less ambiguous. The best and worst thing you can do in fashion is brand. A shirt that says the name on it is valuable to the tourist and devalued to the purist. You don't want a Prada shirt with Prada on it but the one that sells the most is the one that says Prada on it. So you end up with this conundrum of the designer with a public facing role to make the brand cool, but also the internal role on the business side of production to not upset the brand. If you put the brand name on a t-shirt and that shirt then ends up being detrimental, it can kill a brand by making too much of what you don't want to see. That's when I came up with the 'tourist and purist' for the MCA show—how do I build on that? That idea, the exhibition, is like the looking glass to understand what fashion is—but you can apply it here to your book. What's admirable, especially [OMA NY's] work in the US, is that they all challenge. They all have a language that's not even consistent. But they all, at one level, to both the tourist and the purist, challenge some notion.

OMA NY   Virgil Abloh

SS: That's why it's called "Search Term." In a way, we're putting everything out on the table, so we can search ourselves by looking at a subconscious path. Do you find it strange that the firm is searching for its own identity?

VA: Like searching your own self? That's funny. To me, even just the concept of the book— OMA, New York—is its own canon. I would say that it's critical that you research yourself as a means to understand the logic that drives the firm. And to make your own book like this is marketing, but doing it in a way that's critical, with full knowledge of what you're doing and why, is another tier of it.

SS: We definitely have a penchant for self-analysis or self-criticism, which in itself is an interesting challenge because the book reveals a collective of individual voices, decisions, and representation across the different projects. This experiment feels appropriate especially in a moment when the whole world is searching for answers about the future or trying to define it. You often use the word renaissance, and it's been circulating during this crisis. How would you define it now? Do you feel a renaissance, or a movement where everyone is sharing artistic and intellectual ideas and redefining what came before?

VA: I've been using the word since before the Trump era and the disillusion of overt racial classism amplified by the internet. It always exists but there was a moment after year 2000 where kids realized they didn't need a white picket fence, get married after school, work, have a kid. They just needed a passport and they were free to break the notion of the 9 to 5. That's when I started saying my generation is a new renaissance.

With the turbulence in the last four years— Brexit in the UK and Trump at the same time brought issues like overt racism that previous generations had to overcome back to the surface. The reckoning has changed contemporary society. I think we need to get back on track and get further out to dictate what happens in the years to come. But the word renaissance is applicable, because I'm inspired by the social change that's happened. I am having conversations internally within Off White and Louis Vuitton, and my community of artists who are great young provocateurs. What are we making? What are the art exhibits? What new buildings are coming off? What did we take back in the protests? Who is in a position of power that rose from the unrest? Who is the new photo editor at Vogue? If all that was for nothing, that to me is the most frustrating part. It should be a renaissance with more

voices and it takes a particular set of chess pieces to really make sure that the next years head in the right direction. My career is basically to show and prove that collaboration is ok. Louis Vuitton made the radical move by putting me in Paris three years before 2020. I hold the values of the house. I didn't come in and make t-shirts, and that is so that when they think about the future they now know they don't have to do what they always did in the past because now we have an example on paper that showcases it's not dangerous. It doesn't upset the flow.

Virgil Abloh is an artist, architect, and fashion designer with an interdisciplinary practice. He founded Off-White in 2012 and is the artistic director of Louis Vuitton's menswear collection since 2018. He obtained a master's degree in Architecture at the Illinois Institute of Technology.

OMA NY   Virgil Abloh

3233

The Plaza at Santa Monica

The Plaza at Santa Monica

The rise in the mixed-use typology is one byproduct of urbanization, in which stacking a variety of programs into a hermetic box for efficiency felt like a necessity. While this model can be seen as a way to provide an experience of multiple entities within a single building—as in a city—capitalizing on mixing as a virtue has alarmingly become the norm.

Our hypothesis is that the mixed-use will be prosaic. Paradoxically, a market economy is now pushing for maximum efficiency of individual programs, and packing them into a singular container has started to become somewhat counterproductive because each program has its own ideal, efficient form. By surrendering to the market pressure of individual programs, can we create an architecture that truly cultivates a new potential and expression of the mix?

Our approach for The Plaza at Santa Monica is to make the unknown from the known. An "ideal" volume per program—retail, residential, office, and hotel—is created based on the developer's standard dimensions per pro-forma. The resulting volume bars appear the same, but are slightly different based on the optimal organization for their respective programs. Each bar is perfect in its own way, but the way they are stacked and arranged creates a new, horizontal gesture. This stacking manages to make more open space than the site itself and provides vertically continuous amenities that embrace Santa Monica's culture of inside and outside living.

The building contributes to Santa Monica's diverse network of public spaces, from the recreational plazas at the Santa Monica Pier and Palisades Park to contained commercial centers like Third Street Promenade and Santa Monica Place. We wanted each program volume to have its own distinct open spaces, terraces, and plazas. What would be a single, vertical building facing a plaza is unhinged and a cascade of programs offers a new public realm—a stepped building that achieves a strong interaction between interior program and exterior environments.

The angled placement of the bars creates dynamic relationships to the surrounding streets. A large plaza facing Arizona Avenue provides flexibility for year-round outdoor events, from a farmer's market to an ice skating rink. Smaller wedge-shaped plazas on

Fourth and Fifth streets and covered areas around the building offer more intimate open spaces. The multiple scales and characters of open spaces on all sides of the building maximize the potential of the super block. On top of the retail bar that defines the plazas is an outdoor terrace that overlooks the public activities below.

The pivoting positions of the program bars create a central zone on the ground floor for a special program. Within, a cultural venue is embedded into the heart of the building, with street-level access and a dedicated park. Together, the ground-level plaza and elevated terraces provide an additional 56,500 square feet of programmable open space compared with the original site.

At the intersection of each bar is a programmatic hinge that acts as an interface between the specific programs. Each hinge responds to the needs of the two different programs that it connects, while providing a space where people meet and activities mix together.

In June 2021, after eight years of design iterations, environmental impact assessments, and a series of community and council meetings, the Santa Monica City Council voted to overturn the decision to proceed with the project. Santa Monicans deemed the intensity of the mixed-use unnecessary for their village-like city of low density. The mixed-use is a symbol of urban density but, contrarily, our premise was to provide more open space for the city's unique outdoor beach culture. We attempted to make the unknown but the unknown was unfamiliar and unwanted.

Location	Santa Monica, CA, USA		
Status	Unbuilt, 2013–2021		
Typology	Re-Mixed Use		
Program	Office	172,000 ft²	16,000 m²
	Hotel	127,000 ft²	11,800 m²
	Residential	86,000 ft²	8,000 m²
	Public space	56,500 ft²	5,250 m²
	Retail	40,000 ft²	3,700 m²
	Services	11,000 ft²	1,000 m²
	Total Area	492,500 ft²	45,750 m²

OMA NY   The Plaza at Santa Monica

3234

The Plaza at Santa Monica

3235

The Plaza at Santa Monica

OMA NY   The Plaza at Santa Monica

3236

The Plaza at Santa Monica

OMA NY

The Plaza at Santa Monica

3237

The Plaza at Santa Monica

3238　Santa Monica and the Greater Los Angeles area

3239　Between the mountains and the ocean, Santa Monica sits on top of a natural plateau at the edge of the continent. Due to its prime location along the water and proximity to Los Angeles, the city was developed as a port-terminus for the Los Angeles and Independence Railroad in the late 1800s and prospered as an ocean-side resort town.

3240　Santa Monica Pier (2014)

3241　Santa Monica Beach

3242　Downtown Santa Monica (1875)

3243　Promotional photo for Santa Monica beach in the early 1920s.

3244　The city boasts views toward both the ocean and the mountains.

3245　Santa Monica Mountains

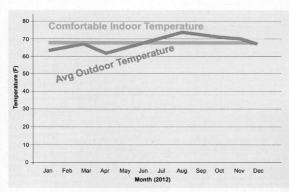

3246　With minimal annual variation between outdoor and indoor temperatures, Santa Monica's temperate climate enables a comfortable indoor/outdoor lifestyle.

3247　Beach camping in 1887, an early example of indoor/outdoor culture.

3248　Bathhouses, like the North Beach Bath House (pictured, 1894), provided amenities for seaside visitors to enjoy changing facilities, showers, and heated pools year-round.

3249　Arcadia Bath House (1887)— bathhouses, many of which were located just steps from the beach, became representative of the region's indoor/ outdoor lifestyle.

3250　Meeting of building and landscape

3251　The city and landscape are juxtaposed in a way that creates a unique urban environment.

3252　Meeting of landscape and city

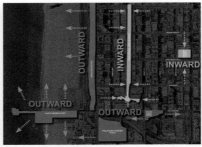

3254 Existing network of open spaces, both outward-facing and inward-facing

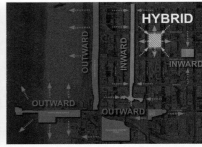

3255 The site represents a potential hybrid open space.

3256 Outward-facing open space—Santa Monica Pier

3257 Outward-facing open space—Palisades Park

3258 Inward-facing open space—Third Street Promenade

3253 The site of the Plaza at Santa Monica is located near downtown Santa Monica's diverse network of open space, from the pier to Palisades Park to the Third Street Promenade. It presents an opportunity to expand on this network.

3259 Site view from 5th Street

3260 Site view from the intersection of Arizona Avenue and 4th Street

3261 The site sits at the boundary of Santa Monica's tourist-friendly commercial heart and its unique residential area.

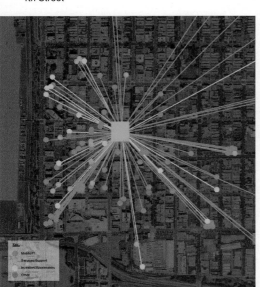

3262 In addition to its geographic advantages, Santa Monica has the highest concentration of creative individuals in the United States, and has become a prime destination for entrepreneurship and the tech sector.

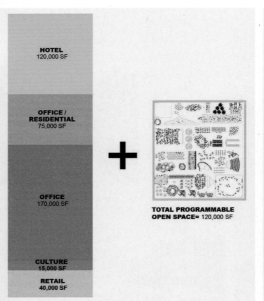

HOTEL 120,000 SF

OFFICE / RESIDENTIAL 75,000 SF

OFFICE 170,000 SF

CULTURE 15,000 SF

RETAIL 40,000 SF

+

TOTAL PROGRAMMABLE OPEN SPACE= 120,000 SF

3263 Comprised of retail, cultural programming, office and residential spaces, and a hotel, the Plaza at Santa Monica will host programs that mix and foster the city's unique creative capital and entrepreneurial spirit, while allowing flexibility for future evolution.

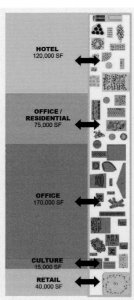

HOTEL 120,000 SF

OFFICE / RESIDENTIAL 75,000 SF

OFFICE 170,000 SF

CULTURE 15,000 SF

RETAIL 40,000 SF

3264 The main ambition of the project is to preserve open space at the heart of Santa Monica's culture and make sure each program maximizes engagement with outdoor areas.

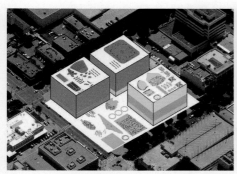

3265 In the city of Santa Monica's visioning scenario, buildings and open space are separate entities, isolating some building areas from the open space.

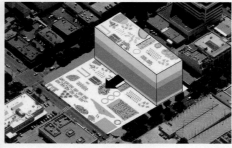

3266 A more radical binary relationship between building and Plaza will isolate the open space from the upper levels of the building. How can the building be designed to bring accessible open space to all of the program parts?

3267 Study models

3270 Open space scoops

3271 Scoops for views and pedestrian activity

3272 Stacked masses with multiple terraces

3273 Center pivot

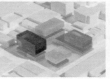

3268 Lifted buildings

3269 Multi-scale plazas

3274 Central voids and perimeter terraces

3275 Porous terraces

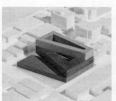

3276 Shifted frames

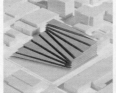

3277 Sweeping terraces

3278 We took inspiration from the Hanging Gardens of Babylon. Legend holds that the king built them for his wife, who missed the mountainous landscape of her homeland.

3279 Compared to the Tower of Babel, which was a monument to the sky, the Hanging Gardens were a monument to the ground, literally covered by the landscape.

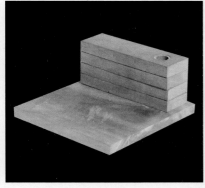

3280 The approach to the development is a celebration of indoor-to-outdoor culture—rather than isolating the building and plaza as separate entities, the design should integrate the two and thereby multiply the number of exchange opportunities for indoor/outdoor continuity.

3281 The proposal is deployed as a series of block-length bars that step up from Arizona Avenue to the southern edge of the site.

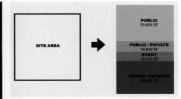

3282 Diversity of outdoor space

3283 Site area

3284 Typical plinth-and-plaza condition

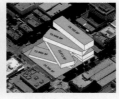

3285 The elevated terraces provide a greater amount of open space than the site area would normally allow.

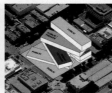

3286 A variety of open space types, determined by their program adjacency

3287 Instead of following the typical plinth-and-plaza condition, the form creates four elevated terraces that span the width of the lot and overlook a public plaza along Arizona Avenue. Each block—retail and culture on the ground floor, office and mixed office/residential blocks above, and hotel at the top—has its own outdoor terrace. The resulting volume is not a monolithic mass but a dynamic elevation permeable to Santa Monica's unique light and air qualities.

The Plaza at Santa Monica

3289 Final concept model—northeast (5th and Arizona)

3288 The form, composed of staggered blocks, allows all of the building programs to spill out onto adjacent elevated terraces, embodying Santa Monica's indoor/outdoor lifestyle.

3290 The mass sets back to a slender bar at the top, maintaining an urban presence that adds to the city's icons while respecting its skyline.

3291 The project's main approach from the Third Street Promenade is anchored by a flexible open space that can be used year-round.

3292 Final concept model—Arizona elevation

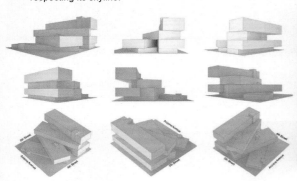

3293 Form rotation

3294 The building's mass steps back toward the south as it rises, framing the plaza along Arizona. On the ground floor, the plaza is framed on one side by retail and a market hall. A spiraling stair allows access to the first terrace, which is open to the public.

3295 One can see every program and open space cascade down toward the plaza.

3296 The form and scale of the building respond to both the mountainous side of Santa Monica and the lower beach side.

3297 The Plaza at Santa Monica aims to create a community destination as well as a central gateway to Santa Monica from the broader region.

3288–3297

The Plaza at Santa Monica

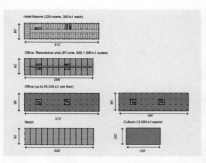

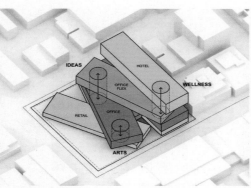

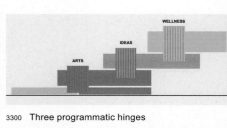

3300　Three programmatic hinges

3298　In addition to the core concept of optimizing public space, the form also ensures that every program is efficiently designed. The dimensions of each block are fine-tuned per programmatic element with maximum flexibility.

3299　Individual blocks are connected via three distinct programmatic hinges, each dedicated to exchange between different programs.

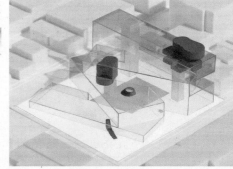

3301　Study model—programmatic hinges as connectors

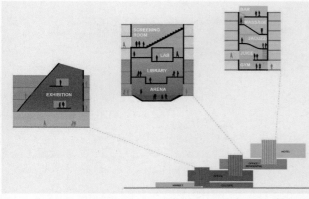

3302　At the intersection of the cultural space and office floors, an Arts Hinge creates new vantage points for large-scale exhibition and connection. At the intersection of the office and residential levels, an Ideas Hinge is dedicated to the testing, presentation, and exchange of ideas. Where hotel and office/residential programs meet, a Wellness Hinge is dedicated to health, fitness, and nutrition and culminates in the rooftop bar.

3303　Ideas Hinge model

3304　While the mass of the building creates a strong impact on the skyline, the terraces extend the surrounding small grain of the city onto the building by a series of pavilions and amenities.

3305　Geographical scale of the bluffs and its surrounding buildings above and below

3306　Urban scale of downtown Santa Monica

3307　Intimate scale of the surrounding neighborhoods

3308　By supporting a smaller scale of buildings on its terraces, the building operates at two scales—an urban scale and an intimate, more human scale.

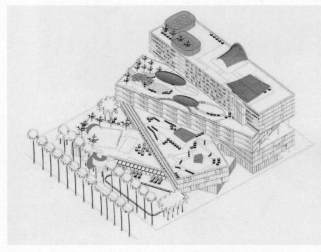

3309　The terrace pavilions act as architectural follies that respond to specific purposes—a spiraling stair to connect the ground-floor plaza to the second-floor terrace, a band shell and a lunch cafe on the second-floor terrace, a shading device on the hotel lobby terrace, and a gondola station on the rooftop.

3310　Arts Hinge atrium as folly

3311　Bandshell pavilion on F2 terrace

　　　The Plaza at Santa Monica

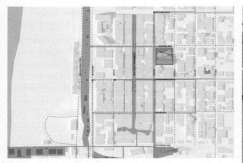

3312 The building also ties into the network of downtown's open spaces, and lifts them vertically to new vantage points.

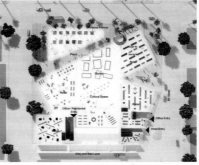

3313 F1 model—plaza, retail, and cultural space

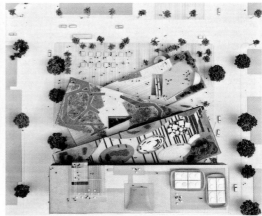

3314 Roof plan with landscaped terraces and pavilions

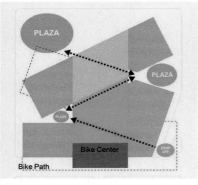

3315 Pedestrian flow through the ground level is anchored by a series of smaller plazas.

3316 The F1 plaza is the most flexible and public open space and expands the project into the community.

3317 Aerial view of terraces and ground level plaza

3318 Plaza activation

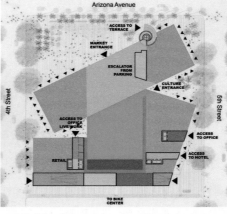

3319 Building access from ground-level plazas

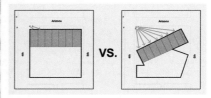

3320 Pedestrians access the site from the commercial heart of downtown, the Third Street Promenade. The retail facade is thus rotated to face oncoming pedestrian flow, exposing storefronts more than it would if the facade aligned with Arizona.

3321 The plaza facing Arizona Avenue offers 20,000 square feet of open space.

3322 Plaza programming scenarios—an embedded system can easily shift from a summer fountain to a winter skating rink, or to a dry plaza that can host concerts or markets.

3323 Plaza as ice rink

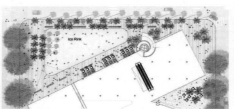

3325 F1 plan—integrated ice rink on the plaza

3326 Plaza view from 4th Street

3324 Indoor food and market hall

3328 Utilization of the facade for cultural festival projections

3327 The plaza also functions as a venue for cultural events, like Santa Monica's Glow Festival.

3329 Aerial view of the plaza and terraces

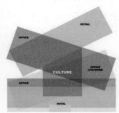

3330 A 12,000-square-foot cultural space lies at the heart of the ground floor, with access to the programmable outdoor spaces as well as a dedicated entry at the pocket park on 5th Street.

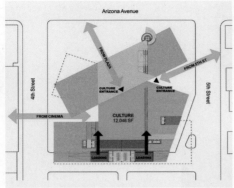

3331 Access points to the central cultural space from 4th Street, Arizona Avenue plaza, and 5th street

3332 Programming of the cultural space can spill out into the plaza along 5th Street.

3333 Culture at the heart of the building

3334 Cultural space scenario as a children's museum

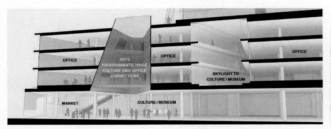

3335 The Arts Hinge vertically connects the culture and office bars and encourages interaction between the two.

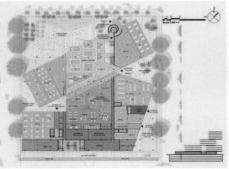
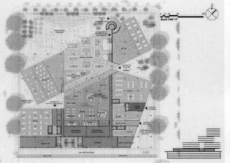

3336 F1 plan—circulation and flow create a porous condition throughout ground-level retail and cultural programs.

3337 Cultural space scenario as an arts institution

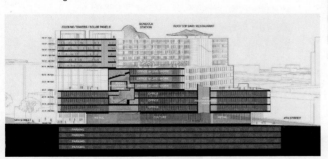

3338 Section through F1 cultural space and Arts Hinge

3341 On the office floors, bridges on F2 and F3 cross through the atrium, providing visual connections to the cultural space below and to the sky above.

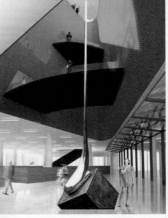

3340 The Arts Hinge atrium creates a dramatic moment at the meeting point of the cultural space and the market on the F1 level. This space poses a unique opportunity for art installations and aims to provide a memorable experience for pedestrians crossing through the building.

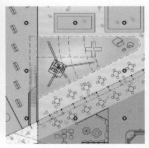

3342 On F1, the Arts Hinge manifests itself as a four-story-high atrium that channels natural light into the cultural space.

3339 Potential uses for the ground floor cultural space include areas for art production, education, and a children's museum.

3327–3342   The Plaza at Santa Monica

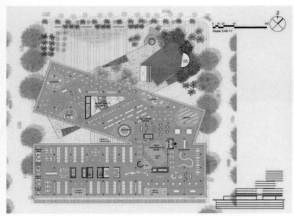

3344 The F2 terrace is open to the public and can be accessed from the ground-floor plaza. This terrace also connects to the F2 office space, providing a place of exchange within the community.

3343 F2–4 have large floorplates and a 30 by 30–foot structural grid that respond to the downtown's need for large office areas. The building's unique indoor/outdoor attitude, abundant access to outdoor landscaped terraces, and the flexibility afforded by the structural grid make it a prime office space for many kinds of office typologies—from more conventional corporate headquarters to creative and entrepreneurial offices.

3345 Office meeting room

3346 The interior of the F2 office break area opens up to the terrace level, blurring the line between indoors and outdoors.

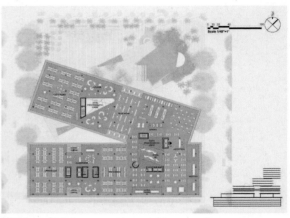

3347 The floorplate can be configured in a multitude of ways to meet various workspace needs—from casual to more formal.

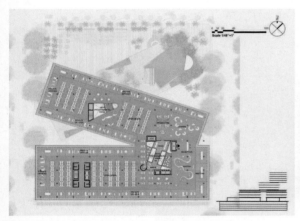

3348 A more efficient layout is also possible to accommodate a conventional corporate fit-out.

3349 The office terrace is essentially an extension of the workplace, allowing users to meet, work, and socialize outdoors.

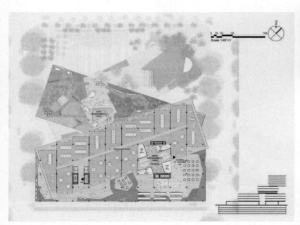

3350 F5–7 are thinner 90-foot-wide floorplates that can be subdivided into smaller offices, live/work spaces, or even residential units if the downtown market so demands. These floors spill out on the F5 terrace to the north and a large covered terrace to the south.

3351 The F5 South Terrace is a covered space that can host large events, such as banquets, and can be used by both the office and the hotel.

3352 The Terrace provides ample indoor and outdoor areas for reception and gathering.

3353 In the daytime, the same F5 South Terrace can be transformed into a work space or social space.

3354 The expansive terrace adds porosity to the building, creating openness toward downtown Santa Monica.

3343–3354   The Plaza at Santa Monica

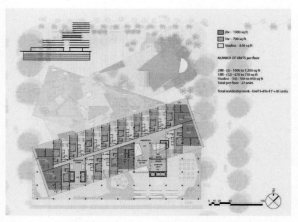

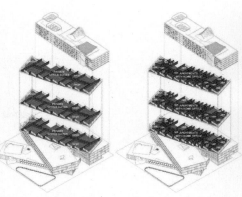

3356 F5–7 axonometric view of office to live/work transformation

3357 East view from 5th Street

3358 Detail model view of office and terrace

3355 F5–7 can easily be transformed from an office to a live/work floorplan without modifying the structure or facade.
This allows the building to respond easily to changes in downtown Santa Monica over time.

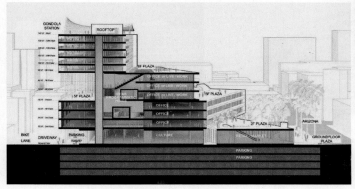

3359 Section through the Ideas Hinge

3360 Final concept model—west elevation

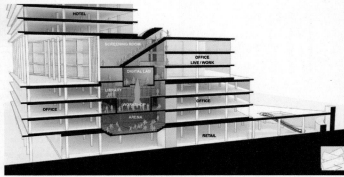

3361 Connecting the various office and residential tenants, the Ideas Hinge is a stack of spaces dedicated to testing, experimenting, and building. A series of workshops, a screening room, and a presentation space interlock, creating double-height spaces in between that visually connect the different offices.

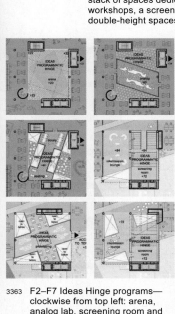

3363 F2–F7 Ideas Hinge programs— clockwise from top left: arena, analog lab, screening room and lounge, screening room and lounge (lower level), prototyping studio, library.

3364 Southeast view

3365 Ideas Hinge model

3362 A library in the Ideas Hinge is shared by various office and residential tenants and fosters creative research and interaction.

3355–3365   The Plaza at Santa Monica

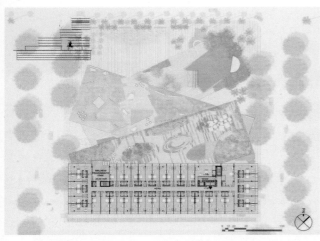

3366 F8–12 house a 225-room hotel with unobstructed views of the city, beach, and mountains.

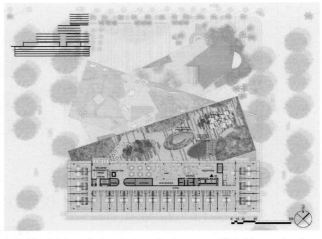

3367 The hotel overlooks a lush garden terrace on F8 that is an extension of its lobby and bar.

3368 The hotel lobby spills out onto the adjacent terrace, creating a more inviting environment than the typical interior hotel lobby.

3369 The terrace extends the lobby's activities, providing guests with views of both the ocean and the mountains.

3370 All of the hotel rooms have balconies and operable windows.

3371 Hotel room view with balconies and operable windows, taking advantage of Santa Monica's exceptional weather.

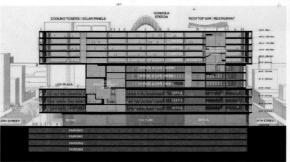

3372 Section through Wellness Hinge

3373 Wellness Hinge view looking down to the gymnasium

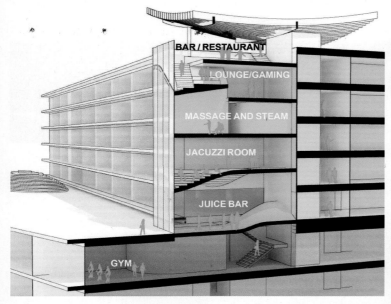

BAR / RESTAURANT

LOUNGE/GAMING

MASSAGE AND STEAM

JACUZZI ROOM

JUICE BAR

GYM

3374 The Wellness Hinge supports the hotel levels fully and the office tenants partially. A series of interconnected floors house a gym, spas, and a breakfast station, and culminate in a rooftop bar.

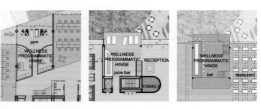

3375 Wellness Hinge plans—from left to right: F7, F8, F13

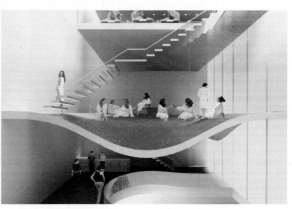

3376 The vertical stack of wellness spaces is located on the facade and is flooded with natural light as it leads up to the roof.

The Plaza at Santa Monica

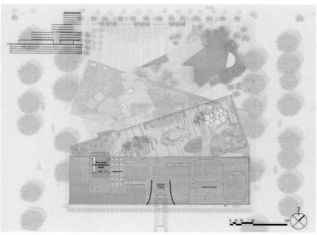
3377 F13 rooftop amenities

3378 Aerial view of model

3379 The rooftop terrace has a pool that seamlessly connects with a view toward the beach.

3380 Model view of rooftop pool and bar

3381 Historic Ocean Skyway on the pier

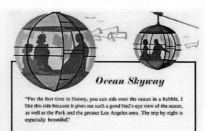
3382 Ocean Skyway advertising

Ocean Skyway

"For the first time in history, you can ride over the ocean in a bubble. I like this ride because it gives me such a good bird's-eye view of the ocean, as well as the Park and the greater Los Angeles area. The trip by night is especially beautiful!"

3383 Taking a cue from Santa Monica's historic Ocean Skyway, which operated along the pier until 1966, the building could potentially receive the landing of a gondola connecting the rooftop to the Expo Line station.

3384 The Expo Line (now E Line) follows the historic railroad right-of-way of the Los Angeles and Independence Railroad. Opened in 2016, the long-awaited public transit route reconnected downtown Los Angeles to Santa Monica. The rooftop gondola could connect the building to the Expo Line as well as to the pier and parking stations on Lincoln Boulevard. It would offer transportation alternatives, as well as spectacular views of Santa Monica.

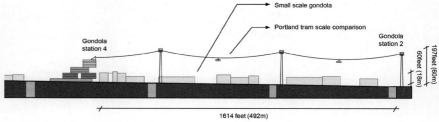

3385 The uppermost terrace could then become the terminus of an elevated experience of the city that would further add to the public nature of the elevated plaza.

3386 Gondola departure

3387 Southwest view

3388 The landscape for the open spaces was designed by OLIN.

3389 Landscape concept model

3390 The landscaping of the building is influenced by the layers and strata of Santa Monica's regional diversity.

3391 The building itself becomes an integrated component of the city's urban and natural landscapes.

3392 The plaza and terrace levels have distinct physical characteristics, ranging from urban park to lush vegetation to a water landscape.

3393 Layers of landscape elements and their program counterparts

3394 The plant material selected for this project represents a diversity of vegetation, both native and adapted, to provide habitats and promote biodiversity.

3395 Irrigation requirements are tailored to meet the project goal of LEED Silver certification or surpass it.

3396 The building's design inherently suggests an attitude regarding sustainability. The stepped form allows for green roofs, and every terrace is at least partially landscaped.

3399 Solar exposure

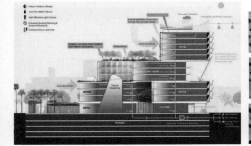

3397 Terraces are also irrigated with treated gray water from the building.

3398 The mass is highest at the southeast, ensuring that the sidewalks and plazas enjoy maximum amounts of sunlight during peak hours of use.

The Plaza at Santa Monica

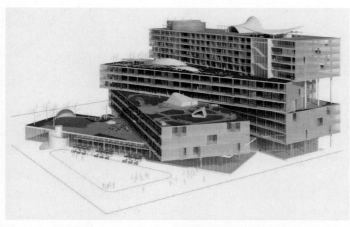

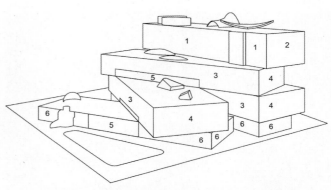

3401 Facade types—1. Hotel, folding glass doors; 2. Hotel, folding glass doors and external shutters; 3. Office, sliding glass doors; 4. Office, sliding glass doors and external shutters; 5. Garage doors; 6. Retail storefront

3400 The facade is both pragmatic (simple systems that span from slab to slab) and radical (blurring the boundary between interior and exterior). In all cases except the ground floor, the envelope is recessed. This creates a 4-foot-deep balcony around the perimeter of each floor. Perforated operable screens on the ends of the bars reinforce the reading of a frame.

3382 Closed office facade

3403 Open office facade

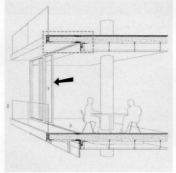

3404 1. Sliding glass door, open position; 2. glass balustrade; 3. sliding glass door, recessed sill

3405 Closed facade

3406 Open facade—almost every part of the facade is operable; the building can become "outdoors."

3407 Hotel facade

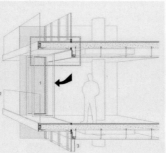

3408 1. Folding glass door, open position; 2. glass balustrade; 3. curtain

3409 External shutters

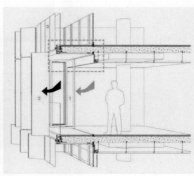

3410 1. Folding glass door, open position; 2. Folding shutter, open position; 3. Folding shutter, closed position

3411 External shutters

3413 West elevation—4th Street

3414 East elevation—5th Street

3416 South elevation

3412 Facade model

3415 North elevation—Arizona Avenue

The Plaza at Santa Monica

3417 Animation stills

3418 Santa Monica site and beach

3419 Program bars

3420 Stacked programs

3421 Hinged bars and terraces

3422 Ground level programs

3423 Entry points

3424 Landscaped terraces

3425 F2 terrace

3426 Spiral staircase from F1 to F2

3427 Arts Hinge

3428 Ideas Hinge

3429 Wellness Hinge

3430 Rooftop terrace

3431 View from 4th Street

3432 View up into the Arts Hinge

3433 External shutters

3434 View from Arizona Avenue

3435 Plaza at Arizona Avenue

3436 Indoor market hall

3437 Bridges in the Arts Hinge atrium

3438 5th Street pocket park

3439 F2 terrace

3440 Ideas Hinge

3441 Ideas Hinge arena

3442 F2 bridge through Arts Hinge

3443 Indoor/outdoor space

3444 Great Lawn on the F2 terrace

3445 Aerial view from east

3446 Arts Hinge folly

3447 F8 Hotel lobby/lounge

3448 Folding glass doors

3449 View into the Wellness Hinge

3450 Rooftop terrace and pool

3451 View toward Pacific Ocean

3452 The Plaza at Santa Monica

3417–3452

The Plaza at Santa Monica

3453   Design workshop (2013)

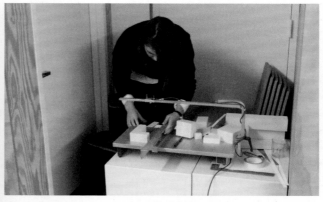

3454   Design workshop (2013)—Caroline Corbett produces new massings in real time.

3455   Design workshop (2013)

3456   Design workshop (2013)

3457   Design workshop (2013)

3458   Shohei Shigematsu presents at a public hearing in 2014.

3459   Public hearing (2014)—Shohei presenting

3460   Public hearing (2014)

3461   Because of the public nature of the project and the large impact it would have in the community of Santa Monica, we had to work closely with city and community stakeholders, meeting with them frequently throughout the design process.

3462   Public hearing—Shohei explaining the model to a Santa Monica resident

3463   Neighborhood meeting presentation (2020)

3453–3463

The Plaza at Santa Monica

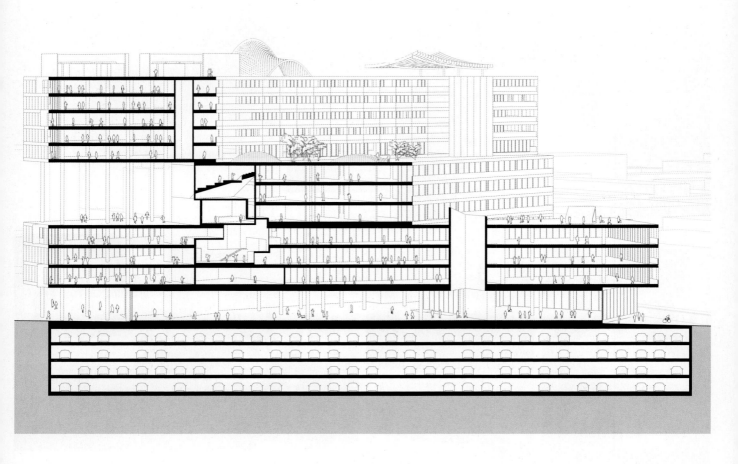

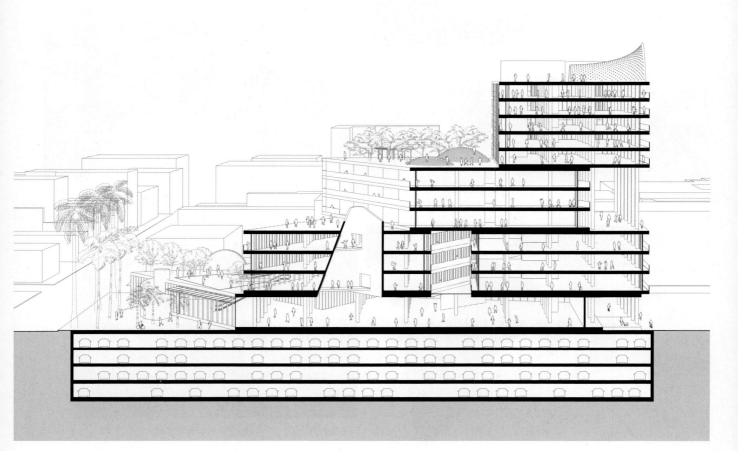

The Plaza at Santa Monica

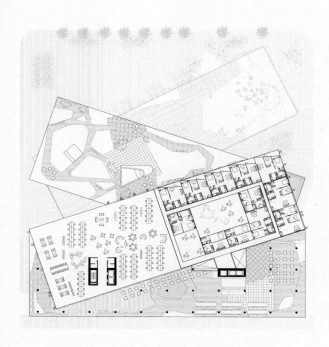

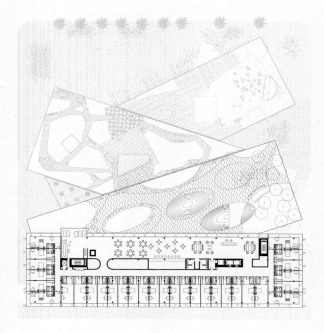

The Plaza at Santa Monica

Tenjin Business Center

OMA's only built project in Japan up until 2012 can be found in Fukuoka. The Nexus World Housing complex was completed more than twenty-five years ago. Local developer Fukuoka Jisho commissioned Arata Isozaki to develop a masterplan that introduces a "new urban lifestyle," for which OMA was invited as one of six architects to design a freestanding housing block.

Fukuoka is the seventh biggest city in Japan, known for its distinct cultural identity. Its central location among major cities of East Asia positions the city as a gateway into Japan, contributing to its standing as the economic center of Kyushu Island. The city has been thriving over the last decade, ranking highly in livability, ratio of younger population, and percentage of start-ups.

Following the Nexus World Housing complex, Tenjin Business Center signals a newfound ambition for urban renewal and growth. It also marks the next generation of collaboration between OMA, the city of Fukuoka, and Fukuoka Jisho. We believe this project was made possible by the fortuitous alignment of three people of the same generation—Shohei Shigematsu, a Fukuoka native; Ichiro Enomoto, the new CEO of Fukuoka Jisho (son of Kazuhiko Enomoto, former CEO who commissioned Nexus World Housing); and mayor Soichiro Takashima.

Tenjin Business Center will be the first development under the mayor's Tenjin Big Bang initiative to stimulate the district's formation as an Asian business hub and startup city. We wanted to create a building that is not just a symbol of success but also an incubator and space for discourse that harnesses the energy and activities of the neighborhood. How can we make an office building that suggests a new generation and reflects Fukuoka's existing urban context?

The site is located at the intersection of two major axes: Meiji-dori—the city's established avenue of commerce lined with financial offices—and Inabacho-dori—an organic pedestrian corridor linked to the City Hall Plaza and Galleria and lined with intimate cafes. Below ground, the site connects to a subway station and shopping concourse. The building program is predominantly workspace, within a given massing that is neither low-rise nor tower.

Office buildings are often quite sober and withdrawn from public life. The introverted typology internalizes its atriums and lobbies, shrouding its best assets. Our approach was to excavate the facade on the corner of Meiji-dori and Inabacho-dori to articulate the convergence of two different urban activities. This gesture enhances two conditions simultaneously—they reveal the internal activity of the office and draw in public activity at the new entry plaza.

Within the carved out corner is a six-story atrium that reinforces the inside/outside visual connection and draws natural light down to the lower-level concourse linked to the area's underground pedestrian, retail, and transit network. The excavation is calibrated as three-dimensional pixels that break down the building to a human scale. The pixelated facade forms a series of soffit surfaces above, activated with signage and lighting that reinforce a sense of place at the convergence point.

Setbacks at the opposing upper level provide green terraces for offices. In respect to the nature in the city, we symbolically introduce terraces with panoramic views to the often-overlooked Naka River and Hakata Bay. Together, the two pixelated edges round out the building to create a sense of softness like that of a melting ice cube.

The eroded corners soften the edge between the public domain and the private office building, generating an openness for the activity along Fukuoka's main civic and commercial thoroughfares. As the first development in the Tenjin Big Bang initiative, we wanted it to set a precedent for the adjacent buildings to come—activated intersections and plazas at each building creating a network of public zones that knit the new district together.

Location	Fukuoka, Japan		
Status	Completed, 2021		
Typology	Re-Mixed Use		
Program	Office	494,600 ft²	45,950 m²
	Financial Services	98,100 ft²	9,110 m²
	Retail	21,300 ft²	1980 m²
	Parking	26,300 ft²	2,440 m²
	Total Area	640,300 ft²	59,480 m²

3471

Tenjin Business Center

3472

Tenjin Business Center

OMA NY

Tenjin Business Center

3473

Tenjin Business Center

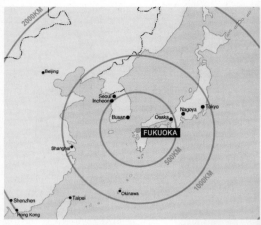

3474   Fukuoka is Japan's seventh largest city and is centrally located among major cities in East Asia.

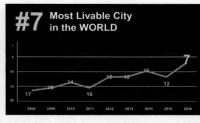

#7 Most Livable City in the WORLD

3475   In the past ten years, Fukuoka has consistently ranked in the top twenty global cities for livability.

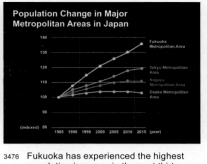

Population Change in Major Metropolitan Areas in Japan

3476   Fukuoka has experienced the highest population increase in the past thirty years compared with other major Japanese cities.

GDP / GRP per capita
Fukuoka vs Major Global Capitals

3477   In terms of GDP/GRP per capita, the city is comparable with other global metropolitan capitals.

3-4 Function-Specific Ranking

Fukuoka ranked higher than Tokyo in livability

3480   Livability ranking (2017)

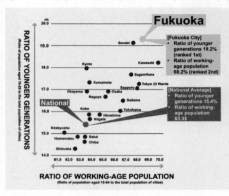

3478   Fukuoka also leads the way in growth rate for younger generations and the working-age population.

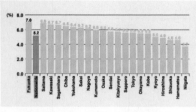

3479   In 2015, Fukuoka had the highest percentage of start-ups in major urban areas of Japan, significantly higher than Tokyo.

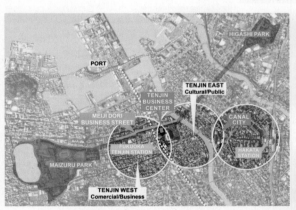

3482   The site of Tenjin Business Center is located at the intersection of three different areas with distinct characters. Centered around Fukuoka Tenjin Station, Meiji-dori, and Watanabe-dori, the business and commercial area sits to the west of the site, while civic and cultural amenities are located immediately to the east. The building volume is also visible from across the river at Canal City, an earlier development by Fukuoka Jisho, that links the Tenjin and Hakata districts.

3483   Civic and cultural amenities east of the site

3484   Fukuoka Jisho's Canal City development

3486   The site is at the crossing of two streets with different characters—Meiji-dori, the main business street lined with financial offices, and Inabacho-dori, a small-scale pedestrian connection linking with City Hall Plaza and Galleria to the south.

3481   In 1989, Arata Isozaki invited one Japanese architect (Osamu Ishiyama) and five non-Japanese architects (Oscar Tusquets, Christian de Portzamparc, Mark Mack, Steven Holl, and OMA) to define a superblock with freestanding perimeter buildings for Fukuoka Jisho (same client as Tenjin Business Center) in order to introduce a "new urban lifestyle" in Japan.

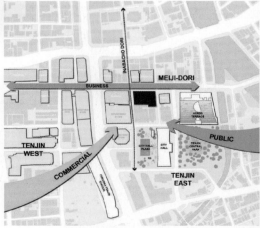

3487   At the intersection of the business, public, and commercial paths, the site is close to public amenities and transportation options.

3485   Business and commercial areas are located around Meiji-dori, one of Fukuoka's main axes and major thoroughfares.

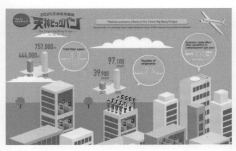

3490 Northeast aerial

3492 View from Meiji-dori and Watanabe-dori

3488 In 2015, mayor of Fukuoka, Soichiro Takashima announced the Tenjin Big Bang Project. The initiative increased buildable capacity (1.7 times the existing floor area ratio limit) and planned a series of developments that would improve civic amenities with the goal of bringing more global companies, employees, and economic benefits to the city by 2024.

3489 Basic massing on the site

3491 View from Hakata Station

3493 View from Meiji-dori on the Naka River

3494 Inabacho-dori has many small cafes and outdoor terraces

3495 As the first Big Bang project, how can Tenjin Business Center create a model for future projects? How can a private building begin to have a public interface?

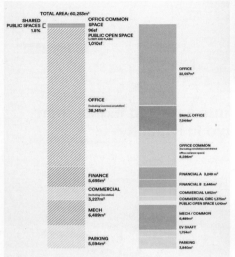

3496 The majority of the building's program is office space, with a limited need for open public and common zones.

3497 However, the building's location—at the intersection of Meiji-dori, Inabacho-dori, the underground shopping district, and City Hall Plaza—requires a credible public interface.

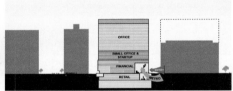

3498 East–west section through site with connection to underground

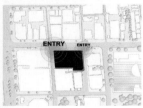

3499 Entry points at two corners along Meiji-dori

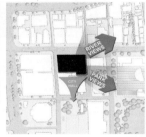

3500 Orientation and views to the river and park

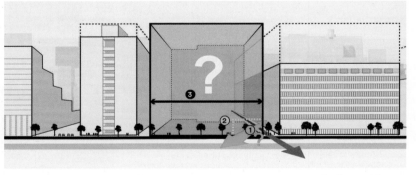

3501 How can Tenjin Business Center maintain its business identity yet emphasize a public openness at the connection between Meiji-dori and Inabacho-dori?

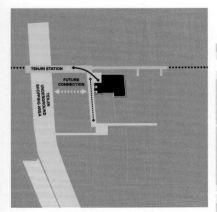

3502 Underground pedestrian network connected to the site's northwest corner

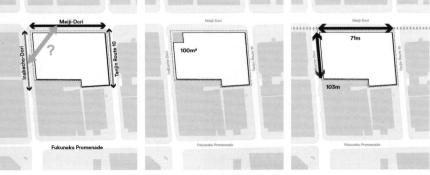

3503 How can the strategy accommodate a seamless connection between the two streets, integrate a need for public open corners, and project a human scale to offset the length of the facade?

3488–3503

Tenjin Business Center

3504 Early concept studies explored ways in which the building could respond to its urban context and open up to the public.

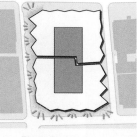

3505 Pleated scheme

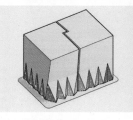

3506 Pleats create a series of openings toward the sidewalks.

3507 The pleated openings partially reveal the activities within the building.

3508 Stepping scheme

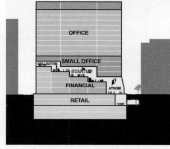

OFFICE

SMALL OFFICE

CO-WORKING START-UP

FINANCIAL ATRIUM

RETAIL

3509 The stepping atrium separates the upper offices from the financial base.

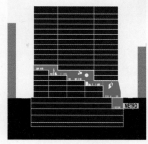

METRO

3511 The steps extend below to connect to the underground subway station.

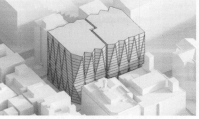

3512 The pleated base is mirrored on the top of the building.

3510 Stepping scheme elevation along Meiji-dori

3513 Double pleated scheme elevation along Meiji-dori

3514 The pleats fold in and out, visually drawing the city into the building and creating a dynamic presence on the street.

3515 Courtyard scheme

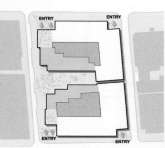

ENTRY ENTRY

ENTRY ENTRY

3517 Four corner entries and a stepped frame of retail draw the public into a courtyard.

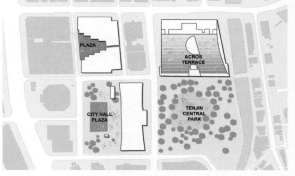

PLAZA

ACROS TERRACE

CITY HALL PLAZA

TENJIN CENTRAL PARK

3516 The courtyard plaza adds to the network of public spaces of the neighborhood.

3518 Two L-shaped office buildings frame the courtyard public space along Inabacho-dori.

3519 The final scheme adds a series of excavations to the volume that react to different characters around the site.

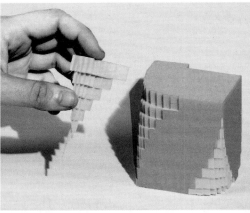

3520 Each excavation reveals a new public face—an entry corner and atrium for the underground pedestrian network and a series of collective terraces and common spaces for the offices.

3521 Crystal formation as reference for facets of three-dimensionality.

3522 "Softening" of form

3523 The resulting pixelation introduce a "softness" to the form— the building mass is reduced and the granular erosion establishes a continuous facade instead of abrupt corner conditions.

3524 Pedestrian scale along Inabacho-dori

3525 Continuous facade

3526 The building concept works with Fukuoka Jisho's logo

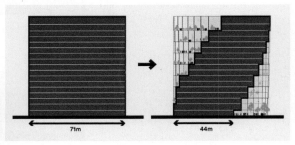

3527 The mass of the building is visibly reduced and avoids the typical curtain-wall condition on the street.

3528 Small-scale terraces at the top and large pedestrian plaza at the ground

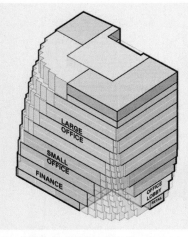

3529 Within the building, the office program is organized as a series of shifting bars. The bars step back at the base to create a large atrium and establish the underground connection. On the opposite corner, the bars step back at the top to give way to a series of terraces.

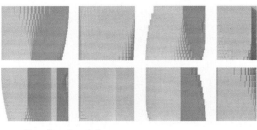

3530 Pure form in rotation

3531 Final concept model

3532 Carving away the corner at Meiji-dori and Inabacho-dori addresses the need for public space and connectivity between the two streets. The resulting plaza is large enough to provide a lively meeting spot for office tenants and pedestrians alike.

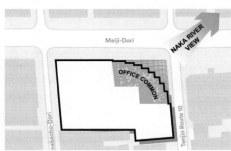

3533 Carving away and pixelating the opposite corner at the building's upper levels creates terraces and amenities for the office floors while offering views of the Naka River and Hakata Bay.

3519–3533   Tenjin Business Center

3535 Northwest aerial

3537 Model—view from north

3538 The corner establishes a distinct identity that is recognizable from afar.

3536 Model—view from west

3534 The three-dimensional pixelated corner creates a canopy over the large public entry plaza at the ground level.

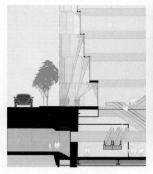

3539 Underside of canopy signage

3540 The three-dimensional facade forms a series of soffit faces that can integrate signage and lighting to provide a dynamic entry.

3541 Daytime view of pixelated corner

3542 Evening view of pixelated corner

3543 Facade visual mock-up with soffit lighting, April 2019

3544 Entry points to ground level programs

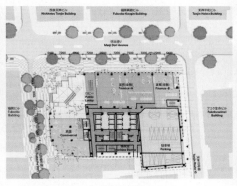

3545 F1 plan—atrium, lobby, office, parking

3546 The pixels set back at the ground level, creating an expansive plaza on the corner and dramatic sense of arrival with the entry atrium.

3547 Plaza event scenario—Hakata Gion Yamakasa festival on the plaza

3548 The corner can become a contemporary Christmas tree at the urban scale.

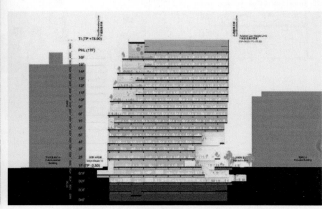

3549 A large atrium located at the corner of Meiji-dori and Inabacho-dori starts from the B2 underground shopping area and rises up to F7.

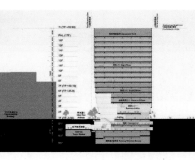

3551 North–south section through atrium

3552 F2 business lobby

3550 While most atriums in private buildings are internalized, here the atrium is embedded into the facade. Directly facing the street, natural light reaches down into the public underground level.

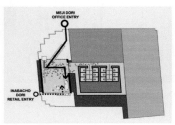

3555 Office entry sequence

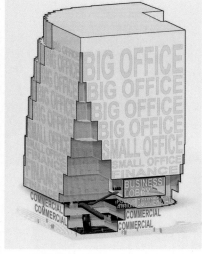

3553 Initial atrium concept—every program within the building has access to the atrium.

3554 The public entry atrium connects the underground commercial spaces with the office lobby.

3556 Entry to the business lobby

3557 Business lobby

3558 Business lobby

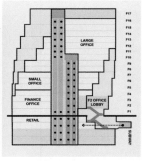

3559 Vertical circulation

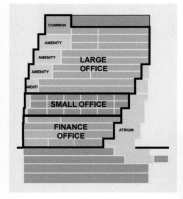

3560 Program distribution

3561 A simple structural grid allows for easy subdivision of the office floorplates, providing flexibility to accommodate a variety of tenant sizes.

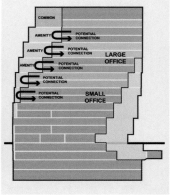

3568 Initial concept—the double-height amenity spaces created by the upper pixelation allows connection from one office floor to another.

3562 Large office

3563 Two tenants

3564 Three tenants

3565 Four tenants

3566 Six tenants

3567 Eleven tenants

Tenjin Business Center

3569 The office common area is consolidated into a large space at the top of the building. Together with the entry atrium, it offers a series of amenities anchoring the opposite corners of the building.

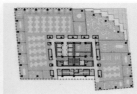

3570 F16 common area

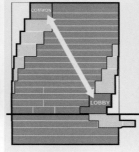

3571 Amenities anchoring opposite corners

3572 Northeast street view of office terraces

3573 Northeast aerial view

3574 Model view of office common areas

3575 Final concept model

3576 Looking down the series of office terraces

3578 The pixelated office terraces also introduce dynamic views toward the Naka River and Hakata Bay.

3579 From the inside, the pixelation offers multiple corner views.

3580 View of office terraces from Nakasu

3577 Model view from Meiji-dori

Tenjin Business Center

3581 The streetscape is designed to create further intersections between the building and street life. A checkerboard pattern emanates from the pixelated form, visually extending the facade onto the streets to merge interior with exterior.

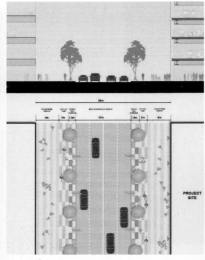

3582 Meiji-dori is an imposing boulevard lined with financial buildings. It is a necessary asset for the coexistence of cars, bicycles, pedestrians, and green space.

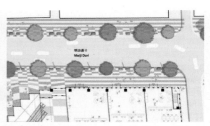

3583 Street pattern along Meiji-dori

3584 The streetscape aims to subdivide and diversify the experience of walking down long streets while maintaining unity.

3585 Inabacho-dori is a narrow pedestrian street that contrasts with Meiji-dori.

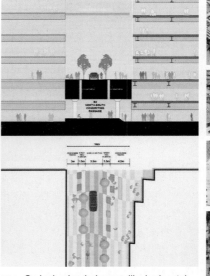

3586 On Inabacho-dori, wave-like horizontal bands correspond to the slow speed at which people move along the street.

3587 Paving pattern references

3588 We also proposed a future development of the Inabacho-dori Galleria.

3589 Inabacho-dori Galleria

3590 The ground-floor entry and retail activate the street life of Inabacho-dori.

Tenjin Business Center

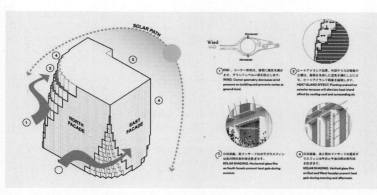

3591 Both the shape and facade of the building are optimized for high energy efficiency. The facade is organized into two broad categories reflecting the specific type of program and use.

3592 North facade pop-out—because solar shading is not required, the windows project out from the facade, creating a series of cells that articulate the flat facade.

3593 East and west facade frame—a series of fins surround the windows to act as solar shading and prevent heat gain in the morning and afternoon.

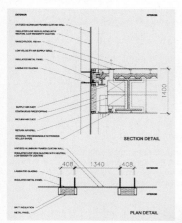

3594 Initial facade louver detail—section and plan

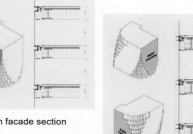

3595 North facade section

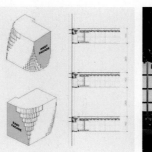

3596 East/west facade section

3597 North facade construction, 2021

3598 West facade construction, 2021

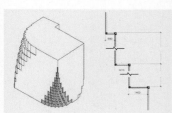

3599 Entry pixelation detail

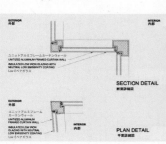

3600 Pixelation detail section and plan

3601 A high-performance reflective film coating on the glass ensures minimal solar transmittance.

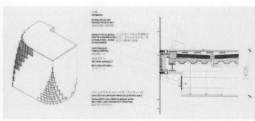

3602 Office terrace detail

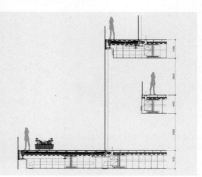

3603 Office terrace section

3604 View looking up at the office terraces, 2021

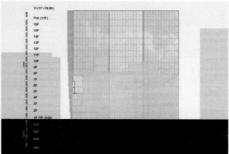

3605 South elevation

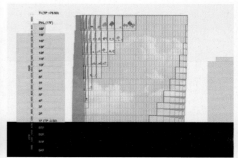

3606 North elevation

Tenjin Business Center

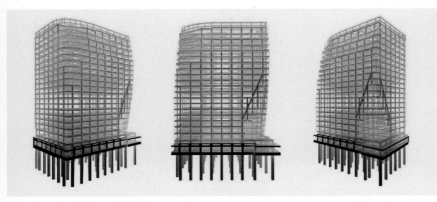

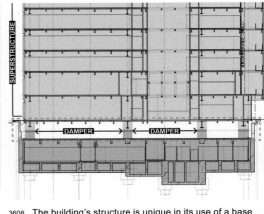

3607 The structure consists of an eccentric core and long column-free spans on the office levels. To achieve the long spans (54 to 62 feet in depth), concrete-filled tube (CFT) columns are used to increase horizontal rigidity in the frame.

3608 The building's structure is unique in its use of a base isolator at the B1 level. Within the base isolator, a plate shifts in response to earthquakes, allowing the entire building above ground to maintain stability.

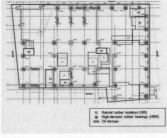

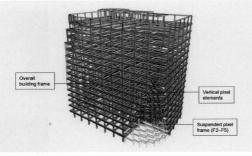

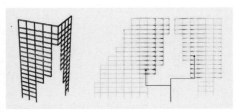

3609 Seismic isolation—high-damped rubber bearings (HRB) and oil dampers are placed at the outer periphery of the building, while natural rubber isolators (NRI) are placed at the center.

3610 The structural components of the pixels in the northeast and northwest corners can largely be divided into two features: vertical pixel elements that are attached to the overall building frame, and a suspended pixel frame in the lower levels of the northwest entry atrium.

3611 Lower corner transfer structure—distributed damping offers redundancy and allows the structural performance of the building to be optimized to suit the seismic demands.

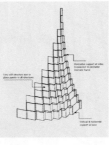

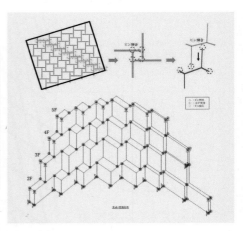

3612 Lower corner—stress in glass panels under wind loading

3613 Lower corner forces in steel sections—the 3D form gives stiffness in all directions.

3614 Multi-story window frame–due to the atrium, the facade cannot be attached to floors in the lower corners. The substructure consists of a 3D moment frame of solid steel sections with glass panels (vertical) and opaque panels (horizontal).

3615 The lower pixel structure is a multi reciprocal grid system and spans a large area through a repeating pin welding. A built-box cross section is used to resist complex stresses.

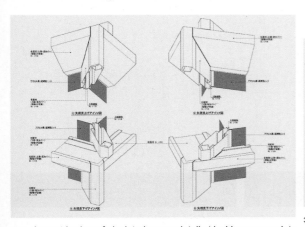

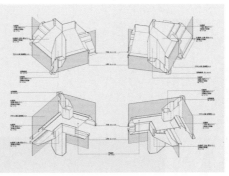

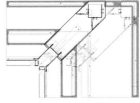

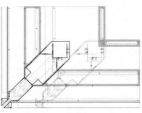

3616 Isometric view of pixelated corner detail at inside corner points

3617 Isometric view of pixelated corner detail at outside corner points

3618 Inside corner detail plan

3619 Outside corner detail plan

3620 In 2018, a new height regulation changed the building's height from 243 feet to 285 feet, adding three more floors and introducing zoning setbacks at the top of the building.

3621 The additional height creates a prominent addition to Fukuoka's cityscape.

3622 The pixelated corner becomes a new meeting point in the Fukuoka streetscape.

3623 Zoning setbacks blend into the upper corner pixels on the northeast corner.

3624 West facade along pedestrian Inabacho-dori

3625 North facade along commercial Meiji-dori

3626 The zoning setbacks subtly shape the building's form.

3627 The overall form is "softened" through the pixels and setbacks.

3628 North elevation, February 2021

3629 Rendered view of building at new height and zoning setbacks

3630 Pixelated northwest corner with entry atrium and zoning setbacks, February 2021

3631 The project broke ground in January 2019 with the The project broke ground in January 2019. Representatives of the city of Fukuoka, including mayor Soichiro Takashima, and of the developer, Fukuoka Jisho, were in attendance.

3632 The groundbreaking ceremony in Japan is known as *jichinsai*, a purification rite held to appease gods or spirits in anticipation of construction's inherent disturbance of the land.

3633 Fukuoka mayor Soichiro Takashima and the president/CEO of Fukuoka Jisho, Ichiro Enomoto.

3634 The ceremony is typically performed by a Shinto priest with the sacred space marked by branches of bamboo. Water, sake, and salt are poured on the symbolic land, which is cleared with a wooden tool to "break" the ground.

3635 Tenjin groundbreaking ceremony reception events in January 2019

3636 Shohei Shigematsu speaking at reception

3637 The project will be completed in fall 2021.

3638 It will be the first development under Mayor Takashima's Tenjin Big Bang initiative to stimulate the neighborhood as a business hub and startup city.

3639 The building aims to be the new focal point of the district.

3640 Inabacho-dori view, February 2021

3641 Meiji-dori view, February 2021

3642 The openness generated at the corner will hopefully set a precedent for the buildings to come and create lively civic activity in the new district.

3643

Tenjin Business Center

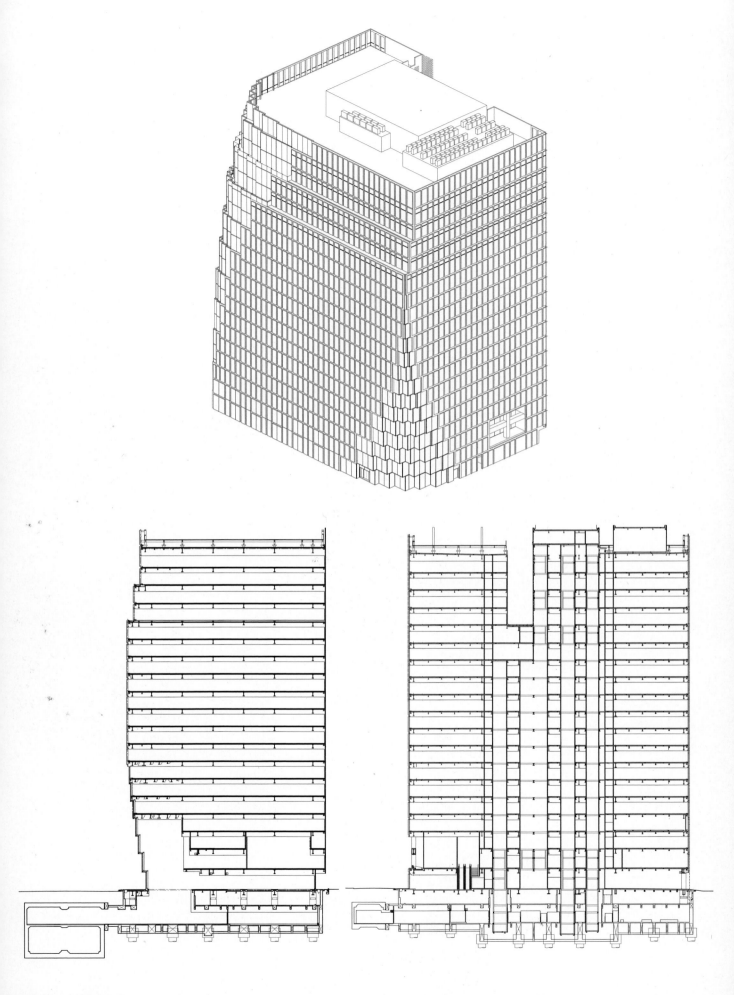

Tenjin Business Center

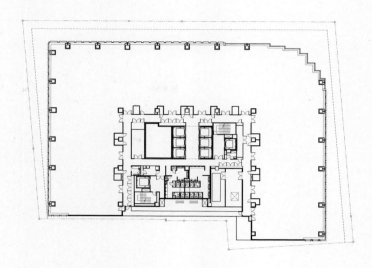

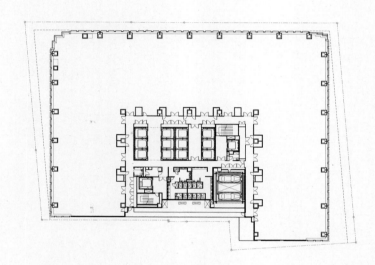

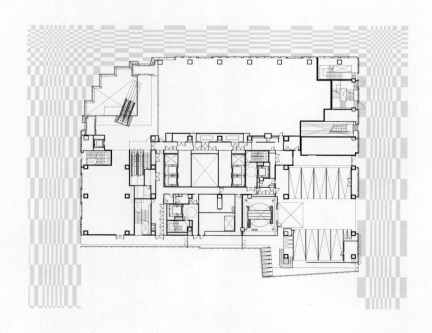

3650

Toranomon Hills Station Tower

Toranomon Hills Station Tower

Tokyo is a large city that has been cultivating areas with distinct characters. The experience of the city is diverse and dynamic, like an à la carte–style dinner, where people share different dishes and make conversation across the table. But recent large-scale mixed-use developments across the different neighborhoods seem to share an all too similar assembly of programs within an efficient container— a bento box as opposed to à la carte. The bento boxes have been multiplying, and what used to be a very diverse experience within the city is becoming increasingly homogeneous and predictable.

In the proliferation of the bento box, no matter how much architects try to differentiate the character of mixed-use buildings through form and facade, we're faced with a dilemma: if the ingredients are the same, the experience within the container is inherently the same. How can we design a mixed-use building that embodies the maximum potential of the mix and stimulates an unexpected affair between building and the city?

Our site lies at the junction of two zones—Toranomon Hills (a global business center) and ARK Hills (a lifestyle cultural center). The tower will stand at the terminus of Shintora-dori Avenue, Tokyo's newly configured axial thoroughfare connecting Tokyo Bay to the city center. In the vicinity of the site, a series of freestanding mixed-use developments have begun to establish the Toranomon Hills Area as a place to live, work, and play. How can we make a tower dedicated to connections—one that forms a new network of mixed-use towers and reflects the energy of the surrounding neighborhoods? How can the high-rise integrate public amenities into known office, hotel, and retail programs for an unexpected experience of the mixed-use?

Our approach is a highly public interface to the tower. The core is lifted and split to either side of the tower's base, opening up the heart of the building and drawing the public inward. The nature and activities of Shintora-dori Avenue extend into and through the tower via an elevated pedestrian bridge, emphatically linking the area's towers together to create a network of activities and greenery.

The bridge sectionally divides the base into two retail zones. The lower zone provides direct access to the new Hibiya Line subway station (Toranomon Hills Station), connecting the tower to the greater region. Within, a grand atrium and subway station concourse flooded with natural light, the first of its kind in Tokyo, provides an exciting sense of arrival.

The public activity at the base extends vertically to form a central band of special areas for tenants throughout the tower. The building form is shaped to reveal the band from multiple vantage points, making it visible from anywhere in Tokyo. Two slabs sandwiching the central band are formed in inverted symmetry. The north slab begins wide at the base and narrows as it reaches the top in deference to the Imperial Palace. The south slab is narrowest at its base and widens as it rises, maximizing views of the Roppongi Hills skyline and Tokyo Tower.

In balance with the highly public base, we capped the tower with an additional public amenity. The Cultural Center (tentative name) is a new type of program we devised in collaboration with Mori Building—a hybrid of flexible event space and innovative forum. The media center/museum-like entity anchors the tower as a global business center that engages the innovative and creative networks in the area and beyond. On the roof, a landscaped terrace provides a lush garden with an infinity pool and a flexible event space accommodates private or public gatherings.

By inserting highly public and dynamic environments at the base and at the top, we wanted to make the experience both within and around the tower less predictable, unboxing the bento box and remixing the mixed-use.

Location	Tokyo, Japan		
Status	Construction, 2015–Ongoing		
Typology	Re-Mixed Use		
	Toranomon Hills Station Tower		
	Total Area	2.54 million ft²	236,000 m²
	East Block Total Area	94,500 ft²	8,780 m²

3651

Toranomon Hills Station Tower

3652

Toranomon Hills Station Tower

OMA NY

Toranomon Hills Station Tower

3653

Toranomon Hills Station Tower

OMA NY

Toranomon Hills Station Tower

3654–3655   Toranomon Hills Station Tower

OMA NY

Toranomon Hills Station Tower

3656

Toranomon Hills Station Tower

3657 Toranomon, once considered a district without a strong identity, is becoming known as Tokyo's premier destination for business, culture, and living.

3658 Declared a National Strategic Special Zone, Toranomon is set to become a central business district home to global corporate headquarters. This reflects a time when Tokyo's ambitions are geared toward increasing international competitiveness through urban development.

3659 Historically, Toranomon's cultural and historical significance comes from its distinction as the southern gate of the Edo Castle (Imperial Palace).

3660 Toranomon is among Tokyo's oldest neighborhoods. The Imperial Palace, along with a number of shrines, coexists with new developments and brings historical significance to the neighborhood.

3661 The Atago Shrine, built in 1603

3662 Kotohiragu Shrine, dating back to 1660

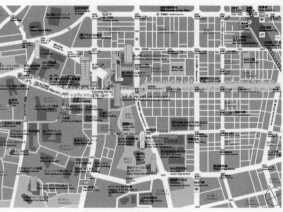

3663 With the development of Shintora-dori Avenue and several commercial and residential buildings—both completed and under construction, mainly through Mori Building—Toranomon is becoming an urban center for landscape, culture, and business.

3664 Landscaped public spaces in the city

3665 Neighborhood spaces for retail and interaction

3666 Vibrant outdoor spaces for public art and activity

3667 Active business district

3668 Tohoku Rokkon Festival Parade along Shintora-dori Avenue

3669 The site for Toranomon Hills Station Tower is located at the junction of two projected zones by Mori Building: the Toranomon Hills Area (THA), a global business center, and the ARK Hills Area, a lifestyle cultural center. It represents the ideal destination for the confluence of international exchange and local activity.

Toranomon Hills Station Tower

3670 Toranomon Hills is situated along Shintora-dori Avenue, the axis that links the commercial center to the Olympic Village for the 2020 Summer Olympics (postponed to 2021), bridging Tokyo's Bay Zone with its Heritage Zone.

3671 Toranomon Hills along Shintora-dori Avenue axis

3672 Base massing view aligned with Toranomon Hills Mori Tower

3675 Bass massing view from Tokyo Tower, situated along National Route 1

3673 Toranomon Hills also stands alongside Route 1, the main transit axis to the Imperial Palace east of the site.

3674 Base massing view from Roppongi Hills

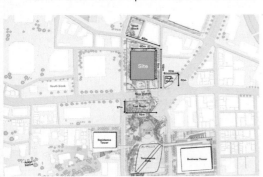

3676 The Station Tower is part of a new cluster of mixed developments that include a brand new transit station, Toranomon Hills Mori Tower (completed 2014), Business Tower (completed 2020), and the planned Residential Tower.

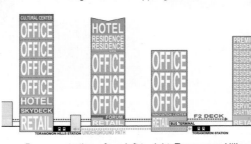

3677 Program section—from left to right: Toranomon Hills Station Tower, Mori Tower, Business Tower, Residential Tower. The new Toranomon Hills Station is next to the Toranomon Hills Station Tower, with connections to the neighboring developments via an underground path and a raised exterior deck and bridge.

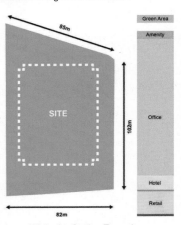

3678 While the Station Tower is primarily occupied by office tenants, the program is mixed and proposes a variety of spaces that invite the public into the site.

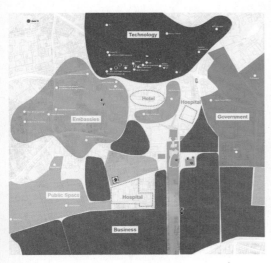

3679 The Station Tower is positioned at the center of a series of key infrastructural and green networks, as well as multiple distinct neighborhoods.

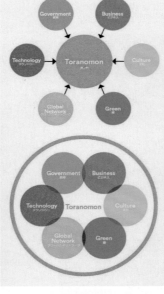

3680 The Station Tower's prime location at this intersection provides a unique opportunity to establish a new type of business hub at the center of Tokyo.

3681 Along with ongoing plans to transform Shintora-dori Avenue into a major pedestrian boulevard, can the Station Tower facilitate enhanced public character as a key landmark along that axis?

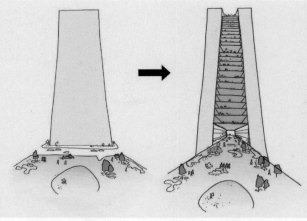

3682   The Station Tower opens up to the city, pulling both green space and activity into the site. An elevated pedestrian bridge runs through the Station Tower's base and defines a vertical central zone of activities.

3683   This gesture extends, rather than terminates, Shintora-dori Avenue and its activities.

3684   Toranomon Hills

3685   Station Tower

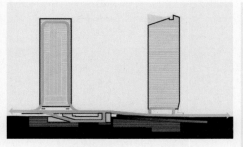

3686   Continuous activity from Shintora-dori Avenue extends vertically down to the underground transit station and loops up through the tower.

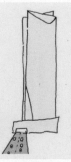

3687   A link for people and cars

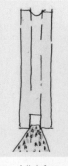

3688   A link for people and landscape

3689   This central zone also acts as a signature gateway, indicating the orientation of the Shintora-dori Avenue axis visible throughout Tokyo.

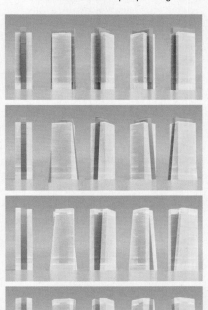

3693   Tower and activity band form studies

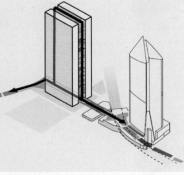

3690   To enable the tower to open up to the city, the building is split into three bars. An activity band at the center continues the shared amenities and acts as an extension of Shintora-dori Avenue and Toranomon Hills Mori Tower.

3694   The final form is composed of two office bars, one an upside-down reflection of the other.

3691   Tower form study models

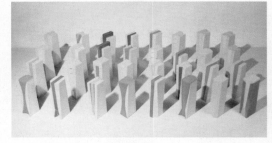

3692   Activity band form studies

3695   Final form rotation—the opposing shapes of the outer bars create a twisting activity band that is visible from various angles.

3682–3695   Toranomon Hills Station Tower

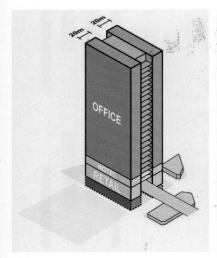

3696   The bars on either end of the activity band house the building's programs— office, hotel, and retail.

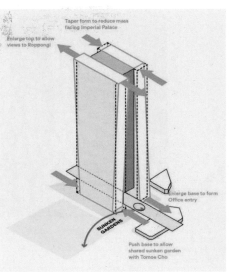

3697   A series of opposite adjustments are made to the top and base of the two office bars.

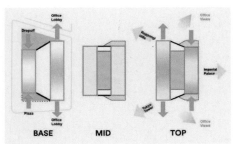

BASE   MID   TOP

3698   The bars are pinched and enlarged in opposite directions to address the urban context while maintaining a consistent leasable office area throughout the tower.

3699   Pinched office bars   3700   Twisting central band

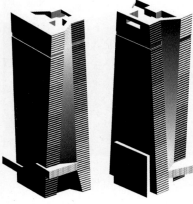

3701   One side pyramidal, the other inverted— the two bars create a dramatic form.

3702   The resulting form exposes the twisting activity band from all angles while maintaining symmetry in elevation.

3703   Looking up to the twisting activity band

3704   Office bars   3075   Activity band   3706   Public amenity   3707   Green bridge

3708   Program organization

3709   Program bar

Green Area

Business and Cultural Facility

Office

Hotel
Sky Lobby
Retail
Parking

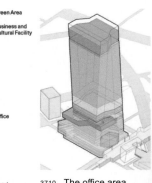

3710   The office area sandwiched by public programs

3711   The Station Tower is dynamic and inviting in form, while the distribution of public programs from the base to the top establishes an office building that draws the activities of the city in.

3696–3711   Toranomon Hills Station Tower

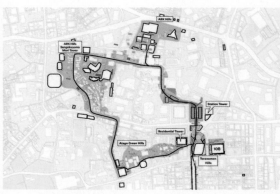

3712 The Station Tower provides a link to complete the new Toranomon-Azabudai Project Area and establish a green loop of pedestrian activity, connecting Toranomon Hills, Atago Green Hills, ARK Hills Sengokuyama Mori Tower, and ARK Hills. It would take approximately forty-five minutes to walk the green loop.

3713 Toranomon Hills Area

3714 Shintora-dori Avenue green belt

3715 Within the network is an elevated, programmed bridge that spans from Toranomon Hills Mori Tower to and through the Station Tower.

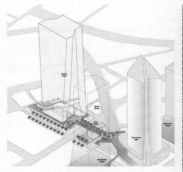

3716 The bridge is on F2 and connects to the Toranomon plinth, forming a green datum.

3717 The elevated green connects Toranomon Hills Mori Tower, Station Tower, and the adjacent buildings.

3718 The F2 connection extends the Shintora-dori Avenue "boulevard" ambition, bridging over Route 1 to create a new pedestrian corridor for landscape and activity.

3719 The pedestrian bridge, designed by Nei & Partners, carries the programmed landscape from Mori Tower's green plaza, through the East Block, into the Station Tower's retail atrium.

3720 F2—bridge, retail atrium, and garden

3721 F2 bridge view toward the Station Tower retail atrium

3722 Landscape draws visitors up from the street level onto the pedestrian bridge and retail base.

3723 View from street level

3724 Pedestrian bridge section

3725 Where the bridge meets the Station Tower, we wanted to create an inviting presence that draws the city into the building.

3726 Central atrium study models

3727 Funnel entry study model

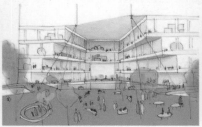

3728 Funnel entry concept sketch

3729 The building form opens outward toward Sakurada-dori Avenue (Route 1), forming a gateway at the base of the tower that draws visitors from the bridge into the retail atrium.

3730 The funnel entry leads into a retail base, a shared space for both office employees and the general public.

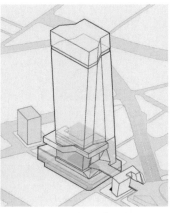

3731 Retail programs include shops, dining, and fitness.

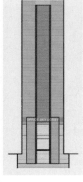

3732 Split core

3733 The core of the building is split at the retail base—shifted to the sides, it allows the public thoroughfare to extend in and through the center of the tower.

3736 The split cores create a retail atrium and a public arcade, inviting the city into the building. The rose gold core has a three-dimensional texture that subtly reflects the activities within.

3734 Retail atrium entrance from F2 bridge

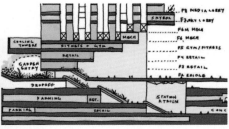

3735 Program section with F2 bridge extending into the retail atrium

3737 The F2 pedestrian bridge sectionally divides the base into two distinct retail zones. The lower retail is arranged in a series of highly efficient retail plates with direct connection to the new Toranomon Hills Station, while the upper retail zone consolidates retail and office lobby programs into two bars on either side of a dramatic atrium.

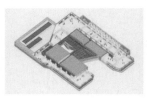

3738 F5—gym/wellness

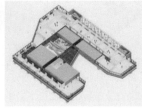

3739 F4—cafe/fine dining

3741 Urban activity from Shintora-dori Avenue defines retail programs.

3742 Landscape from the bridge extends into the retail base.

3743 Upper level retail atrium

3744 Retail atrium palette

3740 B2—retail/market

3745 The vertical circulation—escalators and elevators—has a clear, highlighted presence characterized by custom gradient-colored glass in both warm and cool tones by Sabine Marcelis.

3746 The retail base uses circulation coming from the underground station and carries it through the stepped upper level retail.

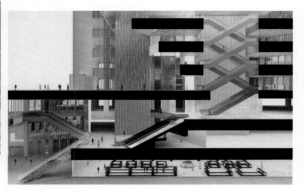

3747 Pedestrians are drawn into the building from above and below the F2 bridge through the funnel of activity and views.

3730–3747

Toranomon Hills Station Tower

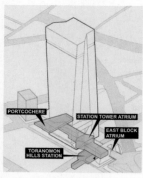

3748 A new station and its underground concourse connect the Toranomon Hills Area to greater Tokyo.

3749 Toranomon Hills Station will be the first new stop added to the Hibiya Line in more than fifty years.

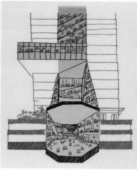

3750 The station atrium becomes the arrival gate of the activity band, as well as the underground subway.

3751 Station atrium studies

3752 Station atrium connection from B2 to F1

3753 Station section—the station atrium connects three public datums: B2 subway concourse, F1 vehicular road, and F2 pedestrian bridge

3754 Faceted ceiling study model

3755 The ceiling of the B2 station atrium is the underside of the pedestrian bridge. The luminous faceted form extends the structural expression of the bridge into the concourse, enhancing the axial quality of the bridge.

3756 Station section—B2 station atrium, B1 station platform, F1 street level, and F2 pedestrian bridge.

3757 Balancing the verticality of the atrium, the B2 level extends laterally with surrounding retail and office lobby spaces to highlight a horizontal datum. Colored-glass escalators clearly define the vertical circulation up from the B2 to F2 levels.

3758 Light from the skylights floods the concourse, washing the walls that define the atrium. White fritted glazing surrounding the atrium enhances the natural light and creates a space that does not feel underground. Views to and from the station platform establish a visual connection between commuters and the station atrium.

Toranomon Hills Station Tower

3759 At the heart and center of the Toranomon Hills complex is the East Block building.

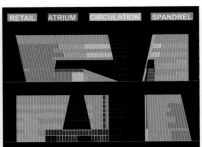

RETAIL   ATRIUM   CIRCULATION   SPANDREL

3760 The East Block provides a highly public center to the neighborhood. It is a retail space that provides added access to the pedestrian bridge and underground station.

3761 East Block study models—how can the East Block establish a formally and programmatically cohesive relationship to the Station Tower?

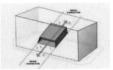
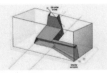

3762 Massing—to create a central hub for public activity, circulation is carved into the block.

3763 Approaching from the Mori Tower on the pedestrian bridge, the East Block frames the entrance to the Station Tower.

3764 Bridge connection through the building

3765 East Block model

3766 Access to the bridge is integrated into the facade

3767 Retail and atrium

3768 Street level view with faceted bridge ceiling

3769 East Block underground connection to the station concourse

3770 The west facade is angled at 13 degrees, establishing synergy to the angle of the main tower's funneled entry. The curved facades on the north and south ends react to the public space below.

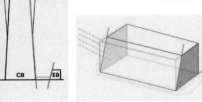

3771 The block's massing is further enhanced in relationship to the Station Tower.

3772 The north facade curves away from the tower, allowing more natural light into the atrium.

3773 The three-dimensional curved facade is composed of cold-bent glass and is fritted to match the facade of the Station Tower's sky lobby.

3759–3773   Toranomon Hills Station Tower

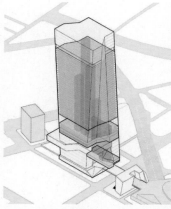

3774 The office levels provide flexible floorplates with efficient 65.6-foot lease spans, connected by the shared activity band.

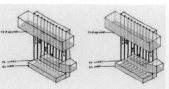

3775 There are three lobbies with access to the offices—B2 concourse lobby, F1 bridge lobby, and F7 sky lobby. Shuttle elevators on the east side of the tower connect the three.

3776 B2 concourse lobby

3777 B2 concourse lobby provides a direct connection from the new station to the office floors.

3778 The F1 office entrance brings employees from the street level to the F7 sky lobby.

3779 F1 lobby

3780 View of shuttle elevators from F1 lobby

3781 F7—sky lobby

3782 F7 sky lobby office elevator banks

3783 F7's sky lobby transitions employees from the shuttle elevators to the office elevator banks.

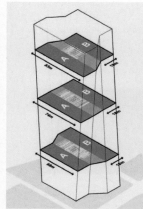

3785 Unique and efficient floorplates

3786 The floorplate dimensions ensure tenant efficiency and flexibility.

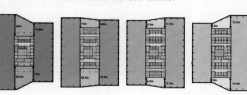

3787 Although the plates are diverse, every level has the same amount of leasable space.

3784 View southeast toward F1 office entrance and shuttle elevators.

3788 Single-tenant open office

3789 Floorplate flexibility—one, two, three, and four tenants.

3790 The activity band creates special floors for office tenants.

3791 Activity band

3792 The special floors provide double-height atriums, staircases, and flexible open spaces for more creative office spaces or amenities.

3793 Business lounge

3794 Cafe/cafeteria

3795 One of the key goals of the project was to bring Tokyo's business and cultural activities into the Toranomon Hills Area and establish a public amenity for global innovation.

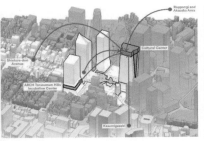

3796 At the top of the tower is a new public program—a place to discuss, debate, and learn—relating to the network of innovative and creative entities within the area.

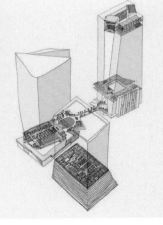

3797 The Station Tower amenity space integrates into the existing network for technology and social interaction, namely the Toranomon Hills Forum, ARCH Toranomon Hills Incubation Center in the Business Tower, and the THA Plaza and Bridge.

3798 Concept collage—merging landscape, art, knowledge, and gathering

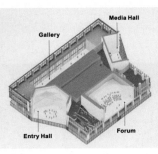

3799 A series of assembly spaces, one on each side of the tower.

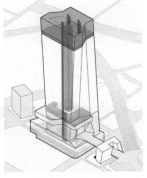

3800 The new public amenity has its own core, allowing visitors direct access to the top of the building.

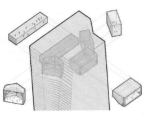

3801 A gallery, the Forum, and two flexible event spaces are inserted against the outer surface of the upper volume like a kit of parts.

3802 The organization of the individual rooms, pushed up against the facade, reveals the diversity of the upper volume program. It is a symbolic ending to the tower that communicates the identity of the Toranomon Hills Area.

3803 The axis of activity that runs through the base extends vertically and wraps the tower along the central band, culminating at the top of the tower with a new public program.

3804 F45 Arrival Hall

3805 F46 prefunction

3806 The Entry Hall on the east side of the tower is a double-height space that can be used for events or large-scale installations.

3807 A long corridor-like gallery provides a more traditional setting for displaying art.

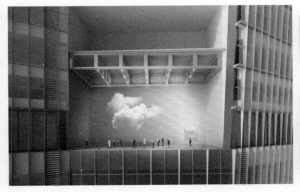

3808 The Media Hall on the west side is another double-height space equipped for events and installations.

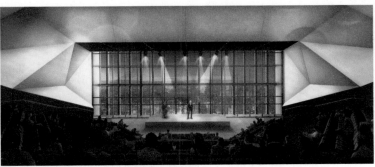

3809 The north-facing Forum auditorium is oriented toward Tokyo's skyline and the Imperial Palace and is suitable for multifunctional events, such as performances, talks, and galas. The room is wrapped with a projectable surface, providing a customized immersive experience.

3795–3809   Toranomon Hills Station Tower

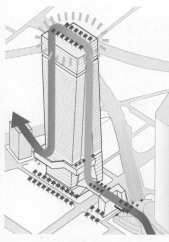

3810 On the roof level, the green landscape of the pedestrian bridge extends up and over the tower to create an outdoor amenity.

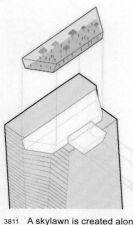

3811 A skylawn is created along the activity band axis and a pool is inserted on the northern end.

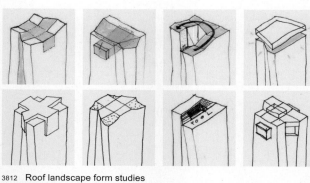

3812 Roof landscape form studies

3813 Skylawn

3814 The skylawn and pool are accessible through the disparate public amenity programs that define the landscape.

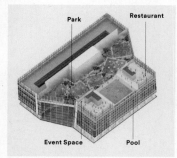

3815 The roof landscape is punctuated by an event space and restaurant.

3816 The mix of indoor and outdoor programming establishes a diverse range of activities.

3817 Evening event

3818 An oasis in the middle of Tokyo

3819 Restaurant

3820 Event space

3821 Rooftop pool

3824 Together, the F2 bridge, East Block, retail atrium, and Toranomon Hills Station create a highly public base and are vertically connected through the activity band to the Cultural Center and rooftop park at the top of the building.

3822 The event space and restaurant are enclosed in glass, enhancing the connection between interior and exterior.

3825 The quartet of Toranomon Hills Mori Tower, Business Tower, Residential Tower, and Station Tower form a highly urban mixed-use development.

3823 A large opening provides an expansive view of the Imperial Palace and Tokyo skyline.

3826 Situated at the intersection of business, culture, and transit, the Station Tower becomes a literal and a symbolic gateway for the Toranomon Hills Area and a global business center for Tokyo.

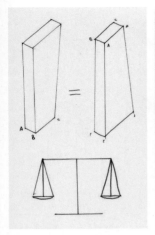

3827   Although the bars are upside down from each other, overall they create a symmetrical balance.

3828   Full model analysis

3829   Axial load paths—office bands and central band

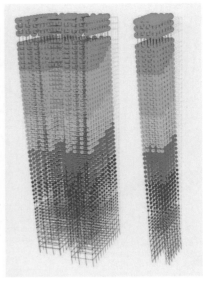

3830   Wind deflections—office bands and central band

3831   Structural frame overview

3832   Structural frame components—diagonal columns crossing over the bridge at the retail base; skybox and MEP box structural appendages

3833   Structural frame components—variable hydraulic dampers located around the core; F44, F14, F10 truss frames

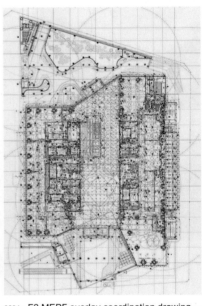

3834   F2 MEPF overlay coordination drawing

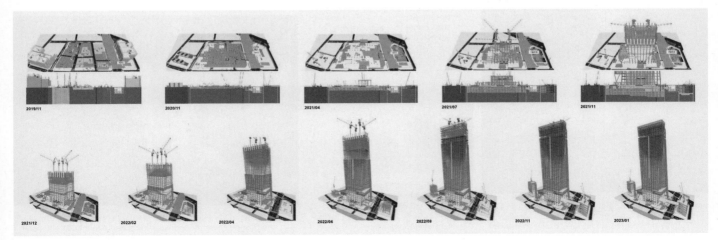

3835   The Station Tower utilizes an inverted construction method to simultaneously build below and above grade, shortening the overall construction period.

3827–3835

Toranomon Hills Station Tower

3836 100 percent DD model

3837 100 percent DD model of Toranomon Hills Area

3838 100 percent DD model

3839 Final model in site

3840 Toranomon Hills Area

3841 Final model—southwest elevation

3842 Final model—north elevation

3843 Final model—northeast elevation

3844 Final model—south elevation

3845 Final model—Toranomon Hills Station Tower, East Block, Mori Tower, Residential Tower, Business Tower

3846 Toranomon Hills located in the 1:1000 Tokyo city model at Tokyo Urban Lab, a theater and workshop space designed by OMA NY

3847 Facade performance test, January 2021

3848 Full scale facade mockup, March 2020

3849 Construction, January 2021

3850 Site view from West Block, January 2021

3851 The Toranomon Hills Station Tower is expected to be completed in 2023.

3836–3851

Toranomon Hills Station Tower

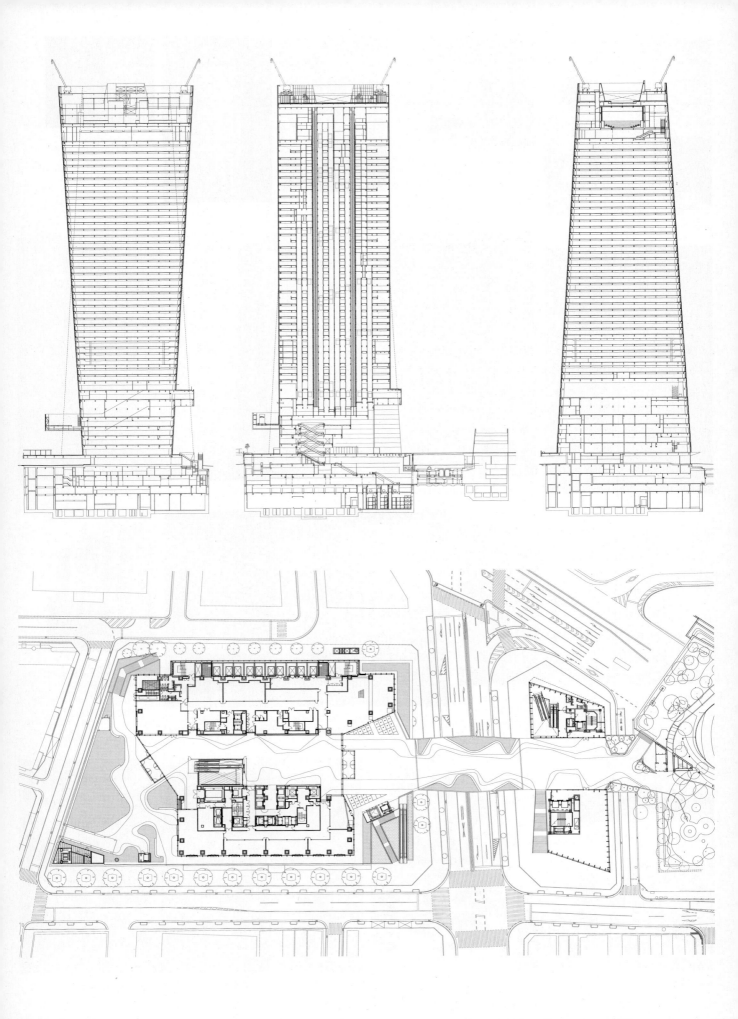

3852–3855

Toranomon Hills Station Tower

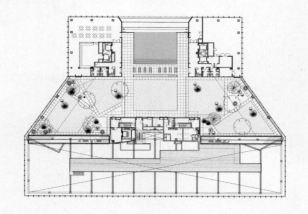

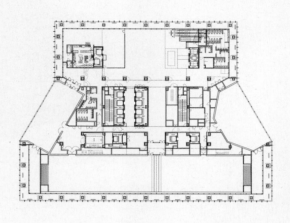

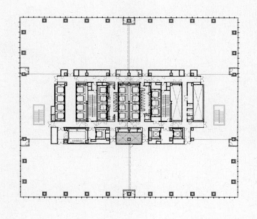

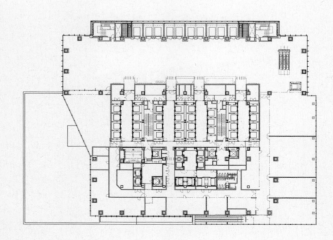

Toranomon Hills Station Tower

Houston, called the "Bayou City," is cut through with verdant swaths of land made resistant to development by their propensity to flood. Its downtown sits where two of these bayous, the Buffalo and the White Oak, cross. At the northern end of downtown—across the Buffalo Bayou from the core of 1970s and 1980s office towers, the vibrant theater district, and major civic institutions—a 500,000-square-foot concrete warehouse and office building sits on the site of what was once Houston's Grand Central Station.

Formerly Houston's main center for the United States Postal Service (USPS), the building was built in 1962 by Wilson, Morris, Crain & Anderson, the architects of the Astrodome. While the Astrodome housed nine men playing a ballgame watched over by 66,000 spectators, the Barbara Jordan Post Office housed 2,000 mail sorters watched over by a handful of men walking through "spy tunnels" above them.

When the USPS closed the facility in 2015, it was purchased by a local Taiwanese-American developer, Frank Liu. Other bidders had all immediately and unquestionably considered the site a potential tabula rasa, but Liu and his sons planned to keep and reimagine the warehouse. The building's scale and solidity offered potential, but also posed questions and contradictions. How can we preserve it but avoid fetishizing its "industrial" character? How can we break its fortress-like relationship with its context without dismantling the building? How can we preserve its scale and aura when those qualities are precisely the elements that disaffect the building from downtown Houston? How do we tame the undifferentiated field of columns within it without creating a maze of dead-ends?

Our approach balanced wholesale preservation with surgical interventions. To integrate the 16-acre site into the fabric of the downtown without dividing it, we focused on a series of connections from the south. Like farmers working on concrete soil, we raked a series of horizontal thoroughfares into and through it. Along each line we cut an interior void. The cuts bring light into the deep floorplates and intersect the building's three levels: a commercial ground plane; a second level of expansive offices; and a 6-acre rooftop park above. They also establish three bands across as zones for different programs—cultural and retail, food market, and collaborative work-space. Within the bands are three atriums—named X, O, and Z—each of which contains a monumental staircase that leads visitors up to the roof-scape and vistas back to downtown. The stairs are distinct in character, structure, and material, but all are designed to encourage interaction. Their paths are doubled, intertwined, and expanded to provide not just trajectories up to the roof but places for accidental encounter—each is an instrument to bring people together.

On the eastern wing of the warehouse we carved out a fourth void to insert the Terminal, the 5,500-capacity music venue and cultural anchor of the complex. The venue features a large, flat general assembly like those of more nimble dance halls, with a tribune of tiered seating hanging over it. The flat floor allows for limitless arrangements. The tribune provides more traditional seating and a sheltered space where visitors can gather away from the performance, like students hanging out under the bleachers.

Like other areas of POST Houston, the Terminal required cutting a void into the existing warehouse. While the three atriums in the main building were introduced to bring in light, the cut for the venue allows for a 95-foot column-free span over the general assembly. Its new roof supports a "Texas-sized" urban farm that, together with an additional zone for large performance, a shaded garden, recreation areas, and two restaurant pavilions, will assemble 170,000 square feet of new public realm for downtown Houston. The building is as much a gateway as a destination. It is a link to a new public space within the city and dramatic view out over its juxtapositions—of infrastructure, business ambition, and natural vitality.

Location	Houston, TX, USA		
Status	Construction, 2016–2021		
Typology	Re-Mixed Use		
	Cultural	45,200 ft²	4,200 m²
	Venue	100,100 ft²	9,300 m²
	Office	130,200 ft²	12,100 m²
	Retail/Market Hall	105,500 ft²	9,800 m²
	Hotel	70,000 ft²	6,500 m²
	Public Space	220,700 ft²	20,500 m²
	Total Area	671,700 ft²	62,400 m²

3861

POST Houston/Live Nation

POST Houston/Live Nation

3863

OMA NY

POST Houston/Live Nation

3865 Houston, Texas, is both a major metropolis and a center of the oil industry.

3866 The city is extremely young. Much of the outer sprawl (yellow on map) was constructed after 1945.

3867 Houston has a "no rules" approach to zoning. As nothing guides what types of programs can be built alongside others, it is inherently a place of radical juxtapositions.

3868 Urban collage— an erotic shop next to a mall and an office tower

3869 The Barbara Jordan Post Office is also a site of juxtaposition, located between the dense high-rise area of Houston's downtown and a sprawling highway interchange that connects the city with its airport.

3870 Although situated along the Buffalo Bayou, the post office site itself is disconnected from the Bayou Greenway, a continuous park system that runs through the city.

3871 Houston's Grand Central Station previously occupied the site.

3872 The Downtown Houston Post Office under construction (1959)

3873 Downtown Houston Post Office on opening day (1962)

3874 The mail sorting warehouse prior to beginning operations

3875 Visitors in the mail sorting warehouse (1971)

3876 The post office was renamed in 1984 to honor U.S. Representative Barbara Jordan.

3877 Postcard of the Barbara Jordan Post Office

3878 In 2015, the post office was closed and bought by Lovett Commercial with the foresight to imagine its transformation into a new type of commercial and workspace for Houston, despite—or perhaps because of—its sheer scale.

3879 The former mail-sorting warehouse covers more than 53,000 square feet.

3880 The warehouse is the length of four 747s laid wing to wing.

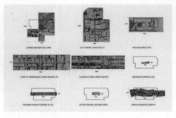

3881 Scale comparisons

3882 Loading dock existing conditions

3883 Warehouse existing conditions

3884 Rooftop existing conditions and skyline views

3885 Downtown Houston developed at the point where White Oak Bayou feeds into Buffalo Bayou, where the POST Houston site now sits.

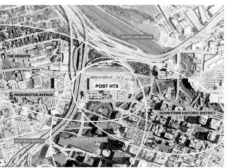

3886 POST Houston is located at the intersection of three key areas in the city—the Theater District, the Downtown Historic District, and the Washington Avenue neighborhood.

3887 POST Houston also lies adjacent to Market Square, University of Houston Downtown, and the Buffalo Bayou Greenway. Our task with this building was to transform the site into something that could better integrate with the city around it.

3888 Concept collage—keyboard

3889 While its scale is its greatest asset, its sheer breadth minimizes penetration of both daylight and the city.

3890 Farming the building

3891 Two potential bayou connections—a bridge over and a tunnel under Franklin Street—link the building and its roof to the greenway.

3892 Buffalo Bayou and Franklin Street, with the POST site beyond

3893 Proposed programmatic bridge and lookout over Franklin Street

3894 Bayou lookout and tunnel connections

3895 Franklin tunnel connection

3896 The proposed bayou connection main stair is placed on axis with the POST building, creating a new gateway from the bayou to downtown.

POST Houston/Live Nation

3897 New development within the former post office's parking lots can extend toward Franklin Street and reintegrate the site with the downtown grid.

3898 Existing road terminations

3899 Road connections through the site and existing post office

3900 Vehicular streets and pedestrian arcades alternate across the site.

3901 A diagonal avenue cuts through the site at the angle of the downtown city grid.

3902 A monumental stair could connect the rooftop directly to the ground, combining circulation and gathering space through a large-scale topographic gesture.

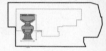

3903 Scale comparison—Spanish Steps, Rome, Italy

3904 Houston's "Spanish Steps"—a social space that makes the rooftop park truly public

3905 New development in a potential long-range masterplan surrounds the warehouse, creating a transition from low-rise Houston to the high-rise downtown skyline.

3906 Long-range model with future residential and office towers

3907 Phase 1 massing

3908 Phase 2 massing

3909 Site plan—long-range masterplan

3910 Existing skyline vs. Phase 2 skyline

3911 Built-out neighborhood bands with Phase 2 high-rises

3897–3911

POST Houston/Live Nation

3913 Three cuts create atriums to bring in light, break up the scale of the space within, and create a series of links from the city to the rooftop.

3914 Each atrium defines a programmatic zone within the building with a dedicated entry, creating multiple connections to downtown.

3912 Following the initial concept, the client found historic preservation tax credits that made keeping the building financially viable. But with this benefit came new limits on how the post office could be modified. We had to be strategic in our interventions, removing discrete volumes rather than radically altering the building's form or making extensive modifications to its facade.

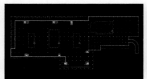

3915 Atrium cutouts

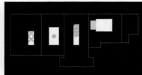

3916 Atrium plan

3917 Each atrium has a signature stair tailored to its individual program and connects the F1 programs, the F2 offices, and the roof.

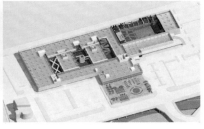

3918 F2 office spaces

3919 The building is divided into north-south programmatic bands.

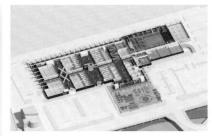

3920 F1 public programs

3921 The three stairs are distinct in material and structure: a concrete stair spanning between existing columns, a metal stair erected as a tower from the floor, and a wooden stair suspended from the roof.

3922 Atrium punchout, March 2020

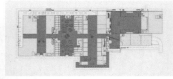

3923 F1 Public circulation

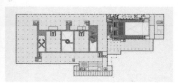

3924 F2 Public circulation

3925 Atrium punchout, April 2020

3926 During the day, the three atriums bring light into the warehouse. At night, their ETFE roofs and a series of skylights glow within the rooftop park.

3927 In the Theater Atrium, a zigzagging stair is reflected to create a double "X" with two floating intersections.

3928 Rather than just a path from the ground to the roof, the atrium stairs are designed to be instruments for bringing people together in chance encounters.

3929 X stair sketch

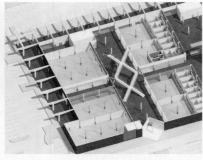

3930 Storefronts line either side of the atrium

3931 The Theater Atrium combines retail, art, and performance.

3932 Theater Atrium section

3935 Precast planks are embedded with steel plates that allow each individual tread to be placed, adjusted, and welded to angles on the box beams.

3933 The box beams that support the stair range from 62 to 77 feet in length. They were delivered in sections and welded on site.

3934 The stair is supported on new beams placed between the existing columns.

3936 Construction, September 2020

3937 Jason Long standing on the X stair

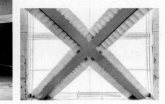

3938 Color tests, October 2020

3939 Below the X stair

3940 Lighting and grate mockup

3941 A backlit grate above the storefronts surrounds each atrium, providing light and shielding mechanical vents.

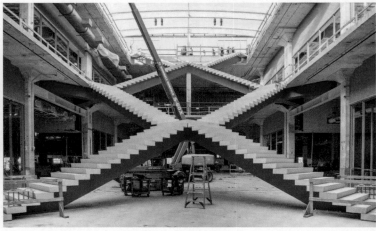

3942 The steel is painted green, drawing from the color of the original columns and the industrial equipment that once navigated the warehouse.

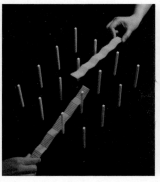 

3943 To maximize the density of food stalls and kiosks in the Market Hall, the O stair intertwines two long staircases to create a double helix.

3944 Early concept rendering of the Market Hall, a flexible system of steel grids

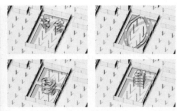

3945 Atrium studies, clockwise from top left: two towers; grand stairs; central tower; double helix

3946 Studies—square tower, round tower

3950 Panel types

3947 O stair sketch

3948 The twin paths up the O stair diverge twice: once to connect to the office level, then again at the roof.

3949 Vertical lighting is embedded in the steel mesh guardrails

3953 O stair and Market Hall roof from below

3956 Double-helix stair, December 2020

3951 O stair under construction in May 2020

3952 O stair plan

3954 The O stair was shop-fabricated in fully welded aluminum sections, then erected and connected on site.

3955 Salome Nikuradze on-site with Thomas Bett, Kirby Liu, and Brandon Roberts of Lovett Commercial

3957 Aluminum posts support both steel mesh guardrails and vertical lights that wrap the stair.

3958 O stair view from the F2 offices, November 2020

3959 Illuminated stair

3960 O stair and the Market Hall construction, April 2021

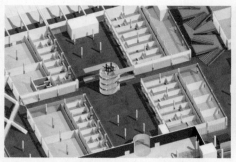

3961 Perimeter stalls line the sides of the Market Hall, with space in the center for island kiosks.

3962 Ridley Scott, *Blade Runner* (1982)

3963 Sample kiosk elevation and plan

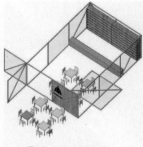

3964 Early concept kiosk

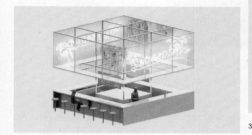

3965 Monolithic stainless steel bases provide all essential services, while grids of steel mesh and neon signage hover above the kiosks to broadcast each vendor.

3966 The largest kiosk incorporates seating into its interior, layering preparation, community, and dining into a single element.

3967 Market Hall kiosk concept collage

3968 The matrix of kiosks, a mix of bar seating, "grab-and-go," and larger vendors, generate unexpected view corridors and establish multiple potential social configurations.

3969 Market Hall under construction, April 2020

3970 Perimeter stall vendor configurations

3971 Gae Aulenti, Altana Palazzo Pucci (1972)

3972 Kiosk mock-up

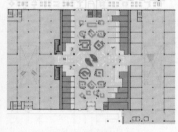

3973 Small kiosks line the north and south entries, with larger kiosks located at the center of the hall.

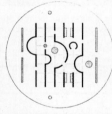

3974 Aldo Van Eyck, *Sonsbeek Pavilion* (1966)

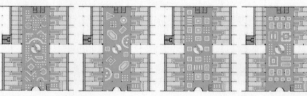

3975 Kiosk layout studies

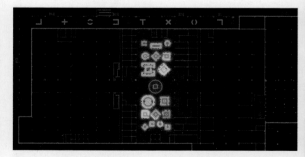

3976 The kiosks' mesh armatures will be integrated with lighting and individualized neon signage for the vendors.

3977 During the day, the kiosks' porosity takes advantage of the ETFE skylight to maximize daylighting. In the evening, the layers of reflective metal and neon recall the aura and energy of night markets.

3961–3977   POST Houston/Live Nation

3978　In the Coworking Atrium a series of enlarged platforms are lifted to create places to sit, work, and meet: a "social stair" big enough for collaboration.

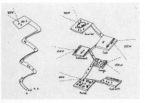

3979　Initial concept sketch

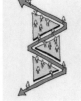

3980　Z stair sketch

3981　Concept sketch

3982　Concept collage

3983　Z stair with straight side panels and hanging structure

3984　The Z stair landings are extended to create three meeting and work areas, one at F2 and two floating between the floors.

3985　Z stair underside stained oak panelization

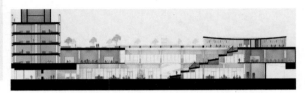

3986　The Coworking Atrium and Z stair act as the main connection from the lobby entrance directly up into the rooftop restaurant.

3987　The former post office lobby serves as the entry point to the Coworking Atrium.

3988　Cafe kiosk

3989　Vista from the platforms

3990　The Z stair is hung from the roof structure, creating additional workspaces in the shade of each of its landings.

3991　Underside of the stair and landings

3992　Z Stair and amphitheater seating construction, March 2021

3993　The Coworking Atrium provides areas for a variety of work: individual and group, casual and concentrated.

3994 Early facade studies clockwise from top left: media facade; Texas flag; gold brise soleil; polycarbonate

3995 In order to receive tax credits for the renovation of the Barbara Jordan Post Office, the fundamental character of the building's original facade had to be preserved. Any alterations to bring light into the building paradoxically would have to reinforce the monolithic character of the building.

3996 North facade existing condition

3997 Lucio Fontana, *Le Jour* (1962)

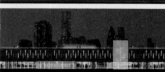

3998 Early facade studies: vertical windows; apertures; randomized; staggered

3999 Loading dock existing condition

4000 Long term plan—aperture facade and roof connections

4001 Early aperture concept

4002 Elevation detail

4003 Facade construction, October 2020

4004 The final apertures transform existing vents into windows, interspersing the existing openings with floor-to-ceiling windows of the same width.

4005 A Morse code facade

4006 The new windows, combined with a network of circular skylights, bring ample daylight into what had once been a dimly lit space.

4007 Skylight cutout, July 2020

4008 Skylight illumination, November 2020

3994–4008

POST Houston/Live Nation

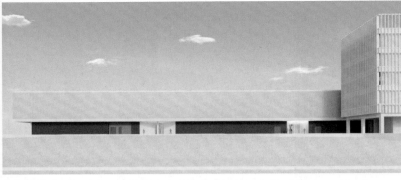

4009 While the Coworking Atrium lines up with the former post office lobby, accessing the Theater Atrium and Market Hall required new entries in the warehouse's south facade.

4010 At an early stage, the entries replicated the internal geometry of the signature stair in each corresponding atrium, a diamond for the X and a semi-circle for the O.

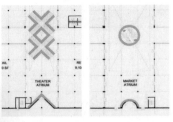

4011 X entry   4012 O entry

4013 In response to historic concerns, the final cuts were simplified. Less permanent marquees were introduced to echo the geometry of the spaces within.

4014 At night, the geometric marquees light up to highlight the points of entry to the two atriums.

4015 Precast panels that line the X atrium entry match the geometry of the atrium stair inside.

4016 When the warehouse was used to sort mail, a series of elevated "spy tunnels" allowed supervisors to watch over the work of mail sorters.

4017 Early site tour with client Frank Liu, 2016

4018 Spy tunnel existing conditions

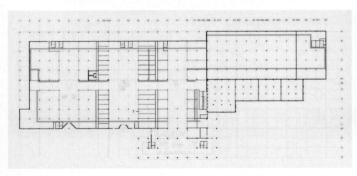

4019 The network of spy tunnels will remain and will be adapted into opportunities for art, light, signage, and graphics.

4020 Spy tunnels that were cut by the new atriums will be activated by new artworks from South Korean light artist Chul Hyun Ahn.

4021 Chul Hyun Ahn, *Void* (2011)

4022 Infinite mirror artworks will be inserted into the severed spy tunnel.

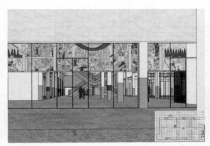

4023 Signage and advertising opportunities

4024 Super graphics

4025 Carsten Höller, *The Prada Double Club* (2017)

4026 Articulated geometry through internal light installations

4027 Administration lobby at the post office's opening, 1964

4028 Ludwig Mies van der Rohe, *Theater Project* (1947)

4029 Lobby desk seen from the plaza

4030 In addition to serving as the primary entry to the Coworking Atrium, the Administration Lobby also serves as reception for a future hotel housed in the former post office tower above.

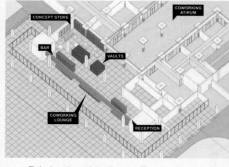
4031 Echoing the original post office service counter, a single long counter runs the length of the lobby and includes a bar, co-working space, and the hotel reception desk.

4032 Camaleonda (Bellini) campaign featuring Rudolf Nureyev (1980)

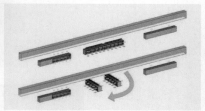
4033 The long counter rotates to become a focal point for events.

4034 Lobby seating

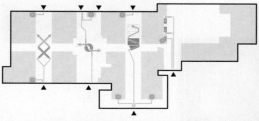
4035 New cabs within the existing elevator shafts create accessible routes around the building and its roof.

4036 Elevator existing conditions

4037 Otto Piene, *Lichtraum* (1961-1999)

4038 The updated elevators will be lined with backlit perforated panels, forming an infinite grid.

4039 The public restrooms on F1 reference the stainless steel materiality of the nearby Market Hall.

4040 Donald Judd, *untitled* (1968)

4041 F2 restrooms in yellow and purple

4042 Colored lighting test, March 2021

4043 The F2 workplace restrooms: bi-colored lighting

4044 Leandro Erlich, *The Swimming Pool* (2004); 21st Century Museum of Contemporary Art, Kanazawa.

4045 Rooftop restroom color study

4046 Rooftop restroom color study

4047 The rooftop restrooms: swimming pool palette

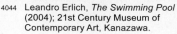

4048   The POST Houston rooftop adds 170,000 square feet of park space to downtown.

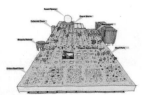

4049   The rooftop consists of a raised park, urban farm, two restaurants, and an event space.

4050   Roberto Burle Marx, Iberapuera Park (1953)

4051   Piet Oudolf, walled garden at Scampston Hall (2004)

4052   The rooftop park is divided up into three principal segments— garden, plaza, and farm

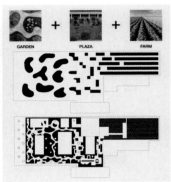

4053   Concept study of three zones

4054   Pattern studies

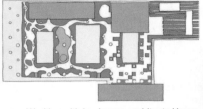

4055   Working with landscape architects Hoerr Schaudt, we developed a strategy for the rooftop that transitions between the linear rows of the farm to a tropical geometry at the lawn and promenade.

4056   Rooftop programs

4057   Concept rendering

4058   OMA and Lovett Commercial on the rooftop, groundbreaking 2019

4059   Jason Long at the POST Houston groundbreaking

4060   Rooftop event space with view of downtown

4061   A series of shading structures tailored to different programs provide shelter from the sun.

4062   ChromatiNet farm netting

4063   Study—bulkheads with canopies

4064   Shade structures and seating

4065   Downtown Houston seen from the rooftop park

4066   Each of the three atriums is capped by a roof of Novum ETFE, lightweight air-filled plastic pillows that let large amounts of natural light through to the offices, shops, and food stalls.

4067   Theater atrium ETFE roof, October 2020

4068   ETFE pillows

4048–4068

POST Houston/Live Nation

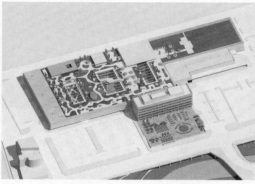

4069   Two restaurants sit within the rooftop park.

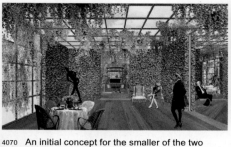

4070   An initial concept for the smaller of the two rooftop restaurants created a hidden garden.

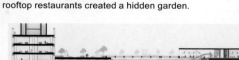

4071   Hidden Garden concept rendering

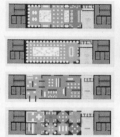

4072   Hidden Garden schemes

4073   Hidden Garden concept rendering

4074   The main restaurant anchors the end of the axis established by the Administration Lobby and the Coworking Atrium.

4075   The grid pattern first found on the exterior plaza continues through each space, further emphasizing the axis.

4076   Rooftop restaurant concept rendering, with a direct view down into the Coworking Atrium and Administration Lobby

4078   To provide shading, ceramic frit on the restaurant's glass walls echoes the vertical brise soleil of the post office tower facade.

4079   Lee Ufan, *From Line* (1978)

4080   The frit pattern is denser at the top of the window, with greater transparency at the bottom.

4077   The larger restaurant from the southwest

4081   View into the restaurant

4082   View toward the Z stair entry and adjacent bar, looking out to the rooftop park

4085   Downtown Houston skyline

4083   Restaurant frit construction view, March 2021

4084   Rooftop park view, April 2021

4086 POST Houston is located along the Houston Theater District. An event space was originally proposed for the roof of the warehouse to expand the theater district into the site.

4087 The proposed 1,000-seat event space would offer views to the city while connecting to the rooftop park. Its sloping roof would create a secondary exterior amphitheater for the rooftop park.

4088 Event space section

4089 Banquet

4090 TED Talk

4091 POST Houston has already been used for music festivals, such as Day for Night (2015–2017).

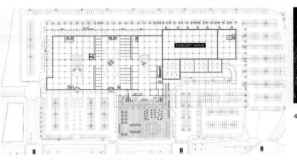

4092 Eventually, the POST Houston event space moved off the roof into the warehouse space to allow for a larger venue.

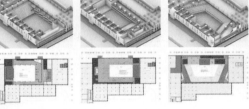

4093 Live Nation Entertainment, one of the country's largest events promoters and venue operators, will occupy the eastern wing of the POST Houston warehouse.

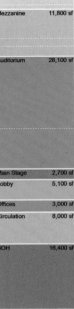

VIP	2,925 sf
Balcony	10,750 sf
Mezzanine	11,800 sf
Auditorium	28,100 sf
Main Stage	2,700 sf
Lobby	5,100 sf
Offices	3,000 sf
Circulation	8,000 sf
BOH	16,400 sf
Total	**88,775 sf**

4095 Construction view, September 2020

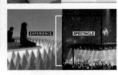

4096 Initial studies of stage placement: west, east, south

4094 Concert venue program breakdown

SOLID VOID BACK OF HOUSE

4097 The final scheme brackets the auditorium (void) with a band of circulation and smaller gathering spaces to the west and back-of-house to the east.

4098 Specific vs. adaptable; experience vs. spectacle

4099 To create the clear span for the venue, the original roof is replaced by a new roof supported by trusses.

4100 Views through the castellated columns

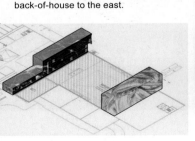

4101 The two solid spaces are defined with their own distinct characteristics and surround the open auditorium space.

4102 Auditorium void construction view, July 2020

4103 Auditorium view with new roof, structure, mezzanine seating, and balcony tribune seating construction, March 2021

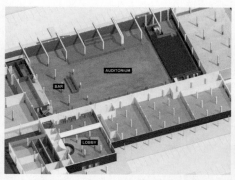

4104 The Lobby creates an entry from the rest of POST and the exterior.

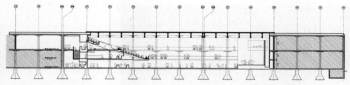

4105 Auditorium section

4106 The tribune of fixed seats on the west side of the auditorium anchors potential reconfigurations.

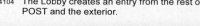

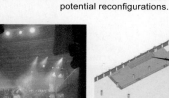

4109 Three bars on F1 surround the auditorium

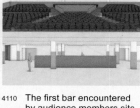

4110 The first bar encountered by audience members sits below the mezzanine.

4107 Audience members enter from the lobby (top left in the model view) to the back of the auditorium opposite the stage. Mezzanine and balcony levels above provide additional viewing space.

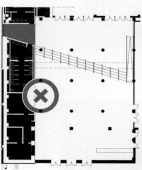

4108 View from the stage

4112 An early concept for furniture pieces designed to pivot around the existing columns, allowing the Lobby configuration to change between concerts.

4113 Early concept for carved wood rotating furniture

4114 Concert merch wall

4115 Lobby wall internal mockup—3 by 3-inch stainless steel mesh supported by cattle fence insulators over industrial heat-shield aluminized fabric

4116 Heat-shield fabric

4117 The ticket desk and coat check

4118 Full-scale lobby wall mockup, March 2021

4111 The only space in the existing building with circular columns, the Lobby is anchored by a circular bar.

4119 View to the entry from POST

4120 Lobby bar ring clad with custom resin by Sabine Marcelis

4121 Stadium lighting

4122 Custom resin initial test sample

4123 Lobby view, Friday Night Lights

4124 Just beyond the lobby and behind a double-height polycarbonate wall lit from within, an X-shaped stair takes audience members up to the mezzanine and balcony levels.

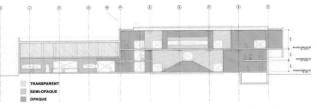

TRANSPARENT
SEMI-OPAQUE
OPAQUE

4125 Varying levels of opacity and transparency along the polycarbonate wall hide and reveal movement and back-of-house spaces beyond.

4126 Stair material— yellow painted OSB

4127 The stair to upper levels within polycarbonate wall

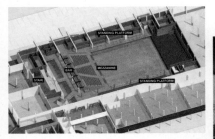

4128 The main stair brings audience members up to additional bars, standing platforms, and the tribune seats.

4129 Mezzanine bridges and bar

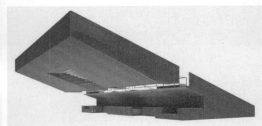

4132 "Under the bleachers"—behind the tribune are a series of discrete social spaces.

4130 Castellated columns

4131 Lighting test, March 2021

4133 Balcony bar and casual seating below the tribune

4134 Audience members sitting in the highest tribune seats enter through a trapezoidal cutout in the balcony.

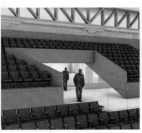

4135 Cutout from the balcony bar to the tribune seats

4136 Material— fiberglass grate

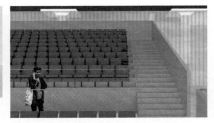

4137 Tribune seating

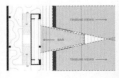

4138 Balcony bar funnel

4139 View from balcony bar to the stage through the tribune

4140 View from the tribune

4124–4140   POST Houston/Live Nation

4141   Three rooms on the balcony level and one underneath the stairs are designated as special areas: a Hidden Club, a Balcony Lounge, a VIP Room, and a Backstage Room for performers.

4142   Mood and material strategy

4143   An early concept for a Hidden Club made use of the space below the X-shaped stair.

4144   Hidden Club scenarios

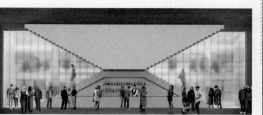

4145   Hidden Club

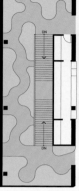

4146   Balcony Lounge plan

4147   Balcony Lounge model—the top of the stair empties out into the Balcony Lounge.

4148   Bernard Govin, Asmara Modular Sectional (1967)

4149   Balcony Lounge

4150   Balcony Lounge

4151   VIP Room plan

4152   VIP Room study

4153   Cut-out semicircular niches create seating in the walls of the VIP Room.

4154   VIP Room

4155   VIP Room materials

4156   VIP Room bar

4157   Stephen Frears, *High Fidelity* (2000)

4158   Backstage Room view from the balcony seats across the stage

4159   The private Backstage Room is carved out from the wall north of the stage, giving performers a view of the audience before the show begins and guests a unique view during the show.

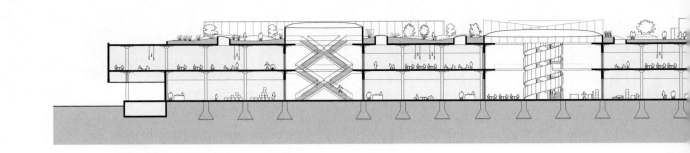

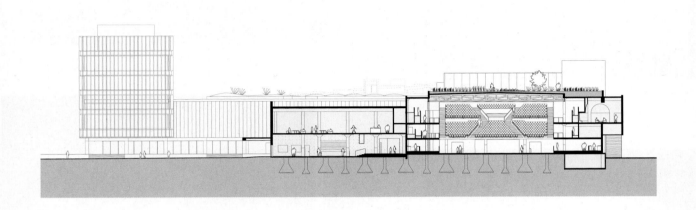

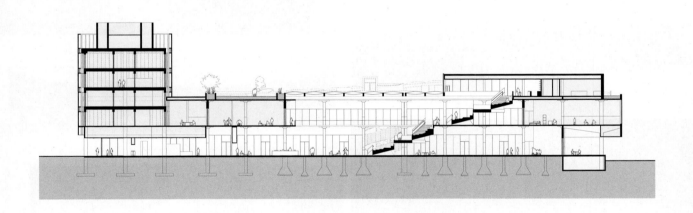

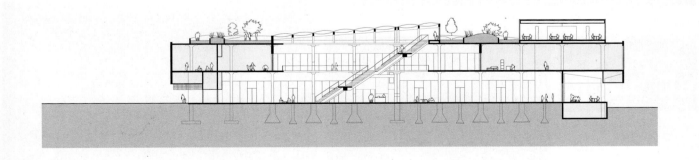

POST Houston/Live Nation

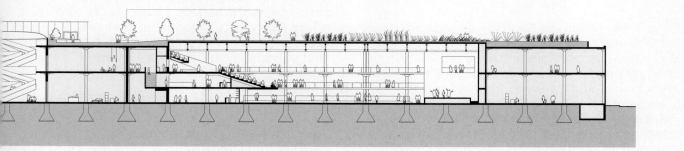

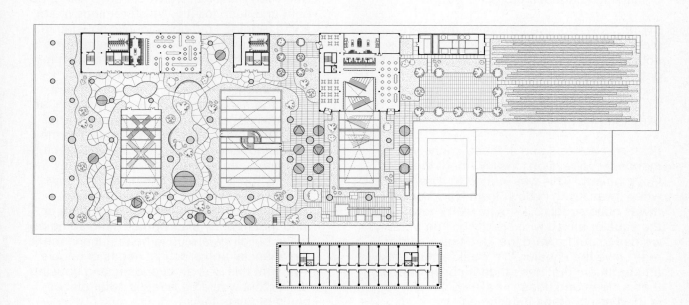

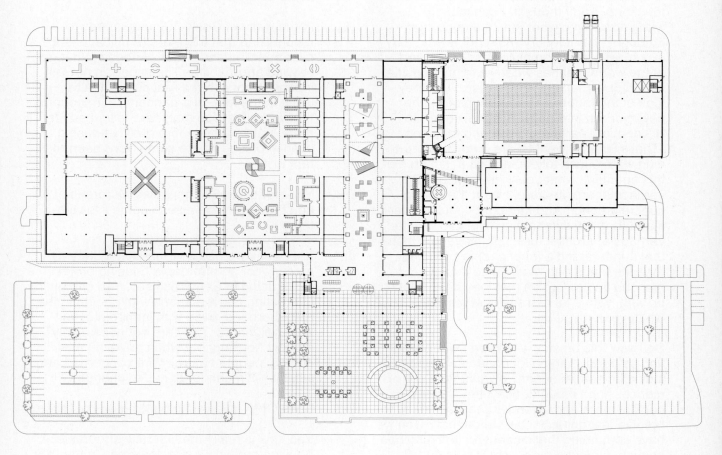

POST Houston/Live Nation

Interview David Byrne

Jason Long: From songs like "Don't Worry About the Government" to "Everybody's Coming to My House," architecture and even urbanism often play a role in your music. Beyond that, in your extra-musical work, from set designs to immersive works like *Neurosociety* and *Playing the Building*, I think there's also a thread of architectural thinking. Have you ever worked with architects, in a private way or in thinking about a project of yours?

David Byrne: Wow, No. I've renovated my apartment and house many years ago, but that's not the same thing. In those cases you don't get to imagine it from scratch. You don't get to question what it should be, how it should be. You're very much restricted—that's okay too.

I can go back to some of those songs you mentioned, like "Don't Worry About the Government." This was written at a period when I was living in downtown New York. It was quite squalid. It's quite well known—the squalor mixed with creativity. I perversely wanted to put forward the idea that we don't really love the squalor. We would actually like an apartment that has modern conveniences, that is clean and doesn't have cockroaches in it, where the taps function and the heat functions. And I thought, I can identify with people who want that. Going further, I thought I can identify with people who may live in, let's say, a small town in some part of the world that has what we might consider beautiful vernacular architecture. But they look at the modern apartment block—the new modern international style, concrete residential apartment block and they go, "That's where I want to live. They have running water, flush toilets, and wi-fi. I'm tired of this beautiful, what you think is nice, cute vernacular architecture. I want the boring concrete thing." And I thought I could understand that. My sympathies might lie with the vernacular architecture, but I have to admit that I understand a lot of people's longing for a life that's free of all those inconveniences and struggles that they have to put up with, with a lot of traditional buildings or whatever it might be.

So I saw this tension—between what I might find as beauty, and a lot of people's longing, including sometimes my own, for just convenience. And I thought, okay, that's a real conflict there and I wonder if there's a way to resolve that conflict. Can we do that? Can we have something that's beautiful that also has convenience and meets our daily needs?

JL: So you were undercutting the romantic attitude that squalor is necessary for a certain kind of creativity. I think you've also referenced before though that cheapness is essential. Or that being free from a certain kind of financial burden of real estate is maybe important to be able to get somewhere creatively early on. But that doesn't have to mean a cold-water-flat.

DB: Yes, absolutely. We took those places out of necessity and because they were cheap. But given a choice, we would have rather had heat and flush toilets. Which reminds me of some reading I did about public housing in Vienna. I think it was about a hundred years ago, when there was a big influx of people into the city. The city had a very leftist government at that point, and they took it upon themselves to build public housing for all these people who were coming into the city. They hired the best architects that they could find, and each architect or architectural firm made these huge edifices in spaces that the city found and brought up around town. They were scattered all over the place. They weren't relegated to the periphery or land that nobody else wanted. And some of these buildings are quite beautiful and meet the financial and practical needs of people. I thought this was an economic and housing model that would be lovely if other places could emulate this.

JL: In the wake of Covid-19, people are recognizing that there are ramifications to overcrowding and a lack of housing that go beyond affordability. The impact is not just inconvenience, but a real public health issue in the face of a pandemic. I'm hopeful that we will realize that there is a need for more housing, and more quality housing, even in places where some have been resistant to it.

DB: You mean like Silicon Valley. Where they don't want anyone else to come live with them.

JL: Last week we had a virtual community meeting for an affordable housing project we're doing in San Francisco. You end up in interesting conversations with people in the neighborhood, even with immediate next-door neighbors. They are not necessarily against housing, but when anything new comes, people naturally are concerned about what it will mean for things to change.

DB: So is OMA involved in building any of those?

JL: Yes, this is really the first fully affordable housing project we are designing in the U.S.

DB: I could see then that part of your work is not just building stuff, it's navigating all the bureaucracy and public perceptions, dealing with all those meetings and the implications that they might have. So sometimes you have to make adjustments.

JL: In some ways we rely on encounters with other people—the public, the client—or difficulties and contradictions in the site or the program to inspire something surprising in the design. So, on one hand you really welcome that sand in the oyster shell, but on the other hand, you have to balance and understand when to put up a fight. If you just say yes to everyone, then you end up with nothing.

DB: Exactly. That's where a bunch of the skill lies, I think. Figuring out how to navigate all that. That to some extent applies to me too, as far as figuring out how to put together a tour, a show. How much can I afford? How much can fit into a truck? How many trucks do I need? That's too many trucks, so we're going to have to cut something. But within financial limits, you have to design something that works. There are a lot of restrictions and pressures that you have to work around, which I don't mind at all. I find that a nice challenge. I'm sure that's part of what you guys do, too.

JL: You probably also need limits to gain any traction. But I feel like some of the things you've done, especially with the latest *American Utopia* set, are trying to get rid of limits in some ways.

DB: In some ways, yes. In that show, I discovered that using wireless technology, harnesses, and a certain number of musicians, I could have the entire band be mobile. Everybody is playing like a marching band carrying their instruments, whether it's drums or guitars. That in turn meant that I could clear the stage. I could have a completely empty stage that didn't need risers or cables, no lighting gear on stage, no platforms. I thought, wow, this is incredibly liberating. Of course there was an awful lot of tech going on backstage to allow that to happen, but what the audience sees is freedom and the liberating feeling that we have. It's not limitless possibilities, but it opens up a whole new set of possibilities.

JL: We're designing a performance venue in Houston and I've been thinking recently that it's a shame we didn't get to talk to performers as part of the design process. Of course, we had a lot of input from people who operate venues and put on shows, but not from musicians directly. A golfer like Jack Nicklaus ends up designing golf courses, but you never hear about a performer or musician designing a performance venue. Have you ever thought about how you might design a venue yourself?

DB: Well, some years ago I noticed that certain venues, certain buildings and spaces, are very suitable to one kind of music and not suitable to another kind of music. Carnegie Hall, for example, is a beautiful place for acoustic music. It has a natural reverberation that amplifies the music and adds warmth to it, to a certain kind of music. But then if you go in with very percussive electric music, it ends up being chattery and chaotic—it's a complete nightmare. The building wins and the music loses and that's not the building's fault. It was designed for a different kind of music. In some cases, with all sorts of baffles and acoustic things, you can add a certain amount of flexibility, but you can never have 100 percent flexibility. That's just not possible. So yes, it would be great to talk to musicians of different kinds about what they would like. But then I think you might get ten different buildings from ten different people. If it's a different kind of music, they're going to have their own dreams and desires.

JL: Sharing a building or a space—allowing it to function for different purposes for different people—always means some negotiation and compromise, I guess. We try to engineer flexibility into all of our buildings, but even that flexibility can create its own specificity, its own limits.

DB: I recently read a review of some books on Japanese postwar photography. One of the claims was that because the Japanese house in general did not have lots of wall space, the idea of making art that you would frame and hang on the walls was just not going to fly. You have the tradition of screens and scrolls where people bring out a scroll and unroll it to look at it. It said that the kind of architecture that they lived in might have determined the kind of work that photographers made. They rarely had exhibitions and would make lots of books, small editions—sometimes 500 copies or as few as 100. I thought this was really interesting—how the physical space that people live in determines the kind of art that gets made. Of course, you just go, of course it does! We just don't think about it because we assume that everybody lives like us.

JL: It's clear that architecture can shape our lives and how culture develops, but it's really rare that you can see it happen. When I was younger, just out of college, I actually lived in

OMA NY

David Byrne

Japan for a couple of years, and I stayed in a small house. That house, just as you described, had almost no walls, or at least walls that didn't move, The experience of living in that house really influenced my decision to try to become an architect because it was such a radically different way of being in a house than I had experienced before. I even wrote in my application to grad school about how I would hit my head constantly on the low doorframes and how that was a way of architecture telling me something.

DB: I think once it's pointed out, it seems very obvious. Of course this kind of music works in a cathedral and this other kind of music does not. It's always fun to find examples where one thing affects another, whether it's architecture or something else, and in ways that you may not first expect.

JL: When you're touring, you're having to fit your foot into many different shoes, so to speak. How do you adjust to those different settings?

DB: In the case of *American Utopia*, I designed a show that requires a lighting truss and a truss to hold this three-sided chain curtain that I designed and the venue would have to accommodate that. Every time restrictions appear, a certain number of venues go out the window. For instance, a lot of symphony halls have the symphony partly thrust out into the audience and the audience to some extent surrounds the symphony, like the Disney Concert Hall. But there are a lot of venues that do that. The show really demands a proscenium stage rather than that kind of stage, so I would've said, no, I can't do it there. We might be able to physically do it, but it's not going to work aesthetically very well. Then some of those restrictions are just about acoustics and the technical aspects of the show.

But I think there are other things that have to do with the experience of the audience. What's the first thing they encounter when they enter the theater? How do they arrive? You guys deal with this all the time, the arrival. What do they experience when they arrive? What is the lobby experience like? Can they have a drink and a conversation or are they just funneled in and funneled right back out, which is the traditional Broadway model of, "get them in, give them a sippy cup, then get them out again." Other theater people that I work with have said the show starts when they enter the door. It's not just what they see on stage, it's the whole thing.

JL: I saw *American Utopia* at the Kings Theatre in Brooklyn, which is a very ornate, older theater, whereas the venue we're working on in Texas is much more like a black box. Whether it's the organization of the space or ornamentation, when you're trying to put on a very specific kind of presentation can the whole architectural narrative of the venue get in the way?

DB: Sometimes. I feel like a contemporary hall and a more traditional hall like gilded Rococo halls, other than acoustic properties, what they have in common is that they make the audience feel special. You're about to have a special experience. There's a tinge of luxury. You're going to get to sit in a nice comfy seat. You're going to relax and we're going to treat you well. So it's that whole social aspect of what you're experiencing as opposed to the visual and audio experience.

JL: In *How Music Works*, you show two sketches of CBGB before and after its configuration was shifted around. In the original plan there was a pool table in the back, actually behind the stage. The later plan has the audience all in front of the stage, with dressing rooms behind. The first plan seems to offer the possibility of a much more complex relationship between the performer and the audience. CBGB was a tiny, almost informal space. Do you think it's possible to orchestrate that same complexity of social experience within a bigger venue?

DB: I suppose there is. I don't have the answers. But I notice that in one case the architecture, the way things are arranged in the room— in CBGBs—it's saying at the gate, you don't have to pay attention to the musicians all the time. You can go over and play at the pool table, halfway behind the musicians, and they become this part of the ambience of the whole place, which they may not appreciate, but that's a valid way of experiencing something too. Then the other thing, it's really designed... Everything is focused toward the stage. You're told by the design of the room that that's what you're here to do. You're here to watch what goes on, on that stage, and not to walk past it and start playing pool with your friends. But they're all equally valid.

Years ago, I finished a tour in Japan and I went to see a lot of Japanese theater— kabuki, noh, bunraku—and I noticed that some of the performances are really long. They can be six hours long, which beats Shakespeare. The audience, like opera audiences, sometimes dozes off. Sometimes they'll wander out in the middle of the show and have lunch or talk with their friends and go back in. The experience is that the show is this ongoing thing, this world that they can step in and out of. I've never thought of what I do in that sense, but it's equally valid.

JL: I once saw an Indonesian shadow puppet performance and noticed people wandering in and out, and even behind the puppeteers. For something that initially seems two-dimensional, with cut paper casting shadows on a screen, it suddenly became much more complex.

DB: Yes, I saw that too and I noticed that sometimes people would wander around the back and they would feel like part of the show was seeing the skill of operator. And so you can break the illusion of the shadow then come back to the front and you see the illusion reasserts itself. So there's all sorts of ways of making theater and performance. We limit ourselves in some ways and sometimes we're limited by the spaces and buildings that we make for our performances.

JL: This book started as a way of taking PowerPoint presentations that we developed for lectures, client presentations, and internal updates, and trying to use the format to investigate what we were doing. With PowerPoint we are presenting almost like a film, as a series of images one after the other, and typically the viewer only gets to see one image at a time. Here, we are unfurling that to see it all together at once.

I was intrigued by your interest in manipulating corporate communication techniques. You've experimented with the PowerPoint format yourself. What do you think about PowerPoint and that way of communicating?

DB: I was fascinated by PowerPoint for a couple of years. I saw it as an art medium. It was this software where you could dump all sorts of things into. You could dump in text, graphics, photos, videos. It was like a catchall, like a basket, and you could throw all that stuff in there. Of course I ended up doing it in a very abstract, humorous way. The slides would advance without the operator so the show would roll by itself. I like to think of a PowerPoint presentation as a form of theater. It's a theater with generally one performer and the screen or slides behind it. It's a kind of theater that has its rules and restrictions. Sometimes you get to a TED Talk and it's expanded to a proper theater, but most of the time it takes place in a conference room or in a very bland space where it doesn't announce that it's a kind of performance. But we all know that we've seen people who are really good at it—great PowerPoint performers. There should be an award for great PowerPoint performers, like the Emmys and

Oscars. I think a lot of the performers would be embarrassed to be considered great PowerPoint performers.

JL: Did exploring that change the way you thought about other types of presentations, staging, or performance at all?

DB: I think we all do that to some extent. When I would see somebody give a talk I would maybe unconsciously, or maybe sometimes a little bit consciously, think about, how did they structure that? How did they talk? What kind of voice did they use? Did that work? You realize that sometimes you're sucked in and engaged by completely irrelevant things that they're doing. They might use a personal anecdote to make a point and you realize that's not really proving the point, that's just a story—they're just a great storyteller.

You start to notice all sorts of things. You start to notice the connection with standup comedians, which is again, a one-person performance where you're just naked on stage. It's just you talking and you're directly connected to the audience. A lot of standup comedians came to see *American Utopia* and I wasn't sure exactly why. I think it might have been because, to some extent, I was getting laughs and sometimes dealing with pretty serious subjects but getting laughs. I think they thought, "Oh, he's putting a toe in our water here. He's walking into our territory. We know a little bit about this and want to see what he's doing." And sometimes they would help me out.

JL: I think standup comedy shares with music the need to convey the appearance of spontaneity for something that's actually quite well worked out.

DB: Exactly. And the only way they can refine it is by doing it in front of an audience. To some extent they know they have skills they can fall back on, but to some extent they have to do it in front of an audience in order to learn what's working and what isn't. You guys can't do that I would say. I mean, you can use PowerPoints, models, computer renderings and things like that, but people really can't experience a space until they're in it.

JL: That's one of the most difficult things. Now you have virtual reality, or you can build as big a model as you can manage. But at the end of the day you're estimating what the final experience will be. There's a real moment of joy when you finish a building and you go and see that it really did work or even worked better than we thought.

DB: For *Playing the Building*, I had certain ideas about how I wanted to do it. I wanted it all to be mechanical and nothing be computer generated. It wasn't until the thing was up and running that I realized what it really was about was democratizing a music experience. You see people waiting to play this thing and going, "Oh well, I didn't have piano lessons. I'm not really a musician. I don't know how good I'm going to be on this." Then they witness a ten-year-old kid joyously banging away on this thing and they realize, if that kid can do it, I can do it. So it puts everybody on the same level playing field and I realized that's what it's about. I didn't know that coming in. Have you had that happen in a space you guys have made—where it's really surprised you and people experience it or use it in a very different way than what you might have imagined?

JL: The project that comes to mind is the first we built after starting this New York office, a building for architecture design studios at Cornell. At the time, the architecture school was in a couple of older buildings from the nineteenth and early twentieth century, so the students were separated into different rooms. We wanted to give them a larger, more open space—a big flat plate that would erase all the limits that the older buildings created. But the plate had to cantilever out over a road, and that forced us to introduce a series of very large trusses into the studios. We worried that the structure—big sloped steel columns—would interrupt our universal ideal. In the end, though, the structure we thought would compromise the plate actually made it something different and better. Those sloped columns became exhibition surfaces or even places for creative vandalism. One student went as far as to string a hammock across the beams and made a small camp for himself. It's like when a ship sinks in the middle of an ocean and corals make a home there. So a space that we planned to be universal actually turned out to be—at the same time—very specific.

Sophia Choi: Unintended consequences are pretty much inevitable. Social media and Instagram have let us see how the buildings are used in ways that you can't plan for—from James Bond bar mitzvahs in a gallery to skateboarding on a concrete dome. I think those surprising and sometimes funny moments are good to witness because they remind us to not take ourselves so seriously all the time.

JL: I think humor or playfulness is important to our office and our designs—the willingness to accept or even amplify awkwardness, but also simply having a sense of humor.

You mentioned comedians coming to *American Utopia*, but humor is in a lot of your work. I'm interested in what draws you to use humor, or maybe more poignantly, did you ever think about doing standup?

DB: Standup seems terrifying. As close as I got to it, I realized how brave and fearless these people are. To a large extent it's very clear whether they're succeeding or failing. They're getting laughs or reactions, people paying attention or not. Whereas a lot of the other things we're doing, like what you guys do and a lot of what I do, the reaction is much more subtle. It's not as binary. It's not "I succeeded" or "I failed." It's something more nuanced.

In American Utopia, I mentioned dada artists and poets and how they use a lot of nonsense and non-rational things. I was similarly attracted to nonsense and humor pretty early on as a way to break the mold or break the restrictive thinking—a way to try and discover new ways of thinking and looking at things by shattering the mold through humor. It's often a disruptive way of making you see things in a different way, cracking through our perceived rationality.

JL: And has that ever been received negatively?

DB: Oh, yeah. There have been times when a lot of the humor that I was attracted to was very ironic humor. Not so much now, but for a while yes, and I think that can be very risky. A good example is Bruce Springsteen's "Born in the U.S.A." song, which sounds like a rah-rah patriotic anthem sonically, but what it's saying is something quite different. So there's this ironic tension between what it's actually saying and what it sounds like it's saying, which I'm sure was all intentional. But it's really difficult because people can hear it in a very different way than what might be intended. They maybe don't get that and that's certainly been the case with that song. That can be dangerous, I think, if it's not perceived the way you intend. I think occasionally you see that with buildings, where somebody has done something that's meant to be ironic architecture.

JL: We've been working recently within the realm of public space, and I think one thing that's interesting to me about some of your non-musical work is how you're engaging with the banal elements of public space, like your bike rack project. And in some of the works that are collected in *Your Action World* you placed collages of explosions onto ad space on bus stops. I'm curious what your thinking was behind engaging with those elements of public space.

OMA NY   David Byrne

DB: I think it goes back to that dada attitude and humor. You hope that by taking something out of a gallery space, you allow the work to be actually taken more seriously and have it be more disruptive and more engaging. When it's in a gallery people say it's art, it's just saying this, it's that, and it's already got a conceptual frame around it. When you take it out into the world, and you do something that looks like it might be a billboard or a bus stop ad, there's this jarring effect where people realize that's not a billboard. What is it? How did that get there? What's it about? I like if it I can find a balance where it looks like it could be an ad or it doesn't announce itself as some kind of artwork. Sometimes things can have more of the impact that you actually intended when they're moved to a different context.

JL: A context that you can't control or don't control.

You named your latest tour and show *American Utopia*, and one thing I wanted to talk about is the idea of utopia. When you think about utopian architecture or utopian urbanism, I think a very particular thing comes to mind—buildings that levitate in the air or structures that are so huge they can envelope a whole city. Utopian architecture is linked to fantastical structures or scales, but also a belief that technology solves its own problems with efficiency. It holds its own weight. But I wanted to ask you, what do you think is a utopian music?

DB: Wow. Utopian music. Well, I'm going to be a little bit immodest, but honest. In that show, because the entire band was mobile and could move around, it meant that the usual hierarchy of musicians could be broken. Usually it's me, the singer, in front, then maybe another layer behind me and another layer behind that. That hierarchy rarely changes. But in this case, everything can be flipped around. There could be moments where it's drummers in front, I'm in the back. Any order would work. It becomes much more democratic as far as what the audience experiences. You get to hear each one shine and what their contribution is to the whole. So, that to me was maybe a little utopian. We're also a very diverse band as far as gender and race. People could witness that and see that here was, in effect, a little tiny society that was working together and achieving something that's very joyful, not only for themselves but for the audience.

It seems to me that some kinds of music are less hierarchical than others. A lot of music that has its roots in Africa is less hierarchical.

You have parts where you have these many little parts that form an intricate machine. The whole thing only comes into existence when each little part is doing its thing. There is no one instrument that's playing, say, the melody. The melody is composed of an aggregate of what different people are doing. This is very much a cliché and probably an exaggeration, but a lot of Western music, Western classical music, let's say, is traditionally very hierarchical. And it would be very tempting to say that that's a mirror of social roles. I'm not sure that's true. It would be very tempting to look for that correlation.

JL: Some of my favorite moments in your music are when, for example, two guitar lines are playing at the same time in a very intricate way that feels almost uncoordinated, but at the same time effortlessly together. And to me those passages evoke joy, because of that vibration, almost, between freedom and meaning,

DB: I agree. I might be wrong but I like to think that the joy we experience in those kind of moments is because those are like musical analogues to a social structure. That we see a structure of collaboration and cooperation that produces something where the sum of the parts is more than the individual parts. And you witness it and experience it. It's not just an idea that's presented to you intellectually. It's something that when it's in musical form, you actually experience it. It comes to life.

David is a singer, songwriter, producer, actor, author, illustrator, filmmaker, and orchestrator of a diverse range of performances. He was a founding member of the Talking Heads. David's recent works include *American Utopia*.

23 East 22nd Street

23 East 22nd Street

23 East 22nd Street is one of the only projects in this book that we worked on pre-2007 recession. In a moment when New York was experiencing a boom in development, we wanted to provide an intuitive resolution to the challenge of creating a luxury residential tower in a culture of congestion. We were asked to design an unequal twin to One Madison Park, a sixty-story tower on 23rd Street that was reaching completion at the time we were commissioned. The shorter, more demure, residential tower would include a shared lobby and screening room connecting to One Madison Park.

Located on a site merely 33 feet wide just off Madison Square Park, the tower had to respond to a number of complex demands: in addition to negotiating zoning law and its neighbors, it had to avoid blocking the views from its taller sibling. At that moment (and even today), architects were being deployed to use every possible method to boost per-square-foot price. We tested a great number of funky forms but, in the end, were reminded by the neighboring Flatiron Building that blatancy—straightforwardness of simply extruding the unique shape of the site—can produce something pristine yet iconic.

We looked at the existing condition again and decided to reflect on the brief and the givens. What we faced was a seemingly unresolvable contradiction between the developer's desired FAR (floor area ratio), and the height limit it set to preserve the views of pre-sold units in One Madison Park. For a tower to meet both requirements was physically impossible—maximizing FAR would result in exceeding the height limit. Luckily, the developer owned the air rights of the adjacent building, which allowed us to cantilever the tower slightly. What if we, like the Flatiron, "extruded" the contradictions of the givens? Could that obedience produce something simultaneously improbable and seemingly inevitable?

The building's external form and internal organization deliberately react to the immediate context. Rising to a height of 355 feet, the tower stretches up to the east and steps away from One Madison Park, gaining additional area as it cantilevers 30 feet over its neighbor. By stepping to the east gradually, rather than in one dramatic push, we were able to extend beyond the expected "slight" cantilever, covering nearly the same distance as the width of the tower's base.

This asymmetrical form simultaneously provides views of Madison Square Park around our taller twin (and preserves views south from its units) while maximizing light penetration to the neighbors below. The building form mirrors a typical New York set-back. From the north, the tower appears like a shy child hiding behind its parent. From the south its dynamic asymmetry creates an iconic silhouette.

The swaying tower is supported by a structural facade: a set of shear walls with openings for light and air. In areas under greatest stress, the window spacing is modified to provide increased structural area and rigidity, supporting the building like a cinched corset. The resulting facade transitions vertically, generating a gradient from punched windows to transparent curtain wall.

Using the complexity—even strangeness—of the site, unusual qualities were introduced to the apartments: irregular ceiling heights, views around the tower to the north, and overhangs with windows to the city below. As the building steps out to the east and then back from the west, the area of every other floor differs. The stepping creates balconies in the upper units and windows placed in the floors of the lower units. Loft-like scenarios play out at the highest and lowest portions of the building, while in the larger middle floors, lower ceilings reinforce the units' panoramic breadth and help establish a more intimate scale.

Despite our efforts, the tower ultimately fell victim to the Lehman Brothers bankruptcy and financial collapse. The tower's form is ironically symbolic of its unfortunate history—the steps that climb up parallel the upturn of the 2007 building boom that conceived the project, and the steps that go down parallel the stock market crash of 2009, which led to its death.

Location	New York, NY, USA		
Status	Unbuilt, 2007–2009		
Typology	Residential		
Program	Residential	48,400 ft²	4,500 m²
	Screening Room	1,600 ft²	150 m²
	Total Area	50,000 ft²	4,650 m²

OMA NY   23 East 22nd Street

4167

23 East 22nd Street

4168

23 East 22nd Street

OMA NY   23 East 22nd Street

4169

23 East 22nd Street

OMA NY

23 East 22nd Street

4170

23 East 22nd Street

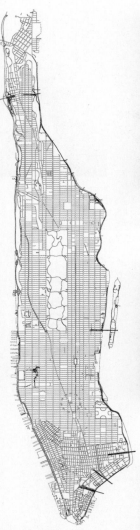

4171 The site for 23 East 22nd Street is located in Manhattan's Flatiron District.

4172 Where Midtown meets Downtown, the Flatiron District is characterized by a series of towers higher than 500 feet. This ensemble of buildings rises above the typical datum of lower Manhattan.

4174 23 East 22nd Street would be the final phase of Slazer Enterprises' One Madison Park (OMP) development, which also includes a sixty-story residential tower on 23rd Street.

4173 Panoramic site view—One Madison Park, Met Life Building, and 41 Madison

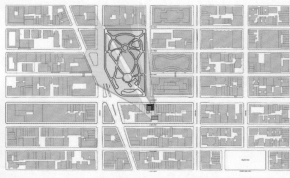

4175 The proximity to Madison Square Park, combined with unobstructed views to the south, give the site a unique opportunity within the city. However, One Madison Park's adjacency to our twenty-two-story building blocks potential views to the park.

4176 Existing building seen from 22nd Street

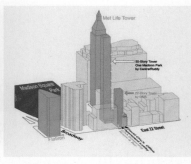

4177 The project as a whole would use the more intimate scale of 22nd Street to serve as the residential entry for the entire development.

4178 23 East 22nd Street aims to complete the client's existing and adjacent One Madison Park.

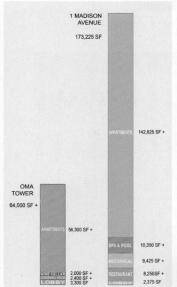

4179 23 East 22nd Street and One Madison Park program

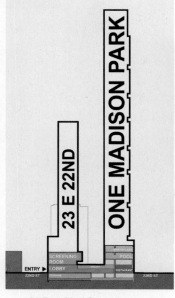

4180 23 East 22nd Street links to One Madison Park through shared lobby and amenity spaces.

4181 Located on a narrow site (33 by 90 feet) with adjacent buildings to the east and west and One Madison Park to the north, 23 East 22nd Street is defined by the presence of its neighbors.

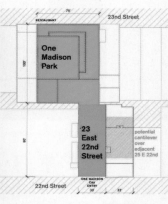

4182 Agreements with the neighbors allow the building to cantilever to the east, expanding the potential for larger floor areas and improved views to the north. However, as the building increases in height and width, it threatens to compromise light and views to and from its neighbors.

4183 Study—brute force cantilever

4184 Study—attachment

4185 Study—bubble

4186 Study—sponge

4187 Study—garden terraces

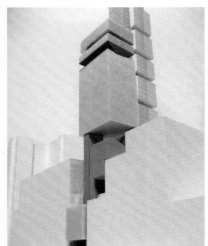

4192 Study—program insertions and stacks

4188 Study—oversized terrace boxes

4189 Study—irregular extrusions

4190 Study—pixel

4191 Study—stepping

4193 Study—stacked villas

4194 Study—stacked loops

4195 Study—tilted townhouses

4197 Study—carved zoning envelope

4198 Study—cantilevered wedge

4199 Study—twist

4201 23 East 22nd Street exhibition at the Center for Architecture (2009)

4202 Study models on display at the Center for Architecture

4200 Study models

4196 Study—supertall

4183–4202

23 East 22nd Street

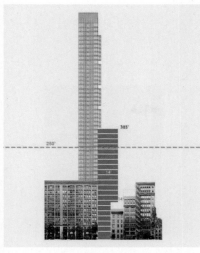

4203 If it stayed within the bounds of an "expected" cantilever, the tower would rise above a 250-foot limit set by the developer and block views from One Madison Park.

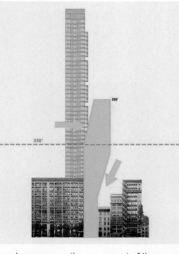

4204 In response, the upper part of the building steps back at the west, preserving southern views from One Madison Park. At the east, it gradually steps out, maximizing light penetration to the neighbors below.

4205 Mirroring the traditional New York setback, the building's form is at once familiar and unique.

4206 New York "ziggurat"

4207 Mirrored

4208 Elevations from 22nd and 23rd Streets

4209 The stepping of the top volume at the west not only preserves views out of One Madison Park, but also preserves views of the building itself.

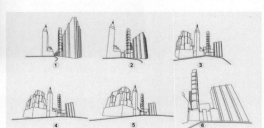

4210 Tower visibility from Madison Square Park

4211 The vertical stepping of the lower volume allows light to penetrate into the lower units.

4212 One Madison Park, 23 East 22nd Street, and the Metropolitan Life building form a trio of towers that provide a new skyline for the Flatiron District.

4213 At times counterpoint, at times complement, the building's relationship to its neighbors changes as one moves through the city.

4214 View from the southwest

4215 View from Met Life clock tower

4216 View from the south

4217 The building is selectively obscured by One Madison Park's slender profile, a vertical datum that is its constant foil.

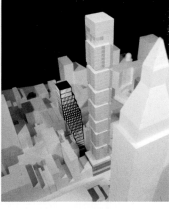

4218 It rises to 355 feet and strategically balances around One Madison Park.

4219 From the east, the two towers stand back to back.

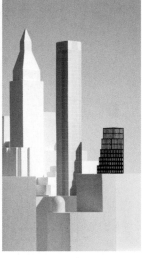

4220 When partially obscured, 23 East 22nd Street can appear almost ordinary.

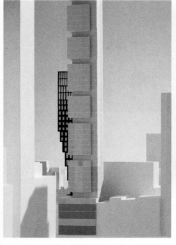

4221 From the north, it is a shy child hiding behind its parent.

4222 When viewed from the south, the three towers seem to align intimately.

4223 Panoramic view from 22nd Street

4224 View from 23rd Street

4225 Residential entrance along 22nd Street

4226 View from 23rd Street

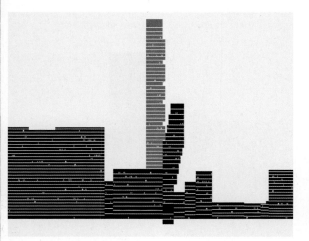

4227 Floor-to-floor heights are compressed toward the middle of the building, increasing structural rigidity.

4217–4227   23 East 22nd Street

4228 The 30-foot cantilever to the east is supported by a structural facade—a set of shear walls with openings for light and air.

4229 Corsets

4231 The seemingly contextual punched window is harnessed for spectacular ends.

4232 Structural stress diagram

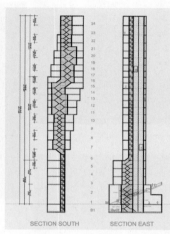

4230 In areas under greatest stress, the window spacing is modified to provide increased structural area, supporting the building like a structural corset.

4233 Model highlighting window spacing throughout the facade

4234 Due to its shifting geometry, only a slender area of the building is continuous throughout the floors.

SECTION SOUTH   SECTION EAST

4235 The core rotates and shifts as it rises through the tower.

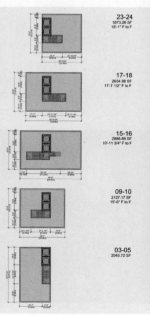

23-24
1873.26 SF
18'-1" F to F

17-18
2634.98 SF
11'-7 1/2" F to F

15-16
2688.89 SF
10'-11 3/4" F to F

09-10
2127.17 SF
15'-6" F to F

03-05
2045.72 SF

4236 The core's position is optimized for each floor plate.

4237 As the egress stair moves vertically up the building, it rotates around the central core.

4238 Model highlighting the shifting egress stair

4239 At the top of the building, the facade thins, approaching curtain wall proportions.

4240 A grid of highly polished stainless steel wraps the facade—a composite of metal and glass fiber reinforced concrete (GFRC) that underlines the building's solidity and reflects the shifting life of the city.

4241 Concrete is always a hybrid of cementitious material and steel. The facade uses a similar composite to create a counterpoint to the solidity of the structure that supports it.

4242 Facade study model

4243 One-inch bands of stainless steel are embedded in GFRC panels during the casting process, allowing for maximum integration of the two materials.

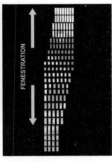

4244 The grid formed by the bands minimizes the reading of panel joints that would otherwise undermine the monolithic nature of the building.

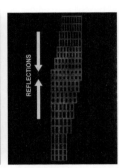

4245 Gradient fenestration

4246 Gradient reflections

4242 Facade study model

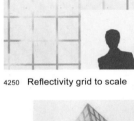

4250 Reflectivity grid to scale

4247 Full-scale mock-up

4248 Facade buildup

4249 Full-scale facade grid study

4251 Facade reflectivity at various times of day

4252 Projection tests on model

4253 Reflection study

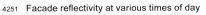

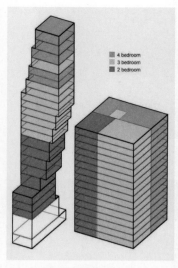

4254 23 East 22nd Street features eighteen luxury residences, including fifteen full-floor residences, two duplexes, and one quadruplex penthouse.

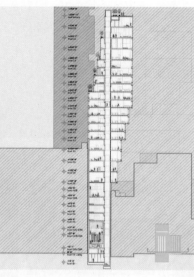

4255 While the units differ in area, smaller floor plates have higher ceiling heights, creating a near-constant volume for each unit. Equality through difference.

4256 Panorama—F13 and F14

4257 Loft—F23 and F24

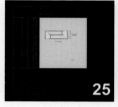

4258 F25 (terrace)

4259 F24 (penthouse)

4260 F23 (penthouse)

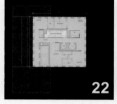

4261 F22 (penthouse)

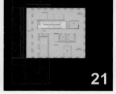

4262 F21 (penthouse)

4263 F15

4264 F7

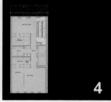

4265 F4

4266 A wide range of finish options allows residents to customize their interiors, ensuring that each unit is unique.

4267 Custom resin sink mock-up

4268 Blue resin sink

4269 Bathroom finishes— aluminum, walnut ecoresin, polished concrete

4271 The four top floors are combined into a quadruplex penthouse. A double-height (30-foot) great room serves as the penthouse entry. An acrylic-bottomed rooftop pool above doubles as a skylight.

4270 Finish options—aluminum and walnut

4254–4271

23 East 22nd Street

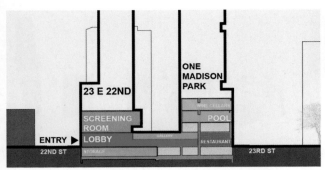

4272 23 East 22nd Street and One Madison Park link through the shared lobby and amenities. The Creative Artists Agency (CAA) Screening Room is located within 23 East 22nd, while a pool, spa, wine storage/tasting room, and restaurant are in the base of One Madison Park.

4273 At the building's base, the Creative Artists Agency (CAA) Screening Room provides an important cultural anchor for the building.

4274 Reference—Samuel Goldwyn Theater, Academy Screening Room, Los Angeles

4275 Reference—MGM United Artists Screening Room, New York

4276 Reference—Paramount Studios Screening Room, Los Angeles

4277 Reference—Universal Screening Room, Los Angeles

4278 Thao Nguyen (CAA) and Jason Long at the CAA Screening Room, Los Angeles

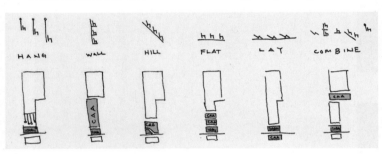

4279 Screening room seating typology studies

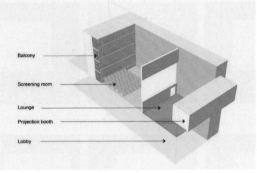

4280 An initial screening room study proposed a balcony wall and flat seating in order to maximize flexibility.

4281 Balcony wall concept collage

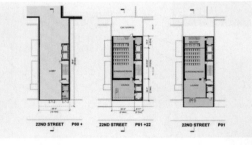

4282 Screening room plans

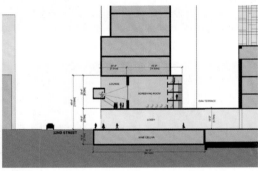

4283 Balcony and screening room section

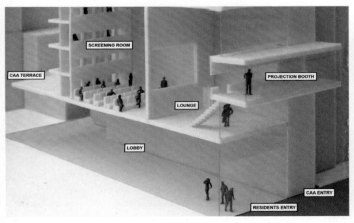

4284 The screening room is placed between two social spaces: a lounge and an outdoor terrace. Projections pass through the lounge to the front of the screening room, allowing seating to occupy the typical projector location at the back.

4285 Cantilevered projection booth over the residents' entry

4286 Balcony wall model

4272–4286   23 East 22nd Street

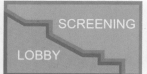

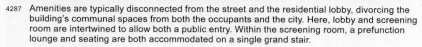

4287   Amenities are typically disconnected from the street and the residential lobby, divorcing the building's communal spaces from both the occupants and the city. Here, lobby and screening room are intertwined to allow both a public entry. Within the screening room, a prefunction lounge and seating are both accommodated on a single grand stair.

4288   The slope of the screening room actively engages the ground level, connecting the building's most prominent and public feature to the street.

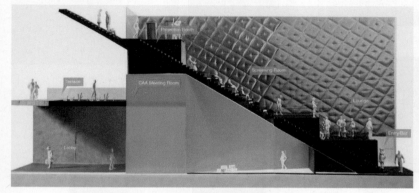

4289   Larger steps within the grand stair accommodate gathering areas for the prefunction lounge. Spaces that serve the screening room—bar, cloakroom, casual seating, and projection—are embedded within.

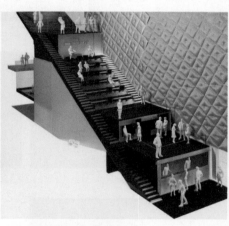

4290   Grand stair screening room

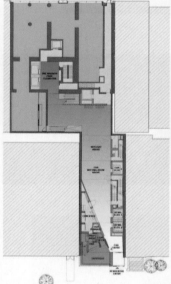

4291   23 East 22nd Street and One Madison Park lobby connection

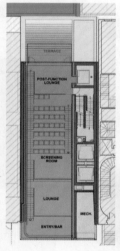

4292   Grand stair plan

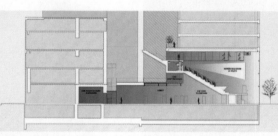

4293   Screening room above, residents' lobby below

4294   Stair reference—Cannes Film Festival

4295   Stair reference in film—*Battleship Potemkin* (1925)

4296   Stair reference in film—*Roman Holiday* (1953)

4297   Acoustic pillow wall

4298   Screening room lounge

4299   Connection to 22nd Street

4300   Lobby view

4301   At the street level, the CAA Screening Room and the building's residential entrance together form a seamless identity for the building.

4287–4301   23 East 22nd Street

4302 Street view of sloping screening room

4303 Street level bar

4304 Prefunction

4305 Screening

4306 Operable full-length curtains open and close to provide a controlled continuity to the street level.

4308 Lecture configuration—stage and closed curtain

4311 The slope of the screening room spills out, playfully connecting the building's most prominent and public feature to the street.

4307 The lobby is shaped by the slope of the screening room seating, creating a funnel that leads residents to 22nd Street.

4309 Lobby study—illuminated

4312 Lobby section with sunken courtyard and CAA meeting room

4310 Study model—illuminated cone

4313 Study model—monochromatic

4314 Study model—reflective panels

4315 Study model—single material in travertine

4316 The building's lobby provides access not only to 23 East 22nd Street, but also to One Madison Park. The presence of the screening room above creates a tapered ceiling that forms a dramatic entry.

4302–4316   23 East 22nd Street

4317 In addition to sharing a common lobby, the two residential towers share two full floors of amenity spaces located on the second and third floors of One Madison Park. We designed the initial interiors for the amenities within the taller tower.

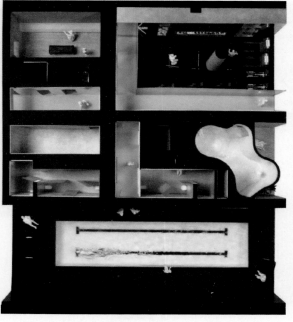

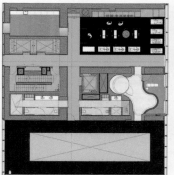

4320 F2 amenity materials are a combination of luxury and playfulness.

4319 F2 plan

4318 F2 amenity level model—gym, spa and shower, pool, and changing rooms

4323 The gym is kept as porous as possible, with a black-stained wood floor with rubber build-up to contrast with the green circulation corridor.

4322 Gym model

4321 Green circulation corridor

4325 Pool model

4326 The pool is surrounded by Absolute Black Granite, providing a strong yet mute backdrop for swimmers.

4324 Changing room

4328 The spa sauna and shower are dual curved shapes directly across from each other.

4329 Spa lounge

4327 Spa and shower

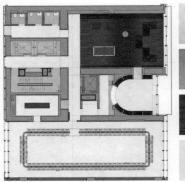

4330 F3 plan

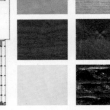

4331 F3 amenity materials feature a more muted palette.

4332 F3 amenity model—wine cellar, tasting room, bar, and club room

4333 F3 corridor toward wine cellar

4334 Custom wine cellar model

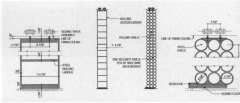

4335 Wine storage—mobile elements

4336 Wine storage full-scale mock-up

4337 Wine storage full-scale mock-up

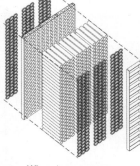

4338 Wine storage axon

4339 The wine cellar features walls lined with an industrial glass tube system for bottle storage.

4340 F3 tasting room

4341 F3 bar

4342 Wine cellar view

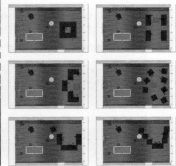

4343 Club room seating configurations—furnishings are designed to be highly configurable.

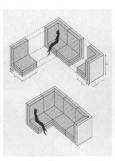

4344 Club room seating modules

4345 F3 club room configurable seating modules

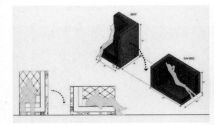

4346 Custom club room furniture flexibility—from seating to daybed

4347 F3 club room

4348 F3 club room model

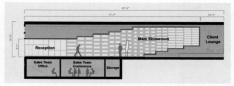

4349 The design of the 23 East 22nd Street sales gallery made it possible for visitors to experience the unique form of the building in a new perspective by walking through the height of the tower.

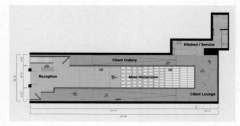

4352 Visitors enter the sales office and immediately enter the tower showroom.

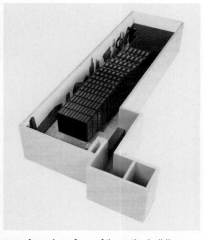

4350 A mock-up form of the entire building was inserted into the existing sales office space, but with the tower on its side.

4351 The 23 East 22nd Street sales office transformed the exterior building elements into an interior space.

4353 The idea was to flip the building on its side so visitors could look and walk through the tower.

4354 Showroom model—view from entry

4355 Showroom model—view from display

4356 Model

4357 Model

4358 The orientation posed a unique opportunity to experience the design of the building.

4359 Different elements of the building's design were adapted to fit the functions of the sales office.

4360 Windows became shelves, and the building's cantilevers and balconies acted as stepped seating, display space, and lighting.

4361 Visitors at the sales office opening

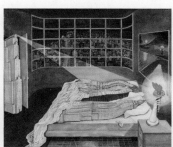

4362 23 East 22nd Street in bed with Madelon Vriesendorp's *Flagrant Délit* (1978)

4363 Mirrored facade wallpaper

4365 The project's inception was a direct result of the 2007 building boom.

4364 Visitors at the sales office opening

4366 But as a result of the 2009 financial crisis, the project was canceled.

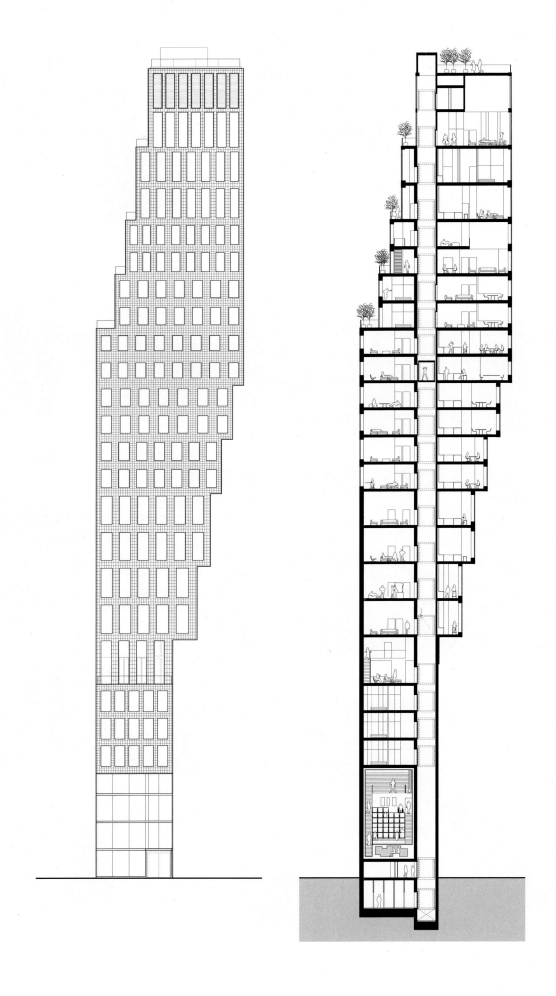

4367–4368

23 East 22nd Street

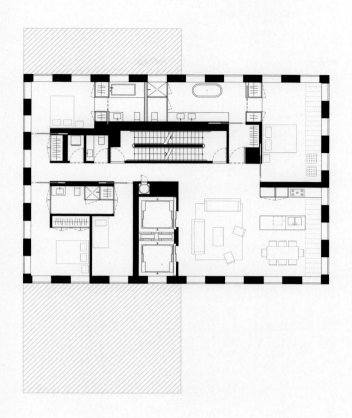

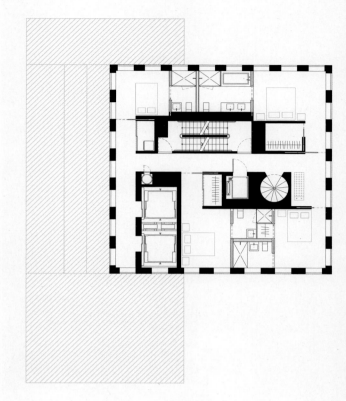

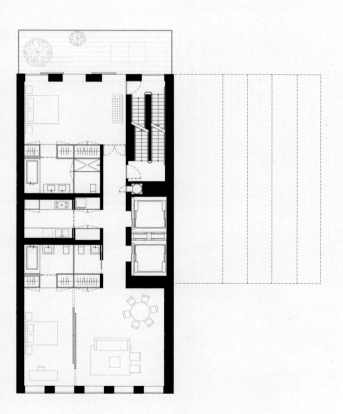

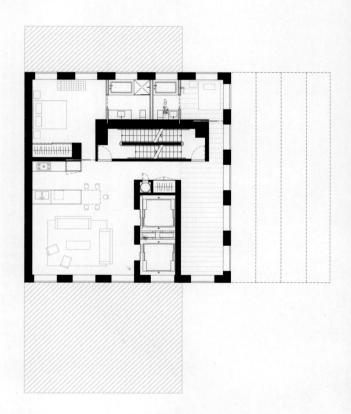

4369–4372   23 East 22nd Street

Park Grove

Park Grove

On our first site visit for Park Grove, we met with a historian and learned about Coconut Grove's development history. One of the first and oldest permanent settlements in Miami, it was once an independent city, later annexed by Miami in 1925. With a history of migration from the Bahama Keys, it has its own bohemian culture, opposite in character to the more dazzling Miami lifestyle. It offers an alternative to metropolitan downtown.

Miami's recent influx of new culture and commerce has resulted in a sea of luxury residential towers that are often disengaged from the subtle historic and cultural contexts of their neighborhood. Rather than surrendering to the "case of the newness" in Miami, we wanted the design to be driven by the essence of the place, which might not always be a guiding principle for the luxury condominium typology.

Coconut Grove has seen its own emergence of vertical density—a string of large-scale condos, offices, and hotel buildings along the waterfront and the main thoroughfare, Bay Shore Drive. Park Grove is located on what was the last developable site along the waterfront. This rare break in an otherwise impenetrable wall of towers was the only remaining connection point between Coconut Grove's community scale and a series of civic assets along Biscayne Bay. Located in a strategic point at the nexus of Miami's urban grid and the bay's edge, the towers posed an opportunity to seamlessly connect the city and coast. Can the development draw in the quality of public life from the city, park, and waterfront while offering the intimacy of a private retreat?

The competition brief proposed a chunky, twin tower arrangement, following the local trend of high-density massing along the waterfront that paradoxically blocked the continuity from the city to the water. We took an idealized approach, simultaneously creating porosity and verticality, but immersed in the natural setting of Coconut Grove. We broke the two towers down into six unusually slender towers that house two units per floor and one unit on the top. The field of slim towers was formed by vertically stacking individual retreats at the scale of Coconut Grove's homes. We won the competition. Immediately after, the scheme was rejected—the six towers were not commercially viable. We tested options for fewer towers. How many towers and what kind of configurations would satisfy the market without sacrificing our intentions?

Our solution was to keep the slender towers but merge them together. Like a reverse mitosis, we combined two sets of two towers into a single tower with two cores. Two undulating towers and one slender tower distribute one million square feet of living space across a five-acre lot and preserve the site's porosity. Like the islands of Biscayne Bay, the three towers have an organic edge that is synergistic with the lush nature around them.

The conjoined cylindrical towers provide a variety of unit floorplans, arranged on axis with the bay. The two cores banish the long corridor and enable direct access to units. The curved plates optimize views for all units while decreasing wind-loads and improving facade-to-area ratios. The cinched centers of the conjoined towers establish floor-through transparency. The panoramic views merge the interior with the exterior—an attribute of the local cottages that once populated Coconut Grove.

Sculptural perimeter columns frame waterfront and city views, freeing the units from interior columns and ensuring future flexibility. From the outside, the tapering columns create a destabilizing, mirage-like effect that resonates with the organic language of a tropical environment. The towers are embedded within an undulating plinth, a programmatic landscape that forms a continuous grove of tiered amenities. Sinuous paths through the three towers across the site weave the waterfront and public park with the city, establishing a continuity of activities and green throughout.

Location	Coconut Grove, FL, USA		
Status	Completed, 2020		
Typology	Residential		
Program	Residential	880,000 ft²	81,800 m²
	Raised Plinth Landscape	86,000 ft²	8,000 m²
	Amenities	138,200 ft²	12,800 m²
	Retail	10,500 ft²	980 m²
	Parking	238,500 ft²	22,200 m²
	Total Area	1.35 million ft²	125,780 m²

4374

Park Grove

Park Grove

OMA NY.

Park Grove

Park Grove

OMA NY   Park Grove

Park Grove

OMA NY

Park Grove

4378

Park Grove

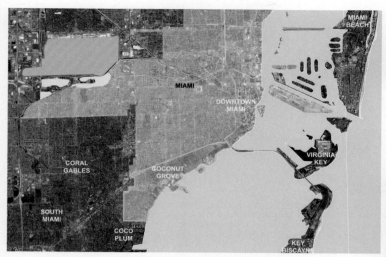

4379 Coconut Grove is located south of Miami proper and is a distinct community within the city's patchwork of neighborhoods. More quiet and intimate, it offers an alternative to metropolitan downtown.

4380 Historically, the neighborhood grew from a new typology that was centered around the local community while offering the intimacy of a private retreat.

4381 Peacock Inn, Coconut Grove (1880s)—the first hotel in Biscayne Bay

4382 Gatherings such as this picnic hosted by Isabella Peacock helped form a close-knit community in Coconut Grove.

4383 Site visit (2013)

4384 Coconut Grove waterfront (1945)

4385 Coconut Grove waterfront (2012)

4386 Existing site (2013)

4387 Existing site (2013)

4388 Site plan and program breakdown—parking, amenities, Coconut Grove Bank, and residential

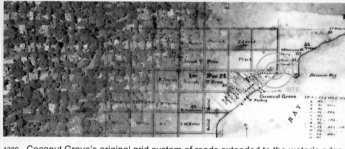

4389 Coconut Grove's original grid system of roads extended to the water's edge. The site lies where the grid meets the waterfront.

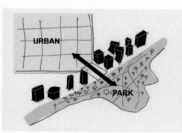
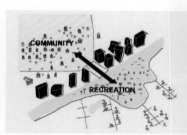
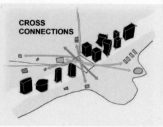

4390 The undeveloped site was the only break in an otherwise impenetrable wall of towers that separated the cultural community of Coconut Grove from a series of key assets to the South. The site has an opportunity to act as a point of connection between the Coconut Grove community and the civic park and waterfront.

4391 The site sits in proximity to many of Coconut Grove's key cultural and leisure attractions.

4392 How could we reinstate the intention of the original grid of roads to forge a better connectivity between the city and the waterfront?

4393 The typical development model along Bayshore Drive is derived to achieve maximum views, generating a wall of towers with minimum permeability.

4394 Park Grove investigates the typical real estate formula—the densest (15,000 square feet per floor), tallest (20 stories), and longest (180 feet) slabs allowable by code. Following this formula would generate two slabs of maximum size, placed at right angles to take advantage of the views to the city and the bay.

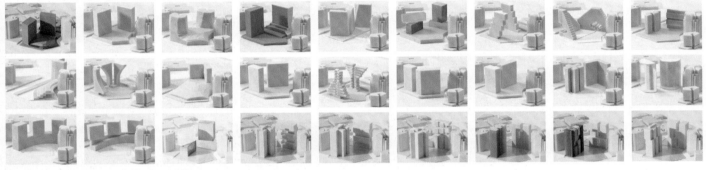

4395 Study models for two-slab tower configuration

4396 Rather than retaining the two-tower condition, the two slabs are decoupled. The "field" scheme proposes a series of six identical towers. Sized according to the ideal unit layout, the towers are slender enough to maximize porosity between the city and waterfront, while placed carefully in relation to one another to achieve maximum views.

4397 Initial massing collage for the "field" six-tower scheme

4398 Study models for six towers

4399 The tower ultimately represents the vertical stacking of individual retreats at the scale of Coconut Grove's homes, thus connecting the residential community while still maintaining intimacy and privacy for the residents.

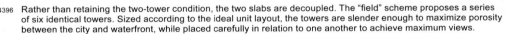

4400 The six slender towers introduced a scale similar to that of the adjacent neighborhoods, like a vertical extrusion of houses.

4401 This decoupled scheme of six towers maximizes views from each individual unit and provides a greater number of units with views to the water and the city.

4402 Dispersing square footage of livable area across the site in multiple towers optimizes views as well as porosity through the site. Structural perimeter columns support the slenderness of the towers.

4403 Like a forest of towers, the residences are immersed in the nature and lush open space around them.

4393–4403   Park Grove

4404 While the six-tower configuration provided permeability through the site, it left efficiency and privacy between the residences lacking, requiring further studies in tower quantity.

4405 Tower quantity studies for site

4406 Tower quantity studies

4407 Various options for tower quantity and configuration were explored to reduce the total number of towers while maintaining views and porosity through the site—clusters of two towers, three towers, and four towers.

4408 Two towers are merged into one another, creating one peanut-shaped tower.

4409 The resulting concept quite literally showed the design process, transforming the six slender towers into merged, organic forms.

4410 The slender columns of towers from the field scheme were merged to optimize privacy between the residences, increase landscaped open space on the ground level, and expand view corridors to the bay beyond from residences and adjacent buildings.

4411 The merging of the towers was informed by reverse mitosis.

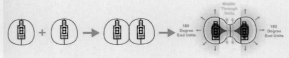

4412 The merged towers have two cores that allow the end units to enjoy panoramic views and create "middle through" units that have views out to two sides. The two cores allow direct access to each unit, eliminating interior corridors.

4413 A concept sketch of Bertrand Goldberg's Marina City— two towers are attached as one.

4414 Six-tower model

4415 Three-tower model

4416 Coupling the towers created clearer, wider view corridors.

4417 Distance between six towers

4418 Optimized privacy and increased open space in the three-tower scheme

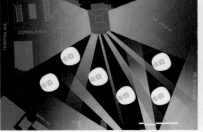

4419 The merged towers increase "good neighbor" views from the adjacent Ritz-Carlton Hotel as well.

4420　Site plan

4421　Tailored by its context, each island is uniquely independent in form and character, yet they maintain a linked intimacy as a continuous whole.

4422　The tower forms are inspired by Florida's Barrier Islands. The residences' organic shapes respond to the surrounding landscape while enhancing it.

4423　Christo and Jeanne Claude, *Surrounded Islands* (1983)— 6.5 million square feet of pink woven polypropylene fabric extended and enhanced eleven small islands in Biscayne Bay.

4424　Collage—island forms emerging from the bay onto the Park Grove site

4427　Three towers on the bay

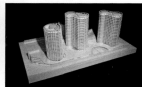

4428　Final model

4425　The massing and placement of towers optimize view corridors to both the bay and the city.

4426　The organic forms soften the relationship between the three towers and respond to the adjacent Regatta Park.

4429　View from the waterfront and porosity through the site

4430　As a gestural extension of the park and the waterfront, a lush landscape weaves around the buildings and through the site. A pedestrian path maintains access from the neighborhood to the waterfront.

4420–4430　　　　　　　　　　　　　　　Park Grove

4431 One million square feet of living is distributed between three towers across the five-acre lot. Tower 1 is a single slender construction and Towers 2 and 3 are peanut-shaped. The towers' organic forms establish a synergy between them and the landscape.

4432 By pinching a typical building slab at its center, more light can penetrate into the middle units.

4433 The sides of the tower facing the water are lined with balconies for serene bayfront living.

4434 The three towers are embedded in a plinth of amenities and landscape that extends to the waterfront park.

4435 Aerial view over the bay

4436 Tower 2 under construction

4437 Tower 2 view from the pool deck

4438 From certain angles, each peanut-shaped tower appears as one slender tower.

4439 Night view of Towers 2 and 3

4440 The roof decks of the three towers resembles an archipelago.

4441 The towers' forms respond to one another.

4442 The towers' siting and orientation create open spaces in between towers that are defined by the building's organic forms.

4443 Sculptural perimeter columns bind each tower, directing views toward the bay and providing column-free living within the residential units.

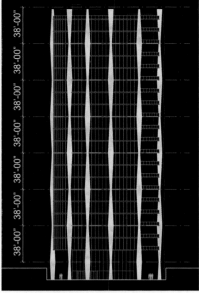

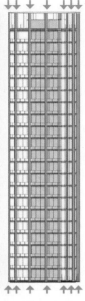

4446 The towers are reminiscent of the grove trees of Florida's ecology.

4444 The tapering column profiles are staggered to create a destabilizing, mirage-like effect, while optimizing the column's connection to the faceted-glass facade on a construction detail level.

4445 The column system combines perform-ance with utility.

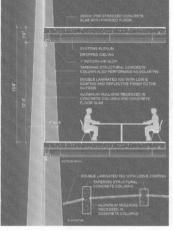

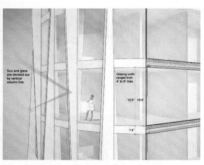

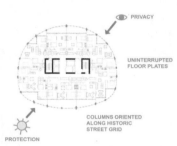

4447 Model

4448 Facade section detail

4449 Facade section

4450 Interior columns are minimized, allowing for maximum flexibility.

4451 Raw concrete columns

4452 Construction view

4453 Tapered columns

4454 Rendering of raw concrete option for columns

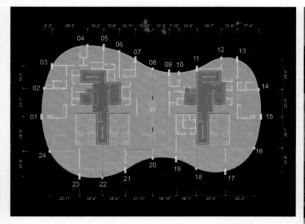

4455 The columns are placed in the skins of the buildings, oriented to allow for maximum views and providing privacy where appropriate.

4456 Columns optimized for views and privacy between units

4443–4456

Park Grove

4457   The spacing of the columns addresses privacy requirements between the units as well as the towers.

4458   The curved form of the building and its perimeter columns establish a dynamic set of balconies.

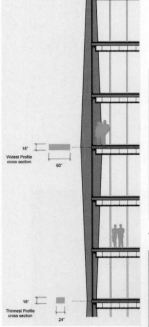

4459   Column section profile— the perimeter columns shield the balconies from the wind, creating comfortable exterior living spaces.

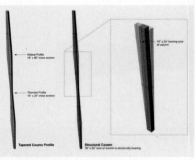

4460   Tapered structural column detail

4461   Looking up Tower 2

4462   View of Tower 2 from Tower 1

4463   Private balcony

4464   The organic form is enhanced by the columns.

4465   The undulation of the perimeter columns creates a subtle organic silhouette.

4466   The tapering columns frame views to the bay from every unit facing the water.

4467   The organic towers are befitting to the natural landscape of the site and of Coconut Grove.

4468   The vertical column fins mitigate solar exposure and glare.

4469   Tower 2 balconies

4470   Columns on the non-balcony side

4457–4470

Park Grove

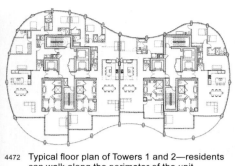

4472 Typical floor plan of Towers 1 and 2—residents can walk along the perimeter of the unit.

4471 The perimeter columns and a split core in Tower 1 and Tower 2 provide a unique layout for living. Residents have direct access to units from the elevator as a result of the split core.

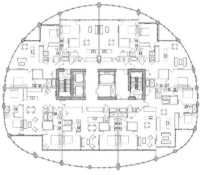

4475 Typical floor plan of Tower 3—every unit has a balcony facing the water

4473 By pinching the form in the center, light penetrates deeper into middle units and multi-directional, floor-through views are provided in the living spaces.

4474 The end units enjoy panoramic views.

4476 Continuity from the living room to the balcony establishes indoor/outdoor living.

4477 Panoramic view from penthouse living room and balcony

4478 Living room with view toward waterfront and Tower 1

4479 Dining room

4480 Balcony with view to Regatta Park

4482 On the lower levels, rooms open up to views of the site's lush landscape.

4483 Living room with garden view

4481 Every room maintains views out onto the city or the waterfront.

4471–4483   Park Grove

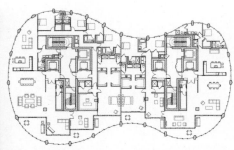

4485 F20 penthouse plan—the demising walls of the penthouse floors allow for flexibility between one or two tenants.

4484 Penthouse units are divided for use by one or two tenants, who enjoy a panoramic backdrop with access to half or all of the tower's perimeter.

4486 Penthouse living room rendering—the bay becomes a natural backdrop.

4487 Every room—from bedroom to living room to kitchen—has expansive views out to the bay or the city.

4488 The upper penthouse has access to a private rooftop walkway around the perimeter of the tower.

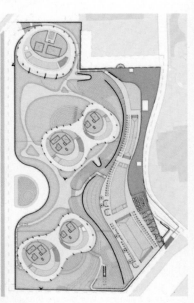

4489 The rooftop levels on all three towers provide shared amenity spaces for the residents.

4490 Landscape projected onto model

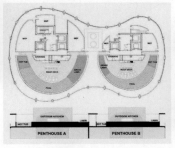

4491 Roof deck plan and section— pool, lawn, and deck

4492 Pools and landscape on the roof aim to bring the natural environment of the neighborhood onto the building.

4493 Rooftop pool rendering

4494 Rooftop pool

4495 A panoramic walkway is located on the boundary of the roof deck.

4496 Curved enclosures for the mechanical and core bulkheads read as objects distinct from the tower massing.

4497 Water and landscaped amenities take advantage of the panoramic views and connect to the surrounding lush landscape of Coconut Grove.

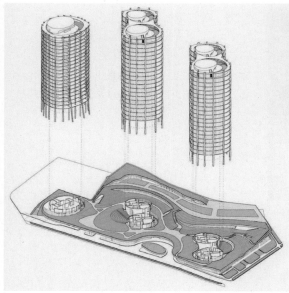

4498 The three residential towers are connected by a lower-level amenity plinth that houses retail spaces, offices, the Coconut Grove Bank, and a clubhouse/restaurant.

4499 Tiers of amenities are enveloped by a programmatic and natural landscape that creates a continuous grove. Natural circulation through the site further preserves its lush conditions.

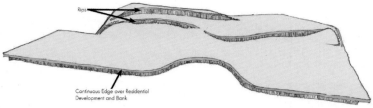

4500 Rather than creating disconnected platforms of programs, rips and tears in the landscape "blanket" provide natural light down to the plinth while maintaining a continuous park-like surface.

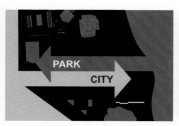

4501 The site's plinth is defined by a lush grove shaped by a meandering pedestrian path that weaves through the three towers from South Bayshore Drive to Cornelia Avenue.

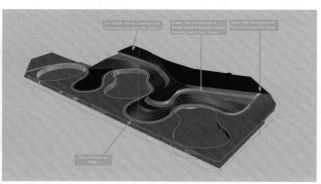

4502 The resulting topography of programs and landscape serves as a dynamic landscape that stitches the elements of the city with the park.

4503 From park to plinth

4504 A public passage preserves access through the site from the city to the bay.

4505 Rendering of drop-off area and adjacent public passage

4506 View toward drop-off area

4507 The goal was to extend the landscape of adjacent Regatta Park onto the plinth, bringing nature closer to the residents.

4508 View from Regatta Park

4509 The plinth concept aims to establish a continuity from the waterfront and park.

4498–4509   Park Grove

4510 F1 is a porous amenity layer that houses the main tower lobby, the Coconut Grove Bank, parking, and retail space for the public, such as a restaurant.

4511 Main entrance at the plinth

4512 The plinth houses the Coconut Grove Bank, which originally existed on the site.

4513 Coconut Grove Bank

4516 The facade is angled at the drop-off area and residential entry, creating a dynamic and inviting interface.

4514 The plinth follows the curves of the tower, continuing the organic language.

4517 Main entrance and stair access to the amenity plinth

4515 Tigertail + Mary, restaurant by chef and restaurateur Michael Schwartz.

4518 Residence lobby reception area

4519 F1 lobby and lounge interior designed by Meyer Davis Studio

4520 F2 of the amenity plinth houses the screening room, fitness room, spa, and lounge. The amenity interiors were designed by Meyer Davis Studio.

4521 F2 spa and sauna

4522 F2 yoga room

4523 F2 screening room

4524 View from tunnel entry

4525 Two tunnels from F2 lead visitors up to F3 of the amenity plinth.

4526 The tunnels provide direct access to the outdoor pool deck from the spa and fitness amenities.

4510–4526

Park Grove

4527 F3 amenity deck plan

4528 Topography—programmatic contouring

4529 Landscape becomes a connective tissue that integrates residences with the amenities.

4530 The amenity deck landscape and pool act as an extension of the waterfront and Regatta Park onto the site.

4531 Lush, green paths and a long, winding series of pools are punctuated by bar and lounge spaces.

4532 Amenity deck pool and bar rendering

4533 The pool deck has unimpeded views out to the water. The pools align to the topographic contours of the amenity deck, shaping the meandering leisure spaces.

4536 Dining room and kitchen

4537 Cabanas

4534 Tower 2 view from the pool deck

4535 Along the pool are a series of amenities: bar and outdoor dining, cabanas, and an indoor dining room and kitchen.

4540 View of Tower 2

4538 Residential balconies enjoy views of the landscape and pool.

4539 Tower 2 evening view

4527–4540

Park Grove

4541 The plinth's landscape enhances the stepped topography of the amenity programs, using natural elements to weave the levels together to create a green space within Park Grove.

4542 Stepped bands of plantings and trees screen the amenity deck activity from the residences.

4543 An expansive park-like surface envelops the towers, acting as an extension of Regatta Park, which lies between Park Grove and the waterfront.

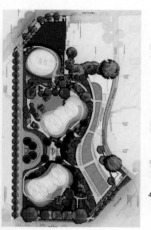

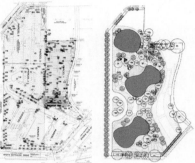

4545 The 182 trees found on the site were catalogued by species and replanted on the new site.

4544 The site is protected as part of Coconut Grove's Environmental Preservation District.

4546 The landscaped plinth unifies the three towers while establishing a convenient path to access various amenities.

4550 The amphitheater can be used for gatherings and events and aims to create a sense of community within Park Grove.

4547 The undulating plinth shapes a green, outdoor amphitheater at Tower 2.

4548 Construction, 2017

4549 The amphitheater faces the double-height lobby of Tower 2 and can be used as steps for access to F2 and beyond.

4552 Tower 1's lobby faces a lush, stepped landscape garden and patio.

4551 View of landscaped amphitheater, looking down Tower 2.

4553 Tower 1 lobby garden—connective layers of programs are knit together by landscape, bringing the bay and green into the site.

4541–4553

Park Grove

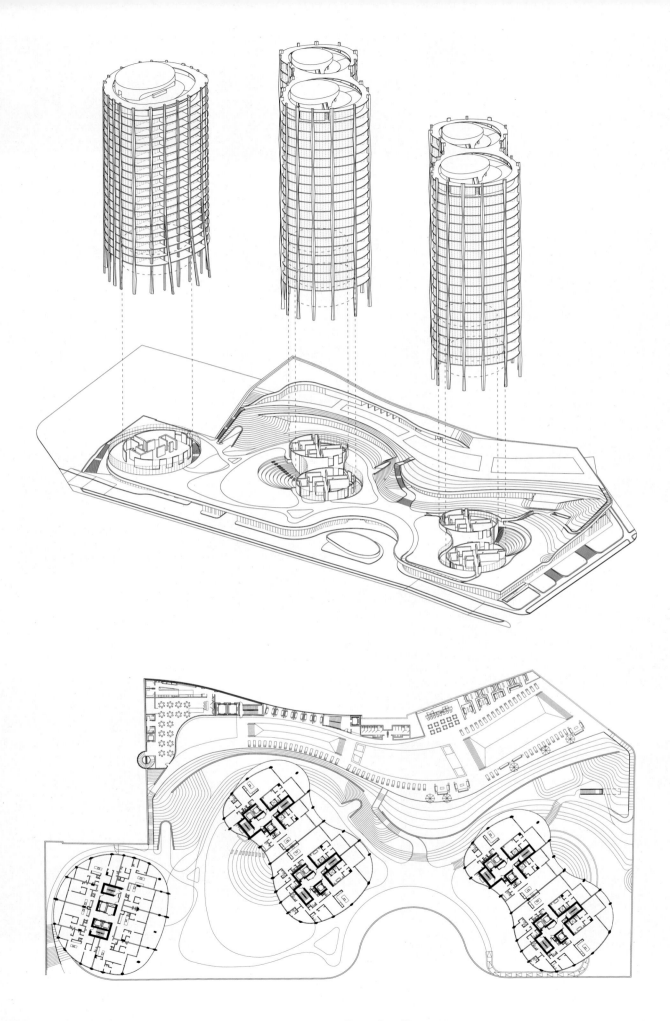

4554—4555

Park Grove

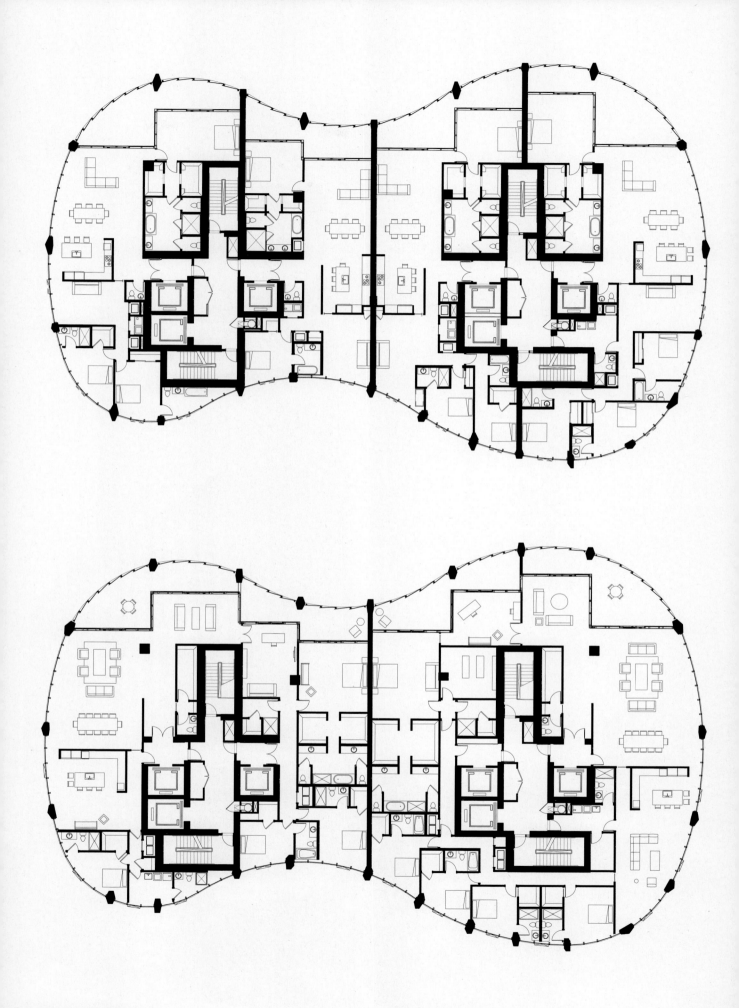

4556–4557   Park Grove

4558

Transbay Block 8 / The Avery

Transbay Block 8 / The Avery

For nearly forty years, the Embarcadero Freeway, a double-decker concrete expressway constructed in the early 1960s, cut San Francisco off from its waterfront. The Freeway ran along the city's eastern edge before turning inward, suffocating the north side of Folsom Street from San Francisco Bay to Second Street in a tangle of interchanges connecting downtown to the Bay Bridge and highways leading south. In 1989, the Loma Prieta earthquake destroyed large sections of the freeway, and in the years that followed its removal the city seized upon the fallow land around the former expressway as an opportunity to create a new district for high-rise density in a city famous for resisting it.

In the span of a decade, new towers by SOM, Arquitectonica, Handel, Goettsch Partners, Pelli Clarke Pelli, Studio Gang, and OMA were built around a new Transbay Transit Center. Thanks to regulations from the city, this sudden influx of high-rises and contemporary architectures would provide a mix of much-needed housing, including condos, market rental, and an average of 30 percent affordable units in most of the blocks. Together, the new developments would transform San Francisco's skyline, but within the apparent carte blanche, we discovered unique complexities that turned our focus from the sky to the ground.

Our site was located at the neighborhood's center, bound by two streets identified by the city as its main east-west connectors. To the south was Folsom, a street planned as an urban boulevard and retail spine. The city envisioned Clementina Street, the street that bounds the site to the north, as Folsom's counterpoint, a quiet pedestrian corridor lined with smaller-scale townhouses. Clementina was to link two new parks: Under Ramp Park, reclaiming as a public space an area underneath what remained of the highway infrastructure; and Transbay Park, a more traditional park closer to the Bay.

We realized early on that traffic from a Bay Bridge offramp planned to run parallel to Clementina would make it impossible for pedestrians to cross toward the bay, leaving the ambition for connection at a dead end. Our masterplan for the block began with a simple urban gesture to solve this problem: a diagonal cut across the site that could simultaneously re-establish the city's desired link and open our development to the new neighborhood around it.

While residential towers are often closed off from the life of the city around them, the cut would allow the public to pass through the site by introducing a new lane connecting Folsom with Clementina. Splitting the building's podium in two, the lane would transform a required courtyard—an internal open space initially doomed to lie in shadow due to the required location of the tower on the southwest corner of the block—into an urban living room. Lined with shops, amenities, landscape, and opened to early morning and late afternoon sunlight, the lane and the courtyard it pierced could serve as a meeting point for the divergent populations living in the tower and around the lane in the lower podium. The lower buildings, designed by San Francisco's Fougeron Architecture, responded to the cut of the lane and were shaped to maximize daylight within it while establishing a more intimate scale at the street.

Our fifty-six-story tower at Transbay Block 8, later named the Avery, combines condos, market-rate apartments, and affordable housing. The logic of the tower typically governs the logic of the podium, but here we wanted to flip that relationship. The same urban gesture that generates the lane slices vertically up the lower half of the tower, tapering its form and creating a series of cantilevered, stepped projections that reorient residences to downtown and the bay. On the upper half of the tower, the southern face is sculpted to mirror the stepped lower facade at the north.

The cut from the ground on the north side and cut from the sky on the south side together form an uneasy, dynamic symmetry—a direction we had first explored at 23 East 22nd Street. Like the lower cut, the upper cut's facade is crenellated to maximize corner windows, looking out to the stretch of waterfront that the city had once forgotten.

Location	San Francisco, CA, USA		
Status	Completed, 2019		
Typology	Residential		
Program	Residential	778,000 ft²	72,280 m²
	Parking	111,300 ft²	10,340 m²
	Retail	16,900 ft²	1,570 m²
	Total area	906,200 ft²	84,190 m²

Transbay Block 8/The Avery

4560

Transbay Block 8 / The Avery

OMA NY

Transbay Block 8 / The Avery

4561

Transbay Block 8/The Avery

4562　San Francisco (1854)

4563　The 2nd Street Cut through Rincon Hill (1869)—in the late 1800s the city began to build more intra-city roads.

4564　The Transbay Terminal opened in 1939 as a train station serving San Francisco's downtown and Financial District. In 1959, it was converted into a bus depot, which later connected to the Embarcadero Freeway.

4565　The Embarcadero Freeway once carried 70,000 vehicles daily toward the Ferry Building.

4566　The 1989 Loma Prieta earthquake caused the freeway to collapse. It was later demolished, with the exception of the ramp to the Bay Bridge, which was rebuilt and retrofitted.

4567　While the freeway had prematurely choked the area south of downtown, its absence offered new potential. The site is blocks from the San Francisco Bay and at the nexus of local and regional transit in the developing Transbay District.

4568　The site is positioned with views of the bay to the north and Twin Peaks to the south.

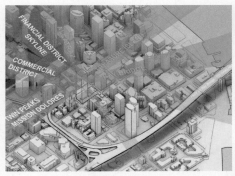

4569　Views from the site extend to the bay and city.

4570　Linked by views and transport to the wider Bay Area region, Block 8 is an important anchor for the neighborhood.

4571　The site lies adjacent to a major junction, with previously undeveloped blocks surrounding the roadway network slated to become a major new district near downtown San Francisco.

4572　Areas along the waterfront near the Bay Bridge are concurrently being redeveloped and will bring a new level of residential density to a city in desperate need of housing, but with a longstanding aversion to change.

4573　Simulated views before completion of in-progress neighborhood buildings

4574　Simulated views after completion of new developments

4575　Site—the intersection of 1st Street and Folsom Street

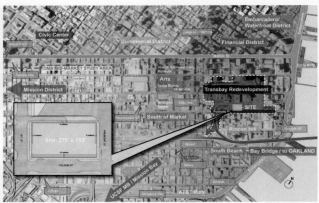

4576　The Transbay Redevelopment is located at the nexus of the Financial District, the Arts District, SoMA (home to many office headquarters and a University of California, San Francisco campus), South Beach, and Rincon Hill. Its transformation will create a new link and a new amenity for multiple neighborhoods.

4562–4576　　　　　　　　　Transbay Block 8/The Avery

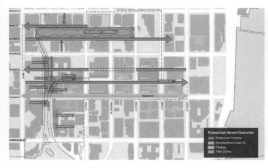

4577 The city's masterplan for Transbay envisioned a series of pedestrian corridors running west to east throughout the neighborhood. To the south, Folsom Street serves as the neighborhood's retail spine. To the north, Clementina Street provides an important pedestrian connection between two new green spaces.

4578 Walking around the site, we realized that traffic from the freeway offramp makes crossing Freemont Street along Clementina Street impossible, severing the city's desired link.

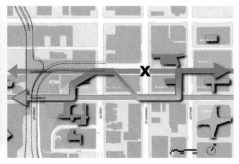

4579 We proposed a paseo, a cut through the site connecting Clementina and Folsom. This cut could provide a shortcut around the pedestrian dead-end and link the site to a network of other neighborhood corridors.

4580 The paseo aims to create an activated passage at human scale, much like Belden Place in San Francisco.

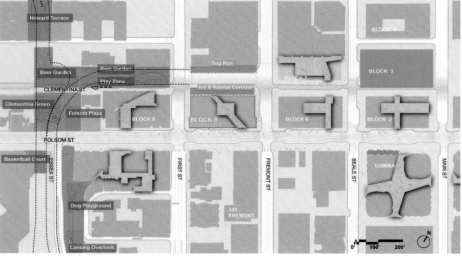

4581 The cut of the paseo extends the streetlife and retail into the interior of the block, activating a required courtyard.

4582 The paseo echoes similar mid-block links in the neighborhood and transforms the center of the block into a place of urban activity.

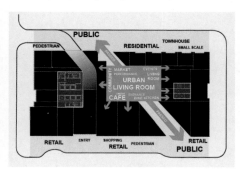

4583 The ground floor is activated on all sides with retail, residential entries, and community amenities.

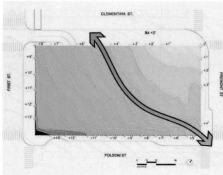

4584 The route of the Paseo aligns with the site's topography, creating a flat passage.

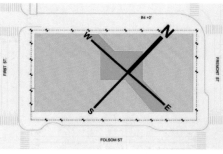

4585 The tower's required southwest location blocked daylight from entering the required courtyard. The Paseo cut, oriented east-west, allows light to penetrate the site in the morning and afternoon.

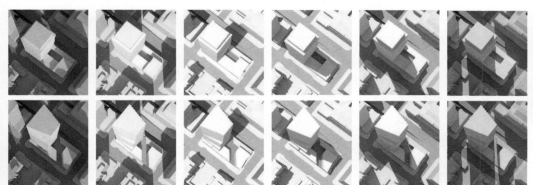

4586 By creating a passage aligned to true east-west, our scheme opens up the courtyard to daylight in the morning and the afternoon, improving the conditions within the courtyard while introducing it as a new public passage along Folsom.

4587 Interior courtyard view

4577–4587   Transbay Block 8/The Avery

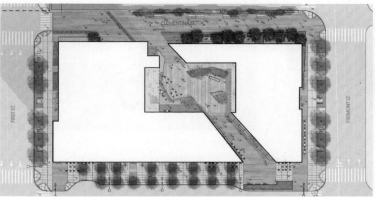

4588 The courtyard within becomes an urban living room, a vibrant center for the diverse community within the block and for the neighborhood as a whole.

4589 The central courtyard in Block 8 adds to the network of proposed green spaces in the neighborhood.

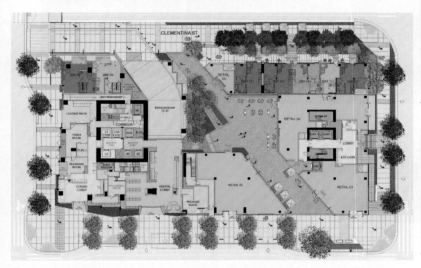

4590 The edges of the courtyard are programmed with retail, entrances, amenities, and temporary market stalls, plus opportunities to spill out into the informal open space.

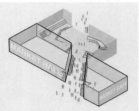

4591 Courtyard scenario—outdoor market

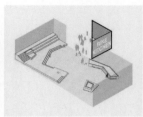

4592 Courtyard scenario—bike and kitchen workshop

4593 Courtyard scenario—outdoor film screening

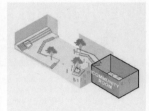

4594 Courtyard scenario—community room activity space

4595 Potential retail programs

4596 A new retail corridor along Folsom

4597 Retail is continued at the B1 level.

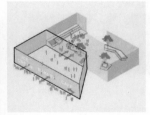

4598 Courtyard scenario—retail and cafe terrace

4599 Creating a clear and direct passage through the courtyard not only brings in light, but also draws activity from the adjacent retail corridor, allowing pedestrians to filter between Folsom and the Under Ramps Park to the northwest on Clementina.

4600 Urban activation along the site and through the paseo

4588–4600   Transbay Block 8/The Avery

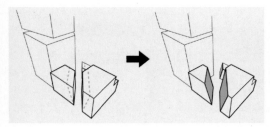

4601 At the podium level, the buildings flanking either side of the paseo gently slope back to enable more light and air to enter the central space.

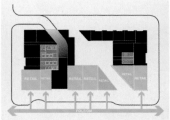

4602 Retail access from Folsom

4603 Paseo entrance from Folsom

4604 The two podium buildings were designed by Fougeron Architecture and contrast with the transparency and lightness of the glass tower. The buildings echo the character of midrise buildings along Folsom Street and SOMA through articulated facades and punched openings.

4605 Podium buildings designed by Fougeron Architecture

4606 Paseo activity

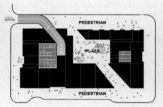

4607 Pedestrian and vehicular access

4608 Entrance to the paseo

4609 The centerpiece of the courtyard is a public art installation, *Absorption* (2018) by Alicja Kwade

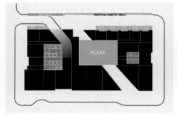

4610 Landscape potentials

4611 Townhouses at Clementina

4614 Courtyard and paseo

4612 Urban living room

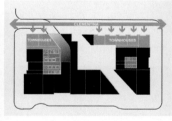

4613 Townhouse access from Clementina

4615 Early elevation—tower base and podium

4616 Podium townhouses along Fremont and Clementina

4617 Aerial view from the southeast

4618 Towers typically dominate everything below.

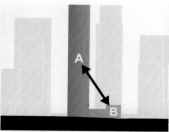

4619 We wanted to invert that typical relationship and create a tower that is defined by its podium.

4620 Study models

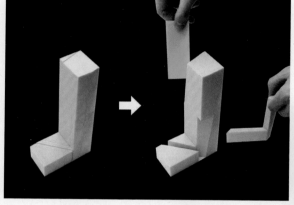

4621 The urban gesture that shapes the podium continues as a vertical slice along the lower half the tower. On the south side of the tower, an equal and opposite cut shapes its upper half.

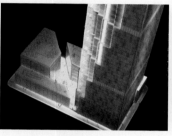

4622 The slice not only creates a formal continuity, but also brings light down to the paseo and the urban living room.

4623 Narrowing the face of the plan toward the bay expands the number of units with views of downtown San Francisco and the bay.

4624 Study model— bayside tapering

4625 Study model— cut extending from podium

4626 Study of maximum potential area at the top of the tower, resulting in an asymmetrical tower that extends out at its midpoint.

4627 Asymmetrical scheme model

4628 An early formal study included setbacks that extend up the full height of the tower

4629 Maximizing views to Bay Bridge

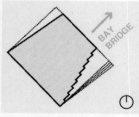

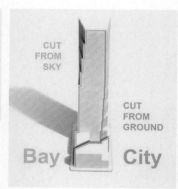

4630 The final form creates a mirrored symmetry between the top and bottom of the tower.

4631 The cuts align with the different residential types within the tower and create setbacks at amenity levels.

4618–4631

Transbay Block 8/The Avery

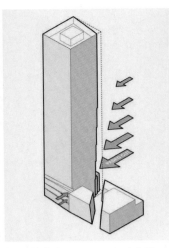

4632 While the tower responds to the Paseo cut, its base steps in and out to meet the ground.

4633 Prismatic tower

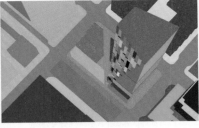

4634 The cut faces of the tower are stepped, or crenelated, creating multiple corners for the units within.

4635 Massing model

4638 Crenellation study

4639 Crenellation detail model

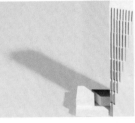

4640 Plaster study model

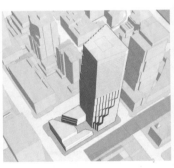

4636 Crenellation study—full tower

4637 Crenellation study view from Transbay Salesforce Park

4641 Continuity of scale from Paseo to tower

4642 Paseo cut and crenellation along Clementina

4643 Tower view from courtyard

4644 Tower view from Clementina

4645 The subtle fanning and crenellation of the facade optimizes views for the residential units while breaking down the scale of the tower.

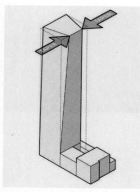

4646 Tapering the upper level increases the amount of frontage with views of the San Francisco Bay

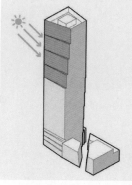

4647 Cutting the upper part of the tower along Folsom also reduces the tower's shadow on the podium.

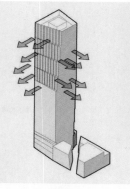

4648 Crenellating the facade at the top of the tower echoes the fanned base.

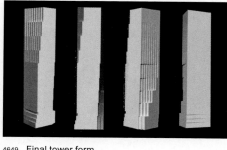

4649 Final tower form

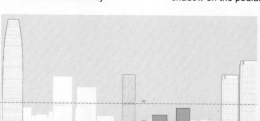

4650 Amenity floors are placed at key levels, responding to the urban context.

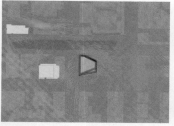

4651 Preliminary wind analysis—wind from west

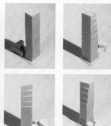

4652 360-degree views

4653 The tapered and crenellated facades create distinct views of the tower from all sides and diverse views out.

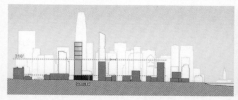

4654 Condo floors are optimized to provide views over the surrounding buildings.

4655 At the thirty-third floor, above the datum established by adjacent buildings, the south face is sculpted to mirror the stepped facade at the north.

4656 Crenellation along Folsom

4657 View from the southeast

4658 Crenellated south face

4660 Tower view from Folsom

4659 View from the southeast at dusk

4661 The project defines a residential tower with an urban gesture.

4646–4661

Transbay Block 8/The Avery

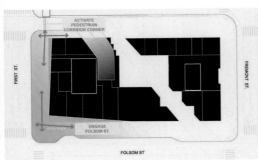

4662　At Folsom and 1st Streets, the tower base is pulled away to expand the sidewalks at the street corners.

4663　When the tower meets the ground, it twists to create a base.

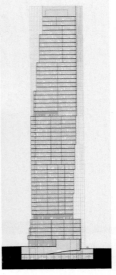

4664　Tower base

F5 plan
4666

4665　The steps of the base align and resonate with the adjacent podium building.

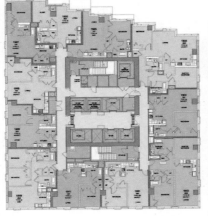

4667　Amenity floor terrace overlooking Folsom Street

4668　The rental portion of the tower and podium includes 150 affordable units distributed throughout.

THE ATHLETIC

Sunday Randomness (with a twist): A heart-warming random act of kindness by Warriors forward Glenn Robinson III

By Marcus Thompson II Oct 27, 2019

4669　When Glenn Robinson III, at the time a Golden State Warrior, was living in one of the tower's condo units, he met affordable housing resident Celia Roberts and her family on the shared amenity terrace, and they struck up a friendship. Later, Robinson bought the family the furniture they needed for their new home.

4670　F19 plan—market-rate and affordable rental floor

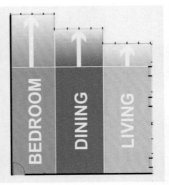

4671　The crenellations define the organization of spaces within the units.

4672　Dining/living spaces

4673　Crenellated living space

4674　Rental kitchen bay view

4675　Crenellations spaced 12 feet apart create subtle divisions between dining and living rooms in common areas and provide corner views for bedrooms.

4662–4675

Transbay Block 8/The Avery

4676   The 118 market rate condominium units span F33 to
       F56.

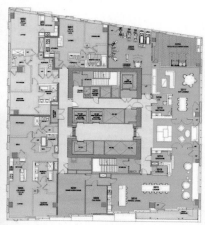

4677   F32 plan—condo and amenity floor

4678   The crenellation offers multiple corner
       views within a single unit.

4679   Penthouse master bedroom, with views toward
       both the bay and the city

4680   F52 plan

4681   Penthouse master bedroom bridge view

4682   Penthouse great room with panoramic bay views

4683   Upper-level tower
       crenellation

4684   View from the Bay Bridge

4685   View of the Transbay District

4686   View toward Glen Canyon, Twin Peaks, and Mount Sutro

4687   The tower is a dynamic addition to the developing Transbay District and the San
       Francisco skyline.

4676–4687   Transbay Block 8/The Avery

4688–4689

Transbay Block 8/The Avery

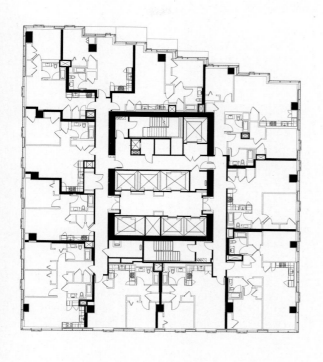

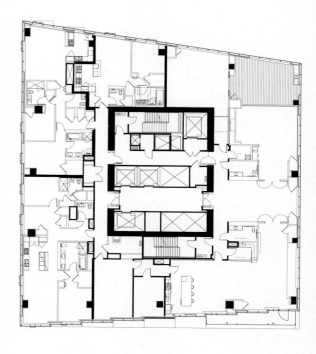

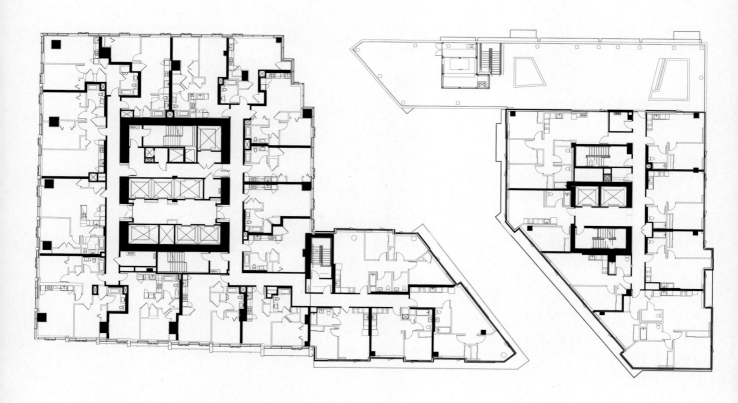

4690–4692

Transbay Block 8/The Avery

4693   121 East 22nd Street

121 East 22nd Street

Almost a decade following the tragic death of the 23 East 22nd Street residential tower, we completed 121 East 22nd Street, our first ground-up residential building in Manhattan. It is ironically located on the same street as the prior project, a mere block away. It was a rare opportunity to build the same typology in a familiar neighborhood, but with unfamiliar complexities—a second chance.

The L-shaped site sits within an ambiguous block that was surprisingly never branded with a neighborhood name. It straddles two separate and different neighborhoods: a quiet residential area surrounding the enclosed private garden that is Gramercy Park, and the bustling commercial space around Madison Square Park, a public park that hosts an array of activities. This context also created two different zoning conditions within a single site—a shorter, more intimate scale South Tower facing Gramercy; and a taller, more commercial scale North Tower facing both 23rd Street and Lexington Avenue.

The undefined threshold between Gramercy and Flatiron posed an opportunity to be informed by their distinct characters while activating three street fronts. We were drawn to the confused identity of the corner at 23rd Street and Lexington Avenue and wanted to represent the convergence of the two neighborhoods. Our formal expression emerges from the dual condition referencing Cubist artwork, in which objects are viewed from a multitude of viewpoints rather than a single one, to represent the subject in a greater context.

At the North Tower, two interlocking planes that come together at 23rd and Lexington form a distinct, three-dimensional corner that embodies the unstable identity. The corner emphatically stitches the two streets together, forming a series of planes that bend in and out vertically up the tower. From the exterior, it evokes a collage assembled from various reflections of street life and neighboring buildings. From the interior, it creates unimpeded views up to the sky and down to the streets.

On the street level, the corner is carved inward, widening the sidewalk and establishing a clear entry point to the ground-floor retail. (Since the beginning of the Covid-19 pandemic, the ground floor has been occupied by the FRIENDS Experience, an interactive installation of set recreations from *FRIENDS*, an iconic TV show that perhaps offers the quintessential image of life in New York.)

From the expressive corner, the building's two facades become more contextual as they near the neighboring prewar buildings. Its black precast panels become bolder as the facade transitions away from the corner, seamlessly establishing a visible gradient from new to historic. Depending on the time of the day, the black concrete works both as a background to the windows accentuating the gradation and a foreground that gives the building a graphic appearance.

On 22nd Street, the South Tower resonates more subtly with the three-dimensional articulation of the North Tower. A grid of punched windows form an undulating facade that conveys the same expression as the North Tower, but more subdued in response to the narrower street and the quieter Gramercy neighborhood.

The South Tower houses the main residential entry, from which a funnel-shaped lobby leads to an enclosed breezeway and central valley connecting the two towers. In the valley, we wanted to create a calm oasis amid the bustle of 23rd Street and Lexington Avenue. Centered around residential amenities and unit balconies, it establishes an inside-outside living space within the complex.

The interior facades of the two towers facing the courtyard echo the three-dimensionality of the exterior facade—a ribbon of volumetric balconies add a sculptural dimension framing the valley. Although similar in language, the materiality of light, perforated aluminum enhances daylight; it provides a healthy contrast to the towers' dark exterior and a third character within the complex emerges. While the complexity of the site drove our ambition to forge a new identity for the ambiguous neighborhood, the block remains unnamed.

Location	New York, NY, USA		
Status	Completed, 2019		
Typology	Residential		
Program	Residential	242,200 ft²	22,500 m²
	Amenities	10,600 ft²	990 m²
	Parking	6,100 ft²	560 m²
	Total Area	258,900 ft²	24,050 m²

4694

121 East 22nd Street

4695

121 East 22nd Street

121 East 22nd Street

4696

121 East 22nd Street

OMANY

121 East 22nd Street

4697

121 East 22nd Street

OMA NY

121 East 22nd Street

4698

121 East 22nd Street

4699　121 East 22nd Street is located at the boundary of two distinct New York neighborhoods, Gramercy Park and the Flatiron District.

4700　Manhattan neighborhoods on a map created by a developer

4701　The site is in a small area that is part of neither Gramercy nor Flatiron.

4702　The unique L-shaped site presented an opportunity for 121 East 22nd Street to be informed by two neighborhoods while activating three street fronts.

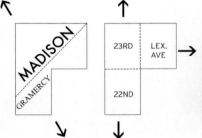

4703　The site faces three streets—Lexington Avenue and, 22nd and 23rd Streets.

4704　Statue of Liberty torch display in Madison Square Park (1876–1882)

4705　Gramercy Park

4706　Programs of neighborhood buildings include residential, mixed-use, public facilities/institutions, commercial/office, and industrial/manufacturing.

4708　Gramercy Park

4709　Gramercy Park is a quiet, lush garden exclusive to neighborhood residents.

4707　While Gramercy Park is often associated with exclusivity and history as an oasis for private residential buildings, Madison Square is anchored by a public park with activities and commercial programming, surrounded by iconic buildings like Daniel Burnham's Flatiron Building and the Metropolitan Life Insurance Company Tower.

4710　Madison Square Park is centrally located within a commercial area.

4711　Madison Square Park and Flatiron Plaza

4712　The park is public and bustling with activities.

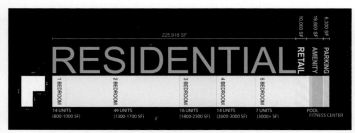

RESIDENTIAL | RETAIL | AMENITY | PARKING

225,916 SF — 10,000 SF — 19,800 SF — 6,300 SF

1 BEDROOM / 2 BEDROOM / 3 BEDROOM / 4 BEDROOM / 5 BEDROOM

14 UNITS (800-1000 SF) / 49 UNITS (1300-1700 SF) / 16 UNITS (1800-2500 SF) / 14 UNITS (2600-3000 SF) / 7 UNITS (3000+ SF)

POOL FITNESS CENTER

4713   Required program distribution—the residences of 121 East 22nd Street range from one- to five-bedroom options.

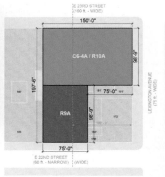

4714   The site lies within two separate zoning districts.

4715   Zoning envelope—corner of Lexington and 22nd

4716   23rd Street looking west (north tower)

4717   22nd Street looking east (south tower)

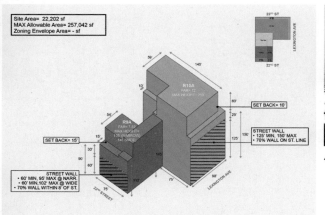

Site Area= 22,202 sf
MAX Allowable Area= 257,042 sf
Zoning Envelope Area= - sf

4718   The zoning for the South Tower is at the more intimate scale of Gramercy, while that of the North Tower allows for higher floor area ratio at the commercial scale of the Flatiron District. Due to the zoning constraints, there was not enough room to create the kind of special form or height that typically attracts buyers in New York.

4719   Team design charrette with client Toll Brothers City Living (2014)

4720   How can the site bring the contrasting spirits of the Gramercy Park and Madison Square Park neighborhoods into the building?

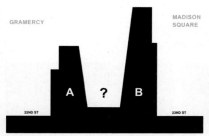

4721   What does a two-tower condition look like on an L-shaped site?

ANGLED   TERRACES

4722   We looked at creating a valley condition that would allow the two towers to relate to one another while forming a shared open space.

4725   Preliminary schemes sought to optimize the form within the given zoning envelope through key elements—form and facade.

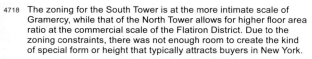

4723   Preliminary scheme—embedding an organic element into the zoning envelope

4724   Preliminary scheme—embedded cluster

4713–4725   121 East 22nd Street

4726 We were drawn to the confused identity of the site's corner and chose to take an urbanistic approach where the design is informed by existing assets.

4727 An initial idea was to create an interlocking form.

4728 The building would express the tension between the two neighborhoods.

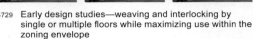

4729 Early design studies—weaving and interlocking by single or multiple floors while maximizing use within the zoning envelope

4730 Pablo Picasso, *The Guitar Player* (1910)—we referenced Cubist artwork, in which the subject is analyzed, broken up and abstractly reassembled.

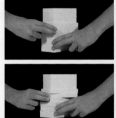

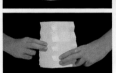

4731 Similarly, here, a single volume is broken up by floor and rotated in alternation.

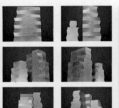

4732 We wanted to translate the dualism in the building's form and proposed a zig-zagging facade that would "weave" the two neighborhood identities across both towers.

4733 Concept model

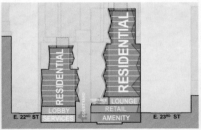

4734 The facade wraps in toward the courtyard "valley."

4735 The warped facade would be composed of a series of interlocking trapezoids.

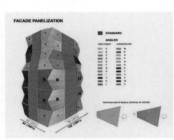

4736 Proposed facade panelization for the interlocking scheme

4737 Upon further study, we wanted to ensure that the building was referential to its neighbors while articulating a new corner identity.

4738 The intersection of two neighborhoods at the corner of 23rd Street and Lexington Avenue is manifested in a dynamic corner.

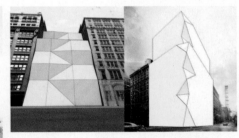

4739 The South Tower facade subtly adopts the three-dimensionality of the North Tower's corner, incorporating larger folds with respect to the quiet residential street it faces.

4740 The straightforward facades on 23rd Street and Lexington Avenue carry the walls from their neighbors and converge at a zig-zagging corner.

4741 Three-dimensional corner

4742 North Tower model

4743 The North Tower's massing takes cues from its adjacent historic buildings while "stitching" the two neighborhood identities at the corner.

4726–4743   121 East 22nd Street

4744 The final design for 121 East 22nd Street is composed of two distinct yet unified towers that share a courtyard.

4745 Rendering—view south on Lexington Avenue

4746 View south on Lexington Avenue

4747 The three-dimensional articulation breaks from the typically abrupt corner conditions of New York City streets and visually marks the meeting place of Gramercy and the Flatiron District at an urban scale.

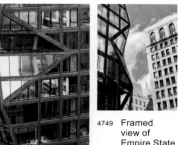

4749 Framed view of Empire State Building

4748 Bending in and out vertically creates unique corner views from the interiors up to the sky and down to the streets.

4750 Reflection of the street

4751 The corner can be spotted from afar.

4752 View west down 23rd Street

4753 View west down 23rd Street

4754 The corner articulation evokes a collage assembled from various reflections of its surroundings.

4755 Looking up the corner

4756 On the street level, the corner carves inward, widening the sidewalk and establishing a clear entry point to the ground floor retail.

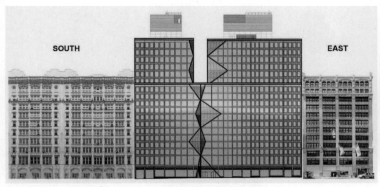

SOUTH   EAST

4758 C.B.J. Snyder's School of the Future (1915)

4759 Met Life North Building (1950) and Met Life Tower (1909) in the Flatiron District

4760 Stepped windows of the neighboring Church Missions House (now home to Fotografiska) by Robert Williams Gibson and Edward Neville Stent (1892)

4757 The facade of the North Tower aims to be contextual to its surroundings. It is defined by the neighboring facades of C.B.J. Snyder's School of the Future (1915) to the south and an art deco building to the east.

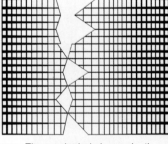

4761 The punched windows echo the facade of the North Tower's pre-war neighbors and seamlessly transition toward a contemporary, more open corner.

4762 Consistent spandrels

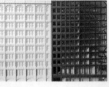

4763 Model view—day

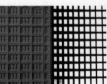

4764 Model view—night

4765 Facade stepping references

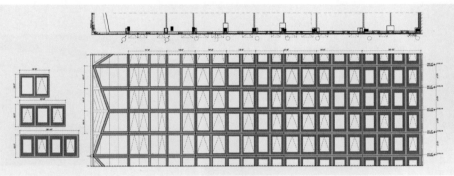
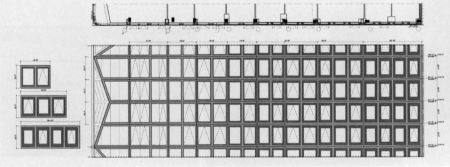

4766 A gradient facade is established.

4767 23rd Street facade

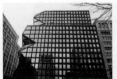

4768 View up the facade from 23rd Street

4769 Looking up from Lexington Avenue

4770 Expressive corner and window gradient

4771 From afar, the punched windows emphasize the building's three-dimensionality.

4772 Detail view of punched window stepping

4773 Gradually becoming more expressive toward the corner, the building's facade adds a new presence to the street, one that is both contextual and contemporary.

4774 On the narrower and quieter 22nd Street, the South Tower resonates more subtly with the corner articulation of the North Tower.

4775 Model view from the intersection of 22nd Street and Lexington Avenue

4776 View from the corner of 22nd and Lexington

4777 It maximizes full use of the smaller zoning envelope on the Gramercy frontage.

4778 The South Tower responds to the more intimate scale of 22nd Street.

4779 View west down 22nd Street

4780 The massing is separate and distinct from its more public faces on 23rd Street and Lexington Avenue.

4781 South Tower rendering

4782 The facade is an unstable grid with three-dimensional "movement."

4783 The grid is composed of punched windows.

4784 The residential lobby entry is located in the South Tower.

4785 The undulating facade of the South Tower is a more subdued interpretation of the three-dimensionality informed by the intersection of two distinct neighborhoods. The subtlety allows the tower to remain respectful to the neighboring buildings.

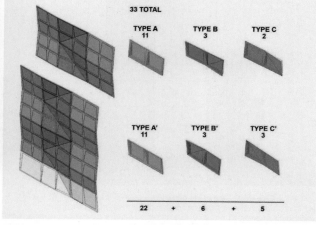

4786 The South Tower showcases a similar facade system using modules that alternate and undulate, creating a three-dimensional essence on a two-dimensional facade.

4787 There are three distinct panel types, each with a sub panel type based on the undulation. There are a total of 33 window panels.

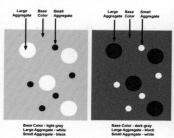

4788 Aggregate color studies

4789 The front face (top) is acid-etched, while the interior steps (bottom) are sandblasted.

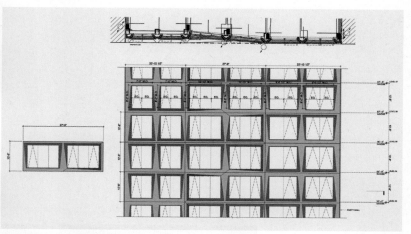

4792 South facade plan and elevation drawing

4790 Test rendering of acid-etched front face and sandblasted stepping

4791 Pre-cast mock-up

4793 Pre-cast mock-up

4794 Pre-cast mock-up

4795 Pre-cast panel on site

4798 South facade in context

4799 South facade detail

4796 Facade under construction before window installation

4797 South facade detail

4800 The undulating facade sets the tower apart from its more classical neighbors and the stepping within each panel resonates with the punched windows of its neighboring buildings.

4786–4800   121 East 22nd Street

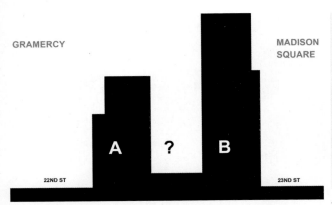

GRAMERCY

MADISON SQUARE

A ? B

22ND ST   23RD ST

4801 1 project, 2 buildings—the presence of two towers facing different streets prompted a need for connections through an internal amenity area and courtyard.

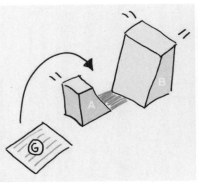

4802 Tucked away from the busy streets, the internal courtyard links the complex's two towers and provides a valley-like retreat.

4803 "Valley" geometry— Gustavo Torner, *Brancusi Column* (1925)

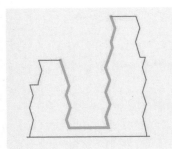

4804 The same geometric concept is employed to the courtyard-facing facades of the two buildings.

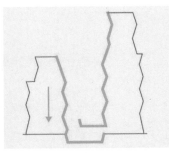

4805 Shifting the facade brings light down into the courtyard

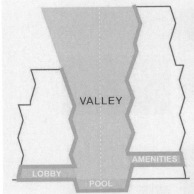

VALLEY

LOBBY

AMENITIES

POOL

4806 In an effort to unify the two volumes, a third identity is born.

4807 Czech Cubism— Pavel Janak, *Crystalline Box* (1911)

4808 Facade study— flat versus shifted

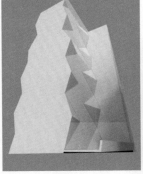

4809 Valley geometry— alternating peaks

4810 Valley concept model—shifting the interior facade allows light to penetrate all the way to the basement level amenities.

4811 Valley concept model—a shifted yet continuous facade

4812 Study—extending the facade down into the valley

4813 Concept collage of extending the interior facade down vertically through the valley

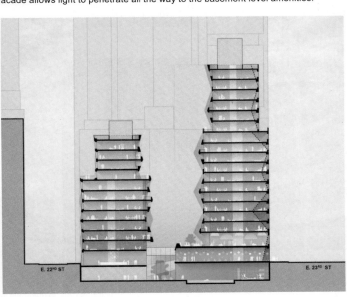

E. 22ND ST   E. 23RD ST

4814 The shared amenity spaces on either side of the courtyard create a connection between the two towers.

4801–4814   121 East 22nd Street

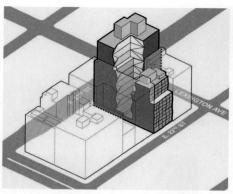

4815 The courtyard also mirrors the urban park conditions of Gramercy Park and Madison Square Park, adding an additional leisure space for the residents to complement the series of open spaces in the neighborhood.

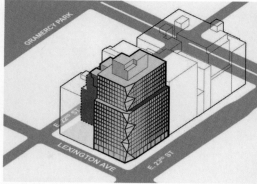

4816 The unique L-shaped site secludes this private open space from the street.

4817 Rather than filling a single courtyard space for outdoor respite, the amenities are split between levels to take advantage of light and open space.

4818 Courtyard and private residential balconies

4819 The terraces provide residents with quiet outdoor moments.

4820 View up the South Tower residential balconies facing the courtyard

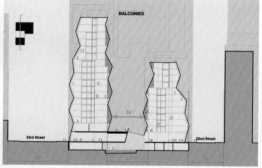

4821 The alternating triangular forms of the courtyard-facing facades create a dynamic set of balconies.

4823 The perforated aluminum balustrade dynamically reflects light at different angles.

4822 The balustrade is perforated aluminum. The light materiality enhances daylight while giving the courtyard its own unique identity, contrasting with the darker materiality of the street-facing facades.

4824 View south from balcony

4825 Balcony view looking into the courtyard valley

4826 Sculptural balustrade

4827 Balcony view

4828 View of South Tower

4829 View up the courtyard valley

4830 Rendered view down into the courtyard

4831 Bird's-eye view of courtyard and split amenity levels

4815–4831   121 East 22nd Street

4832 Wrapping around the central courtyard is an interior corridor, or breezeway.

4833 The breezeway is accessed from the ground-floor lobby and leads up to the F2 amenities and down to the B1 amenities.

4834 View into the courtyard from the breezeway

4836 Courtyard view toward mechanical parking

4837 Courtyard view toward pool

4838 Circulation within the courtyard allows creative vantage points to the activities in the B1, F1, and F2 amenities.

4835 The breezeway establishes access and connections between the two towers while maintaining uninterrupted views into the shared courtyard. The glazing is operable, allowing both air and light into the towers themselves.

4839 Floor-to-ceiling, operable doorways allow amenity spaces such as the gym and pool to extend outdoors.

4840 The B1 level pool enjoys a connection to the outdoor courtyard, establishing a seamless transition from inside to outside.

4841 Swimming pool and courtyard connection

4842 View down to the courtyard and breezeway from the amenity terrace

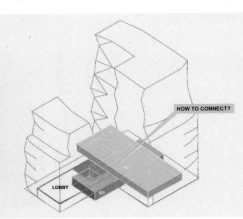

4843 The amenities are spread across three levels. The distinct plates on B1, F1, and F2 establish further connections between the two towers.

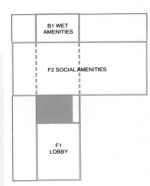

4844 The three plates of amenities are stacked, staggered, and connected centrally, while expanding out to the extents of the two buildings.

4832–4844

121 East 22nd Street

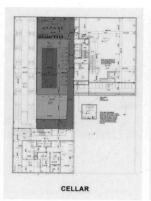

CELLAR

F1

F2

4846 F2 amenity terrace rendering

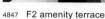

4845 Lower-level amenities include a pool, gym, and courtyard. On the second floor are indoor and outdoor lounges, a catering kitchen, a private dining room, a children's playroom, and a screening room.

4847 F2 amenity terrace

4848 F2 amenity terrace

4849 On F2 are the social amenities, including the lounge and dining room, which connect to an expansive outdoor terrace that can accommodate resident activities, such as dinner parties and other social gatherings.

4850 The terrace provides a seamless connection from the interior amenities to the outside courtyard.

4851 F2 children's playroom rendering

4852 The light pink of the children's playroom contrasts with the gray-to-black gradient tones of the building.

4853 View into screening room from the residential lounge on F2

4854 The monochromatic orange palette of the screening room provides a punch of color.

4855 Panel discussion with Shohei Shigematsu (OMA), Adam Rolston (INC Architecture), Michael Duff (Toll Brothers City Living), and James Davidson (SLCE), moderated by Chris Yoon (OMA)

4856 Additional terraces on the building's setback and the roof offer views down to the activities below as well as out toward Gramercy and Flatiron.

4857 The shared roof terrace establishes indoor/outdoor living within the complex while reconnecting residents to the two different neighborhoods in which the building lies.

4858 Shared roof terrace rendering

4859 Shared roof terrace completed view

4860 Residences in both the North and South Towers are accessed through the entrance located on 22nd Street.

4861 Lobby rendering framing the courtyard

4862 The main residential entry consists of a funnel-shaped lobby that narrows toward the breezeway and is centered on the courtyard below.

4863 The lobby funnel is composed of 500 pieces of superwhite travertine, placed in alternating bands of honed and polished finishes to create a sense of directionality as one moves through the lobby toward the amenity spaces.

4864 F2 plan—across the two towers, the units range from studios to five-bedroom apartments.

4865 The corner and form of the building give way to unique units in the North Tower, with views onto the Lexington and 23rd Street intersection or private terraces facing the quiet central valley.

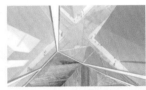

4866 The corner units boast unique vantage points down to the bustling streets of the two neighborhoods.

4867 Typical living room in the North Tower corner units—in this one, the corner window slopes outward, providing views down to activity on the street.

4868 Completed North Tower corner unit with window sloping inward

4869 Completed view of North Tower unit—living room with balcony and courtyard views

4870 Custom automatic shading for sloped, corner unit windows

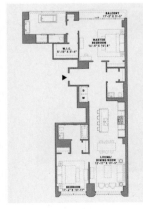

4871 The South Tower has units that look out onto both 22nd Street and the courtyard.

4872 South Tower penthouse living room

4873 South Tower penthouse kitchen

4874 South Tower private terrace overlooking the central courtyard

4860–4874

121 East 22nd Street

4875　4876　4877　4878　4879　4880
4881　4882　4883　4884　4885　4886
4887　4888　4889　4890　4891　4892
4893　4894　4895　4896　4897　4898
4899　4900　4901　4902　4903　4904
4905　4906　4907　4908　4909　4910
4911　4912　4913　4914　4915　4916

4875–4916　　　　　　121 East 22nd Street

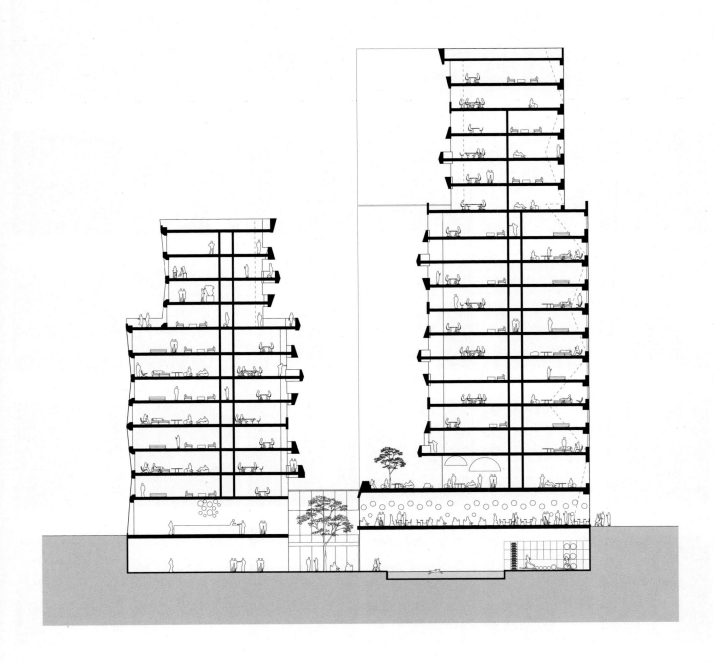

4917

121 East 22nd Street

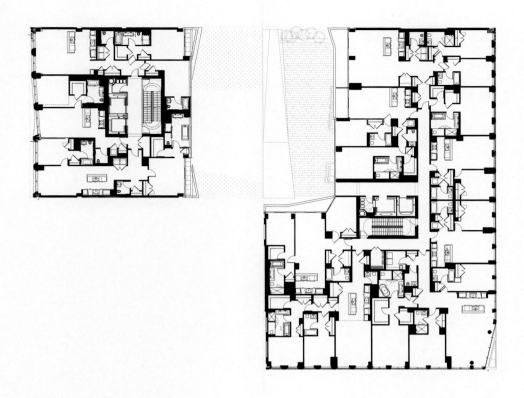

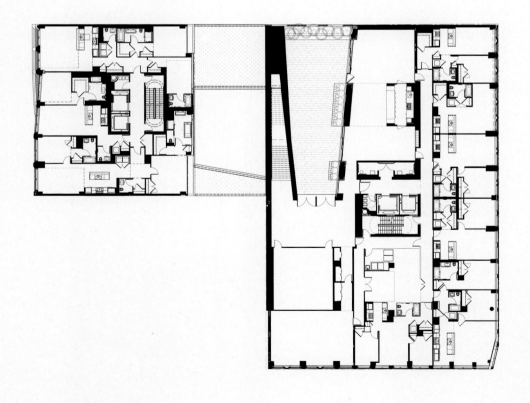

4918–4919   121 East 22nd Street

4920

Greenpoint Landing Block D

Greenpoint Landing Block D

Greenpoint lies at the northernmost tip of Brooklyn where Newtown Creek meets the East River. The neighborhood—sometimes called "Little Poland"—has historically consisted of low-rise townhouses with industry at its waterfront edges. The industrial border, which included shipbuilding, rope-making, and more toxic activities such as petroleum refinement, cut the neighborhood off from the East River.

As part of a sweeping rezoning of both Greenpoint and Williamsburg in 2005, our site and blocks to the north and south were identified as an area for new residential density—introducing pairs of thirty- and forty-story towers to include market-rate and affordable housing (30 percent of units to be affordable). In exchange, this new development would open access to and along the East River. Our site sits at the conjunction of Greenpoint's primary grid and a secondary grid that extends perpendicular to Newtown Creek. This hinge-point provides panoramic views of Manhattan, but also cuts the western end of the site, creating a trapezoidal outline and constraining the size of the block. Our challenge was to fit the desired amount of housing into a site and a neighborhood that both seemed too small to accommodate it.

The zoning allowed for a maximum floorplate of 11,000 square feet. We quickly found that this scale and required setbacks would result in only 40 feet of separation between our two towers—an uncomfortable proximity that undermined the potential of the site and would create a wall from the neighborhood. We began by reducing their footprints to allow for 60 feet of open space, more akin to the scale of a typical street. We could then strategically expand and contract the towers for zones of maximum efficiency within each.

The two towers simultaneously lean into and away from one another. The taller tower widens toward the east as it rises, maximizing views and creating a dramatic face to the neighborhood. The shorter tower, a fraternal twin, widens toward the ground to face a new waterfront park to the north. The two towers are shaped to create terraces and overhangs that emphatically link them together as if they were broken apart from a single block. A ziggurat and its inverse, the pair are distinct yet intimately connected by the void between them. The stepped forms of the towers and the articulation of their facades mediate the inevitable contrast in scale between the two towers and the existing neighborhood. The stepping divides the tower into seven- to eight-story blocks that echo the scale of the neighboring buildings. The facade reinforces this subdivision.

While The Avery's glass curtain wall was rising in San Francisco, our proposal here sought to embrace solidity. Incorporating large 8-foot-by-8-foot windows into a grid of precast concrete maintains expansive views while making the complex negotiations between unit interiors and facade easier to accommodate. The solidity also creates a set of buildings that emerge more seamlessly from the neighborhood. Much like the shingled facades seen on Greenpoint's townhouses, the precast panels are carved by a series of angled planes. The shingling of each "block" of the tower alternates in orientation to emphasize the finer scale of the towers' mass—a dynamic relief that reacts to the movement of the sun.

Waterfront towers typically try to both maximize the views to the water and establish a distinct, even iconic frontage within the skyline. Too often that means turning away from the neighborhood, creating a "back" side and disengaging the tower from its context. Here, a set of cantilevers—extending the building 48 feet from its base—faces east toward Greenpoint and presents our most dramatic facade to the neighborhood.

Echoing Greenpoint's pastoral origins as a neighborhood of family farms, two levels of green space open to the waterfront. Terraces are framed by a collection of common spaces. Above them, the towers are linked by an amenity bridge looking over the Manhattan skyline. Altogether, Greenpoint Landing aims to be a platform for living: connecting past and future, indoor and outdoor, urban streetscape and waterfront.

Location	Brooklyn, NY, USA		
Status	2017–Ongoing		
Typology	Residential		
Program	Residential	801,000 ft²	74,400 m²
	Parking	51,800 ft²	4,800 m²
	Retail	7,900 ft²	730 m²
	Total Area	860,700 ft²	79,930 m²

4921

Greenpoint Landing Block D

4922

Greenpoint Landing Block D

4923

Greenpoint Landing Block D

4924

Greenpoint Landing Block D

OMA NY

Greenpoint Landing Block D

4925

Greenpoint Landing Block D

4926 Greenpoint is located at the northern tip of Brooklyn, bordered by the East River and Newtown Creek.

4927 Originally named for its lush topography, Greenpoint has changed character over time, transforming from pastoral farmlands to industrial hub.

4928 Greenpoint became a major shipping center in the nineteenth century. Its grid, which extended directly to the East River, diverted at its northern edge to meet Newtown Creek.

4929 Industries like shipbuilding and petroleum refining changed the character of the Greenpoint waterfront.

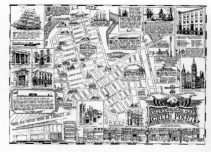

4930 During that time, the neighborhood also established itself as a center for printing, pottery, glassworks, and foundries.

4931 View of Greenpoint and Newtown Creek (1982)

4932 By the late nineteenth century, Greenpoint also saw a rise in Polish immigrants moving into the neighborhood, earning it the nickname "Little Poland."

4933 Because of its geographic location and heavily industrial waterfront, the residential neighborhood was always cut off from the water's edge.

4934 Greenpoint Terminal Warehouse, location of the Donnie Paduana assassination, *The Sopranos* season one, episode twelve

4935 Wedding at Greenpoint Terminal Warehouse, 2018

4936 Together with other areas of North Brooklyn, the Greenpoint waterfront was rezoned for residential development in 2005.

4937 Over the last decade, the Brooklyn and Long Island City waterfronts have been transformed by a wave of high-rise residential development.

4938 Williamsburg North 4th/The Edge

4939 Williamsburg Waterfront, Domino

4940 Away from the waterfront, the fabric of the neighborhood is composed of low-rise multifamily townhouses.

4941 Three layers

4942 In addition to new residential development, the neighborhood's industrial edge will be transformed into a public promenade with views of Manhattan.

4943 Greenpoint Landing marks the area along the river that our clients, Park Tower Group and Brookfield, are transforming.

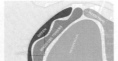

4944 Zones

4945 Programs

4946 Public transit

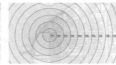

4947 Walkability

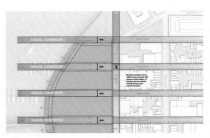

4948 The masterplan calls for the re-extension of the street grid to the East River.

4949 Greenpoint's east-west streets will lead to a newly greened and connected waterfront.

4950 A commercial overlay along Green and West Streets promotes street-level retail and activates the public space along the East River.

4951 Planned waterfront North Brooklyn

4952 Newtown Barge Park, north of our site

4953 The site's zoning allows for a series of 300-foot and 400-foot residential towers along the waterfront. Each tall tower has a shorter sibling.

4955 Within the Greenpoint grid, the blocks south of Dupont Street can become a collection of interrelated twins.

4956 Greenpoint Landing masterplan

4954 Tower proximity study

4957 Site visit walking down Eagle Street toward Block D, 2017

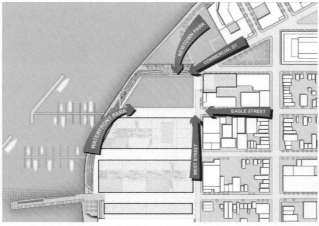

4958 Our focus was Block D, a site at the hinge-point between the East River and Newtown Creek. It is the shortest site south of Dupont Street, but arguably has the best potential for views.

4959 Greenpoint Landing Block D site

Greenpoint Landing Block D

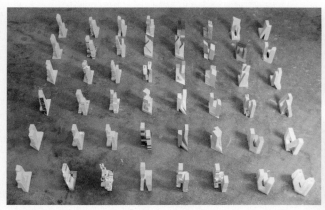

4960   Initial Block D massing studies

4961   Initial studies

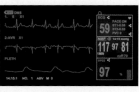

4962   Block D lies at the connection point between the grid and the waterfront.

4963   Can the block open up to provide a connection through the site?

4964   Electrocardiogram

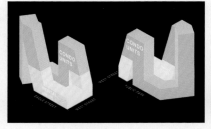

4965   The early Gate scheme creates a continuous band of residential units while inviting circulation through the site.

4966   Gateways connect the new paths through the site

4967   Early Gate scheme viewed from the East River Ferry

4968   Tango

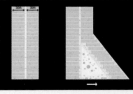

4969   The early Tango scheme split the buildings along their central corridors to create stepped plinths and vaulted lobbies.

4970   Exposing the lobby

4972   Model

4973   Early Tango scheme viewed from the East River Ferry

4971   The two towers form a valley through the site.

4974   The early Blocks scheme stepped and divided the building according to potential unit types.

4975   Distinguishing the blocks breaks down the scale of the towers.

4976   Concept collage

4977   Blocks scheme viewed from the East River Ferry

4960–4977   Greenpoint Landing Block D

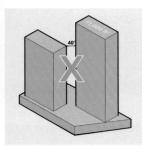
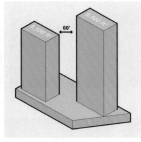
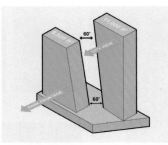
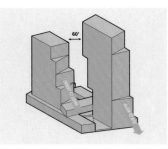

4978 Our final scheme began with the problem of proximity. If we maximized the floorplate sizes, the towers would only be 40 feet apart.

4979 If we expanded the gap to 60 feet (the width of a typical street), we could not accommodate the potential floor area.

4980 So we extended the shorter building at the ground, along the adjacent Newtown Barge Park, and expanded the upper levels of its taller sibling.

4981 The towers taper back and step out, creating terraces and overhangs while maximizing floorplate size, park frontage, and city views.

4984 Breaking bread

4985 Stepping in and out, the building's form appears different from all angles.

4982 Like a single slab...

4983 ...broken in two.

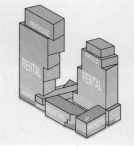

4987 Market rate and affordable housing units are dispersed throughout, with amenities connecting the towers and commercial spaces lining the street.

4988 The pair of towers, while distinct, are intimately linked.

4989 Void as figure

MARKET RATE
HOUSING

AFFORDABLE

AMENITIES
COMMERCIAL
BOH
CIRCULATION
PUBLIC

4986 Program bar

4993 The 300-foot tower (D2) is characterized by balconies facing the waterfront.

4990 The balconies and plinth terraces bring the waterfront park landscape up onto the building.

4991 As the taller tower gets higher, its floorplates become larger and more efficient.

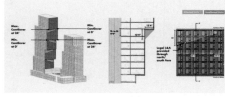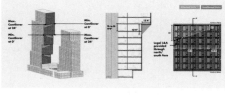

4992 Overhang impact study

4994 The 400-foot tower (D1) is composed of 24-foot cantilevers

4995 The project's most dramatic feature faces the neighborhood.

4996 View from the east

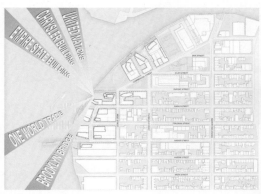

4997 Views to Manhattan from the site.

5000 By subtly angling the towers, we can bias toward the best views.

4998 The most dramatic views are north to Midtown and south to Downtown.

4999 Jason Long and Yusef Dennis present tower configurations to the Brookfield and Park Tower Group team.

5001 Initial view study

5006 The towers step back and forth in unison

5002 D1 massing development, multiple fanning steps

5003 D1 massing development, multiple parallel steps

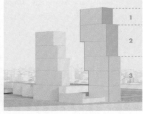

5004 D1 massing development, two parallel steps

5005 D1 massing development, one parallel step

5007 D2 bulkhead development, stepped top

5008 D2 bulkhead development, notched penthouse

5009 D2 bulkhead development, penthouse setback

5010 Model construction

5011 ⅛ inch = 1 foot physical model

5012 Jason Long with Block D model

5013 View from the East River Ferry

5014 View from the East River

5018   Wave facade panel study

5016   Early brick facade studies with balconies and pop-out windows

5017   Early wave facade study

5015   The building is divided into sets of seven- and eight-floor blocks. We wanted the facade to enhance that division and help break down the scale of the towers.

5021   Razzle dazzle camouflage

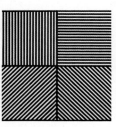

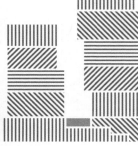

5023   The typical horizontal shingle can be rotated, becoming diagonal or vertical from one block to the next.

5019   Unlike the brownstones of southern Brooklyn, many of Greenpoint's townhouses are clad in shingled siding.

5020   If one goal of our building's form was to respond to the scale of the neighborhood, perhaps we could also use its shingles to subtly differentiate the towers' blocks?

5022   Sol LeWitt, *A Square Divided Horizontally and Vertically into Four Equal Parts, Each with a Different Direction of Alternating Parallel Bands of Lines* (1982)

5024   Full-scale blue foam facade mock-ups

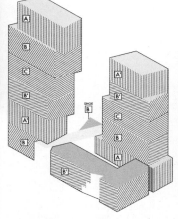

5025   Facade pattern axonometric

5026   Diagonal and vertical shingles

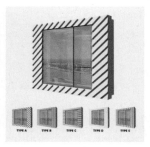

5027   The same material and profile, rotated in a number of orientations, creates a variety of effects under shifting light conditions.

5028   Facade panel physical model

5029   Large 8 by 8-foot punched windows preserve expansive views out to the city and waterfront.

5030   Mock-up of a punched window paired with a queen-sized bed

5031   Window glass review

5032   Full-scale plaster mock-up

5015–5032

Greenpoint Landing Block D

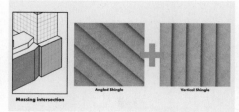

5033 We wanted to create a distinctive pattern to define specific moments on the ground floor.

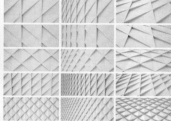

5034 "Fish-scale" shingle studies

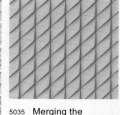

5035 Merging the shingle orientations produced a new, more three-dimensional pattern.

5036 Full-scale notch mock-up

5037 This three-dimensional pattern is deployed at each of the building entries and divisions between the volumes.

5038 Precast aggregates

5039 Shingle tests using various concrete aggregates

5040 Shingle mock-ups testing aggregate, finish, and shadow patterns in daylight conditions on-site

5041 Panel shadow study

5042 Twenty-four-hour timelapse with a south-facing visual mock-up on site

5043 Facade panel inspection, Kingston, New York

5044 Jason Long, Chris Yoon, and Sam Biroscak at the panel storage site, Kingston, New York

5045 Full-size performance mock-up (PMU), Montreal, Canada

5046 Nonmitered shingle corner treatment

5047 Mitered shingle corner treatment

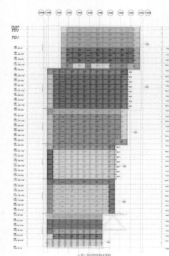

5048 D1 facade panelization

5049 A single facade panel spans two windows.

5050 D3 megapanels

5051 D2 tower construction view, February 2021

5033–5051

Greenpoint Landing Block D

5053 Could we extend that diverse streetscape around the lower floors of our building?

5054 Early concept sketches introduced cuts leading up to the raised courtyard

5055 Ground-floor cut access points

5052 Along Greenpoint's characteristic long blocks, we noticed a variety of scales and building heights that made for a dynamic streetscape.

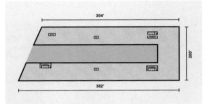

5056 The building occupies a full block.

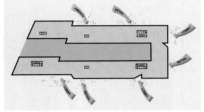

5057 We introduced a series of notches to define different programmatic sections within the building, create spatial variety from the street, and denote entries.

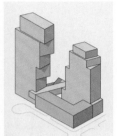

5058 Straight street wall

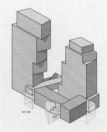

5059 Defined entry points

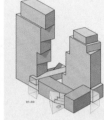

5060 Folded entry notch at the podium

5061 Podium with notches, view from Eagle and West Streets

5062 Stepped notch at podium entry

5063 Sliced notch at junction between podium and lower tower (D2)

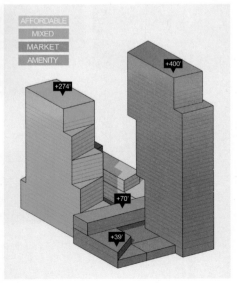

AFFORDABLE
MIXED
MARKET
AMENITY

5066 The podium houses a portion of the affordable units on the project, with a total of 30 percent affordable units in the three buildings.

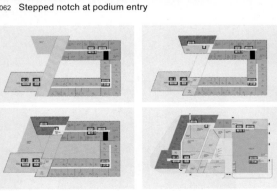

5064 Lower-level floor plans

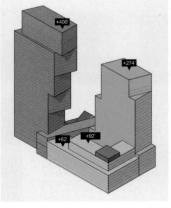

5065 In addition to the two towers, the podium acts as an independent building.

5052–5066

Greenpoint Landing Block D

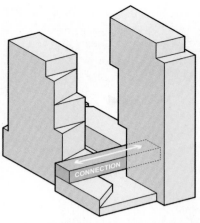

5067 Located above the residential podium, an amenity bridge links the two towers at the fourth and sixth floors.

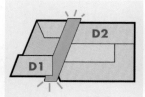

5068 Tower connection

5069 Leviton Factory and Warehouse, Greenpoint

5070 Early concept sketch of amenity bridge from the waterfront park

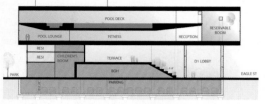

5071 A gym, pool, and a reservable Great Room occupy the two floors of the bridge.

5072 F4 amenity bridge reception, early sketch

5073 Physical model view of amenity bridge

5074 An early concept of the double-height gym space on F4 offered views into the lap pool above

5075 F4 gym with articulated lap pool above, January 2021

5076 Amenity bridge truss and waterfront view

5077 The F6 pool looks out to Manhattan and the East River.

5078 Bridge above lobby, model view

5079 View from the Great Room, March 2021

5080 Bridge view from the F4 pool deck, January 2021

5081 The reservable Great Room, a triple-height multipurpose space, terminates the bridge at the south end, extending out over the D1 lobby and entry.

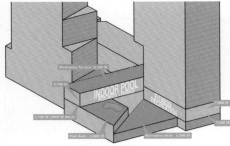

5082   The amenity bridge and terrace complete a loop between the different programmed levels.

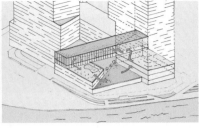

5083   Amenity terrace loop

5084   Large terraces extend adjacent to and below the bridge.

5085   The pool terrace

5086   Amenity terrace

5087   Outdoor and indoor amenity levels from F2 to F6

5088   Within the courtyard, the windows of one facade are adjusted to create a visual terminus.

5089   Courtyard construction view, February 2021

5090   Amenity bridge view from the recreation deck, February 2021

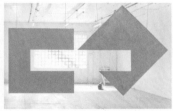

5091   Roland Gebhardt, *Untitled* (2017)

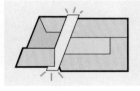

5092   The south end of the bridge is expressed by notching the plinth and shifting the tower back, exposing the D1 lobby entrance with a hovering canopy above.

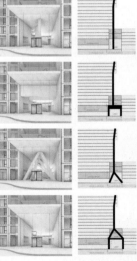

5093   Lobby entrance along the south facade

5094   Amenity bridge cantilever

5095   Four megacolumns holding up the tower's cantilevers terminate directly above the D1 lobby. Various studies were conducted to split the columns at the base to preserve an open lobby space.

5096   The resulting lobby space is triple-height and column-free. The angled split megacolumns are articulated in the Great Room above and are integrated into the walls of the lobby below.

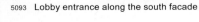

5097 Visitors and residents can pass directly from the lobby to the terrace through a stepped garden. On the left, an interior stair leads up to the amenity levels.

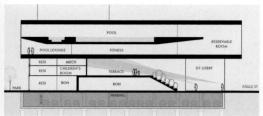

5098 D1 lobby section, with an uninterrupted view from the entrance to the F2 terrace

5099 D1 lobby circulation concept sketches

5100 Jardin de Reuilly, Paris, France

5101 A terraced garden provides a lush backdrop for the lobby, drawing visitors up to the raised courtyard.

5102 Terraced garden construction, January 2021

5103 Interiors, designed by Marmol Radziner, highlight the amenity stair portal adjacent to the garden.

5104 The D2 lobby fronts West Street.

5105 D2 lobby entrance

5106 Matt Simmonds, *Trilogy* (2010)

5107 D2 lobby with view to adjacent park

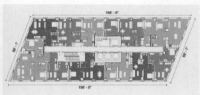

5108 D1 tower F29–35 floorplan

5109 D1 tower interior with angled column

5110 D1 tower corner column study

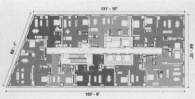

5111 D1 tower F28 floorplan

5112 The units within the building are organized to provide large living spaces with multiple windows at each corner.

5097–5112

Greenpoint Landing Block D

5113 The taller tower steps out in 24-foot increments one side at a time (two per side) for a total cantilever of 48 feet.

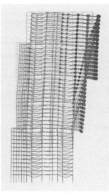

5114 Deflections resulting from cantilever

5115 The structural loads of the cantilever need to be brought to the ground without compromising the units throughout.

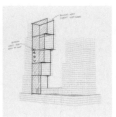

5116 Structural option, structural demising walls

5117 Structural option, moment frames

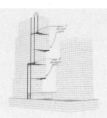

5118 Structural option, transfer beams

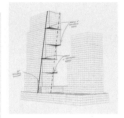

5119 Structural option, inclined columns

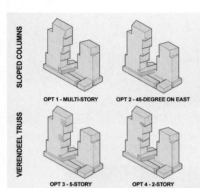

SLOPED COLUMNS

OPT 1 - MULTI-STORY   OPT 2 - 45-DEGREE ON EAST

VIERENDEEL TRUSS

OPT 3 - 5-STORY   OPT 4 - 2-STORY

5120 From the initial structural concepts, we focused with Desimone on two strategies: multi-story sloped columns and Vierendeel trusses.

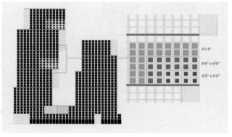

5121 Vierendeel facade impact study

5122 Vierendeel trusses would create reduced window sizes on the cantilevered units and slow construction.

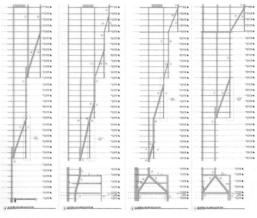

5123 Using high-angle sloped columns, there is minimal architectural impact and reduced horizontal forces, resolvable within the slab thickness.

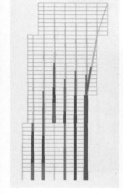

5124 The shear load from the cantilevers culminates in the building's main entrance.

5125 A-frame megacolumns at the base of the tower divide the cantilever load to either side of the lobby.

5126 Structural megacolumn

5127 Two two-story steel trusses allow the amenity bridge to span between the towers.

5128 Amenity bridge pool structure studies

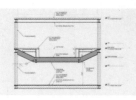

5129 A 23-inch-deep kinked "belly beam" hints at the pool's presence to the floor below while minimizing impact on the facade.

5130 Bridge construction on the pool level with a view toward the A-frame megacolumns, December 2020

5131 The project is supported by a foundation composed of more than 1,200 open steel pipe piles and drilled tension caissons.

5132 With affordable housing projects deemed essential, construction continued during the 2020 Covid-19 shutdown.

5133 D1 cantilever construction, May 2021

5134 D1 entry and lobby

5135 Workers installing steel platforms to support initial stages of cantilevered concrete slabs.

5136 Facade panels

5137 D2 tower terraces

5138 Courtyard view of D1 tower

5139 Construction, May 2021

5140 Construction, May 2021

5141 Construction, May 2021

5142 The pair of towers topped out on April 28, 2021, with D1 reaching 400 feet and D2 at 300 feet. The project is expected to be completed in 2023.

5131–5142   Greenpoint Landing Block D

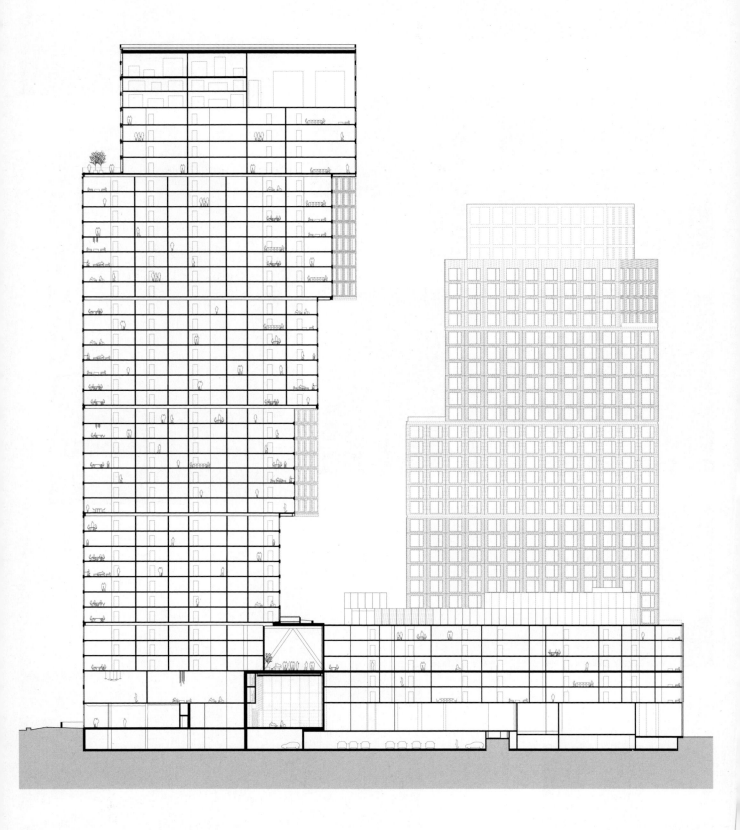

5143–5147   Greenpoint Landing Block D

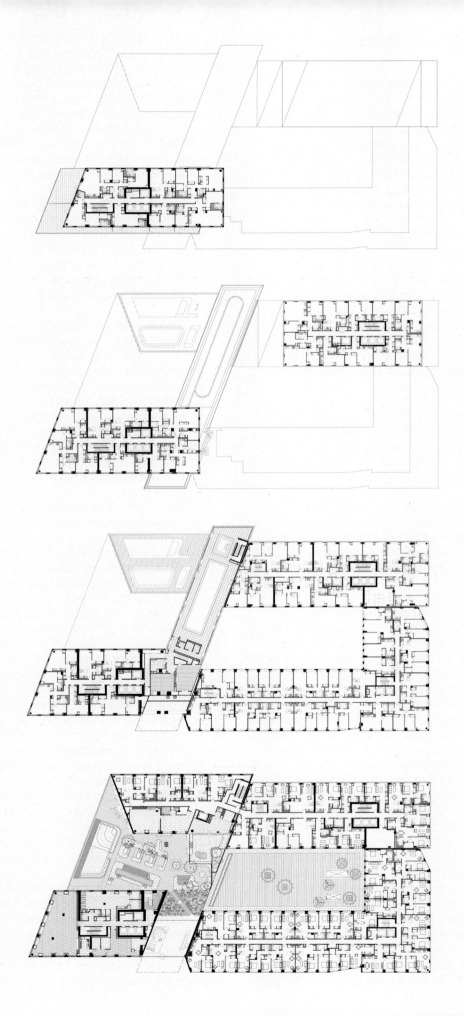

OMA NY

Greenpoint Landing Block D

Interview Alice Waters

Shohei Shigematsu: I taught a studio called Alimentary Design for a number of years at Harvard GSD [Graduate School of Design] because I am interested in looking at architecture and urbanism through the lens of food. We did three years of research with students, and this brought about a basic knowledge of the food industry, food production, and its issues as well as opportunities.

One of the reasons that I picked food as a topic for research at Harvard is that, within the three fundamental needs for human beings—shelter, food, and clothing—both architecture and fashion have been globalized very quickly. But food somehow manages to be both local and global at the same time. I think architecture should learn more from that. What do you think about the role of food in this moment, post-globalization?

Alice Waters: There's no question that our future is local. Eating local, seasonal food is the only way that we're going to address the climate and the health of communities. I really am convinced about that.

SS: What is the role of food in America and its culture and identity? One of the most shocking results from our research was how American nutritional guidelines are compromised by lobbying from big food corporations.

AW: We have been indoctrinated by fast food values since the 1950s. For decades now, we have been fed the message that everything should be fast, cheap, and easy; that cooking and farming are drudgery; that we should have everything we want, all the time, with no regard for season or place or the environmental cost. I don't believe the definition of fast food begins and ends with fast food restaurants—it's any food that's been produced by the industrial agricultural system. It's not just that the food we digest may not be good for us; every time we eat fast food, we digest these insidious fast food values, and it's really changed the world. We have been sold a false cultural understanding. So I'm trying to think about fighting against those fast food values in everything that we do, especially in kitchens of restaurants and in deciding how food comes to those kitchens. It's incredibly important to foster a regenerative way of thinking.

We're in the process of designing a restaurant for the Hammer Museum in Los Angeles.

What really interests me is that the Hammer is part of UCLA, which is similar to Chez Panisse and its proximity to UC Berkeley. We are constantly in this place of teaching— about cooking, about regenerative farming, about seasonality and ripeness. I think when we create spaces that accommodate that kind of communication and education, they encourage people to come into the kitchen, and to come into a new relationship to food.

I believe it's also vital to design a food system where there is no middleman. That's how we operate at Chez Panisse, where regenerative local farmers connect directly with the restaurant. Not only are farmers paid the true cost of their food; it brings the earth-bound values from the farm into the kitchen.

SS: The systematic issue you bring up about the food chain is what we address in our Food Port project in Louisville, Kentucky. We were trying to create a system that supports the local farmers—not just creating a farmer's market, which tends to be business-to-consumer—but to encourage a business-to-business distribution so that local food reaches a much wider audience. What do you think of the farmer's market and the current system of seemingly supporting local food? In our research we discovered that many farmer's markets are not actually maximizing the real potential of local food.

AW: Most of the local food in this country is not organic and regenerative. And it really needs to be. People have to understand what they are buying. When I lived in France in the 1960s it was a slow food culture, with a huge central marketplace where food went from there straight to the farmer's markets. There were local farmer's markets in all the neighborhoods. There weren't supermarkets anywhere at that time and you just went to your local market. I loved shopping like that and living in that world. I ate only seasonally and the food was as beautiful in the winter as it was in the summer. When I came back to the United States, that's what led me to open my own restaurant: because I couldn't find that taste, and I wanted to recreate it back in Berkeley. In pursuit of that taste, I ended up at the doorsteps of local organic farmers who grew the best-tasting fruits and vegetables. We bought directly from them, and that's how our network grew. We gave all the money to the farmers, not the middleman. It's very critical that that happens, because farmers can't make it without a reliable buyer. Chez Panisse was able to be that reliable buyer and create restaurant-supported agriculture. In that same way, I am thinking about school-supported agriculture. What could be more reliable than the public school system? It's the perfect economic engine for this. But there really needs to be a food hub in Berkeley for that to happen here in the public school system, and I've been thinking about what that looks like for a long time. The San Francisco Ferry Plaza Farmers Market is the best market I know of in the United States, because they do give some priority to people who are buying whole-sale—but there could be even more support for that. Maybe it's another pier nearby that does that.

SS: I think your point about cutting off the middle-man and bringing the market back to the city is very critical. I'm from Japan, and Tokyo once had a very beautiful market that was recently demolished and moved a bit out of town. It's probably difficult to bring back the market as it was, but maybe it could return to city life but in different forms. Lately I've been observing more crossovers between agricul-tural land and the city, in which a rapidly growing population in urbanized areas and the subsequent need for increased food pro-duction trigger the two to merge. Have you thought of any ideas for bringing food produc-tion back into the city?

AW: I truly believe that nourishment is in the soil, and it's very hard to create a rich soil life in an urban space. I profoundly believe that the soil can make us well again. Nature is hard to rep-licate, so I'm skeptical, but it's not to say that there aren't ways to bring food production back into the city. I've seen what's happened with Will Allen's urban farms up in Milwaukee. I'm impressed with the way he farms in the urban environment and uses brewery waste that's mixed up there in the soil.

I've also been involved with some museum projects in cities. At the California Academy of Sciences in San Francisco's Golden Gate Park, we're trying to build a big edible education landscape outside. I'm definitely a believer in decentralization. I would like to see the creation of food hubs in different places on the periphery of cities. When we have the buying power of big institutions like universities and environmental businesses that care, it's going to create the demand for regenerative agriculture. I think architects and people involved need to get out ahead of that to think about all of the real needs. And it's definitely about localization. Decen-tralization and localization is the key.

There are some other exemplary farmer's markets in cities around the country, like the one in Detroit that's being built with the Ford Foundation. When the old market was no longer useful, they carefully took it down and saved all the pieces of it, and they are now recreating the historic open-air market and a new hub centered around food. It's so mind-blowing to me that it's both beautiful and useful.

SS: I think building a market as the heart of urban activity could transform it into place that serves more than just food. Given the recent pandemic, there is also a chance to rethink the city through the lens of food. Maybe humans will migrate closer to the ground and closer to the soil, as you say. High-rises that were built exclusively for human occupation could become towers for food production with hydroponics and aquaponics—which of course, might not be ideal as you mention the difficulty of creating rich soil life in cities. But for me, there is something symbolic about the skyscraper, an emblem of human civilization, being given over to food production.

AW: I think it's a matter of where the water comes from, ensuring the purification and enrichment of the water. It's also about being specific about choosing produce that grows more naturally in water, like maybe watercress that is naturally full of water. Conceivably, some kinds of fish that are used to being in confined areas could really enrich the water for hydroponic agriculture.

I always think of Spain and the streets that are lined with Seville orange trees. The idea that cityscapes could have edible land-scapes. I helped with a food project at Yale where the landscape on campus integrates edible plants. After twenty years the garden is still thriving.

Sophia Choi: You work with institutions and museums, which are both inherently educational spaces, to nurture the next generation's food literacy. But have you ever thought about the role or potential of food in other types of spaces, such as the corporate office?

SS: We investigated different examples of can-teens, which, of course, is a model where food can act as a social bond, but is now deployed into the most capitalistic environ-ments like in offices of tech giants.

AW: It's what Google thinks it's doing. Call it a canteen, but it's a fast food dispensary. I had the opportunity to talk with David Adjaye when his firm was designing the Obama Presidential Library, and he asked me how I thought their food space should be designed. I said it really needs to be a place where everybody can gather to eat—not just the executives, but the people who wash dishes and clean up. And you need to think about creating a kitchen that can be used during the day for the business, and then maybe it could be a catering kitchen in the evenings—an open kitchen that invites people in.

What we don't want is people eating at desks in little alcoves by themselves. If you don't sit down and eat with your families—without the computer on the table—you're missing that important punctuation in the day. When does your day stop? I really worked on that at Yale. They have the huge opportunity because they have dining halls already set up for that, big beautiful dining halls with long communal tables. When you're coming together at a table and you're eating good food, you're having a different kind of conversation.

SS: Food literacy seems to be improving in the U.S., due to the ideas that you and others in the slow food movement have been advocating for—more people are recognizing the importance of what you eat and where you eat. At the same time, the distribution and movement of food in urban environments are changing, due to services like food trucks, Uber Eats, and Amazon Fresh. What do you think about this new industry of food mobility?

AW: They should call it Amazon Not Fresh.

SS: What is your notion of fresh then?

AW: Fresh means seasonal. That's what it means. Absolutely. Fresh, of course, means just picked off the branch, but we can't do that unless we're growing the food ourselves, or on the farm. But we certainly can eat food completely in season. We've done it before; we did it until sixty years ago. We preserved the summer harvest for the winter, and we did most of that without chemicals. But after World War II, we were particularly lost in this country and vulnerable to the ideas and values of fast food. We felt like it was too hard to cook, and we didn't know how to do it, and then somebody said, "Hey, freeze all the food." We didn't know what was really happening; it even felt hopeful, like women were liberated from the labor of cooking.

And then those fast food values grew and grew. Terms like "fresh" become meaningless when they're appropriated by fast food culture—"fresh" is used to describe a peach that's been industrially grown, shipped 8,000 miles, and sold in the middle of winter. The dishonesty is really a Trump kind of

dishonesty: it is just flat-out lying about the consequences of living in a fast food culture. In order to come back to our senses, I think it's really going to take a concerted and deliberate effort, particularly on the part of architects and food people who have the right motivation to dream this up. Landscape architects are also important, and the people who are thinking about pathways from the farmer's market to the cities. City planning is so critical right now.

SS: I agree that we could use more imagination to plan cities that are food-centric. Manhattan is surrounded by water and its piers used as ports to receive food from farmers. Parts of the shore itself were oyster reefs and had local markets selling oysters. The city has been turning piers into parks, but it could be more interesting if some of them became markets and edible landscapes.

AW: There are a couple that are trying to be ambitious, but in the end it's a bit sold out. Space in New York is pretty valuable. I'm thinking about what we can do with those big old towers, like you said. At least we could grow food up the sides of them and make them into green monuments.

SS: We are definitely up for that if you are!

AW: But think about the gift of Central Park to New York. That is without question how every city needs to be designed. It's like the town square. Historically, marketplaces brought neighborhood businesses back to life. Because I've spent a lot of time in Rome, I think the more pure the market, the more successful it can be—a place for a lot of small, like-minded businesses with shared values to exist. That kind of a space in the city will bring those people together naturally, because they want to be a part of it. It's happened up in Seattle, too, and it affected the way that hotels were built, where they wanted to take advantage of the local fish they could buy at the corner. I think it does bring back urban life in a great way.

In New York, I always go to the Union Square Greenmarket. The market there has educated New Yorkers like nothing else. Then there are a lot of satellite projects, but what is most important again is decentralization and supporting local people. I think it's important that the message be: you can't have a stall at the market unless you believe in stewardship, organic growing practices, and building community.

SC: The pandemic has definitely highlighted the importance of decentralized, local pockets of public space but also the use of streets. Restaurants are taking over parking spots with outdoor dining—it's created a new urban life but also makes us reassess how streets were used before.

AW: I hope the city really takes note of this. We need streets that are devoted to the public. And with the limitations we need to put on cars to make them electric, we're going to just need to get on our bikes. Strangely, I don't see that people are unwilling to do that. They simply don't have the place where they feel comfortable doing that in the city.

We're working with the city to let us take over in front of Chez Panisse, because it's almost like a little piazza. But we're also thinking about the post office right next door to the restaurant and how people can get in and out. So it's all about interconnectedness. This affects this, that affects that. I always think that architects can help desperate city planners who know nothing about this. They know nothing about designing schools, or even designing parks. It's something that has been industrialized. You get the guy who designs parks for all the cities, and they all look the same.

SS: There needs to be a shared vision across the different stakeholders. I do feel that the food domain has been expanding, creating a baseline understanding of its issues and potentials—I'm optimistic that we can work with the city to build consensus. Zooming in now from the city to domesticity… At a smaller scale of food in everyday life, where would you find design to be effective?

AW: I'm particularly interested in the design of kitchens that can respect the values of cooking. There should never be a back of house. That means that every space where somebody is working has to be desirable. It can be as simple as having the right light or windows or art. Whatever it is, it really needs to inspire them.

Whenever I do an event, I want to be able to invite people everywhere. Where the cooks are cooking, I want the compost to look good, I want every table to have a tablecloth on it. I want fruit to be displayed beautifully. I don't want people to feel a disconnect between the kitchen and what they're eating.

SS: It's all front-of-house.

AW: All of those jobs are valuable in the kitchen. Whether it's the cooks in the kitchen or the people cleaning up at night, everybody needs to be thought about ahead of time.

SS: I think that's a very important issue, seeing how kitchens are one of the most evolving parts of the house. A kitchens used to be tucked away at the back of the house, but now it's the center for social activities and made visible.

AW: I know someone who is currently designing a composter for the home. I told him, don't make it out of stainless steel. Make it out of something that makes you want to have it in your kitchen. Something that represents the earth.

SS: Lastly, what do you think about architects?

AW: I have lots of wishes for architects. They have such power to teach us about nature and building communities. We're all hungry for beauty—really hungry. We can't think about designing factories the way that Amazon has, with a disregard for humanity. I would love to design a factory.

In your book, I saw a bridge that had trees on it going across a river. I think when you are designing and building beautiful public spaces, you have the opportunity to inspire people to think about the world differently. We're doing a big event in Sacramento centered around food, climate, and hope in the spring of 2022. It's a Slow Food event, and we're going to create a table that goes from the capitol building to the Sacramento River. It will be a long table for teachers and farmers to eat together, and we'll take up the whole street, both sides and center.

Alice Waters is a chef, restaurateur, activist, author, owner of Chez Panisse restaurant (est. 1971) and founder of The Edible Schoolyard, both in Berkeley, California. She's a pioneer of the slow food movement and an advocate for universal access to local and regenerative organic foods.

OMA NY

Alice Waters

5148

West Louisville Food Port

West Louisville Food Port

Our research on food was in part a reaction to the global homogeneity we began to observe in architecture and urbanism. Within the three fundamentals of human life—clothing, shelter, and food—both shelter (architecture) and clothing (fashion) were globalized and thus homogenized. Food, on the other hand, manages to be both global and local. It embodies the ultimate specificity to local culture, livelihood, soil, and climate, much like terroir, but can be widely distributed to have a global presence and identity. Can architecture be viewed through this lens of food to learn and evolve?

Food is also inherently diverse. It is multi-processed, touching upon different areas of our lives. We looked into the relationship between food production and urbanism, as in Frank Lloyd Wright's Broadacre City, which imagined an antithesis to the city by merging suburbia with agriculture. Food is related to mobility, from drive-thrus to app-based delivery services. Food also shapes our social environments—like the canteen, a model for dining where food is a bond (or not), used in various settings from schools, churches, and museums to tech companies, military bases, and prisons.

Through this research, we were asked to design a new type of public building that precisely addresses the multi-faceted issues around the food chain—a Food Port for West Louisville, Kentucky, that consolidates a community center, distribution center, and a shared agricultural aggregation center.

The development of cities has been inextricably connected to the production, supply, and distribution of food. But with the migration of rural communities to cities, people have become removed from agricultural production and less aware of how their food is made. The direct producer-to-consumer relationship is now separated by middleman entities: distributors, processors, and retailers. Individual and commercial consumers are increasingly looking to buy directly from the producer, but the scale of most local farms and their distribution networks make it difficult to meet the growing demand. Food hubs can alleviate this bottleneck by consolidating supplies into shared facilities for local farmers and locating them strategically within cities.

The site for the West Louisville Food Port (Food Port), is located within an area classified as a food desert, where nutritious and affordable food is scarce due to its history of disinvestment after the Great Flood in 1937. The food hub sought to revitalize the local Louisville community. The Food Port operates as more than the typical food hub with the addition of key programs that serve and provide for all stages of the food chain: farming to processing, shared community kitchen spaces, retail, and recycling. It provides the much-needed infrastructural connection between farmers and suppliers and meets the growing demand for local food. Referencing the street grids of the city, which are rotated at different angles from neighborhood to neighborhood to maintain orientation to the Ohio River, we conceived a masterplan that stitches together the urban fabric.

Programs are organized by shared needs and facilities of tenants. The northeast corner of the site is anchored with retail, coffee roastery, and juicery production facilities. Aggregation and processing facilities are located at the center of the site, connected to offices and the kitchen incubator. A research facility for a local university is lifted to form a strong connection to its demonstration farm below, and directly connected to the Urban Farm. The recycling facility at the southwest corner of the site provides ease of access. Corresponding outdoor spaces include a market plaza, food truck plaza, and edible garden. The efficient building plan supports systematic growth, allowing the building and its tenants to develop over time.

The Food Port provides a comprehensive survey of the food industry and its processes, to make food widely accessible for local individuals and businesses. But it also creates a platform for learning and discourse to equip communities with a better understanding of the diverse social implications of food. Can this typology be applied to cities globally, while enhancing the locality of each place?

Location	Louisville, KY, USA		
Status	Commissioned Study, 2015–2016		
Typology	Public Realm		
Program	Open Space	852,100 ft²	79,160 m²
	Retail	15,500 ft²	1,440 m²
	Production/Urban Farm	84,500 ft²	7,850 m²
	Office/Education	42,300 ft²	3,930 m²
	Industrial/BOH	90,100 ft²	8,370 m²
	Total Area	1,084,500 ft²	100,750 m²

5149

West Louisville Food Port

5150

West Louisville Food Port

OMA NY

West Louisville Food Port

5151　West Louisville Food Port

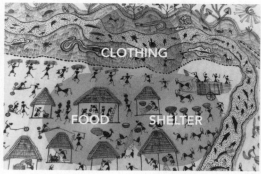

CLOTHING

FOOD   SHELTER

5152   The history of human evolution is directly connected to three fundamental needs for life: food, clothing, and shelter. As opposed to fashion and architecture, both of which have been globalized and homogenized, food remains diverse.

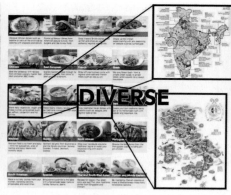

DIVERSE

5153   The world of food is extremely varied. It is global and local, in line with the concept of *terroir*.

$15 trillion

FOOD + BEVERAGE

$6 t   ENERGY

$2 t

TOURISM

5154   Food and beverage makes up one of the world's largest industries.

ARCHITECTURE AND URBAN DESIGN

FOOD

NEW TYPOLOGIES

5155   How can food be a way to rethink architecture and urban design typologies?

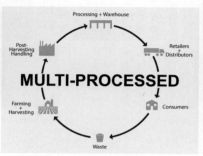

MULTI-PROCESSED

5156   Food as a multi-processed industry

TRADE ROUTES AND GREAT EMPIRES OF THE FIRST CENTURY A.D.

5157   Trade between the Roman Empire and Asia defined the global spread of food and culture as early as the first century.

SUPER FARM

5158   The globalization of food brought new models for global food production—such as the Jilin food zone super farm, where an entirely new city with an area twice the size of Singapore is dedicated to food production.

Housing is individual: not apartments, but private houses with at least four acres of property each, land which the proprieter uses for agriculture and for different leisure activities.

5159   The growth of cities and coincident shrinking of agricultural land became a catalyst for urban and suburban development crossovers, such as the Broadacre City proposed by Frank Lloyd Wright in 1934.

5160   While Wright's proposal mainly focused on food production, it projected a futuristic model for living.

5161   Merging agriculture with living on plots of land, one acre per person, this model seemed unrealistic at the time considering the level of urban growth taking place.

5162   Wright's vision has been unintentionally realized today, where places like the Zhejiang Province in Eastern China have developed directly along plot lines of arable land. While 40 percent of the Earth's land is used for agriculture, land for food production continues to decrease.

In 2011, for the first time in modern history, the global production of farmed fish exceeded beef production.

5163   In 2011, for the first time in modern history, the global production of farmed fish exceeded beef production.

5164   Bo'ao floating village in Hainan China—urban development as a byproduct of the fishing industry

5165   The first McDonald's, in San Bernardino, California (1940s)—the fast food industry gained popularity for its mobility and speed.

DONUT HOLE

5166   The drive-in has been on the decline due to increased real estate premiums. What new models of food retail can be considered based on future ideas of mobility?

grubHub

GRUB $2.36 billion financing in food-related investments in 2014 RUB

5167   Food-related startups are one of the fastest growing areas in the financial market.

FOOD LIVE + WORK

5168   MVRDV's Markthal Rotterdam, where an arch of apartments surrounds a colorful market hall—how can food-related functions be brought back into the city?

amazon fresh

5169   The availability of food has changed because of delivery services like Amazon Fresh.

5170   Googleplex canteen—at IT and tech companies today, the canteen plays a crucial role in recruiting potential employees and sustaining production.

5171   Major kitchen appliance manufacturers are investigating the changing role of the kitchen. What is the future for the design of food spaces?

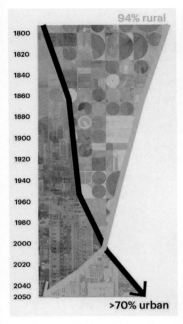

94% rural

1800
1820
1840
1860
1880
1900
1920
1940
1960
1980
2000
2020
2040
2050

>70% urban

5172 In a trend that can be traced back to the movement of large groups of people to cities during the Industrial Revolution in the eighteenth and nineteenth centuries, the rural population has continued to fall as the urban population has grown.

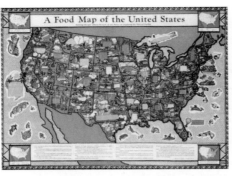

5173 Historically, the development of communities and cities has been connected to the production, supply, and distribution of food.

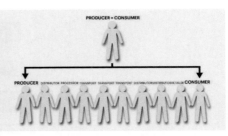

5174 People have become increasingly separated from sites of agricultural production and less aware of where their food comes from. Where the producer and the consumer were once the same person, today they are separated by numerous other entities, including distributors, processors, and retailers.

I ♥ EATING LOCAL FOOD

5175 There has been a counter-trend in the twentieth century toward increasing consumers' desire to understand where their food comes from and how it has been handled.

5176 In the past twenty years, the number of farmer's markets in the United States has grown nearly five times, and they currently number over 8,000.

AGGREGATOR

DISTRIBUTION

STORAGE

MARKETING

5177 Although food hubs nationwide vary widely, they all contain four typical core components.

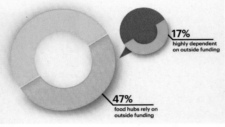

17% highly dependent on outside funding

47% food hubs rely on outside funding

5178 Many food hubs rely on outside funding, such as startup funding from philanthropic institutions and the USDA, according to the results of a 2013 national food hub study.

NO TRANSPARENCY

NO PUBLIC INTERFACE

5179 Food hubs serve an important purpose to connect the producer with the consumer, but are typically opaque industrial facilities with little to no public interaction.

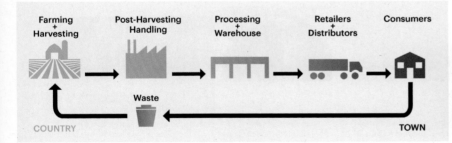

Farming + Harvesting → Post-Harvesting Handling → Processing + Warehouse → Retailers + Distributors → Consumers

Waste

COUNTRY   TOWN

5180 The typical food chain includes many entities and separates the growing urban population from the typically rural producers.

"SKYROCKETING CONSUMER DEMAND FOR LOCAL AND REGIONAL FOOD IS AN ECONOMIC OPPORTUNITY FOR AMERICA'S FARMERS AND RANCHERS. FOOD HUBS FACILITATE ACCESS TO THESE MARKETS [AND] FOOD HUBS KEEP MORE OF THE RETAIL FOOD DOLLAR CIRCULATING IN THE LOCAL ECONOMY."
— USDA Secretary Tom Vilsack, May 2013

5181 A food hub is not only a way to create access to fresh food; it has the potential to reinvigorate the local economy while building a sense of connected community through food.

A FOOD HUB FOR WEST LOUISVILLE

A FOOD STATION FOR WEST LOUISVILLE
A FOOD CENTER FOR WEST LOUISVILLE
A FOODTOPIA FOR WEST LOUISVILLE
A FOOD FIELD FOR WEST LOUISVILLE
A FOOD INTERCHANGE FOR WEST LOUISVILLE
A FOOD LINE FOR WEST LOUISVILLE
A FOOD PARK FOR WEST LOUISVILLE

5182 How can the West Louisville Food Port re-imagine the typical food hub to provide a new model for food production, distribution, and consumption?

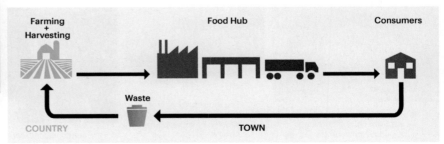

Farming + Harvesting → Food Hub → Consumers

Waste

COUNTRY   TOWN

5183 A food hub reconnects the producer to the consumer and relocates integral components of the food industry back into the city.

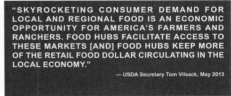

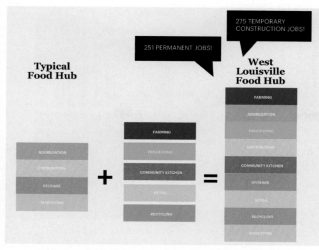

Typical Food Hub

251 PERMANENT JOBS!

275 TEMPORARY CONSTRUCTION JOBS!

West Louisville Food Hub

5184 A food hub, as defined by the USDA, includes four main program components: aggregation, distribution, storage, and marketing. The West Louisville Food Hub, or Food Port, goes beyond the typical programmatic mix with the addition of several key programs that serve and provide for all stages of the food chain—farming, processing, shared community kitchen spaces, retail, and recycling.

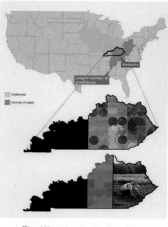

5185 The West Louisville Food Port is located in Louisville, Kentucky, which lies at the junction of the Heartland and Eastern Uplands agricultural regions, combining the most fertile region in the United States with the country's largest number of small farms.

5186 Tobacco field near Louisville, Kentucky—the state has a long legacy of agriculture.

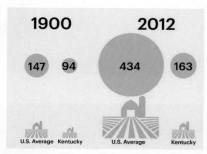

1900   **2012**

147   94   434   163

U.S. Average   Kentucky   U.S. Average   Kentucky

5187 Farm sizes in acres—US average vs Kentucky

THIS LAND IS YOUR LAND

5188 Approximately 55 percent of Kentucky's total land area is made up of farms. Of those farms, 60 percent are classified as small with annual sales of ten thousand dollars or less.

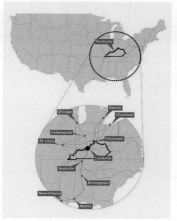

5189 Connectivity to the south

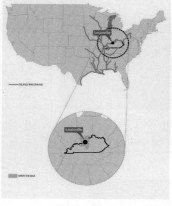

5190 Louisville is centrally connected through inland waterways.

5191 Louisville's food history—1883 Southern Exposition agricultural display

5192 Louisville is located close to many small and local farms.

5193 Local farms at a short distance produce a variety of crops and products and would have access to aggregation facilities of the food hub

5194 Map of food deserts in the United States. Despite the expanse of agriculture within the state, regions within Kentucky are food deserts.

SEED CAPITAL KY

5195 "We're looking at ways to do just what the tobacco economy did; take the produce from hundreds of Kentucky farmers around the state, bring it here to West Louisville, process it and create hundreds of jobs, send it out, and make money that stays in the tax and employment base of Louisville and Kentucky."
—Stephen Reily, Seed Capital Kentucky

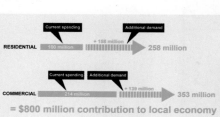

RESIDENTIAL: Current spending 100 million + 158 million Additional demand → 258 million

COMMERCIAL: Current spending 214 million + 139 million Additional demand → 353 million

= $800 million contribution to local economy

5196 The food culture and the legacy of agriculture of Louisville extends to a high demand for local food, with unmet demands outstripping supply for both residential and commercial consumers.

5197 The current demand for local food from both the individual and the commercial consumer is impeded by the lack of market connections, which has created a bottleneck of inefficiency. The West Louisville Food Port will alleviate this bottleneck.

5198 The site for the food port was formerly occupied by a four-story building belonging to the American Tobacco Company, which was founded in 1890 and acquired by Lucky Strike in 1905.

5199 Historic Louisville street grids

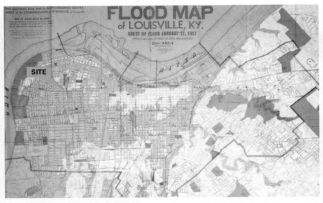

5200 As a result of the Great Ohio River Flood of 1937, future development in Louisville was directed east, out of the flood plain to the west. This move continues to affect the economy and demographics of Louisville today.

5201 The Great Ohio River Flood of 1937

5202 A number of initiatives and developments have been completed and are currently underway to reconnect the urban fabric of Louisville. Located at the junction of many of these initiatives, the site for the West Louisville Food Port has the potential to supplement the given program and serve the surrounding neighborhoods and greater community.

5203 Louisville divisions

5204 Urban connections

5205 Cultural connections

5206 West Louisville demographics

5207 The site for the West Louisville Food Port is located at the intersection of three neighborhoods.

5208 The site spans 23.86 acres.

5209 Existing site conditions

5210 Possibilities and challenges

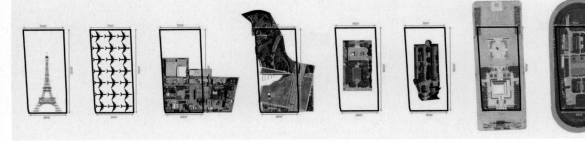

5211 Scale comparisons—Eiffel Tower, Boeing 747, Brown-Foreman, Louisville Waterfront Park, Bryant Park, Faneuil Hall, Tiananmen Square, Churchill Downs

5199–5211   West Louisville Food Port

5212 Food Port is a unique combination of programs and tenants that provides a comprehensive survey of the industry.

5213 "[This project] is unique in its collaborative approach. Businesses coming together in this project, while having seemingly disparate individual objectives... together they achieve benefits which both further their individual goals and result in added benefits for the community. This makes this project a true social investment project." —Seed Capital Kentucky

AGGREGATION
STORAGE
DISTRIBUTION
MARKETING

5214 The addition of programs to a typical food hub allows the producer to reconnect with the consumer in an urban environment.

5215 The programmatic mix of tenants is seen as one continuous loop and can be arranged on site to maximize shared resources, amenities, and collaboration.

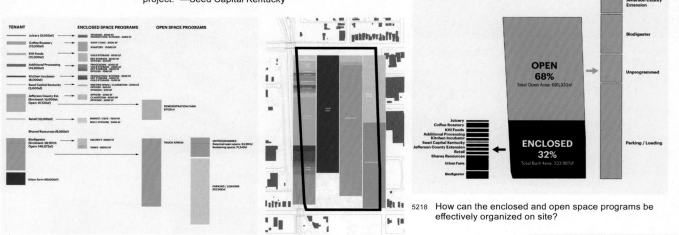

5216 Program breakdown of enclosed and open spaces by tenant (1,084,525 square feet total area)

5217 Overlay of all tenant program square footages on the site.

5218 How can the enclosed and open space programs be effectively organized on site?

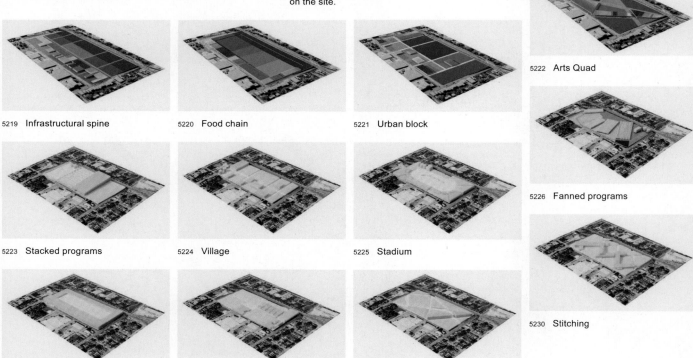

5219 Infrastructural spine

5220 Food chain

5221 Urban block

5222 Arts Quad

5223 Stacked programs

5224 Village

5225 Stadium

5226 Fanned programs

5227 Giant courtyard

5228 Warehouse cluster

5229 Diagonal paths

5230 Stitching

5212–5230

West Louisville Food Port

5231 If the program were to be considered in its most efficient layout, it could form a long bar dividing the logistically heavier programs along the elevated highway to the west. This would, however, recreate the conceptual and physical barrier between East and West Louisville.

5232 Instead, the linear bar is subdivided based on programmatic adjacencies and compressed into the site boundaries, referencing the rotated street grid of the Portland neighborhood, as well as creating opportunities for public interface along 30th Street and the corners of the site.

5233 Concept collage—1883 Southern Exposition building reconfigured

5234 Downtown and West Louisville street grids

5235 Portland neighborhood grid

5236 Food Port stitches the two adjacent neighborhoods of Shawnee and Russell together by addressing the streets from both areas.

5237 The angled bars are aligned to connect the existing street grids to the east and west, weaving the site into the urban fabric.

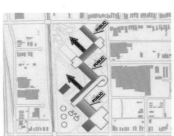

5238 Logistics-heavy programs are shifted toward the west side of the site, while more public programs face toward the northeast and the corner of 30th and Market.

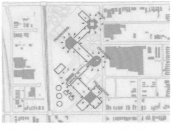

5239 Collaborative intersections in Food Port's continuous campus create new programmatic efficiencies that enable tenants to interact with each other in ways not possible at typical food hubs or similar facilities.

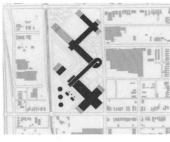

5240 The flexibility of the bars accommodates future growth into the unprogrammed zones.

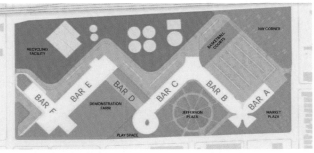

5241 Open and undefined program

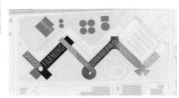

5242 Six program bars

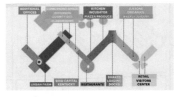

5243 Tenant layout

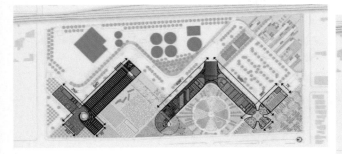

5244 Ground-level plan

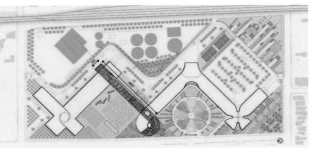

5245 Upper-level plan

5231–5245

West Louisville Food Port

5246 Bars A and B connection—pinch, pasta

5247 Visitor Center studies

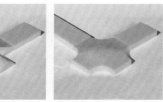

5248 Intersection of Market Plaza, Congress Street, and parking

5249 Visitor Center entry

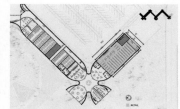

5250 Bar A—retail

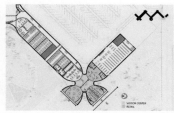

5251 Intersection—Visitor Center

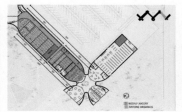

5252 Bar B—juicery, cafe

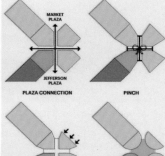

5253 Visitor Center concept diagram

5254 Visitor Center concept—squeeze, juicer

5255 Visitor Center entry from Market Plaza

5256 The Visitor Center is the first entry point from the north and represents an intersection with access points from four main zones of pedestrian activity.

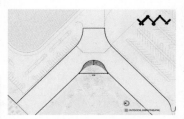

5260 Intersection—outdoor amphitheater

5257 Visitor Center—event use

5258 Bars B and C connection—hinge, wishbone

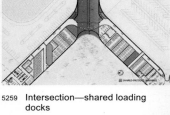

5259 Intersection—shared loading docks

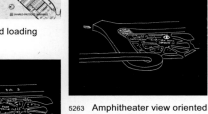

5263 Amphitheater view oriented down Jefferson Plaza and Jefferson Street

5262 Shared loading dock between Bars B and C

5261 The amphitheater opens up to the orange slice-shaped Jefferson Plaza. Acting as the cultural heart of the project, the plaza's centerpiece is a large water tank in the shape of a location pin. The pin acts as a landmark at the end of West Jefferson Street, which directly connects to City Hall and downtown Louisville.

5264 View from Jefferson Plaza with the amphitheater beyond

5246–5264

West Louisville Food Port

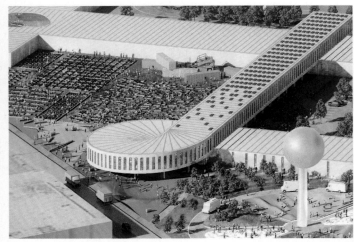

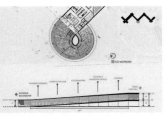

5266 Co-working space configuration

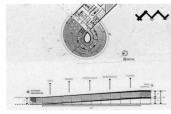

5267 Retail/dining configuration

5265 Adjacent to Jefferson Plaza is a curved ramp that connects Bar C (kitchen incubator) and Bar D (offices and classrooms). The continuous ramp can be flexibly programmed and creates a dynamic open space beneath it that extends toward Jefferson Plaza.

5268 Co-working loop on the curved ramp

5269 Retail/dining on the curved ramp

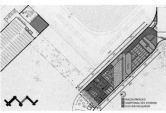

5270 Bar C—kitchen incubator

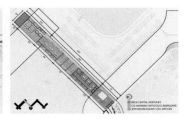

5271 Bar D—offices and classrooms

5272 Bar D—co-working offices/classrooms

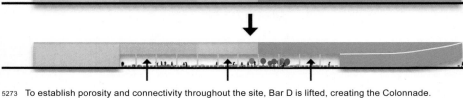

5273 To establish porosity and connectivity throughout the site, Bar D is lifted, creating the Colonnade.

5274 Colonnade Walk in Central Park, Louisville

5275 The historic colonnade at the site of the 1883 Southern Exposition in Louisville

5276 Lifting Bar D to create the Colonnade harkens back to historic Louisville references while creating a unique connection between the Jefferson County Extension tenant spaces, outdoor recreational spaces and the Demonstration Farm.

5277 The Colonnade becomes a covered outdoor space for additional activity and exchange.

5265–5277

West Louisville Food Port

5278 Bars E and F connection—swirl, penguin pool at the London Zoo

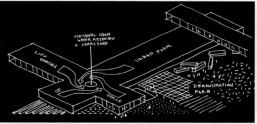

5279 Intersection—Urban Farm and office tenants

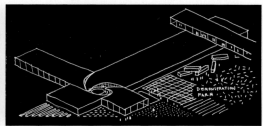

5280 Shared outdoor courtyard

5281 Potential Urban Farm method—aeroponics

5282 Potential Urban Farm method—aquaponics

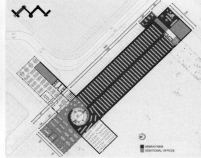

5283 Bar E—Urban Farm

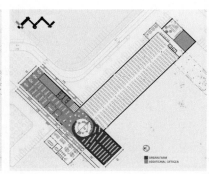

5284 Bar F and Urban Courtyard

5285 The Urban Courtyard that is created at the intersection between Bars E and F blends together farming and office spaces to provide a shared outdoor amenity for both tenants.

5286 The West Louisville Food Port is a continuous linear campus.

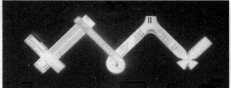

5287 Plan view of model

5288 Model view from south

5289 Programming model

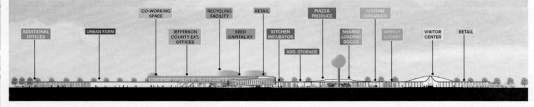

5290 Program gradient from south to north—private to public

5291 The West Louisville Food Port re-imagines the typical food hub into a community space within a food desert, providing connectivity between food production, consumption, and community education.

West Louisville Food Port

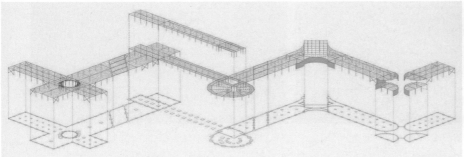

5293 Physical model

5292 Structural framing system—to provide the most economical structural system, conventional framing systems are employed for the Bars, while unique layouts support the Intersections.

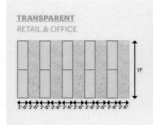

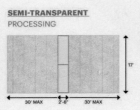

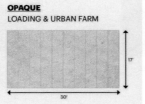

TRANSPARENT
RETAIL & OFFICE

SEMI-TRANSPARENT
PROCESSING

OPAQUE
LOADING & URBAN FARM

5295 Facade types—transparent (light blue), semi-transparent (dark blue), and opaque (black)

5294 Tilt-up concrete facade panels are spaced in correlation to the structural grid and have a wide variety of texture, aggregate, pattern, and color options.

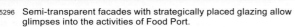

5297 Facade study—graphic concrete pattern

5298 Graphic concrete texture

5296 Semi-transparent facades with strategically placed glazing allow glimpses into the activities of Food Port.

5302 Polished graphic concrete

5299 Polished concrete

5300 Exposed aggregate

5301 Curved formlined concrete

5303 Local soil aggregate

5304 Mixed concrete panels

5305 Opaque facades are used for back-facing logistical programs.

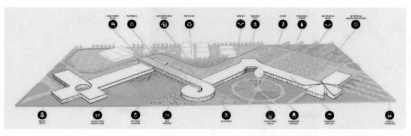

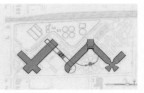

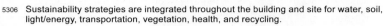

5306　Sustainability strategies are integrated throughout the building and site for water, soil, light/energy, transportation, vegetation, health, and recycling.

5307　The stormwater management plan studies areas to capture and infiltrate on-site, while exploring strategies for rooftop re-use and rainwater storage.

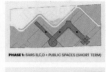

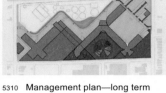

5310　Management plan—long term

5308　Phasing plan

5309　Management plan—short term

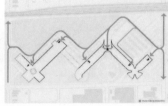

5312　Loading circulation path

5311　Parking circulation path

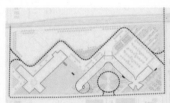

5314　Bicycle loop

5313　Mayor's Mile running loop

5315　Visitor's map

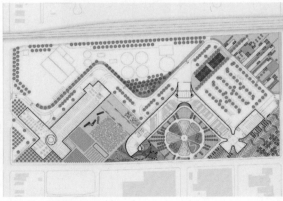

5316　Long-term landscape plan

5317　Planting types

5318　The diverse landscape reflects West Louisville Food Port's ambition to be a jobs-producing resource for the community and a variety of business tenants.

5306–5318

West Louisville Food Port

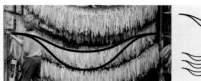

5320 Market Plaza paving pattern—tobacco

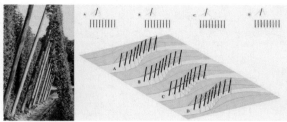

5319 The Market Plaza is conceived as an entrance and extension of the adjacent retail. Wooden trellises provide organization for market tents as a flexible event space.

5321 Market Plaza planting pattern—hops growing on pole

5322 Market Plaza trellises

5323 Market Plaza entry axis

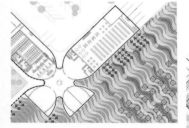

5324 Market Plaza layout

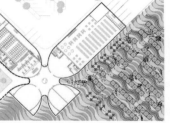

5325 Programming—market tents

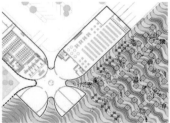

5326 Programming—large event

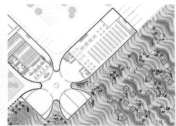

5327 Programming—small event

5328 Demonstration Farm

5329 Demonstration Farm programming—raised beds, cut flowers, cover crop/flowers, nursery trees

5330 Play Space

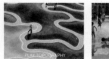

5331 Play Space programming—play topography, splashpad, play furniture

5332 The Play Space and the adjacent Demonstration Farm are intended to provide areas for activity, exploration, and recreation without the use of typical play equipment.

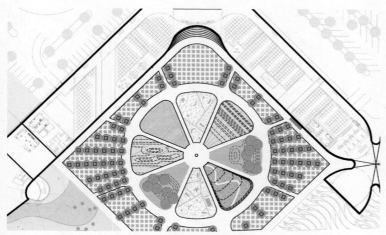

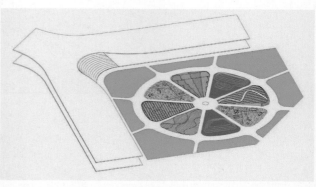

5334 The plaza can be used for community gatherings, including multiple small or single large events, performances, and food/cooking related demonstrations, and food trucks.

5333 The Jefferson Plaza strategy, proposed by the landscape architecture firm Stoss, aims to reflect and support a range of active and passive activities by establishing wedge-shaped spaces with unique materiality and landscape characteristics.

5335 Jefferson Plaza programming—food trucks, food-related events, fitness classes

5336 Materiality—rubber play surface

5337 Materiality—orange textured concrete

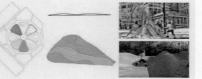

5338 Materiality—rubber play surface

5339 Landscaping—grassy slope

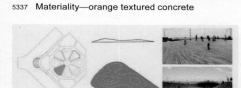

5340 Materiality—formed hardwood

5341 Landscaping—flower beds

5342 Landscaping—grassy slope

5343 Private event

5344 Food trucks

5345 Event/temporary tent structures

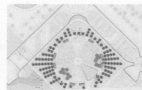

5346 Kitchen incubator-related event

5347 Small event

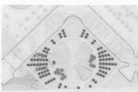

5348 Simultaneous events

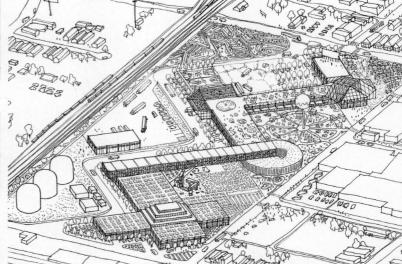

5349 The West Louisville Food Port is a new model for defining the relationship between consumer and producer, addressing uncaptured market demand and inefficiencies within the local food industry. It combines infrastructure, education, retail, urban farming, and community gathering spaces to establish a network of connections and address the growing demand for local food.

5333–5349

West Louisville Food Port

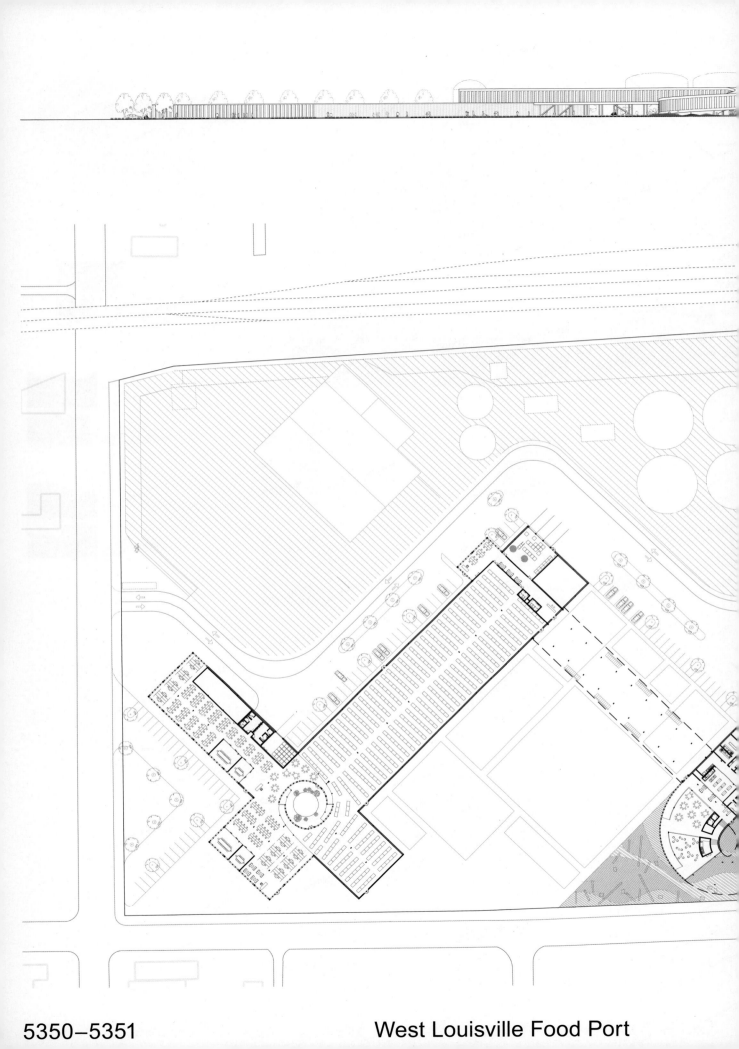

5350—5351   West Louisville Food Port

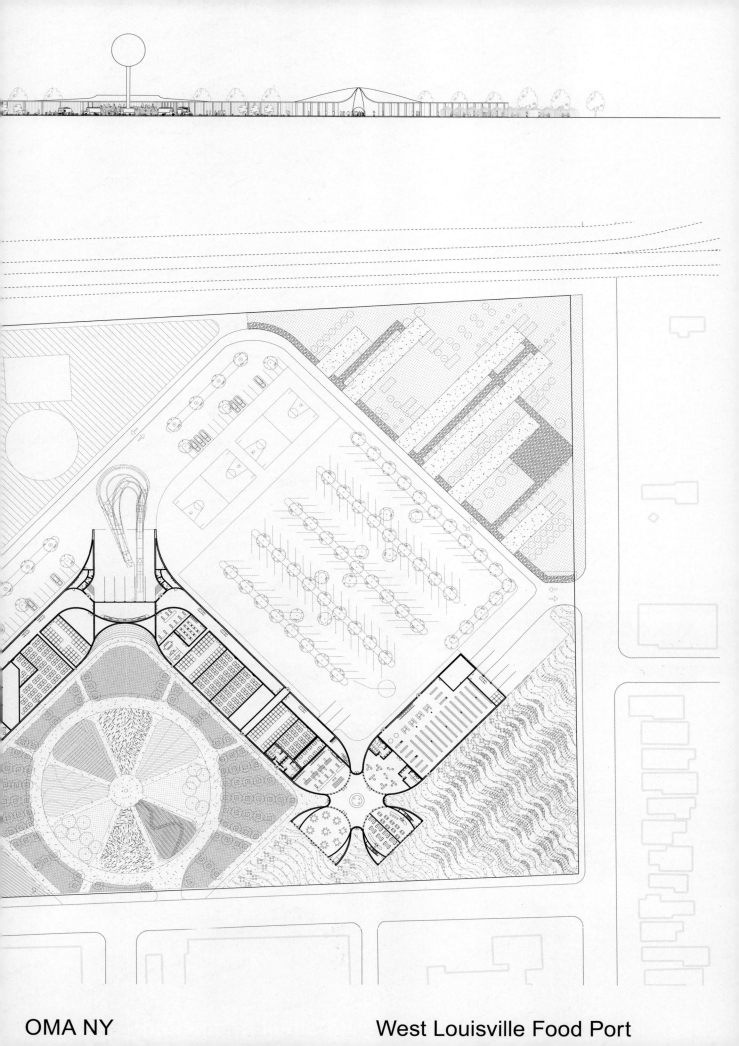

OMA NY

West Louisville Food Port

5352   11th Street Bridge Park

11th Street Bridge Park

The 11th Street Bridge Park in Washington, D.C., confronted us with a set of entrenched divisions that dominate many cities—disparities of income and investment that all too often align with race and are reinforced by geography. D.C. was planned around the confluence of two rivers, the Potomac and the Anacostia. While the more recognized Potomac defines its organic southwestern edge with Virginia, the Anacostia cuts through the city, dividing its southeastern quadrant from the rest.

The west side of the Anacostia River is defined by Pierre Charles L'Enfant's classical plan, crisscrossed with diagonal avenues whose intersections—called Reservations—mark the locations of civic buildings and public spaces. The east side is less formally organized, with a terrain of hills that fragment its street grid and a riverfront that is bucolic in comparison to the industrialized western bank. The west is dominated by D.C.'s practical and symbolic role as the nation's capital, while the largely African-American east side is home to more native D.C. residents than any other neighborhood. Today, the west is high income while the east has the lowest income levels in the district. Over the last fifteen years, the post-industrial Capitol Riverfront along the west bank has become a thriving mixed-use area, while the east side has long been excluded from the city's economic progress.

The idea behind the 11th Street Bridge Park was to utilize abandoned infrastructure—a set of piers from a now-defunct vehicular bridge—to create a pedestrian link between east and west. As its name implies, the park would be at once a thoroughfare across the river and a gathering place over it. This improbable proposal led to a design competition we entered together with landscape architects OLIN in the spring of 2014.

Our approach was not to create a singular and symbolic connector, but rather a multilayered place formed by the literal extension of two paths over the river. The two trajectories extend through and past each other, creating a gathering space where they intersect. The resulting form—an X—is an iconic encounter, an intersection that, like L'Enfant's Reservations, marks a shared civic space in the city. The X shape provides a number of practical benefits. Its upper decks lift visitors high above the river, providing a vantage point from which they can orient themselves and look out to both the monuments of D.C. and the hills of Anacostia. Where the upper and lower decks overlap, the gaps between them provide depth for the bridge's structure. The decks also provide covered zones that, together with OLIN's carefully orchestrated landscape, offer a continuous shaded path—a relief from D.C.'s famously swampy summers.

The most straightforward way to ensure that the investment in the Bridge Park would benefit the east side of the river was to simply make the bridge wider on that side, allowing for a concentration of programs and space. An Environmental Education Center, cafe, and playspace are located on this wider east side, with a performance space and a hammock grove on the west. The layering of the bridge also allows us to temper the potential for it to be—like some contemporary parks—too fixed with specific programs. While we can provide dedicated spaces for attractors like the cafe and amphitheater on the lower decks, above them we can allocate spaces for more casual and open-ended areas, such as a walkway and a lawn.

Almost immediately after the competition, we began to see our renderings used by real estate agents in Anacostia. What we saw as an unquestioned benefit could clearly have more sinister, unforeseen impacts. Having won the competition in 2014, we finally entered the final phases of design in 2021. That seven-year lag has provided space for our client (Building Bridges Across the River led by Scott Kratz), to conceive and fund an equitable development plan. The goal of the plan is to ensure that the park will be a driver of inclusive development. From educating residents about tenants' rights and facilitating homeownership to investing in Black artists and businesses, these efforts have helped extend the project of the Bridge Park far beyond its physical limits—even before it exists.

Location	Washington, D.C., USA		
Status	2014–Ongoing		
Typology	Public Realm		
Program	Landscape	80,000 ft²	7,360 m²
	Recreation	30,000 ft²	2,700 m²
	Restaurant/Cafe	5,200 ft²	490 m²
	Education	6,100 ft²	570 m²
	Total Area	121,300 ft²	11,120 m²

5353

11th Street Bridge Park

11th Street Bridge Park

OMA NY

11th Street Bridge Park

5355

11th Street Bridge Park

OMA NY

11th Street Bridge Park

"I expose slavery in this country, because to expose it is to kill it. Slavery is one of those monsters of darkness to whom the light of truth is death."

5356

11th Street Bridge Park

5357 While the Anacostia River is a connector for the region, it also divides two very different parts of Washington, D.C. Pierre Charles L'Enfant's original plan for the capital (pictured) did not include the areas east of the river, including the neighborhood of historic Anacostia.

5358 Single bridge built 1907

5359 Two bridges built 1965-69

5360 Bridges' end of life 2008

5361 Replacement spans 2009

5362 New spans completed

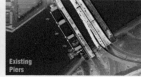

5363 Remaining bridge piers

5364 Navy Yard development on west bank of the Anacostia River (1972)

5365 Frederick Douglass House in Anacostia (1972)

5366 The omission of Anacostia from the L'Enfant plan left the two sides of the river to develop independently. Engraving of Anacostia and the future Navy Yard (William J. Bennett, 1834).

5367 The construction of the Anacostia Freeway (I-295) imposed a barrier between the community of historic Anacostia and the riverfront (1960s).

5368 West versus east

5369 D.C. natives

5370 Pedestrian casualties

5371 Anacostia is home to much of D.C.'s black community.

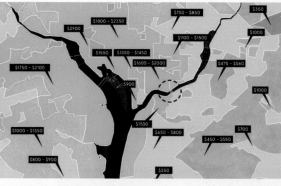

5372 Economic disparity within the D.C. region, as illustrated by mapping median rent values.

5373 The west side of the river is changing from what had been an industrial area into a mixed-use district of residential buildings, offices, and parks.

5374 East of the river in historic Anacostia there has been a history of neglect.

5375 Anacostia also sees signs of gentrification.

5376 How can a park floating above a river overcome historic and economic disparity?

5377 The bridge park will create new pedestrian connections (pink) to the waterfront and the city.

5378 View of Washington Monument

5379 View of U.S. Capitol

5380 The remnant piers of the old 11th Street Bridge will be the foundation for a new connection. A bridge that is also a park will link east and west.

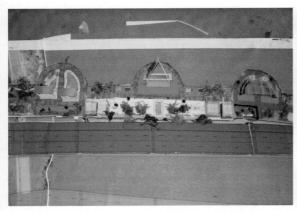

5382 Programmatic diversity

5383 Programmatic platforms

5381 Models of the park from community visioning sessions with local schoolchildren revealed a desire for the bridge to be a destination above the river and not just a passage over it.

5384 Pyramid references

5385 Our first scheme, like the childrens' model, extended a pier from the middle of the bridge.

5386 Widening the bridge to facilitate real programs

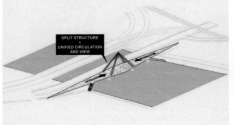

5387 The extra width is hung from four columns joined together to form the outline of a pyramid.

5388 Pyramid scheme model

5389 Landscape and program activities line the bridge.

5390 Pyramid scheme Navy Yard view

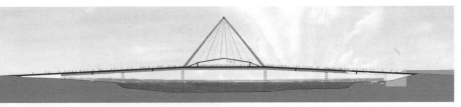

5391 The midspan structure of the Pyramid scheme becomes a visual landmark.

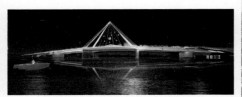

5392 Night view

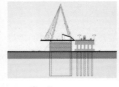

5393 Section

5394 Evening event view

5395 The Pyramid scheme created an icon in the middle of the river, but its engagement with the riverfront on either side was anemic.

5396 Could we create a platform that would facilitate a diverse range of programs throughout the day, located where they have the most impact?

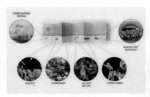

5397 Annual events calendar, linking with activities throughout the city.

5398 We wanted the program to engage with both land and river, and to respond to the conditions on either side.

5399 Widening the bridge toward the east locates the most active programs where they can best serve the Anacostia community.

5400 Early program distribution

11th Street Bridge Park

5401 Our final concept for the Bridge Park begins with two paths, independent trajectories that launch from either side of the river.

5402 The two trajectories extend past each other, creating a gathering space where they intersect.

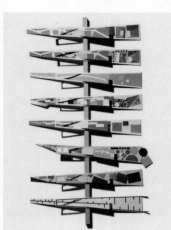

5403 Study models

5404 The resulting form creates a gateway from the west...

5405 ...a civic roof that shelters programs on the Anacostia side...

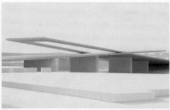

5406 ...and a simple iconic form over the river.

5407 The "X" interconnects two neighborhoods and combines park and bridge.

5408 Physical model

5409 Where the two planes converge, a flat flexible space becomes a new public plaza hovering over the river.

5410 Model view from Anacostia

5411 A new icon

5412 A civic monument for Washington, D.C.

5413 The bridge echoes L'Enfant's "Reservations"—X's that create public squares and mark the sites of Washington, D.C.'s most important places.

5414 Two "Reservations," Stanton Park and the White House

5401–5414

11th Street Bridge Park

5415 The west side of the river is hard and urban while the east is lined with under-utilized green space.

5416 The Bridge Park complements either side with its opposite.

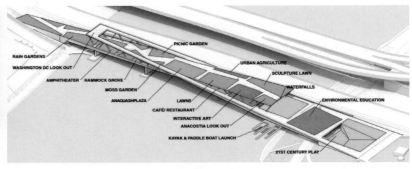

RAIN GARDENS
WASHINGTON DC LOOK OUT
AMPHITHEATER HAMMOCK GROVE
MOSS GARDEN
ANAQUASHPLAZA
CAFÉ/ RESTAURANT
INTERACTIVE ART
ANACOSTIA LOOK OUT
KAYAK & PADDLE BOAT LAUNCH
21ST CENTURY PLAY
PICNIC GARDEN
URBAN AGRICULTURE
SCULPTURE LAWN
WATERFALLS
LAWNS
ENVIRONMENTAL EDUCATION

5417 Landscaped and programmed spaces located along the bridge

1. Rain Garden
2. Amphitheater
3. Hammock Grove
4. Picnic Garden
5. Moss Garden
6. Anaquash Plaza
7. Urban Agriculture
8. Lawns
9. Interactive Art
10. Sculpture Park

5420 Navy Yard trajectory plan

1. 21st Century Play Space
2. Environmental Education Center
3. Waterfall
4. Cafe Restaurant + Gift Shop
5. Flexible Terrace / Art Workspace
6. Plaza

5421 Anacostia trajectory plan

GATHER   RELAX   ACTIVE

5418 Active and passive program distribution

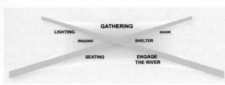

GATHERING
LIGHTING   SHADE
RIGGING   SHELTER
SEATING   ENGAGE
THE RIVER

5422 Unlike a single arcing plane, the X creates an overlapping topography of spaces within which activities and programs can take place.

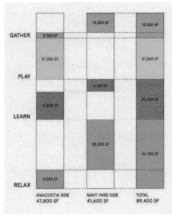

5419 Program: gather, play, learn, relax

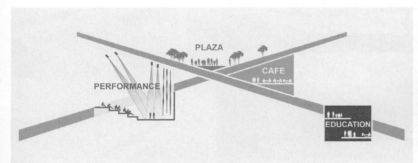

PLAZA
CAFE
PERFORMANCE
EDUCATION

5423 Things don't occur only "on" the bridge: they happen over, under, and inside it.

5424 View from the Navy Yard promenade

5425 The Bridge Park's activated spaces start on the shore, mixing landscaped paths and programmed spaces to bring the community together over the Anacostia River.

5426 Like Venice's Rialto Bridge...

5427 ...with a twist.

11th Street Bridge Park

5430 Forth Bridge, Scotland (1882)

5429 Cantilever bridge system concept demonstration, Forth Bridge, Scotland

5428 The bridge's form creates the depth for two tapering trusses that meet at its midpoint, an efficient strategy similar to a cantilever bridge system.

5431 Structural concept axon

5432 Structural elevation (Arup)

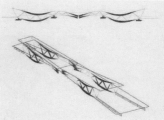

5433 Deflection diagram (Arup)

5434 Axial load diagram (Arup)

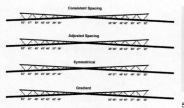

5435 The cantilever bridge and steel truss system allow for lighter bridge construction and ease of constructibility, while adding to the variety of spaces along it. (Arup)

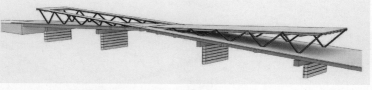

5436 The bridge trusses are supported on the remaining piers from the former 11th Street Bridge. (Arup)

Consistent Spacing
Adjusted Spacing
Symmetrical
Gradient

5437 Truss spacing options

5438 The lower chord of the trusses was updated to a box girder to reduce depth and simplify the framing. (WRA)

5440 Structural overview (WRA)

5439 To reduce loads on the existing structural piles, solid piers above the water are to be replaced with columns. Column form studies: rotated square, angled for views, fixed datum, continuous with edge, concentrated load.

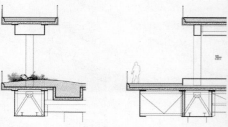

5442 The sheathing was later removed to express the bridge's structure rather than cover it up.

5443 Bridge edge sheathing study

5441 Initial edge concept: sheathing conceals the structure

5444 Deck depth and 3½-foot cantilever

5445 Physical model

5428–5445   11th Street Bridge Park

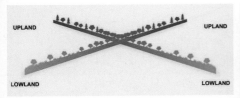

5446 We worked with Landscape Architect OLIN to develop a bridge that is also a park.

5447 A network of planted zones on the bridge harvests and filters stormwater.

5448 A rain garden acts as a pastoral entrance to the bridge from the Navy Yard to the west.

5449 As stormwater runs down the sloped bridge, it is intercepted by rain gardens and patches of softscape populated with native or adaptive vegetation.

5450 Navy Yard side waterfalls and rain gardens

5451 Waterfalls on both ends of the bridge contribute to education and ecology.

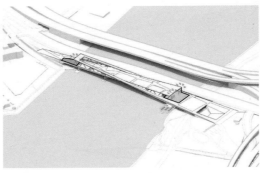

5452 The waterfalls act as attractors, sound buffers, and cooling devices.

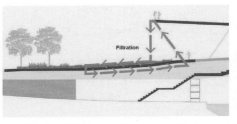

5453 The Navy Yard waterfall becomes a filtration system for the adjacent rain garden

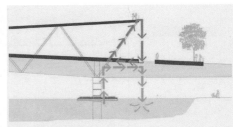

5454 The waterfall on the Anacostia side employs a double waterfall system that helps clean the river and enhance the flow of water through the surrounding wetlands.

5455 The waterfalls can also be used for interactive media displays celebrating the region's rich history.

5456 Potential backdrops for projections

5457 The bridge creates shade to protect visitors from D.C.'s swampy summers.

5458 The bridge's form and landscape create a shaded path from one side to the other.

5459 Heat map

5460 Physical model—waterfront terrace with shade canopy and waterfall

5461 The waterfall porch on the east side creates a covered terrace for open-air events programming. Projections on the waterfall act as a dynamic backdrop.

5462 In the daytime, the terrace acts as a location for outdoor markets and performances and a spill-out space for the adjacent cafe.

5463 The overhang on the west side shades the hammock grove and amphitheater.

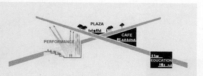
5464 The amphitheater anchors the western end of the bridge.

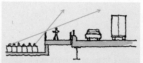
5465 Sinking the amphitheater mitigates roadway noise. (Threshold Acoustics)

5466 Acoustic barrier

5467 An early amphitheater orientation had audience members facing west.

5468 Performances were framed with a waterfall backdrop and a view toward the Navy Yard in the background.

5469 Visitors walking on the upper bridge paths could look down into the activity of the submerged amphitheater.

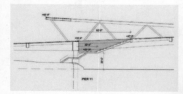
5470 West-facing amphitheater

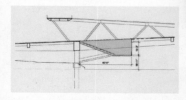
5471 The amphitheater was flipped to allow for better access from the western end of the bridge, and to orient audiences toward a view of the river below.

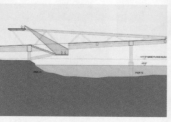
5472 The Capitol Lookout becomes a balcony for the amphitheater.

5473 The upper walkways above the performance space provide unique vantage points and create anchor locations for lighting and speakers.

5457–5473   11th Street Bridge Park

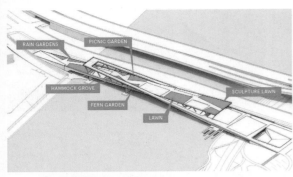

5474 Larger landscaped spaces throughout the Bridge Park facilitate programs while handling stormwater runoff.

5475 The Hammock Grove

5476 The Picnic Garden

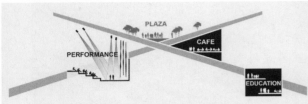
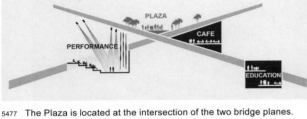

5477 The Plaza is located at the intersection of the two bridge planes.

5478 The Plaza is a central space for gathering—more destination than elevated thoroughfare—where two sides of the river converge and coexist.

5479 Plaza view

5480 Focal point

5483 Fashion show

5484 Film screening

5485 Green market

5481 A destination with a dramatic view of the river

5482 Waterfront wedding

5486 Wedding ceremony

5487 Live performance

5488 Ice skating rink

5489 Lawn view

5490 The Lawn occupies the upper deck on the bridge's east side.

5491 Fitness on the Lawn

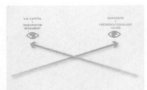

5492 At the top of each path, lookout points provide views of prominent landmarks on both sides of the river.

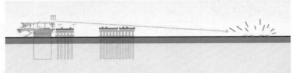

5493 The extra height at the lookouts allows for views of activities on the river.

5494 The bridge can become a viewing platform for rowing events, engaging the river and providing new access to the water.

5495 Anacostia Hockey Championships

5496 Capitol Sprints Regatta (any sport with sticks works)

5474–5496

11th Street Bridge Park

5497 The bridge visually links to the entire city.

5498 View of the Capitol Lookout, with historic Anacostia in the background

5499 Unlike a flat bridge that is as low to the river as possible, the bridge features high points that create a new way to appreciate the river and the neighborhoods on either side.

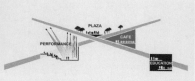

5500 The Bridge Park Café is located to the east of the Plaza.

5501 The café has space for up to 80 seats inside and an additional 2,300 square feet of external shaded dining area.

5502 The shaded porch space can also be used for a variety of programs, including book fairs and arts-related workshops.

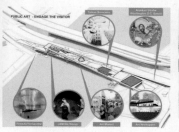

5503 Public art location study

5504 An early concept for interactive art occupied voids in the bridge.

5505 Interactive art installation located above the river

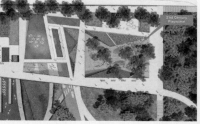

5506 A children's playspace is the gateway to the bridge from the east.

5507 View of the bridge from the Playspace

5508 Playspace access at the bridge entry

5509 The kayak and canoe docks on the Anacostia shore encourage interaction with the river.

5497–5509   11th Street Bridge Park

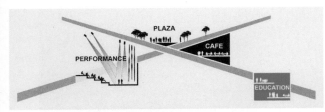

5510 The Environmental Education Center (EEC) is located where the bridge meets the river's edge.

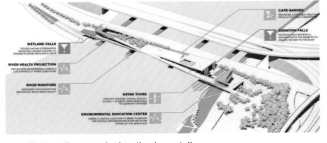

5511 Early wellness and education impact diagram

5512 Saloua Raouda Choucair, *Composition in Blue Module* (1947-51)

5513 Terra firma concept—EEC as a collision between the bridge the riverbank.

5514 Early diagram

5515 Early study with an occupiable EEC roof

5516 Landform studies

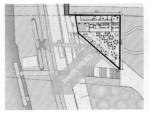

5517 The EEC classroom is angled toward river views.

5518 EEC classroom with a river backdrop

5521 The Anacostia Watershed Society will utilize the two classrooms, atrium, and plaza to orchestrate an educational program for local school groups.

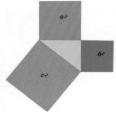

5519 Pythagorean theorem

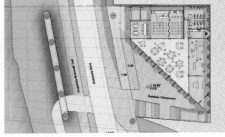

5520 Classrooms, a gallery, and an outdoor plaza surround a central atrium

5522 The Flex Hall opens up to a plaza and garden, extending educational opportunities outdoors.

5523 The double-height atrium brings light to both the classrooms and the exhibition hall.

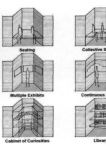

5524 Exhibition hall gallery niches

5525 Exhibition hall gallery

5526 The Bridge Park offices are located on F2, with views of both the EEC atrium and the bridge waterfall beyond.

5527 The EEC anchors the Anacostia entrance to the Bridge Park.

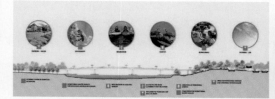

5528　The Bridge Park integrates with local ecology through water-and air-quality enhancements, habitat creation, stormwater management, and urban heat reduction.

5529　The park offers various paths that bring people down to the river and provide spaces for shade, education, recreation, and relaxation.

5530　Path entry at Good Hope Road

5531　Exploded axonometric of planting, ecology, and hydrology

5532　Planting zones

5533　Pattern studies—paths

5534　Pattern studies—patches

5535　Early view from the east

5536　A year-round destination

5537　View from the urban agriculture plots—the integration of architecture, landscape, and infrastructure allows for the creation of a socially sustainable civic experience.

5538　View from Anacostia Riverwalk Trail

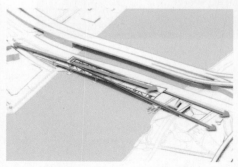

5539　The west platform and its path extend to form the Anacostia Lookout on the east, while paths from the opposite side form a loop around it. The Central Plaza creates an interchange between both routes.

5540　Half-mile running loop

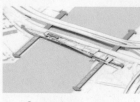

5541　Connections to the riverwalks

5542　The loop creates an extension of the Anacostia Riverwalk Trail, providing runners and hikers with a spectacular view over the river.

5528–5542　　　　　　　　　　　　　11th Street Bridge Park

5543 Two platforms—materiality

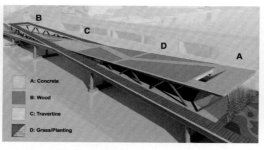

A: Concrete
B: Wood
C: Travertine
D: Grass/Planting

5544 Material strategy axon

5545 The Navy Yard Deck is finished with concrete pavers.

5546 The Anacostia Deck is finished with wood decking.

5547 View from Capitol Lookout over the Bridge Park

5548 Two platforms—guardrails

5549 The Navy Yard Deck uses horizontal light gray guardrails.

5550 The Anacostia Deck uses vertical dark gray guardrails.

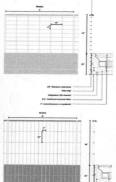

5551 Guardrail details

5552 Bridge profile and guardrail contrast from the east

5553 Bridge Park lighting, glowing X

5554 Bridge Park lighting, 4th of July

5555 View at night

5556 View from Marine 1 (fictional)

5557 $X

5543–5557

11th Street Bridge Park

5558

11th Street Bridge Park

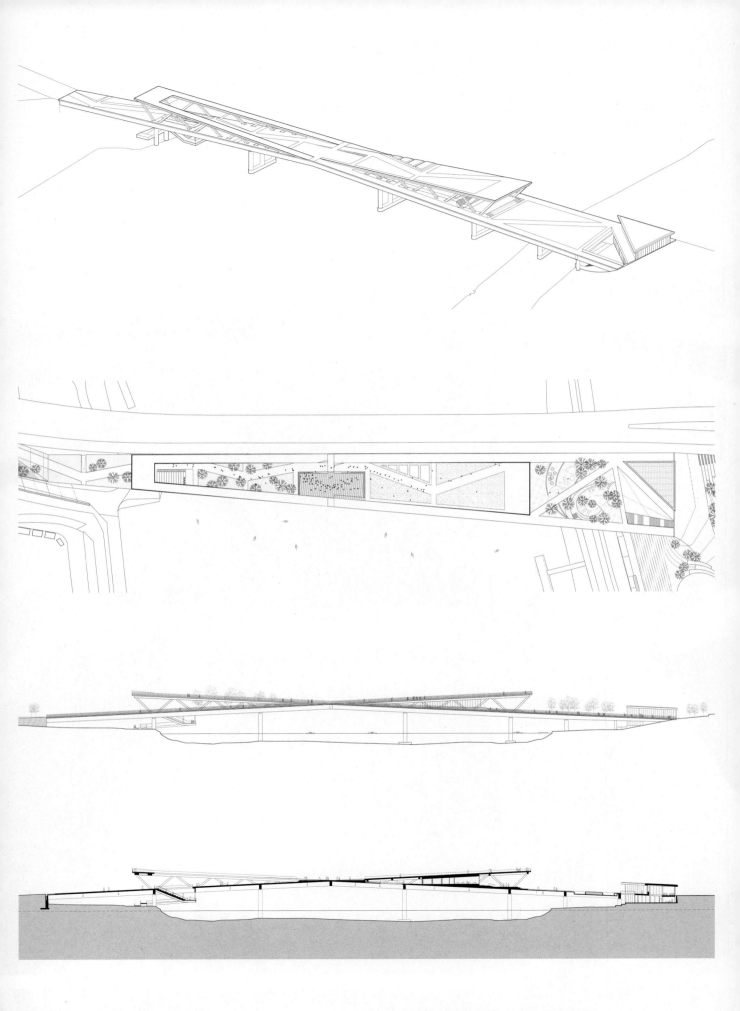

5559–5562

11th Street Bridge Park

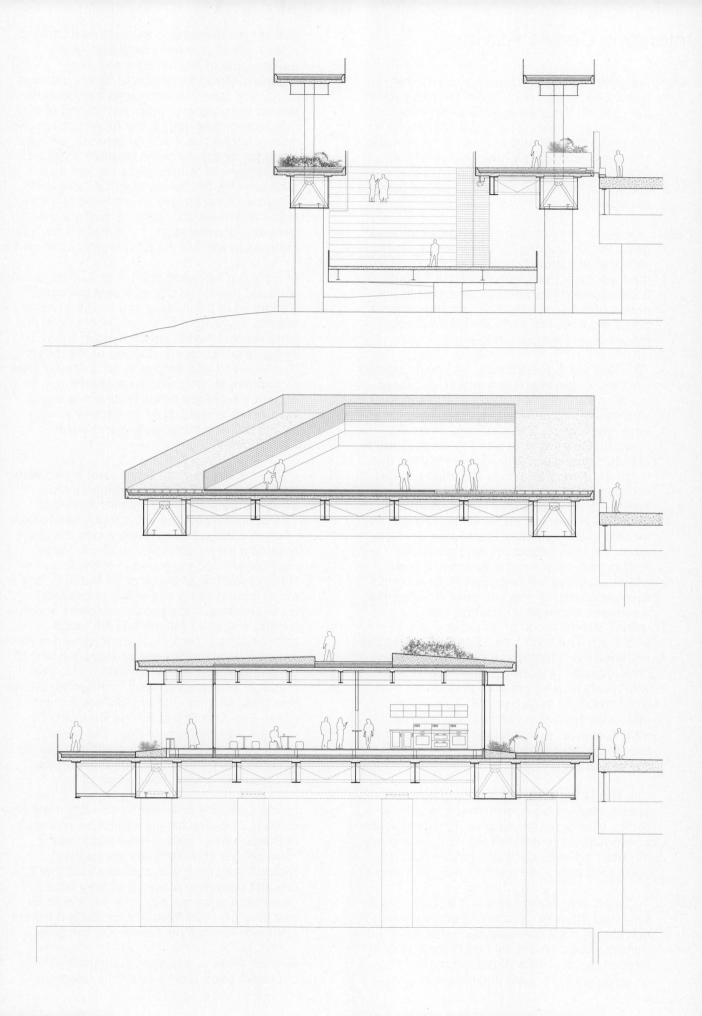

5563–5565

11th Street Bridge Park

Interview Cecilia Alemani

Jason Long: From the High Line to curating Art Basel Cities, your work has often focused on bringing art to public spaces in different cultures and cities, and I'm curious about the perspective that gives you on how public spaces function. How have you seen the role of public space differing across the various cultures and cities that you've been engaged in?

Cecilia Alemani: The first thing that comes to mind as an Italian working in New York City is the lack of what I naturally think of as public space— the traditional European piazza or square. It's something I immediately connect to the notion of public space. This is different from parks, squares are explicitly urban public places, the real nexus of the city.

This was the biggest challenge when I started working for the High Line, which, of course, is also a very specific architectural space with its linear nature that doesn't allow for large gatherings. The challenge truly was how to rethink my own more traditional notion of public space and allow for something that is much more of a hybrid. The High Line is an interesting case because it has so many layers: it's an example of industrial infrastructure reuse, but at the same time it's located in the middle of brand new development. You can't avoid thinking about the relationship between the new and the old, which is always troubling. But when it comes to artists creating new site-specific artworks, it's always an inspiring starting point to rethink the definition of public space and public art. The High Line forces one to do this because it is a hybrid creature constructed on a recycled steel bridge from the 1930s, with newly built layers and gardens to welcome eight million people a year. I'm interested in thinking of this multilayered stratification of public space that comes from the site's own history, its uses, and also its surroundings.

JL: The High Line is clearly a unique public space. Has engaging with that space as a territory for art changed your thinking about how public art functions? Do you see the role of public art in a new way, compared to how you saw it when you were working in Europe?

CA: To be honest, when I was in Italy I had never fully paid attention to contemporary public art. Maybe it's a generalization, but when I think of public art in Italy I don't think of contemporary art: I think of bronze monuments on pedestals. It's quite inspiring that there

has been a discussion in the United States and in other countries about the social-political role of monuments and their meaning. Until this relatively recent moment of consciousness monuments had become almost invisible to people. Rethinking public monuments has helped me reconsider public space, not just as a site for artwork, but as a place for people to come together. I've been able to think of public space not just as a physical site, but as a place that exists only because of the people who inhabit it. It's a place where art can facilitate gathering and generate conversation, but it doesn't necessarily exist without the people who activate it.

In a project I curated in Buenos Aires in 2018, we used the entire city as a vast pedestal: we looked at the history and architecture of the city in trying to fill the niche of public art, which hadn't particularly thrived in Buenos Aires up to that point. But one of the things that I missed was engaging on a deeper level with different communities around the project. These are relationships that might take years to build, but I do believe art is a way to achieve cohabitation and build communities.

JL: Using the city itself as a pedestal for art also implies that the two have a relationship, in which one informs or reveals the other. The pedestal puts the art in a position to be seen, but the art also draws you to the pedestal and reshapes how you see it. I was really interested in your idea of the Buenos Aires project as a "hopscotch" with a linked set of itineraries. We're trying to use this book as a way to diagnose ourselves and find trends, and one of the things we found throughout our projects were diagrams with arrows connecting zones or zippers trying to close gaps. You see a consistent effort to create links across spaces, connecting disparate programs, or crossing divides within cities. The 11th Street Bridge Park in D.C. is one literal example of that. The idea of using art to also create links within a city is in some ways similar. Do you think art can successfully create those kinds of links?

CA: I think it has the potential to do so, but not on its own. The idea for the exhibition I curated in Buenos Aires called *Hopscotch* was to have people choose their own journey through the city. It was successful in that it brought people to places that they would never otherwise go, and they were able to see their own city from a completely different perspective—the perspective of the artist.

Buenos Aires is a fantastic city for that kind of project because it's so rich in history and has wonderful architecture but is still unexplored by artists when it comes to public space. It felt almost like New York City in the 1970s, when the city was a big arena for artistic experimentation. Art can bring people to places they would never visit on an ordinary day—think of the West Side piers in Manhattan in the 1970s and 1980s. Art can add something visually compelling and intellectually exciting to the fabric of the city, but you need more than art to create bridges, you need community. These relationships can be built over time and sometimes they manifest themselves at a very slow pace, which at times seems to stand in opposition to the model of the festival, which is becoming more and more popular in the art circuit.

JL: One thing that has always struck me about successful public art is its potential to allow us to engage with the city in a new way, not just with its physical presence, but also with the invisible forces that organize it. I'm thinking about Christo and Jeanne-Claude, where the work is 90 percent the struggle to get the necessary approvals. Through that process they unearthed the byzantine bureaucracy that exists unseen all around us. As we're engaging with more public projects, our process is also shaped by public agencies and that same bureaucracy. And I have to say it's less entertaining to do it than to observe from outside. How has that kind of engagement shaped your work as a curator?

CA: On one hand, you have to be able to navigate the bureaucracy, whether that's in a museum or working in public space. Something I've learned over the years is the difference between commissioning temporary versus permanent art, which, of course, is an issue you also face because, as architects, you're doing things that are much more permanent than an artwork, which can be moved. For us, as public art curators, very often these objects can be removed within a year, so the cities themselves aren't as stressed out about making big decisions about the afterlife of these artworks.

I always tell people to go and attend community board meetings because that's actually when things get real. It doesn't matter where you went to school, what artist you're proposing, the meaning of a work: certain questions always come up. Is this artist local? Are you doing something for the community? On the other hand, the project in Argentina was a collaboration between Art Basel and the City of Buenos Aires, which hired the Swiss company as a consultant to execute an event that would also attract international visitors while highlighting the local art scene. That meant two different places working together: the private sector and public administration.

JL: I once heard you say that one challenge for artists working on the High Line is the extreme level of specificity they have to contend with. It's obviously not a generic or flexible situation, and artists have to adapt to multiple factors, from the varied conditions along it, to the structure and even the vegetation. How do artists react to the burden—or the inspiration—of that specificity?

CA: When I take an artist for a site visit their first reaction is a mix of excitement and incredulity: to hear everything that could possibly happen to an artwork, including being touched or climbed on by eight million people or being shaken by hurricane winds, is quite intimidating! But then, when the exhibition opens and you actually witness the extreme weather and the force of the visitors, at that point artists understand why we are so cautious at first. In spite of the many limitations, we are getting good at finding and working with artists who don't necessarily say, Okay, so then I have to make something out of bronze." We've had works of ceramic, textiles, and other delicate materials, and we like to give artists the platform to explore other methodologies and mediums—using the High Line as an opportunity to experience something they have never done before, not only in terms of materials, but of the audience and context, as well. There are also other limitations that have to do with the physical nature of the park: it's elevated 30 feet in the sky, it has only a narrow path for people to walk, and most of it is covered by a lush garden. All of these restrictions can turn into opportunities to create a dialogue with the surroundings because there is no way the artwork will be a self-standing isolated piece. The work needs to be in the context of the High Line, and that context is the vegetation, the people, the cityscape—so many factors you don't have in a white cube. At the High Line we like to work with artists who haven't done public art before. In spite of all the physical and logistical challenges, your work will be seen by millions of people: there is no other place in the world where you get that visibility.

JL: Has anyone ever thrown their hands up in frustration?

CA: No, I think we're very clear when we first talk to artists. We show them the High Line is not like Storm King; it's not a beautiful park with big green lawns. We aren't going to cut anything, not even a single blade of grass, to accommodate artworks, so if you install a sculpture in the vegetation, in the summer it might be completely invisible because the vegetation grows and overtakes it. But that's the beauty of it. Since everything we do stays on the High Line for twelve months, the sculpture will change with different backdrops and the community returns to see a completely different artwork every three or four months. The seasons, the plant life cycles, and the city around us change so fast. The High Line has been designed to invite people back over and over again.

JL: I remember when I first talked to you in the initial competition stage of the 11th Street Bridge Park, you mentioned that one of the difficulties of the High Line was that it wasn't originally designed for art. As we've been furthering the design of the Bridge Park, we've been having conversations about where art can go, and planning for it. As the High Line has expanded, it seems that there are now places that are more clearly designated for art, at the Spur, for example. Those new settings must operate differently for both the artist and the audience than the initial areas of the High Line where art is released into an existing park. How has that affected how you plan for art within the context of the High Line?

CA: I think the success of the Spur and the Plinth is that they're not just empty spaces that can be used for art. Art engages with other elements of the overall design. The idea that we put a pedestal—the most traditional way to show a work—in the middle of the only square we have on the High Line creates a piazza, but also a space that's of a more human scale. You're surrounded by new towers and skyscrapers—it's a very masculine environment. So how do you make the space feel like a park, like you're in a different place in the city? It's actually the first time at the High Line that art was involved in the design process: collectively, we decided to make the space rather simple, so that the focal point would be the art itself.

The Spur has also become a wonderful place for hosting public programs and events. Of course, the High Line Plinth was not necessarily our idea. We were inspired by the famous Fourth Plinth program in London's Trafalgar Square. I think what's successful here is that it really allows for so many different kinds of art to be shown. You can engage with it even from the avenue below because the artwork is so visible from the street. When you walk the High Line you tend to look down and parallel. You look at the vegetation or into peoples' homes. When you get to the Spur, because of the geography of the city at that very point, all of a sudden you stare up. With that in mind, we wanted to create something that could actually command the space.

And it's not always going to be a bronze sculpture! We might do something that is much more ephemeral, and invite artists to push the definition of public art beyond what we normally think. But I think the centrality of the space was really important in that specific section of the Spur: we couldn't have done a project like this anywhere else on the park. I always complain we have too many benches and every time there's a bench it means I cannot put a sculpture there. But benches are fundamental for our visitors. So, I believe what contributed to the success of this space was having a conversation that brought together the design team and the programmatic team at the High Line, to conceive a space where art could facilitate the design itself of the piazza: a monument in the middle of the space that functions as a focal point, facilitating circulation and fruition.

JL: While buildings or artworks can be popular or unpopular, that doesn't always determine whether they are "successful" or not. Success and popularity don't have a necessary correlation. But that logic operates differently for public space; it has to be popular. If it's empty it can feel dangerous. If the High Line had one hundred visitors a year versus eight million, I don't think anyone would call it a success.

But the necessity for popularity can also impact how public spaces are planned. Recently there has been a trend of injecting a multitude of specific programs into public space, saturating them with sports or recreation programs. How do you think the popularity of the High Line, or of public spaces in general, relates to how they are programmed today versus how public spaces were designed previously?

CA: That's an interesting question, because right now we have 2,000 visitors a week, when normally we would have 50,000 people in one day. That's shocking. The first time I went back to the High Line after we reopened in July, I was the only person in the park. The High Line is a particular case in that we are a victim of our own success, meaning nobody ever foresaw having millions of visitors. When they did initial visitation studies, they expected 300,000 people would visit in a year. Now, in the summer, we get 300,000 people in two weeks.

OMA NY   Cecilia Alemani

So clearly, there is something that has more to do with the city—I always find that New York City is able to embrace novelty in such an effervescent way. The High Line is a new kind of public space and people coming from abroad have not seen anything like it and want to see it. Also, sometimes people don't realize that being popular—unlike a museum that gets richer from the admission fees—for us means more expenses, because we have to pay for extensive cleaning, more repairs, more staffing. I'm not complaining, we all love it, but there is something counter-intuitive when it comes to its success, and that's what's been very hard. We're trying to change certain perceptions, for instance, that it's overcrowded so locals don't want to visit. That was very true at the beginning, but I think through programming and other events it has changed radically. If you come on a Saturday afternoon, it's extremely busy, but if you come on a Wednesday afternoon, you can actually enjoy the park.

JL: New York's density can act like a compressor. A decade ago, the city started painting over median areas in places like Times Square to make informal plazas. One of these "plazas" was in an area of the Lower East Side, near where I lived at the time, that was a complete no-man's land. It was just two benches and an umbrella sitting in a wasteland at the foot of the Williamsburg Bridge, but you would still see people there hanging out, even relaxing. Somehow, despite the noise and the absence of almost any appealing quality, it still found an audience through the power of density.

Covid obviously has had an impact on that density and for some, even called into question the viability of the inherent density of a city like New York. This feels like on the one hand a moment of instability—of shifts that question our assumptions—but at the same time an era of entrenched divisions. How can we as artists or architects respond to a zeitgeist that's in flux? How do you think as a curator, or as an artist, one can engage with a unique moment like this?

CA: As a curator I always look to the artists because they are the ones who are able to quickly absorb the changes and re-contextualize them within their own language. I don't have an answer yet because it's too fresh, so that's also one of the main challenges. But there's also some excitement to be found in these new conditions. I'm putting together the Venice Biennale basically from my apartment. I'm still able to have thoughtful and very personal conversations with artists via Zoom because we're all in our own

studios or offices or homes. We have yet to see what will come out of this moment, but I do think it will have a deep effect on art production. In 2020 because of Covid the Architecture Biennale was postponed to 2021, leaving a void to be filled. The new president of the Venice Biennale, Roberto Cicutto, decided that the six curators of the different sectors of the Venice Biennale—art, architecture, cinema, music, dance, theater—should do a show about the history of the Biennale itself. Together then we decided to present the Venice Biennale through the lens of crisis, looking back at times of war, revolution, and social unrest that characterize the twentieth century. The exhibition was titled *The Disquieted Muses*.

So, how can art be a way of supporting the community, and how can institutions like the Venice Biennale be a beacon of hope for society? I think there has been a certain degree of exponential acceleration in the past decade when it comes to art production. This might be the time to take a break, to look back to what our predecessors did in similar moments, and to ask deeper existential questions. It is certainly a traumatic time, but it can also be seen as an exciting time to restore ourselves.

JL: At a moment like this it's helpful to see other moments of crisis and understand how people managed and reacted.

CA: It was an amazing experience because I learned so much about the history of the Venice Biennale. There is an incredible archive in Venice that was founded in the 1920s and it has documents, videos and photos, and artworks capturing the history of that incredible place. We were able to do this exhibition because we didn't have to ship anything except ourselves.

JL: In addition to the impact from Covid, this summer has also been a time of widespread public protest in the wake of the murder of George Floyd. The scale of those protests and the painful reaction to them have high-lighted that the most public of public spaces is infrastructure and the street. I think that is part of why the High Line is successful, because it is infrastructure, it's a street but not a street. What do you think about the issue of protest as it relates to public space, or art's relationship to politics and protest?

CA: I think what's happening to communities of color is, of course, completely horrifying. What is incredible, and hopeful, however, is to see people come together in the streets to protest in the aftermath of these tragic events. Sometimes I feel like our cities are so controlled and they rarely allow for spontaneous gatherings, unless the situation is so extreme, like now. Between surveillance and social media, our public space seems to act almost like private space, and it is really hard to reclaim it. This might be a turning point in how these spaces can become sites for change and action, collectively, without the barriers private spaces impose.

JL: I was once walking down a closed street and someone mentioned that anytime they were able to walk down the middle of the street freely, it meant something good or special was happening. I thought about that during the protests. They were, of course, an expression of exasperation and anger or even rage, but you felt that something special was taking place. It made me think of the High Line because it is also a piece of infrastructure that has been taken over by the public. There's an element of joy inherent in that kind of transgression.

It would be great to hear about your process as a curator in that context. Often, a museum curator is trying to establish an intellectual agenda, figuring out a script within a controlled context. You're involved in a more urban setting that maybe requires a more unscripted approach.

In many ways the role of the curator in your position has parallels to the role of the architect—it is highly collaborative and engages with the public and public space and all the unpredictability that comes with that territory. How do you begin, and how does your research process play out when entering into a project?

CA: I always start with the artist, whether I know them or not. The best way to start a project is to take a walk on the High Line, to sit on a bench for an hour listening to people. In that hour, you will hear at least ten different languages. It's that intangible component, the people, that makes the space so unique and vibrant. It also needs to feel like the artwork belongs there. Considering 90 percent of what you see has been commissioned by us for that site on the High Line, the artworks are very responsive to a set of geographic and human factors.

And then it is definitely a process. Artists always start with an idea and we work with our production team to make sure the project maintains its soul and integrity while checking the engineering and architectural elements. Some artists are more interested in having a dialogue with nature, while others want to use the High Line as a platform for looking onto the city. You can do both, and that richness of opportunities for engagement is what is so fascinating for artists.

Sophia Choi: It must be also be surprising for you to see how those dialogues evolve over time in the changing context of a city. For us, documenting the immense amount of process and output in this book has sometimes revealed the fluidity of a project's original intent by putting it against what came before and what's happening now. In considering the archive, or a larger context in your research, do you have any tricks for navigating an overwhelming amount of diverse information? You mentioned dealing with quite a massive archive for *The Disquieted Muses*.

CA: I'm quite analog, actually! I have binders with hundreds of pictures, and I flip through them all day and night. For the exhibition on the history of the Biennale the archive in Venice was particularly helpful, because first of all, I was on a different continent and second of all, even the team in Venice couldn't visit. So, we really had to do everything remotely with whatever they had in digital form. We are definitely at a turning point in terms of how we work, having realized that working remotely is actually okay and that a lot of things can be done through technology. But there is nothing like handling a document or flipping the pages of a book, or seeing art in person. I try to stay intentionally attached to the physical experience of seeing and reading.

SC: It's funny because our book was inspired by the search engine. So we applied a very digital logic to a printed matter.

CA: I wish I could do something like that. I can't even imagine what that would look like for my own profession! It's an incredible model that can serve as inspiration for others. I look at your book and imagine all the different stories one might tell by using the individual elements and rearranging them like the words of a poem.

Cecilia Alemani is the artistic director of the upcoming 59th International Art Exhibition (2022) in Venice. Since 2011, she has been the director and chief curator of High Line Art, the public art program presented by the High Line in New York.

OMA NY   Cecilia Alemani

Architecture, Art Inspiration, Big Model, Borrowed Iconography, Cantilever, Circle, Collage, Color Splash, Concrete, Crowd, Day in the Life, Dichotomy, Dome, Facet, Food, Funnel, Geology, Gradient, Hand-Job, Hand Sketch, Lantern, Model Army, Opening, Over and Under, Pair, Pattern, Pixel, Playtime, Program Diagram, Projection, Question Mark, Reflection, Romance, Sandwich, Science, Silhouette, Skeleton, Solitude, Square, Stepped, Stress, Sunset, Timeline, Translucency, Truss, Undulation, Wedge, Wellness, White, Wood, X

Architecture

386   439   558   559

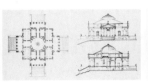    

561   605   1275   1922   1923   2229   2231

2236   2239   2240   2248   2298   2771

2826   3111   3278   4028   4413   4758

Art Inspiration

615   1294   1516   1811

1812   2044   2772   2872   2873   3997

4021   4025   4040   4044   4050   4079

4423   4730   4793   4807   5022   5091   5105   5512

Big Model

24   78   78   78   80

446   450   766   772   827   830

1301 1327 1410 1522 1523 1667

1801 1802 2295 2643 2565 2681 3012

3170 3289 3292 3360 3462 3531

3836 3842 3843 3921 3921 3926 4290 4318

4428 4740 4741 4742 4922 4923 5084 5010 5012

Borrowed
Iconography

TEMPLE

DOME ARCH

383 385 388 2242

2243 2369 2773 2774 2775 2837

3209 3210 3231 4205 4206 4207

5384

5392 5409

5412 5413 5557

Cantilever

23 66 74 140

1082 1090 2316 2321 2324 4211

4228 4232 4921 4924 4991 4992 5124 5127

Circle

167 168 263 468

471 495 496 2240 2241 2249

2267 2271 2291 2390 2445 2446 2447

  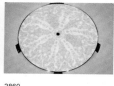
2452 2459 2775 2824 2841 2860

  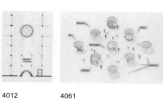  
3474 4006 4012 4061 4100 4120 4308

  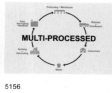 
4337 4409 5149 5156 5166 5343

Collage

351 422 607 1681

2242

3210

3216

3798

3888

3890

4205

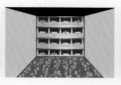
4281

4424

4724

4955

5427

Color Splash

457

463

479

491

908

919

1649

1679

1684

1686

1687

1709

1712 2287

2422

2424

2427

3224

3340

3440

3745

3768

3941

4042 4043

4131 4145

4147

4137

4154

4289

4321 4322

4854

Concrete

172

173

223

234

245

538

910

914

2057

2090

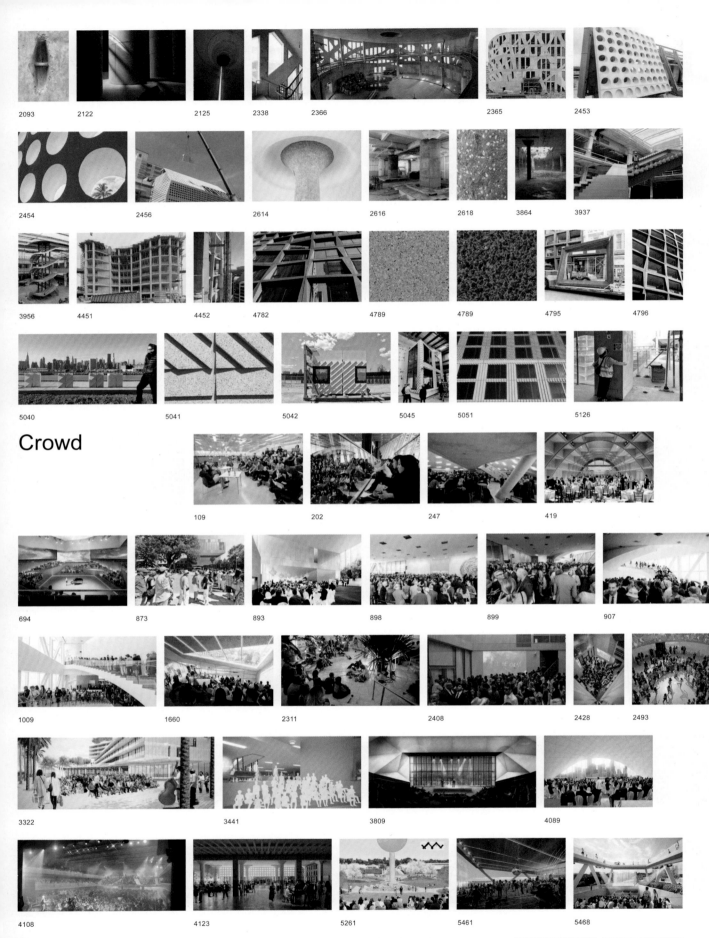

2093   2122   2125   2338   2366   2365   2453

2454   2456   2614   2616   2618   3864   3937

3956   4451   4452   4782   4789   4789   4795   4796

5040   5041   5042   5045   5051   5126

Crowd

109   202   247   419

694   873   893   898   899   907

1009   1660   2311   2408   2428   2493

3322   3441   3809   4089

4108   4123   5261   5461   5468

Day in the Life

112   117   220   220   220

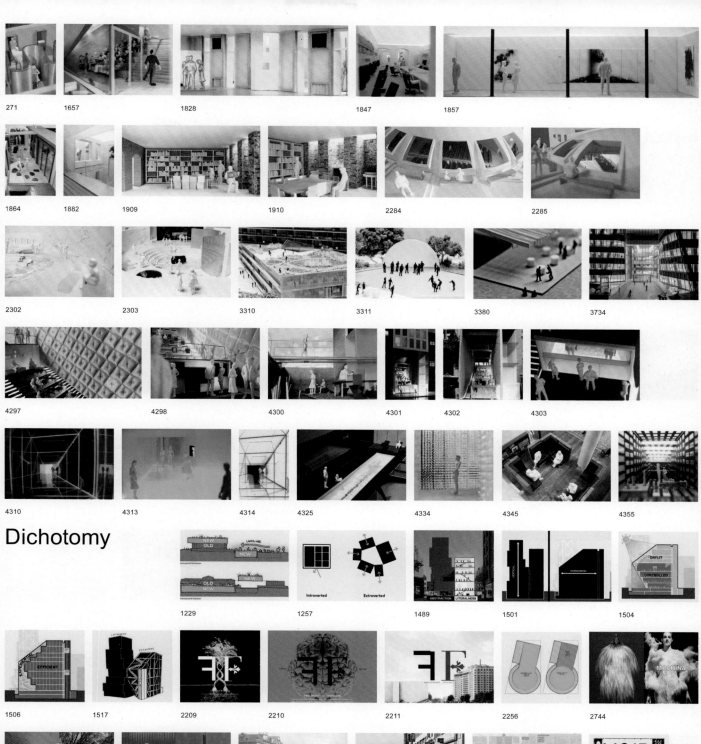

271   1657   1828   1847   1857

1864   1882   1909   1910   2284   2285

2302   2303   3310   3311   3380   3734

4297   4298   4300   4301   4302   4303

4310   4313   4314   4325   4334   4345   4355

Dichotomy

1229   1257   1489   1501   1504

1506   1517   2209   2210   2211   2256   2744

3205   3206   3250   3252   3261   4097

4098   4098   4623   4630   4726   5416   5543

Dome

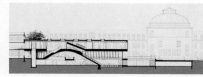
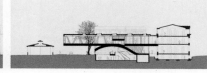

328   329   385

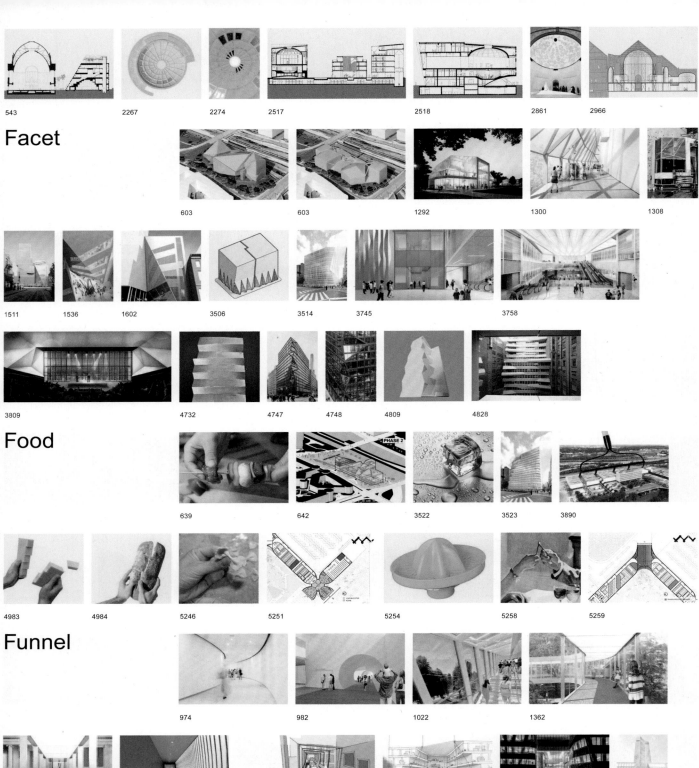

543 2267 2274 2517 2518 2861 2966

Facet

603 603 1292 1300 1308

1511 1536 1602 3506 3514 3745 3758

3809 4732 4747 4748 4809 4828

Food

639 642 3522 3523 3890

4983 4984 5246 5251 5254 5258 5259

Funnel

974 982 1022 1362

1363 2422 2560 3728 3734 3763

4310 4313 4315 4321 4359 4832 4862

Geology

824 1064 1067 1499 3521

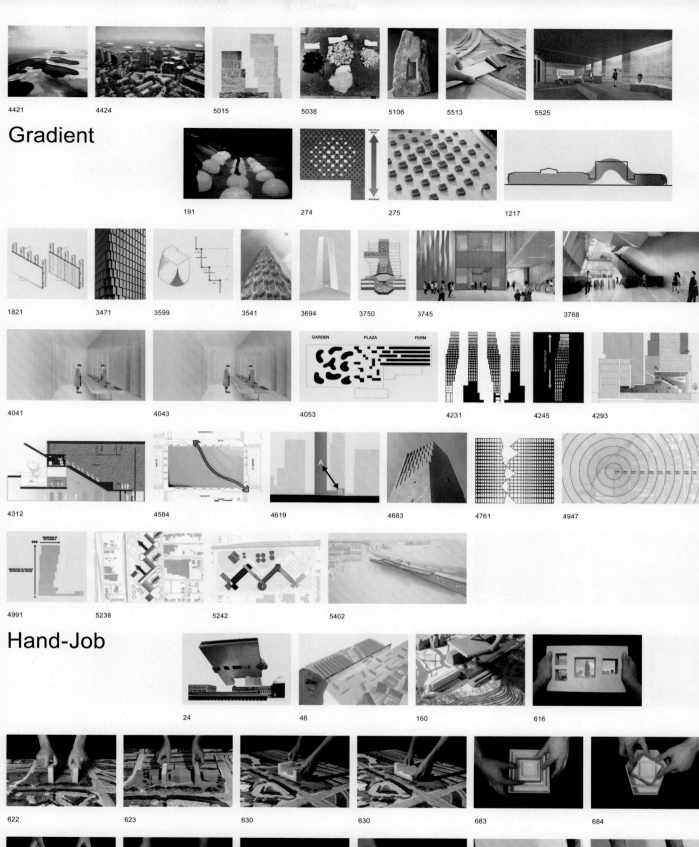

4421 4424 5015 5038 5106 5513 5525

Gradient

191 274 275 1217

1821 3471 3599 3541 3694 3750 3745 3768

4041 4043 4053 4231 4245 4293

4312 4584 4619 4683 4761 4947

4991 5238 5242 5402

Hand-Job

24 46 160 616

622

623

630

630

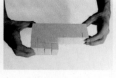
683

684

686 715 716 717 806 807

824

967

1215

1238 1239

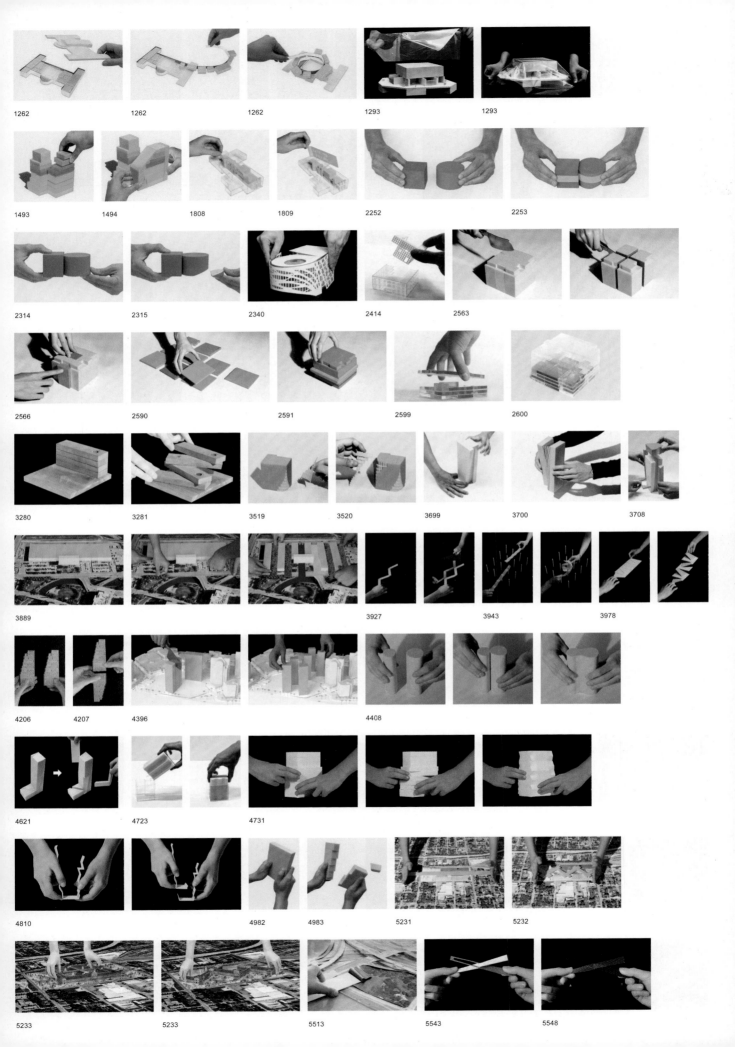

1262　　　　　　1262　　　　　　1262　　　　　　1293　　　　　　1293

1493　　　　　　1494　　　　　　1808　　　　　　1809　　　　　　2252　　　　　　2253

2314　　　　　　2315　　　　　　2340　　　　　　2414　　　　　　2563

2566　　　　　　2590　　　　　　2591　　　　　　2599　　　　　　2600

3280　　　　　　3281　　　　　　3519　　　　　　3520　　　　　　3699　　　　　　3700　　　　　　3708

3889　　　　　　　　　　　　　　　　　　　　　3927　　　　　　3943　　　　　　3978

4206　　　4207　　　4396　　　　　　　　　　　4408

4621　　　　　　4723　　　　　　4731

4810　　　　　　　　　　　4982　　　4983　　　5231　　　　　　5232

5233　　　　　　5233　　　　　　5513　　　　　　5543　　　　　　5548

Hand Sketch

606

620

641

652

656

660

662

670

671

672

707

736

737

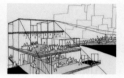

739

746

1270

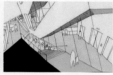

1296

1566

1571

1575

1644

2559

2565

2568

2571

2573

2574

2601

2603

3212

3218

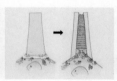

3588

3686

3750

3797

3895

4049

4087

4971

5263

5279

5349

Lantern

191

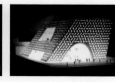

508

508

539

748

869

1081

1095

1303

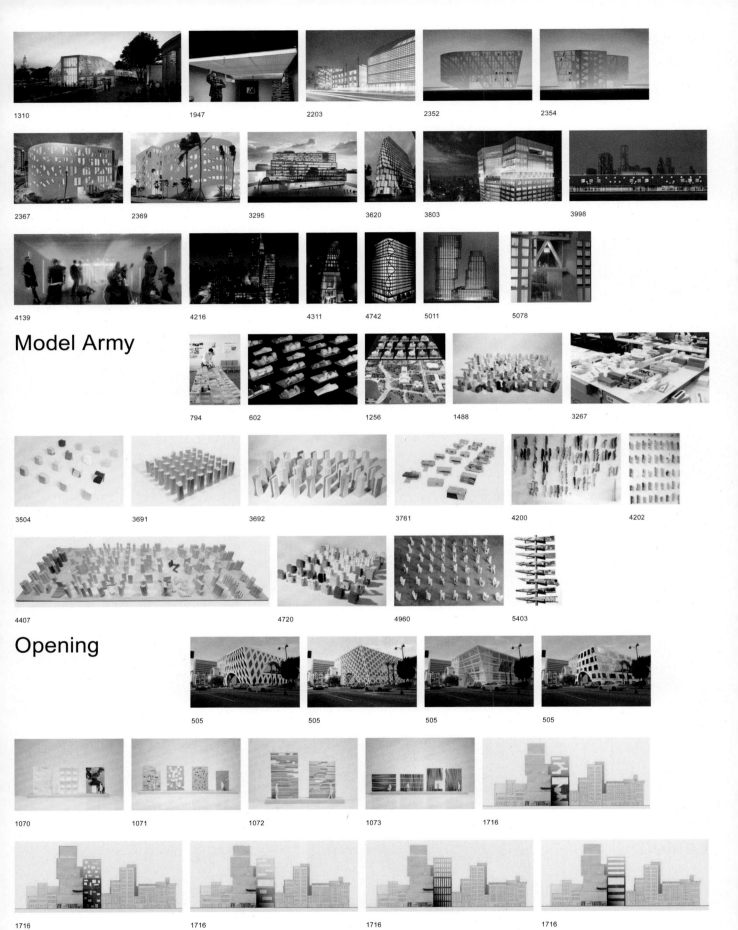

1310 1947 2203 2352 2354

2367 2369 3295 3620 3803 3998

4139 4216 4311 4742 5011 5078

Model Army

794 602 1256 1488 3267

3504 3691 3692 3761 4200 4202

4407 4720 4960 5403

Opening

505 505 505 505

1070 1071 1072 1073 1716

1716 1716 1716 1716

1717 1717 1717 1723 1723 1723 1723

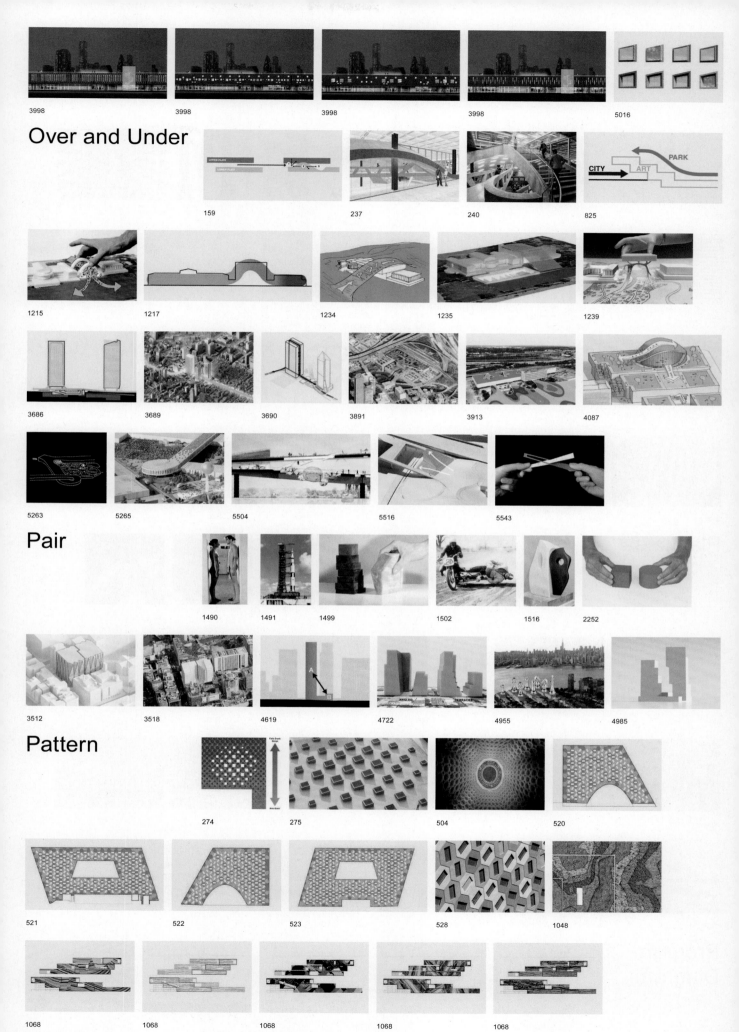

3998 3998 3998 3998 5016

Over and Under

159 237 240 825

1215 1217 1234 1235 1239

3686 3689 3690 3891 3913 4087

5263 5265 5504 5516 5543

Pair

1490 1491 1499 1502 1516 2252

3512 3518 4619 4722 4955 4985

Pattern

274 275 504 520

521 522 523 528 1048

1068 1068 1068 1068 1068

2347

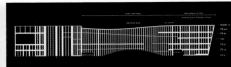

2348

2349

3389

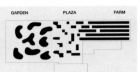

4053

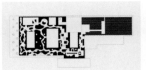

4053

4054

4231

4360

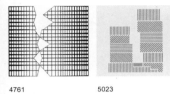

4761

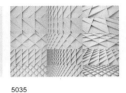

5023

5035

5403

5533   5534

Pixel

805

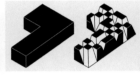

808

812

1046

3470

3534

3546

3578

3615

4190

4645

4683   4971

Playtime

99

125

126

189

191

1033

1378

2483   3323

3332

3334   4044   4508

4852

5276

5332

5456

5475

5505

5507

5509

Program
Diagram

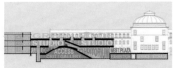

158

423

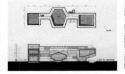

618

642

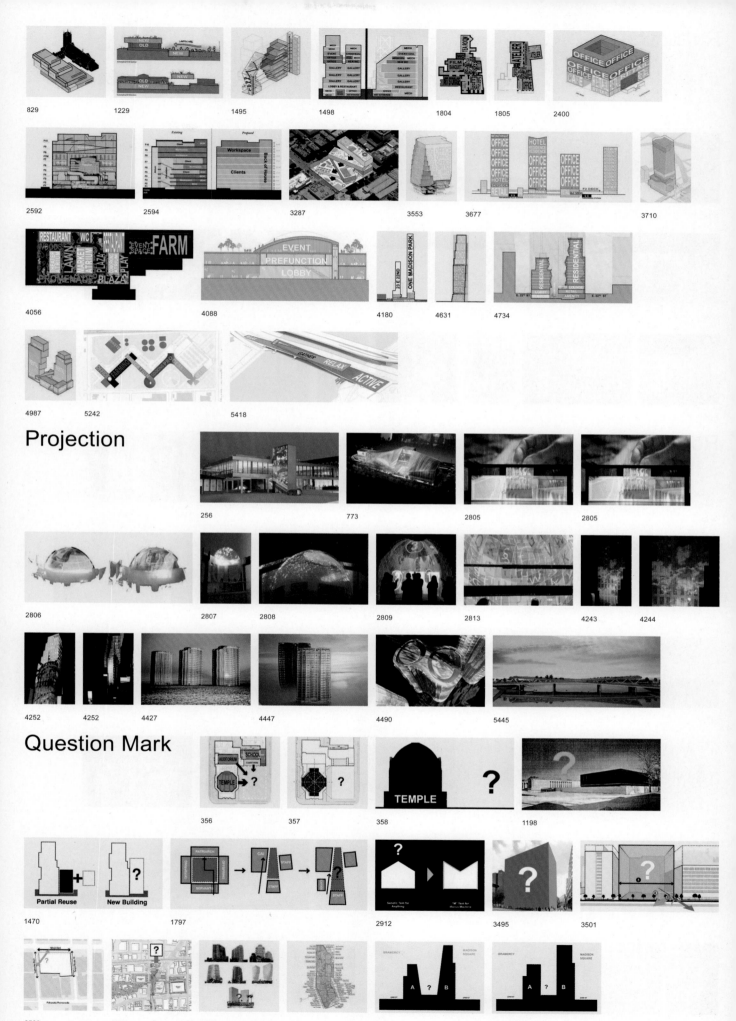

829 1229 1495 1498 1804 1805 2400

2592 2594 3287 3553 3677 3710

4056 4088 4180 4631 4734

4987 5242 5418

Projection

256 773 2805 2805

2806 2807 2808 2809 2813 4243 4244

4252 4252 4427 4447 4490 5445

Question Mark

356 357 358 1198

1470 1797 2912 3495 3501

3503 3681 4393 4701 4721 4801

Reflection

110 113 272 1025 1115

1939 1956 1958 3016 3018 3068 3139 3202

3223 3768 3780 3804 3977

4039 4117 4118 4244 4247 4655 4656 4754 4900

Romance

72 154 905 917 1490 1516 1574

2252 2253 2395 2664 2900 3337

3450 3451 4327 4362 4408

4412 4493 5258 5499

Sandwich

 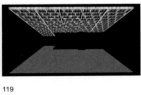  

24 119 129 637 679

 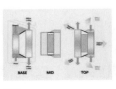 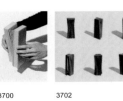

1725 3693 3694 3698 3700 3702 3787 3790 4184 4806

Science

714

718

1075

1076

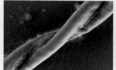

2271

2269

2274

2891

2892

2893

2894

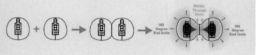

2902

4229

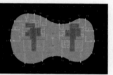

4230

4403

4411

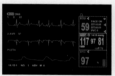

4412

4437

4455

4765

4772

4964

4965

5519

5520

Silhouette

433

436

808

1257

1517

1641

2226

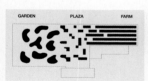

2228

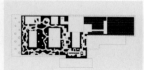

2250

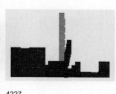

3684

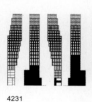

3685

3701

4053

4053

4227

4231

4761

4801

5023

5412

Skeleton

 38
 394
 826
 831

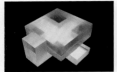 1276
 1277
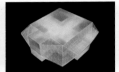 1278
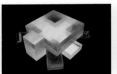 1351
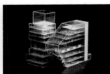 1496
 1497

 1519
 1521
 1540
1721
 3301
4403

Solitude

 100
 188
 286
 300
 313
 314

 322
 483
 881
 1028
1007
 1091
 1110

 1684
 1686
 1689
 1967
2124
 2159

 2164
 2166
 2469
 2511
 2661
 2856
 4042
 4326

Square

 38
 149
 372
 616

 683
 690
 807
 1201
 1206
 2421
 2590

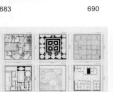 2608
 2643
 2867
 3216
 3221
 3265
 3270

3966   4001   4038   4247   4261   4793   5022   5044

Stepped

427   660   911   921

1095   1237   1492   1495   1508   3231   3274

3281   3287   3301   3511   3736   3741

4199   4209   4211   4626   4631   4663   4791   4985   4989   5137

Stress

75   76   168   169

766   1084   1746   1747   2341   2342

2350   3454   3611   3612   3613   3829   3830

4230   4232   5010   5114   5115   5124   5433   5434

Sunset

     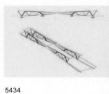

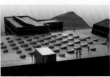    

277   831   854   1375   2430

2495   3295   3296   3297   3339

3379   3434   4048   4060   4400

4471   4533   4659   4686   4996   5445

Timeline

13   552   569   593

595   1179   1180   1190   1436

2528   2529   2530   2541   2545

2983   3866   5187   5358   5359   5360

5361   5362   5363   5396

Translucency

714   731   786   1086

1088   1090   1090   1093   1600   1715

1724　1730　1731　1821　1825　1826　1834　1841

1844　1845　2792　2793　2795　2796　3994

4066　4081　4127　4267

Truss

75　76　79　81

83　843　844　845　1082

1083　1084　1087　1092　5076

5077　5080　5429　5436

Undulation

159

222

269

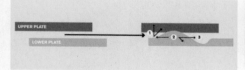

270

593

714

718

3015

3034

3122

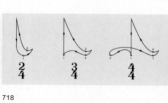

3140

4146　4147　4444　4462　4469

4501

4514

4544

4724

4729

5321

5396

Wedge

816

818

1512

1536

1679

2314

2315

2316

2437

3519

3520

4621

4924

4991

4994

5059

5500

Wellness

99

1776

1954

2480

3248

3323

3373

3376

3429

3822

4323

4324

4325

4326

4327

4329

4494

4533

4840

4841

5074

5077

5424

5456

5475

5491

5509

5537

5542

White

223 999 1006 1007 1019 1131

1831 1835 1837 1838 2258 2275

2283 2332 2661 2669 2682 2793

2829 2847 2855 2876 4001 4314

Wood

253 418 428 693

717 942 946 947 1336 1687

2634 2645 3276 3702 3984 3985

   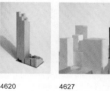  

4126 4127 4345 4620 4627 5542

X

55 389 1478 2804 4404

4978 5427 5446 5517 5553

Image Credit/ Source

Photography